Exploring the Dynamics of Consumerism in Developing Nations

Ayantunji Gbadamosi
University of East London, UK

A volume in the Advances in Marketing, Customer Relationship Management, and E-Services (AMCRMES) Book Series

IGI Global
DISSEMINATOR OF KNOWLEDGE

Published in the United States of America by
IGI Global
Business Science Reference (an imprint of IGI Global)
701 E. Chocolate Avenue
Hershey PA, USA 17033
Tel: 717-533-8845
Fax: 717-533-8661
E-mail: cust@igi-global.com
Web site: http://www.igi-global.com

Library of Congress Cataloging-in-Publication Data

Names: Gbadamosi, Ayantunji, editor.
Title: Exploring the dynamics of consumerism in developing nations / Ayantunji Gbadamosi, editor.
Description: Hershey PA : Business Science Reference, [2019] | Includes bibliographical references.
Identifiers: LCCN 2018037396| ISBN 9781522579069 (hardcover) | ISBN 9781522579076 (ebook)
Subjects: LCSH: Consumer behavior--Developing countries--Case studies. | Consumption (Economics)--Developing countries--Case studies.
Classification: LCC HF5415.33.D48 E97 2019 | DDC 339.4/7091724--dc23 LC record available at https://lccn.loc.gov/2018037396

This book is published in the IGI Global book series Advances in Marketing, Customer Relationship Management, and E-Services (AMCRMES) (ISSN: 2327-5502; eISSN: 2327-5529)

British Cataloguing in Publication Data
A Cataloguing in Publication record for this book is available from the British Library.

Advances in Marketing, Customer Relationship Management, and E-Services (AMCRMES) Book Series

Eldon Y. Li
National Chengchi University, Taiwan & California Polytechnic State University, USA

ISSN:2327-5502
EISSN:2327-5529

Mission

Business processes, services, and communications are important factors in the management of good customer relationship, which is the foundation of any well organized business. Technology continues to play a vital role in the organization and automation of business processes for marketing, sales, and customer service. These features aid in the attraction of new clients and maintaining existing relationships.

The Advances in Marketing, Customer Relationship Management, and E-Services (AMCRMES) Book Series addresses success factors for customer relationship management, marketing, and electronic services and its performance outcomes. This collection of reference source covers aspects of consumer behavior and marketing business strategies aiming towards researchers, scholars, and practitioners in the fields of marketing management.

Coverage

- Social Networking and Marketing
- Web Mining and Marketing
- Telemarketing
- CRM and customer trust
- CRM strategies
- Data mining and marketing
- B2B marketing
- Relationship marketing
- CRM in financial services
- Electronic Services

IGI Global is currently accepting manuscripts for publication within this series. To submit a proposal for a volume in this series, please contact our Acquisition Editors at Acquisitions@igi-global.com or visit: http://www.igi-global.com/publish/.

The Advances in Marketing, Customer Relationship Management, and E-Services (AMCRMES) Book Series (ISSN 2327-5502) is published by IGI Global, 701 E. Chocolate Avenue, Hershey, PA 17033-1240, USA, www.igi-global.com. This series is composed of titles available for purchase individually; each title is edited to be contextually exclusive from any other title within the series. For pricing and ordering information please visit http://www.igi-global.com/book-series/advances-marketing-customer-relationship-management/37150. Postmaster: Send all address changes to above address.

Titles in this Series

For a list of additional titles in this series, please visit: www.igi-global.com/book-series

Evaluating the Gaps and Intersections Between Marketing Education and the Marketing Profession
Margarida M. Pinheiro (University of Aveiro, Portugal) Ana Estima (University of Aveiro, Portugal) and Susana Marques (University of Aveiro, Portugal)
Business Science Reference • copyright 2019 • 252pp • H/C (ISBN: 9781522562955) • US $190.00 (our price)

Advanced Methodologies and Technologies in Digital Marketing and Entrepreneurship
Mehdi Khosrow-Pour, D.B.A. (Information Resources Management Association, USA)
Business Science Reference • copyright 2019 • 818pp • H/C (ISBN: 9781522577669) • US $315.00 (our price)

Multifaceted Explorations of Consumer Culture and Its Impact on Individuals and Society
David J. Burns (Kennesaw State University, USA)
Business Science Reference • copyright 2019 • 318pp • H/C (ISBN: 9781522561200) • US $215.00 (our price)

The Role of Language and Symbols in Promotional Strategies and Marketing Schemes
Manuela Epure (Spiru Haret University, Romania) and Lorena Clara Mihăeş (University of Bucharest, Romania)
Business Science Reference • copyright 2019 • 333pp • H/C (ISBN: 9781522557784) • US $205.00 (our price)

Application of Gaming in New Media Marketing
Pratika Mishra (Presidency University Bangalore, India) and Swati Oberoi Dham (New Delhi Institute of Management, India)
Business Science Reference • copyright 2019 • 312pp • H/C (ISBN: 9781522560647) • US $215.00 (our price)

Strategic Perspectives in Destination Marketing
Mark Anthony Camilleri (University of Malta, Malta)
Business Science Reference • copyright 2019 • 411pp • H/C (ISBN: 9781522558354) • US $215.00 (our price)

Corporate Social Responsibility and Strategic Market Positioning for Organizational Success
Carlton Brown (University of Plymouth, UK) and Uzoechi Nwagbara (Sunderland University, UK & Cardiff Metropolitan University, UK)
Business Science Reference • copyright 2019 • 301pp • H/C (ISBN: 9781522554097) • US $195.00 (our price)

Optimizing Millennial Consumer Engagement With Mood Analysis
Sabyasachi Dasgupta (O.P. Jindal Global University, India) and Priya Grover (Symbiosis International (Deemed University), India)
Business Science Reference • copyright 2019 • 351pp • H/C (ISBN: 9781522556909) • US $215.00 (our price)

IGI Global
DISSEMINATOR OF KNOWLEDGE

701 East Chocolate Avenue, Hershey, PA 17033, USA
Tel: 717-533-8845 x100 • Fax: 717-533-8661
E-Mail: cust@igi-global.com • www.igi-global.com

Editorial Advisory Board

List of Reviewers

Table of Contents

Detailed Table of Contents

Consumption is a global phenomenon that permeates virtually every walk of life in developed and developing nations. Consequently, extant literature is awash with postulations on consumer behavior in these contexts in varying forms. Most of the perspectives relating to developing nations explicate various issues that revolve around how the lower economic development in these nations affects their consumption when compared to what is in place in developed countries. Nonetheless, this chapter which classifies the key influences on consumer behavior into three factors, namely personal factors, socio-cultural factors, and marketing stimuli, argues that the consumption pattern of consumers in the contemporary developing nations tend to mirror that of developed nations in many ramifications. Thus, the chapter suggests that the consumption pattern of consumers in these nations is changing significantly by the day from what it used to be in response to the pace of changes in the global marketing environment such as the interconnectedness of people through technological advancement.

Neuromarketing is providing the leverage for marketers to delve into consumers' subconscious minds to determine behavior. Marketers, economists, and other consumer-related disciplines are looking to science to accurately determine consumer behavior. The purpose of this chapter is to provide insight into a burgeoning field of study, neuromarketing, documenting various research studies and applications of mechanisms in determining brain activities and other uses of science to benefit marketing research. Data for the study is derived from impartial cross-referencing of conceptual and empirical articles published in major journals. The application of neuroimaging technique in research have provided marketers with concrete evidence of brain activation that signal increased activities during stimulation. Further, the implication and causes of concern in using neuroscience methods in marketing are highlighted. Developing country studies on neuromarketing are examined to determine its application and use as a marketing research tool.

This chapter examines the impact of consumer ethnocentrism and country of origin of a low involvement product on consumer brand perception and purchase behavior in a transitional market setting of Central and Eastern Europe. Data were collected from 317 respondents from an urban population in three large cities in Romania. The results show that country of origin has a significant impact on the consumers' perception of the Danish beer brand Tuborg. The results show statistically significant associations between consumer ethnocentrism taxation and buying Romanian products as well as between demographic characteristics and brand perception.

Perfumes have been important in India for millennia and so have the stories connected with them. The perfume business in India is worth billions ($). A background from which the Indian perfume industry can be understood in terms of the Berger's STEPP model, the consumers' cognitive schemas, consumers' behaviors, and the story of the product, brand, and their customers' stories. Three sets of themes—product perceptions, concerns, and consumers' lifestyle—are identified, each with their own sub-themes that are antecedents to perfume purchasing behavior. Segments in the Indian perfume market are also identified. Each consumer segment has their own behavioral nuances and they consider different aspects of the perfume product taking into account their own income and aspects of the three themes and 19 sub-themes. It is important for perfume marketing managers to consider each aspect of the STEPPs modeland for the Indian government to locate and develop a "Place of Perfume" within India that will eventually challenge the region of Grasse in France as the global perfume marketplace.

The purpose of this chapter is to highlight the implications of the marketing activities undertaken by tobacco companies in Sub-Saharan Africa (SSA) and especially as it pertains to vulnerable groups such as children. Using illustrative cases of two SSA countries—notably Malawi and Nigeria—with disparate economic sizes but nonetheless critical for the discussion in question. Consequently, the chapter posits that the marketing practices of tobacco giants (i.e., Big Tobacco), exploiting the weak regulatory environment in SSA, is worthy of scholarly and policy attention. The chapter focuses primarily on the promotion element of the traditional marketing-mix (which also includes the production and its packaging and branding attributes, pricing strategies, and distribution/place elements) as well as the public policy implications of these four Ps. It also touches upon some of the institutional elements that handicaps governments from undertaking necessary corrective measures/action such as in the case of Malawi where tobacco accounts for a substantial part of the GDP.

The chapter explores the growing importance of children as consumers. The chapter would first discuss the importance, growth, and views on consumer socialization theory. The chapter would then take the discussion forward by introducing the change in the role of children not just as learners but as influencers. This section of the chapter concludes by initiating a discussion to understand the similarity and differences in the two theories: consumer socialization and reverse socialization. The theoretical overview provides the researchers a premise to integrate consumer socialization theory and reverse socialization to understand how children and parents acquire learning properties to be a consumer. Based on the two theories, a conceptual model was developed by the author to understand and indicate the process of children and parents becoming consumers. The chapter further discusses the changing social and economic scenario in developing nations with a special focus on India.

One of the strategies that are used by companies to differentiate their cosmetic products is celebrity endorsement. Despite this popular advertising technique, researchers and advertisers have not agreed as to which celebrity source characteristics are most effective in influencing consumers' purchase intention. Another important factor that affects consumers' purchase intention is the consumer ethnocentrism level. Consumers in different countries have different preference over local and international products. Thus, the objective of this chapter is to examine the source credibility theory with the moderating role of ethnocentrism. The result suggests that celebrity endorsers' trustworthiness (TR), attractiveness (AT), and expertise (EX) had a significant positive influence on cosmetic product purchase intention (CPPI). The moderating role of ethnocentrism between AT, TR, and CPPI were examined and found to be significant. This indicates that AT and TR are stronger when consumers' ethnocentrism is high.

Advertisers engage celebrities to endorse their products. This chapter hinges on the meaning transfer theory of McCracken that says that celebrity image can be transferred to items that users buy. Using the survey method, this work examined if celebrity endorsements affect buying. Copies of the questionnaire were administered on 1,516 residents drawn from urban, suburban, and rural areas of Lagos and Ogun States, Nigeria. The Pearson correlation found positive relationships between celebrity endorsements and buyers' decisions. The tests show that celebrity endorsements influence the purchase decisions of the residents, and these buyers' avoidance of a product is more clearly influenced by celebrity endorsements. People buy products because of the celebrities that endorsed them. However, some respondents, especially those in the rural areas, were not as influenced into buying these products as are those from the urban and sub-urban areas. It is advised that advertisers pursue other avenues to draw patronage from this area.

The development around social class evolvement in sub-Saharan African market dated back to pre-colonial era when traditional African institution operated on the basis of royalty, land ownership, subjugation of weak tribe, and superiority of strong and powerful tribes. The advent of slavery and migration of white settlers and traders (slaves and goods) further entrenched social class structure in the system. The advent of colonial rule greatly impacted social class system whereby new strata were created based on the new administrative system that colonial system introduced into sub-Saharan Africa. Largely, acquisition of formal education, salary and wage-collection jobs, business opportunities, Western religion, clothing styles, and new roles to the traditional chiefs opened doors for new social class strata. Social class has witnessed development and improvement that has further improved marketing system and consumer understanding in the society through design of products and services for the market.

This chapter investigates the influence of country of origin's reputation on the notion of place brand and vice versa. Employing a case study methodology, cases of Lagos (Nigeria) and Dubai (UAE) are examined to generate a model of place brand/branding. This model highlights the flow of causality between a nation brand and a city brand. Four themes are highlighted as matters of interest to focus on when recommending a way forward for Lagos city to generate and improve its global reputation in order to increase the footfalls of visitors and expats.

This chapter examines the diffusion and adoption of electronic governance systems (e-government) in South Africa. The purpose of the chapter is to determine how the supply side in South Africa has facilitated consumers' adoption of e-government. To achieve this objective, an extensive review of the literature encapsulating e-government, South African public services, information communication technologies (ICTs), and commerce was conducted. Findings revealed interesting results. First among many was that e-government is viewed by the government as a panacea to a plethora of socio-economic problems facing the country. It was further revealed that e-government initiatives at the municipality level are quite instrumental in driving the e-government agenda in South Africa. Of note, municipalities have rolled out various e-government programs. As a result, the country's overall e-government rankings were observed to have significantly improved in the recent past. The chapter concludes by highlighting several opportunities through which e-government could be further strengthened.

Preface

Consumer behaviour is notably the bedrock of marketing discipline. It focuses on the process of consumption, elucidating the stages involved both before and after the decision in relation to the market offerings and the associated factors that underpin this act. So, the consumers are at the centre of marketing activities as they engage in the exchange of something of value to satisfy their needs. Interestingly, what constitutes value to these consumers vary in many ways and it is in a state of flux. So, what a group of consumers considers valuable as market offerings a couple of decades ago may have lost its vantage position in their consumption pattern this day and age. Similarly, as postmodernism emphasises, these consumers could also be driven by fragmentation, de-differentiation, hyperreality, chronology, pastiche, pluralism, and anti-foundationalism (Brown, 1999; Parsons et al., 2018). It is particularly interesting to note the wider relevance of this phenomenon in that consumption permeates every facet of human endeavours. The wealthy and the poor, the old and the young, introverts and extroverts, rural residents and urban dwellers; and several other categorisations of people we could think of engage in one consumption act or another. Accordingly, the variations associated with consumption acts could take different forms such as ethnicity, income, age, usage pattern of a product or service, and geographical settlement to mention but few. These idiosyncrasies that depict consumption behaviour constitute part of what make marketing enigmatic in nature. Essentially, they determine which type of products or services consumers buy and their perception and interaction with price as a marketing stimulus. Similarly, these factors provide explications of various channels of distribution that are applicable to the consumer groups and the nature of the marketing communication system that could effectively communicate the value of those offerings to the target audience.

The variation of consumerism and marketing stimuli in relation to consumers' age is an example of consumption pattern that demonstrates diversity among people. Clearly, it has been an issue of significant scholarship effort for a long time in the extant literature (Ward, 1972; Carlson & Grossbart, 1988; Burt & Gabbort, 1995; Ward, 1972; Gbadamosi et al., 2012; Yang et al., 2014; Gbadamosi, 2018a). As an example, one study conducted by Burt and Gabbort (1995) on the elderly consumer and non-food purchase behaviour found gender to be more important attribute propelling their shopping traits than age. They even found that this consumer segment have preference for locally operated rather than nationally operated stores. In the contexts relating to research around children (See for example, John, 1999; Chan, 2006; Lawlor & Prothero, 2011; Gbadamosi et al., 2012, 2018b) the main arguments revolve around children's roles in family consumption behaviour, showing their incremental involvement at different age categories and their socialization. In the discourse on children socialization, the agents that aid children's learning in terms of consumption activities are their peers, marketing communication messages, and their parents. Meanwhile, there are two broad perspectives on their roles and involvement in the marketplace. One considers them to be active, in that they are consumers themselves consuming various products and services with or without their family members. On the other hand, the second perspective emphasises the fact that they are vulnerable consumers that are not adequately competent to relate to the marketing strategies of businesses. With this degree of diversity around consumers' age and consumption behaviour, it sounds logical to also explore the consumption dynamics of consumers in developing nations as a specific consumer group.

It is also interesting that culture plays pivotal role in human consumption in different ways. Essentially, the literature is replete with studies that show how it differentiates the consumption pattern of consumers in a particularly cultural setting in relation to their norms, mores and values from those in other cultural contexts. Culture tends to be prescriptive in various ways. The type of fashion items worn by people and how they use them, colour preference of specific market offerings, food consumption and a plethora of other consumption decisions are influenced by people's cultural orientations. Interestingly, one of the salient characteristics of culture is that it is learnt as the norms and values that typify a particular cultural group are passed down from one generation to another. Similarly, as more and more people move from their countries of origin to settle in others; they engage in cross border activities including consumption and these are being influenced by various factors (Luedicke, 2011; Gbadamosi, 2012; Schau et al., 2017). An example is the study about Black Africans women's consumption of clothing in the UK showing that they are influenced by weather condition, social factors, personal factors, and religion (Gbadamosi, 2012). The finding concerning the influence of social factors is particularly exciting in that the influence works in different dimensions. These women are driven to consume in order to fit into the social fabric of the host cultural environment. This is tied to their interactions with others at their places of employment, local communities, schools, and other social gatherings. On the other hand, their social affiliation to their host cultural heritage still propels them to consume clothing consistent with their home cultural system. This is because they use such consumption behaviour to interact and integrate with other consumers of their ethnicity resident in the host country to show that they are socially connected with them during special occasions of celebration in manners reminiscent of what they used to experience in their countries of origin. Findings of another study also show that teenage ethnic consumers in the UK are influenced by the interaction of personal, social, cultural, psychological and commercial factors as reported in a study that explored their consumption vis-à-vis brand personification and symbolic consumption (Gbadamosi, 2015). Similarly, research around the experience of international students and expatriates in the UK, US and various other countries (Friedman et al., 2009; Goldstein & Keller, 2015; Gbadamosi, 2018c) corroborate the contention that, more often than not, acculturation continues to occupy a centre part of the human consumption system. Accordingly, a research focus on the dynamics of consumerism in developing nations is justifiably a worthy course of action that will enrich knowledge about the associated specificities.

Furthermore, religion as one of the key factors under culture offers us some useful clues in relation to people's decisions around their value-oriented activities. More specifically, the nexus between religion, consumption and entrepreneurship takes the discourse of culture to a whole new level (McRoberts, 1999; Casanova, 2001; Gbadamosi, 2015, 2018d). In these various studies, ethnic consumers in host cultural environments develop special preference for products and services offered by entrepreneurs that belong to similar faith-based organisations. These emphasise the interplay of bond shared by members, consumption, and social capital as underpinning arguments in these contexts.

While there are several other postulations around diversity in consumer behaviour vis-à-vis other internal and external factors that influence consumption, the aforementioned cases and studies, to a great extent, provide interesting dynamics about the differences in consumer behaviour pattern in various contexts. Accordingly, there are stereotypes around consumerism and consumer behaviour in relation to developing nations. It is often easier to simply dismiss the need for further rigorous studies about consumption in developing nations on the ground that the preconceived perspectives would suffice to enlighten us on the issues. Nonetheless, some of the existing assumptions and theories about consumption in various societies are being displaced by the day due to the dynamic nature of the marketing environment. Evidently, research attention has not been adequately devoted to exploring the developments in consumer behaviour in developing nations as there are still numerous unanswered questions about buying behaviour in this milieu. Hence, research endeavours in such academic terrain, as those featured in this book, will be significantly beneficial.

Moreover, the extant literature is replete with contributions which indicate the increasing relevance of developing nations in the global marketplace. While there are many indicators that corroborate this standpoint, arguably, the most notable of them all is the growing consumer power in this marketing context which cannot be ignored. This in turn is substantiated by the changes in socio-cultural dimensions of the marketing environment and the trend of globalisation. Accordingly, devoting research attention to consumer behaviour in this context will be invaluable towards enriching our knowledge in this academic domain.

OBJECTIVE OF THE BOOK

This publication is intended as a compendium of research materials that will constitute an essential reference source by building on the existing consumer behaviour literature and contributing to the field of marketing in general. It is comprehensive in nature, and positioned to illuminate the field and provide the resources necessary for researchers, managers, and policy makers for insight into consumption practices in developing nations and the relevance of this for globalisation.

TARGET MARKET

This book primarily targets researchers, advanced- level students, and managers. Moreover, it will also be invaluable to policy makers with interest in developing nations.

STRUCTURE OF THE BOOK

This book, *Exploring the Dynamics of Consumerism in Developing Nations*, significantly extends understanding in the field of consumer behaviour especially in relation to its predecessor, *The Handbook of Consumerism and Buying Behaviour in Developing Nations* published in 2016. Apart from significantly strengthening and repositioning the existing chapters that feature in this book towards increasing their value to readers, this new publication also has seven new chapters which extend the frontier of knowledge in this research domain. Essentially, this book has sixteen chapters and focusses on exploring the dynamics of consumer behaviour in developing nations as related to individuals and those linked to societal members. By and large, the chapters explore a variety of consumption activities touching on perception, learning, attitudes, motivation and involvement, personality, and the self as synthesized to be within the developing nation's context. Similarly, the chapters address consumer behavior in social settings contextualized to developing nations ranging from culture, sub-culture, children as consumers, income and social class to family. Apart from consumerism, the book also covers contemporary issues in consumer behaviour such as neuromarketing, consumption of nation brand, and celebrity endorsement. A brief overview specific to of each of the chapters is given below:

Chapter 1 of the book is titled "An Overview of the Consumer Behavior in the Contemporary Developing Nations." Most of the postulations relating to developing nations discuss various issues that revolve around how the lower economic development in these nations affects their consumption when compared to what is in place in developed countries. However, this chapter which classifies the key influences on consumer behaviour into three namely Personal factors, Socio-cultural factors, and Marketing stimuli; shows that the consumption in the contemporary developing nations tend to mirror that of developed nations in many areas. As shown severally in the chapter, these changes in the status quo are significantly facilitated by the changes in global marketing environment including advancement in technology that permeates virtually every society in recent times.

The key focus in Chapter 2 of the book is Neuromaketing which revolves around various mechanisms that are being used to determine brain activities in relation to consumption decisions. By the nature of the topics covered, the chapter shows how marketers are using science to accurately determiner consumer behaviour. Apart from discussing the implications of using neuroscience methods for marketing decisions, it also highlights areas of concerns about this method. The authors also discuss studies on this important topic in relation to developing countries.

Chapter 3 is a robustly presented examination of the impact of consumer ethnocentrism and country of origin of a low involvement product on consumer brand perception and purchase behaviour in a transitional market setting of Central and Eastern Europe. The study reported is based on data collected from respondents resident in 3 large cities in Romania. The results show statistically significant associations between consumer ethnocentrism taxation and purchasing Romanian products; as well as between demographic characteristics and brand perception.

Bamber and Grandsen's chapter contribution, Chapter 4, is focussed on Perfume Consumption in a developing country, India. According to them, Perfumes have been important in India for millennia and so have the stories connected with them.. Three sets of themes: product perceptions, concerns, and consumers' lifestyle are identified in the chapter,. Each of these themes also has its own sub-themes that are antecedents to perfume purchasing behavior. Segments in the Indian perfume market are also identified. Interestingly, the chapter shows that each consumer segment has its own behavioral nuances and considers different aspects of the perfume product taking into account their own income and aspects of the three themes and nineteen sub-themes. A number of interesting and valuable marketing implications are discussed.

The purpose of Chapter 5 is to highlight the implications of the marketing activities undertaken by tobacco companies in Sub-Saharan Africa (SSA) with specific reference to vulnerable groups such as children. The chapter is mainly underpinned by two illustrative cases of two SSA countries – notably Malawi and Nigeria – with disparate economic sizes, but nonetheless critical for the discussion in question. The argument advanced in the chapter by the authors is that marketing practices of tobacco giants (i.e. Big Tobacco), exploiting the weak regulatory environment in SSA – is worthy of scholarly and policy attention. The chapter focuses primarily on marketing communications as an element in the marketing mix It also touches upon some of the institutional elements that handicaps governments from undertaking necessary corrective measures/ action.

Chapter 6 explores the growing importance of children as consumers. It discusses the importance, growth and views on consumer socialization theory. The chapter introduces the change in role of children not just as learners but as influencers and emphasises the need to understand the similarity and differences in the theories of consumer socialization and reverse socialization. Based on these two theories a conceptual model was developed by the author to understand and indicate the process of children and parents becoming consumers. Overall, the chapter discusses the changing social and economic scenario vis-à-vis children in developing nations with special focus on India.

Issues on the relevance of celebrity in consumer behaviour and marketing in general has been a popular topic for some time. As argued in this chapter, it is one the strategies that are used by marketers to differentiate their cosmetic products from competing offerings. Nevertheless, it has been noted in this chapter that scholars and advertisers are yet to agree as to which celebrity source characteristics are most effective in influencing consumers' purchase intention. Hence, the objective of this seventh chapter of the book is to examine the source credibility theory with the moderating role of ethnocentrism. Findings of the study suggests that celebrity endorser's trustworthiness (TR), attractiveness (AT) and expertise (EX) had a significant positive influence on cosmetic product purchase intention (CPPI). The moderating role of ethnocentrism between AT, TR and CPPI were examined also found to be significant.

Although Aririguzoh, Mogaji, and Odiboh's chapter contribution is also based on celebrity endorsement, their contribution to the literature is from a different perspective compared to what is reported in Chapter 8. The study reported in the chapter is based on a survey of 1,516 residents of urban, suburban and rural areas of Lagos and Ogun States in Nigeria, a developing country. By and large, the study shows that celebrity endorsements influence the purchase decisions of the residents; and these buyers' avoidance of a product is more clearly influenced by celebrity endorsements. The chapter also shows interesting contracting findings concerning respondents from rural and those in urban and sub-urban areas and discussed the implications of the study.

Chapter 9 discusses Social Class and Consumer Behaviour in Sub-Saharan Africa and specifically explores the implication of this for cross cultural marketing. It synthesises issues like the development of social class in sub-Saharan African, the pre-colonial era and slavery. It is interesting to note also that the chapter explores this topic vis-vis acquisition of education, wages and salaries, business opportunities, societal roles and consumption. The author argues that the impact of social class on consumption in the area used as the contextual platform is significant and the implications are far-reaching than the scope previously imagined.

Places, nations, and cities are increasingly becoming popular issues in consumption literature. Chapter 10 of this book contributes to this discourse by investigating the influence of country of origin's reputation on the notion of place brand and vice versa. The arguments in the chapter are underpinned by the use of two cases of Lagos, one of the states in Nigeria and Dubai (UAE) and a model is developed from this synthesis. Four key themes are highlighted in the chapter. Overall, the chapter presents some useful recommendations on how global reputations of cities could be improved upon based on the analysis of the cases explored for the study.

The focus of Chapter 11 is on facilitating Consumers' Adoption of E-government in South Africa. The author examines the diffusion and adoption of electronic governance system in South Africa. The chapter features a critical and extensive review of the extant literature around the key themes on the topic. The findings reported in the chapter suggests that e-government is noted by the government as a panacea to a plethora of socio-economic problems facing the country. A number of useful opportunities through which e-government could be enhanced are presented in the chapter in a comprehensive form.

Chapter 12 shows that while some efforts have been made to understand green market, the inadequacy of information on how enhance consumers' green behaviour is slowing the growth of this market. Using Malaysia as the contextual platform, this chapter examines the impact of environmental knowledge and cultural values on consumers' green purchase intentions. It is based on data collected from 200 respondents and the results are quite interesting. The study suggests that knowledge is not a significant factor influencing buying intention of green products. The managerial and theoretical implications of these findings are comprehensively discussed in the chapter.

The context of the study reported in Chapter 13 is also on South Africa but the focus of the study is on sustainable consumption and social institutions. Purushottam expands the research agenda to examine the role and potential of social institutions in facilitating sustainable consumption in a developing country like South Africa through this chapter. The chapter argues that it is important to ensure equitable growth in developing countries without degradation of natural and social environment and resources. It is argued in the chapter that examination of institutional actors shows gap which can be filled by social institutions. The contention in this chapter is that these social institutions are active and growing in South Africa and could promote sustainable consumption through cooperation, collaboration and partnerships.

Chapter 14 of this book reports the results of an exploratory qualitative investigation into buying behaviours and growth challenges within the solar energy industry in Ghana. The premise of the authors' contention in the chapter is that customers doubt that capabilities of African firms concerning producing and installing renewable energy products developed in the West. The study shows that Ghanaian consumers tend to evaluate the capabilities of foreign solar energy providers as superior to those of local firms. Hence, Kuada et al, in the chapter, content that market-driven growth of the solar energy sector in Ghana requires firm level capability development through institutional support that promotes effective cross-border inter-firm collaborations as well as trust-building relationships with local customers.

Consistent with the main theme of this book, that authors of Chapter 15 decry the paucity of research on consumption behaviour in developing societies. Accordingly, the chapter explores how Nigerian immigrants in information entrepreneurship in Ghana responds to consumers' needs and demand in this specific marketing environment. By and large the chapter provides a deep understanding on the dynamics of consumption practices that make the existence of these businesses to thrive in the developing nation. The implications of this study especially in relation to globalisation are comprehensively discussed in the chapter.

Chapter 16 authored by Abinusawa is entitled Consumerism and Entrepreneurial Opportunity: The Case of MMM. MMM that is used as the underpinning case for this chapter stands for Mavrodi Mundial Movement. The chapter fills a palpable gap in the extant literature by examining the connection between consumerism and entrepreneurial opportunity. The diversity of the sources of the information used in the synthesis of the ideas in the paper is an area of strength that aids the chapter in fulfilling its promise.

Overall, the book features contemporary and comprehensive discourses on the changing landscape of consumerism in developing nations. It is hoped that the compendium will be as thought-provoking on this research domain to readers as purposed while putting the ideas together.

Ayantunji Gbadamosi
University of East London, UK

REFERENCES

Brown, S. (1998). *Postmodern Marketing 2: Telling Tales*. London: ITP.

Burt, S., & Gabbott, M. (1995). The elderly consumer and non-food purchase behaviour. *European Journal of Marketing*, *29*(2), 43–57. doi:10.1108/03090569510080941

Carlson, L., & Grossbart, S. (1998). Parental Style and Consumer Socialization of Children. *The Journal of Consumer Research*, *15*(1), 77–94. doi:10.1086/209147

Casanova, J. (2001). Religion, the New Millennium, and Globalization. *Sociology of Religion, 62*(4), 415-441.

Chan, K. (2006). Consumer socialization of Chinese children in schools: Analysis of consumption values in textbooks. *Journal of Consumer Marketing*, *23*(3), 125–132. doi:10.1108/07363760610663286

Friedman, P., Dyke, L. S., & Murphy, S. A. (2009). Expatriate Adjustment from the Inside Out: An Ethnographic Account. *International Journal of Human Resource Management*, *20*(2), 252–268. doi:10.1080/09585190802670524

Gbadamosi, A. (2012a). Exploring Children, Family, and Consumption Behaviour: Empirical Evidence from Nigeria. *Thunderbird International Business Review*, *54*(4), 591–605. doi:10.1002/tie.21486

Gbadamosi, A. (2012b). Acculturation: An Exploratory Study of Clothing Consumption among Black African Women in London (UK). *Journal of Fashion Marketing and Management*, *16*(1), 5–20. doi:10.1108/13612021211203005

Gbadamosi, A. (2015a). Brand Personification and Symbolic Consumption among Ethnic Teenage Consumers: An Empirical study. *Journal of Brand Management*, *22*(9), 737–759. doi:10.1057/bm.2015.40

Gbadamosi, A. (2015b). Exploring the Growing Link of Ethnic Entrepreneurship, Markets, and Pentecostalism in London (UK): An Empirical study. *Society and Business Review*, *10*(2), 150–169. doi:10.1108/SBR-11-2014-0053

Gbadamosi, A. (Ed.). (2016). Handbook of Research on Consumerism and Buying Behaviour in Developing Nations. Hershey, PA: IGI Global.

Gbadamosi, A. (Ed.). (2018a). Young Consumer Behaviour: A Research Companion. Oxfordshire, UK: Routledge.

Gbadamosi, A. (2018b). The Changing Landscape of Young Consumer Behaviour. In Young Consumer Behaviour: A Research Companion (pp. 3-22). Oxfordshire, UK: Routledge.

Gbadamosi, A. (2018c). The Anatomy of International Students' Acculturation in UK Universities'. *Industry and Higher Education*, *32*(2), 129–138. doi:10.1177/0950422218760335

Gbadamosi, A. (2018d). Women Entrepreneurship, Religiosity, and Value-co-creation with Ethnic Consumers: Revisiting the Paradox. *Journal of Strategic Marketing*. doi:10.1080/0965254X.2017.1344293

Gbadamosi, A., Fletcher, K., Emmanuel Stephen, C., & Olutola, I. C. (2018). Consumerism and Consumer Protection: A Focus on Young Consumers. In Young Consumer Behaviour: A Research Companion (pp. 391-413). Oxfordshire, UK: Routledge.

Gbadamosi, A., Hinson, R., Eddy, T. K., & Ingunjiri, I. (2012). Children's attitudinal reactions to TV advertisements: The African experience. *International Journal of Market Research*, *54*(4), 543–566. doi:10.2501/IJMR-54-4-543-566

Goldstein, S. B., & Keller, S. R. (2015). US College Students' Lay Theories of Culture Shock. *International Journal of Intercultural Relations*, *47*, 187–194. doi:10.1016/j.ijintrel.2015.05.010

John, D. (1999). Consumer Socialization of children: A Retrospective Look at Twenty-Five Years of Research. *The Journal of Consumer Research*, *26*, 183–213. doi:10.1086/209559

Lawlor, M., & Prothero, A. (2011). Pester Power – A Battle of Wills Between Children and their Parents. *Journal of Marketing Management*, *27*(5-6), 561–581. doi:10.1080/0267257X.2010.495281

Luedicke, M. K. (2011). Consumer acculturation theory: (crossing) conceptual boundaries. *Consumption Markets & Culture*, *14*(3), 223–244. doi:10.1080/10253866.2011.574824

McRoberts, O. M (1999). Understanding The "New" Black Pentecostal Activism: Lessons From Ecumenical Urban Ministries in Boston. *Sociology of Religion, 60*(1), 47-70.

Parsons, E., Maclaran, P., & Chatzidakis, A. (2018). *Contemporary Issues in Marketing and Consumer Behaviour* (2nd Ed.). London: Routledge.

Schau, H. J., Dang, Y. M., & Zhang, Y. G. (2017). Learning to navigate the American retail servicescape: Online forums as consumer acculturation platforms and consumer gift systems. *Journal of Business Research*, *72*, 178–188. doi:10.1016/j.jbusres.2016.08.031

Ward, S. (1972). Children's reactions to commercials. *Journal of Advertising Research*, *12*, 37–45.

Yang, Z., Kim, C., Laroche, M., & Lee, H. (2014). Parental Style and Consumer Socialization among Adolescent: A cross Cultural Investigation. *Journal of Business Research*, *67*(3), 228–236. doi:10.1016/j.jbusres.2013.05.008

Acknowledgment

As the editor of *Exploring the Dynamics of Consumerism in Developing Nations*, I am greatly indebted to numerous people for their contributions in one way or another for the successful completion of this project.

Special thanks go to all the authors of the chapters whose strong commitment and enthusiasm at every stage of this project contributed significantly to the success. Their expertise and time dedicated to contributing to the work are invaluable. Similarly, the time, advice and contributions of the reviewers regarding the improvement of quality, coherence, and content presentation of the chapters are greatly appreciated. Most of the authors also served as reviewers of some of the chapters. Clearly, this great support has contributed immeasurably to the work.

I also would like to specially appreciate the support and words of encouragement of the Editorial Advisory Board members. To them, I say thanks a lot! Also, the great support of the IGI team on this project from the proposal to the final stage is well appreciated. They are great people to work with. The gesture is very helpful.

I would like to acknowledge my wife, Sarah Remilekun Gbadamosi, and my children, Miracle, Favour, and Joy, for their support. Their constant understanding for the time I spent on the computers and arriving late contributed to the success of this project. To several others who have helped in one form or another but have not been specifically named, I think of you and thank you nevertheless. Above all, I would like to greatly appreciate God who empowers, strengthens, and inspires me. Without this special inspiration to work on the project, the book could not have seen the light of the day.

Ayantunji Gbadamosi
University of East London, UK

Chapter 1
A Conceptual Overview of Consumer Behavior in the Contemporary Developing Nations

Ayantunji Gbadamosi
University of East London, UK

ABSTRACT

Consumption is a global phenomenon that permeates virtually every walk of life in developed and developing nations. Consequently, extant literature is awash with postulations on consumer behavior in these contexts in varying forms. Most of the perspectives relating to developing nations explicate various issues that revolve around how the lower economic development in these nations affects their consumption when compared to what is in place in developed countries. Nonetheless, this chapter which classifies the key influences on consumer behavior into three factors, namely personal factors, socio-cultural factors, and marketing stimuli, argues that the consumption pattern of consumers in the contemporary developing nations tend to mirror that of developed nations in many ramifications. Thus, the chapter suggests that the consumption pattern of consumers in these nations is changing significantly by the day from what it used to be in response to the pace of changes in the global marketing environment such as the interconnectedness of people through technological advancement.

INTRODUCTION

One of the established perspectives in the extant consumer behaviour literature is that consumers could be categorised in various ways using different bases (Gbadamosi, 2018a, Saleem *et al.,* 2018; Kotler & Armstrong, 2018). In its basic form, this could be done with respect to geography, behaviour, psychographics, and demography. As a matter of fact, each of these broad categorisations also has further sub-factors such age, income, gender, and ethnicity that could give further explication around the issue of what consumers buy, where they buy them from, how they buy them, and when they do so. Accordingly,

DOI: 10.4018/978-1-5225-7906-9.ch001

this line of reasoning offers a robust justification for having a discourse around consumer behaviour in developing nations. To put the discussion in the right perspective, we will make reference to a definition of developing countries. They are often defined statistically by the Word Bank in relation to Gross National Income (GNI) per capital. Currently, these are countries with less than US $12,275 Gross National Income per capital (The Balance, 2018). It is relevant to note that the World Trade Organisation (WTO) often gives developing countries certain favourable differential treatments over other WTO members. These special provisions are stated on the organisation's website as follows:

- Longer time periods for implementing Agreements and commitments,
- Measures to increase trading opportunities for developing countries,
- Provisions requiring all WTO members to safeguard the trade interests of developing countries,
- Support to help developing countries build the capacity to carry out WTO work, handle disputes, and implement technical standards, and
- Provisions related to least-developed country (LDC) Members (WTO, 2018).

Meanwhile while this definition is very helpful statistically to define these nations, another simple perspective that will also be needed to provide background for this chapter is to note that these countries have lower economic development compared to industrialized countries (Akam and Muller, 2013). So, it is not outlandish to suggest that there will be some differences in consumption pattern of consumers in these nations and those in the developed countries especially in relation to values and attitudes to consumption (Wang and Chen, 2004). However, increasing evidence continues to point to the increasing value of these nations vis-à-vis marketing activities of various organisations in relation to the sales of various products and services. It is notable to indicate that consumers in these developing countries constitute more than three-quarter of the world population (Rand, 2018). Similarly, a specific example of prospect in this region is the case of average household spending in India which is expected to reach rupees 61,500 in the year 2025, representing an increase of over 70% compared to the figure of rupees 34, 552 recorded for 2005 (Kathuria & Gill, 2010). Also, report indicates that economic growth of one third of Sub-Saharan African countries is expected to increase from 2.8% for 2017 to 3.4% for 2018 (IMF, 2018). This information cannot be ignored in terms of scale and significance. So, the landscape of consumption activities in the contemporary developing nations is changing and it could be fallacious to rigidly rely on the preconceived and dated perspectives on consumption pattern of consumers in these nations. Apart from showing how consumption is a universal culture vis-à-vis developing nations, this chapter discusses the major influences on consumers with specific reference to the context of this book. We will now explore these factors in turn.

INDIVIDUAL CONSUMER BEHAVIUOR

In their consumption activities as individuals for personal gratification and household use; decisions of consumers in developing countries are influenced by a plethora of factors which can be categorized as shown in Figure 1 below. As the diagram shows, these factors are akin to what we read and know about the mainstream consumer knowledge. Nonetheless, while we use this as the thread to weave the discussion, specific reference will be made to cases and illustrations from the context of developing countries which is the focus of this book.

Figure 1. Major influences on the consumer in developing nations

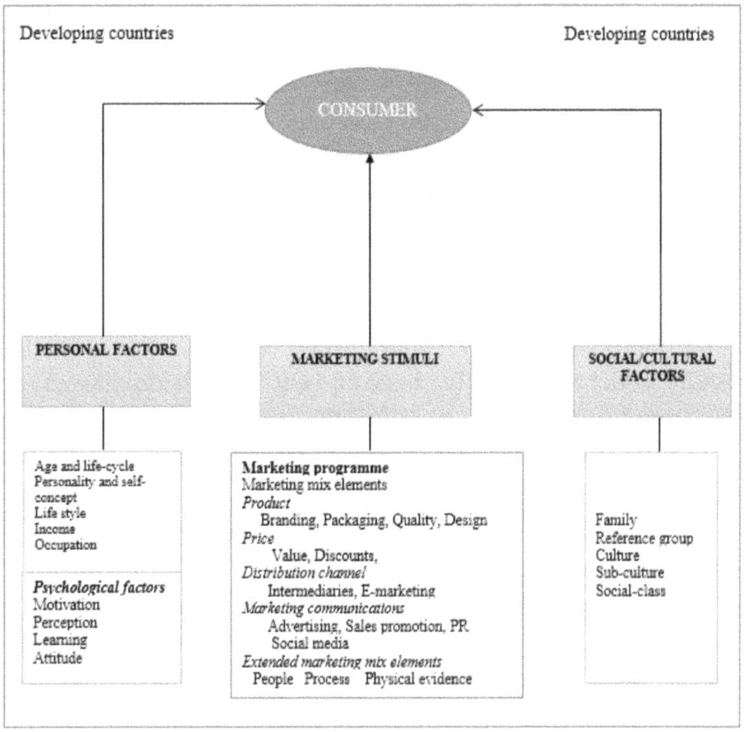

PERSONAL FACTORS

As consumers of goods and services, our needs are often driven by many factors which could be specifically categorized as personal. So, in this category, factors such as age and life-cycle, income, occupation, and self-concept are good examples. We would have noticed that some certain products or services that used to be at the top of our mind when we were a lot younger may no longer appeal to us again. Similarly, there are some market offerings that we now cradle for but would not have caught our attention during our childhood stage of life. As consumers of different age groups, our needs and wants are dissimilar in many contexts. Children's food consumption as an example has been a well discussed topic in the marketing literature and has generated kin interest (Robert & Pettigrew, 2013; Deming *et al,* 2014; Pettigrew *et al.,* 2015). But, in the context of the focus of this chapter, it has been shown that many developing countries suffer from malnutrition and obesity; and consequently, high childhood mortality (The World Bank, 2006; McLeay & Oglethorpe, 2013). This is noteworthy and partly explains the strong presence and activities of NGOs and social marketers dealing with these issues in these countries. This seems to also strengthen the prevalent competition among these businesses in various ways. Furthermore, it is also relevant to the claim that transition to adulthood is shaped by societal context as various societies have role definition and what are expected of their young people (Fatusia & Hindin, 2010). Accordingly, consumption of the young consumers in turn could be linked to the society as this will provide a very rich discussion of what are bought, how they are bought, where, how often, and when. As stated by Fatusia and Hindin (2010), a number of young people in developing countries are confronted with the dilemma of their transitory life stage and the clash between their strict societal traditional values and the many forces of westernization as evident in the global youth culture. In a study that examines the cosmetics buying behavior of young UAE female consumers, Khraim (2010) found that older consumers tend to compare prices of these products more than their young counterparts. He also found that these young consumers rank cosmetics that are sold at specialty store as better in quality than the ones sold at discount store. This dynamics around age and consumption has huge implications for marketing in this context.

An interesting addition to the discussion of consumer age is the family life cycle. It is common to classify consumers as individuals and households into different stages of life cycle. Early consumer research on consumer life cycle including Wells and Guba (1966); Murphy and Staples (1979) and Wilkes (1995) have underscored the importance of this issue to consumer behavior. Essentially, it looks into how an individual and household change over time taking into consideration factors like age, marital status, number of children in the family, ages of those children, retirement and death of spouses in the households and other relevant factors. If done effectively, this could enrich decision makers' understanding of the development of suitable marketing offerings to satisfy the target markets. Meanwhile, as far back as the 70s, Murphy and Staples (1979) advocate a need for a review of the existing life cycles conceptualization and suggest looking into the relevance of divorce in relationships. Similarly, the cultural divide between the developing countries and developed nations on family compositions is a good pointer for why it is important to look at life cycle differently for developing nations' context while using the phenomenon to make sense of marketing transactions in these marketing environments.

Income is a defining factor in how consumers in developing nations make their consumption decisions. To a great extent, the financial capability of the consumer determines his or her choice of products. Conventionally, it is expected that affluent consumers would buy products that project their status which in most cases attract relatively high financial commitment while low-income consumers would favour cheap alternatives. Evidence of this is shown in a claim that working women who have high disposable income spend more on cosmetic and beauty product (Khraim, 2010). Nonetheless, this may not always be the case for a number of reasons. Firstly, there can be considerable differences within countries or contexts. For example, Sun and Collins' (2006) study shows that despite the low-income state, some Chinese prefer more expensive imported fruit to domestic type which is relatively cheaper. Moreover, the notion of consumer *self-concept* and symbolic consumption further echoes the view that income and consumption may not necessarily follow the same pattern for every consumer nor apply in similar way for all societies. Some people, though may be on the lower end of the income spectrum, might still buy moderately expensive products to enhance their identity and self-esteem. *Self-concept* or self-image describes an individual's thought of himself or herself. It is believed that individuals have a concept of self-based on who they think they really are, known as *the actual self* and another concept of who they would like to be – *the ideal self.* The seminal papers of Solomon (1983), Belk (1988); and Sirgy and Johar (1999) are some of the examples that constitute the increasing body of knowledge that emphasizes that consumers' decisions are not only driven by functional benefits associated with products but also the symbolic meanings they connote and the value to the buyer. In extending this further, Solomon *et al.* (2013) emphasise that we as consumers have many different selves and use different products or services to fulfil or actualize these selves. To corroborate this stance, Amine and Lazzaoui (2011) explore the symbolic consumption issue in relation to modern retailing systems in Morocco. Their findings indicate that there are differences in shopping strategies exhibited by consumers based on social classes, and that differences in social classes generate singular symbolic representations of shopping experiences.

Personality, lifestyle, and occupation are other interesting factors personal to the consumers that influence their consumption decisions. In a simple form, Armstrong and Kotler (2018) define personality as the unique psychological characteristics that distinguish an individual or group. It is the way we respond to the world around us as consumers. A strong body of literature (Kassarjian, 1971; Aaker, 1997; Guthrie, *et al.*, 2008; Hamidizadeh *et al.*, 2014) has provided very useful postulations on personality. But essentially, it is important to acknowledge that consumers are often identified by specific traits. So, an individual may be described as aggressive, an introvert, an extrovert, competitive, gregarious, and authoritative. One of the key areas of applications of personality to consumer behavior is the anthropomorphism, which involves metaphorically describing brands with some kind of human behaviour (Delbaere *et al.*, 2011). One of the major contributions on the application of personality to consumer behaviour is the work of Aaker (1997) which draws on the 'Big Five' human personality structure. The study shows that brands have five distinct personality dimensions which are Sincerity, Excitement, Competence, Sophistication, and Ruggedness. With reference to Micklethwait and Woodbridge (2005), Brown (2011) draws attention to joint stock companies as an example of anthropomorphism. According to him, these organisations are artificial persons that have obligations and rights. Evidently, the phenomenon is wide-spread. Hence, it has been widely applied in developing countries. An example is evident in the work of Opoku *et al* (2006) that investigated the application of brand personality in relation to Business programmes in some South African universities. They found that many of the dimensions used for describing the MBA programmes mirror those previously found for consumer brands. Their study suggests that there is a need for Business schools to carefully manage their online marketing communication messages, constantly update their websites and incorporate brand personality into their scheme of things for attracting students into the university.

Consumer lifestyle is about their pattern of living which shows their preferences, values, how they spend their resources, and interact in their environment. They are usually referred to as an individual's *AIO,* which stands for activities, interests, and opinion (psychographics). As consumers of many product items, each of us makes relevant consumption decisions that help define a unique lifestyle. It has been argued that consumers' personality and self-concept are reflected in their lifestyles, which are also very useful for segmenting and targeting consumers (Lamb *et al.*, 1999). Festervand and Sokoya (1994) studied consumer ethnocentrism in developing economy and report that most of the consumers in their study show ethnocentric characteristics. In other words, they show preference for domestic products over the imported types as they think the importation of products into their country could have negative effect on their country's economy. This is partly down to the consumers' lifestyle. Meanwhile, the role of occupation as a personal factor that influence consumers' choices could not be overlooked. People's occupation could be conceptualized in many ways in the society. For example, while some consumers could be self-employed others may be employed in various private and public organizations. We can even consider consumers' occupation on the basis of whether they are blue collar or white collar jobs. To a great extent, income and occupation tend to be related. Some job types attracts more income than others, so a good understanding of the existing occupation structure in various societies of developing nations will be of great value to marketers as they will be able to plan and position their offerings provided in these settings.

SOCIAL/CULTURAL FACTORS

From the viewpoint of Grønhaug and Kleppe (2010), the consumer as an individual does not operate in a vacuum but is embedded in the surrounding social context. Hence, some of the factors that influence consumers' decisions lie within their interactions with other people. Commonly noted factors in the social and cultural factors include family, reference groups, culture, and social class. These factors can have a very intriguing differential impact on consumption pattern of consumers in developing countries.

Family as a social factor constitutes a fundamental phenomenon in marketing and consumer behaviour and a significant buying and decision making unit in the recent society (Xia et al, 2006; Bassett et al, 2008). One good example is the importance of *Ubuntu* in African context. There is a consistent claim that African philosophy and culture is significantly underlined by *Ubuntu* which underscores family atmosphere and emphasises that it is the community that recognises an individual as a person (Shutte, 1993; Karsten & Illa, 2005). This togetherness influences consumers' consumption decisions for various products and services. We could think of families in different forms. For example, we can have nuclear, extended, orientation, and procreation types of family conceptualisations. The dynamics of each of these in relation to the members can offer explanation for peoples' consumption patterns. A nuclear family consist of a husband, wife, and their children whereas an extended family consists of members of the nuclear family with at least one grandparent within the household (Schiffman *et al.*, 2010). While a family of orientation is the family into which one is born, the family of procreation is the family which one helps create by reproduction (Kotler, et al, 2008). Marketers often show keen interest in the roles being played by each members of the family in their purchases. These roles are initiator, gatekeeper, influencer, decider, buyer, and user as shown in Figure 2 below. In a family, while the *Initiator* initiates the idea to acquire a type of product or service, the *Gatekeeper* control the flow of information about a product or service into the family, and the *Influencer is the family member* whose influence carries a lot of weight in supporting the idea to buy the said the product or service. The *Decider is the family* member who has the authority to make the buying decision by himself or herself, while the buyer makes the actual purchase of the product, and the Users are those family members who consume the product or service.

Due to many factors such as civilisation, culture, finance, globalisation, the relative economic power in the family, and the nature of the product involved; the pattern of these roles is dynamic and could vary from society to society like when comparing developing to developed nations. For example, there is a claim that the importance of tribal loyalty, obedience to elders, and group orientation are among the main factors that typify the work values and motives of sub-Saharan African countries (Lamb 1990; Harvey *et al.,* 2000). The logic in this argument in relation to the family buying roles is that while the purchase decisions in developed countries could give room for children in the family to play key roles in the family purchases, this freedom may not be prevalent or so freely applicable in many developing countries due to cultural factors.

Meanwhile, despite this claim, it is also important to note that with civilization and globalisation at play, this dictatorial role of parents in family consumption which presents children as passive stakeholders in the consumption system in Africa, is now diminishing. For example, Gbadamosi (2015a) shows that children in African context are becoming more focal in family consumption system than it used to be in the past as they now have more access to socialization agents like TV, radio and the internet which subtly introduce foreign cultural values and mores into their society. In fact, in an empirical study (Gbadamosi, 2012a), it was shown that children in Nigeria have opportunities to be involved in family consumption decisions, especially in cases related to routinely-consumed products.

As consumers, we belong to one group or another at any particular time. Group members could be classmates, co-workers, neighbours, family members, members of the same faith-based organisation and many others. For instance, a university professor working among other scholars in her institutions may

Figure 2. Family buying roles in developing nations

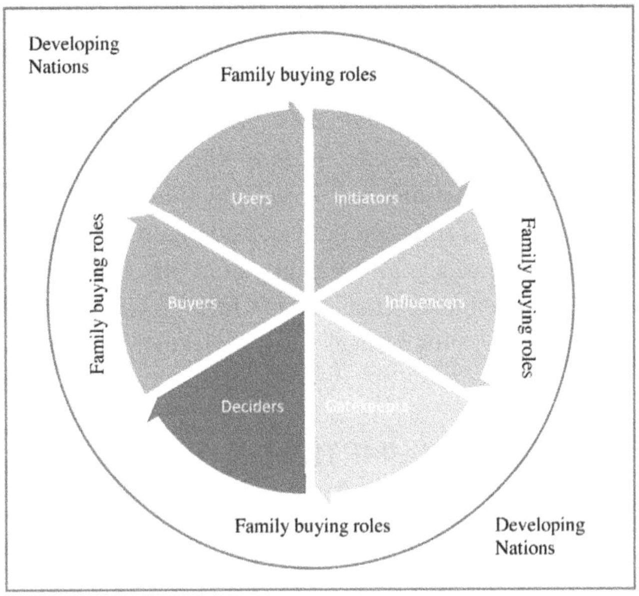

have a strong network outside her institution, and could also belong to a religious organisation as well as playing a prominent role in her family. Setting these in context, this group formation and its dynamics, have considerable implications for our consumption activities.

A *reference group* may be defined as a group which someone uses as a basis of comparison or point of reference in his or her evaluations, aspirations, decisions, and behaviour. It is important to state here that an individuals' reference group can be a group in which he or she is already a member or a group which he or she is longing to join. Reference groups have quite far-reaching implications for consumer behaviour and this links is well established in the relevant literature (Escalas & Bettman, 2005; Ramanathan & McGill, 2007). This is because consumers often buy certain goods and services, or even particular brands of certain items based on their reference groups. Some buy a type of product to be seen by others as belonging to the group. An example of this is shown Gbadamosi (2015c) on symbolic consumption of ethnic minority teenagers in a new environment.

Reference groups vary in many ways. For instance, a reference group for a consumer might be small or large, formal or informal. However, there has been an argument that the smaller and more intimate a reference group, the stronger its influence it likely to be on the individual (Lancaster & Reynolds, 2002, 94). Schiffman *et al.* (2012) identify some of the major consumer reference groups as family, friends, social class, selected subcultures, one' own culture, and other cultures. As explained by Peter and Olson (2010: 350), the reasons why people identify and affiliate with particular reference groups can be classified into three namely:

- To gain useful knowledge,
- To obtain rewards or avoid punishments, and
- To acquire meanings for constructing, modifying, or maintaining their self-concepts.

While reference group can be very useful for marketing programmes especially for segmentation, targeting, and positioning based on the presumption that it influences what people buy, it is also noteworthy to acknowledge that its impacts on purchases could vary in degree for products and brands. Ooi *et al* (2011) found that social groups, as an influence, have a stronger impact on Malaysian consumers for broadband adoption than secondary information sources such as newspapers and magazines. Meanwhile, marketers focussing on developing countries also need to know the effective means of targeting and reaching the *opinion leaders* who, by definition are people within a reference group whose views and opinions are important and respected. They exert quite considerable influence on others. This is usually because they have special skills, knowledge, personality, or other characteristics that enables them to influence others' attitudes and behaviour about a market offering. Given the weight of their influence, targeting opinion leaders in marketing programmes can be effectual for marketing in these settings.

CULTURAL FACTORS AND CONSUMPTION IN DEVELOPING COUNTRIES

Culture

The significant role of culture in consumption activities and its role in how consumers in developing countries approach their purchase decisions is a worthy research endeavour. It can be defined as the set of beliefs, attitudes, and behaviour pattern shared by members of a particular society and passed on from one generation to the next. So, the content of a culture will include beliefs, attitudes, goals, and values held by most members of the society, as well as the meanings of characteristics behaviours, rules, customs and norms followed by most of the people (Peter & Olson, 2010). They represent what the society considers as desirable and permeate virtually everything we do including consumption. In that sense culture is prescriptive and plays significant roles in the society. Interestingly, cultural values are not static but continually evolving. They change from one generation to the next. This explains why culture is described as the personality of a society (Solomon *et al.,* 2013) and without cultural patterns to follow it will be difficult for people to live together (de Mooij, 2013). Like in other societies, most, if not all of the cultural values in developing countries have undergone several changes. Dressing habits, the type of food eaten and how they are consumed, the services subscribed to, language, and many other numerous issues are encapsulated in the narrative of culture. Some of the challenges confronting international marketers is managing how their offerings could be successful in different cultural contexts they operate. The activities of multinational firms like Coca-Cola, McDonald, Procter and Gamble, and HSBC offering goods and services internationally show example of how culture is paramount in the toolkits required for managing operations across different cultures.

In explaining culture and consumption in developing nations, the notion of ethnocentrism cannot be glossed over. As stated by Festervan and Sokoya (1994), ethnic groups in developing countries are interested in establishing national identities, and consequently enjoy the benefit of a new world order prompted by the free market. In this study, conducted decades ago on consumer ethnocentrism in a developing economy, these authors found that most of their respondents exhibit ethnocentric characteristics regarding certain areas. Meanwhile, face saving has been reported as the strongest influence on the consumption of East Asian consumers in respect of conspicuous and hedonic dimensions of luxury products while group orientation is noted as the strongest factor that predict extended self, exclusivity, and quality dimensions (Monkhouse *et al.,* 2012). This further directs our attention to how cultural values can pattern consumption in specific cultural settings. One of the major long established view about culture is that fact that it is learnt. The term *enculturation* is used to explain the process by which consumers learn their own culture whereas *acculturation* is the term that explains learning a foreign culture. Evidence shows that more and more developing countries are learning consumption practices from the developed societies through globalisation (Penaloza 1994; Gbadamosi, 2015c; Gbadamosi, 2018b). Gbadamosi (2012b) provides an interesting account of acculturation of Black African women in respect of their consumption decisions for clothing as they make sense of their host cultural environment in the UK. He posits that these women's acculturation is aided by the combination of a number of factors which are: whether condition, religion, social, and personal factors, Durvasula and Lysonski (2008), for instance show that Chinese and Indian consumers' concern for their physical appearance and professional achievement is on the increase and this is most likely caused by the rising living standard, and exposure to Western media, and its culture. Similarly, Hooper (2000) quoting from New China News Agency, reports an incidence of a Chinese official being sentenced to five years' imprisonment and 'having a fondness for Coca-Cola' was one of the allegations levied against him, which were described as imperialist attitudes in February 1951. Recent evidence all around now is not only showing an acceptance of Coke by the Chinese consumers but of many other international products. Moreover, the use of credit card were only for professionals and Business people in Malaysia several decades ago, but by the end of 1970, the usage has become significantly widened (Ahmed *et al.*, 2010). So, globalisation and acculturation have some interesting links to explain how cultural values are learnt. The seminal work of Hofstede (1984) and its several extensions on national culture are very important to the discussion of culture and consumption in developing nations. While Hofstede (1980; 1984) emphasised a typology of four dimensions by which countries could be compared culturally, a fifth dimension, long-term orientation was added in Hofstede and Bond (1988). They are namely:

- Power distance,
- Individualism,
- Masculinity,
- Uncertainty avoidance,
- Long-term orientation.

This typology has been applied widely in various areas of marketing including consumer behaviour. For example, it has been shown that people from collectivist cultures, had lower propensity to trust external partners as this culture shows a bias towards out-groups (Huff & Kelley, 2003 in Biachi & Saleh, 2010). From a broad perspective, this typology/postulation on culture provides insight into the diversity which exists among countries and further reinforces that there is value in acknowledging the peculiarities of different societies so that appropriate marketing plans could be put in place to ensure successful activities in the cultural environments.

Subcultures

There are also identifiable smaller groups within each dominant culture. These are known as subcultures. These groups also have beliefs, and experiences that make them distinct from other members of the society. The extent to which an individual conforms to unique subcultural values depends greatly on the extent to which he or she identifies with that subculture (Hawkins *et al.*, 2001). Their points of difference within the larger group may be geographical settlement, race, religion, age, or other factors. Specifically targeting consumers in subcultural groups can be very rewarding for marketing practice especially when the subgroup is substantial. Gbadamosi (2015b) explains the dynamics of subcultures in a study on how people in Pentecostal faith based religious organisations use their network and entrepreneurial activities to get prospects, provide value to their customers, and satisfy them. Identifying and analysing the subcultural groups give room for a closer targeting of the consumer and ultimately may lead to higher satisfaction rate and loyalty. An example of this is demonstrated by Sun and Collins (2006) who conducted a study in Guangzhou, a highly developed city within China and Urumqi which is a relatively underdeveloped Chinese city on the five intended uses of imported fruits. Interestingly, there were noted significant differences between the two cities concerning the relative importance of these five uses. While the best intended use of fruit in Guangzhou is self-consumption, for Urumqi, it is to purchase it as a gift. One of the key areas of application of the culture and subculture in marketing is in the global marketing as organisations involved have to operate in different cultural settings. To what extent will the existing marketing programmes of a firm be extended to a new cultural milieu? From a broad perspective, organisations are often confronted with the question of whether to engage in standardisation or adaptation of the marketing tools in the new environment. In standardisation, the marketing programmes are directly extended to a new cultural system without any change but on the other hand, adaptation involves changing the marketing programmes such as the product, price, channels of distribution and marketing communications to fit the cultural systems of the new marketing environment. Although the latter approach requires the commitment of more resources, it caters for the cultural differences and needs of the target markets and ultimately leads to customer satisfaction.

Social Class and Consumption in Developing Countries

Social class classification refers to the division of members of the society in hierarchical order based on the combination of some factors in such a way that members of the same class have approximately the same social standing in the community compared to others outside this class. Social classes among societal members have been a recognised phenomenon. The distinction between developing countries and developed nations in itself is a form of acknowledgement that wealth are unequally available in different societal settings. The criteria for the classification of members into social classes include income, education, wealth, and occupation. Understandably, the social class patterns differ from society to society. Previous studies have shown several patterns of social class that could be used as examples but not a typical case for all societies because of the society-specific variables involved. Some of the existing classifications distinguish among social classes by denoting each class with different letters such as A, B, C, D, E, etc while others conceptualise the classes in the forms which range from Upper-upper to Lower-lower, and there will be classes in the middle. Durvasula and Lynsonski (2008) report the significant change in the middle class in China and India in the last couple of years. In a study on social class and body weight among Chinese urban adults, Bonnefond and Clément (2014) identify four groups which are *the elderly and inactive middle class, the old middle class*, and *the lower middle class* and *the new middle class*. According to them, there is a strong homogeneity in the urban middle class, and these classes within the middle class also show specific features that compare them to the poor and the rich. The study specifically shows that the *New middle class* is to be relatively well-protected against obesity. It was also argued that by 2025, the middle class in urban India would account for over three quarter of urban expenditure on food (Kathuria & Gill, 2013). Doku *et al.* (2010) also found some socioeconomic differences in tobacco use in Ghana. They found that adolescents that are expected to end up in a lower socioeconomic status than their families when they reach their adulthood stage or remain stable in low socioeconomic status are more likely to use tobacco than their counterparts who are stable in the high socioeconomic status. There are huge marketing implications associated with these various findings for market targeting and segmentation strategies in developing nations ranging from mainstream marketing activities to social marketing.

PSYCHOLOGICAL INFLUENCES ON CONSUMPTION IN DEVELOPING COUNTRIES

Motivation

As consumers, we are influenced by a group of factors which are though personal, could be further categorised as psychological, going by the way they function. These are motivation, perception, learning, beliefs and attitudes, and learning (Kotler & Armstrong, 2018). In the words of Kimmel (2010: 123) 'the application of knowledge derived from systematic research in psychology…is crucial to the ongoing evolution of the hybrid field of marketing'. *Motivation,* one of the salient topics in this field, explains the 'whys' of behaviours. It is the reason behind what we do as consumers. It can be described as the drive or arousal that impels consumers to exhibit certain behavioural pattern towards a goal-object. In that sense, it could be conceptualised as having two components, namely: (a) drive or arousal, and (b) goal-object (Sheth *et al.,* 1999). The drive is the inner state of tension that produces actions that supposed to reduce the tension while the goal-object is the something in the external world (e.g. product or service) whose acquisition will reduce the existing tension. As individuals, we all strive to reduce tension by choosing behaviour that we anticipate will fulfil the needs in our lives, and solve the problem of deprivation that we experience. Specifically, needs are the outcomes of the discrepancy between consumers' desired and actual states. Motivation as a topic, and its application to marketing have attracted considerable attention in the relevant literature. One of these which is commonly discussed is the Maslow hierarchy of need (Maslow, 1943). It views human's needs in hierarchical order beginning from physiological needs to Self-actualization as shown in Figure 3.

Figure 3. Hierarchy of needs

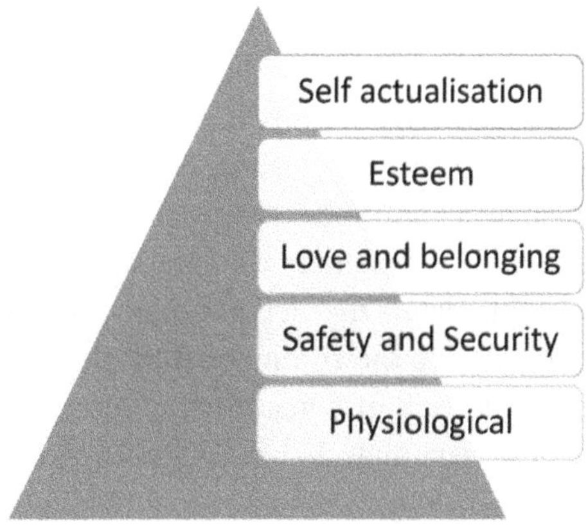

Maslow (1943) postulates that human needs can be arranged hierarchically in such a way that the physiological needs comes first, the safety and security next followed by social needs. The fourth on the hierarchy is the esteemed needs while self-actualization needs come last on top of the pyramid. In this postulation, examples of physiological needs are foods, water, and shelter while needs for protection will be for safety and security. Love and affection needs emphasise need to love and be loved, while esteem needs revolve around self-esteem which is believed leads to self-confidence, attention, recognition, and respect from others. The self-actualisation need is the need for one to become actualised and fulfil his or her potential (Self-fulfilment). The application of this long-standing contribution cut-across both developed and developing nations to a great extent. The application of various marketing stimuli in the marketplace such as sales promotional programmes appeal to different levels of consumer needs on the hierarchy. As a specific example, Varman and Belk's (2012) study shows a clear case of how consumers in India, a developing country, handle their need for esteem. In this study, the young middle class consumers use post-colonial retail shopping malls to disguise their Third Wold realities. This is intriguing. It could be argued that with the constant struggle between the values and priorities typically associated with developing countries and those of developed nations in the consumption pattern of consumers in the former shows that some of the assumptions about consumer behaviour in the developing nations' context could be spurious.

Perception

Perception could be defined as the way people select, organise, and interpret stimuli to make sense of the world around them. As we make various value-oriented consumption decisions, we act on the basis of our perceptions. Interestingly, each consumer perceives in an individual way. The basic perceptual process could be explained as encompassing three steps namely, sensation, organisation, and interpretation.

Sensation involves attending to stimulus in the environment with one or a combination of five senses of seeing, hearing, smelling, touching, and tasting. Seeing a colourful package of a new brand of chocolate on the supermarket shelf could be an example here. *Organisation* entails categorizing by matching the sensed stimulus with similar object categories in ones' memory. For this same example given, organisation in that context could be that the consumer who sees the new chocolate brand associate the colour of the package with the colour of another product, like biscuit which is her favourite. At the stage of i*nterpretation*, the person attaches information to the stimulus, and checks whether it is an object that will be of value to her. As consumers, we regularly encounter numerous and different stimuli but tend to manage them through different means namely selective exposure, selective attention, and selective retention, and selective interpretation. When a consumer uses *Selective exposure,* she chooses what to see, listen to, taste, smell, or touch and avoid others based on the influence of her needs, beliefs, or interest. For instance, consumers that are interested in houses and mortgages are likely to seek out for publications that contain such information by visiting the sellers' websites, exploring the relevant ad pages in newspapers, and magazines and other means specific to this product for the information required to guide their choices. Similarly, consumers who are not interested in automobiles would most likely skip the newspaper or magazine pages that feature marketing communications on this product or decide to change the TV channels during the commercial breaks featuring such particular products.

Selective attention explains the tendency of consumers to screen out certain parts of the information to which they are exposed. Consumers may choose to ignore marketing communication messages, internet pop up ad messages, other marketing communication messages, cold calls, and salesmen visits considered as not of value to the satisfaction of his or her needs. The onus is on the business organisation to ensure that its particular stimuli receive the individual consumer's attention. Consumers can also apply selectivity to the retention of the messages, which is known as *selective retention* (Jobber & Ellis-Chandwick, 2013), and interpretation given to stimuli. Selective interpretation describes the act of consumers interpreting stimuli in conformity with their prior beliefs and attitude. In other words, the quality of information may be altered by the buyer to make them congruent with his own frame of reference, as determined by the amount of information he has already stored (Howard & Sheth, 1968). For instance, some consumers might choose to belief the ad that stresses that a particular carbonated drink refreshes rather than the published warnings concerning the health problems associated with consuming too much of it. Given that the product image is only as good as how consumer perceive it, marketers are concerned with influencing buyers' perception in relation to factors like price, quality and risk (Lancaster & Reynold, 2002).

There are several areas of application of perception in marketing and a good number of these relate to developing countries context. These include perceived risks, quality perception, perceived price, reference price, and perceptual mapping. As an example, the notion of Country of origin (COO) serving as a cue for consumers' decisions has been a valuable topic in international marketing for a long time (Paradapoulos & Heslop, 1993; Kaynak *et al.*, 2000). This relates closely to consumer perception. Yamoah (2005) found that Ghanaian consumers perceive foreign brands of rice to be of better quality than Ghanaian brands; hence they show no strong loyalty to the latter. Accordingly, there is a claim that products that are coming from countries that are less wealthy need be targeted at consumers at low and middle income categories while those coming from developed countries such as Europe and North America will be a good fit for the 'new rich' consumer markets (Kaynak et al, 2000). Moreover, the perception of consumer in developing countries for market offerings could also be affected by patriotism and ethnocentrism (Han, 1988; Shimp & Sharma, 1987; Festervand & Sokoya, 1994). Consumers' tendency to act on this is a function of their perception. In a study of South African consumer perception of drug quality, respondents felt that the medicine supplied free by government under the South Africa's Medicine policy were inferior and viewed with suspicion, and they particularly avoid this so that they would not be labelled second class citizen (Patel *et al.,* 2010). Clearly, the perception of the consumers in developing countries plays a pivotal role in how they weigh a market offering and react to it.

Learning

Learning, a change in behaviour which arises as a result of experience is a backbone of most of human actions. As consumers, our attitudes, preferences, tastes, and behaviours are acquired through learning, which is an indication that learning is very essential to consumption processes. We learn through various experiences of our purchases and consumption activities. Besides, our social interactions at various social settings such as workplaces, schools, religious organisations, family circles, and cultural settings provide experiences which serve as platforms for learning that significantly influences our consumption styles. A relevant example here is the growing knowledge of consumerism among developing countries, which was not the case several decades before now. This observation was noted by Darley and Johnson (1993) in their study which examined consumer attitudes towards consumerism in four developing countries. As consumers in developing countries become aware of products offered from Western countries, they also may form Western expectations (Darley and Johnson, 1993). Similar point is noted by Wabwile (2010) that in spite of the macro-economic disadvantages, developing nations can improve the process of implementing the economic and social rights of children. So, learning is changing the landscape of consumption in developing countries.

The two main perspectives on the discussion of learning are the Behavioural perspective and the Cognitive Perspective. The behavioural theory of learning is of two types which are the classical conditioning and the instrumental conditioning. Classical conditioning is a process by which a neutral stimulus becomes capable of eliciting a response because it was repeatedly paired with a stimulus that naturally causes the response (Peter & Olson, 2010). The Pavlov experiment which showed the dog salivated to an unusual stimulus has been a common platform for explaining this theory. Examples of classical conditioning abound in human lives and marketing settings including in developing nations. For instance, when marketers use a popular musical tune to promote a product or brand repeatedly, this could lead consumers to develop positive attitude towards the products and show preference for it over others during purchase even in the absence of the tune.

Although the instrumental conditioning also involves developing a connection between the stimuli and responses, it is different in that it is based on reinforcing the appropriate response discovered by the learner. Whereas classical conditioning used an existing stimulus-response connection, operant conditioning gives the learner to attempt trial-and-error to get a reward or avoid punishment (Blythe, 1997). An example of instrumental conditioning in marketing is consumers' trial of a particular product and if they find it satisfying, then they repeat the purchase act and possibly become loyal. However, if the purchase leads to unpleasant experience, then the buyer would switch to another brand due to the dissatisfaction.

In contrast to Behavioural theory of learning, the cognitive learning perspective involves the use of all mental activities to solve a problem. It involves consumers actively processing information before making a decision. Some purchase decisions are not made until the consumer explored virtually all basic opportunities such as reading newspaper ads, exploring the internet, asking experienced users of the products, seeking clarifications from salespeople. With the influx of various market offerings into developing countries and the increasing sources of information these days, it is reasonable to expect that consumers in this context would exhibit cognitive learning in relation to their decisions especially for products that are of high value and considerable perceived risks in some cases.

Attitude

Attitude is defined as a learned predisposition to respond in a consistently favourable or unfavourable manner with respect to a given object (Fishbein & Ajzen, 1975). In view of the overall value of doing so, researchers and practitioners have long been interested in the genesis of consumer attitude towards marketing, and how they affect consumers' experiences in the marketplace (Treise, *et al.*, 1994). We have attitudes towards virtually everything. In marketing terms, consumers can develop attitudes to any marketing stimuli. Our attitudes to these stimuli as consumers are closely linked to our beliefs about them. In linking attitude to belief, Armstrong and Kotler (2015) describe belief as a descriptive thought that an individual hold about something. This belief may be based on so many factors which include real experience, faith, and opinion.

It is widely discussed to consider attitudes as having three components which are *cognitive, affective,* and *behavioural*. While the cognitive component part refers to the beliefs an individual holds about an object, the affective component relate to feelings of a positive or negative nature towards an object, and the conative which is also known as behavioural is one's tendency to respond in a certain manner towards an object or activity. Clearly, all these three components of an attitude are important but their relative importance will vary depending on the level of motivation of the consumer in respect of the attitude object in question (Solomon, 2013). Attitudes held about something could be positive, negative or neutral and is quite enduring but due to so many reasons attitude about something may still change. Knowing the massive impact of attitude on purchases, marketers often try to generate favourable attitude for their products through various means such as product modification and Public Relation (PR) activities. Durvasula and Lysonski (2010) found that unlike those of older generation, the attitude of young Chinese toward money has taken a new dimension. They regard money as a source of power and prestige, hence their consumption pattern are likely to mirror those of young people found in the post-industrial societies, seeking fulfilment from consumption of latest products and trends (Durvasula & Lysonski, 2010). Similarly, it is shown that Malaysian consumers in large cities of the country are becoming more brand-conscious and seeking products that could be of good fit for their life-styles. From a different perspective, attitude of people from a particular developing country to specific product or service from another country could be influenced by affinity or animosity towards that country. Wongtada *et al's* (2012) study found that Thai consumers could be prompted to trust the quality of the products from a foreign country, if that country has friendly and likeable people, educational advancement, and business achievements. So, they emphasise that acrimony towards foreigners could make people to make negative judgment about a product. All of these lay credence to the claim of Kimmel (2010) that the power of attitude is especially noticeable in the issue of customer brand loyalty. A study in this direction, Pinar *et al.* (2011) on Consumer-based brand equity (CBBE) in Turkish Banking Industry, gives some useful and remarkable findings. They found significant differences in Consumer-based brand equity (CBBE) for the three bank types which are states, foreign, and private; as consumers' perceived quality and brand loyalty were higher for private than for the other two bank types. Their study shows further that female customers, and customers with higher education and higher income perceived higher quality service for private banks and also felt more loyal to this bank category.

Marketing Toolkit and the Consumer Decisions: Integrative Perspectives

While all of the factors examined so far influence decision making of consumers in developing nations in various ways, the key roles of marketing stimuli orchestrated by firms to get the desired result from consumers are also pivotal to the explanation of consumption in these countries. This is shown as such in Figure 1 above. These influences are submerged within the firms' marketing programmes. Astute firms are continuously preoccupied with the thought of how to effectively manage their marketing mix elements to create value for their target markets.

Factors like brand names, packaging, price, store image, distribution channels, advertising, and sales promotion to mention but few are examples of the marketing jigsaw that make consumers 'tick'. Apart from maintaining that consumers' brand knowledge determines how they think about a brand and responds to different stimuli regarding the brand, O'Cass and Lim (2002) also state that brand awareness, reflected by a consumer's ability to identify a brand under different conditions, is related to the strength of the brand trace in memory and influences how a brand is perceived by consumers when considering which offering to buy. In the study conducted by Kathuria and Gill (2013) on the purchase of branded commodities in India, it was found that brand recall for branded rice and sugar was more among higher income category consumers than as found among their low-income counterpart. Similarly, while exploring differences between genders and consumer behaviour, Yousaf and Huaibin (2013) report that men were more quality conscious than women in Pakistani context. These are interesting findings, especially for the research contexts and could be very helpful for segmentation, targeting, and positioning in developing countries. Moreover, from the general viewpoint, packaging can provide information that enhances cross-selling of other related products. For instance part of the information that the package of a product shows can suggest the use of another product that is related to the one purchased. Davies and Wright (1993) argue that the use of packaging will be one of the criteria for the choice of products for food related items. As consumption pattern in developing countries is not in a static state but keeps evolving, businesses will need to scan the target environment to acquire information that will serve as input to their marketing strategies.

The influx of various brands to developing countries in recent times is considerable. Many global brands now appear in these countries to appeal to the local consumer. In some cases, the products are modified to suit local and cultural needs and *prices* adjusted to match the purchasing power in the region. Clearly, distribution of products is taking diverse sophisticated modes these days, but not all developing nations have fully embraced the digital boom in the world of business due to limited infrastructure. Hence, the scope of e-marketing in such contexts will have to be managed to suit the local infrastructural capability. For instance, Adnan (2014) highlights the challenges of low internet usage in Pakistan which could be due to factors such as high unavailability of the internet, high cost of PCs, and low rate of education for the use of the computer and internet facilities. Nonetheless, he stresses that this trend is now improving and from a broader perspective, online retailing activities in developing countries is expected to improve in the near future.

The influence of marketing communications in consumer decisions is also of great significance. After all, no good product will sell itself, if it is neither known nor communicated to the target market. The role of marketing communications is quite diverse ranging from achieving cognitive to behavioural changes such as building credibility, introducing a new attribute for a new product, changing misunderstanding, changing perception of competitors' offerings, and changing product beliefs (Dahlen *et al.*, 2010). Sales promotional tools like sampling, coupon, discount, and contests influence consumers' product choices. For instance in a study of the efficacy of sales promotions, Gilbert and Jackaria (2002) investigated consumer response to some promotional deals and observed that, though not all consumers were influenced by the four promotional tools to the same degree; their findings indicate that price discounts promotion proved to be statically significant on consumers' reported buying behaviour and buy-one-get-one-free was found to be influential at making consumers to switch brand and stockpile. Gbadamosi (2009) also found that low-income consumers prefer monetary promotion such as buy-one-get-one free to non-monetary such as contest for their purchase of low-involvement products. The significant development in social media for marketing communications has had considerable influence on people's choices. This is especially interesting as it breaks geographical barriers in terms of how consumers both in the developed and developing nations interact and could be reached. Increasing number of global organisations now communicate the benefits of their offerings and brands on Facebook, YouTube, Twitter and many other social media platforms. As an example, evidence shows that online sales in china for the year 2009 were noted to be about $36.6 billion (Forbes, 2010; Adnan, 2014). Indeed, online communications between businesses and their target markets is increasing and opening unprecedented and pronounced opportunities in various developing countries.

CONSUMER DECISION MAKING PROCESS

It is well established that as consumers, we pass through certain stages concerning our purchase actions. These stages, shown in Figure 4 are need recognition, information search, evaluation of alternatives, purchase decision, and post-purchase evaluation.

The first stage in the buying process is need recognition. This is a stage where the consumer feels the discrepancy between his or her ideal state and the actual state. So, the consumer recognizes a need. This need recognized by the consumer can be prompted by either *internal* or *external* stimuli. The greater the disparity between the consumers' ideal state and the desired state, the more likely it is for need recognition to occur. As Ooi *et al* (2011) highlights the problem of slow IT infrastructure and low broadband adoption in Pakistan, Bangladesh, and Malaysia; need recognition for a consumer in this region will develop with the continuous frustration of a need for highly functional internet facilities that could satisfy his daily appetite for these services. It has been suggested that companies can activate need recognition through the use of marketing strategies such as marketing communications by simply reminding consumers of the need or through product innovation (Engel *et al.,* 1995).

Having recognized the need to be satisfied, consumers' attention now turns to searching for information relating to the potential products or services applicable. At this stage, they could use either *internal* or *external search.* Sometimes, a combination of the two may be deemed necessary. In internal search for information, consumers search their memories for recollection of past experiences which might provide adequate information to make the present purchase decision. External sources of information can be in the form of *commercial sources*, *public information*, and *word-of-mouth communications.* Walle and Ryans (1992) describe developing countries as a desert of documentation and laments the inadequacy of information in these countries. While this challenge still remains to an extent, the scale of this problem appears to have reduced with the spread of civilization, thus consumers in these environments are becoming exposed to increasing information sources that could help their consumption decisions.

During the search for information, consumers usually have information regarding numerous competing brands. In deciding which to buy, they rely on their evaluation of the alternatives. At this stage, they often start by reducing the list of all products that can satisfy a given need to a smaller set of acceptable options

Figure 4. Consumer decision making process

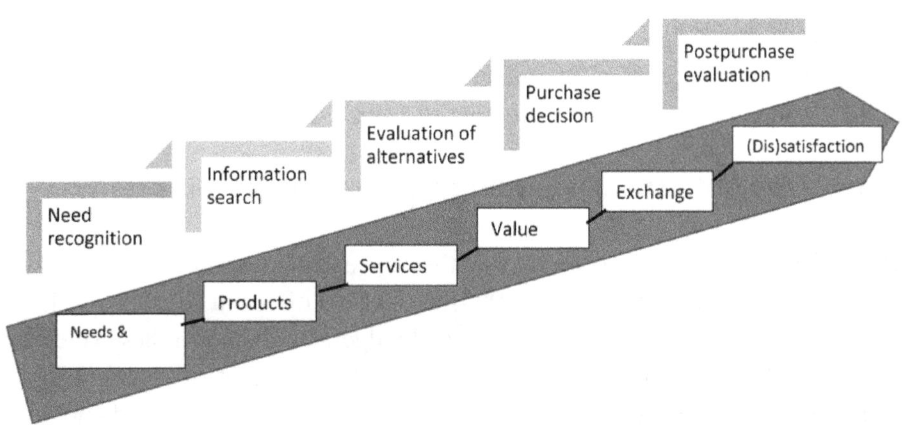

to be considered for decision making known as the *evoked set*. Depending on the product involved, the criteria for the evaluation of alternatives could be technical, economic, social and personal (Jobber and Fahy, 2003). If the firm understands the choice criteria that are mostly preferred by consumers, they can design their stimuli accordingly, and this will save them the hassle of concentrating too much on what consumers will consider as non-salient attributes or criteria. As it is the case in the study of Sun and Collins (2006) in which it was found that Chinese consumers prefer imported fruits, which are labelled as such to domestic produce, Country of origin (COO) of the products could also be a major criteria for evaluation of what to buy.

At the purchase stage, the real exchange of something of value, takes place between the consumer and the organisation. Nonetheless, the consumption process does not end at the purchase stage but extends beyond to the evaluation of the consumption experience. Basically, at the stage of post-purchase evaluation, consumers compare their expectations prior to the purchase with what they think the product has offered. This evaluation could result in satisfaction or dissatisfaction. The feeling of dissatisfaction or unease that consumers sometimes have after the purchase decision is known as *cognitive dissonance*. This theory of Cognitive dissonance, proposed by Festinger (1957) holds that "when an individual holds two or more elements of knowledge that are relevant to each other but inconsistent with one another, a state of discomfort is created. This unpleasant state is referred to as 'dissonance'" (Harmon-Jones and Harmon-Jones, 2008; p.1518). This dissonance can be reduced by seeking constant information, attitude change, and trivializing (Festinger, 1957; Lindsey-Mullikin, 2003). Applying this in the marketing parlance, Lindsey-Mullikin (2003) states that when consumers have unexpected price encounter, they tend to engage in biased and filtered search for information that will support their prior belief. They might search for information about another retailers, and substitute products that is consistent with their state, they could re-evaluate the price in relation to the external reference prices, or trivialize the importance of saving money, shopping around, and receiving a good deal. Although it has been argued that this relates to purchases involving high valued items (Seeney *et al,* 2000), Gbadamosi (2009) shows that this phenomenon is also applicable to low involvement products for low-income consumers. Hence, it is context specific and may as well have different format for some of the developing nations. Given that the post-purchase evaluation stage impacts on future patronage and loyalty for the business, it is necessary to take actions to build the consumers' confidence regarding the choice they have made. This is achievable by engaging in a well-co-ordinated after sales-services. Marketing communication messages that provide positive reinforcement about the purchase decision could also be provided. Above all, businesses should build long term relationship that transcends the current transaction. It is therefore understandable that Donoghue and de Klerk (2009) posit that for consumers to be heard in emerging economies, it is very imperative for the manufacturer, retailers, consumer consultant, and those that handle customer complaints to understand the whole process involved including how consumers perceive justice and satisfaction.

Consumer Involvement: Are Developing Nations Really Different?

Beharrell and Denision (1995) traced the root of the concept of 'involvement' to the early work of Sherrif and Cantril (1947) and Sherrif *et al.* (1965) in the field of social psychology. It was discussed as the relation between ego and an object, and as social judgement theory in these studies respectively. However, it was the publication of Krugman (1965) on advertising that first popularised this concept in marketing. In this context, Krugman argues that by the term involvement 'we do not mean attention, interest, or excitement but the number of conscious "bridging experiences" connections, or personal references per minute that the viewer makes between his own life and the stimulus (p.355)'. So, we can define involvement as the perceived relevance of a purchase to the consumer (Szmigin & Piacentini, 2015). Consumers can be involved with various goal objects which could be product categories, specific brands, advertisements, media types, or decisions.

Whichever is the goal object the consumers' involvement, it could be different in degree. People have high involvement for purchases of some products and low involvement for others. Hence, if consumers are highly involved in certain products they tend to engage in extensive search for information and do a thorough evaluation of alternatives before making a choice. Products like cars and houses, could be good examples of high involvement products. On the other hand, when consumers have low involvement in a market offering they tend to devote very little efforts to search for information and may not even bother to evaluate the alternatives but act on the basis of habit or might use only one or very few criteria to determine the choice. Usually for these products, the risk of getting the wrong choice is very low. Examples of this category of products will include table salt and toothpaste. However, Gbadamosi (2013) contends that the issue of consumer involvement is better viewed differently for different cultural contexts as some products that are considered to be of high involvement in one society might be viewed differently in another context. Using Africa as the platform, he cites cases of some products such as Life insurance products that a western based study (Ratchford, 1987) identifies as a high involvement product but was not considered as important by Nigerian consumers (Yusuf et al., 2009). Similarly, Hinson *et al.* (2009) in their study on the key motivations for bank patronage in Ghana, a developing country note that in spite of high rating given to word of mouth communications in the mainstream marketing literature, Ghanaian consumers considered this as the least important factor in their choices. Logically, it will be misleading to approach the explication of consumer involvement with undue generalisation without looking closely at the context specific of developing nations.

SUMMARY AND CONCLUSION

The growing impact of globalisation in the society, and the plethora of changes in various parts of the world have made the ned to understanding what people buy, how and why their decisions are patterned as exhibited increasingly compelling for marketing decisions. Meanwhile, specifically focussing on exploring the consumption behaviour of consumers in developing nations is significantly beneficial because it focuses our attention on a specific context thereby enriches our understanding of that milieu.

Like every other consumer, the consumer in developing nations is influenced by a myriad of factors which could be categorised as personal, social and cultural factors, and the marketing stimuli. The impacts of these influences on consumption are wide-ranging. The psychological factors (motivation, perception, learning, and attitudes) play prominent roles in the explanation of consumer behaviour. These are in addition to the significant influence of the combination of other personal factors including age and lifecycle, income, occupation, lifestyle, and self-concept; in the consumer decision making process. Similar considerable impact of social and cultural factors covering culture and subculture, social class, family, and reference group is also noteworthy; as well as the marketing stimuli orchestrated by the organisation.

It is a common knowledge that developing nations are characterised with relatively lower development in several areas than the developed nations including politics, economy, and sociocultural issues.

Examples include limited purchasing power, and limited access to current developments in the world of technology. Moreover, while their cultural values and mores are fairly heterogeneous, they present interesting patterns locally and nationally for the explication of their consumption activities. Interestingly, there are some issues on the differences between developing and the developed nations that cannot be dismissed as merely theoretical. These pinpoint the need for stakeholders such as firms interested in this context to not only embrace sound marketing research programmes to enrich their knowledge, but also to do so continuously because of the dynamic nature of these environments. For instance, what is the degree of consumer involvement in the various developing countries for specific products? What is the perception of product quality in relation to whether produced locally or imported in these contexts? What is their view on ethnocentrism and national animosity? What are the dynamics of the family buying decision system in these countries? These and many more related questions are thought-provoking and focussing them is relevant for success in the marketplace these days and will also extend our knowledge of consumer behaviour in the developing nation's context. Interestingly, the trend in the literature seems to suggest that consumers in this region are becoming more informed through various socialisation agents. More and more of these consumers are now having access to the foreign media, internet, and social media in various forms that enrich the society with information from other parts of the world including the developed countries. Hence, the consumption pattern in developing countries is taking different outlook than it used to be. The market structure and taste for products and services are changing; the tension between the local culture and globalisation is becoming more critical and perceptible. Consequently, as marketing plans for targeting developing countries are contextualised to fit the peculiarities of these societies, it is important to see these consumer needs and markets as dynamic that should be approached as such.

AVENUE FOR FUTURE STUDIES

This chapter is conceptual and exploratory in nature and has provided a synthesis of issues pertaining to consumer behaviour in developing nations. While it is enlightening in relation to the scope it is designed to cover, it also suggests avenues for future scholarship efforts on this important topic. It is fair to acknowledge that significant research attention has been done in this areas in the past couple of years as shown in the citations used for this chapter and indeed the entire book. Nonetheless, given the dynamic nature of marketing environment, it is very imperative and will be greatly beneficial if further studies, both conceptual and empirical of different methodological stances, could be conducted to update what we already know on this issue. For example, it will be greatly valuable to know how consumer in developing countries would react to latest developments in the world of business such as new products and services. As shown in this chapter, consumption pattern of consumers in developing countries now mirrors what has been noted in most developed countries to a great extent, ranging from fast moving consumer goods (FMCG) to luxurious products. But, how sustainable is this trend? This is a clear and noteworthy research agenda that could enrich our knowledge. The significant interaction of factors within the classifications of Personal factors, Socio-cultural factors, and Marketing stimuli (See Figure 1) is emphasised in this chapter. However, constantly interrogating the impact of the mix and the pattern in which they trigger specific actions from this consumer segment is a worthy research endeavor for future studies.

REFERENCES

Aaker, J., & Fournier, S. (1995). A Brand as a Character, A Partner and a Person: Three Perspectives on the Question of Brand Personality. *Advances in Consumer Research. Association for Consumer Research (U. S.), 22.*

Aaker, J. L. (1997). Dimensions of Brand Personality. *JMR, Journal of Marketing Research, 34*(August), 347–356. doi:10.2307/3151897

Abbad, M., Abbad, R., & Saleh, M. (2011). Limitations of e-commerce in developing countries: Jordan case. *Education, Business and Society, 4*(4), 280–291. doi:10.1108/17537981111190060

Adcock, D., Bradfield, R., Halborg, A., & Ross, C. (2001). *Marketing Principles and Practice* (4th ed.). Essex, UK: Pearson Education Limited.

Adnan, H. (2014). An Analysis of the Factors Affecting Online Purchasing Behavior of Pakistani Consumers. *International Journal of Marketing Studies, 6*(5), 133–148.

Ahmed, Z. U., Ismail, I., Sadiq, M., Sohail Tabsh, I., & Alias, H. (2010). Malaysian consumers' credit card usage behavior. *Asia Pacific Journal of Marketing and Logistics, 22*(4), 528–544. doi:10.1108/13555851011090547

Akamp, M., & Müller, M. (2013). Supplier management in developing countries. *Journal of Cleaner Production, 56*, 54-62.

Alfadl, A. A., Izham, M., Ibrahim, M., & Hassali, M. A. A. (2013). Scale development on consumer behavior toward counterfeit drugs in a developing country: A quantitative study exploiting the tools of an evolving paradigm. *BMC Public Health, 13*(829), 1–9. PMID:24020730

Al-Khatib, J. A., Stanton, A. D., & Rawwas, M. Y. A. (2005). Ethical segmentation of consumers in developing countries: A comparative analysis. *International Marketing Review, 22*(2), 225–246. doi:10.1108/02651330510593287

Amendolagine, V., Boly, A., Coniglio, N. D., Prota, F, & Seric, A. (2013). FDI and Local Linkages in Developing Countries: Evidence from Sub-Saharan Africa. *World Development, 50*, 41–56.

Armstrong, G., & Kotler, P. (2000). *Marketing: An Introduction* (5th ed.). Upper Saddle River, NJ: Prentice-Hall Inc.

Bianchi, C., & Saleh, A. (2010). On importer trust and commitment: A comparative study of two developing countries. *International Marketing Review, 27*(1), 55–86.

Blythe, J. (2001). Essentials of Marketing (2nd ed.). Pearson Education Limited.

Bonnefond, C., & Clément, M. (2014). Social-Class and Body Weight among Chinese Urban Adults: The Role of the Middle Classes in the Nutrition Transition. *Social Science & Medicine, 112*, 22–29. doi:10.1016/j.socscimed.2014.04.021 PMID:24788113

Boyd, H. W. Jr, Ray, M. L., & Strong, E. C. (1972). An Attitudinal Framework for Advertising Strategy. *Journal of Marketing, 36*(April), 27–33. doi:10.2307/1250974

Boyd, W. B. Jr, Walker, O. C. Jr, Mullins, J., & Larréché, J. C. (2002). 'Marketing Management', A strategic Decision-making Approach', New York: McGraw-Hill. *Higher Education*, 122.

Celsi, R. L., & Olson, J. C. (1988). The role of Involvement in Attention and comprehension Processes. *The Journal of Consumer Research*, *15*(September), 210–224. doi:10.1086/209158

Chari, M. D. R., & Dixit, J. (2014). Business groups and entrepreneurship in developing countries after reforms. *Journal of Business Research*. doi:10.1016/j.jbusres.2014.12.006

Chen, T. B., & Chai, L. T. (2010). Attitude towards the Environment and Green Products: Consumers' Perspective. *Management Science and Engineering*, *4*(2), 27–39.

Cheng, H., & Patwardhan, P. (2010). One region, two worlds? Cultural values in Chinese and Indian TV commercials. *Asian Journal of Communication*, *20*(1), 69–89. doi:10.1080/01292980903440863

Chiu, W., Lee, K., & And Won, D. (2014). Consumer Behavior Toward Counterfeit Sporting Goods. *Social Behavior and Personality*, *42*(4), 615–624. doi:10.2224bp.2014.42.4.615

Coleman, R. P. (1983). The continuing significance of Social class in Marketing. *The Journal of Consumer Research*, *10*(December), 265–280. doi:10.1086/208966

Combes, J., Ebeke, C. H., Etoundi, S. M. N., & Yogo, T. U. (2014). Are Remittances And Foreign Aid A Hedge Against Food Price Shocks In Developing Countries? World Development, 54, 81–98.

Dahlen, M., Lange, F., & Smith, T. (2010). *Marketing Communications: A Brand Narrative Approach*. Chichester, UK: Wiley & Sons Ltd.

Darley, W. K., & Johnson, D. M. (1993). Cross-National Comparison of Consumer Attitudes Towards Consumerism in Four Developing Countries. *The Journal of Consumer Affairs*, *27*(1), 37–54. doi:10.1111/j.1745-6606.1993.tb00736.x

Davies, M. A. P., & Wright, L. T. (1993). The Importance of Labelling Examined in Food Marketing. *European Journal of Marketing*, *28*(2), 57–67. doi:10.1108/03090569410055283

Day, E., Stafford, M. R., & Camacho, A. (1995). Opportunities for involvement research: A scale-development. *Journal of Advertising*, *24*(3), 69–75. doi:10.1080/00913367.1995.10673484

de Mooij, M. (2011). *Consumer Behaviour and Culture* (2nd ed.). London: Sage.

Deming, D. M., Briefel, R. R., & Reidy, K. C. (2014). Infant Feeding Practices and Food Consumption Pattern of Children participating in WIC. *Journal of Nutrition Education and Behavior*, *46*(3), s29–s37. doi:10.1016/j.jneb.2014.02.020 PMID:24809994

Donoghue, S., & de Klerk, H. M. (2009). The right to be heard and to be understood: A conceptual framework for consumer protection in emerging economies. *International Journal of Consumer Studies*, *33*(4), 456–467. doi:10.1111/j.1470-6431.2009.00773.x

Durvasula, S., & Lysonski, S. (2008). A double-edged sword: Understanding vanity across cultures. *Journal of Consumer Marketing*, *25*(4), 230–244. doi:10.1108/07363760810882425

Durvasula, S., & Lysonski, S. (2010). Money, money, money – how do attitudes toward money impact vanity and materialism? – The case of young Chinese consumers. *Journal of Consumer Marketing*, *27*(2), 169–179. doi:10.1108/07363761011027268

East, R. (1997). *Consumer Behaviour: Advances and Applications in Marketing Hertfordshire*. Prentice Hall.

Engel, J. F., Blackwell, R. D., & Miniard, P. W. (1995). *Consumer Behavior* (8th ed.; pp. 364–365). Orlando, FL: The Dryden Press.

Escalas, J. E., & Bettman, J. R. (2005). Self-construal, reference groups and brand meaning. *The Journal of Consumer Research*, *32*(3), 378–389. doi:10.1086/497549

Fatusia, A. O., & Hindin, M. J. (2010). Adolescents and youth in developing countries: Health and development issues in context. *Journal of Adolescence*, *33*(4), 499–508. doi:10.1016/j.adolescence.2010.05.019 PMID:20598362

Festervand, T. A., & Sokoya, S. K. (1994). Consumer Ethnocentrism in a Developing Economy: A Preliminary Investigation. *The International Executive*, *36*(1), 95–105. doi:10.1002/tie.5060360107

Festinger, L. (1957). *A Theory of Cognitive Dissonance*. Stanford, CA: Stanford University Press.

Foxall, G. R., & Goldsmith, R. E. (1994). *Consumer Psychology for marketing*. London: Routledge.

Gbadamosi, A. (2018a). The Changing Landscape of Young Consumer Behaviour. In Young Consumer Behaviour: A Research Companion. Oxfordshire, UK: Routledge.

Gbadamosi, A., Fletcher, K., Emmanuel Stephen, C., & Olutola, I. C. (2018). Consumerism and Consumer Protection: A Focus on Young Consumers. In Young Consumer Behaviour: A Research Companion. Routledge.

Gbadamosi, A. (2018b). The Anatomy of International Students' Acculturation in UK Universities. *Industry and Higher Education*, *32*(2), 129–138. doi:10.1177/0950422218760335

Gbadamosi, A. (2015a). Family Consumption Systems in Africa: A Focus on Children. In S. Nwankwo & K. Ibeh (Eds.), *Routledge Companion to Business in Africa* (pp. 146–159). Oxfordshire, UK: Routledge.

Gbadamosi, A. (2015b). Exploring the Growing Link of Ethnic Entrepreneurship, Markets, and Pentecostalism in London (UK): An Empirical study. *Society and Business Review*, *10*(2), 150–169. doi:10.1108/SBR-11-2014-0053

Gbadamosi, A. (2015c). Brand Personification and Symbolic Consumption among Ethnic Teenage Consumers: An Empirical study. *Journal of Brand Management*, *22*(9), 737–759. doi:10.1057/bm.2015.40

Gbadamosi, A. (2013). Consumer Involvement and Marketing in Africa: Some Directions for Future Research. *International Journal of Consumer Studies*, *37*(2), 234–242. doi:10.1111/j.1470-6431.2012.01096.x

Gbadamosi, A., Hinson, R., Eddy, T. K., & Ingunjiri, I. (2012). Children's attitudinal reactions to TV advertisements: The African experience. *International Journal of Market Research*, *54*(4), 543–566. doi:10.2501/IJMR-54-4-543-566

Gbadamosi, A. (2012a). Exploring Children, Family, and Consumption Behaviour: Empirical Evidence from Nigeria. *Thunderbird International Business Review*, *54*(4), 591–605. doi:10.1002/tie.21486

Gbadamosi, A. (2012b). Acculturation: An Exploratory Study of Clothing Consumption among Black African Women in London (UK). *Journal of Fashion Marketing and Management*, *16*(1), 5–20. doi:10.1108/13612021211203005

Gbadamosi, A. (2009). Cognitive dissonance: The implicit explication in low-income consumers' shopping behaviour for 'low-involvement' grocery products. *International Journal of Retail & Distribution Management*, *37*(12), 1077–1095. doi:10.1108/09590550911005038

Gilbert, D. C., & Jackaria, N. (2002). The efficacy of sales promotions in UK supermarkets: A consumer view. *International Journal of Retail & Distribution Management*, *30*(6), 315–322. doi:10.1108/09590550210429522

Grønhaug, K., & Kleppe, I. A. (2010). The Sociological Basis of Marketing. In Marketing Theory: A Student Text. London: Sage Publication Ltd. doi:10.4135/9781446280096.n7

Guthrie, M., Kim, H., & Jung, J. (2008). The effects of facial image and cosmetic usage on perceptions of brand personality. *Journal of Fashion Marketing and Management*, *12*(2), 164–181. doi:10.1108/13612020810874863

Hamidizadeh, M. R., Alavije, M. R. K., & Rezaee, M. (2014). The Effect of Perceived Business Ethics on Brand Personality Dimensions & Creation of Brand Equity in Developing Countries. *Central European Business Review*, *3*(3), 46–53. doi:10.18267/j.cebr.93

Harmon-Jones, E., & Harmon-Jones, C. (2008). Action-Based Model of Dissonance: A Review of Behavioral, Anterior Cingulate, and Prefrontal Cortical Mechanisms. *Social and Personality Psychology Compass*, *2/3*(3), 1518–1538. doi:10.1111/j.1751-9004.2008.00110.x

Haub, C. (2012). *World Population Data Sheet, 2012: Population Reference Bureau (PRB)*. Retrieved from http://www.prb.org/Publications/Datasheets/2012/world-population-data-sheet.aspx

Hawkins, D. I., Best, R. J., & Coney, K. A. (2001). *Consumer Behavior: Building Marketing Strategy* (8th ed.). New York: McGraw-Hill Company Inc.

Hofstede, G. (1980). *Culture's Consequences: International Differences in Work-Related Values*. Beverley Hills, CA: Sage.

Hofstede, G., & Bond, M. H. (1988). The Confucius connection: From cultural roots to economic growth. *Organizational Dynamics*, *16*(4), 4–21. doi:10.1016/0090-2616(88)90009-5

Hofstede, G. (1984). The cultural relativity of the quality of life concept. *Academy of Management Review*, *9*(3), 389–398. doi:10.5465/amr.1984.4279653

Hooper, B. (2000, December). Globalisation and Resistance in Post-Mao China: The Case of Foreign Consumer Products. *Asian Studies Review*, *24*(4), 439–470. doi:10.1080/10357820008713286

Howard, J. A., & Sheth, J. N. (1968). A Theory of Buyer Behaviour. In H. H. Kassarijan & S. T. Robertson (Eds.), *Perspectives in consumer Bahavior* (pp. 467–468). Glenview, IL: Scot, Foresman & Co.

Howard, J. A., & Sheth, J. N. (1969). *Theory of Buyer Behavior*. New York: Wiley.

IMF. (2018). *Regional Economic Outlook: Sub-Saharan Africa*. Retrieved from https://www.imf.org/en/Publications/REO/SSA/Issues/2018/04/30/sreo0518

Jobber, D., & Fahy, J. (2003). Foundations of Marketing. London: McGraw-Hill Education (UK) Limited.

José, A., & Cobas, J. A. (1987). Ethnic Enclaves and Middleman Minorities: Alternative Strategies of Immigrant Adaptation? *Sociological Perspectives*, *30*(2), 143–161. doi:10.2307/1388996 PMID:12315137

Kassarjian, H. H. (1971). Personality and Consumer Behaviour A review. *JMR, Journal of Marketing Research*, *8*(November), 409–419. doi:10.2307/3150229

Kathuria, L. M., & Gill, P. (2013). Purchase of branded commodity food products: Empirical evidence from India. *British Food Journal*, *115*(9), 1255–1280. doi:10.1108/BFJ-08-2011-0209

Kaynak, E., Kucukemiroglu, O., & Hyder, A. S. (2000). Consumers' country-of-origin (COO) perceptions of imported products in a homogenous less-developed country. *European Journal of Marketing*, *34*(9/10), 1221–1241. doi:10.1108/03090560010342610

Kaynak, E., Kucukemiroglu, O., & Odahasi, Y. (1992). Consumer Complaint Handling in an Advanced Developing Economy: An Empirical Investigation. *Journal of Business Ethics*, *11*(11), 813–829. doi:10.1007/BF00872359

Khraim, H. S. (2010). Cosmetics Buying Behavior of Young UAE Female Consumers: The Influence of Demographics. *Skyline Business Journal*, *6*(1).

Kirkpatrick, E. L., Cowls, M., & Tough, R. (1934). The Life cycle of the Farm Family in Relation to Its Standard of Living (Research Bulletin No. 121). Madison, WI: University of Wisconsin Agricultural Experiment Station.

Kimmel, A. J. (2010). The Psychological Basis of Marketing. In M. J. Baker & M. Saren (Eds.), *Marketing Theory: A Student Text* (pp. 121–144). London: Sage Publication Ltd. doi:10.4135/9781446280096.n6

Koh, L. P., & Lee, T. M. (2012). Sensible consumerism for environmental sustainability. *Biological Conservation*, *151*(1), 3–6. doi:10.1016/j.biocon.2011.10.029

Kotler, P., & Armstrong, G. (2016). *Principles of Marketing* (16th ed.). Essex, UK: Pearson Education Limited, Inc.

Kotler, P., & Armstrong, G. (2018). *Principles of Marketing* (17th ed.). Essex, UK: Pearson Education Limited, Inc.

Kotler, P., Armstrong, G., Saunders, J., & Wong, V. (2001). *Principles of Marketing*. Essex, UK: Pearson Education Limited.

Krugman, H. E. (1965). The Impact of Television Advertising: Learning without Involvement. *Public Opinion Quarterly*, *29*(Fall), 349–356. doi:10.1086/267335

Lamb, C. W. Jr, Hair, J. F. Jr, & McDaniel, C. (1999). *Essentials of Marketing*. South-Western College Publishing.

Lancaster, G., & Reynolds, P. (2002). *Marketing: the one semester introduction*. Oxford, UK: Butterworth-Heinemann.

Lindsey-Mullikin, J. (2003). Beyond Reference Pricing: Understanding Consumers' Encounters with Unexpected prices. *Journal of Product and Brand Management*, *12*(3), 140–153. doi:10.1108/10610420310476906

Lowe, H. D. (1965, Fall). Doing Business in Developing Countries. *Business Horizon*, 25-33.

Lu Wang, C., & Xiong Chen, Z. X. (2004). Consumer ethnocentrism and willingness to buy domestic products in a developing country setting: Testing moderating effects. *Journal of Consumer Marketing*, *21*(6), 391–400. doi:10.1108/07363760410558663

Lutz, R. (1985). *Affective and cognitive Antecedents nof Attitude Toward the Ad: a conceptual Framework. In Psychological Processes and Advertising Effects: Theory, Research and Application* (pp. 45–63). Lawrence Erlbaum.

Lysonski, S., Durvasula, S., & Zotos, Y. (1996). Consumer decision-making styles: A multi-country investigation. *European Journal of Marketing*, *30*(12), 10–12. doi:10.1108/03090569610153273

Madichie, N. O., & Yamoah, F. A. (n.d.). Country Image and Consumer Food Quality Perception: A Developing Country Perspective. *The Consortium Journal, 10*(2), 89-100.

Maslow, A. (1943). A Theory of Human Motivation: The basic needs. *Psychological Review*, *50*(4), 370–396. doi:10.1037/h0054346

Mcleay, F. J., & Oglethorpe, D. (2013). Social marketing, parental purchasing decisions, and unhealthy food in developing countries: A Nigerian typology. *Journal of Consumer Behaviour*, *12*(3), 232–242. doi:10.1002/cb.1426

Meschi, E., & Vivarelli, M. (2009). Trade and Income Inequality in Developing Countries. World Development, 37(2), 287–302.

Monkhouse, L. L., Barnes, B. R., & Stephan, U. (2012). The influence of face and group orientation on the perception of luxury goods A four market study of East Asian consumers. *International Marketing Review*, *29*(6), 647–672. doi:10.1108/02651331211277982

Murphy, P. E., & And Staples, W. A. (1979). A Modernized Family Life Cycle. *The Journal of Consumer Research*, *6*(June), 12–22. doi:10.1086/208744

O'Cass, A., & Lim, K. (2002). Understanding the Younger Singaporean consumers' View of Western and Eastern Brands. *Asia Pacific Journal of Marketing and Logistics*, *14*(4), 54–79. doi:10.1108/13555850210764954

Ooi, K., Sim, J., Yew, K., & Lin, B. (2011). Exploring factors influencing consumers' behavioral intention to adopt broadband in Malaysia. *Computers in Human Behavior*, *27*(3), 1168–1178. doi:10.1016/j.chb.2010.12.011

Penaloza, L. (1994). Atravesando Fronteras/Border Crossings: A Critical Ethnographic Exploration of the Consumer Acculturation of Mexican Immigrants. *Journal of Consumer Research*, *21*(1), 32-54.

Peter, J. P., & Olson, J. C. (2010). Consumer Behavior and Marketing Strategy (9th ed.). Boston: McGraw-Hill Companies, Inc.

Pettigrew, S., Jongenelis, M., Chapman, K., & Miller, C. (2015). Factors Influencing the Children's Consumption of Soft drinks. *Appetite, 91*(August), 393–398. doi:10.1016/j.appet.2015.04.080 PMID:25953597

Pinar, M., Girard, T., & And Eser, Z. (2011). An Exploratory Study Of Consumer-Based Brand Equity In Turkish Banking' Industry. *Services Marketing Quarterly, 32*(4), 282–301. doi:10.1080/15332969.2011.606760

Rahman, S., & Azhar, S. (2011). Xpressions of generation Y: Perceptions of the mobile phone service industry in Pakistan. *Asia Pacific Journal of Marketing and Logistics, 23*(1), 91–107. doi:10.1108/13555851111100012

Rajarathinam, V. (2013). Internet Banking Users' Competence and its Influence On Usage Satisfaction – A View from India. *Journal of Internet Banking and Commerce, 18*(3), 1–13.

Ramanathan, S., & McGill, A. L. (2007). Consuming with others: Social influences on moment-to-moment and retrospective evaluations of an experience. *The Journal of Consumer Research, 34*(4), 506–524. doi:10.1086/520074

RAND. (2018). *Developing Countries*. Retrieved from https://www.rand.org/topics/developing-countries.html

Rand, J., & Tarp, F. (2002). Business Cycles in Developing Countries: Are They Different? *World Development, 30*(12), 2071–2088. doi:10.1016/S0305-750X(02)00124-9

Roberts, M., & Pettigrew, S. (2013). Psychological Influences on Children's Food Consumption. *Psychology and Marketing, 30*(2), 103–120. doi:10.1002/mar.20591

Roper, S., & Shah, B. (2007). Vulnerable consumers: The social impact of branding on children. *Equal Opportunities International, 26*(7), 712–728. doi:10.1108/02610150710822339

Rossi, N. (1989). Dependency Rates and Private Savings Behavior in Developing Countries. *International Monetary Fund, 36*(1), 166-181.

Rossiter, J.R., Percey, L., & Donovan, R.J. (1991, October). A better advertising planning grid. *Journal of Advertising Research*, 11-21.

Rothschild, M. L. (1979). Advertising Strategies for High and Low Involvement situations. In J. C. Maloney & B. Silverman (Eds.), *Attitude Research Plays for High Stakes* (pp. 74–93). Chicago: American Marketing Association.

Saleem, M. A., Eagle, L., & Low, D. (2018). Market segmentation based on eco-socially conscious consumers' behavioral intentions: Evidence from an emerging economy. *Journal of Cleaner Production, 193*, 14–27. doi:10.1016/j.jclepro.2018.05.067

Schiffman, L. G., & Kanuk, L. S. (2004). *Consumer Behavior* (8th ed.). Pearson Education, Inc.

Schiffman, L. G., Kanuk, L. S., & Hansen, H. (2012). *Consumer Behavior: A European Outlook* (2nd ed.). Essex, UK: Pearson Education Limited.

Sheth, J. N. (1967). A Review of Buyer Behavior. *Management Science, 13*(12), 718–786. doi:10.1287/mnsc.13.12.B718

Sheth, J. N., Mittal, B., & Newman, B. I. (1999). *Customer Behaviour. In Consumer Behaviour and Beyond* (pp. 343–355). Orlando: The Dryden Press.

Skowron, L., & Kristensen, K. (2012). The impact of the recent banking crisis on customer loyalty in the banking sector. *The TQM Journal, 24*(6), 480–497. doi:10.1108/17542731211270052

Solomon, M., Bamossy, G., Askegaard, S., & Hogg, M. (2013). *Consumer behaviour: A European perspective* (5th ed.). Harlow: Prentice Hall.

Solomon, M. R. (2013). *'Consumer Behaviour: Buying, Having, and Being* (10th ed.). Harlow: Pearson Education Ltd.

Srinivasan, S. S., & Till, B. D. (2002). Evaluation of search, experience and credence attributes: Role of brand name and product trial. *Journal of Product and Brand Management, 11*(7), 417–431. doi:10.1108/10610420210451616

Statt, D. A. (1997). *Understanding the consumer: A psychological Approach.* London: Macmillan Press Ltd. doi:10.1007/978-1-349-25438-5

Sun, X., & Collins, R. (2006). Chinese consumer response to imported fruit: intended uses and their effect on perceived quality. *International Journal of Consumer Studies, 30*(2), 179–188.

Sweeney, J. C., Hausknecht, D., & Soutar, G. N. (2000). Cognitive Dissonance after Purchase: A Multidimensional Scale. *Psychology and Marketing, 17*(5), 369–385. doi:10.1002/(SICI)1520-6793(200005)17:5<369::AID-MAR1>3.0.CO;2-G

Szmigin, I., & Piacentini, M. (2015). *Consumer Behaviour.* Oxford, UK: Oxford University Press.

The Balance. (2018). *What is a Developing Country? Developing Countries classification.* Retrieved from https://www.thebalance.com/what-is-a-developing-country-1978982

Treise, D., Weigold, M. F., Conna, J., & Garrison, H. (1994). Ethics in advertising: Ideological correlates of consumer perception. *Journal of Advertising, 23*(3), 59–69. doi:10.1080/00913367.1994.10673450

van der Boor, P., Oliveira, P., & Veloso, F. (2014). Users as innovators in developing countries: The global sources of innovation and diffusion in mobile banking services. *Research Policy, 43*(9), 1594–1607. doi:10.1016/j.respol.2014.05.003

Vaughn, R. (1980). How Advertising Works: A planning model. *Journal of Advertising Research, 20*(5), 27–33.

Vaughn, R. (1986, February). How Advertising Works: a planning model revisited. *Journal of Advertising Research*, 57-66.

Wabwile, M. (2010). Implementing the Social and Economic Rights of Children in Developing Countries: The place of International Assistance and Cooperation. *International Journal of Children's Rights, 18*(3), 355–385. doi:10.1163/157181810X494308

Walle, A. H., & Ryans, J. K. (1992). SIA, Developing Countries and Marketing Opportunities: A Primer. *Management Decision*, *30*(7), 25–29. doi:10.1108/00251749210019405

Wells, W., & Gubar, G. (1966). Life Cycle concept in Marketing Research. *JMR, Journal of Marketing Research*, *3*(4), 355–363. doi:10.2307/3149851

Wicker, A. W. (1969). Attitude vs Actions: The relationship of verbal and overt behavioural responses to attitude objects. *The Journal of Social Issues*, *25*, 41–78.

East, R. (1997). *Consumer Behaviour: Advances and Applications in Marketing*. Hertfordshire: Prentice Hall.

Wilke, W. L., & Dickson, P. R. (1991). Shopping for Appliances: consumers' Strategies and pattern for Information search. In Perspectives in Consumer Behaviour (4th ed.). Englewood Cliffs, NJ: Academic Press.

Wilkues, R. E. (1995). Household Life-Cycle Stages Transitions And Product Expenditures. *The Journal of Consumer Research*, *22*(1), 27–42. doi:10.1086/209433

Wongtada, N., Rice, G., & Bandyopadhyay, S. K. (2012). Developing and Validating AFFINITY: A New Scale to Measure Consumer Affinity toward Foreign Countries. *Journal of International Consumer Marketing*, *24*(3), 147–167. doi:10.1080/08961530.2012.682037

World Bank. (2015). Global Economic Prospect, Middle East and North Africa. World Bank.

WTO. (2018). *Special and differential treatment provisions.* World Trade Organisation. Retrieved from https://www.wto.org/english/tratop_e/devel_e/dev_special_differential_provisions_e.htm#legal_provisions

Yamoah, F. A. (2005). Role and Impact of Product-Country Image on Rice Marketing: A Developing Country Perspective. *The Journal of American Academy of Business, 7*(2), 265-276.

Yousaf, S., & Huaibin, L. (2013). Profiling Consumer Behavior in the Context of Involvement Level and Demographic Factors: Evidence of Within-Country Differences From a Developing Economy. *Journal of Global Marketing*, *26*(1), 1–17. doi:10.1080/08911762.2013.779404

Zaichkowsky, J. L. (1985). Measuring the Involvement Construct. *The Journal of Consumer Research*, *12*(3), 341–352. doi:10.1086/208520

Zaichkowsky, J. L. (1986). Conceptualizing Involvement. *Journal of Advertising*, *15*(2), 4–14. doi:10.1080/00913367.1986.10672999

KEY TERMS AND DEFINITIONS

Attitude: A person's learned consistent evaluation of people or something such as an object, an idea, or issues.

Culture: The set of beliefs, attitudes, and behavior pattern shared by members of a particular society and passed on from one generation to the next.

Marketing Stimuli: Factors orchestrated by marketers that influence people's consumption choices.

Personal Factors: Those factors that relate to the consumer as an individual and influence his or her consumption choices.

Social Factors: Factors that relate to the consumer's interaction with other people and influence his or her consumption choices.

Chapter 2
Measuring Consumer Behavior Using Neuroscience Methods in Marketing

Cynthia A. Bulley
Central University, Ghana

Veronica Adu Brobbey
University of Education – Winneba, Ghana

Esther O. Duodu
ABL Intel Consulting Ltd., Ghana

ABSTRACT

Neuromarketing is providing the leverage for marketers to delve into consumers' subconscious minds to determine behavior. Marketers, economists, and other consumer-related disciplines are looking to science to accurately determine consumer behavior. The purpose of this chapter is to provide insight into a burgeoning field of study, neuromarketing, documenting various research studies and applications of mechanisms in determining brain activities and other uses of science to benefit marketing research. Data for the study is derived from impartial cross-referencing of conceptual and empirical articles published in major journals. The application of neuroimaging technique in research have provided marketers with concrete evidence of brain activation that signal increased activities during stimulation. Further, the implication and causes of concern in using neuroscience methods in marketing are highlighted. Developing country studies on neuromarketing are examined to determine its application and use as a marketing research tool.

INTRODUCTION

The medical environment and its numerous usage of imaging have found its way in marketing. Medical imaging basically provides a visual scan (still pictures) or video of any part of the body for analysis. It noninvasively reproduces image of the internal aspects of the human body. Moreover, this aspect of science research applied in neuroscience, behavioural economics, human psychology (to mentions a few)

DOI: 10.4018/978-1-5225-7906-9.ch002

have brought to the fore methods that marketers can explore to arrive at reliable conclusions on human behaviour and reactions to products and services. Marketers have to deal with consumer behaviour especially the decision making process and activities of the human brain.

Neuromarketing is a discipline that applies a purely scientific process to measure and analyse consumer brain activity to determine decisions and choices made in buying products and services. It is a synthesis of neuroimaging techniques in neuroscience and marketing. The transdisciplinary nature of neuroscience provides a platform that allows marketers to better understand consumer decision making process and personal choices. Marketers are making use of this scientific process in monitoring and analysing consumers. Clinical information and observations about the functions and movements in the brain facilitates explanation of the human mind and thought process to explain consumer behaviour. It is all about reactions of neurons in our brain and other parts of our human body. Neurons are cells that form part of the human nervous system whose chief function is to send messages to and from the brain. Marketing stimuli is transferred through or along the neurons by means of electrical impulse.

The nervous system is made up of the brain, spinal cord and other peripheral nerves. These are nerve cells named neurons and other supporting cells called glial cells. The neurons are nerve cells that act in unison in transferring electrical and chemical stimuli in or to the brain. Neurons are complex cells that are the pathway for transmitting information in the nervous system. There are three main neurons – the sensory neurons, the motor neurons and interneurons. The sensory neurons are attached to receptors that detect and respond to various stimuli internally and externally. The receptors are very sensitive to stimuli and other internal and external changes. For instance, variations in sound, light, and other chemical and mechanical stimuli affect hearing, vision, touch, skin responses (pain), smell and taste. The motor neurons are the chief controllers of human muscles and therefore are responsible for movements and behaviour (even speech). The interneurons are cells that particularly populate the human brain (almost 80%). Interneurons are responsible for the highest functions of the brain and support optimal processing of information of any stimulus (Rawlins, 2005; Bear, Connors & Paradisco, 1996). This preamble provides a basic understanding of activities and functions of aspects of neuroscience that play a role in consumer research and methods applied in marketing studies.

Consumer behaviour is embodied in the “dynamic interaction of affect and cognition, behaviour and the environment” that influences human decisions and choice (Schiffman & Kanuk, 2007). These reactions and interactions are a function of the brain (neurons in the nervous system) responding to internal and external stimuli. Marketing researchers are now looking to clinical information and measurement of brain functions and its mechanisms to explain behaviour and decision making. Although the method involves imaging and scanning equipment that may hinder frequent usage, the rise of neuromarketing firms like Neurofocus, Brighthouse, EmSense, SalesBrain, Sands Research, Beckley Cali, Mindlab International and Neurosense (now Nielson) are contributing to its popularity as a more reliable and concise technique of data collection especially on consumer behaviour. There is a platform online - Neuromarketing Business Association - that encourages research, research firms and others interested in this discipline to network.

Research interest in neuromarketing has grown exponentially and the potential application of such scientific methods in measuring consumer behaviour is a positive and necessary endeavour. Neuromarketing as a field has the potential of showing consumer behaviour that can be tapped in advertising, target/profit branding, and consumer influencing communications. The purpose of this chapter is to provide insight and document various research studies and application of mechanisms in determining brain activities and other uses of science to benefit consumer research. Selected studies are analysed accordingly to highlight the current state of research and areas of further possible inquiry to bring to the fore this burgeoning method. The usage of such methods in developing countries particularly in Africa is a question that needs to be examined to throw more light on the discipline and increase its future deployment as a method of choice in consumer studies.

The chapter is organised in five sections. This section introduces the chapter focusing on a general overview of neuromarketing. The background information follows examining related works that provide the main foundation for the review (under quest for in-depth literature). It includes other subtopics relevant to building a body of knowledge on neuromarketing. An analytical section that reviews tools and techniques used in neuromarketing research follows with relevant findings, discussions and recommendations. It takes a look at what is going on in developing countries in terms of brain imaging techniques and consumer research. Furthermore, ethical issues and its implications emerging from neuromarketing research are evaluated. Finally, future research directions and conclusion end the chapter.

THE NEUROMARKETING DISCIPLINE

Until recently, the discipline and study of consumer behaviour using neurons under neuromarketing has been conceptually under studied. The word neuromarketing is derived from neurology or neuroscience and marketing. Martinez (2011) attributes neuromarketing to the integration and usage of aspects of three disciplines – neurology, psychology and marketing in the processes and procedures of the discipline. Neuromarketing taps into neuroscientific methods of examining changes in the brain to understand consumer reaction and decision process. This view is shared by many in the field of marketing, psychology, economics and science (Fugate, 2007; Rawlins, 2005; DeFelipe and Farinas, 1992). Defining neuromarketing basically delineates the effect of neuroscience imaging on marketing subjects that is, consumers. It seeks to map out brain processes in response to stimulus, choices and decisions made thereof. Calvert and Brammer's (2012) definition of neuromarketing dwell on applying neuroscientific techniques to measure *unconscious* reactions and responses of consumers to marketing stimuli. It measures consumers' actual feelings.

Neuromarketing mainly focuses on the complex interactions in the brain. Neuroscience and marketing in this sense share a common concern that is, finding out how consumers react to stimulus and decisions made in this regard. It measures consumer 'sensorimotor', cognitive and affective responses to marketing stimuli. Hence marketing researchers have defined neuromarketing in simple terms as the research activity that uses methods, techniques and tools from the field of neuroscience (Genco et al., 2013).

The word neuromarketing is attributed to Smidts, a professor of marketing research at the Rotterdam School of Management, Erasmus University. Although the works of Plato, Adam Smith, Rene Descartes, Engel, Kollart and Blackwell focused on rational thinking and decision making, laying foundation for the development of science to address everyday issues (Glimcher, 2003; Fugate, 2007). These philosophers examined the human mind, human behaviour and rational and emotional thinking (the "economic man" – Adam Smith). Further, mental activities in relation to the nervous system (Rene Descartes) and thought process were used to articulate deeper subconscious rational thinking. The relevance of these studies promoted scientific inquiry into neuroscience. Significant progress was made in the area of structure and functioning of the brain in relation to marketing efforts. However, neuroeconomics began the scientific inquest followed by neuropsychology, then neuromarketing and neuroethics. The implication of neuromarketing is that there will be a balance between science and marketing in seeking and determining consumer subconscious motives. The scientific tools and techniques ensure a bias free and accurate measurement of human subconscious thinking and reasoning. Marketers can now reliably and empirically measure, observe and predict behaviour. In other words, quantitative data can be derived from constructing inferential models from consumer behaviour outcomes and observations using neuroscience techniques. Neuromarketing research is capable of determining emotional and rational thoughts which in fact, depend on each other in the human mind (brain).

In neuromarketing studies, rational activity in the human brain (*Neocortex*) and the unconscious mind can be measured, evaluated and used to reveal human decisions. For instance, emotional impulse decisions (especially impulse buying decisions) can be activated because humans have three distinctive brain functioning system (Zarã & Tuţã, 2013; Renvoisé & Morin, 2005). The *Neocortex*, the *Limbic system* and the *Reptilian* brain. The *Neocortex* also known as *Neopallium* is typically peculiar to humans and it enables the most complex mental activity. It is the main rational and thinking aspect of the brain. The *Neocortex* has four other subdivisions – the *frontal*, the *parietal*, *occipital* and *temporal lobes.* The *frontal lobe* is located at the front and upper portions of the brain hemisphere (cortex), where decision making and other high level human analysis occur. It enables reasoning, judgement and language among others. The *parietal lobe* is at the upper but back portion of the brain. It responds to sensory stimuli (taste, touch, feelings – temperature) and may be an important area for neuromarketing research (Swenson, 2006). The *occipital lobes* can be found at the bottom back portion of the cortex and it controls sight (the eyes and seeing). It is responsible for rapidly processing visual data from the eyes. The *temporal lobe* is for hearing and listening. It processes auditory information. The *temporal lobe* is for processing what the ears absorb. It processes and recognises auditory information. The lobe is an integral part of the cortex that is, key to comprehension and understanding. It is associated with memory and speech (Renvoisé & Morin, 2005).

The *Limbic system* is the middle inner surface portion of the brain. It is made up of interconnected structures (lobes, cortex, nuclei and others). It adjusts autonomic responses especially in relation to internal and emotional aspect of behaviour. It is the emotional brain (for arousal, motivation and reinforcement behaviour) and performs other important functions linked to learning and memory. The *reptilian brain* is the upper brain stem and it is made up mainly of the fore brain. It is the central system that controls the autonomic nervous system and regulates the body's total functioning. Also known as the *R-complex,* it controls breathing, the heart rate, body temperature and the total balance of the human being. The *reptilian brain* is in charge of reflexive and instinctive behaviours therefore decision – making processing and rational decisions are processed in that part of the brain. Hence consumer behaviour and purchase decision processing and other impulses are the fundamental function of the brain.

The use of neuroscience to find out the actual insights and brain functions of consumers provide marketers with a better tool to predict subsequent buyer behaviour. Besides, this has been discussed at length by neuroscience, neuroeconomics, and neuromarketing researchers like Fugate (2007), and McDowell and Dick (2013). The argument that has been propounded is the view that consumers as rational human beings will seek their interest and therefore decisions made would follow rational thinking that examines all other available options in any situation. However, this kind of classic economics premise is not usually followed by consumers in critical decisions. Rather emotional intuitions overtake or sometimes are put aside in consumer decisions. Pop and Lorga (2012) and Genco et al. (2013) have on these grounds concluded that research point to 'strong emotions' overtaking rational decisions made by consumers. The researchers compare and contrast the *intuitive consumer model* against the *rational consumer model* to emphasize on emotions playing a major role in decisions and behaviour. The intuitive consumer model emphasizes the use of "emotions, habits and experience" in consumer decision – making and choice rather than using rational logical evaluations. The rational consumer model places emphasis on rational thinking which drives decision – making, and product and service decisions instead of intuition (Du Plessis, 2011; Damasio & Bechara, 2005). The two models play a critical role in decision making but it is the symbiosis relationship that drives choices and decisions that is important to consumer researchers. Damasio (2006) and Damasio and Bechara (2011) have argued that human rational decisions actually rely on prior processing of intuitions and emotions. This is a fact that drives marketing researchers to want to know more about the brain and its functions to understand consumer perceptions, behaviour and decision – making.

Neuromarketing encourages researchers to conduct studies on consumer behaviour that are transparent to increase the 'generalisablity' of findings and understanding of consumer decisions. The sizable research and literature on neuromarketing creates a fundamental foundation for the full application of scientific methods in marketing research.

THE QUEST FOR MORE IN-DEPTH LITERATURE ON NEUROMARKETING

Marketing research methods have come a long way and any addition that would deliver concise and more accurate understanding of consumer behaviour should receive positive acclaim. The extensive research in the field of neuromarketing indicate that the scientific research method is going to expand the scope of the traditional consumer behaviour studies (Mucha, 2005; Lee, Broderick & Chamberlain, 2007; Lindstrom, 2009). Neuromarketing research avoids rational interpretation and applies scientifically derived results of the subconscious areas of the brain to explain consumer behaviour, decision making and choice. This makes the discipline a more precise research method for understanding human behaviour. The acceptance of neuromarketing methods requires extensive conceptual and theoretical analysis of research in the field. Further empirical company specific research using neuromarketing tools and techniques should be replicated to affirm its acceptance and usage. Empirical studies where specific cases were researched by neuromarketing companies are geared toward predicting consumer reactions and behaviour with specific products. These studies focus on particular methods and tools. Nielsen's Neuro-Focus Company uses a specially developed EEG device and other eye and skin monitoring tools in their studies. Other research firms use different metrics to measure brain and skin changes to determine consumer response to stimuli and subsequent choices made. The practical application of these methods and techniques will *revolutionalize* the field and promote its acceptance. The use of imaging techniques provides marketers with an alternative research method that can lead to further mind targeting communications. The question that needs to be addressed is that – is there adequate literature to move neuromarketing to the next level of development? There is the need for more literature especially on interpreting and reading results of neuromarketing tests.

Some sceptics like Booth and Freeman (2014) have challenged the interpretations of the brain imaging scans and reports on the grounds that it produces *abstract* reports that can only tell one brand from the other. Their argument is that external cues (marketing related) and product variables influence decisions. The researchers conclude that individual behavioural mapping based on psychological responses can be more beneficial, and cognitive responses can produce better results. The study on consumer *choice processes* examine the *conceptual-sensory interaction in a marketing place*. Further it goes to prove that individual cognitive responses provide the necessary cues for preferences and choice making. For instance, information provided to the consumer is analysed and the resulting decisions made reflects the interaction between that consumer and any cues (advertisements) they come into contact with during the process.

There is a dearth of research papers on different aspects of neuromarketing and the use of neuroimaging technique. Although such literature provides detailed understanding of the underlying concepts and processes, there is the need for more literature on the subject. This calls for more empirical studies that creatively use the scientific process, concepts and framework to make its application more beneficial for better interpretation and advancement of the field and method. Theorising in neuromarketing is largely a matter of relying on neuroscience, social psychology, behavioural and biological science, economics and marketing. It is important to note that neuroscience research seeks to develop scientific knowledge to a higher level to simplify complex problems. This means complex issues can be defined, explained, and used in resolving future problems. There is the need for in-depth literature to add to the current array of literature to facilitate development of models and strategies for the discipline.

REVIEW OF STUDIES IN THE FIELD OF NEUROMARKETING

This review outlines the direction of prior research to stimulate new and innovative ideas that will promote neuromarketing studies. The section pulls together disparate research studies to present some of the articles on the current state of knowledge in the field. The research studies were selected from well-known databases such as "EBSCO host", "emerald", "science direct" "WileyInterscience" and Google scholar. For the purpose of this evaluation, publications between 1995 and 2015 were reviewed. The impartial cross – referencing of conceptual and empirical articles published in major journals were targeted and used. The articles selected were essentially based on its academic background and scientific grounding. It is important to emphasize that the journal articles chosen were not limited solely to one particular field but rather an interdisciplinary approach that is directed at marketing research was the focus. The review regrouped the articles into two based on the methodology applied. Literature review studies and empirical papers indicating the actual tools applied are examined. The major conclusion and authors (as shown in Table 1) summarises important objectives, research methods and primary areas emphasized in these articles. The publications also addressed other objectives. This is a semi-systematic inquiry and the main objective is to provide information.

In all the literature review articles, information provision discourse is paramount. This is interspersed with definitions, history, brain structure and attributes of neuromarketing and its relevance to consumer behaviour studies. Furthermore, imaging techniques and tools are emphasized in the research papers (Perrachione & Perachione, 2008; Lee et al. (2007; Fugate, 2007; Pechman et al., 2005). Paramount in all the articles is the description and purpose of the field. In all the articles reviewed, neuromarketing has been described as a scientific field under neuroscience (Perrachione & Perrachione, 2008), as a research method in marketing (Fugate, 2007; Fisher, Chin & Klitzman, 2010; Wilson et al., 2008), as part of psychology under consumer behaviour and perception (Butler, 2008; Pechmann et al., 2005), as part of economics (Hubert & Kenning, 2008) and as a new academic field (Garcia & Saad, 2008; Godwin, Kothai & Saranya, 2012).

Wilson et al. (2008), da Rocha et al (2013) and Burgos – Campero et al. (2013) provide a brief report on neuromarketing methodologies that comprehensively provide a gist of tools that can be used in the field. The electro encephalography (EEG), functional magnetic resonance imaging (fMRI) and other

Table 1. Synopsis of neuromarketing publications

AUTHOR/YEAR/ Journal COUNTRY	TITLE/MAJOR OBJECTIVES/TYPE OF PAPER	METHODOLOGY APPLIED	MAJOR CONCLUSION
Perrachione, T. K. and Perrachione, J. R. (2008). Journal of Consumer Behaviour Vol. 7 no. 4/5 pp. 303-318. DOI: 10.1002/cb.253 USA	**Topic:** "Brains and Brands: Developing mutually Informative Research in Neuroscience and Marketing". **Objective**:"to develop a synthesis of the theoretical interests of marketing and neurology to bring out an educative study" **Type**: Research paper.	Literature Review	1. The need for collaboration between neuroscientists and marketers to 'align" this aspect of researching emphasised 2. All marketing mix variables were on the whole more likely to have correlations with neuroscience methods but calls for a strong scientific mindset.
Lee, N.; Broderick, A. J. and Chamberlain (2007). International Journal of Psychophysiology (Science Direct) Vol. 63 pp 199 – 204. DOI: 10.1016/j.ijpsycho.2006.03.007. UK	**Topic:** What is Neuromarketing: Discussion and Agenda for Reseearch. **Objective**: to provide knowledge of neuromarketing to go beyond application. **Type**: Research Paper	Literature Review	Issues of trust, pricing and negotiation should be given more attention in neuromarketing studies
Fugate, D. L. (2007). Journal of Consumer Marketing, Vol. 24 (7) pp. 385–394. http:dx.doi.org/10.1108/073637607/0834807 accessed on June 17, 2015.	Topic: Neuromarketing: A layman's Look at neuroscience and its potential Application to Marketing Practice. **Objective:** Examine the origins of neuromarketing, its processes in simple terms and documenting findings for future research **Type:** General Review	Content Analysis of Literature	There is the need to operationalise neuromarketing experiments, and construct models to measure and determine brain activities' overall contribution to decision making.

imaging applications are presented describing the processes involved and the sample size that can be utilized in such research. The studies agree that small samples are necessary due to the process and the procedure of the neuroscience research method. Reports by Morin (2011), Lang, Forson and Rothschild were used in majority of these studies to illustrate the use of EEG and fMRI tests especially. Some of these tests indicate that despite millions invested in brand emphasis and all advertising campaigns, research methods applied do not present actual reports of emotions and the deciding factor when consumers are exposed to promotions. Hence neuromarketing research has come to bridge that gap to provide in-depth analysis of consumer unconscious reactions.

Various case specific studies done by Gladwell (2005), McClure, Li, Tomlin, Cupert, Montague and Montague (2004), Lindstom (2010) and others about the subconscious image effects on consumers provide the base studies for neuromarketing. Consumer preferences for Coca Cola and Pepsi and the effects of advertisements on the subconscious mind research was a major step forward in the advancement of the field (McClure, Li, Tomlin, Cupert, Montague and Montague, 2004; Gladwell, 2005). Lindstom's (2010) research on the effect of cigarette packs advertisements on consumers, and the media time slots survey horn in the use of neuromarketing research. This study provided more specific responses based on images from particular areas of the brain to determine positive and negative reactions, emotional effect and, final choice and purchase decisions. Research companies and industry empirical studies outnumber academic studies (per the review conducted). This can be attributed to the elementary stages of the method and the cost involved in conducing such survey.

In terms of theorising, consumer behaviour theories are the main driving force for quantitative studies. The synopsis of journal articles delves into areas that touch on various theories. Leslie (2005) and others use cognitive and affective constructs of consumer behaviour which is rooted in psychology. Garcia and Saad (2008) dwell on *evolution* and *Darwinising* the neuromarketing methods. Resource – based theories featured in Burgos – Campero (2013) studies. Da Rocha et al (2013) focus on consumer satisfaction while Wilson and Gaines (2008) point out the ethical issues and challenges that arises from using neuroimaging methods. Concepts have been explored by all the studies examined (Table 1), and the issue of trust, cost, sampling and techniques, and tools to apply were major huddles that must be addressed in conducting research using neuromarketing methods. Literature reviews outnumber empirical studies (reflected in the analysed articles), and researchers such as Fugate (2007) have advocated that theoretical and qualitative studies should be forthcoming since that would highlight the field and encourage model development by marketers.

The first attempt at model development was initially muted by Butler (2008). He integrated views from academic studies and applied company specific empirical research and reporting to derive his *model of Co-Production in Organisational Cognitive Neuroscience.* The model indicates the interconnection of scientific research, knowledge and practice and the different perceptions generated in the marketing field. It brings together the various groups who have vested interest in the methodology, and use neuroscience knowledge. Waldman (2013) and Butler (2008) point to a strategic fit between academic research (scientific rigorous research), practical commercial agencies application and the clients' satisfaction with the reporting. And emphasis is placed on the scientific rigorous process done under ethical considerations. The model has been criticised for various reasons. Edwards (2013) pinpoints how in reality the *mental processes* that come into contact with stimulus to result in consumer behaviour are dynamic processes hence would be difficult to determine. This may cause over simplification of the reporting of the findings. Lindebaum and Zunndel (2013) and Becker (2013) in their critique concluded that neuroscience and neuromarketing may not be able to stand on its own as a field *theoretically or empirically* but more research needs to be done. Butler (2013) further re-examined the model and added that a behavioural model alongside the *Organisational Cognitive Neuroscience* would be the answer to the criticisms.

Two researchers whose systematic reviews proposed frameworks for brand psychology and preferences are Schimtt (2012) and Plassman, Ramsoy and Milosavljevic (2012). Plassman et al. (2012) used consumer decision – making construct developed by psychologist (Wirtz, Kruger, Scallon & Diener, 2003; Rangel, Camerer & Montague, 2008; Kahneman & Snell, 1992) to arrive at their *value signals important for brand decisions* construct. The construct in four stages indicates the components needed to form brand preference. The stages are a) *representation and attention*, b) *prediction of value*, c) *experience the value* and d) *remember the value and learn* respectively. The first stage tackles the information consumers are exposed to, and the specific brand that catches their attention. The identification of a specific brand follows a *prediction of the value* and qualities of the item. The purchase and experience precedes memorisation of a particular brand. The area of the brain where this process takes place is indicated. Various studies support every stage of this assertion (Payne, Bettman & Johnson, 2003; Koch, 2004; McClure et al., 2004; Plassman et al., 2008). The review concludes that consumer psychology is supporting neuroscience in an interdisciplinary way to promote theorising and improve neuromarketing studies. This is in line with Perrachionne's (2008) article which examines neuroscience concepts and modelling the process of neuromarketing research.

Perrachionne (2008) emphasizes *that location, connection and representation* are the main components in neuroscience that neuromarketing must focus on. The *location* that is, focusing on a particular region of the brain that indicates areas that is more metabolically active. *Connectivity* is the means by which neurons in the located cerebral areas of the brain react to process data while *representation* is the *encoding process* that stores the information being processed. Based on research in neuroscience, the brain functions and maps can provide such information and research must pinpoint the exact area that are active in decision making that must be analysed. The use of imaging provides the functioning and necessary information in particular areas of the brain and its interpretation for further analysis. These studies validate and give credence to neuromarketing's relevance and studies. However, it is important to note that researchers must decipher and interpret results to arrive at credible reporting.

The articles point to a collaboration between scientists and marketing researchers to arrive at reliable results.

Using Neuroscience in Marketing Surveys/Research

Even though in the 1990s Dawkins' "meme" and Zaltman's Metaphor Elicitation Technique were the first methods used for eliciting information to understand consumers' mind, currently other more sophisticated methods abound. The "meme" are analogous to genes and unit information that is stored in the human brain is measured. Memetics is a field of study that seeks to empirically provide understanding of human behaviour and cultural process by measuring genes in the brain. Zaltman Metaphor Elicitation Technique is a research method that builds statements that are used to probe and identify deeper feelings that motivate consumer behaviour. There are different tools and methods in neuroscience that can be applied in marketing to determine consumer reactions and decisions making. Some of the tools and techniques include: functional Magnetic Resonance Imaging (fMRI), electroencephalography (EEG), magneto encephalography (MEG), Positron Emission Tomography (PET), Steady State Topography (SST), Transcranial Magnetic Stimulation (TMS), eye tracking, facial coding and other biometrics that observe and measure autonomic arousal and movements. The fMRI, EEG and SST measures activities in specific areas of the brain to determine its response to changes in the respondent's physiological state and the portion of the brain that is affected. Other responses and technique include heartbeat, respiratory rate, skin responses (galvanic skin response - GSR) to observe consumers' reaction, thoughts and the decisions that follow. Figure 1 provides a grouping of the tools and techniques applied in neuromarketing research.

The neuroscience tools used in neuromarketing studies can be grouped into three based on the purpose for which it is used. The fMRI and PET record metabolic reactions in the brain. The process is able to localise and image the neural activity in the brain, measuring the changes that occur in the blood flow.

The EEG, MEG, SST and TMS monitor and document electric activity in the brain. The process involve using electrodes (EEG), electrical helmet (magnetometer), to measure the frequency of electrical current and the electro-chemical changes and signals (Figures 2, 3, 4). The biometric and other body

Figure 1. Neuromarketing tools and instruments applied in data collection

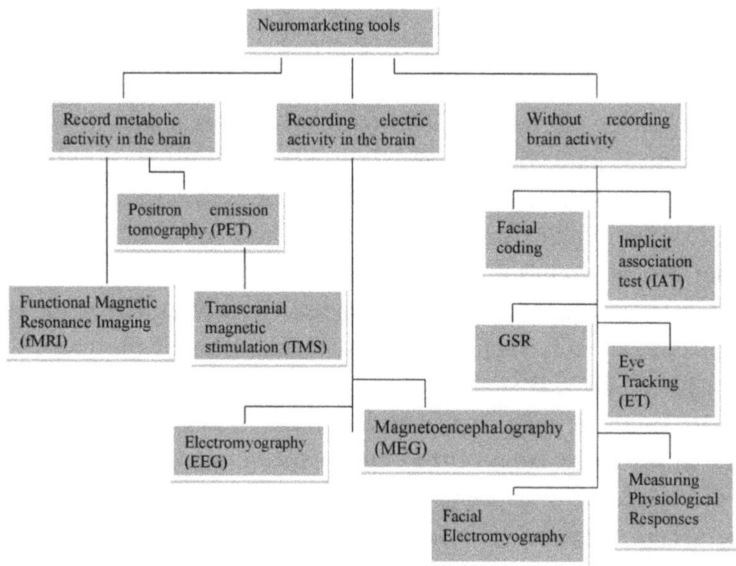

response tools are non – neurological tools that measure specific portions of the body like the skin, face eye to read its responses to stimuli.

Marketing research can make use of these tools in numerous studies These tools can be applied in brand differentiation determination and product perception research, advertising and promotion research, and other studies that evaluates emotions, interests, trust, customer loyalty, decision – making and choice. Neuromarketing is a field of inquiry that is growing. The scientific methods if applied and the corresponding results call for expert interpretation and marketing researchers would have to gear up to take up the challenge.

Marketing Research or Neuromarketing Research

Research has reported a total of 80% of failures particularly in the effectiveness of advertising campaigns due to lack of precise information on consumer thought process (Morin, 2011; Pradeep, 2005). In conducting marketing research, respondents' willingness to provide truthful responses particularly in relation to feelings and reactions lie on the consumer. Evaluations of cognitive and affective processes are at a level that marketing researchers cannot determine but rather depend on consumers to provide answers. Marketing research methods like surveys, focus group discussions and interviews are not suitable for evaluating brain functions to determine feelings that can only be determined from the subconscious mind. Traditional marketing methods are not explicitly able to model what takes place in the brain or subconscious mind of the consumers when exposed to stimuli. Hence neuromarketing research which uses neuroscience imaging is able to map or scan consumer brain when activation takes place. Activation involves the introduction of any marketing related stimuli. The choice of methods in this sense sways toward meuromarketing. This demonstrates that neuroscience fills the gap in providing critical inputs for marketing research.

The question of samples and procedure needs to be addressed. Neuromarketing research uses smaller sample size and real time studies are recorded to provide a better understanding of the subconscious mind and its processes. The issue of sampling and the process is due to the equipment involved and the cost of imaging. Is marketing researchers ready to take on the challenge? Are consumers who mostly make up research respondents ready to go through such surveys? The respondents in most neural research cases may not be conscious of the actual process of the study though their consent is sought to avoid any contention. The non-invasiveness of neuromarketing methods allow the researcher to measure consumer physiological reactions. Direct benefits of neuromarketing research have been tabled by Zarã and Ţuţã (2013) and these include consumer behaviour, decision process and choice particularly in field of marketing. The research method is able to process information using scientific tools to provide detailed knowledge about consumers.

Academic researches mostly dwell on qualitative and theorising with a few specific landmark studies while company specific surveys have made use of neuromarketing tools and methods. *Neurorelay* and the *Neuromarketing Science and Business Association* (NMSBA) have a list of neuromarketing research companies worldwide for 2014 and this is compiled to provide information on the tools available to these companies (the list is not as comprehensive since new companies are added from time to time). It provides the continent, country, the company and the technology available to the firms as listed in Table 2.

MEASURING CONSUMER BEHAVIOUR USING NEUROMARKETING METHODS

Consumers' true unconscious feelings that arise during decision making are beyond reckoning since it provides information that help in understanding human behaviour. The use of neuromarketing methods and techniques in measuring consumer behaviour implies that marketers are hoping to locate information within the brain that would reveal the true human preferences.

Neuroimaging technology is able to detect the portions of the brain where neurons are activated during marketing stimuli leading to increased blood flow and blood oxygenation or activity levels (waves/ electrical activity). The evaluation maps out the brain's reaction of consumers at the time of processing marketing stimuli such as selecting a product or viewing advertisements of a product. The three main applications credited with creating unbiased consumer thought mapping process are:

- Measurements of blood flow and blood oxygenation,
- Measurement of electrical activity, and
- The physiological reaction measurement

The measurement of blood flow and blood oxygenation is a procedure for detecting oxygen levels during brain activity. In active brain areas more oxygen is required. The process involves the measurement of blood oxygen saturation changes in active areas of the brain in response to external stimuli. Blood flow and oxygen delivery to the brain of humans during functional and induced activity is a systemic procedure of oxidation and de-oxidation of the body. During prolonged visual stimulation (as in neuromarketing experimentation), oxygen consumption and ATP (adenosine triphosphate) production is activated in the visual cortex. It is the most commonly used technique in fMRI imaging. The results are captured using specific software packages - Brain Voyager QX (Levy et al., 2011); Statistical Parametric Mapping (SPM_5) – (Falk et al., 2009). The results are transformed to generate blood flow images that

Table 2. A compilation of neuromarketing companies and technology available

CONTINENT	COUNTRY	COMPANY	TECHNOLOGY AVAILABLE
Europe	Milan, Italy	1to1 Lab	EEG, Eye tracking
	Milan, Italy	Behaviour and Brain Lab	EEG, Eye tracking, GSR, Heart rate, respiration rate, Electromiography
	Milano - Modena, Italy	Fondazione Organismo di Ricerca & Innovazione	EEG, Eye tracking
	Milan, Italy	SR Labs	Eye tracking
	Milano, Italy Barcelona, Spain	SalesBrain	Pain Probe (voice layering analysis) **Brand Names**: NeuroMap™ , PAIN Probes ™
	Milan, Italy	NeuroBiomarketing	EEG, EMG, ECG, GSR, Eye tracking,
	Rome, Italy	Brain Signs	EEG, Heart rate, GSR, Eye tracking
	Rome, Italy	Brain Trends	EEG, Thermography, fMRI, Eye tracking, 3D Virtual reality
	Trento, Italy	NeurExplore	EEG, GSR
	Marsa Malta	AAT Research Limited	EEG, GSR, Eye tracking, Virtual reality tracking
	Bruxelles, Belgium	Brain Impact	fMRI, EEG, Eye tracking, IAT priming test
	Heverlee, Belgium Amsterdam, The Netherlands	Haystack	EEG, GSR, Eye tracking
	El Passo (TX), USA	Sands Research	EEG, eye tracking, biometrics (GSR, heart rate), fMRI, **Brand Name**: NeuroiEngagement Score (NES™), Emotional Valance Score (EVS™)

provide insights into consumers' mental reactions and actions. The test assesses how consumers think and respond to marketing stimuli (for instance, product advertisement). The advantages of using this method for data collection in consumer research range from localising neural processing to high spatial resolution of images that permits the viewing of more detailed brain structures for interpretation. It produces valid measures for cognitive and affective responses.

The measurement of electrical activity of the brain involves the use of electrodes placed on the scalp of a respondent in particular spots to measure and record amplitude of the waves in specified areas (cortex) in relation to specific situations or circumstances. Most of these devices are simple and portable allowing for easy transportation and usage (EEG in the appendix - Figure 4). It is able to measure variations and changes in the electrical activity in the brain. Its advantage lies in the high temporal resolution in the images produced that can precisely detect changes in the brain activity during continuous consumption experience. The difficulty in locating the exact electric conductivity is a disadvantage that may hinder the results. Also, only positive and negative emotions can be determined.

The physiological reaction measurement provides information on emotional response to marketing stimuli. Devices monitors heart rate, blood pressure, skin conductivity (arousal response levels or sweat inducements), facial responses and eye tracking devices. These devices are important common attitude measuring tools. The pace of technological changes is enabling marketers to use advanced devices and equipment to conduct physiological reaction measurements. An excellent method for testing responses to advertisements.

Another application is the use of magnetic helmets placed on the head to record brain activity. There is the need to demagnetise the research room when using such devices (MEG, TMS).

All these applications make use of multiple processes in data analysis. The pre-processing, processing, statistical analysis and interpretation, and the final triangulation to validate the research and arrive at meaningful results are the standard procedure. Neuromarketing research focuses on causal effects (cause and effects) to make predictions on consumer behaviour. Both quantitative and qualitative methods are applied but the intersection of the two validates and gains in-depth understanding of research problem while offsetting inherent weaknesses. Although neuromarketing research cannot make use of large samples, images produced are objective to a large extent.

Applying Neuromarketing to Business Practices

Marketers are now making useful correlations with results from neuromarketing studies than before in major aspects of consumer research and business practices. Neuromarketing research provide more probabilistic predictions about consumer behaviour. This makes neuromarketing more attractive to marketing practitioners and business organisations whose interest lie in its applications to influence or determine consumer behaviour. In the business world, consumer behaviour is paramount to firms' decisions. The major areas that neuromarketing is applied falls under three aspects: consumer product management, advertisements (ad) effectiveness and experiential marketing. Neuromarketing research can be used to measure consumer reactions to new products, test packaging designs and brand heuristics (brand preferences, brand recall brand loyalty, brand repositioning). In the advertising world neuromarketing is making strides in testing new product campaigns, identifying key moments and other sensory perceptions to directly generate information that can be used to influence consumer choice decisions. Adopting neuromarketing research perspective in measuring experiential marketing effectiveness could track rapid changes in the speed of neural processing in different parts of the brain in such exercises. Advance technology is promoting virtual web experiences and experiential marketing activities and neuromarketing research can facilitate its use.

The application of scientific method to identify needs and predict choices using computation and advance technology is pushing the limits of research into many fields of study. Neuromarketing research is influencing business strategy and practices especially in product development, launching, pricing, promotions (consumer advertisements), distribution and location decisions, and service experiences.

Currently neuroscience methods in research is transcending economics, psychology and marketing to finance and management. Neurofinance is challenging the status quo to look at neural functions, investment behaviour and finance. The business world is ready for neuromanagement. Cognitive neuroscience can focus on exploring mental and brain processes in solving management problems and decision making.

IMPLICATION OF NEUROMARKETING RESEARCH

The consumer in marketing is the prime focus of every marketing activity. The aim of neuromarketing research is to understand consumers, how and why they make buying decisions, the choices they make and the portion of the brain that support this process. The implication is that there will be a balance between science and marketing in seeking and determining what really is going on with consumers. However, the consumer may be inconvenienced in such surveys and ethical issues bothering on consumer rights and abuse may hinder the attractiveness of the method.

Nevertheless, the information from neuromarketing research using scientific tools provides a bias free and accurate measurement of human subconscious thinking and reasoning. Marketers can now reliably and empirically measure, observe and predict behaviour. The *Pepsi Challenge* by McClure et al. (2004) demonstrates the potential to use external information to trigger particular choices and brand decisions.

From 2005 to date, the advertising industry has moved to the next level in conducting consumer behaviour studies. Neuroscience techniques are supporting the industry in its efforts to critically examine consumers and brand engagement. In addition, promotional campaigns and other communications that call for more effective and detailed knowledge of consumer preferences and decision making can benefit from neuromarketing studies. The industry mainly uses sensory tools like the fMRI, EEG and Eye tracking tools in measuring consumer response to advertising message. Overall, marketing and public policy stand to benefit from the implication of neuromarketing research.

Ethical Concerns and Its Implications

Many concerns have been raised by consumer advocates about the intrusiveness of neuromarketing techniques. The first issue raised is the privacy and rights of consumers. The research method requires the consent of consumers and fundamentally consumer advocates could argue on the evasiveness of the procedures and interpretation of the results. The potential abuse of consumer rights and consent in acquiring information from brain activities to interpret behaviour and the end use of the data which influence decisions is the main issue. And this may lead to a breach of confidentiality of thought that can be challenged legally. Moreover, neuromarketing methods and techniques may be criticised because it induces and interprets consumer behaviour at a subconscious level within the brain. Arguments developed by consumer and ethical advocates are on the basis of circumventing consumer rational decision and choice. The key issue (especially with advertising) is the potential to mislead consumers into believing that a purchase decision is a rationally motivated choice when in fact there may be a stimulant influencing their subconscious impulses and thinking. This means marketers and advertisers could go beyond inquiry to unlawfully coercing consumers into believing that they desire or want particular products and services for which they do not need. Based on this premise, the vulnerable populace could be disadvantaged and consumer laws need to be tightened or promulgated to protect consumers. The European Union's *Unfair Commercial Practices Directives* and other country-specific consumer protection laws need to be pronounced particularly if the neuromarketing technique should gain universal application.

In the United States, the Federal Trade Commission Act, Section 5 protects consumers against *unfair and deceptive trade practices* and the Act has spelt out offenses that could emanate from trade practices against consumers especially failure to provide needed information. Neuromarketing studies could face various claims as the method override consumer rational decision – making process in favour of impulse propensity in brain activity in purchase choice. In Africa, the African Yamoussoukro decision on consumer protection, Article 9.6, ensures that consumer rights are protected. But by and large some African countries do not have any consumer protection laws or regulations (Consumers International, 2015). The fundamental rights of consumers are entrenched in other country-specific equality and unfair practices laws and acts. And investigating trade practices particularly marketing and advertising issues may not be given much attention or dealt with sceptically. In 2008, South Africa passed its consumer protection law, Act 68, and the number one declaration spells out equal rights to the consumer and protects against *discriminatory marketing practices* and privacy. Under this act, managing neuromarketing ethics issues adequately would not be a challenge.

Another ethical controversy is the assumption that firms could identify and spark brain mechanisms that would influence choices and purchase behaviour. This clearly would expose consumer thoughts and could be a dangerous direction ethically. Companies would be able to take advantage of the process and knowledge for commercial purposes (Javor et al., 2013; Morin, 2011; Senior & Lee, 2008; Fugate, 2007; Lee et al., 2007). There is the need for principles guiding the use of neuromarketing research. The global acceptance of a regulatory body like the Neuromarketing Science and Business Association (NMSBA), as the overall professional and trade group for protecting the interest of the field and consumers would be the way forward.

The third ethical challenge has to do with reliability of neuromarketing research results. This aspect of ethics questions the degree of predictability of the results of neuroimaging scans and reports, and the potential to misuse the information derived. Critics foresee a future of marketing research manipulating and coercing consumers to take decisions and make choices that promote particular products or services and thus are skeptical about the new field. There is the need to impose standards, boundaries and code of ethics for which researchers would have to abide by at all times.

The use of high and inflexible technological machines like the MRI scanners (as in Figure 2) and imaging instruments (Figure 3 and 4) may cause serious setback. These imposing instruments

could affect research respondent in different ways. The nature and size of the medical instruments used in research may deter respondents or intimidate and influence them. The machines and gadgets may scare research respondents. The laboratory setting also may pose serious problems that may influence responses. Is it ethically right to subject consumers to stressful procedures in the name of research and solving problems? Research respondents should be briefed on the instruments and techniques of data collection to overcome this challenge.

Are ethical concerns looking for regulations to guide and monitor neuromarketing application or restrictions that would prevent negative illegitimate practices? Ethics in neuromarketing should address the procedural and interpretational implications and the social ramification that could emerge from negative practices. Consumers must be informed about the purpose of the data collection, the process and potential end use of the information. This has been articulated by several researchers (Wilson, Gaines and Hill, 2008; Lee et al., 2010). Neuromarketing studies as it stands must focus on the advantages of using neuroscience research methods while solving business problems. As a discipline and research choice, neuromarketing studies have been criticised but in all, its reliability, benefits and measures make it more popular. In view of the fact that its indirect measurements addresses marketing and brand choice questions better than ordinary consumer surveys it must be encouraged under strict ethical considerations.

Developing Country Studies on Neuromarketing

In the last decade, information technology and medicine have made strides in imaging techniques that have moved diverse fields like psychology, marketing and engineering into using this scientific method in resolving and delving into the consumer mind to find reasons for decisions and choices made. Currently, the human brain activities' reaction to external stimuli can be captured to know what drives consumer behaviour. Championing research and the field of neuromarketing are studies from more advanced countries like the United States, Europe and Asia. These countries have more advanced markets and products. Industry and company promotions are geared toward consumers who have a myriad of product and service to choose from to satisfy their needs. Products and service communications are moving toward investigating consumer decision process and what drives certain brand choices. And neuroscience methods aptly provide the process for digging deeper to understand consumer thought process and decision making. Indeed, researchers and communication agencies are seeking information to comprehend and find ways to coerce and encourage buying. Studies emerging from scholars from developing countries are limited to particular countries that are more technology advanced. Neuromarketing research from developing countries search yielded 523, 000 results (Google search as at 4/6/2015) but further probing revealed that most of these studies are not from African countries. Developing countries are making their mark in the field in terms of interest and academic research but empirical studies are lacking as per review for this chapter. Industry specific consumer advertising and brand research by international marketing firms in some developing countries are introducing this innovative research procedure gradually into their studies. Associations and groups are sensitising and providing knowledge on theory and practice. The Neuromarketing Science and Business Association (NMSBA) for example, is a professional trade group for disseminating information about the field. The association has established code of ethics and definition of neuromarketing terms for use by its members. Currently, there are 40 chairs globally (Appendix) with South Africa (SA) being the only African country. South Africa (SA) is now taking bold steps in neuromarketing research with the *beer and mind control* and other *consumer responses to advertising* studies (Moerdyk, 2013; Neurogadget, 2012). Two notable neuromarketing firms in South Africa are HeadSpace SA and Neural Sense, SA. The South Africa Marketing Research Association (SAMRA) in 2013 formalised neuromarketing research through its maiden conference that year to provide more insight into burgeoning field. du Plessis of Millward-Brown, SA spearheaded the introduction and sensitisation key note discussions at the conference. Other developing countries have their fair share of theoretical reviews. The challenge will be the cost of conducting neuromarketing surveys and availability of tools. Research companies so far are going global and taking on jobs that require the use of scientific tools and the advantages of this new field will endear itself to every country.

The question that must be addressed is that - Is Africa ready for the challenging? Future research on neuromarketing in Africa particularly will provide the answer to address this question.

FUTURE RESEARCH DIRECTIONS AND CONCLUSION

The knowledge of the world around us depends on the human thinking and perception. Neuroscience is breaking grounds in connecting research and practice with other important fields that study the human being. Consumer behaviour studies are moving toward the mapping of the thought process. And further studies could explore what consumers are thinking and what drives that process. The potential of neuromarketing lies in its ability to go beyond determining the effect of marketing campaigns and brands on consumers and the decisions they make thereafter to predicting future choices.

Neuromarketing is concern with generating knowledge which is verifiable by observation (direct or indirectly), or experiences. The tools and techniques are rooted in neuroscience and measurements derived indirectly provide responses that marketing researchers can use to gain a better understanding about consumer attitudes, behaviour, decision making and choice. These tools measure portions of the brain and its response to stimuli. Theories and methodologies of cognitive neuroscience is utilised by researchers to measure marketing activities. The meaningful interpretation of these tests are the dilemma that marketers will need to sharpen to accurately present the factual information. This calls for special training to equip and prepare for in-depth interpretation of scientific imagining and other methods of neuromarketing. From all indications, neuromarketing advocates are increasing in number but the emphasis on the benefit of neuroscience in promoting the field.

The major controversy with the field has to do with intrusion on consumers and the ability to influence consumer decision making and choice. Also the invasive tools and techniques can be misused by marketing researchers to their advantage. Another challenge with neuromarketing research is adequately interpreting information from neuroimaging (fMRI, EEG and others). Ethical questions may be the biggest challenge that neuromarketing would have to address for the field to flourish. But all in all, consumer laws, advocates and associations would be able to protect consumer interest and guide best practices.

From the review, it can be posited that theoretical studies in neuromarketing is trending. The effort at developing models that can be used in this new territory is grow rapidly. In all, 120 articles were selected for review based on neuromarketing specifically. The convenient sampling method was applied in this case. The articles selected had 95% (114) being theoretical based review and 5% (6) were empirical. Empirical documentation studies abound but it is more on industry specific studies for organisations done by marketing research firms. This makes Garcia and Saad (2008) assertion that all empirical surveys are 'one-shot empirical studies' focusing on a single research worth reviewing. The NMSBA is gradually building a base that would monitor neuromarketing practice and activities.

Consumer behaviour and consumers are the focus of neuromarketing practice and research but this chapter delimits itself to the thematic issues relating to the topics discussed. In regard to the articles reviewed, it is important to note that it is not a representative of articles and empirical research of the whole arena of studies on neuromarketing but rather an optimization that encouraged an extensive analysis of the articles chosen.

In conclusion, it can be said that despite concerns raised by sceptics about the intrusiveness of the methods of enquiry on consumers, neuromarketing techniques will go a long way in providing more accurate information. Neuroimagining as a survey instrument cannot easily be over turned, but the question of acquiring some of the equipment may be a disadvantage to its usage. It is an important area of study and its application and tools for monitoring, measuring and possibly manipulating and knowing what is on the minds of consumers is the next colossus in marketing. Neuromarketiing research is here and the opportunity to determine consumer behaviour and measure actual responses is the way forward.

Neuroscience methods usage in research are now more multidisciplinary. The power of its technical and statistical computation ability to study human neural functions to determine behaviour promises to have a wide implication for business practitioners in the twenty first century.

REFERENCES

Bear, M. F., Connors, B. W., & Paradisco, M. A. (1996). *Neuroscience: Exploring the Brain*. London: Williams & Wilkins.

Booth, D. A., & Freeman, R. P. J. (2014). Mind-reading versus Neuromarketing: How Does a Product make an impact on the Consumer? *Journal of Consumer Marketing*, *31*(3), 177–189. doi:10.1108/JCM-08-2013-0674

Butler, M. J. (2008). Neuromarketing and the Perception of Knowledge. *Journal of Consumer Behaviour*, *7*(4-5), 415–419. doi:10.1002/cb.260

Butler, M. J. (2013). Operationalising Interdisciplinary research – a model of Co-Production in Organisational Cognitive Neuroscience. *Frontiers of Human Neuroscience, 7*, 720. Retrieved on 4/06/2015 from: www.ncbbi.nlm.nih.gov/pmcparticles/PMC3893564/

Consumer Protection Act. (2009). *I know my rights. Do you know Yours*. The Department of Trade and Industry, Republic of South Africa. Retrieved on 20/06/2015 from http://www.consumer_protection_pocketguide.pdf

Consumers International. (2015). *Consumer Rights*. Retrieved on 13/06/2015 from http://www.consumersinternational.org/who-we-are/consumer-rights

Dowouna-Hammond, M. C., Atuguba, D. R., & Nabila, D. L. (2006). *Legal and Policy Framework for Consumer Protection in Ghana*. Accra: Friedrich Ebert Foundation, Ghana.

Du Plessis, E. (2011). *The Branded Mind* (1st ed.). London, UK: Kogan Page Limited.

Edwards, P. (2013). *Neuroscience and Reductionism: Some Realist Reflections*. Birmingham Business School. Discussion Paper Series, 2013 – 2008.

Eze, A. G. (2012). Consumer Rights as Constitutional Rights: A comparative analysis of some selected jurisdictions. *Nnamdi Azikiwe University Journal of International Law and Jurisprudence*, 184 – 196.

Fisher, C. E., Chin, L., & Klitzman, R. (2010). Defining Neuromarketing: Practices and Professional Challenges. *Harvard Review of Psychiatry*, *18*(4), 230–237. doi:10.3109/10673229.2010.496623 PMID:20597593

Glimcher, P. (2003). *Decisions, Uncertainty and the Brain: The Science of Neuroeconomics*. London: MIT Press.

Hubert, M. (2010). Does Neuroeconomics give new impetus to Economic and Consumer research? *Journal of Economic Psychology*, *31*(5), 812–817. doi:10.1016/j.joep.2010.03.009

Hubert, M., & Kenning, P. (2008). A current Overview of Consumer Neuroscience. *Journal of Consumer Behaviour*, *7*(4-5), 272–292. doi:10.1002/cb.251

Javor, A., Koller, M., Lee, N., Chamberlain, L., & Ransmayr, G. (2013). Neuromarketing and Consumer Neuroscience: Contributions to neurology. *BMC Neurology*, *13*(1), 1–12. doi:10.1186/1471-2377-13-13 PMID:23383650

Kahneman, D., & Snell, J. (1992). Predicting a Changing Taste: Do people know what they will like? *Journal of Behavioral Decision Making*, *5*(3), 187–200. doi:10.1002/bdm.3960050304

Karmarkar, U. R. (2011). *Note on Neuromarketing*. Harvard Business School.

Koch, C. (2004). *Quest for Consciousness: A Neurobiological Approach*. Englewood, CO: Roberts & Company Publishers.

Lee, N., Broderick, A. J., & Chamberlain, L. (2007). What is "Neuromarketing"? A discussion and agenda for future research. *International Journal of Psychophysiology*, *63*(2), 199–204. doi:10.1016/j.ijpsycho.2006.03.007 PMID:16769143

Lee, N., Butler, M., & Senior, C. (2010). The Brain in Business: Neuromarketing and Organisational Cognitive neuroscience. *Journal of Marketing*, *49*, 129–131. doi:10.100712642-010-0033-8

Lewis, D., & Briader, D. (2005). Market Researchers make increasing use of Brain Imaging. *Advances in Clinical Neuroscience & Rehabilitation: ACNR*, *5*(3), 35.

Lindebaum, D., & Zundel, M. (2013). Not quite a revolution: Scrutinizing Organisational Cognitive Neuroscience in Leadership Studies. *Human Relations*, *66*, 857–877. doi:10.1177/0018726713482151

Martinez, P. (2012). *The Consumer Mind: Brand Perception and the Implication for Marketers* (1st ed.). London, UK: Kogan Page Limited.

McClure, S. M., Li, J., Tomlin, D., Cypert, K. S., Montague, L. M., & Montague, P. R. (2004). Neural correlates of Behavioral preferences for culturally familiar drinks. *Neuron*, *44*(3), 379–387. doi:10.1016/j.neuron.2004.09.019

Moerdyk, C. (2013). *Synopsis of Neuromarketing*. South Africa Marketing Association (SAMRA). Retrieved on 20/06/2015 from: www.erikdup.com

Morin, C. (2011). Neuromarketing: The New Science of Consumer Behaviour. *Society*, *48*(2), 131–135. doi:10.100712115-010-9408-1

Neurogadget. (2012). *HeadSpace Agency brings neuromarketing Studies to South Africa*. Retrieved on 20/06/2015 from: http://www.neurogadget.com/2012/08/28/headspace-agency-brings-neuromarketing-studiesto-SA/4603

Payne, J. W., Bettman, J. R., & Johnson, E. J. (1993). The Adaptive Decision Maker. Cambridge, UK: Academic Press. doi:10.1017/CBO9781139173933

Plassman, H., O'Doherty, J., Shiv, D., & Rangel, A. (2008). Marketing actions can modulate neural representations of experienced pleasantness. *Proceedings of the National Academy of Sciences of the United States of America*, *105*(3), 1050–1054. doi:10.1073/pnas.0706929105

Rangel, A., Camerer, C., & Montague, P. R. (2008, July). Value-based Decision making. *Nature Reviews. Neuroscience*, *9*(7), 545–556. doi:10.1038/nrn2357 PMID:18545266

Rawlins, N. (2005). The Nervous System. In M. Hewstone, F. D. Fincham, & J. Forster (Eds.), *Psychology* (pp. 42–72). Blackwell Publishing.

Schaefer, M., Berens, H., Heinze, H. J., & Rotte, M. (2006). Neural correlates of culturally familiar brands of car manufacturers. *NeuroImage, 31*(2), 861–865. doi:10.1016/j.neuroimage.2005.12.047

Senior, C., & Lee, L. (2008). A Manifesto for Neuromarketing Science. *Journal of Consumer Behaviour, 7*(4-5), 263–271. doi:10.1002/cb.250

Waldman, D. A. (2013). Interdisciplinary Research is the key. *Frontiers in Human Neuroscience, 7*, 5. doi:10.3389/fnhum.2013.00562 PMID:24062664

Wilson, M., Gaines, J., & Hill, R. (2008). Neuromarketing and Consumer Freewill. *The Journal of Consumer Affairs, 42*(3), 389–410. doi:10.1111/j.1745-6606.2008.00114.x

Wirtz, D., Kruger, J., Scollon, C. N., & Diener, E. (2003). What to do on spring break. *Psychological Science, 14*(5), 520–524. doi:10.1111/1467-9280.03455 PMID:12930487

Zaltman, G. (1997). Rethinking Marketing Research: Putting people back in. *JMR, Journal of Marketing Research, 34*(4), 424–427. doi:10.2307/3151962

Zaltman, G. (2003). *How Consumers think: Essential Insights into the Mind of the Markets*. Boston: Harvard Business School Press.

KEY TERMS AND DEFINITIONS

ATP (Adenosine Triphosphate): Molecule found in the cells of living organisms that transport energy necessary cellular metabolic activities.

Brain: A soft organ made up of blood vessels, interconnected nerves (neurons), and fluid-filled ventricles.

Galvanic Skin Response (GSR): Also known as skin conductance. It is a method applied to measure the skin responses to stimuli.

Glial: Cells that support neurons in their tasks and contribute to the development of the nervous system and its activities.

Receptors: Special spots or areas in the nervous system (like the brain) where neuron transmitters have their greatest effects.

APPENDIX

Figure 2. The Tamale Hospital in Ghana's MRI scanner

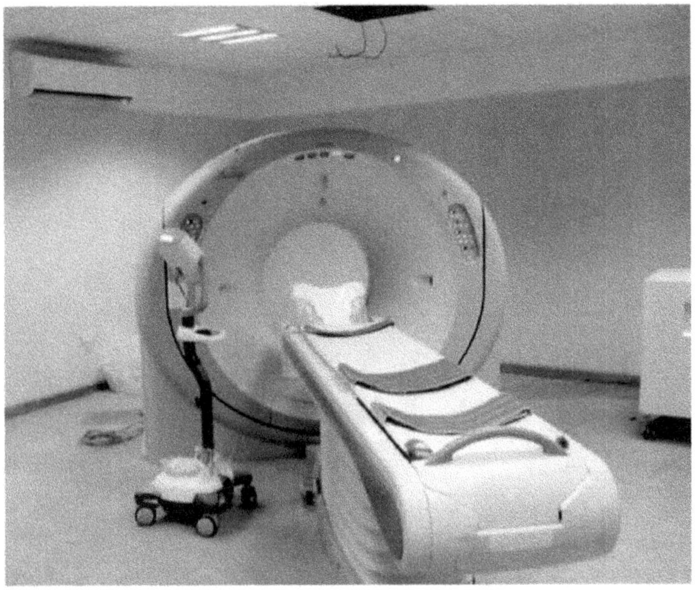

Figure 3. The Tamale Hospital in Ghana's computed tomography
Source: www.ghanahealthnet.com

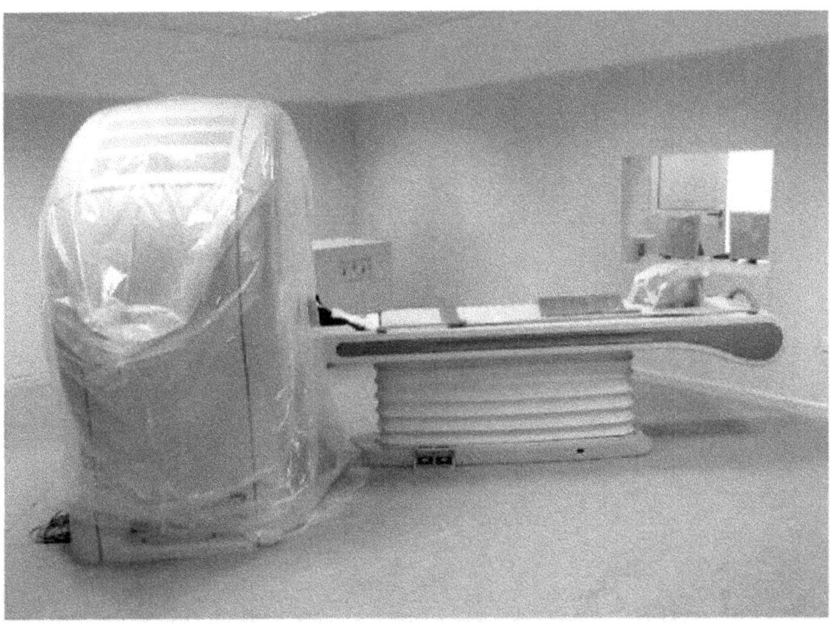

The NMSBA local chairs are in the following countries: Argentina, Australia, Belgium, Brazil, Canada, China, Colombia, Costa Rica, Croatia, Denmark, Ecuador, El Salvador, Finland, France, Germany, Guatemala, India, Italy, Japan, Korea (Republic of Korea), Luxembourg, Malta, Mexico, Netherlands, Panama, Peru, Poland, Portugal, Romania, Russia (Federation of Russia). Singapore, South Africa, Spain, Sweden, Switzerland, Turkey, United Arab Emirates, United Kingdom and Venezuela

Figure 4. Courtesy of Kaidi Reedi, TNS Emor, Neuromarkeing presentation
Source: www.07-kaidi-Reedi-neuromarketing.pdf

Eye - Tracking device

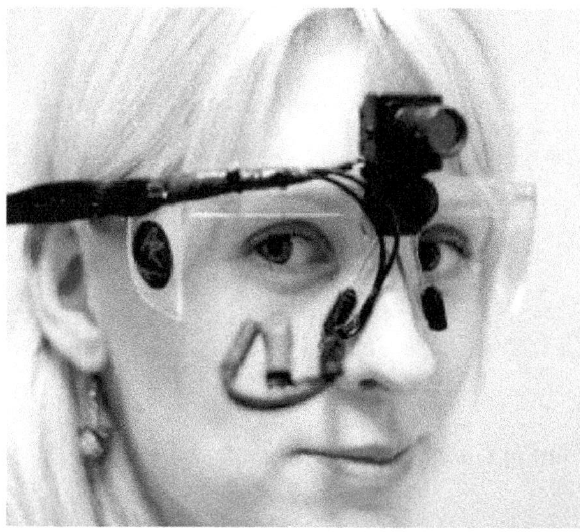

EEG

Chapter 3
Country-of-Origin Effect and Consumer Ethnocentrism:
The Brand Perception of Romanian Consumers of a Danish Beer Brand

Andreea I. Bujac
Aalborg University, Denmark

Lartey G. Lawson
The Ministry of Transport, The Danish Road Directorate, Denmark

ABSTRACT

This chapter examines the impact of consumer ethnocentrism and country of origin of a low involvement product on consumer brand perception and purchase behavior in a transitional market setting of Central and Eastern Europe. Data were collected from 317 respondents from an urban population in three large cities in Romania. The results show that country of origin has a significant impact on the consumers' perception of the Danish beer brand Tuborg. The results show statistically significant associations between consumer ethnocentrism taxation and buying Romanian products as well as between demographic characteristics and brand perception.

INTRODUCTION

International marketing research has long been concerned with examining whether consumers prefer domestic products, as opposed to foreign products and how the country of origin of the foreign product is perceived (Evanschitzky et al., 2008). Marketing scholars have also long argued that the cause of the appearance of country-of-origin (COO) effect can be found in consumer ethnocentrism (CE) (Stoltman et al., 1991; Lantz & Loeb, 1996; Lee & Ganesh, 1999; Chryssochoidis et al., 2007; Ding, 2016). There has also been substantial research interest in country-of-origin effects on foreign and domestic brands (Klein et al., 1998; Balabanis & Diamantopoulus, 2004; Liu & Johnson, 2005; Verlegh et al., 2005; Hong & Kang, 2006; Maheswaran & Chen 2006; Pappu et al., 2007).

DOI: 10.4018/978-1-5225-7906-9.ch003

Recent studies in the field of the country-of-origin effect and ethnocentric perceptions show consumer behavioural tendencies not only towards local and foreign products in general but more specifically brands (Kinra, 2006; Chryssochoidis et al., 2007; Ferguson et al., 2008; Alden et al. 2013; Guo 2013). Kinra (2006) for example investigated the Indian consumers' attitudes towards local and foreign brands and found that foreign brands were perceived as being more reliable and safe than local brands, thus displaying a low level of ethnocentric tendencies. On the other hand, some scholars suggested that CE has no influence on the COO effect (Yagci, 2001; Sharma, 2011). For example Sharma (2011) investigated the role of CE in COO effects for consumers from the USA and the UK with regard to cars and found that ethnocentrism does not interact with COO and has a weak negative effect on the consumers' product evaluation and behavioural intentions for imported products. On the other hand, Ding (2017) examined whether consumer ethnocentrism in China is prevalent and its impact on Chinese consumers' product preferences between local and foreign products. He found that Chinese consumers display a low level of ethnocentric tendency, but that CE did affect product preferences amongst Chinese consumers and that the availability of domestic alternative is a key factor that cannot be ignored.

All in all, the body of knowledge on the link between COO and CE and their effect on brand perception produced some inconclusive results. Scholars like Kinra (2006), Liu et al. (2006), Chryssochoidis et al. (2007), Ferguson et al. (2008), Zolfagharian and Sun (2010) found that in connection with the country-of-origin effect, the ethnocentric perceptions indeed showed an influence on consumer behavioural tendencies, not only towards local and foreign products and services in general, but more specifically towards brands. On the other hand, some scholars suggested that CE has no influence on the COO effect (Yagci, 2001; Sharma, 2011), and consumer ethnocentrism becomes a significant predictor only when the product is manufactured in less-developed/liked countries. The main reason behind this contradictory evidence may lie in the differences in product involvement. Studies which included low involvement products showed a greater relationship between CE and COO, than studies which used high involvement products.

Since there are mixed views on whether a developed country of origin has an impact on how consumers perceive low involvement local products, authors like Kwok et al. (2006), Kumar et al. (2009), Pentz et al., (2016), Siamagka and balabanis (2015) and Balabanis and Siamagka (2017) call for additional research to be undertaken with low involvement products in the field of COO and CE. This study will try to bring additional insights into the impact of consumer ethnocentrism and country of origin of a low involvement product on consumer brand perception and purchase behavior.

BACKGROUND

According to Han and Terpstra (1988) country of origin is defined as "the country of manufacture or assembly" identified by "made in" or "manufactured in" labels. But due to multi-national companies evolving into trans-national companies and the emergence of hybrid products coming from different countries, the image of the made-in label has been blurred (Baker & Michie, 1995; Ahmed et al., 2004).

Siamagka and Balabanis (2015) describe consumer ethnocentrism as a means to understand the moral concerns arising from the consumption of foreign and domestic products. In addition to this, it has also been shown that consumers usually perceive products made in developed countries to be of higher quality compared with products made in emerging markets (Pappu et al., 2007; Josiassen & Harzing, 2008; Usunier & Cestre, 2008, Ding, 2017). In a study conducted by Hamin & Elliott (2006) in countries such as Mexico, the Philippines, Jordan and Nigeria, the consumers seemed to rate products from more developed countries more highly than domestic products. That said, these authors also noted that alongside the generalised preference for products originating from developed countries, there is also evidence to suggest that some consumers will always prefer to buy products manufactured in their home country (Beverland, 2001; Pecotich & Rosenthal, 2001; Dmitrovic, Vida & Reardon, 2008; Acikdilli *et al.*, 2017). Furthermore, people displaying ethnocentric tendencies view their own in- group as the center of the universe and this results in negative out-group attitudes (Park and Yoon, 2017)

Previous research into the relationship between COO and CE included both low and high involvement products. While studies involving high involvement products have dominated this stream of research (Magnusson et al. 2011 (TV's); Diamantopoulus, 2011 (refrigirators); Jimenez and Martin, 2012 (cars); Sinrungtam, 2013 (cars)), a few scholars have also introduced low involvement products as being prone to COO and CE effects (Ahmed et al., 2004; Chryssochoidis et al., 2007; Balabanis and Diamantopoulos 2008, 2011). For example, Chryssochoidis et al. (2007) evaluated the level of ethnocentrism of Greek consumers, and investigated the CE-COO effect relationship and implications on consumers' perceptions regarding imported food products, like beer, ham and cheese. The results showed that CE affects consumer beliefs and how the perceived quality of domestic and foreign products are evaluated, culminating in the appearance of COO-effects. On the other hand, Kwok et al. (2006) conducted a study on Chinese consumers and investigated the impact of COO of different grocery brands on purchase behaviour and found out that Chinese consumers prefer to buy local Chinese grocery brands rather than foreign ones, although this preference for local brands was not reflected in their purchase behaviour, due to the possibility that the Chinese consumers did not know the true origin of the brands, and perhaps they were unable to act according to their preferences.

Until the turn of this century, limited empirical studies have been conducted on the impact of COO and CE on consumer behaviour in emerging market economies (Kinra, 2006; Liu et al., 2006; Chryssochoidis et al., 2007; Ferguson et al., 2008; Zolfagharian & Sun, 2010; Siamagka and Balabanis, 2015). The systemic political and economic changes in the Central and Eastern European countries during the past two decades have provided both academic and strategic marketing management justifications for the increasing number of studies in the field (Beverland, 2001; Pecotich & Rosenthal, 2001; Dmitrovic et al., 2009). Furthermore, Siamagka and Balabanis (2015) argue that the investigation of consumer ethnocentrism is essential for global marketers to provide guidance for global positioning, branding and market entry decisions to and from developing nations.

The transition1 markets from Central and Eastern Europe (CEE), which have also been considered of great interest by Western countries, especially after the collapse of the communist regime in 1989, will add another US$95 billion of consumer spending to the global economy per year. The decrease in economic growth of developed countries compared to emerging countries has provided Western marketers a convincing justification for expanding their business to emerging markets. Thus, Western brands have been encouraged to bid aggressively for market share in these countries, by drawing on the positive COO effects that these developed countries bring with them (Kinra, 2006).

Furthermore, the political developments in the EU, mentioned above, along with the increase of interest in CEE countries in the current global economy, have opened up questions about how consumers in CEE countries perceive Western brands. According to Dmitrovicet al., (2009) there is an emergent ethnocentric tendency among consumers in CEE countries, which becomes a major concern for Western companies which are operating in these markets. As Chryssochoidis et al. (2007) and Chu et al. (2010) suggest a more thorough examination of COO effect and consumer ethnocentrism with reference to brand names is an interesting area for future research. In addition, in the current global economy, there is increased interest in CEE countries, especially Romania (Central and Eastern European Development Institute Report 2012), in terms of their attractiveness for FDI and the growth in consumer spending over the next three years. This has opened up questions about how consumers in CEE countries perceive Western brands (Beverland, 2001; Pecotich and Rosenthal, 2001; Dmitrovic et al., 2009).

The low involvement product chosen for this study is beer. Previous studies involving beer have been undertaken by Schaefer (1997), Phau & Sunttornnond (2006) & Chryssochoidis et al., (2007), who found that beer is a good denominator of COO and CE effects. Schaefer (1997) investigated the relationship between dimensions of consumer knowledge and the use of COO cues on beer from Germany, Belgium, UK, The Netherlands, Australia, and Denmark. The findings suggested that brand familiarity has a significant effect on the use of the COO cue in product evaluation, while subjective product knowledge and personal experience with a brand were not found to have a significant effect on the use of COO in product evaluation. Phau and Sunttornnond (2006) wanted to determine how different dimensions of consumer knowledge can affect COO cues and found that COO information actually affects Australian consumers in their evaluation of beer products.

The brand chosen for this study is Tuborg, which is a Danish beer brand. The reason why Tuborg was chosen is due to its popularity and familiarity among European consumers.. Belonging to the Carlsberg Group, Tuborg is Denmark's best-selling lager beer, present in more than 70 countries worldwide (Carlsberg, 2017). Since Eastern Europe is regarded as the biggest potential growth market alongside Asia (Carlsberg Group, 2017), Romania was chosen as the country of research due to the fact that beer consumption in Romania has become very popular in the last few years (see Research Context section).

As laid out above, this study examines the level of consumer ethnocentrism (CE) and its implication on the consumers' evaluation of a specific foreign beer brand. Furthermore it seeks to test whether country of origin matters in connection to the consumers' brand perception and what kind of impact demographic characteristics exhibit on brand perception. Thus, the study seeks to make additional contributions to the limited empirical research knowledge about the links between COO, CE and brand perception involving internationally acknowledged brands. Furthermore, by situating the study in the transitional economy of Romania, it provides additional evidence on how rapid systemic changes in economies impact consumer attitudes and behaviour.

The rest of the paper is structured as follows: In section 2, the extant literature on consumer ethnocentrism, country of origin and brand perception is briefly reviewed and hypotheses are formulated for the empirical investigation in section 3. Here, a presentation of the methodological approaches used for the empirical investigation is presented and the results of the empirical analyses are reported. Finally, section 4 discusses the findings and provides conclusions.

LITERATURE REVIEW AND MODEL DEVELOPMENT

Previous studies have suggested that the country-of-origin effect can be observed in two ways: halo effect and summary construct (Jaffe & Nebenzahl, 2001).The halo effect comes into play when consumers are not familiar with the products of a country, then the country image acts as a "halo" that directly affects consumers' beliefs about these products. This means that stereotypes about that specific country come into the consumer's mind. A general understanding provided by the extant literature is that economic, social, and cultural systems of countries as well as their relative stage of economic development are used by consumers as stereotypical cues in their evaluation of products and choice behaviour (Bilkey & Nes, 1982; Tse & Gorn, 1993). On the other hand, when consumers are familiar with a country's products, the summary construct model comes into play, in which consumers infer a country's image from its product information, which then indirectly influences brand attitudes (Han, 1989).

As mentioned above, previous research on the COO effect on consumer behaviour also introduced the term of consumer ethnocentrism as being the cause of its appearance, thus presenting a close relationship between the two terminologies. CE represents an individual tendency to view the purchasing of imported products as wrong as it hurts the domestic economy and is not congruent with their in-group feelings of patriotism and belongingness to their societies (Shimp & Sharma, 1987; Granzin & Olsen, 1998). It may lead to overestimating the quality of locally made products while underestimating the quality of foreign-made products (Huddleston et al., 2001; Suh & Kwon, 2002; Erdogan & Uzkurt, 2010). These perceptions tend to be guided by rational, emotional and even moral considerations. Watson & Wright (2000) believe that in connection with the country-of-origin effect these perceptions represent consumer behaviour not only towards local and foreign products in general but more specifically, brands.

Consumer ethnocentrism is affected by many factors. One of them is the product type, where previous research found out that the impact of CE varies among product categories. Sharma et al. (1995), argued that low involvement products, are more prone to ethnocentric tendencies. Also, Javalgi et al. (2005) found that the impact of CE on purchasing intentions of a particular product is moderate when this product is perceived as absolutely necessary. One other factor which has shown a direct impact on consumer ethnocentrism is the level of development of the consumers' home country. According to Wang & Chen (2004), consumers from a developed country tend to appreciate domestic products more favorably than imported ones, leading to a greater degree of ethnocentrism and thus a higher tendency to reject foreign products. The reverse has been observed in developing countries, where consumers perceive Western products as superior. It has also been shown that consumers typically view products made in developing countries less favourably than the ones manufactured in developed countries (Cordell, 1993; Lin & Sternquist, 1994; Kinra, 2006; Hu et al., 2008; Wang & Yang, 2008). Furthermore Balabanis & Diamantopoulos (2004) argued that CE is mostly related to consumers showing a preference for domestic products but not necessarily rejecting foreign ones. Finally, they assert that the CE impact varies significantly among different product categories and countries of origin.

Past literature has also shown that demographic characteristics have an influence on the impact of COO and CE on brand perception. The literature on COO has long indicated that consumer demographics, like age, gender, income, and occupation, play a significant role in country perceptions, and since marketing scholars call for additional research in these fields, further investigation is required (Schaefer (1997; Balabanis et al., 2001; Wang et al., 2004; Samiee et al., 2005). Schaefer (1997) for example, suggests that consumers' age and socio- economic group affects the extent to which they are influenced by the country of origin in product evaluations of lager and sparkling wine. While Ahmed et al. (2004) suggest that gender does not seem to affect the magnitude of country-of-origin effects, other studies suggest that men are more prone to be biased against foreign products (Schooler, 1971; Samiee et al., 2005). Furthermore, the existing literature suggests that young people are less ethnocentric and less influenced by country-of-origin effects. According to Javalgi et al. (2005) and Josiassen et al. (2011) the most common use of demographic variables in studies regarding consumer ethnocentrism are age, gender, education and income. Due to this inconsistencies Pentz et al. (2014) call for additional research into the impact of demographic characteristics like age, gender, education on the CE and COO relationship.

Based on the discussion above, a conceptual model is proposed (see Figure 1), in order to test the relationships between COO, CE and demographics and their impact on brand perception. The model has also guided the hypothesis formulation.

HYPOTHESES

The Country-of-Origin Effect on Brand Perception

From an information-processing perspective it is argued that consumers evaluate a product based on both intrinsic cues (e.g., taste, design, and other product features) and extrinsic cues (price, brand, and warranty) (Ahmed & d'Astous, 2008). As an extrinsic attribute, COO is used by consumers in the absence of information about tangible attributes (Han, 1989; Han & Terpstra, 1988).

When reviewing the literature on COO effects, one can acknowledge that there exists a huge body of empirical research. Schooler (1965) was the first to conduct an empirical study about COO and proved that consumers rate identical products based on their country of origin. Previous research depicted that COO has an impact on brand/product perceptions (Etzel & Walker, 1974; Han & Terpstra, 1988; Leonidou et al., 1999; Paswan & Sharma, 2004), beliefs and attitudes (Lee & Ganesh, 1999; Knight & Calantone, 2000), perceived quality (White & Cundiff, 1978; Han & Terpstra, 1988; Teas & Agarwal, 2000; Baldauf et al., 2009) and evaluations (Hong & Wyer, 1989; Roth & Romeo, 1992; Verleghet al., 2005), and that certain aspects interact to moderate the COO effect on product evaluation (Gürhan-Canli & Maheswaran, 2000). COO has also been shown to influence consumer preferences (Knight & Calantone, 2000) and purchase intentions (Roth & Romeo, 1992; Nebenzahl & Jaffe, 1996; Ghalandari & Norouzi, 2012).

A number of scholars have observed that consumers from developing countries perceive Western products as superior and seek to emulate Western consumption practices and lifestyles and purchase foreign brands (Cordell, 1993; Lin & Sternquist, 1994; Kinra, 2006; Hu et al., 2008; Wang & Yang, 2008). For example, Kinra (2006) found out in a study conducted in India, towards local and foreign brands, that consumers do evaluate foreign Western brands more favourably than local ones. On the other hand, the study conducted by Saffu & Scott (2009) in Malaysia and Papuan New Guinea (PNG), showed that consumers from Malaysia evaluated their home country products higher than Western ones, while PNG consumers rated their home country product quality as the lowest one.

Based on the discussions above, the following hypothesis is drawn:

Figure 1. Conceptual model
Source: Own Creation

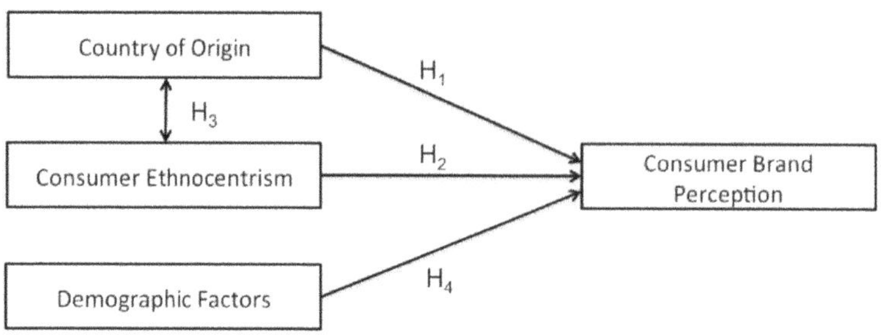

Hypothesis One: A Western country of origin will have a positive impact on Romanian consumers' beer brand perception.

Consumer Ethnocentrism and Brand Perception

Wang & Chen (2004) state that consumers from a developed country have a tendency to evaluate domestic products more favorably than imported ones, thus increasing the impact of ethnocentricity when it comes to buying the local brand/product over the foreign one. When looking at consumers from developing countries this phenomenon is reversed, they tend to perceive foreign products, especially the ones coming from Western countries, as superior in quality to local products. Furthermore, Balabanis & Diamantopoulos (2004) argue that CE is a more of a "consistent predictor" of preferences for locally-made products rather than foreign products, thus asserting that consumer ethnocentrism leads to the preference of domestic products but not necessarily to the rejection of foreign ones.

One of the predominant factors which affect CE is the type of product. The less important the product category is, the higher the ethnocentric tendency of the consumer (Sharma et. al, 1995; Balabanis & Diamantopoulos, 2004). Previous research explored the ethnocentric tendency of consumers concerning food products (Sajdakowska, 2003) or clothing (O'Cass & Lim, 2002). Emerging economies are becoming increasingly interesting for marketing scholars in terms of CE. The focus in recent years has leaned towards Eastern Europe (Parts, 2007 in the Baltic States; Vida & Damjan, 2000 in Slovenia; Cumberland et al., 2010 in Poland), India (Bawa, 2004; Khan & Rizvi, 2008), Turkey (Dedeoglu et al., 2005), Russia (Puzakova et al., 2010), and China (Hsu & Nien, 2008). Based on the above, the hypothesis is as follows:

Hypothesis Two: The higher the degree of ethnocentric tendencies of the Romanian consumers, the higher their negative perception of Tuborg beer brand will be.

Relationship Between Country of Origin and Consumer Ethnocentrism and Their Effect on Brand Perception

The relationship between COO and CE was also proven to be significant by a number of scholars: Kinra, 2006; Chryssochoidis et al., 2007; Zolfagharian & Sun, 2010. Kinra (2006) for example investigated the Indian consumers' attitudes towards local and foreign brands, by looking at the COO effect and ethnocentric tendencies. The findings suggested that foreign brands were perceived as being more reliable and safe by Indian consumers, than their local brands. COO credibility was rated high for foreign brands, particularly for consumer durables and the ethnocentricity level was rather low. Liu et al. (2006) examined how CE relates to the Chinese consumers' brand evaluation across 3 brand naming strategies of a store sign: Chinese name, English and Chinese name and English and Chinese name with the brands' COO, and found that a high ethnocentric level has a negative impact on the evaluation of a store sign containing a foreign brand name and a foreign COO. Thus, the interaction between COO and CE on foreign brand evaluation was significant. Furthermore, Chryssochoidis et al. (2007) investigated the CE-COO effect relationship and implications on consumers' perceptions regarding imported food products, like beer, ham and cheese. The results showed that CE affects consumer beliefs and how the perceived quality of domestic and foreign products are evaluated, culminating in the appearance of COO-effects. Based on these findings, the hypothesis is as follows.

Hypothesis Three: There is a positive association between the COO-CE relationship and the Romanian consumers' beer brand perception.

Demographic Characteristics and Brand Perception

The conceptual model presented above depicts the most frequently investigated demographic factors of gender, age, education and income. These factors generally reflect what could be termed as an individual's time line for demand or consumption of a particular good. These factors form the core of the consumer market segmentation that is of interest for the marketing manager. The extent to which these demographic factors might influence brand perception may be due to their country specific ethnocentric tendencies or country-of-origin (COO) influences.

With respect to gender, empirical investigations have produced contradictory results. Schooler (1971) & Samiee et al. (2005) found that females are less ethnocentric than their male counterparts and are hence more prone to rate foreign-made products more favorably. However, the studies by Vida & Fairhurst, (1999), Balabanis et al. (2001), as well as by Javalgi et al. (2005) found women to exhibit more ethnocentric tendencies in their consumption decisions than men. For COO effects, the research conducted by Ahmed et al. (2004) found no significant differences between males and females in their mean likelihood of purchasing each product from different countries. These mixed results may be partly explained in terms of the age, education or income of the consumer involved in the studies.

Research reports evaluating the role of age suggested that older consumers are more ethnocentric than younger consumers, which suggests that older consumers find it more difficult to switch to other brands, including foreign brands (Han & Terpstra, 1988; Balabanis et al., 2001; Wang et al., 2004). However, the exact opposite has been suggested by Bannister & Saunders (1978) as well as Mittal & Tsiros (1995), that is, that younger consumers are more ethnocentric,. Similarly, research studies reported that older people show stronger country-of-origin effects (Schellinck, 1989; Wall et al., 1991; Schaefer, 1997), while others suggested that younger rather than older consumers exhibited a greater COO effect for Mexican and US consumers (Insch & McBride, 2004).

The level of education could alter consumer perception of product brands. However, this needs to be linked to the length or the type of educational level attained prior to the specific purchase decision making. A well-educated consumer with less ethnocentric tendencies is expected to exhibit a positive attitude towards foreign or imported product brands, suggesting that COO is less important for their purchasing decisions. These are the views reported by Festervand et al. (1985), Ueltschy (1998) & Erdogan and Uzkurt (2010). However, one cannot exclude the possibility of the opposite view. Consumers with a high level of education may be exposed to the need for acting to support domestic production biasing them against foreign products and making them exhibit more ethnocentric tendencies and negativity towards the positive impact of COO effect. This might especially be the case if the quality of the domestic product matches the foreign one.

Generally, it is expected that consumers with a high level of income would be more attracted to foreign products, with high price levels and positive COO effect. Wall et al. (1990) reported positive attitude towards foreign products when income is high, Good & Huddleston (1995), and Bailey & Pineres (1997) also showed that if the consumer's income is high, the probability of buying domestic products is lower. However, McLain & Sternquist (1991) found no such relationship between the income level and product brand perception. The general conclusion from these studies is that the influence of consumer ethnocentrism and COO on brand perception is dependent of demographic factors. Hence, the hypothesis is as follows:

Hypothesis Four: The Romanian consumers' perception of a foreign beer brand is dependent of demographic factors such as age, education and income.

RESEARCH CONTEXT

The Romanian Beer Market

With a population of 21.5 million people, Romania is one of the bigger former communist countries in Eastern Europe that joined the European Union in 2007. The GDP per capita (PPP) is around 25,840.836 $ (World Bank, 2018), which is only 47% of the average EU-27 income. During the first years of the financial crisis, 2008-2009, the national GDP dropped 9.4%, but the World Bank (2018) predicts an annual average growth of 2.5%. The unemployment rate is lower than in the EU-27 countries with 4,2% (Eurostat, 2018).

Beer consumption in Romania has become very popular in the last few years. Between 1996 and 2001, beer consumption per capita increased from 37.4 liters to 56.9 liters, but still slightly below the average Eastern European consumer consumption of 60.6 liters (Larimo et al., 2006). In 2016 beer consumption/per capita amounted to 80 liters (Beer Statistics, 2017). Revenue in the beer segment amounts to US$1,731m in 2018, in comparison In global comparison, most revenue is generated in the United States (US$76,916m in 2018) (Statista, 2018). In relation to total population figures, per person revenues of US$89.50 are generated in 2018 (Statista, 2018).

The key players on the Romanian market are: SABMiller (South Africa) with a 26% market share, Heineken (Netherlands) with a 24% market share, Anheuser-Busch InBev (USA) with a 14% market share, Carlsberg (Denmark) with a 12% market share, and European Drinks (Romania) with a 5% market share. While only one main player in the market is Romanian, other big international brands buy local brands, like Ursus acquired by SABMiller, or Bergenbier acquired by InBev. The only foreign beer company that did not acquire a local brand is Carlsberg, which entered the market through a license agreement, with popular beer brands such as Tuborg, Carlsberg and Skol.

METHODOLOGY

Data Collection Process

The questionnaire was first written in English and then translated into Romanian by one of the authors and then back-translated by another Romanian fluent in both English and Romanian to make sure that all idioms and Romanian expressions were correct. It was then pretested on Romanian students studying at Aalborg University, to check for any misunderstandings. The questionnaire was administered to an urban population in Bucharest, Cluj-Napoca and Sibiu – three major cities in Romania, using the mall intercept method, leaving 317 questionnaires usable for the analysis.

Survey Instrument

The questionnaire was developed containing three major sections. The first section covers the demographic data, specifically gender, age, education and monthly income. The second section contains questions relating to the Tuborg beer. Each of the items was evaluated using a 5 item Likert-type scale), ranging from strongly disagree (coded 1) to strongly agree (coded 5). The third section of the questionnaire consists of questions related to consumer ethnocentrism using the CETSCALE (Consumer Ethnocentric Tendencies Scale), a 17-item questionnaire, developed by Shimp & Sharma (1987) to measure consumer ethnocentrism which is based on the same 5 ranged Likert-type scale as described earlier. Table 1 shows the demographical distribution of the respondents.

Data Analysis

The Analysis of the data was done using the statistical analysis from the SPSS version 19. First, a descriptive analysis is carried out to gain an overview of how the respondents perceive the Tuborg beer brand through 3 survey instruments, which represent our dependent variables and one of the independent variables, the country of origin, Denmark. Furthermore, a description is provided of the 3 deconstructed components of the CETSCALE from a principal component analysis. The components were classified into 4 levels of consumer ethnocentric tendencies with their respective factor scores. Descriptive statistics of the demographic characteristics of the Romanian respondents were also provided.

Table 1. The percentage distribution of the socio-demographic profile of the 317 respondents

Demographic characteristics	%
Gender	
Female	57.4
Male	42.6
Age in years	
< 26	33.1
26 - 45	42.9
> 45	24.0
Education	
Primary	6.3
Secondary	28.1
University	46.4
Post University	19.2
Income in EUR (netto)	
No income	20.2
≤ 400	38.8
401- 600	23.3
≥ 601	17.7

Secondly, pair-wise descriptive statistics of all independent variables representing COO, consumer ethnocentrism and demographic variables are provided for the 3 dependent variables measuring consumer brand perception of the Tuborg beer. Similarly a pair-wise relationship between the independent variables is also conducted to identify a possible correlation between these variables. Finally, Multiple Analysis of variance (MANOVA) is conducted to investigate the specified hypotheses.

RESULTS

Consumers' Perception Towards the Brand Tuborg and COO Effect

Three characteristics for the perception of the Tuborg brand have been evaluated by the Romanian consumers (see Table 2). A total of 51.7% of the respondents agree that they trust the quality of the brand, while 48.9% believe that the Tuborg brand matches their needs. It further shows that 33.4% of the respondents would choose Tuborg instead of other beer brands, compared to 18.8 who disagree with this statement.

The Pearson and the Spearman correlation coefficients between the 3 instrument items is positive and between 0.4 and 0.71, which is statistically significant ($p<0.001$) and devoid of multicollinearity or singularity, suggesting that the multivariate analysis variance (MANOVA) can be performed on the data. The country-of-origin effect is further presented in Table 3, showing that 36% of the respondents have a positive opinion about Tuborg being a Danish brand, while 26.8% feel that the country of origin has a negative effect on them.

Table 2. Percentage distribution of respondents scores and mean scores for the Tuborg brand perception (n = 317)

Instrument items [a]	Totally disagree	Disagree	Neither agree nor disagree	Agree	Totally agree	Mean	Std
1. I trust the quality of the products of this brand	.9	4.1	43.2	27.4	24.3	3.70	.915
2. I think that this brand is always looking to improve its products to better satisfy consumers' needs.	1.3	2.2	47.6	30.9	18.0	3.62	.847
3. I prefer this brand over other brands in the same product category.	7.9	10.7	47.9	20.2	13.2	3.20	1.057

Note: [a]The response format is a five-point Likert-type scale (1= strongly disagree, 5= strongly agree.)

Table 3. Percentage distribution of respondents scores and mean scores for the country-of-origin effect (n = 317)

Instrument items	Positive effect	Negative effect	No effect	Mean	Std
The beer brand Tuborg is from Denmark. How does this information affect your opinion of the brand?	36	26.8	37.2	2.01	.856

Degree of Ethnocentrism Among Romanian Consumers

The 17 items of the CETSCALE were estimated using an exploratory factor analysis with principle component analysis and varimax rotation. Firstly, it was observed that the factor loadings were at least .5, suggesting a high factorability. Secondly, the Kaiser-Meyer-Olkin measure of sampling adequacy was .864, above the commonly recommended value of .7, and Bartlett's test of sphericity was significant ($\chi 2 = 4335.8$, $p < 0.000$). Therefore, it was considered appropriate to factor analyze the data. The results of our analysis produced 3 factor components, labeled: "taxing imports", "buy Romanian products" and "support Romanian products". Table 4 shows the results of the principal component analysis of the CETSCALE.

Results of the Multivariate Analysis of Variance (MANOVA)

As mentioned earlier, MANOVA models were used to investigate whether a developed country of origin, (in this case Denmark) has a positive impact on how Romanian consumers perceive the brand. The authors also analysed whether a high ethnocentric tendency and demographic variables impact on the perception of a foreign beer brand.

The estimated functional form for our model is as follows:

$$Y_{ij} = \alpha_0 + \alpha_j X_{ij} + \varepsilon_{ij}$$

i represents an individual respondent; Y is a vector of 3 variable scores for Tuborg beer brand perception. The $\alpha 0$, is the mean of the referenced category of the cohort groups, αj are the parameter estimates of the rest of the categories in the group X, and εij is the vector of the error terms assumed to be multinormally distributed $N(0,\sigma^2)$.

The classified levels of the distribution of respondents and mean estimates of the Tuborg brand perceptions by COO, CE and demographics are presented in Table 5.

The 3 dependent variables (Y-vector) represent how consumers perceive the quality of the Tuborg beer, to what extent the beer satisfies consumers' needs and their preference of Tuborg relative to other beers in the same category. The independent variables were consumer ethnocentric tendencies of imposing tax on foreign products, buying Romanian products and supporting Romanian products as well as the demographic variables, gender, age, education and income levels in addition to the country-of-origin variable.

Table 4. PCA and 3 component factor loadings for the 17-items measuring "consumer ethnocentrism" based on CETSCALE (n = 317)

Instrument items	Rotated loading[a] for component1: "Taxing imports"	Rotated loading[a] for component 2: "Buy Romanian	Rotated loading[a] for component 3: "Support
1. Romanian people should always buy Romanian- made products instead of		.809	
2. Only those products that are unavailable in Romania should be imported.		.690	
3. Buy Romanian-made products. Keep Romania working.		.752	
4. Romanian products, first, last and foremost.		.721	
5. Purchasing foreign made products is un-Romanian.	.636		
6. It is not right to purchase foreign products, because it puts Romanians out of work.			.739
7. A real Romanian should always buy Romanian-made products.			.855
8. We should purchase products manufactured in Romania instead of letting other countries get rich by us.			.821
9. It is always best to purchase Romanian products.			.834
10. There should be very little trading or purchasing of goods from other countries unless out of necessity.			.831
11. Romanian people should not buy foreign			.834

The results suggested that:

There was a statistically significant difference between COO effects on the combined dependent variables F (6,582)=18.69; P=0.001; Wilks' Lambda=0.70; partial eta square=0.162 i.e. 16.2%. When the results for the dependent variables are considered separately, with a Bonferroni adjusted alpha level of 0.017, the differences for the 3 scores for Tuborg brand perception are significant F(198,118)=39.3, 32.5 and 4.8 respectively; P=0.001 for all; eta square =21.1%, 18.2% and 9.2% respectively. The inspection of the means show that those positive towards the country of origin, Denmark, consistently score higher means scores compared to those being negative or neutral to the fact that the Tuborg brand comes from Denmark, thus hypothesis 1 is confirmed.

The estimated model results also showed an interaction effect between Taxation and "buy Romanian products" ethnocentric tendencies. F(18,823)=1.87; P=0.015; Wilks' Lambda=0.110; partial eta square=3.7%. When the results for the dependent variables are considered separately, with a Bonferroni adjusted alpha level of 0.017, only the differences between Tuborg brand perception defined as satisfac-

Table 5. Distribution of respondents and mean estimates of Tuborg brand perceptions by COO, CE and demographics

Respondents			"Trust the quality of the brand"		"The Tuborg brand is attentive to consumers' needs"		Prefer Tuborg over other brands	
		%	Mean	SE	Mean	SE	Mean	SE
Total	317	100	3.70	.051	3.62	.047	3.20	.059
COO effect								
Positive effect	114	36	4.152	0.131	3.954	0.127	3.637	0.165
Negative effect	85	26.8	3.058	0.144	2.995	0.140	3.055	0.182
No effect	118	37.2	3.608	0.126	3.523	0.122	2.897	0.159
Ethnocentric Tendencies (CE)								
Tax on Imports, component 1								
High-non-CE	51	16.1	3.784	0.172	3.638	0.167	3.401	0.217
Less-non-CE	118	37.2	3.521	0.117	3.440	0.114	2.980	0.148
Less-CE	94	29.7	3.536	0.145	3.360	0.141	3.195	0.183
High-CE	54	17	3.584	0.187	3.524	0.182	3.210	0.236

tory for consumer needs is significant F(6,118)=2.78; P=0.012; eta square =5.4%. The inspection of the means show that means scores for "Buy Romanian products" (high non ethnocentric) and for Taxation (high non ethnocentric) is higher compared to the other levels of the taxation while for Buy Romanian products (less ethnocentric) it is the Taxation score (high ethnocentric) which is higher compared to the other taxation levels. A possible explanation for these findings is that although Romanian consumers may generally consider the foreign beer brand to be of good quality, this does not necessarily imply that they are likely to buy them. Hypothesis 2 is therefore only partially supported, since only 2 of the three components denoting ethnocentricity are dependent on the consumers' brand perception.

The model results on the relationship between country of origin and consumer ethnocentrism and their effect on the Romanian consumers' brand perception only showed a significant level of 0.04 ($p<0.05$) on the interaction between COO and the CE component "Support Romanian Economy" and how the Romanian consumers perceive the quality of the Tuborg brand, where those respondents who admit that the fact that the country of origin is Denmark has a positive effect are also more inclined towards less supporting the Romanian economy (72%), and thus are less ethnocentric. In this regard hypothesis 3 is only partially confirmed, since the only relationship between COO and the component denoted as "Support Romanian Economy" show a strong (> 95%) relationship with the consumers' brand perception.

The estimated model results also showed an interaction effect between the demographic variables: education and age F(12,770)=3.30; P=0.001; Wilks' Lambda=0.876; partial eta square=4.3%. When the results for the dependent variables are considered separately, the direction of significant difference is not the same for all levels of the 2 items which denote the Tuborg brand perception: "The Tuborg brand is attentive to consumers' needs" and "Prefer Tuborg over other brands". The inspection of the means for the second brand perception item showed that at an age of less than 26 years, the secondary education level mean score is consistently higher compared to the other educational levels. However, at the age group of above 46 years, a university education mean score is consistently higher compared to the other educational levels. For the latter Tuborg brand perception item, the results showed that at an age of less than 26 years age, the post university education level mean score 2.9 is consistently lower compared to the other education levels within this age group. However, for the age group between 26 and 45 years it is the secondary educational level which is consistently lower compared to the other educational levels within this age group. There was also a statistically significant difference between males and females on the combined dependent variables $F(3,291)=3.45$, $P=0.017$; Wilks' Lambda=0.97; partial eta square=0.034 i.e. 3.4%. When the results for the dependent variables are considered separately, with a Bonferroni adjusted alpha level of 0.017, only the difference in how consumer perceive the quality of the Tuborg beer is significant $F(198,118)=9.3$; $P=0.003$; eta square =3.1%. That is to say, males evaluated consumer perceived quality of the Tuborg beer higher compared to females. The direction of difference is the same for how the beer satisfies consumers' needs and the preference of the Tuborg relative to other beers in the same category. Since the brand perception of Romanian consumers is dependent on demographic characteristics as age, education and gender, hypothesis 4 is confirmed.

FUTURE RESEARCH DIRECTIONS

While our study helps illuminate research into consumer ethnocentrism and country of origin –effect, there are limitations that future research should address. Firstly, only respondents from 3 cities in Romania were chosen, limiting the accurate representativeness of the sample. According to Malhotra & Birks, (2003) marketing research that aims to assess foreign markets should consider at least five major cities in order to achieve a representative sample of the population. In a future study it would be interesting to see whether the results differ in a rural context, where educational level as well as familiarity with foreign products is lower. In addition, since the focus of this paper was on brand perception it would be interesting to examine the consumers' purchasing intentions. Finally, future research should consider both low and high involvement products with multiple countries of origin, in order to examine whether a country is regarded as the "benchmark" for each product type or whether all foreign products are being evaluated similarly.

CONCLUSION

Main Findings and Implications

The present study empirically tested the link between consumer ethnocentrism (CE), COO demographics and its implication on the consumers' evaluation of a specific foreign beer brand. The results show that:

1. A developed country of origin has a significant impact on the consumers' perception of the Danish beer brand Tuborg, and the Romanian respondents are more likely to evaluate a low involvement product, in this case a beer, more favorably if it has a Western country of origin.

These findings are consistent with past studies on the effect of COO on the consumers' brand perception. For example, Hu et al. (2008) found out that Chinese consumers consider COO as the most important factor in their wine evaluation, evaluating those wines from Western countries more favourably. Another study conducted by Saffu & Scott (2009) in Papuan New Guinea showed that consumers rated the quality of their domestic low involvement products as being lower than the product from the USA and Australia. Similarly, Chryssochoidis et al. (2007) evaluated the level of ethnocentrism of Greek consumers, and investigated the CE-COO effect relationship and implications on consumers' perceptions regarding imported food products, like beer, ham and cheese and found that CE affects consumer beliefs and how the perceived quality of domestic and foreign products are evaluated, culminating in the appearance of COO-effects. These findings add to the body of research indicating that consumers use country of origin as an informational variable, and reinforce the notion that country of origin plays an important role in consumer product evaluation.

2. When it comes to the level of ethnocentricity of the Romanian consumers, the results suggested that the tendency towards taxation of imports and buying Romanian products were dependent on each other when analysing their impact on how the consumers perceive the brand. Thus, the more non-ethnocentric the consumers are, the more they look favourably upon towards foreign brands and the less they support the taxation of foreign products. Furthermore, they are less inclined to want to buy Romanian products.

These results are therefore consistent with studies by Erdogan & Uzkurt (2010), who found out that those with low-ethnocentricity levels perceive foreign products more favourably than their high-ethnocentricity counterparts. Similarly, Chryssochoidis et al. (2007) evaluated the level of ethnocentrism of Greek consumers and investigated the CE-COO effect relationship and implications on consumers' perceptions regarding imported food products, like beer, ham and cheese. The findings suggested that CE affects consumer beliefs and how they evaluate the quality of domestic and foreign products. These findings add to the body of research supporting the notion that the relationship between country of origin and consumer ethnocentrism plays an important role in consumer product evaluation.

3. The relationship between COO and CE and their effect on brand perception was found to be only partially confirmed, where a clear relationship was shown between positive COO perception and less ethnocentric tendency.

These results are consistent with the findings by Sharma (2011) who investigated the role of CE in COO effects for consumers from the USA and the UK with regards to cars and found that ethnocentrism does not interact well with COO and has a weak negative effect on the consumers' product evaluation and behavioural intentions for imported products. Similarly, Yagci (2001) found that CE affects brand evaluations when the product is manufactured in its home country (i.e., BMW in Germany). In the relationship between CE and COO, consumer ethnocentrism becomes a significant predictor only when the product is manufactured in a less-developed/liked country (i.e. S. Korea).

4. The results of the impact of the demographic characteristics on brand perception showed that in the case of gender, the perceptions were different between men and women. It was shown that men evaluated the quality of the Tuborg beer as being higher when compared to females. An interaction between age and education meant that those respondents who assessed the brand favourably, belong to the age group of lower than 26 years with a secondary educational level, and the age groups of above 46 years with a university education.

The results are, therefore, consistent with studies by other scholars including Sharma et al. (1995), Ueltschy (1998), Watson & Wright (2000), Huang et al. (2010) as well as Erdogan & Uzkurt (2010) who found that younger consumers have more open attitudes towards foreign products, and are less ethnocentrically inclined (O'Cass and Lim, 2002; Wang et al., 2004; Hsu and Nien, 2008; Acikdilli et al., 2017).

The knowledge drawn from the study, which could be useful for scholars and practitioners alike, is that the Western COO effect showed a significant impact on the positive perception of the brand. Furthermore, quality plays an important role in the decision making process of the Romanian beer consumers.

Contributions to Theory and Methodology

Firstly, the study seeks to make additional contributions to the limited empirical research knowledge about the links between COO, CET and brand perception involving internationally acknowledged brands. Previous research on the COO and CE effects on consumers in developed markets (as opposed to emerging markets) has been inconclusive, and thus scholars have called for additional contributions to this emerging stream of research (Ahmed et al., 2004). Some studies have shown the negative effect of consumer ethnocentrism (CET) on the evaluation of foreign products by consumers in emerging markets (Klein et al., 2006). Other studies showed either no significant effect (Huddleston et al., 2001), or different effects based on product type (Hamin and Elliot, 2006), and perceptions of domestic products (Wang and Chen, 2004). It has also been noted that only limited empirical research has been conducted on the impact of COO and CET on consumer behaviour in emerging market economies (Kinra, 2006; Liu et al., 2006; Chryssochoidis et al., 2007). Additionally, previous research into the relationship between COO and CE included both low and high involvement products. While studies involving high involvement products have dominated this stream of research, a number of scholars also introduced low involvement products as being prone to COO and CE effects (Ahmed et al., 2004; Chryssochoidis et al., 2007).

Secondly, the systemic political and economic changes in the Central and Eastern European countries during the past two decades have provided both academic and strategic marketing management justifications for the increasing number of studies in the field (Beverland, 2001; Pecotich and Rosenthal, 2001; Dmitrovic et al., 2009). Consequently, this study provides additional evidence on how rapid systemic changes in economies impact consumer attitudes and behaviour. The Report on Consumer Spending Outlook and Value Creation in the New Global Economy states that between 2012 and 2016, the transitional markets from Central and Eastern Europe will add another US$95 billion per year to the global wealth, which means that the rapid acceptance of capitalism by many Eastern European countries, while presenting a major opportunity, also presents a challenge for marketers. This study is thus aimed at giving additional insights into how the consumers of a transitional CEE economy like that of Romania perceive brands from the "outside".

Managerial Implications

The study holds some implications for marketing practice. When it comes to the low involvement product used, beer, the findings represent some important guidelines for foreign beer companies that wish to enter the Romanian beer market. Romania is the second largest beer-consuming Eastern European country, closely following Poland (European Brewers Statistics, 2012) and therefore, foreign companies operating in Romania's larger cities must consider adapting their marketing strategies to fit local requirements. Firstly, since the Western COO effect showed a significant impact on the positive perception of a Danish beer brand, this cue should be taken advantage of in order to gain market share. Hence, both local and foreign managers should pay attention to the ethnocentric dispositions of consumers in positioning their products and developing advertising messages. In this case, and in contrast to what has previously been suggested, it may be useful to de-emphasise the country of origin of their products and emphasise their quality attributes instead. Thus, by highlighting the quality of their products, foreign firms are most likely to reduce the negative country-of-origin associations that some Romanian consumers may have about the product.

Finally, one lesson that we have drawn from the findings of the paper takes its point of reference from Theodor Levitt's (1983) argument that the world was witnessing the emergence of a global homogeneous culture as a result of global integration. He further noted that by converging value systems of consumers, there will emerge a "Global Village" where products and services would no longer be associated with a specific country. Furthermore, while globalisation has encouraged the expansion of firms' operations into unfamiliar market segments in both developed and emerging markets, this has also exerted a great influence on brands. The issue is not whether to sell products and services in a different market, but rather how to do so. Since then, there have been many developments that have challenged Levitt's earlier perceptions. Globalisation has contributed to the increase in importance of sub-national differences, and the revival of regional identities, rather than a convergence of consumers as Levitt suggested (Orbaiz & Papadopoulos, 2003). There is an increasing degree of regionalisation of markets since the creation of an integrated region creates economic benefits for members (Zahrnt, 2005), and within these regional centers there are political activities that bring these countries together. These trends spill over onto the Romanian beer consumers who follow the trends of the regional European Union environment, and thus, a specific type of homogeneous consumer is created, and foreign companies that wish to operate in Romania should be aware of these communalities of the Romanian beer consumers and the European consumer as such, to a great extent.

REFERENCES

Acikdilli, G., Ziemnowicz, C., & Bahhouth, V. (2018). Consumer Ethnocentrism in Turkey: Ours are Better than Theirs. *Journal of International Consumer Marketing*, *30*(1), 45–57. doi:10.1080/08961530.2017.1361882

Ahmed, S. A., & d'Astous, A. (2008). Antecedents, Moderators, and Dimensions of Country-of-Origin Evaluations. *International Marketing Review*, *25*(1), 75–106. doi:10.1108/02651330810851890

Ahmed, Z. U., Johnson, J. P., Yang, X., Fatt, C. K., Teng, H. S., & Boon, L. S. (2004). Does country of origin matter for low-involvement products. *International Marketing Review*, *21*(1), 102–120. doi:10.1108/02651330410522925

Altintas, M. H., & Tokol, T. (2007). Cultural openness and consumer ethnocentrism: An empirical analysis of Turkish consumers. *Marketing Intelligence & Planning*, *25*(4), 308–325. doi:10.1108/02634500710754565

Bailey, W., & Gutierrez de Pineres, S. (1997). Country of Origin Attitudes in Mexico: The Malinchismo Effect. *Journal of International Consumer Marketing*, 9.

Baker, M. J., & Michie, J. (1995). *Product country images: perceptions of Asian cars*. University of Strathclyde, Department of Marketing, Working Paper Series 95.

Balabanis, G., & Diamantopoulos, A. (2004). Domestic Country Bias, Country-of-Origin Effects, and Consumer Ethnocentrism: A Multidimensional Unfolding Approach. *Journal of the Academy of Marketing Science*, *32*(1), 80–95. doi:10.1177/0092070303257644

Balabanis, G., Diamantopoulos, A., Mueller, R. D., & Melewar, T. C. (2001). The Impact of Nationalism, Patriotism and Internationalization on Consumer Ethnocentric Tendencies. *Journal of International Business Studies*, *22*(1), 157–175. doi:10.1057/palgrave.jibs.8490943

Balabanis, G., & Siamagka, N. T. (2017). Inconsistencies in the behavioural effects of consumer ethnocentrism. *International Marketing Review*, *34*(2), 166–182. doi:10.1108/IMR-03-2015-0057

Bannister, J. P., & Saunders, J. A. (1978). UK Consumers' Attitudes towards Imports: The Measurement of National Stereotype Image. *European Journal of Marketing*, *12*(8), 562–570. doi:10.1108/EUM0000000004982

Bilkey, W. J., & Nes, E. (1982). Country-of-origin effects on product evaluations. *Journal of International Business Studies*, *13*(1), 89–99. doi:10.1057/palgrave.jibs.8490539

Chryssochoidis, G., Krystallis, A., & Perreas, P. (2007). Ethnocentric Beliefs and Country-of-Origin (COO) Effect. *European Journal of Marketing*, *41*(11/12), 1518–1544. doi:10.1108/03090560710821288

De Mooij, M. (2010). *Global Marketing and Advertising: Understanding Cultural Paradoxes*. Thousand Oaks, CA: SAGE Puplications.

Ding, Q. (2017). Chinese products for Chinese people? Consumer ethnocentrism in China. *International Journal of Retail & Distribution Management*, *45*(5), 550–564. doi:10.1108/IJRDM-11-2016-0212

Dmitrovic, T., Vida, I., & Reardon, J. (2009). Purchase behavior in favor of domestic products in the West Balkans. *International Business Review*, *18*(5), 523–535. doi:10.1016/j.ibusrev.2009.05.003

Erdogan, B. Z., & Uzkurt, C. (2010). Effects of ethnocentric tendency on consumers' perception of product attitudes for foreign and domestic products. *Cross Cultural Management*, *17*(4), 393–406. doi:10.1108/13527601011086595

Etzel, M. J., & Walker, B. J. (1974). Advertising Strategy for Foreign Products. *Journal of Advertising Research*, *14*, 41–44.

Evanschitzky, H., Wangenheim, F. V., Woisetschla, D., & Blut, M. (2008). Consumer ethnocentrism in the German market. *International Marketing Review*, *25*, 7–32. doi:10.1108/02651330810851863

Festervand, T. A., Lumpkin, J. R., & Lundstrom, W. J. (1985). Consumers' Perceptions of Imports: An Update and Extension. *Akron Business and Economic Review*, *16*, 31–33.

Ghalandari, K., & Norouzi, A. (2012). The Effect of Country of Origin on Purchase Intention: The Role of Product Knowledge. *Research Journal of Applied Sciences, Engineering and Technology*, *4*, 1166–1171.

Good, L. K., & Huddleston, P. (1995). Ethnocentrism of Polish and Russian consumers: Are feelings and intentions related? *International Marketing Review*, *12*(5), 35–48. doi:10.1108/02651339510103047

Granzin, K. L., & Olsen, J. E. (1998). Americans' choice of domestic over foreign products: A matter of helping behavior? *Journal of Business Research*, *43*(1), 39–54. doi:10.1016/S0148-2963(97)00101-X

Gürhan-Canli, Z., & Maheswaran, D. (2000). Cultural Variations in Country-of-Origin Effects. *JMR, Journal of Marketing Research*, *37*(3), 309–317. doi:10.1509/jmkr.37.3.309.18778

Hamin, & Elliott, G. (2006). A less-developed country perspective of consumer ethnocentrism and "country of origin" effects: Indonesian evidence. *Asia Pacific Journal of Marketing and Logistics*, *18*(2), 79–92. doi:10.1108/13555850610658246

Han, C. M., & Terpstra, V. (1988). Country-of-origin effects for uni-national and bi-national products. *Journal of International Business Studies*, *19*(2), 235–256. doi:10.1057/palgrave.jibs.8490379

Hsu, J. L., & Nien, H. P. (2008). Who are ethnocentric? Examining consumer ethnocentrism in Chinese societies. *Journal of Consumer Behaviour*, *7*(6), 436–447. doi:10.1002/cb.262

Hu, X., Li, L., Xie, C., & Zhou, J. (2008). The effects of country-of-origin on Chinese consumers' wine purchasing behaviour. *Journal of Technology Management in China*, *3*(3), 292–306. doi:10.1108/17468770810916195

Huang, Y.-A., Phau, I., & Lin, C. (2010). Consumer animosity, economic hardship, and normative influence: How do they affect consumers' purchase intention? *European Journal of Marketing*, *44*(7/8), 909–937. doi:10.1108/03090561011047463

Huddleston, P., Good, L. K., & Stoel, L. (2001). Consumer ethnocentrism, product necessity and Polish consumers' perceptions of quality. *International Journal of Retail & Distribution Management*, *29*(5), 236–246. doi:10.1108/09590550110390896

Insch, G. S., & McBride, J. B. (2004). The impact of country-of-origin cues on consumer perceptions of product quality: A binational test of the decomposed country-of-origin construct. *Journal of Business Research*, *57*(3), 256–265. doi:10.1016/S0148-2963(02)00323-5

Jaffe, E. D., & Nebenzahl, I. D. (1996). *National Image & Competitive Advantage: The Theory and Practice of Country-of-Origin Effect*. Copenhagen Business School Press.

Javalgi, R. G., Khare, V. P., Cross, A. C., & Scherer, R. F. (2005). An Application of the Consumer Ethnocentrism Model to French Consumers. *International Business Review*, *14*, 325–344.

Josiassen, A., & Harzing, A. W. (2008). Descending from the Ivory Tower: Reflections on the Relevance and Future of Country-of-Origin Research. *European Management Review*, *5*(4), 264–270. doi:10.1057/emr.2008.19

Kaynak, E., & Kara, A. (2002). Consumer perceptions of foreign products: An analysis of product-country images and ethnocentris. *European Journal of Marketing*, *36*(7/8), 928–949. doi:10.1108/03090560210430881

Kinra, N. (2006). The effect of country of origin on foreign brand names in the Indian market. *Marketing Intelligence & Planning*, *24*(1), 15–30. doi:10.1108/02634500610641534

Klein, J. G., Ettenson, R., & Krishnan, B. C. (2006). Extending the construct of consumer ethnocentrism: When foreign products are preferred. *International Marketing Review*, *23*(3), 304–321. doi:10.1108/02651330610670460

Knight, G. A., & Calantone, R. J. (2000). A flexible model of consumer country-oforigin perceptions A cross-cultural investigation. *International Marketing Review*, *17*, 127–145. doi:10.1108/02651330010322615

Lee, D., & Ganesh, G. (1999). Effects of partitioned country image in the context of brand image and familiarity: A categorization theory perspective. *International Marketing Review*, *16*(1), 18–41. doi:10.1108/02651339910257610

Levitt, T. (1983, May). The globalization of markets. *Harvard Business Review*, 92–102.

McLain, S., & Sternquist, B. (1991). Ethnocentric Consumers: Do They Buy American? *Journal of International Consumer Marketing*, *4*(1-2), 39–57. doi:10.1300/J046v04n01_03

Mittal, V., & Tsiros, M. (1995). Does Country of Origin Transfer Between Brands? *Advances in Consumer Research: Association for Consumer Research*, *22*, 292–296.

Nebenzahl, I. D., & Jaffe, E. D. (2001). Measuring the joint effect of brand and country image in consumer evaluation of global products. *International Marketing Review*, *13*(4), 5–22. doi:10.1108/02651339610127220

O'Cass, A., & Lim, L. (2002). Understanding the Younger Singaporean Consumers' Views of Western and Eastern Brands. *Asia Pacific Journal of Marketing and Logistics*, *14*(4), 54–79. doi:10.1108/13555850210764954

Orbaiz, L. V., & Papadopoulos, N. (2003). Toward a model of consumer receptivity of foreign and domestic products. *Journal of International Consumer Marketing*, *15*(3), 101–130. doi:10.1300/J046v15n03_06

Paswan, A. K., & Sharma, D. (2004). Brand-country of origin (COO) knowledge and COO image: Investigation in an emerging franchise market. *Journal of Product and Brand Management*, *13*(3), 144–155. doi:10.1108/10610420410538041

Pentz, C., Terblanche, N., & Boshoff, C. (2017). Antecedents and consequences of consumer ethnocentrism: evidence from South Africa. *International Journal of Emerging Markets*, *12*(2), 199-218.

Sajdakowska, M. (2003). Consumer ethnocentrism -Factor influencing consumers' purchasing decisions in the food market. *Acta Scientiarum Polonorum. Technologia Alimentaria*, *2*, 177.

Samiee, S., Shimp, T. A., & Sharma, S. (2005). Brand origin recognition accuracy: Its antecedents and consumers' cognitive limitations. *Journal of International Business Studies*, *36*(4), 379–397. doi:10.1057/palgrave.jibs.8400145

Schaefer, A. (1997). Consumer knowledge and country of origin effects. *European Journal of Marketing*, *31*(1), 56–72. doi:10.1108/03090569710157034

Schooler, R. D. (1965). Product bias in the Central American common market. *JMR, Journal of Marketing Research*, *2*(4), 394–397. doi:10.2307/3149486

Sharma, S., Shimp, T., & Shin, J. (1995). Consumer Ethnocentrism: A Test Antecedents and Moderators. *Journal of the Academy of Marketing Science*, *23*(1), 26–37. doi:10.1007/BF02894609

Shimp, T., & Sharma, S. (1987). Consumer Ethnocentrism: Construction and Validation of the CETSCALE. *JMR, Journal of Marketing Research*, *24*(3), 280–289. doi:10.2307/3151638

Siamagka, S., & Balabanis, G. (2015). Revisiting Consumer Ethnocentrism: Review, Reconceptualization, and Empirical Testing. *Journal of International Marketing*, *23*(3), 66–86. doi:10.1509/jim.14.0085

Beer Statistics. (2017). *Beer Statistics 2017 edition*. The Brewers of Europe, December 2017.

Teas, R. K., & Agarwal, S. (2008). The effects of extrinsic product cues on consumers' perceptions of quality, sacrifice, and value. *Journal of the Academy of Marketing Science*, *28*(2), 278–290. doi:10.1177/0092070300282008

Tse, D. K., & Gorn, G. J. (1993). An experiment on the salience of country-of-origin in the era of global brands. *Journal of International Marketing*, *1*, 57–76.

Ueltschy, L. (1998). Brand perceptions as influenced by consumer ethnocentrism and country-of-origin effects. *Journal of Marketing Management*, *8*, 12–23.

Vida, I., & Damjan, J. (2000). The role of consumer characteristics and attitudes in purchase behavior of domestic vs. foreign made products: The case of Slovenia. *Journal of East-West Business*, *6*(3), 111–131. doi:10.1300/J097v06n03_06

Vida, I., & Fairhurst, A. (1999). Factors underlying the phenomenon of consumer ethnocentricity: Evidence from four central European countries. *International Review of Retail, Distribution and Consumer Research*, *9*(4), 321–337. doi:10.1080/095939699342444

Vida, I., & Reardon, J. (2008). Domestic consumption: Rational, affective or normative choice? *Journal of Consumer Marketing*, *25*(1), 34–44. doi:10.1108/07363760810845390

Wall, M., Hofstra, G., & Heslop, L. A. (1990). *Imported Versus Domestic Car Owners: Demographic Characteristics and Attitudes*. Paper Presented at the *Conference of the Administrative Sciences Association of Canada*.

Wall, M., Liefeld, J., & Heslop, L. (1991). Impact of country-of-origin cues on consumer judgments in multi-cue situations: A covariance analysis. *Journal of the Academy of Marketing Science*, *19*(2), 105–1. doi:10.1007/BF02726002

Wang, C. K. (1978). *The Effect of Foreign Economics, Political and Cultural Environment on Consumers' Willingness to Buy Foreign Products* (PhD Dissertation).

Wang, C. L., & Chen, Z. X. (2004). Consumer ethnocentrism and willingness to buy domestic products in a developing country setting: Testing moderating effects. *Journal of Consumer Marketing*, *21*(6), 391–400. doi:10.1108/07363760410558663

Wang, C. L., Siu, N. Y. M., & Hui, S. Y. (2004). Consumer decision-making styles on domestic and imported brand clothing. *European Journal of Marketing*, *38*(1/2), 436–447. doi:10.1108/03090560410511212

Watson, J. J., & Wright, K. (2000). Consumer ethnocentrism and attitudes toward domestic and foreign products. *European Journal of Marketing*, *34*(9/10), 1149–1166. doi:10.1108/03090560010342520

World Bank. (2018). *The World Bank Statistics*. Retrieved from www.data.worldbank.org

Zahrnt, V. (2005). *Enhancing the internal legitimacy of WTO negotiations: Representations of member states through common interest groups and integrated regions*. Working paper.

KEY TERMS AND DEFINITIONS

Brand Perception: Consumers' beliefs and attitudes towards a brand.

Central Eastern Europe: Group of countries comprising Albania, Bulgaria, Croatia, Czech Republic, Hungary, Poland, Romania, Slovak Republic, Slovenia, and the three Baltic States: Estonia, Latvia, and Lithuania.

Country-of-Origin Effect: The effect that the country of manufacture or assembly of a product has on consumer behavior.

Ethnocentrism: A belief that one's own culture is superior to other cultures.

Tuborg: A beer brand part of the Danish Carlsberg Group.

Chapter 4
Perfume Consumption in India: An Exploratory Study

David James Bamber
University of Bolton, UK

Clay Gransden
Liverpool Hope University, UK

ABSTRACT

Perfumes have been important in India for millennia and so have the stories connected with them. The perfume business in India is worth billions ($). A background from which the Indian perfume industry can be understood in terms of the Berger's STEPP model, the consumers' cognitive schemas, consumers' behaviors, and the story of the product, brand, and their customers' stories. Three sets of themes—product perceptions, concerns, and consumers' lifestyle—are identified, each with their own sub-themes that are antecedents to perfume purchasing behavior. Segments in the Indian perfume market are also identified. Each consumer segment has their own behavioral nuances and they consider different aspects of the perfume product taking into account their own income and aspects of the three themes and 19 sub-themes. It is important for perfume marketing managers to consider each aspect of the STEPPs modeland for the Indian government to locate and develop a "Place of Perfume" within India that will eventually challenge the region of Grasse in France as the global perfume marketplace.

INTRODUCTION

The key objective of the chapter is to show that in the developing market of India there is a product type: "perfume" that contributes in numerous ways to the economy of the country and the market is driven by various consumer behaviors and demands from differing consumer segments. The Indian market is complex and has developed over millennia. It must not be assumed that just because the market is still developing that the consumers' behaviors there are simple, the behaviors are indeed complex and manifold. The consumers of perfumes in India are presented with a vast array of perfume offerings from multinationals, from prestigious brands to fragrances offered by independent manufacturers, with some perfumes produced according to traditional formulae laid out in the ancient Hindu Ayurvedic texts. However, a

DOI: 10.4018/978-1-5225-7906-9.ch004

broad range of consumer behavior literature concerning health issues, halal branding, packaging, gift giving, glocalisation, word-of-mouth endorsements and eco-friendly attitudes, social entrepreneurship coupled with ethical consumption, pricing and celebrity endorsements, that have been well reported in the marketing literature, concern consumers' behaviors in developing nations, like India. There are other product types that contribute directly and indirectly to the India economy, such as *Indian cuisine*, that was arguably further popularised in Europe by Madhur Jaffrey (1992). Other developing nations have important product types; such as China with silk (Silk Road, 2015), that have been and continue to be important to their economies. Due to the historic abundance of natural aromatic resources in the Indian geographic region, there is a plethora of natural raw materials from which India extracts perfumes and scents. Furthermore, that "natural" industry is augmented by the synthetic fragrance industry. All those products are exported from India to the international perfume houses of the world, as well as being used by a broad segment of local manufacturers. The world leading perfume houses of France are considered and their business and marketing practices are presented as basis from which Indian perfumeries may develop their own world leading positions. The region of Grasse is France is the heart-place of perfume and we propose the India will need to identify and develop its own world leading "Place of Perfume" in order that India's perfumery house may begin to challenge on the global perfume stage.

BACKGROUND

Throughout India, from the sole traders of attar (non-alcoholic herbal perfume) on the streets of Hydrabad, to the village of Kannauj's distilleries in the Indian state of Uttar Pradesh and then to the Hindustan Unilever Corporation (HUC) located in Mumbai one does not need to go far to be connected to the perfume industry in India. Arguably, everyone in India has some family member working in the industry or using some perfume. Hence, within the consumer collective each individual consumer has recollections of their own stories: an auntie collecting jasmine flowers, an uncle working in the factory, buying perfume with a friend, or perhaps mother wearing a particular perfume for that special occasion. Each consumer has their own stories within their own cognitive schema: Brewer and Nakamura (1984) and Bartlett (1932) described a (cognitive) schema as "an active organization of past reactions, or of past experiences, which must always be supposed to be operating in any well-adapted organic response", which would include consumer behaviors. Hence, in this chapter we argue that the narrative of the product type, in this case "perfume" is very important, because through that narrative we can understand how the product is not only already positioned in the minds of particular consumers and consumer segments but is historically embedded in the wider cultural psyche. Berger (2013), argues that there are six things that promote products and things become "contagious" through Social Currency, Triggers, Emotions, Public, Practical Value and Stories (placed under the acronym STEPPS). We argue that each of those six antecedents to a product becoming contagious are connected with perfume in general and it is when the manufacturer can position their own specific product or brand in the mind of the consumer (Reis and Trout, 2001) that the product will take off. At the same time it is necessary to ensure that the product position is closely connected within the existing cognitive schema of the target consumers' STEPPS. It is then likely that the particular perfume product will gain completive advantage, the product having been placed not only in the mind of the consumer but also having been placed close to the heart of the positive emotions connected to the stories to which the consumers attach positive value. Thus it is necessary to understand the story of the product type in connection with the cultural melee of the nation, when considering consumers behaviors. Indian consumers, just like consumers worldwide, take into consideration a number of factors when intending to buy perfume, those factors include: the scent of the perfume, the brand, the price, internal (psychological, emotional and health) factors and external factors (social and media) factors. Consumers are not only attracted to the scent of the perfume, the brand and the price but they are also affected by a mix of emotional, practical, public and psychological factors which influence the decision to purchase or to not purchase a particular perfume. Hence, different consumers respond to different perfumes in different ways.

India

The culture of India encompasses the lifestyle of the people of India and includes its complex mix of languages, religions, castes, tribes, cuisine, dance, history and customs, amongst many other things which form the stories that are embedded within the consumers' cognitive schemas. In India there are estimated to be 1365 rationalised mother tongues, 234 identifiable mother-tongues and 122 major languages (Census India, 2011). People from the different religions of India hold a vast range of attitudes, beliefs and practices associated with perfumes. There are six main religions represented in India, with populations as shown in Table 1. Jains advocate "cruelty free cosmetics" (Jainworld, 2015). There is an ongoing debate about whether Muslims could be allowed to wear (externally) perfumes containing alcohol or not (Emirates247, 2015) and the Muslim text of the Hadith exonerates the wearing of perfume, the giving and receiving of perfumes as gifts in certain circumstances. Attar (or ittar) is widely available in India and is a perfume that contains oil derived from botanical sources and when produced without alcohol is certainly permitted for use by Muslims. McMahon (1996) discusses a journey through India to discover the plethora of attars and their manufacture. Some Christians argue that the wearing of perfumes may be wrong (Catholic Forums, 2015), whilst Hindu Sanskrit texts highlight the practice of "sola singar": that women should wear sixteen items, two of which are perfume and sandalwood paste (Hinduism, 2015). McHugh (2012) presents an intriguing account of the pleasant scents (sandalwood) and some repulsive smells (carrion) of South Asia and he presents clear links between the aromatic culture, olfactory aesthetics and the historical trade networks through India and elsewhere, noting that for ancient and modern people the scents of people, goods, reliquary stupas, and places were always important.

Table 1. The six main religions of India

Religion	Population India	Population Worldwide
Hinduism	1 billion	1.1 billion
Islam	258 million	1.6 billion
Christianity	171 million	2 billion
Sikhism	29 million	31 million
Buddhism	24 million	535 million
Jainism	4.2 million	4.2 million

The Indian Perfume Market

In India, there is a build up of local perfume manufacturing companies and many, less well known, perfume houses that operate alongside the noted national and international brands. Some of the local perfume manufacturers in India produce quality perfumes yet remain largely anonymous. Such companies struggle to gain market share against the large well known brands and the world famous French perfume houses. Yet, many Indian perfume manufacturers aim to develop distinct personalities for their perfumes so that the consumers can identify with the brand and buy those branded products (Naresh, 2012). With the support of government opportunities exist for the Indian perfume houses to begin to challenge on the global stage. In India, perfume companies have extended their product ranges and launched products in the same brand line of perfumes but with different varieties of fragrance, for example "Axe" is a men's deodorant that is offered by Hindustan Unilever Limited and has different *blends* of fragrance (Music Star, Wild Spice, Pulse Instinct, Marine and Apollo). Another perfume producer is Raymond Ltd., which is part of an Indian group of companies that is one the world's largest integrated fabric manufacturers and Raymond Grooming produces perfumes, perfume sprays, deodorants and shaving solutions. Additionally, J.K. Helene Curtis Ltd. (also part of the Raymond group) holds a range of fragrancies that include "Park Avenue" and "Premium". However, Park Avenue's perfume market share in India was eaten up by Axe when they launched their products in India, so much so that Axe had 33% market share in Indian Perfume Industry in 2012 (Business Standard, 2012). Due to that, Park Avenue repositioned the brand and launched a new range of men's deodorant. However, because of lack of adequate positioning through the use of promotion and public relations activities from the manufacturer, the product still lost out to the new competitor. Due to India's large population, coupled with economic growth and the rising of income of the lucrative middle class and elite consumer markets, India is targeted by global perfume conglomerates. In particular, France is chosen as the preferential country of origin for perfumes by elite consumers when purchasing perfume for everyday use, for a party, as a gift and as indicator of quality (Khan, Bamber, & Quazi, 2012). France is home to some of the world largest and most prestigious perfume houses. Coty Inc., for example, one of the largest French perfume manufacturing companies, acquired Unilever's fragrance manufacturing unit (Unilever Cosmetics International) in 2005 and so strengthened Coty's brand image further (BBC UK, 2005). Later in this chapter when present an overview of some the prestigious perfume houses of the Grasse region of France: Parfumeries Galimard, Guerlain, Givaudan and Fragonard.

In India, as elsewhere, the middle class and elite consumer markets are well connected to and strongly influenced by the media and social media (Global Outlook, 2012). Furthermore, the Hindu Business Line reported that that the online marketplace "eBay" way India's primary "Perfume Mall" with over one hundred leading perfume brands for sale on their platform (Urs, 2015). The online marketplace has over one thousand stock keeping units for the prestigious international brands, such as Giorgio Armani, Bvlgari, Hugo Boss, Chanel, and Davidoff offering up to thirty percent discounts. Shanbaug (2012), for the Economic Times of India, showed the economic importance of the perfume industry in India and presented details of The Associated Chambers of Commerce and Industry of India's (ASSOCHAM) scoping document: "The Domestic Fragrance Industry: The way ahead". The Indian domestic luxury perfume market is estimated to be around 4.5 billion pounds sterling and in addition to that there has been an annual growth rate of around forty to forty-five percent in an industry that includes fragrances, perfumes, deodorants and roll-ons. The deodorant industry constitutes the forty-nine percent lion's share of the total Indian domestic perfume industry, with about forty percent of the market being devoured by the global and domestic perfume giants. For example, Takasago, the leading Japanese fragrance player targeted the Indian market as part of its strategy for global growth (Pitman, 2012). Scion International, Dubai's perfume giant, has also entered the Indian market (Prayag, 2012). Half the consumer market share is dominated by teenager students and nearly, sixty percent of the whole fragrance industry is devoted to men's products because urban Indian men desire to be "well- groomed", so they buy high end luxury grooming products. Generally, perfume sales are higher in the coastal areas and during the hotter months between March and September: the Indian perfume industry is blooming.

Perfumes and Ancient Brands

Perfumes are a mixture of fragrant essential oils and aromatic compounds, fixatives and solvents that are used to give the human body, animals, food, objects, and living spaces a pleasant scent. The word "Perfume" is used to describe the pleasantly scented mixtures of various substances and originates from the Latin *"per fumus"* denoting "through smoke", as the original base for most fragrances was incense based: the pleasant smelling fragrances were produced by the burning of gums, spices, or other natural substances. Pliny the elder (Bostock & Riley,1855) describes the composition of various perfumes and how fashions changed for different perfumes in Roman times. Perhaps two of the perfumes mentioned by Pliny the Elder in around AD 75 are two of the first *"branded"* perfumes: "regale unguentum" and "megalium" both of which aspired to elite consumers. "Regale unguentum" (Regal unguent) was originally prepared for the Parthian kings and was made from various proportions of myrobalanus, costus, amomum, cinnamon, comacum, cardamum, spikenard, marum, myrrh, cassia, storax, ladanum, opobalsamum, Syrian calamus and Syrian sweet-rush, œnanthe, malobathrum, serichatum, cyprus, aspralathus, panax, saffron, cypirus, sweet marjoram, lotus, honey, and wine. Another perfume "megalium" was said to have held the "very highest rank" and was made from the oil of balanus, balsamum, calamus, sweet-rush, xylobalsamum, cassia, and resin. This chapter essentially deals with fine perfumes and fragrances that are used to give the human body a pleasant scent. Generally, there are now three perfume grades: Eau de Parfum has a higher concentration of essential oils than Eau de Toilette, which in turn has a higher concentration of the essential oils than Eau de Cologne (Hello, 2010). However, the exact concentrations vary between different perfume house and perfume ranges. Women's fragrances are seldom sold as Eau de Colognes and fragrances for men are rarely sold as Eau de Parfums. Perfumes (fine perfumes) sometimes called perfume extracts or extraits are the most expensive versions of any fragrance and they contain the highest concentrations of essences and they provide the longest lasting fragrances. Men tend to use grooming products, deodorants, after shaves and moisturizers rather than body sprays or perfumes as such (Mintel, 2012).

"Chyawanprash" is perhaps the oldest generic botanical branded product that has been used in India since the ancient Vedic period and is still used today (Banyan Botanicals, 2015). This is not a perfume but is consumed as a dietary supplement. Chyawanprash is a cooked jam mixture of sugar, honey, triphala, ghee, sesame oil, berries and other herbs and spices. Although, the main ingredient is the Indian Gooseberry "amla", there are over thirty other botanical ingredients. Chyawanprash is made following the instructions that are written in the in ancient Ayurvedic texts (Pole, 2006). Ayurveda, means "life-knowledge" and Ayurvedic medicine is a system of traditional Hindu medicine handed down the generations through the Hindu Ayurvedic texts and culture. The Ayurvedic texts indicate how to produce perfumes that will benefit royals: there are sixteen ingredients that make up the "Gandharnara" (Perfume Ocean) they should be combined in certain propotions in prescribed ways, with some combinations warned against, making a total of 174720 perfumes possible according to the Brihat Samhita (Panditbhushan, Shastri, & Bhat, 1946).

Multinationals and Modern Brands

There are a number of huge players in the global fragrance business and Ellison and Side (2003) reported on the takeover of Wella by Proctor & Gamble in 2003 for nearly $6 billion US dollars. Fragrance brands Gucci, Mexx, Bruno Banani, Escada and Gabriela Sabatini were all part of the Wella portfolio that was acquired by Proctor & Gamble in 2003. Yet a portfolio of 43 beauty brands, that include "Covergirl" and "Max Factor", are being sold on to Coty: for a reported $15 billion US dollars (Gaurdian, 2015). Some other fragrance brand ranges that Proctor & Gamble have acquired over the years are included in Table 2, but most of these have been sold on to a range of other companies that include Designer Parfums, Fribad, Inter Parfums, L'Oreal Group, Lornamead, Luxess, Maürer & Wirtz, Morris Profumi and Selective Beauty (Osborne, 2015). So, any brand, from India or elsewhere, that is seen as "lucrative pickings" may be well be snapped up to be regurgitated again by the global giants, who become consumers of the growing brands in developing countries; for example, Paul and Bhawsar (2011) note that Ranbaxy raised a "premium share price" when the company agreed to their own acquisition by Dai-Ichi - a Japanese multinational, which in return gained access to India and Ranbaxy's customers, as well as gaining production and management control of Ranbaxy.

Indian Consumers

Culture can be defined as the common sets of beliefs that a group of people within society have about human roles and behavior within that society which is learned by the individual from the immediate family and institutions that are further afield but within that society thereby forming a fairly uniform and homogeneous set of norms, customs and traditions. Culture influences the thoughts, feelings, language, materials and behavior of the society (Czinkota and Ronkainen, 2011). Hence, it is very important to understand the cultural background of the market being targeted before launching a product as culture influences consumer buying behavior to a great extent. Therefore, academic literature cites the importance of cultural awareness in respect to consumer buying behavior thus giving way to the concept of "glocalisation" which means the organisations keep their marketing strategies global by adapting their marketing plan to local cultural conditions (Tai and Wong, 1998). The experience that consumers gather by using a specific product will be different across different cultures depending upon the external factors, and that will influence how and where the cultural diversity will influence the consumers (Overby, Woodruff, & Gardial, 2005). For example KFC, has their own Indian versions of the burgers and their wraps are made exclusively out of the Indian spices and that increased the sales of their products by influencing the consumers' buying behaviors by matching the product to their ethnocentric cultural needs and offering consumers a local taste which they relate to. Additionally, there are sub-cultures, that are referred to as the groups of people, within a broader culture, but with close-fitting value systems based on common life experiences. Demography and religion are the two major factors that create sub-cultures. India has its own broad culture, however every Indian state has its own unique sub-cultures based upon the majority religion, demography, language, values, life style and experiences in those particular re-

Table 2. Brand acquisitions made by Proctor & Gamble then disinvested

Brand Range	Date	Acquired From
Alberta Ferretti	1999	Proteo, after Proteo's bankruptcy
Christina Aguilera	2007	Sarantis
Cover Girl	1989	Noxell
Dolce & Gabbana	2005	Euroitalia
Giorgio Beverly Hills	1994	Avon
Hugo Boss	1991	Betrix from Revlon
Jean Patou	2001	Jean Patou
Lacoste	2001	Jean Patou
Laura Biagiotti	1991	Betrix from Revlon
Max Factor	1991	Revlon
Otto Kern	1991	Betrix from Revlon
Replay	2007	License acquired from Morris
Shulton (Old Spice)	1990	American Cyanamid
Stella McCartney	2013	L'Oreal
Valentino	2003	Unilever
Yohji Yamamoto	2001	Jean Patou
Zirh	2009	Zirh Holdings

gions. Hence, people from certain sub-cultures may prefer brands over the scent of the product whilst others may prefer scent over brand. Hence, it is important to understand such factors in detail so as to understand what really attracts the consumers to a particular product (Lenartowicz and Roth, 2001).

EXPLORATORY INDIAN CONSUMER RESEARCH

We conducted primary qualitative research, using ten focus groups and a total of 103 participants, in order to further our understanding of Indian consumers' perceptions of perfumes and their perfume buying behavior. 51 of the participants were employed and 52 were students who were not employed. 59 participants were female and 44 were male. Each focus group had a mix of participants from the six major religions. We focused our research in one of the metropolitan cities of India: Kolkata, as Kolkata is the most important financial hub of Eastern India. One group of participants were employed and another group were students that represented "Little India", who at the time of the study were full-time students and are likely to become the wealthier and elite consumers of the future.

The moderator was a Hindu and a female graduate resident of Kolkata. The same procedures were followed for each of the focus groups and the moderator asked the same questions to each group.

Kolkata (previously known as Calcutta) is the capital of the Indian state of West Bengal and is India's oldest port that is placed on the east of the Hooghly River in the Lower Ganges Delta of eastern India. Kolkata is India's second largest urban city area with over 14 million people, Delhi is larger with nearly 17 million and Mumbai is third largest with around 12.5 million people (Census India, 2011). Kolkata has a "tropical wet-and-dry" climate with temperatures up to 44°C in the summer and down to 4°C in the winter. Typically, in June the heavy monsoon rain floods the streets and that makes travel awkward. The city can be struck with heavy rains but is also hit by thunderstorms and hailstorms. Bengali is the official language of Kolkata but English is used by the white-collar work force, both Hindi and Urdu are spoken by a sizable minority. According to the Census India (2011) for Kolkata, 78% of the population is Hindu, 20% Muslim, 1% Christian, and 0.5% Jain. The remainder of the population are mainly Sikhs and Buddhists. The ratio of the religions represented in Kolkata is fairly similar to India as a whole, although there are variations in such populations. Kolkata is perceived a "city of creative energy", being the Cultural Capital of India, with a strong scholastic, literary, musical and artistic heritage (Sinha, 1990). Clearly in Kolkata there is a rich mix of people from diverse cultural and sub-cultural backgrounds, as there is across India. Consumers not only practice their own religions but interact daily with people of many other religions.

Feedback from focus group members was recorded manually by the moderator: one participant in the first focus group had expressed a desire that the comments should not be recorded electronically. As the research progressed, we proceeded to reflect on the data in an iterative manner and undertook content analysis of the data collected from all focus groups following the steps identified by Rabbie (2004). Aiming to understand the reasons for perfume purchases and the principles connected with the antecedents to perfume purchase, three broad categories that were antecedents to the perfume purchase, emerged from the data and its content analysis. The Indian consumers made sense of their world through stories connected with the perfume purchase. The three broad categories where 1) perception of the product, 2) concerns, containing both personal concerns and concerns about the perfume company and 3) consumers' lifestyle. The three broad categories each contained sub-themes that are related to components of STEPPS and these are arranged in a model of purchase intentions for Indian perfume as shown in Table 3. Although, each of the sub-themes (discussed below in light of the connected literature) were found to be already latent in the literature, they are presented in a coherent model for the intending Indian perfume consumers.

Health Issues and Fragrance Sensitivity Affecting Consumer Behavior

For some consumers, health issues and skin sensitivity need to be considered when purchasing and using perfumes. Clearly, health issues and skin sensitivity can have a strong effect on consumer buying behavior and can even restrict a buyer from purchasing such goods that have adverse effects on the consumers' health and even on the health of pets. It has been shown that sensitivity to certain fragrances can cause adverse reactions among the consumers such as headaches, migraines and breathing troubles Meggs, Dunn, Bloch, Goodman, & Davidoff, 1996). CREAT India, which is a consumer rights and education awareness trust that encourages consumer education in India has introduced consumer education programs to create more awareness among the consumers about the adverse affects of products on their health and welfare (CREAT India, 2007). So, the fragrance market of India is well aware of the possible harm that perfumes may cause to consumers' skin and health. For some consumers, the wisest choice, most of the time, is to purchase the well-established, safe and trusted branded perfumes which are often expensive. The branded products however, are not affordable to a large proportion of the student market. Very few perfumes list the ingredients on the packaging. Axe deodorant for example contains may man-made ingredients; Aluminum Zirconium Tetrachlorohydrex Gly, Cyclopentasiloxane, PPG-14 Butyl Ether,

Stearyl Alcohol, PEG-8 Distearate, Hydrogenated Castor Oil, Talc and Butylated Hydroxytoluene. As, fragrance sensitivity is on rise in India many beauty products are being launched in India that are without any sort of fragrance and Neutrogena launched a facial sunscreen cream that does not contain any fragrance or alcohol (Shyna, 2010).

Halal Branding and Religious Values

Attars (ittars) are substitutes for perfumes often used at Muslim shrines and other religious places and are considered to be *halal*: any object or an action which is acceptable to make use of, according to Islamic law. Halal is just not a concept or an element but is a strong belief system, a code of conduct, a disciplinary system that forms one of the most important parts of the Islamic life-style and culture and as such is a concept that carries much cultural significance. The Halal approach surpasses Muslim consumers and also attract some consumers who are non-Muslims because it refers to any food or goods produced in pure and ethical terms that could benefit the society (Wilson & Liu, 2010).

Muslims constitute 11% of the total world population and the halal market is estimated to be US$2.1 trillion and is growing (Dubois & Janmohamed, 2011). Haffar *et, al.* (2012) note the important part that religion plays for Muslim consumers. Wilson and Liu (2011) proposed a paradigm in which brand managers could deal with the issue of halal branding and can attract more customers towards their product without damaging religious sentiments and beliefs. However, one of the key issues faced by halal brand

Table 3. A model of purchase intentions for Indian perfume consumers related to STEPPS

<table>
<tr><th>Antecedents</th><th>Intermediate Consequences</th><th>Final Consequences</th></tr>
<tr><td>Perceptions of the Product:
All “public” and potential “triggers” in character:
Brands
Packaging
Gift wrapping
Price
Celebrity endorsement
Scent</td><td rowspan="3">Differing attitudes towards
different perfumes by
different consumers in
different places at
different times
These are dependent of the pre-existing stories within the cognitive schema of the individual</td><td rowspan="3">Consumer purchases a perfume
Consumer recommends a perfume
Consumer disinvests in the perfume
Consumer produces negative word of mouth marketing
Social status maintained
Social status improved
Perfume acknowledged as delightful by others
Perfume rejected by others
These outcomes will be largely dependent on the “social currency”, the “practical value” and the “emotional significance” they afford to the consumer</td></tr>
<tr><td>Concerns:
Personal Concerns mainly related to “social currency”:
Fragrance sensitivity
Religious values
Health
Company Concerns mainly related to “practical value”:
Eco friendly attitudes
Social entrepreneurship
Ethical consumption</td></tr>
<tr><td>Social Lifestyle related to “social currency” and “emotional significance”
Relationships
Gift giving
Friends
Family
Cultural identity
Religious identity</td></tr>
</table>

management is that of having an effective supply chain management that understands the importance of the halal concept at every stage of production. Many companies use the concept of halal branding as a defensive corporate strategy rather than being proactive (Maklan & Knox, 1997).

Packaging

Packaging informing the public perception of the product is an important attribute which has a strong positive or negative influence on consumers' behaviors and is closely linked to gift buying behavior. Packaging lays the foundation for marketing communications and the positioning of the product in the consumer's mind. Effective packaging can turn many consumers that hold purchasing intentions into real purchasers. As Rundh (2005) mentioned, packaging and labelling are "those vital things that cannot be overlooked or ignored" because they attract and capture the attention of potential consumers and they give a shorthand description of the product that helps the consumer to uniquely identify the product. Ampuero and Vila (2006) note that packaging has a direct proportional effect on consumer behavior: good packaging motivates the consumer to go ahead with the product purchase, whilst bad packaging demotes the consumer's purchasing intentions. All the elements of packaging starting from the colour of the external package, to the shape of the bottle, to the colour of the perfume liquid, the font size, the font type and the message should be directed towards the target market (Deliya & Parmer, 2012).

If the target audience are students, then the packaging should be vibrant and sporty, youthful and present a light hearted message thus connecting with the relevant stories that the students have in mind. However, if the middle class and elite consumers are the target market, then the packaging needs to be elegant and suave, connecting with their own stories. Packaging should be different for male and female perfumes; female perfumes should be more feminine with floral patterns and other feminine designs, and in colours like pink or red. When the perfume is targeted at the male population, then the packaging should be funky with block designs primarily using blue or green colours. The quantity of perfume offered should be given importance and again be done based on the target segment: students would prefer more quantity and would expect value for money, whereas high earning consumers would expect compact packaging (Rettie & Brewer, 2000).

Gift Giving

Perfumes are often purchased as gifts in India and, as such, represent high emotional value. Some consumers only use perfumes that are gifted to them. Perfumes are considered to be extravagant and elegant gift options, especially when it comes to giving something special to a woman. Particular perfumes are perceived to suit various occasions and moods. Giving perfume, is perceived as the best way to express one's own feelings towards the person that is receiving the gift. Giving perfume as a gift has been on the rise in India and the Indian perfume industry was estimated to grow by 10000 crores Indian Rupees in 2015 (Shanbaug, 2012). Gift giving and gift receiving behaviors become a habit and a personal characteristic and consumers either tend to purchase the same product or not purchase at all during the entire year (Qian, Razzaque, & Keng, 2007). The consumer's fascination with a particular brand plays a major part and therefore, some gift givers make it a point to give to others based on the brand preference that they assume would suit the gift receivers best. There are various gift options for perfumes in India and, perfume brands launch their newer collections in India to coincide with various festivals. For example, the French perfume brand Canali launched their perfume in India to coincide with Indian Independence

Day, thereby giving people the option to gift perfumes as a gift during the Independence Day and during the ensuing festive time. Many perfume brands in India, such as Axe, recognise the importance of gift giving and offer gift wrapping services for their perfumes. Yet, the consumeristic perspective may at time be superseded in India by Hindu cultural and religious notions of gift giving, whereby the Brahman who receives a gift also takes on some "poison" (the evil and the sin) of the gift giver (Raheja, 1988), thus the gift takes on a public significance and is of practical value.

Glocalisation

Another significant issue that emerged out of the data analysis was that of "Glocalisation": thinking globally and acting locally. Glocalisation is a crucial step towards placing the product at the centre of the consumer's cognitive schema. One of the male earning members when asked "What would be the first thing that he would consider while buying a perfume?", replied that he would always go for those perfumes which are very local and Indian in approach rather than being *"Westernised"*. It is important for perfume manufactures to adopt the local approach with the global attitude in order to be a market leader in the ethnocentric Indian marketplace (Kraidy, 2003). In India, there are many international companies who have adopted the local approach with their global business strategies: international companies like McDonald's India, Starbucks and KFC are in the food industry. Other companies like Revlon, Maybelline, Mac and The Body Shop have introduced cosmetics ranges keeping in mind the Indian skin tone and colour palette. Automobile companies, besides Tata, such as Ford and Hyundai have devised small cars with low budgets in mind: to suit the Indian modern middle class section. International perfume brands like Burberry and Chambor have introduced jasmine perfume ranges in India to suit the preferences of Indian people, as jasmine is a true Indian orchid that is widespread all over Indian and is associated with Indian mythology and culture (Chambor, 2011) with the scent of Jasmine aligning with the Indian ethnocentrism. The Japanese perfume brand Harajuku have introduced a range of coconut perfumes that keep in mind Indian consumers, which are available to purchase online through portals like Amazon, eBay and Myntra (Stefani, 2008) and Hugo Boss launched the "Orange for men" range with a scent that echoes memories of the Indian summer.

Word of Mouth Endorsements

Word of mouth endorsements snowball through social media to make products "contagious", Berger (2013). In India, female consumers often ask friends, family and colleagues (as these are the guardians of social, emotional and public value) about their perfume preferences and based upon that information go ahead and makes her own purchasing decisions. One focus group participant stated she would never purchase a perfume that has been received a negative feedback from her reference group, stating she "would never purchase such a perfume that has received a negative feedback even if she personally has not used it". This feedback indicates that word of mouth endorsements and oppositions are strong influences on perfume consumers purchasing decisions. Additionally, the worthiness of the information and the amount of trust that the consumer has in the person who is giving their word of mouth experience is important (Zamil, 2011). In particular, many Indian women are likely to choose their perfumes based on word of mouth as this gives a certainty about the product and a conviction that the product they are purchasing is a product that offers social value. Success achieved by the local Indian perfume firm Vini group of companies, point to this: Vini's deodorant range "18+" (18+ has variants: Thrill,

Surprise, Dare and Impress - all words that are full of emotional significance) and those variants are popular among the Indian youth because the group facilitated effective word of mouth marketing via social media (Shanbaug, 2012).

Eco-Friendly Attitudes

It is important for Indian consumers to know that the perfume manufacturer is eco-friendly and environment friendly, even when the consumers themselves may not be active environmentalists or strong eco-champions. The notion of *Ahimsa* "do no harm" is one main tenets of three main religions of India: Jainism, Hinduism, and Buddhism. Ahimsa goes beyond doing no physical harm to "causing no injury" through one's deeds, words and thoughts, Corner (2009). The highly valued social and public notion pervades into causing no harm to the environment, as to do harm to the environment would lead to doing harm to living beings. It is however important that for these consumers they use only products which are environmentally friendly. Eco-friendly products are those which are manufactured without causing any harm to the environment.

Two of the female earning members stressed that they would only purchase perfumes which have 100% herbal ingredients and have no artificial chemical content, as they perceived artificial chemicals to pose risks, in particular those chemical might cause skin damage. They *"love"* herbal perfumes because according to them, not only is the scent good but the product also protects their skin from substantial damage: thereby keeping their skin healthy and fresh. They insisted that people should indulge in buying more herbal products than branded ones because it is the herbal products that are the *"best for mind and body"*. Milotic (2006) noted that herbal perfumes have a strong and positive influence on the purchase behavior of consumers over and above the products which have artificial chemical contents. The Body Shop is a case to note, as they have experienced success in India since their launch because of their natural and herbal cosmetics. They have consistently maintained quality and the principle of "no animal testing". Hence, the use of natural and herbal ingredients, along with a local approach like using coconut oil in their perfumes, has been an extremely successful approach in India (Bhattacharya, 2011).

Consumers with better knowledge of the eco-system, environmental crises, and with higher involvement in social issues are found to be more actively involved and concerned about eco-friendly purchases (Phau and Cheah, 2011). According to the National Geographic Society's green index "Greendex", India has shown considerable rise in eco-friendly attitudes and behavior and is ranked as the number one *"greenest"* country (Greendex, 2015). One of the most popular eco-friendly perfume brands available in India includes the French perfume company Acorelle. Acorelle reportedly have 100% eco-friendly perfumes with fragrances ranging from berries to orchids and citrus fruits. Aveda (a US company now owned by Estee Lauder) is another popular company, that offers perfumes and other products made from "the essential oils of flowers and plants gathered from around the world". Aveda adopts procedures that originate from Ayurvedic traditions of the *upaveda* or "auxiliary knowledge" in the Hindu Vedic tradition. Additionally, Pacifica have products across sets of fragrance ranges: fruits, florals, herbs and spices and woods and resins and the Body Shop, is the fourth most popular eco-friendly brand in India. Body Shop and Aveda have their own outlets in India, but Pacifica and Acorelle have designated distributors and additionally rely on online portals for their sales. All these companies are environmentally friendly and hence their popularity is increasing among the environmentally conscious Indian consumers (Wright, 2009).

Social Entrepreneurship and Ethical Consumption

Social entrepreneurship and ethical consumption go hand in hand for many Indian consumers. Ethical consumption means consuming ethically those products from business where the entire business operations have not exploited anyone, where there has been no misuse of natural resources and where environmental regulations have been followed (Harrison, Shaw, & Newholm, 2005). Social entrepreneurship on the other hand concerns entrepreneurs who have taken up a social cause and offer business solutions to alleviate particular social problems. Consumers get inspired by social entrepreneurs and thereby try to offer them support by purchasing their products (Hibbert, Hogg, & Quinn, 2006). Keya Seth is one of the leading social entrepreneurs in eastern India offering aromatherapy products, skin care products and perfumes. Keya Seth's company supports the development of under privileged women, championing the cause of women's welfare. Seth tackles female unemployment and has only under privileged women working for her in her clinics, factories and salons. She has made it a point to take up ethical production and social entrepreneurship together; therefore all her products are eco-friendly, affordable, cater to women's welfare and beauty throughout all aspects of the business. Keya Seth has received a national award for research and development in 2008 and an international Award for Leadership in Quality 2010 (Keya Seth Aromatherapy, 2012) and is highly esteemed publicly. Keya Seth products are now available in many countries like US, Singapore and Bangladesh. The story of Keya Seth intimately connects the stories of individual women that work in the company with the consumers of the company's products.

Pricing

There is a vast price sensitive market in India that includes both teenagers who are students, with little disposable income, and the lower earning class. Hence, there is a vast segment of Indian perfume consumers who take price as the first and foremost factor when purchasing perfumes. They are of the opinion that there is no use looking at the scent or the brand of the perfume unless and until they have the money to buy it. This segment either has very little disposable money or have high financial commitments towards their families. Consumers with low disposable income are the ones who consider price first, and that needs to be considered in the case of all products, not just in the case of perfumes (Moschis & Moore, 2001). Hence, the stories and contexts of Indian consumers in relation to their own families are entwined with the consumers' reactions and behaviors to differently priced products. International perfume brands which offer affordable perfumes in India include Burberry, Chanel, Estee Lauder, Nina Ricci, Lacoste, Hugo Boss and Dior and for those consumers who are not brand sensitive, a wide range of deodorants is available in India with prices as cheap as one hundred rupees (one pound sterling).

Celebrity Endorsements and Brands

Brands and products which are endorsed by celebrities have a higher popularity and therefore, higher chance of having larger sales volumes. Celebrities endorse brands to make consumers perceive them to be more attractive, trustworthy, glamorous and acceptable; thus making celebrity endorsement an effective corporate marketing tool. Consumers identify and aspire to the life stories of the celebrities with which they empathise. A segment of Indian perfume consumers consider celebrity endorsement and do not care about brand, scent or price, because a perfume that is endorsed by their favourite celebrity, is "a must have" for them. Celebrities give their unique characteristics and ally their fame with a brand when they endorse the brand, making the brand a trusted brand for the consumers who are then co-consumers of the celebrity's stardom (Kambitsis, Yvonne, Nicholas, & Giannis, 2002).

In India there are different perfumes that are endorsed by celebrities: Spinz deodorants are endorsed by the Indian female actor Genelia D'Souza and French perfume brand Jeanne Arthes first launched their Indian celebrity endorsed perfume "Zeenat", named after famous Indian female actor Zeenat Aman. Shah Rukh Khan, an Indian film actor, producer and television personality (known as "The King of Bollywood") launched his own perfume "SRK" in India in 1998 under a company with the same name: SRK. French perfume brand Lomani introduced "Amitabh B": endorsed by the famous legendary Indian film actor Amitabh Bachchan (Anamika, 2012). It is well known that Indians are fanatical about their cricket and so it is of no surprise that Indian cricket captain M.S. Dhoni endorses Reebok deodorants and Sachin Tendulkar (former Indian cricket captain) endorses Adidas deodorants. Whereas, the world famous soccer player David Beckham endorsed Emporio Armani and Christiano Ronaldo endorses Georgio Armani (Pagnotta, 2012).

Scent Perceptions

Scent perceptions can be defined as the sensation that people feel in their nose when they smell something pleasant. The way the nose's receptors receive a pleasant odour and responds to it can be broadly termed as scent perception. For most consumers, the most important factor related to perfume is the pleasantness or the unpleasantness of its scent and how that sensation leaves an impression in their mind (Engen, 1982). Scent acts as an olfactory catalyst that triggers memory recall for certain past events with which the scent has previously been associated and acts as trigger to remember important stories.

FUTURE RESEARCH DIRECTIONS

Analysis of the focus group data highlighted certain nuances within various segments of Indian perfume consumers and these are presented below and each consumer segment and sub-segment should be the object of further research. Twenty-five percent of students reported that they would prefer to buy an expensive perfume with a prestigious brand name. All those students had a relatively high level of disposable income (£50 per month provided by parents). Of that 25%, the majority (17% of the total number of students) formed a segment that if faced with a product that was an extension of the brand, felt that they did not need to smell the perfume in order to make a purchase; that is, for them, the brand acts as a proxy for scent. Yet, a second segment (eight percent of the total number of students) stated that fragrance would still matter to them over and above brand and price. For this segment even if faced with an extension of a brand that was well known to them (which they had tested before) they felt they could not rely on the brand identity alone to confirm their purchase intentions. For this segment they would need to smell the perfume before contemplating a purchase. It was clear that there were two distinct segments of consumers: one segment are those who are students and would intend to purchase the brand extension using the presumption that the new product would have a delightful scent, "knowing" that it was an extension of the existing well known brand and the second segment are those students who choose "brand" as the prime influencer while purchasing a perfume, but for whom the fragrance of the perfume remains an important factor, and these consumers are not willing to base the perfume purchasing decision on the presumption that if one product in brand range has a delightful scent that a brand extended product would be equally delightful. Twenty-one percent of students said that they would look for price as the first factor when purchasing a perfume. According to them, it does not really matter how good the fragrance of the perfume is or how popular the brand image might be, as they are not likely to be able to afford the "best" and "branded" perfumes. Hence, price is the overriding factor that influences the purchasing decision. Four percent stated they had never previously considered "brand" when making perfume purchases in the past. All of the students in this segment had little disposable income (about £10 a month or less that was received from their parents). There were two segments who were students with lower purchasing power: the first segment contained students who look for price as the first factor when they go to purchase a perfume but also consider brand as a subsidiary factor. The second segment was that of the students who look for price as the first factor while purchasing perfume but are not at all brand conscious when it comes to perfume but still consider scent to be important purchasing influencer.

Eight percent of the total number of students stated that they used all those perfumes that are endorsed by the celebrities they like. Six percent of the total number of male students were soccer and cricket fans who used products endorsed by sports personalities. One female participant had purchased "Spinz" deodorants which had been endorsed by her favourite female Indian actress. For these consumers, the celebrity represents the aspirations and life-style that they desire. Hence, when the consumer engages with products that celebrity engages with, this eases the dissonance between the consumer's own current reality and their desired state. This, ease of dissonance, of course is based on a series of presumptions and assumptions. One female student said that she is allergic to perfumes and hence she cannot use any perfume products at all. She only uses "oil essences" or talcum powder. This consumer, although being the exception rather than the rule, is likely to represent a considerably sized "niche" market in India. It may well be that the consumer has made an assumption that has become generalised: that the problems caused by one product (or sub-set of products) will be caused by all products in that product class. Whereas, one particular ingredient may be the cause of the problem, there may well be a particular perfume product that does not contain the allergen, but remains unknown to the consumer.

Twenty-five percent of the total respondents, who were employed and earning, said that they would first consider the scent of the perfume, then the brand and lastly the price when intending to purchase perfume. This segment forms the majority of the older respondents who do not base their perfume purchasing decisions using any presumptions that a brand extension of perfume range will have a delightful scent: they always consider the scent first, but supplement their purchasing decisions with the assumption, based on past experience, that the brand is important, although it be a proxy, for guaranteeing product quality and safety. This segment was a high earning group with most disposable income, yet they still expressed a strong degree of social responsibility towards their family and were financially responsible for those family members. Thirty-seven percent of participants, who were full-time earners, said that they would look at the brand of the perfume first before anything else when they intend to purchase perfumes. After the brand, they would consider the scent next and finally the price. They said that price was not a main factor. However, they would still consider the price and use the price information to draw comparison with other perfume brands. For these consumers, purchasing their desired perfume brand is the main consideration without even giving a second thought to price. On probing deeper, it was clearly pointed out that all of these participants had family members that were all finically independent in their own rights. This segment consisted of the highest earners and they clearly formed an elite consumer segment. Here, the affiliation with the prestigious brand confirmed their elite status to others and the maintenance of that elite status overrode almost all other considerations. Sixteen percent of full-time earners who had family members, who were highly dependent on them, said that they would first look at the price of the perfume, then the scent of the perfume and finally the brand. They would first look at the price to see whether they can afford it or not, and if they could afford it, then they would start considering the scent. For them brand did not matter as much as maintaining family responsibilities and they did not consider their own elite status as very important.

Two of the female participants said that the first thing they considered was whether the perfume was herbal one or not. This segment did not use any perfume which had any "artificial chemical ingredient" in it. The "natural nature" of the product was of utmost importance and hence both brand and price were insignificant. One of the female earning participants said that the first thing she looks at while purchasing perfume is whether the packaging of the perfume is attractive or not. If the packaging is not good enough she would not bother buying it even if the scent was delightful, the brand was prestigious and the price was low. Another female participant said that she never purchases perfume on her own, and only buys perfume as gifts for others and she only uses perfumes that are gifted to her by others. She believed that buying perfume for her own personal use would diminish the intrinsic value of the perfume gifts that she had been given and could undermine the friendships between herself and the gift givers. One of the Muslim male earning participants said that he does not use perfumes that are available in the market as they are not halal brands and those perfumes are not permitted to be used as they conflict with his religious values. Hence, he uses ittar or attar (perfumes which are alcohol-free, which are permitted under the Islamic decrees, and are available at the Muslim shrines. Another male earning participant stated that he uses only those perfumes that are produced by social entrepreneurs, as he is a social activist who believes in ethical consumption and does not pay much attention to brands or price but purchases products made by social entrepreneurs provided the scent of the perfume is relatively good. One female earning participant stated that she did not use perfume at all because her pet dog was allergic to perfumes and talcum powders and only uses milk based soaps. One female participant buys only perfumes for which she has received positive word of mouth comments from her friends or relatives and she seeks out comments from her friends, family members and colleagues before she actually going ahead with a purchase. If she receives negative feedback about any particular perfume, she makes it a point to not to purchase that product. Another female participant does not use perfume at all because her mother was very fond of perfumes and, after her mother passed away, the participant stopped using any perfumes as the scent triggered pleasant but painful emotional memories that she found difficult to cope with. One male earning participant was highly ethnocentric, stating that he only used those perfume which had a local or Indian origin, as he was "not fond of westernised products".

Hence, there are a number of design features that need to be considered by perfume manufacturers as they all impact on the consumers' behaviors in different ways depending on the individual consumer and the target market to which they belong. Those features need to embrace stimuli from the perfume design: the branding, the packaging, the container design and the perfume colour which immediately impact on consumer perception of the perfume and hence the decision to purchase or not. Some consumers assume red to be lucky, gold to be luxurious, green to symbolise eco-friendliness and silver to be elite. Flowers are presumed to be feminine and sports themes masculine. Perfume does serve certain functions, and has practical value. Depending on the purchase intentions, the perfume may be a gift, a means to enhance attractiveness of self and thereby the user will be attractive to a partner or potential partner, or the perfume maybe for everyday use, which may vary depending on the geographical location, the seasons and other environmental factors. The positive attribute of the scent used as a delightful fragrance outweighs the use of a scent to mask obnoxious odours. Longevity of the scent is related to the concentrations of the essential oils in the perfume. The interface design is important and different for different perfume uses: whether the perfume has a spray, a droplet applicator, a roll on or is solid. In some cases the consumer will require that the perfume has a strong on-line brand presence with connected social media interfaces. The perfume needs to be not only have a pleasant and delightful scent as perceived by the wearer of the perfume, but also have a pleasant and delightful scent for others. The perfume needs a certain "social design" that focuses on the target market: recommendations by peers and family are important, as are celebrity endorsements. For some consumer segments, the perfume needs to be ethnocentric, natural, eco-friendly with the company displaying a degree of social entrepreneurship. For those consumers with little disposable income or with high family commitments, price and value for money remain important but not necessarily at the cost of a delightful fragrance. However, there is a cautionary note from prestigious multinational brands to the healthy Indian companies that they may become "rich pickings" and that the multinationals may become consumers and consume local brands as and when fashion demands.

CHALLENGES AND OPPORTUNITIES FOR INDIAN PERFUME HOUSES

France is widely considered to be the romantic and economic heart of the global perfumery industry but within France the region of Grasse is considered to be the "World's Perfume Capital". Many of the great perfume houses that flourish in France today were born in Grasse and we argue that to compete on the global stage India will need to identify, develop, brand and sustain its own "Perfume Placebrand" such as Grasse. Grasse has its own iconic scents derived from indigenous flowers such as Roses, Lavenders, Mimosas, Violets, Lilies and Irises. India also has its iconic scents and those scents are equally evocative but are drawn from a different pallet of plants such as Frankincense, Kweda, Lemon Grass, the flower of the Champaca tree (the Hindu and Buddhist monasteries in India and Nepal are still perfumed with incense made from the scent of Champaca and other flowers that is infused into a sandalwood foundation) and Oudh (referred to as "Ud" or "Agar-wood" that originates from the Assam: the tree's dark and fragrant resin protects itself against a fungus (Phialophora parasitica) but holds a scent that is prized by Middle Eastern perfumeries). We present case studies of perfumeries based in the Grasse regions of France that exemplify the unique strength and nature of the global perfume market that India needs to challenge.

Relationship marketing has been shown to be vitally important to businesses in gaining customers and retaining them. The perfume industry has long since known this and indeed relationships are doubly important to the perfume industry because their customers to a large extent trust the industry to facilitate the perfume consumer's own relationships. Emotional attachments are made with a particular perfume, so that the perfume may be connected with a person and a personal event: such as a first romantic date. So much so that many years after the event the perfume may act as a trigger to remember the emotions connected with that person and event. The relationship between mother and daughter is also special, with the mother's perfume evoking found memories of love and affection in the daughter, and these emotions may pass from generation to generation and such relationships, in must be noted, are not at odds with those in India. From the foundation of Guerlain by Pierre-François Pascal Guerlain 1828, to the opening (in 1914) of the flagship store: the House of Guerlain in the Champs-Elysées (Paris), Guerlain has welcomed mothers taking their young teenage daughters for their first perfume to the iconic store: a rite of passage (perhaps), in a location where the young daughter can test the many different luxurious perfumes, before selecting their own: a perfume which distinguishes them from their mother but is well connected with the trusted iconic brand. The challenge for perfume houses in developing nations will be to cultivate their own brand in their own location that matches and supersedes the romance, emotions and emotional attachments that the established perfume houses of France hold.

Jean-Paul Guerlain the third generation perfumer in the House of Guerlain, in an interview with the BBC Four, recognised that the company should gain its customers at young age and keep them for life. This is the best options for "relationships" in general, as noted in the inaugural speech of Professor Dangerfield (Professor of Systems Modelling at the University of Salford, UK). The "golden wedding" option is when the couple make slow progress over many years before committing to engagement and then wedded life with the "integration of love" persisting and increasing over decades. This is best option for the business: slowly developing the relationship with the customer and maintain it, even over generations. Dangerfield (2003) stated that two other kinds of relationships exist but both of these become detrimental and unsustainable over time. The two alternatives are all too common in the fast paced society life: the first is the "boom and bust" relationship where everything is thrown in at the beginning, so much so that the expectations of both parties cannot be maintained and the relationship plummets into catastrophe and the other type of relationship appears to start well then hits a problem and falls below the line of "positive love" then an opportunity of redemption of the relationship (perhaps in terms of gifts such as perfume and flowers) is given and accepted – but this type of relationship begins a "roller coaster romance" of ups and downs with each "down" requiring a greater gift in order to be redeemed each time – this again is unsustainable with the "integration of love" under the curve falling into "negative love equity". The first challenge for perfume houses in developing nations will be to cultivate their own brand and relationships with its customers in a sustainable: using the principle of "slow relationship growth".

Education, training and research are important to the perfume industry, as they are to all industries. Connected with the growth of the perfume industry in developing markets will be the development of training schools in emerging economies for perfumery. However, two schools which may well be classed as the "Iris League" (rather than Ivy League) of the perfume world are "The Grasse Institute of Perfumery" and "The Givaudan Perfumery School" in France. Givaudan's Perfumery School is in Paris and is world renowned and in 2015 opened a Perfumery School in Singapore. The school was opened in 1946 and professes that it has trained one third of all master perfumers worldwide, although courses are open to a only an elite few potential masters perfumers each year that have a love for perfumes and have entry characteristics that vary from the scientific to the artistic. Essentially the mission Givaudan Perfumery School seeks to attract talented young perfumers that align with the school's own values concerning the love and heritage of perfumery as a creative craft using both natural and synthetic ingredients.

The second perfume "Iris League" school is the Grasse Institute of Perfumery (GIP) that first opened in 2002 following thirty years of in house training. It is no mean coincidence that this institute is located in the commune or town of Grasse in the south of France and on the French Riviera, but sheltered inland so that the micro-climate is favourable to the flower farms of the region. The region has over sixty companies employing three thousand produce raw materials for six percent of the global perfume industry and account for half of France's raw material business in flavours and fragrances. GIP acknowledges that Grasse is the birthplace of the global perfume industry and offers professional and technical courses for perfumers, perfumer assistants, evaluators, laboratory assistants and raw materials sourcers as well as offering short summer courses. Close to GIP is the Musée International de la Parfumerie (International Museum of Perfume) that was founded in 1989, and is well worth a visit for readers who are interested in the history of perfumery, manufacturing of perfume and the iconic perfumery houses of France. Three perfumeries in Grasse offer "perfume tours" to visitors:

1. The Parfumerie Galimard was founded by Jean de Galimard lived in Grasse in 1747. Jean was also the founder of the Corporation of Glovemakers and Perfumers, as of that time gloves were scented with perfume and Jean de Galimard was purveyor of gloves and perfumes to the court of Louis the King of France., with olive oil, pomades and perfumes from which he developed the first formulas.
2. The Molinard Perfumery was founded in 1849 by Hyacinthe Molinard, who worked in a small shop in Grasse to sell "Eaux de Fleurs". Maybe Hyacinthe represents a case of "nominative determinism" where her "implicit egotism" drew her to a profession that involved flowers and reminded her of her own name. However, the shop drew in wealthy patrons, one of which was Queen Victoria, who were attracted to high quality of the French perfume that was crafted creatively by Hyacinthe. In the 1930's Molinard co-branded with Rene Lalique, a famous French glass designer who become renowned for art deco glass, and designed glass containers for Molinard's perfume. Molinard is currently head by Célia Lerouge-Bénard a member of fifth generation of the family and the company holds the Entreprise du Patrimoine Vivant ("Living Heritage Company") award presented by the French government in acknowledgement of the proficiency practise throughout several generations.
3. In 1926, in Grasse, Eugène Fuchs named his then newly formed perfumery after the local painter, Jean-Honoré Fragonard (1732-1806): co-branding the company with France's cultural history itself and sold perfumes of the Fragonard Perfumery directly to the customer tourists, who had already, through their arrival there, bought into that region of France and France's culture.

Those three perfumeries in the Grasse region: Fragonard, Galimard and Molinard, we argue use experiential marketing that mirrors the strategic framework of Schmitt (1999): they present tours to visitors and explain the processes involved in making a perfume. The visitors can create their own perfumes, eau de perfumes or eau de toilettes and involve themselves in all production phases: picking flowers to bottling the perfume. Traditional marketing accepts consumers as rational decision-makers who pay attention to the functional features and benefits that products holds, where as experiential marketing posits that consumers value pleasurable experiences along the five domains of sensory experiences, affective experiences, creative cognitive experiences, physical experiences and lifestyle behaviours. The visitor to the perfumery will have their social-identity reinforced through relating very closely to the culture of the perfumery and the perfume experts who become the reference group (see Hammerl et al., 2016). Hence, the perfumeries act as experience providers that apply the visitor experience to create a holistic experience that integrates the individual's experiences into their own "holistic gestalt".

CONCLUSION

We have argued that India perfume consumers' behaviors are influenced by \Berger's (2013) STEPPS and note how consumers value perfume products in India according to the social currency that the perfume carries and the triggers that activate word of mouth marketing and buying behaviors. The emotional value, public value and practical value that are carried by the product and brand are largely dependent on how the product fits in the cognitive schema of each individual consumer and how the stories embedded in those schemas align with the story of the product and the brand. Since India has a long, complex and rich cultural history we have argued that the product needs to be marketed in such a way that the product is well placed within the cognitive schemas of the target market, aligning and being coherent with the stories in those culturally associated schema. The product itself must be an integral part of the consumers' story, if indeed the consumers are to engage with the product. Companies that have been successful in aligning their products with India consumers' requirements ensure the way that they manufacture the products and the philosophy they use to do business, are employed in a way that matches up with the values, behaviors and stories of the consumers themselves. One such successful company is Keya Seth, as Keya Seth (2015) states the company has won "the hearts of millions of people for over a decade", to become "one of the leading brands of beauty and health care in India", while at the same time winning numerous international awards. Undoubtably, Keya Seth knows the mind and heart of her target market and has placed her products in a central position, not only in the cognitive schemas of the consumers' minds but also close to the heart of the positive emotions connected to the stories which the consumers truly value.

The weight of responsibility for the development for an Indian perfume industry that challenges France for first place will be with the National and Regional Governments of India that preserve existing perfumery culture and assets. A region in India could be identified, developed and branded as the "Place of Perfume". However elite skills development will need to be supported, responsible governance guidance given and suitable infrastructure will need to be provided: to use aspects of place branding as means to sustainable development as proposed by Maheshwari et al (2011). The India perfume houses themselves could consider how the French houses continue to prosper through a) relationship marketing, b) emotional marketing that integrates the perfumery house with the customers personal memories, family history and experiences across generations of the perfumery house and the customer and c) "Iris league" education, training and research. Then through its own rich history; the Indian perfumery houses may begin to challenge the notion that France is the sole place for perfumes and by acknowledging the rule of slow growth of business and relationships "the Golden Wedding" of relationship with customers will arrive. The perfume houses of India will need to use not only the historical story of perfume in India in their marketing but also understand and apply, in culturally acceptable ways, the personal history stories of customers and the interconnectedness of those stories and experiences with the generations gone by and of the just born histories of the customers and the perfume house itself.

REFERENCES

Adler, A. (1935). The fundamental views of individual psychology. *International Journal of Individual Psychology*, *1*, 5–8.

Ampuero, O., & Vila, N. (2006). Consumer perceptions of product packaging. *Journal of Consumer Marketing*, *23*(2), 100–112. doi:10.1108/07363760610655032

Anamika, S. (2012). *Indian celebrity endorsed perfumes*. Retrieved July 19, 2015, from http://anamikas.hubpages.com/hub/Indian-Celebrity-endorced-Perfumes-Shilpa-Shetty-Amitabh-Bachchan

Banyan Botanicals. (2015). *Ayurvedic Herbs*. Retrieved from www.banyanbotanicals.com

Bartlett, F. C. (1932). *Remembering*. London: Cambridge University Press.

BBC News UK. (2005). *Unilever parts with perfume names.* Retrieved July 19, 2015, from http://news.bbc.co.uk/1/hi/business/4566831.stm

Berger, J. (2013). Contagious: Why things catch on. New York: Simon & Schuster.

Bhattacharya, P. (2011). The Body Shop gets closer to mass market in India. *GCI Magazine*, *9*(3), 10–13.

Bostock, J., & Riley, B. (1855). *Pliny the Elder, Historia Naturalis* (ca. 77 AD). Retrieved July 19, 2015, from www.scentedpages.com/pdf/historia_naturalis.pdf

Brewer, W. F., & Nakamura, G. V. (1984). The nature and functions of schema. In *Centre for the Study of Reading Technical Report, No. (325)*. University of Illinois.

Business Standard. (2012). *Deo-drama hots up for men*. Retrieved July 19, 2015, from, http://www.business-standard.com/india/news/deo-drama-hotsfor-men/472713/

Catholic Forums. (2015). *Is wearing perfumes wrong?* Retrieved July 19, 2015, http://forums.catholic.com/

Census India. (2011). *2011 Census Data*. Retrieved July 19, 2015, from, http://censusindia.gov.in/

Chambor. (2011). *Corporate Overview*. Retrieved July 19, 2015, from www.chambor.com

Corner, P. D. (2009). Insights from an Eastern Spiritual Tradition. *Journal of Business Ethics*, *85*(3), 377–389. doi:10.100710551-008-9776-2

CREAT India. (2007). *Consumer Education*. Retrieved July 19, 2015, from http://www.creatindia.org/consumer-education-%20clubs-reading-material.pdf

Czinkota, R. M., & Ronkainen, A. I. (2011). *Global business: Positioning ventures ahead*. London: Routledge.

Dangerfield, B. C. (2003). *The pursuit of understanding: Modelling dynamic behaviour in disease, life and love*. Inaugural Lecture: Professor Brian Dangerfield, 12 November 2003, University of Salford. Retrieved August 19, 2018 from http://usir.salford.ac.uk/17837/

Deliya, M. M., & Parmar, J. B. (2012). Role of packaging on consumer buying behavior – Patan district. *Global Journal of Management and Business Research*, *12*(10), 48–69.

Dubois, N., & Janmohamed, S. (2011). *The rise of the young Muslim consumer*. Retrieved July 19, 2015, from http://sparksheet.com/branding-halal-the-rise-of-the-young-muslim-consumer/

Ellison, S., & Sidel, R. (2003). *Procter & Gamble Nears Deal To Buy Wella for $5.9 Billion*. Retrieved July 19, 2015, from www.wsj.com

Emirates247. (2015). *Muslims can spray on alcohol based perfumes*. Retrieved July 19, 2015, from http://www.emirates247.com

Engen, T. (1982). *The perception of odors*. New York, NY: Academic Press.

Gaurdian. (2015). *Procter & Gamble sells 43 of its beauty brands to Coty for $15bn*. Retrieved July 19, 2015, from www.theguardian.com

Global Outlook. (2012). *India targeted by international perfume giants*. Retrieved July 19, 2015, from www.researchandmarkets.com

Greendex. (2015). *Third annual survey*. Retrieved July 19, 2015, from http://environment.nationalgeographic.com/environment/greendex/

Haffar, M., Al-Hyari, K., Muhammed, A., & Al-Weshah, G. (2012). Religious beliefs and consumer behaviour: From loyalty to boycotts. *Journal of Islamic Marketing*, *3*(2), 155–174. doi:10.1108/17590831211232564

Hammerl, M., Dorner, F., Foscht, T., & Brandstätter, M. (2016). Attribution of symbolic brand meaning: The interplay of consumers, brands and reference groups. *Journal of Consumer Marketing*, *33*(1), 32–40. doi:10.1108/JCM-12-2014-1243

Harrison, R., Shaw, D., & Newholm, T. (2005). *The Ethical Consumer*. London: Sage Publication.

Hello. (2010). *Perfume or eau de toilette? What's the difference?* Retrieved July 19, 2015, www.hellomagazine.com

Hibbert, S., Hogg, G., & Quinn, T. (2006). Consumer response to social entrepreneurship. *International Journal of Nonprofit and Voluntary Sector Marketing*, *7*(3), 288–301. doi:10.1002/nvsm.186

Hinduism. (2015). *The heart of Hinduism.* Retrieved July 19, 2015, from http://hinduism.iskcon.org/lifestyle/808.htm

Jaffrey, M. (1992). *The Madhur Jaffrey Cookbook: Over 650 Indian, Vegetarian and Eastern Recipes.* Tiger Books.

Jainworld. (2015). *Cruelty free cosmetics.* Retrieved July 19, 2015, http://jainworld.com/jainfood/crueltyfree.asp

Kambitsis, C., Yvonne, H., Nicholas, T., & Giannis, C. (2002). Sports advertising in print media: The case of 2000 Olympic games. *Corporate Communications*, *7*(3), 155–161. doi:10.1108/13563280210436763

Keya Seth. (2015). *Keya Seth's Aromotherapy Company*. Retrieved Oct 29, 2015, from http://keyaseth.in/about.html

Keya Seth Aromatherapy. (2012). *About us*. Retrieved July 19, 2015, from www.keyaaromatherapy.com

Khan, H., Bamber, D., & Quazi, A. (2012). Relevant or redundant: Elite consumers' perception of foreign-made products in an emerging market. *Journal of Marketing Management*, *28*(9-10), 1190–1216. doi:10.1080/0267257X.2011.635153

Kraidy, M. M. (2003). Glocalisation. *Journal of International Communication*, *9*(2), 29–49. doi:10.1080/13216597.2003.9751953

Lenartowicz, T., & Roth, K. (2001). Does subculture within a country matter? A cross-culture chapter of motivational domains and business performance in Brazil. *Journal of International Business Studies*, *32*(2), 305–325. doi:10.1057/palgrave.jibs.8490954

Maheshwari, V., Vandewalle, I., & Bamber, D. (2011). Place branding's role in sustainable development. *Journal of Place Management and Development*, *4*(2), 198–213. doi:10.1108/17538331111153188

Maklan, S., & Knox, S. (1997). Reinventing the brand: Bridging the gap between customer and brand value. *Journal of Product and Brand Management*, *6*(2), 119–129. doi:10.1108/10610429710175655

McHugh, J. (2012). *Sandalwood and Carrion: Smell in Indian Religion and Culture*. Oxford University Press. doi:10.1093/acprof:oso/9780199916306.001.0001

McMahon, C. (1996). Indian attars. *International Journal of Aromatherapy*, *7*(4), 10–13. doi:10.1016/S0962-4562(96)80023-3

Meggs, W. J., Dunn, K. A., Bloch, R. M., Goodman, P. E., & Davidoff, A. L. (1996). Prevalence and nature of allergy and chemical sensitivity in a general population. *Archives of Environmental Health*, *51*(4), 275–282. doi:10.1080/00039896.1996.9936026 PMID:8757407

Milotic, D. (2006). The impact of fragrance on consumer choice. *Journal of Consumer Behaviour*, *3*(2), 179–191. doi:10.1002/cb.131

Mintel. (2012). *The Men's and Women's Fragrance Market: UK, September*. Retrieved July 19, 2015, from www.mintel.com

Moschis, G. P., & Moore, R. L. (2001). Decision making among the young: A socialisation perspective. *The Journal of Consumer Research*, *6*(2), 101–113. doi:10.1086/208754

Naresh, G. (2012). Do brand personalities make a difference to consumers? *Procedia: Social and Behavioral Sciences*, *37*, 31–37. doi:10.1016/j.sbspro.2012.03.272

Osborne, G. (2015). *All of Procter & Gamble's fragrance acquisitions and divestures 1990 – 2015*. Retrieved July 19, 2015, from http://www.basenotes.net/features/3165-all-of-procter-and-gambles-fragrance-acquisitions-and-divestures-1990-2015

Overby, J. W., Woodruff, R. B., & Gardial, S. F. (2005). The influence of culture upon consumer's desired value perceptions: A research agenda. *Marketing Theory*, *5*(2), 139–163. doi:10.1177/1470593105052468

Pagnotta, K. (2012). *Celebrity endorsed perfumes*. Retrieved July 19, 2015, from www.trendhunter.com

Panditbhushan, V., Shastri, S., & Bhat, V. (1946). *Brihat Samhita of Varaha Mihra (with English Translation)*. Electronic Printing Works, Bangalore. Retrieved July 19, 2015, from https://archive.org/details/Brihatsamhita

Paul, J., & Bhawsar, P. (2011). Japanese acquisition in India's Ranbaxy. *Competitiveness Review*, *21*(5), 452–470. doi:10.1108/10595421111171957

Phau, I., & Cheah, I. (2011). Attitudes towards environmentally friendly products: The influence of ecoliteracy, interpersonal influence and value orientation. *Marketing Intelligence & Planning*, *29*(5), 452–472. doi:10.1108/02634501111153674

Pitman, S. (2012). *Takasago targets expansion into fast growing India fragrance market*. Retrieved July 19, 2015, http://www.cosmeticsdesign-europe.com/Business-Financial/Takasago-targets-expansion-into-fast-growing-India-fragrance-market

Pole, S. (2006). *Ayurvedic Medicine: The Principles of Traditional Practice*. Philadelphia, PA: Churchill Livingston Elsevier.

Prayag, A. (2012). *Dubai's Scion Intl to enter India with fragrances in mid-segment*. Retrieved July 19, 2015, http://www.thehindubusinessline.com

Qian, W., Rszzaque, M. A., & Keng, K. A. (2007). Chinese cultural values and gift-giving behaviour. *Journal of Consumer Marketing*, *24*(4), 214–228. doi:10.1108/07363760710756002

Rabbie, F. (2004). Focus-group interview and data analysis. *The Proceedings of the Nutrition Society*, *63*(4), 655–660. doi:10.1079/PNS2004399 PMID:15831139

Raheja, G. G. (1988). *The poison in the gift: ritual, prestation, and the dominant caste in a north Indian village*. Chigago, IL: University of Chicago Press.

Rettie, R., & Brewer, C. (2000). The verbal and visual components of package design. *Journal of Product and Brand Management*, *9*(1), 56–70. doi:10.1108/10610420010316339

Ries, A., & Trout, J. (2001). *Positioning: The Battle for Your Mind Paperback*. New York: McGraw-Hill.

Rundh, B. (2005). The multi-faceted dimension of packaging. *British Food Journal*, *107*(9), 670–684. doi:10.1108/00070700510615053

Schmitt, B. (1999). Experiential Marketing. *Journal of Marketing Management*, *15*(1-3), 53–67. doi:10.1362/026725799784870496

Shanbaug, A. (2012). *Fragrance industry to cross Rs 10,000 crore in next 3 years*. Retrieved May 12, 2015, from http://articles.economictimes.indiatimes.com/2012-05-9/news/31778108_1_perfume-market-fragrance-market-deodorants

Shyna, N. (2010). *Neutrogena oil moisturizer*. Retrieved July 18, 2015, from http://www.fragrance.org/forum-Fall-Winter-2010/5-profile-indian-fragrance-industry.php

Silk Road. (2015). *History of the silk road*. Retrieved April 19, 2015, from http://www.silk-road.com/artl/silkhistory.shtml

Sinha, P. (1990). Kolkata and the Currents of History. In Kolkata - The Living City: Vol. 1. The Past. Oxford, UK: Oxford University Press.

Stefani, G. (2008). *Harajuku lovers*. Retrieved April 19, 2015, from www.basenotes.net

Tai, S. H. C., & Wong, Y. H. (1998). Advertising decision making in Asia: "Glocal" versus "regcal" approach. *Journal of Managerial Issues*, *10*(3), 318–339.

Urs, A. (2015). *eBay emerges largest online perfume mall in India*. Retrieved July 19, 2015, from http://www.thehindubusinessline.com

Wilson, J. A. J., & Liu, J. (2010). Shaping the Halal into a brand? *Journal of Islamic Marketing*, *1*(2), 107–123. doi:10.1108/17590831011055851

Wilson, J. A. J., & Liu, J. (2011). The challenges of Islamic branding: Navigating emotions and halal. *Journal of Islamic Marketing*, *2*(1), 28–42. doi:10.1108/17590831111115222

Wright, A. (2009). *Eco-friendly perfumes: 4 Top Brands*. Retrieved July 2, 2015, from http://voices.yahoo.com/eco-friendly-perfume-4-top-brands-4677815.html?cat=69

Zamil, A. (2011). The impact of word of mouth (WOM) on the purchasing decision of the Jordanian consumer. *Research Journal of International Studies*, *20*, 24–29.

KEY TERMS AND DEFINITIONS

Cognitive Schema: An active organization of stories, past reactions, and past experiences that operate to affect consumer responses and consumer behaviors.

Emotions: One of the STEPPS. Emotions are the states of feelings that result in physical and psychological changes that influence consumers' behaviors and the tendencies for consumers to operate those behaviors. Emotions drive positive and negative motivations.

Experiential Perfume Marketing: The marketing of a perfume through experiences that connect, create, and maintain emotional attachment to the perfume. Interactive experiences reinforce the perfume offer so that the perfume remains part of the customer's identity.

Grasse: France is widely considered to be the romantic and economic heart of the global perfumery industry but within France the region of Grasse is considered to be the "World's Perfume Capital." Many of the great perfume houses that flourish in France today were born and continue to trade in Grasse.

India: The Republic of India is a developing nation in South Asia and is the most largest democracy in the world with over 1.27 billion people. India has a multi-faith market with six main religions. India's sixteen thousand species of flowering plants account for six percent of the total plant species in the world.

Iris League: (Rather than *Ivy League*) A term applied here to the premier perfume schools of the world: "The Grasse Institute of Perfumery" and "The Givaudan Perfumery School."

Ittar: Originates from the Persian word "Atr" (fragrance) and refers to alcohol-free perfumes that are used by many Muslim men and women.

Perfume (Latin: *Perfumare* "To Smoke Through"): Perfumes were used by the Indus civilization (3300 BC – 1300 BC) and one of the earliest "Ittar" perfume preparations was mentioned in the ancient Hindu texts.

Place Branding: The process of image communication to the target market so that the place can compete with other places for people, culture, heritage, economic resources, and business.

Practical Value: The usefulness of the perfume as perceived by the consumer. One of the STEPPS.

Public: The readily perceived values associated with the perfume and brand including but not limited to the importance of the scent, the celebrity endorsement, and the social and economic responsibilities. One of the STEPPS.

Social Currency: Sharable information that makes the perfume publicly good and worthy of consumers' making remarks. One of the STEPPS.

Stories: The perfume brand makes embedded promises to consumers through stories. The notable perfume brand aligns its own story with the stories embedded in the consumers' cognitive schemas. Every communication should reinforce the perfume brand's story. One of the STEPPS.

Trigger: An experience associated with the perfume or perfume brand that causes consumers to recall a previous memory, story, or emotion that is encoded in the consumer's existing cognitive schema. The trigger may be the scent, the perfume packaging, or word-of-mouth marketing that causes activations of positive or negative product involvement. When the trigger has a positive effect, it is one of the STEPPS.

Chapter 5
Regulatory Challenges in Sub-Saharan Africa and Marketing Malpractices of "Big" Tobacco

Nnamdi O. Madichie
Centre for Research and Enterprise, UK

Promise A. Opute
Independent Researcher, Germany

ABSTRACT

The purpose of this chapter is to highlight the implications of the marketing activities undertaken by tobacco companies in Sub-Saharan Africa (SSA) and especially as it pertains to vulnerable groups such as children. Using illustrative cases of two SSA countries—notably Malawi and Nigeria—with disparate economic sizes but nonetheless critical for the discussion in question. Consequently, the chapter posits that the marketing practices of tobacco giants (i.e., Big Tobacco), exploiting the weak regulatory environment in SSA, is worthy of scholarly and policy attention. The chapter focuses primarily on the promotion element of the traditional marketing-mix (which also includes the production and its packaging and branding attributes, pricing strategies, and distribution/place elements) as well as the public policy implications of these four Ps. It also touches upon some of the institutional elements that handicaps governments from undertaking necessary corrective measures/action such as in the case of Malawi where tobacco accounts for a substantial part of the GDP.

CHAPTER OVERVIEW

The purpose of this chapter is to highlight the implications of the marketing activities undertaken by tobacco companies in Sub-Saharan Africa (SSA) and especially as it pertains to vulnerable groups such as children. Using illustrative cases of two SSA countries – notably Malawi and Nigeria – with disparate economic sizes, but nonetheless critical for the discussion in question. Consequently, the chapter posits that the marketing practices of tobacco giants (i.e. Big Tobacco), exploiting the weak regulatory environment

DOI: 10.4018/978-1-5225-7906-9.ch005

in SSA – is worthy of scholarly and policy attention. The choice of countries is discussed in subsequent sections of the chapter as these countries are the most at-risk and tobacco marketing-prevalent in SSA.

A further rationale and/ or motivation for the chapter was a 2008 BBC documentary, which highlighted the marketing practices of tobacco giants in these countries[1]. The aforementioned countries are used as multiple case studies drawing upon the observation technique (and analysis of the video clip) based on the aforementioned BBC documentary, which prompted the study. The chapter focuses primarily on the promotion element of the traditional marketing-mix (which also includes the production and its packaging and branding attributes; pricing strategies; and distribution/ place elements) as well as the public policy implications of these four Ps. It also touches upon some of the institutional elements that handicaps governments from undertaking necessary corrective measures/ action such as in the case of Malawi where tobacco accounts for a substantial part of the GDP.[2]

In the first section of this chapter, a general background of what to expect is provided – especially in the light of what aspect of consumerism the chapter focuses upon (i.e. consumer protection). The second section provides an overview of the global tobacco industry and its importance/ contribution to the economy of countries used as case illustrations in the chapter. This is followed by a brief review of the literature. In the third section the current marketing malpractices of BIG Tobacco in SSA is documented. The chapter starts off with a brief introduction into consumerism and consumer protection as it pertains to the marketing of harmful products. It then delves into the global tobacco industry in the second section where the "Big 6" players are identified. In section three the literature on consumer buying behavior (notably consumer involved in low-involvement products) as well as Tobacco marketing practices are reviewed. In the fourth section a discussion is undertaken in the light of the key players – British American Tobacco, Japan Tobacco and Imperial Tobacco. This discussion is further reviewed in the light of the regulatory environment across the three countries being investigated – notably Malawi and Nigeria – in section five. Section six concludes the chapter with a discussion of learning points opening avenues for student debates on the subject taken from the purview of tobacco buying behavior and the interactions between markets, consumers and governments.

INTRODUCTION

Consumerism is a social and economic order and ideology that encourages the acquisition of goods and services in ever-greater amounts. Early criticisms of consumerism are present in the works of Thorstein Veblen (1899). Veblen's subject of examination, the newly emergent middle class arising at the turn of the twentieth century, comes to fruition by the end of the twentieth century through the process of globalization. In this sense, consumerism is usually considered a part of media culture – a subject that resonates with the cool exhibited in the marketing of tobacco companies. In the domain of politics, the term "consumerism" has also been used to refer to something quite different called the *consumerists movement*, consumer protection or consumer activism, which seeks to protect and inform consumers by requiring such practices such as 'honest packaging' and advertising, product guarantees, and improved safety standards. In this sense it is a political movement, or a set of policies aimed at regulating the products, services, methods, and standards of manufacturers, sellers, and advertisers in the interests of the buyer.

This chapter is based on the politico-legal dimension of consumerism – notably consumer protection, highlighting how marketers of harmful products have managed to remain on the right side of the law by engaging in *guerrilla marketing* tactics, notably *below-the-line* promotional campaigns in their marketing strategies. Products that are usually marketed in this way tend to include steroids, amphetamines or other drugs such as *speed* and *ecstasy* pills (targeted at young clubbers); tobacco and alcohol etc. However, studies of this nature are very rare especially in the management literature (Van Tosh *et al.*, 2000) and this paucity adds to the value of the study. Moreover, among the existing studies, the focus has mainly been on misplaced marketing in the food and beverage industry/ sector (mostly fizzy drinks) and their contributions to the obesity concerns of their respective governments (see Cassim and Langton, 1996; Skirstad, 2006; Gbadamosi, 2010, 2013; Cui *et al.*, 2012).

Breaking with tradition, therefore, this chapter focuses on how tobacco marketers such as British American Tobacco (BAT) have subjected vulnerable groups in SSA to a laboratory for their 'global marketing' campaigns (see Times Online, 2007; Chironga *et al.*, 2011) – having been banned and literally banished from most parts of the developed world. For instance, cigarettes are not sold in singles in most parts of the world including many emerging markets (e.g. the Middle East), but this is a very common practice in SSA especially in the countries of interest in this chapter – i.e. Malawi and Nigeria.

BIG TOBACCO: AN INSIGHT INTO THE INDUSTRY

Tobacco is the world's most widely cultivated non-food crop and farmers (mostly in the developing world) opting for such cash crop do so because it is hardy, grows well in poor soils and volatile weather, and is known for fetching stable prices. It is not surprising, therefore, to observe that tobacco creates more employment per hectare of cultivated land than any other crop in the world. Furthermore, the tobacco industry produces more than 5,000 billion cigarettes a year globally. The biggest market is China (where the industry is state-owned and controlled) with some 350 million smokers consuming around 1,800 billion cigarettes a year, or 35% of the global total[3]. Outside of China (for a notable article on the scramble for Africa see Chironga *et al.*, 2011; as well as Box 1 for the cases of the UK, Ireland and Australia), stock market quoted international tobacco companies compete and account for more than 51% of the global market.

Described as the most fervent critic of the American tobacco industry Henry Waxman under his Chairmanship of the House Subcommittee on Health and the Environment between 1980 and 1994 is known to have exposed a plethora of lies by the heads of 'Big Tobacco'. In one report (see Rehn, 2014), he grilled the so-called "Seven Dwarves" (the heads of Philip Morris USA, RJ Reynolds, US Tobacco, Lorillard Tobacco, Liggett Group, Brown and Williamson and the American Tobacco Company) on

Box 1. The plain packaging debate/ legislation

In the United Kingdom MPs (Members of Parliament) recently voted by a majority of 254 in favour of introducing standardised cigarette packaging from May 2016 - subject to approval by the House of Lords. The legislation, which is designed to reduce the appeal of cigarettes, was voted for by 367-113, with support from Labour and Liberal Democrats, and opposition from Conservative backbenchers. The packaging of all cigarettes sold in England will have to uniform in size, shape and design, with only the brand name and graphic health-warning images permitted on the front. A dark colour such as olive green is favoured for the packaging. The result of the vote makes England the third country to introduce such a law. Ireland introduced a similar legislation at the beginning of March and Australia did the same in 2012. Although the vote only applies to England, other regions of the UK have said they will introduce similar legislation.

Perraudin, F. (The Guardian, 11 March 2015) MPs pass legislation to introduce standardised cigarette packaging. Retrieved from: http://www.theguardian.com/politics/2015/mar/11/mps-pass-legislation-introduce-standardised-cigarette-packaging areas of health policy, corporate social responsibility and possible racketeering (see Rehn, 2014). Globally, however, the "seven dwarfs" become somewhat insignificant as the number one, China Tobacco, holds about 37.1% market share in the tobacco industry – primarily due to China's 350million smokers (see Table 1). The number two position is held by Philip Morris International with 17.4% of the global tobacco market share.

In third place is BAT, founded in 1902 and currently holding 12.0% global market share. Japan Tobacco International (Geneva) is number four with 9.6% of global market share. Imperial Tobacco (Bristol, UK) is ranked fifth by market share – having clawed their way to 4.9% from a paltry 0.8% in 2000. Recently re-branded as the more benign 'Altria Group, Inc.' Philip Morris US ranks sixth with 2.8% of global market share. In terms of annual revenue, the "Big 6" in 2010 alone was US$346.2 billion with US$35.1 billion in pure profit, equivalent to the combined profits of Coca-Cola, Microsoft, and McDonald's in the same year, which translates to "a shocking 81% of the market share in the global tobacco industry [...] controlled by these six multinational corporations" (see Rehn, 2014). All other tobacco companies made up only 19% of the global tobacco industry in 2008 – down from 32.2% in 2000. This means that the "Big 6" account for 81% of world tobacco production, and have cannibalized 13.2% of the global tobacco industry since 2000 – a brief outline is highlighted below:

1. China Tobacco has US$91.7 billion annual revenue and US$16 billion annual profits, one of the highest margins for any non-financial services company. State-owned China Tobacco manufactures 2.1 of the 5.9 trillion cigarettes made each year.
2. Philip Morris International enjoys US$67.7 billion annual revenue with US$7.5 billion annual profits and is a separate entity from the smaller Altria Group/Philip Morris USA, which only produces products for the US market. As recently as 15 years ago, Philip Morris was the largest tobacco company in the world by a comfortable margin.
3. BAT annual revenue is US$58.1 billion and annual profits total US$4.2 billion[7].
4. Japan Tobacco has US$65.9 billion annual revenue and US$1.5 billion annual profits. Due to stricter regulations in the markets they serve, Japan Tobacco's profits are a fraction of Philip Morris International's despite almost identical annual revenue.

Table 1. The big 6 tobacco firms

Company	Market Share	Annual Revenue (profit)
China Tobacco[4]	37.1%	US$91.7 billion (US$16 billion)
Philip Morris International[5]	17.4%	US$67.7 billion (US$7.5 billion)
British American Tobacco	12.0%	US$58.1 billion (US$4.2 billion)
Japan Tobacco International (Geneva, Switzerland)	9.6%	US$65.9 billion (US$1.5 billion)[6].
Imperial Tobacco (Bristol, UK)	4.9% (from 0.8% in 2000)	US$38.4 billion (US$2 billion).
Altria Group, Inc.	2.8%	US$24.4 billion (US$3.9 billion)
Total	**81%**	**US$350.1 billion (US$35.1 billion)**

Source: Adapted from Rehn, A. (Policy.Mic, 12 February 2014)

Note: Total revenue for the Big 6 in 2010 alone was $346.2 billion with $35.1 billion in pure profit. All other tobacco companies made up only 19% of the global tobacco industry in 2008, plummeting from 32.2% in 2000. This means that the Big 6 own a shocking 81% of world tobacco production and have cannibalized 13.2% of the global tobacco industry since the year 2000.

5. Imperial has about US$38.4 billion annual revenue and US$2 billion annual profits. Imperial Tobacco is the world's largest producer of cigars, rolling papers, and fine-cut tobacco.
6. Altria Group, Inc. with US$24.4 billion annual revenue and a surprisingly high US$3.9 billion in annual profits. Philip Morris International was spun off in 2008 to evade taxes on US operations, and now manages all overseas markets and takes in much more total revenue than Altria. Philip Morris USA is the second most active lobbying organization in the US, having spent US$101 million lobbying Congress between 1998 and 2004 alone.

The market shares of the 'big six' (see table 2) adds up to over 80% of the global total – notably (i) China Tobacco, 37% (ii) Philip Morris 17%; (iii) British American Tobacco 12%; (iv) Japan Tobacco 10%; (v) Imperial Tobacco 5%; and (vi) Altria 3%.

A REVIEW OF THE LITERATURE

In this section the review would cover two broad subjects – consumerism; protection; involvement; and Tobacco marketing. While the former is heavily reliant on elements of consumerism and the nature of products being targeted at vulnerable groups such as children, the latter is more specific on the marketing practices of Big Tobacco.

Consumerism, Consumer Involvement, and Consumer Protection

Consumerism has been a primary concern of developed countries where consumer protection is quite advanced. It is among the fastest-growing social movements in Africa, where the marketplace has been a seller's haven (Njuguna, 2015). In the case of Nigeria, Nkamnebe *et al.* (2009: 89) argue that "consumers' awareness of consumer protection laws is rather low, which results in absence of litigations against sellers even in cases of obvious infringement. These authors consequently proposed the need for intensified consumer education as a strategic choice for enlightenment and empowerment. A similar observation is made in the Kenyan context where Njuguna (2015: 5) points out, the rise of consumerism in Kenya has been marked by registration of consumer organizations and enactment of consumer laws. This author notes, however, that despite these institutional developments, consumerism has not yet picked up momentum to the desired levels in the country. This is mostly due to the observation that most consumers in Kenya, majority of who are vulnerable, remain disorganized and uninformed and often unsuspectingly fall prey to fraudulent practices in the market. Kenyan consumers have been exposed to poor quality of goods and services in the marketplace ranging from food to medicines to services. Again, the consumers' response to calls for nationwide protests organized by COFEK (Consumers Federation of Kenya) in 2011 (dubbed "Unga" revolution), 2010 and 2008 over rising cost of living in Kenya were too low to achieve much in the marketplace.

In both cases, the need for the discussion of consumer involvement seems rather clear. Interestingly, in an unrelated study, Gbadamosi (2013) picks up the mantle in his bid to highlight the missing link in consumer involvement in the SSA region. As he points out, "the scale of international marketing activities among multinationals in Africa is considerable [with examples] in virtually all sectors [...] manufacturing, oil, banking, construction, telecommunication, retailing, entertainment..." (p. 237). This observation provides a good Launchpad to specifically investigating the tobacco marketing activity in that region.

Indeed the attractiveness of SSA markets for global tobacco marketers has long been studied (Nwankwo, 2000), and the sub-region has been demonstrated to be the largest and second most populous continent, after Asia (see Nwankwo, 2000: 144), and "one of the fastest expanding markets in the world [thereby making] the market in this continent for these multinationals is vast and attractive" (Gbadamosi, 2013: 238). Indeed, scholarly discourse (see for example, Jones, 1986; Pratkanis and Greenwald, 1993; Harvey *et al.*, 2000; Madichie, 2010) about SSA popularity vis-à-vis marketing activities have shown increasing evidence that Western management theories need to be adapted to the local culture of SSA countries. Interestingly one study discusses one of the cases being investigated in this chapter – i.e. Malawi, where it was observed that "differences between managers in Malawi and the West in terms of values, attitudes and motives [...] have considerable implications for management education, payment systems, training and development." (Gbadamosi, 2013: 236). An entire section was also dedicated to 'conceptualizing involvement,' but the treatment was not in the context of SSA.

In discussing the levels of involvement, it has also been pointed out that, "at a low level of involvement, the responses of consumers are often characterized as indifference. This indicates a lack of commitment [in other words] consumers take the purchase of low-involvement with levity" (see Gbadamosi, 2013: 237)[8]. Another interesting research consideration has to do with consumer involvement especially as it pertains to high versus low involvement products (see Box 3 for an illustration). Indeed, research points out that such a debate may well be the missing link in the assessment of "*Consumer involvement and Africa*". In his suggestion as to the direction for further studies, for instance, Gbadamosi (2013: 240) called for research that:

[...] products are considered as low and high involvement in nature by Africans would reveal culture-laden reactions and significantly contribute to marketing and consumer behaviour literature [as well as] explore involvement in relation to different demographical variables such as age, gender, educational qualifications and income of consumers in this [...] continent.

Indeed, demographic attributes (such as age, education and income) are evident and directly mapped with young children of pre-teen age, with only primary or at best secondary education, and of low-medium income brackets – being targeted to mini countlines which are readily affordable. Consequently, it extends the extant review undertaken by Gbadamosi (2013) and maps this consumption pattern to Tobacco marketing with its public policy implications. As far as regulating child-related advertising in Nigeria is concerned, there has been a lot of criticism in the efforts to date. Extant research have been undertaken in a range of contexts including South Africa (see Cassim, 2005), Kenya (Darley and Johnson, 1993; Asher and Rijit, 2012; Njuguna, 2015) and Nigeria (Darley and Johnson, 1993; Nkamnebe, 2009; Bello *et al.*, 2012; Halliru, 2012; Okpara and Onah, 2013; Dike and Onah, 2014); and outside SSA – notably the USA (Kotler, 2000; Koester, 2003; Green & Armstrong, 2012); UK (Dresden and Barnard, 2003); Australia (Le Guay, 2003), Canada (Phillips, de Savigny, and Law, 1995; Reed *et al.*, 2003); and more interestingly Switzerland (Hofer & Bieri, 2005).

From the foregoing it is evident that this issue is yet to be explored in the context of the Nigerian marketing environment let alone other contexts such as Malawi. Indeed, as Gbadamosi (2010: 205) points out:

In general advertising has multiple roles in relation to both the sponsor and the target audience. To the sponsor, it is very common to associate advertising with creating awareness of a new product or brand, informing customers of the features and benefits of the product or brand, creating desired perceptions of

Box 2. The consumption of low-involvement products in SSA

Could cigarettes be considered high or low-involvement products? To what extent would this matter for both marketers and the 'buying behaviour' of consumers in the developing world context? Should this impact any scholarly investigation of the practices of tobacco marketers in SSA? In order to answer some of these questions, Gbadamosi (2013) provides a much needed insight – from the extant review of the literature, with two interesting maps based on the studies by Ratchford (1987) and Rossiter et al. (1991) citing the 'major study grid-60 common products' and the 'Rossiter-Percy grid' respectively, where beer was positioned as a low involvement product in both studies. Indeed, beer has been long-conceived as the natural partner and accompaniment to smoking – and because of this association – both products may be persuasively positioned as low-involvement products (see the beer positioning grid in Gbadamosi, 2013). Indeed, in his suggestions on future research directions for understanding "consumer involvement, marketing and Africa," Gbadamosi (2013: 240) opines that "researching on which products are considered as low and high involvement in nature by Africans would reveal culture-laden reactions and significantly contribute to marketing and consumer behaviour literature." It is also pointed out that the exploration of "involvement in relation to different demographical variables such as age, gender, educational qualifications and income of consumers in this [context]" would be yet another area for future research enquiry. Indeed, on this latter note the mention of age (underaged smokers for the purpose of this chapter) is very much related to the level of education (mostly children of primary school age – as young as 8 years old) with very limited or no-income at all (as most of their financial resources are from pocket money for snacks/ food at school). Indeed, marketers in SSA seem to understand these constraints in their devised marketing strategies of making mini-countlines affordable and available for these consumer groups and/ or segments. Although the contentions are not explicit on consumer involvement, they do provide insights into what consumers' buy, when they buy them, where they buy them and how they buy them are useful.

the product or brand, creating preference for the product or brand, and persuading customers to purchase the product or brand [...]To the target audience, advertising provides information about the product, its use, and sometimes reassures them of the efficacy of their choices among the available alternatives.

In Nigeria, a common observation has been made where children, especially in urban centers where advertising media are widely available, to be playing in groups and singing advertising slogans and sharing the humour that accompany many of these messages (see Gbadamosi, 2010). This thus indicates the social benefits associated with the use of advertising. He also opined that ethical questions often enter the discussion of advertising to children especially as marketers are perceived to be only interested in economic motives in the promotional messages (see Madichie, 2010 for promotional insights from the Nigerian movies). As far as advertising regulation in Nigeria goes, there are regulatory efforts in place towards ensuring ethical practice by advertisers on advertising to children in Nigeria – e.g. the Association of Advertising Agencies of Nigeria (AAAN), the Advertising Practitioners Council of Nigeria (APCON)[9], and the Advertising Standard Panel (ASP), but "the relationships between these bodies need be made more harmonious with a common purpose of achieving a socially respectable advertising industry"[10]. However some serious questions still linger and especially in relation to what extent the implementation of these policies have been effected as well as to what impact for the protection of vulnerable groups – notably children .While *a* "considerable level of regulation is available to marketers operating in the Nigerian marketing environment on how to practice socially responsible marketing in respect of advertising to children in Nigeria," these regulations are constantly flouted. For example, and as Gbadamosi (2010: 210) seems to suggest, BAT has been reported as continually circumventing advertising restrictions and violating international marketing standards in Nigeria by subtly targeting children in the sale of cigarettes. Moreover, some advertisers in Nigeria also promote their brands through signage – usually in the form of a public relations gesture to schools with the brand names of these corporations being more conspicuously displayed than even the names of the schools. As Gbadamosi (2010: 206) once put it, "extending the scope beyond food and drink, advertising plays many positive roles in the lives of children such as in their socialization process [...] as it educates children as to the meaning associated with consumption."

Furthermore, and more pertinent to the subject of marketing to children, Gbadamosi (2010: 211) also observes that "the Nigerian case is approximately comparable to the picture depicted about India [...] and possibly South Africa [...] advertisers have more freedom in respect of advertising their goods and services to children than they do in developed countries. The rules are in place, but irregularities are still yet to be totally removed from the system." This prompts the need for a more cohesive regulatory framework in SSA, where in the particular case of Nigeria, the regulation of medical drugs and food has been effective under the National Agency for Food and Drug Administration and Control or NAFDAC (see Nkamnebe, Idoko and Kalu, 2009; Dike and Onah, 2014), but APCON remains fraught with challenges – restricting its ability to adequately and autonomously scan, monitor, and control the advertising environment. A similar trend was also observed in other contexts such as South Africa and India. In the case of South Africa (see Cassim, 2005) it was observed that advertisers have more freedom in advertising to children than what obtained in the developed world, but surprisingly not Switzerland where Hofer and Bieri (2005; cf. Gbadamosi, 2010: 207) reported that advertising to children has not been a topic of much interest to politicians and the industry, as it remains very liberal compared to some other countries. However, some patchy legislation does exist in that country, one example being that alcohol and tobacco advertising both of which are prohibited in books and magazines for the young. From a broader perspective, it is usually argued that advertising messages are sometimes offensive, false, misleading, unfair and/ or socially irresponsible – and even more so in the context of the selected SSA countries in this chapter.

Tobacco Marketing

For illustrative purposes seminal papers from the *Journal of Public Policy & Marketing*, *Young Consumers,* and the *Journal of Consumer Marketing* are provided in boxes across the chapter – notably highlighting front-of-package labelling; need or incidence of mandatory disclaimers in advertising; the behavior and perceptions of College Students with respect to cigarettes; and why policy matters (see Box 3 for an illustrative study). According to Phillips, de Savigny, and Law (1995) although rates of tobacco smoking in Canada have dropped dramatically over the last three decades the same cannot be said for other regions. Indeed Phillips *et al.* (1995) observed that "for every tonne of tobacco that Canadian adults gave up between 1970 and 1990, aggressive marketing by multinational tobacco companies has ensured that an additional 20 tonnes is now consumed in developing countries." The authors describe the dilemma faced by policymakers in their efforts to control the epidemic of tobacco smoking in the developing world: although tobacco consumption leads to increased rates of mortality and morbidity and lost productivity, its production creates employment, generates tax revenue and earns foreign exchange.

Hastings and Aitken (1995) reviewed the evidence for links between tobacco advertisement and children's smoking and concluded that "within the confines of doubt that will always exist in social scientific research, it now has to be accepted that tobacco advertising does influence children's smoking behavior." Cassim (2005) in her research on advertising to children in South Africa, reviewed the demographics of the children's market in that market, discusses current advertising practice, the regulatory environment in which marketers operated. According to her (see Cassim, 2005: 55):

The furore around advertising to children and its impact on children's food choices has not reached yet South Africa. While the developed world hotly debates the issue and implements strict controls on advertising aimed towards children, South Africa with its very young population (nearly half the population under the age of 21) has paid little attention to the issue. As the debate on the effects of advertising on children (and particularly food advertising) rages on, worldwide attention is focused on the activities of marketers. South African marketers will not escape the debate.

Green and Armstrong (2012) examined 18 experimental studies that provide evidence relevant to mandatory disclaimers" and opined that mandated messages increased confusion for consumers and were ineffective or harmful in the 15 studies that examined perceptions, attitudes, or decisions – using an experiment on the effects of a government-mandated disclaimer for a Florida court case, highlight some inconsistencies.

This is rather instructive in the sense that government-mandated disclaimers in advertisements may be lacking in terms of execution and/ or policy implementation even in developed world contexts such as the US. Interestingly, Shultz II *et al.* (2012: 178) pick up on this problem in from the point of view of developing countries, when they opined that:

Developing markets are a challenge for researchers who study them and for governments, business leaders, and citizens who strive to improve the quality of life in them. The limitations of the dominant development paradigm coupled with the need to focus on consumers provide tremendous opportunities to engage in truly transformative research.

Consequently, several interactive forces must be understood and addressed during research design, management, and implementation. The main aim of their study was to "provide a synthesis [...] framework in the form of a conceptual model—with practical applications to transformative research in developing markets and, ultimately, with the broader objective to stimulate new conceptualizations, research, and best practices to transform consumer well-being" (See Shultz II *et al.* 2012: 178) in that context. Be that as it may, the study did not specifically highlight the practices of tobacco marketers in the context of SSA. Taking the discussion from a consumerism perspective, the study of Cui and Cui (2004) provides some indication of significance of such scholarly pursuit. According to these authors, "burgeoning consumerism in transitional economies has significant implications for both multinational corporations and local companies" (see Cui and Cui, 2004). Based on a survey of four cities in mainland China, the authors

Box 3. Public policy studies: College students, regular, light, and ultralight cigarettes

In their exploratory survey, Smith, Stutts, and Zank (2012) *examined the smoking behavior, perceptions, and quitting intentions of 579 college students – arguably an important segment because of their large numbers, their education, and the fact that many of them begin smoking during college. The findings revealed that "most college students in the sample did not perceive that light cigarettes are safer than regular cigarettes or that ultralight cigarettes are safer than light cigarettes, but rather they perceived lights to provide sensory benefits (e.g., milder, lighter taste) over regular cigarettes." This was especially true for former and current smokers. The majority of smokers were nondaily smokers, many of whom have no thoughts of quitting. This is a concern because these nondaily smokers may not consider their smoking behavior risky. In addition, nondaily college student smokers who are primarily social smokers constitute a large group of young adults for which there is little research into the health risks from smoking.* In a follow-on study, Hoek and Dewhirst (2012) questioned Smith, Stutts, and Zank's (2012) conclusion that young adult smokers interpret "light" and "mild" as taste attributes on several grounds. Hoek and Dewhirst examined evidence from industry documents that reveal strategies to use light and mild variants to reassure smokers. These authors also went on to explore the multiple meanings of terms such as "light" and "mild" and illustrate how "light" is commonly used to imply a reduction, particularly in food and alcohol products. Third, they review the extensive consumer evidence documenting smokers' belief that light cigarette variants will deliver less tar and nicotine and reduce the risk of harms arising from smoking. Finally, they suggest that predominantly social smokers, have important cognitive biases – from the measures of risk used; superficiality in risk understanding; considerable potential for harm; and revealed high levels of deception, even among college students, who might be expected to be better educated and more discerning.

sought to examine "consumer attitudes toward marketing [with a view to comparing] the findings with those of previous studies of other economies." Their results tended to suggest that "consumers in mainland China are less critical of marketing than their counterparts in advanced economies." These authors also observed that consumer attitudes toward marketing, beliefs about business, and their interactions have significant effects on consumer satisfaction (see Cui and Cui, 2004).

Indeed Cui, Lui, Chan and Joy (2012) investigated the sources of cross-national differences in consumer attitudes toward marketing using rigorous analyses to improve the accuracy of cultural attribution for international marketing and cross-cultural consumer research. According to these authors, "previous studies have found significant differences in consumer attitudes toward marketing between countries and attributed such variations to differences in the stage of consumerism development and cultural values." Using survey data of consumer attitudes toward marketing from China and Canada, these authors adopted an econometric decomposition to examine the cross-country difference in consumer attitudes toward marketing and posited that (see Cui *et al.*, 2012: 213):

Chinese consumers have more positive attitudes toward marketing than Canadians and the two countries differ significantly across all predictor variables. However, the results of decomposition suggest that consumerism, individualism and relativism do not have any significant effect on the country gap in consumer attitudes toward marketing, while idealism has a significant coefficient effect.

Roberts and Manolis (2000) compared and contrasted "various marketing- and consumer-related attitudes and behavior across the baby boomer (those born between 1946-1964) and baby buster (those born between 1965-1976) generations." Their results suggest that baby busters, compared with baby boomers, are more favorably predisposed toward marketing and advertising. It was also observed that (see Roberts and Manolis, 2000: 481):

Two generations differ in their understanding of the domain of marketing. These findings have important implications for marketing practitioners and academics alike." Possibly the most significant finding of the present study was the generally elevated levels of compulsive buying found across both generations. Using Faber and O'Guinn's compulsive buying clinical screener, we found that 7% of baby boomers and 11% of baby busters were classified as compulsive buyers. These are considerably higher than earlier estimates of the incidence of compulsive buying and warrant further investigation.

Based on their size, disposable income, and purchasing power, Durvasula and Lysonski (2008) pointed out that "Generation Y consumers are viewed as the Holy Grail for marketers." These authors also raised an interesting question for managerial consideration. According to them, the key question for both marketers and policy makers is what is the best way to understand the Gen Y segment? This arose out of what they described as "The vanity concept" as a means of better understanding "the Gen Y consumer segment." This is especially when it comes to dealing with health-related issues such as "... poor financial planning, bulimia and anorexia nervosa." The authors consequently drew upon a sample of approximately 125 young consumers from two eastern and two western cultures in a bid to find support for their proposed vanity perceptions. In conclusion they pointed out that "both males and females are highly concerned about physical appearance and professional achievements. However, self-assessment of physical appearance and professional achievement are significantly lower among females as compared to males" – thus prompting the call for "future studies [...] to study differences among other countries and consumer groups." More interestingly their findings suggested that for "marketers [...] vanity appeals can resonate well with Gen Y especially those in China and India." This summation was also arguably instructive for "consumer protection advocates [especially in the light of understanding] the extent to which importance of vanity is likely to increase, especially in countries that embrace globalization" (see Durvasula and Lysonski, 2008: 230).

Clarke (2005) reported on how an industry funded media literacy programme works in the UK and suggests how it may be replicated in other European contexts. He concluded that (see Clarke, 2005: 32), "[...] the current concern about advertising and marketing to children is not going to go away, and it is in the industry's interest to take an active part in encouraging children to understand fully what advertising, and marketing is all about..." Extending these studies to the specific issue of marketing tobacco products to minors, Strong and Eftychia (2006) probed the influence of family and friends on teenage smoking in Greece. They investigated the influence of family and friends on teenage smoking behavior in Greece, as distinct from tobacco marketing. They thus concluded that smoking among Greek teenagers is strongly influenced by family and friends. According to these authors, roughly one in ten were offered a cigarette by a relative; two-thirds came from families containing at least some smokers, with only two with no friends who smoked. In all these, however, there are hardly any academic studies focused on tobacco marketing in SSA.

TOBACCO MARKETING IN SSA: A DISCUSSION

Inspired by a 2010 BBC-sponsored documentary undertaken by Bannatyne, a British Entrepreneur, and key figure in the popular Dragon's Den (derived from a UK channel 4 documentary in the same year), this chapter profiles tobacco consumption amongst under-aged children and the marketing practices of the tobacco companies. Specifically the documentary highlighted (i) the emotional journey for Bannatyne, who is himself an ex-smoker; who (ii) along the way met children as young as 11 who are not only smoking 10 cigarettes a day, but also trying to make a living selling them; and (iii) uncovers evidence of extraordinary marketing tactics used by a British-based cigarette company and investigates claims that it is encouraging young people to smoke. There are some interesting observations made from an interrogation of policy papers and the regulatory environment as it affects consumer protection in the selected countries: Malawi is obviously reluctant, as that industry happens to be a key source of its GDP (gross domestic product); and Nigeria is fraught with complications (both economic and non-economic). The role of buying behavior remains contentious especially where vulnerable groups such as children (notably below the ages of 12) and young adults are exposed to taking up the habit as their parents either send them out to purchase or even hawk cigarettes just to make ends meet. This is further compounded by the sale of cigarettes in single units which is cheaper than buying in packs of say 10's or 20's as is the case in most parts of the developed world. In the next sub-section, the marketing strategies of the leading players in the market will be outlined drawing upon self-reported excerpts from their respective websites.

British American Tobacco (BAT)

BAT is a world leader and key player in the Africa sub-region with four Global Drive Brands - Dunhill, Kent, Lucky Strike and Pall Mall - are well represented across the segments and since 2001 have together grown volumes by 57 per cent. According to Jimmi Rembiszewski, British American Tobacco's Marketing Director:

While developing our Global Drive Brands is central to our strategy, we are also increasing the profile of Vogue in the super premium segment and Viceroy, a leading low price international brand. We have never believed that 'one size fits all'. Our portfolio of some 300 brands is based on distinct 'must-win' consumer segments - international, premium, lights and adult smokers aged under 30 (ASU30)[11].

This is a clear acknowledgment that BAT's focus on the younger consumer is deliberate. It also confirms that the company is intentionally geared towards consolidating its international markets – notably Africa (one of its largest). But this is not all, as sources close to BAT also disclosed the company recognizes that tobacco is a hazardous product that requires restrictions:

We recognise that our business starts with our consumers and our brands. It's not about encouraging people to start smoking or to smoke more, but about meeting the preferences of adults who have chosen to consume tobacco and differentiating our brands from competitors.... Our aim is to satisfy adult consumers' demands better and more profitably than our competitors. We fully acknowledge that our product has health risks, so there should be restrictions on how it is marketed...[12]

Japan Tobacco

JT International or JTI (a new company, formed by two leading tobacco manufacturers-Japan Tobacco and RJ Reynolds in 1999) is an operating division of Japan Tobacco Inc., handling the international production, marketing and sales of the group's cigarette brands. JT Group has just completed the acquisition of Gallaher Group to become the world's third largest international tobacco manufacturer. Total net sales were US$39.5 billion during the fiscal year that ended 31 March 2006. JT sells 8 out of the 10 top brand styles in Japan, with the top three styles all coming from the *Mild Seven* brand. In Asia, the group has significant presence through JTI, where Mild Seven is the major brand in the portfolio. In the global market, three of the best-selling international cigarette brands: Camel, Mild Seven and Winston, are within JT's product portfolio, along with Salem, one of the world's leading international menthol brands[13].

Imperial Tobacco Group Plc

Imperial Tobacco believes that tobacco products are for adults[14]. We support the enforcement of legal minimum age restrictions by the appropriate authorities for the purchase of tobacco products. According to sources close to the company, it was committed to promoting and selling its products responsibly, within the laws and voluntary agreements of the countries in which it operates. The company also proudly declares that:

Our international standard for the marketing of tobacco products reinforces this commitment and sets out clear rules and principles to ensure that our advertising and promotional activities are directed only to adult smokers in all circumstances. We adhere to these stringent marketing standards at all times, wherever we operate.

The company also claims to encourage governments and other relevant authorities in the markets in which we operate to incorporate the practices laid out in our Marketing Standard into national laws and agreements, respecting the principles of informed adult choice and commercial communication. All national laws, codes of practice and voluntary agreements relating to tobacco products to which Group companies are signatories are always observed. Where such requirements are less stringent than our Marketing Standard, the Standard takes precedence unless otherwise required by law. The adoption or absence of a national code does not in any way relieve our obligation to comply with the Standard.

THE REGULATORY ENVIRONMENT

According to the Centre for Tobacco Control in Africa (CTCA), the WHO Framework Convention on Tobacco Control (FCTC) consists of six key areas (i) Smoke free environments, (ii) Pictorial Health Warnings, (iii) Ban on Tobacco Advertising,[15] Sponsorship and Promotion (TAPS), (iv) legislation, (v) Tobacco Industry Monitoring and (vi) Alternative Livelihoods. The target countries included; Angola, Kenya, Mauritania, South Africa and Uganda (see Box 5). The CTCA has effectively started its phase II (2014-2017) operations, bringing on board a set of five new target countries. The target countries during this phase include Botswana, Ethiopia, Gambia, Gabon, and Niger. The CTCA continues to provide minimal support to the original five target countries covered during phase I which included Angola, Kenya, Mauritania, South Africa and Uganda[16].

Tobacco Control Legislation in Malawi

Malawi is one of the few countries in the sub-Saharan region, which has no tobacco control legislation. The tobacco industry has influenced on the government to resist any attempts to put in place tobacco control legislation and policies. As Kapito (2000) clearly pointed out:

No research has been done so far on smoking prevalence in Malawi but there is evidence that the youth are now picking the habit with the increasing misleading adverts from the tobacco distributors...

The lack of tobacco legislation and policies has enabled the tobacco industry to freely promote cigarette trade and is manifested in the following scenarios. Advertising on tobacco smoking is not regulated in Malawi. BAT Malawi, which is the sole distributor of cigarettes, advertises cigarettes on radio programs targeted at the youth and that BAT promotes and sporting events in Malawi like football, discos, which are frequented by the youth.

Tobacco Control Legislation in Nigeria

The Tobacco Control Bill which was passed by the Nigerian House of Senate on 15 March 2011, clearly states, in Part II section 3(1) that "no person below the age of eighteen years (18 years) shall sell or be sold tobacco or tobacco products." Indeed, the entire section was on legislation on "Supply of Tobacco Products to Young Persons." The responsibility of key stakeholders was also highlighted in sub-section (b) of section 3(1) that it was:

... unlawful for a parent, legal guardian or other person acting in place of a parent or legal guardian or person who is responsible for the care and welfare of a minor under the age of 18 years to knowingly allow that minor to possess any cigarettes made of tobacco or of any other substance which can be smoked, any cigarette paper or tobacco in any form, including but not limited to smokeless tobacco.[17]

Furthermore, in section 4(1) it was explicitly stated that point-of-purchase displays should highlight the regulation related to health warnings and underage smoking restrictions, "the sale of Tobacco products to anyone under the age of 18 is prohibited by law". However, in part III of the bill that would be explored in this chapter as it touches directly upon the focus i.e. promotional activities of tobacco products. Indeed, Part III of the Bill covers regulation over the "Prohibition of Promotion of Tobacco and Products." Section 11(1) specifically states that "No person shall promote a tobacco product by means of a testimonial or an endorsement." Explicit descriptions of phrases such as "person" were stated in Section 11(2) thus:

... the depiction of a person, character or animal, whether real or fictional, including and not limited to literary, dramatic, musical, cinematographic, educational or artistic works, productions or performances that use or depict a tobacco product or a tobacco product-related brand element. Whatever the mode or form of its expression, shall be considered to be a testimonial for, or an endorsement of the product where such is exposed to person under 18 years.

Finally, section 12(1, 2, 3) of the Bill makes it clear that "no person shall promote a tobacco product by means of an advertisement that depicts, in whole or in part, a tobacco product, its package or a brand element or one that evokes a tobacco product or element, or that depicts at tobacco product manufacturer." It also states in 12(2) that:

No person shall advertise any tobacco product on any satellite, electronic and print medium or by any other form of communication including but not limited to newspaper adverts, bill boards, leaflets, posters, point of sale adverts, branding of vehicles, mobile adverts facilities, films, brand placements, Home videos, cultural events, musical events, sports events, events by unions or associations and branding of walls, restaurants.

Indeed, in section 12(3) it was clearly stated that "no person shall promote tobacco or a tobacco product by means of lifestyle advertising." However, such advertising has become the new black in the SSA context (see for example, Lysonski and Durvasula, 2013). The extent to which young urban Nigerians in Lagos (the commercial capital of the country) have become acculturated to global consumer culture and the impact of acculturation on consumer ethnocentrism and materialism has also been investigated in the literature. Basing their study on a total of 165 young Nigerians living in Lagos, Lysonski and Durvasula (2013) developed scales consisting of seven different dimensions of global consumer acculturation, ethnocentrism, materialism and demographics. Following from this, they posited that Nigerians were acculturated to a large degree in terms of cosmopolitan tendency, exposure to marketing activities of multinationals, English language usage, social interactions, and global mass media exposure (see

Madichie, 2010). However, openness to emulate global consumer culture was moderate and identification with global consumer culture was very low. Acculturation affected consumer ethnocentrism and materialism to some extent. In the specific context of Nigeria, the consumerist culture is clearly affected by socioeconomic conditions as identified in the literature (Lysonski and Durvasula, 2013: 493):

Nigerians may be in a state of transition as they adapt to global consumer culture. Nigerians may have some resistance in adapting to global consumer culture given ideological, nationalistic, and socio-economic conditions. International marketers must realize that a level of 'glocalization' is required attuned to the identity and national character of Nigerians.

Overall the afore-stated authors discussed the 'paradox' where Nigerians tended to have low levels of 'identification with global consumer culture' despite being exposed to 'global forces' (Lysonski and Durvasula, 2013). Indeed, such forces have provided avenues for marketing malpractices to flourish in this sector (see Box 4 for an illustrative insight into the Kenyan situation).

SUMMARY

The main aim of this chapter is to provide some insight into how tobacco marketers have subjected SSA to a launchpad for *guerrilla marketing* campaigns especially in the absence of clearly defined consumer protection legislation in these countries – unlike what obtains in other parts of the world. It takes the specific illustration of tobacco marketing and consumer attitude towards these marketing activities as a focus. From the review of the regulatory environment in the three countries investigated in the chapter – i.e. Malawi and Nigeria, it was evident that some regulation, while in place to protect vulnerable groups from the consumption of harmful products, are rarely enforced. Indeed, the prevalent sale of cigarettes are not sold singly in most parts of the world, but this is very common in African countries especially in places such as Malawi and Nigeria – as one documentary undertaken by a rich British Entrepreneur (the key figure in the popular Dragon's Den) showed. Moreover, tobacco companies tend to get readily involved and with the support of African governments in publicity stunts including PR (public relations) and sponsorship manoeuvres such as the *John Players Gold Leaf* music festival – which projects smoking as the new 'cool'.

Box 4. Exposing tobacco marketing malpractices

Only three years ago in a 2012 policy report under the auspices of the World Health Organisation, the International Institute for Legislative Affairs (ILA) published a damning exposition, "Tobacco Industry Tactics to undermine tobacco control must be exposed and resisted". The report coincided with a statement made on the occasion of the World No Tobacco Day, 31 May 2012. Section three of that report interrogates the activities and/or tactics of Big Tobacco Advertising, Promotion & Sponsorship (TAPS) practices, as well as the acclaimed Corporate Social Responsibility practices. It also detailed the rampant "interference with policy and legislative processes", which included a catalogue of malpractices such as intimidation & litigation; use of front groups; and smuggling and illicit trade of tobacco products. From the aforementioned it is evident that Big Tobacco marketers, and especially those with operations in regions with weak regulatory mechanisms in place, have been complicit in flouting consumer protection regulations and business practices. The question therefore remains: who is to blame? Governments (and their respective agencies) or Big Tobacco? Source: ILA (2012) "Tobacco Industry Interference in Kenya: Exposing the tactics." Revised Edition, January 2013. International Institute for Legislative Affairs (ILA).

In times where tobacco firms have been viewed as key culprits of marketing malpractices in SSA having come under enormous pressure from their home country governments (see Crotty *et al.*, 2016), the study goes beyond mere advertising targeted at vulnerable groups – especially children. Overall the chapter thus moves away from the traditional focus on 'fatty foods' and 'fizzy drinks' by presenting evidence of the poor social responsibility records of multinational marketers into order spheres such as tobacco/ cigarettes. In other words, we have moved the discourse on socially responsible marketing away from the clichéd obesity concerns and binge drinking (alcoholic beverages) to a 'clear and present danger' in SSA – underaged smoking. Studies of this nature are very rare especially in the management/ marketing literature and even more so in the SSA context.

This chapter, therefore, adds value to the existing body of knowledge in at least four ways. First, the chapter draws attention to the marketing practices in the tobacco industry of the explored countries – with implications for others in the sub-region. Second, the chapter is a pioneering effort at highlighting the impact on Big Tobacco on the increasing youth smoking culture in SSA. Third, it proffers policy guidelines for curtailing the marketing malpractices by Big Tobacco in weak regulatory environments. Fourth, and finally, the chapter signals a 'call to action' for more quantitative studies either on a country/ regional basis or on a larger scale covering a distinct market – notably primary school children across clearly defined geographical boundaries. The chapter, nonetheless, acknowledges the need to consider the regulatory experiences of select western cultures (e.g. Greece and Switzerland, and especially the latter) and other emerging markets (such as India as already identified in this chapter) in order to benchmark the SSA experience.

LIMITATIONS, IMPLICATIONS, AND FUTURE DIRECTIONS

While this chapter has highlighted the implications of the marketing activities undertaken by tobacco companies in relation to vulnerable groups such as children in SSA – using illustrative cases from two SSA countries (Malawi and Nigeria), there is a need to extend this further. Indeed, a recent report has pitched three SSA countries – Tanzania, Zambia, and Zimbabwe – amongst the largest tobacco producing countries in a space dominated by China, India and Brazil. According to the report (see Statista, 2018), in "the worldwide tobacco production in 2016, by country [...] China was the biggest tobacco producer worldwide with an amount of some 2.8 million metric tons of tobacco produced."

The chapter has also focuses primarily on the promotion element of the traditional marketing-mix (which also includes the production and its packaging and branding attributes; pricing strategies; and distribution/ place elements) and the public policy implications of these 4Ps. Perhaps an extension into the other Ps of marketing (people, process and physical evidence) may be useful in future studies – and especially the people and process. Furthermore, considering that there are various tobacco goods ranging from cigarettes to cigars, chewing tobacco, pipe tobacco and shisha tobacco amongst others, future studies may need to go beyond just the marketing of cigarettes. Overall the chapter discussed a range of learning points opening-up avenues for debates on the subject taken from the purview of tobacco buying behavior and the interactions between markets, consumers and governments. These interactions would need to be probed further using a range of research strategies beyond a qualitative and/ or descriptive lens.

REFERENCES

Andrews, J., Lin, C.-T., Levy, A., & Lo, S. (2014). Consumer Research Needs from the Food and Drug Administration on Front-of-Package Nutritional Labeling. *Journal of Public Policy & Marketing*, *33*(1), 10–16. doi:10.1509/jppm.33.1.10

Barat, S. (2014). Religion in Consumer Society: Brands, Consumers and Markets. *Journal of Consumer Marketing*, *31*(3), 228–230.

Béjot, N., & Doittau, B. (2004). Advertising to children in France. *Young Consumers*, *5*(3), 69–72. doi:10.1108/17473610410814274

Bello, K. B., Suleiman, J. B. A., & Danjuma, I. (2012). Perspectives on Consumerism and Consumer Protection Act in Nigeria. *European Journal of Business and Management*, *4*(10), 72–78.

British American Tobacco targeting African Children with cigarettes. (n.d.). In *YouTube*. Retrieved from: http://www.youtube.com/watch?v=ldbRXAOiwWs

Brunk, M. (1973). The Anatomy of Consumerism. *Journal of Advertising*, *2*(1), 9–46. doi:10.1080/00913367.1973.10672477

Cassim, S. (2005). Advertising to Children in South Africa. *Young Consumers. Quarter*, *2*, 51–55.

Cassim, S., & Langton, R. (1996). Current issues in the regulation of deceptive advertising: Some consequences for South Africa. *South African Journal of Business Management*, *27*(1), 82.

Chan, K. (2006). Consumer socialization of Chinese children in schools: Analysis of consumption values in textbooks. *Journal of Consumer Marketing*, *23*(3), 125–132. doi:10.1108/07363760610663286

Chironga, M., Leke, A., Lund, S., & van Wamelen, A. (2011). Cracking the next growth market: Africa. *Harvard Business Review*, *89*(5), 117–122. PMID:21510523

Clarke, B. (2005). Children get Media Smart in the UK. *Young Consumers*, *6*(4), 29–34. doi:10.1108/17473610510680894

Consumers International. (2011). *A guide to developing consumer protection law. Open Society Initiative for Southern Africa (OSISA)*. Consumers International, May. ISBN No.

Crotty, J., Driffield, N., & Jones, C. (2016). Regulation as Country-Specific (Dis-) Advantage: Smoking Bans and the Location of Foreign Direct Investment in the Tobacco Industry. *British Journal of Management*, *27*(3), 464–478. doi:10.1111/1467-8551.12161

CTCR. (2007). *Tobacco Papers*. The Centre for Tobacco Control Research. Scotland, UK: University of Strathclyde. Available online at: http://www.tobaccopapers.com/

Cui, G., Lui, H.-K., Chan, T.-S., & Joy, A. (2012). Decomposition of cross-country differences in consumer attitudes toward marketing. *Journal of Consumer Marketing*, *29*(3), 214–224. doi:10.1108/07363761211221747

Cui, T.-S., & Cui, G. (2004). Consumer attitudes toward marketing in a transitional economy: A replication and extension. *Journal of Consumer Marketing*, *21*(1), 10–26. doi:10.1108/07363760410513932

Daley, P. (2013). Rescuing African bodies: Celebrities, consumerism and neoliberal humanitarianism. *Review of African Political Economy*, *40*(137), 375–393. doi:10.1080/03056244.2013.816944

Darley, W., & Johnson, D. (1993). Cross-National Comparison of Consumer Attitudes toward Consumerism in Four Developing Countries. *The Journal of Consumer Affairs*, *27*(1), 37–54. doi:10.1111/j.1745-6606.1993.tb00736.x

Dike, O., & Onah, J. (2014). Evaluating Consumers' Protective Measures Against unethical Marketing of Medical Drugs in Nigeria. *International Journal of Business and Management Invention*, *3*(1), 14–21.

DoH. (2008a). *NHS Stop Smoking Services & Nicotine Replacement Therapy*. Department of Health, UK. Available online at: http://www.dh.gov.uk/en/Policyandguidance/Healthandsocialcaretopics/Tobacco/Tobaccogeneralinformation/DH_4002192

DoH. (2008b). *Reducing exposure to second hand smoke*. Department of Health, UK. Available online at: http://www.dh.gov.uk/en/Policyandguidance/Healthandsocialcaretopics/Tobacco/Tobaccogeneralinformation/DH_4080093

Dresden, B., & Barnard, J. (2003). Legal and regulatory controls on advertising and marketing to children in the United Kingdom. *Young Consumers*, *5*(1), 77–83.

Durvasula, S., & Lysonski, S. (2008). A double-edged sword: Understanding vanity across cultures. *Journal of Consumer Marketing*, *25*(4), 230–244. doi:10.1108/07363760810882425

Gbadamosi, A. (2010). Regulating child-related advertising in Nigeria. *Young Consumers*, *11*(3), 204–214. doi:10.1108/17473611011074278

Gbadamosi, A. (2013). Consumer involvement and marketing in Africa: Some directions for future research. *International Journal of Consumer Studies*, *37*(2), 234–242. doi:10.1111/j.1470-6431.2012.01096.x

Green, K. C., & Armstrong, J. S. (2012). Evidence on the effects of mandatory disclaimers in advertising. *Journal of Public Policy & Marketing*, *31*(2), 293–304. doi:10.1509/jppm.12.053

Halliru, M. (2012). The development of consumerism in Nigeria: Prospects and challenges. *International Journal of Arts and Commerce*, *1*(4), 274–285.

Harvey, J., Carter, S., & Mudimu, G. (2000). A comparison of work values and motives among Zimbabwean and British managers. *Personnel Review*, *29*(6), 723–742. doi:10.1108/00483480010296933

Hastings, G., & Aitken, P. (1995). Tobacco advertising and children's smoking: A review of the evidence. *European Journal of Marketing*, *29*(11), 6–17. doi:10.1108/03090569510100678

Hoek, J., & Dewhirst, T. (2012). The Meaning of "Light" and "Ultralight" Cigarettes: A Commentary on Smith, Stutts, and Zank. *Journal of Public Policy & Marketing*, *31*(2), 223–231. doi:10.1509/jppm.11.142

Hofer, P., & Bieri, J. (2005). Advertising to children in Switzerland. *Young Consumers*, *6*(3), 80–81. doi:10.1108/17473610510701232

Jones, M. L. (1986). Management development: An African focus. *Management Education and Development*, *17*(3), 202–216. doi:10.1177/135050768601700306

Kapito, J. (2000). *For a strong and binding framework.* Convention on tobacco Control (FCTC) at the Public Hearing of the World Health Organization. Retrieved from: http://www.who.int/tobacco/framework/public_hearings/tobacco_control_advocate_consumer_association.pdf

Koester, J. V. (2003). Legal briefing: Advertising to children in the USA. *Young Consumers, 4*(1), 65–71. doi:10.1108/17473610310813735

Le Guay, P. (2003). The regulation of advertising to children in Australia. *Young Consumers, 4*(2), 63–67. doi:10.1108/17473610310813834

Lysonski, S., & Durvasula, S. (2013). Nigeria in transition: Acculturation to global consumer culture. *Journal of Consumer Marketing, 30*(6), 493–508. doi:10.1108/JCM-07-2013-0626

Lysonski, S., Durvasula, S., & Zotos, Y. (2004). The Metamorphosis of Greek Consumers' Sentiments Toward Marketing and Consumerism. *Journal of Euromarketing, 13*(4), 5–29. doi:10.1300/J037v13n04_02

Madichie, N. (2010). The Nigerian movie industry "Nollywood"-a nearly perfect marketing case study. *Marketing Intelligence & Planning, 28*(5), 625–649. doi:10.1108/02634501011066537

Madichie, N., & Opute, A. P. (2016). Consumer Protection in Sub-Saharan Africa: An Exploration of "Big Tobacco" Marketing Practices. In A. Gbadamosi (Ed.), *Handbook of Research on Consumerism and Buying Behavior in Developing Nations* (pp. 311–333). IGI Global. doi:10.4018/978-1-5225-0282-1.ch014

Maher, J. K., Lord, J. B., Hughner, R. S., & Childs, N. M. (2006). Food advertising on children's television. *Young Consumers, 7*(4), 41–52. doi:10.1108/17473610610717964

Marquis, M. (2004). Strategies for influencing parental decisions on food purchasing. *Journal of Consumer Marketing, 21*(2), 134–143. doi:10.1108/07363760410525696

Njuguna, P. M. (2015). *Marketing Factors Affecting Consumerism among Urban Household Consumers in Nakuru County, Kenya* (Unpublished PhD Thesis). Jomo Kenyatta University of Agriculture and Technology, Kenya.

Nkamnebe, A. D., Idoko, E., & Kalu, S. E. (2009). Consumer protection in market transactions in Nigeria. *Innovative Marketing, 5*(4), 89–94.

Nwankwo, S. (2000). Assessing the marketing environment in sub-Saharan Africa: Opportunities and threats analysis. *Marketing Intelligence & Planning, 18*(3), 144–153. doi:10.1108/02634500010327935

Okpara, G., & Onah, J. (2013). The Entrepreneurial Challenge of Consumption Complex Syndrome (CCS) in SSA's MDG – Evidence from Nigeria. *World Review of Business Research, 3*(3), 30–46.

Perraudin, F. (2015). *MPs pass legislation to introduce standardised cigarette packaging.* Retrieved from: http://www.theguardian.com/politics/2015/mar/11/mps-pass-legislation-introduce-standardised-cigarette-packaging

Phillips, A., de Savigny, D., & Law, M. (1995). As Canadians butt out, the developing world lights up. *Canadian Medical Association Journal, 153*(8), 1111–1114. Retrieved from http://www.ncbi.nlm.nih.gov/pmc/articles/PMC1487334/pdf/cmaj00080-0061.pdf PMID:7553519

Pratkanis, A. R., & Greenwald, A. G. (1993). Consumer involvement, message attention, and the persistence of persuasive impact in a message-dense environment. *Psychology and Marketing*, *10*(4), 321–332. doi:10.1002/mar.4220100406

Reed, W., Catherine Bate, C., & Simsovic, D. (2003). Kid Law: advertising to children in Canada. In Advertising & Marketing to Children. World Advertising Research Center.

Rehn, A. (2014). *6 Mega Corporations Control Almost the Entire Global Cigarette Industry*. Retrieved from: http://mic.com/articles/81365/6-mega-corporations-control-almost-the-entire-global-cigarette-industry

Roberts, J. A., & Manolis, C. (2000). Baby boomers and busters: An exploratory investigation of attitudes toward marketing, advertising and consumerism. *Journal of Consumer Marketing*, *17*(6), 481–497. doi:10.1108/07363760010349911

Rosenberg, N., & Siegel, M. (2001). Use of corporate sponsorship as a tobacco marketing tool: A review of tobacco industry sponsorship in the USA, 1995-99. *Tobacco Control*, *10*(10), 239–246. doi:10.1136/tc.10.3.239 PMID:11544388

Shultz, C. J. II, Deshpandé, R., Cornwell, T. B., Ekici, A., Kothandaraman, P., Peterson, M., ... Veeck, A. (2012). Marketing and Public Policy: Transformative Research in Developing Markets. *Journal of Public Policy & Marketing*, *31*(2), 178–184. doi:10.1509/jppm.11.007

Skirstad, H. (2006). Marketing to children and young people in Norway. *Young Consumers*, *7*(2), 78–80. doi:10.1108/17473610610701529

Smith, K. H., Stutts, M. A., & Zank, G. M. (2012). An Exploratory Study of the Behavior and Perceptions of College Students with Respect to Regular, Light, and Ultralight Cigarettes. *Journal of Public Policy & Marketing*, *31*(2), 206–222. doi:10.1509/jppm.09.022

Smoke free England. (2007). *A Healthier England*. Available online at: http://www.smokefreeengland.co.uk./

Statista. (2018). *Leading tobacco producing countries worldwide in 2016 (in 1,000 metric tons)*. Retrieved from: https://www.statista.com/statistics/261173/leading-countries-in-tobacco-production/

Times Online. (2007). *Tobacco giants targeted African children to boost flagging profits*. Available online at: http://www.timesonline.co.uk/tol/news/world/africa/article2022928.ece

Vadehra, S. (2004). Advertising to children in India. *Young Consumers*, *6*(1), 75–78.

Van Tosh, L., Ralph, R., & Campbell, J. (2000). The Rise of Consumerism. *Psychiatric Rehabilitation Skills*, *4*(3), 383–409. doi:10.1080/10973430008408630

Veblen, T. (1899). The preconceptions of economic science. *The Quarterly Journal of Economics*, *13*(4), 396–426. doi:10.2307/1883645

Ward, S. (1974). Consumer Socialization. *The Journal of Consumer Research*, *1*(2), 1–14. doi:10.1086/208584

Wimalasiri, J. (2004). A cross-national study on Children's purchasing behavior and parental response. *Journal of Consumer Marketing*, *21*(4), 274–284. doi:10.1108/07363760410542183

World Advertising Trends. (2001). NTC Publications.

KEY TERMS AND DEFINITIONS

Big Tobacco: The "big 6" global tobacco producers and/ or marketers who constitute over 80% of the global market – notably (1) China Tobacco, 37%; (2) Philip Morris, 17%; (3) British American Tobacco, 12%; (4) Japan Tobacco, 10%; (5) Imperial Tobacco, 5%; and (6) Altria, 3%.

Consumerism: A social and economic order and ideology that encourages the acquisition of goods and services in ever-greater amounts.

Consumer Protection: Also sometimes referred to as consumer activism, is a political movement or a set of policies aimed at regulating the products, services, methods, and standards of manufacturers, sellers, and advertisers in the interests of the buyer. It seeks to protect and inform consumers by requiring such practices such as "honest packaging" and advertising, product guarantees, and improved safety standards.

Sub-Saharan Africa: A term with both geographical and political explanation. Geographically, it is the area of the continent of Africa that lies south of the Sahara Desert. Politically, it consists of all African countries that are fully or partially located south of the Sahara (excluding Sudan, even though Sudan sits in the Eastern portion of the Sahara Desert).

ENDNOTES

1 See the YouTube clip at: http://www.youtube.com/watch?v=ldbRXAOiwWs.

2 According to the CIA WorldFact Book (22 August 2018), "Landlocked Malawi ranks among the world's least developed countries. The country's economic performance has historically been constrained by policy inconsistency, macroeconomic instability, poor infrastructure, rampant corruption, high population growth, and poor health and education outcomes that limit labor productivity. The economy is predominately agricultural – a sector that "accounts for about one-third of GDP and 80% of export revenues." Furthermore, the "performance of the tobacco sector is key to short-term growth as tobacco accounts for more than half of exports, although Malawi is looking to diversify away from tobacco to other cash crops."
https://www.cia.gov/library/publications/the-world-factbook/geos/mi.html
Nigeria is Sub Saharan Africa's largest economy and relies heavily on oil as its main source of foreign exchange earnings and government revenues. Nigeria's economic growth has been driven by growth in agriculture (70% of the labour force), telecommunications, and services. Over 62% of Nigeria's over 180 million people still live in extreme poverty. Like Malawi, the country is marred by "inadequate power supply, lack of infrastructure, delays in the passage of legislative reforms, an inefficient property registration system, restrictive trade policies, an inconsistent regulatory environment, a slow and ineffective judicial system…"
https://www.cia.gov/library/publications/the-world-factbook/geos/ni.html

3 Interestingly Beijing (China) only as recently as 1 June 2015 banned smoking in public places.

4 China Tobacco manufactures 2.1 of the 5.9 trillion cigarettes made each year.

5 The company enjoys and is a separate entity from the smaller Altria Group/Philip Morris U.S.A., which only produces products for the U.S. market.

6 Due to stricter regulations in the markets they serve, Japan Tobacco's profits are a fraction of Philip Morris International's despite almost identical annual revenue.

7 As Njuguna (2015) argued, perhaps the earliest consumer organization to emerge outside Europe and North America was the Kenya Consumer's Organization (KCO). Although it did not officially adopt this name until 1974, it existed since 1951 when self-styled "housewives" decided to boycott stores known to overcharge customers. However, the Kenyan consumer has faced a number of challenges that seem to affect its progression; there were scattered pieces of consumer legislations that were "toothless" and provided no or lenient penalties to errant manufacturers; most consumer organizations in the country were lacking resources, political goodwill and suffered from industry influence or corruption; majority of consumer protection institutions have not been effective in addressing the challenges being faced by consumers in the country; and the consumer protection bodies carried out overlapping roles resulting in the reduction in the efficiency of each body. There have been several concerted efforts to revamp the consumer movement in Kenya. One of the major achievements for consumerism in the country was the registration of non-political and independent consumer organizations such as Consumers Federation of Kenya (COFEK), Consumer Information Network (CIN), Consumer Unity Trust Society (CUTS) among others. Consumer organizations fight for fair prices, quality and safety of goods and services. They offer litigation services, consumer education, provision of information on consumer issues and advisory services. They work closely with government agencies such as Kenya Bureau of Standards (KEBS), Competition Authority of Kenya (CAK) and Communication Authority of Kenya (CA) to provide an effective consumer protection regime in the country (see Njuguna, 2015: 3).

8 After decades of strong marketing in Africa, the Nigerian government has filed a massive US$42.4 billion lawsuit against BAT, seeking to cover past and future healthcare costs caused by smoking.

9 However in his 'determinants of consumer involvement' some notable insight is provided by Gbadamosi (2013: 236) in respect to advertising cues "Various factors determine the level of involvement that consumers have towards products, brands, advertisements [and] other stimuli. These factors have been identified to be the characteristics of the consumer making the purchase, the physical characteristics of the stimulus and the situation [...] classified into three broad areas: the background characteristics of the consumer making the purchase (culture and values, demographics, personality, lifestyle and psychographics); product characteristics (attributes, benefits, cost, and the perceived risk of buying and using the product); and situational effects that accompany a particular purchase or usage occasion [that] may arise..."

10 See the Official Website of APCON online at: http://www.apcon.gov.ng/.

11 "APCON is a Federal government agency that is responsible for the regulation and control of advertising [...] to ensure that only substantiated claims are used in ads, stopping ads that are misleading, and stopping claims that are spurious, and carrying out verification exercises on sales promotions [...] advertising for controlled products are mandatory for pre-exposure vetting [to ensure that these] conform to the code of advertising practice." (Gbadamosi, 2010: 209).

12 See BAT (no date) British American Tobacco - Company profile. Retrieved from: http://www.itraineeship.com/profiles/british_american_tobacco/.

13 In December 2006, Japan Tobacco made an agreed takeover bid for UK-based Gallaher which will consolidate the Japanese company's world number three position. Gallaher is thus now part of JT International, whose headquarters is in Switzerland. JT international employs around 24,000 people and operates in over 80 markets. http://www.gallaher-group.com/.

14 With internationally recognized brands, and a comprehensive portfolio of quality American blend cigarettes, JTI is the new global force in the tobacco market. Camel, Mild Seven, Salem and Winston are recognized the world over as leading international brands. All are made of the finest tobaccos and produced to the highest quality standards.

15 In their study, Crotty *et al.*, (2016: 466) point out that "…smoking bans, rather than prompting the relocation of firms, act as an institutional constraint on internationalization. It would appear therefore that FDI in this sector appears to be more prevalent from countries without smoking bans. Thus, smoking bans at home can be seen as a major source of CSA (Country Specific Disadvantage) that impacts upon firm strategy."

16 For the purpose of our International Marketing Standard, we define an adult as someone who is aged 18 years or over, unless a higher minimum age is specified by local law or voluntary agreement. See the Official CTCA Website online at: http://ctc-africa.org/.

17 The National Assembly (no date) Tobacco Control Bill. The Federal Republic of Nigeria. Retrieved from: www.nassnig.org/nass/legislation.php?id=377.

Chapter 6
The New Consumers of India:
Children as Learners and Teachers

Adya Sharma
Symbiosis International University (Deemed), India

ABSTRACT

The chapter explores the growing importance of children as consumers. The chapter would first discuss the importance, growth, and views on consumer socialization theory. The chapter would then take the discussion forward by introducing the change in the role of children not just as learners but as influencers. This section of the chapter concludes by initiating a discussion to understand the similarity and differences in the two theories: consumer socialization and reverse socialization. The theoretical overview provides the researchers a premise to integrate consumer socialization theory and reverse socialization to understand how children and parents acquire learning properties to be a consumer. Based on the two theories, a conceptual model was developed by the author to understand and indicate the process of children and parents becoming consumers. The chapter further discusses the changing social and economic scenario in developing nations with a special focus on India.

INTRODUCTION

Some adjectives used to describe children in the past have traditionally been cute, intelligent, innocent, and naughty among others. Society did not associate the word Consumer with children. Even the marketing world did not see any consumer segment in that group. The interest of the marketers was restricted in knowing and understanding how children learnt consumer skills, acquired market knowledge and became consumers when they grow up. This curiosity, inquisitiveness helped in the development of Consumer Socialization (Ward, 1974) or "the process by which children acquire skills and knowledge to become consumers". Substantial literature on this topic has proved that family, peers and media are important socialization agents (Hota & McGuiggan, 2006; Ghazali, 2011; Minahan & Huddleston, 2010; Fan & Li, 2009) Age too has been identified as an important cognitive factor (Roedder, 1999). Role of family as a socialization agent has been emphasized time and again. The process was unidirectional and children were assumed to have a passive role in the process. Their role was defined and restricted as only learners.

DOI: 10.4018/978-1-5225-7906-9.ch006

In the past few decades the world has witnessed major changes on economic and social scenario. Globalization of economies has ensured interdependence among the nations. Spread of internet has further ensured that the world is a smaller place. Social changes have also changed the societal makeup. The traditional Family Life Cycle witnessed a lot of changes. All the economic, technological and social changes also impacted the role of children in family purchase decisions. Busy life style of parents coupled with easy access to knowledge for children, made them active participants in family decisions. In order to explain the growing importance of children as consumers, researchers have cited the following reasons:

1. "There is a growing market of children's products
2. There is increasing influence of children in purchases of goods and services across categories
3. There is a new trend of accepting and encouraging children as co decision makers in family" (Sharma & Dasgupta, 2009)

The researchers and marketers started questioning the uni- directional process of socialization (Ekstrom et al. 1987). Children were not only learners but were teaching the parents also. A new area, reverse socialization, started gaining strength and importance. It became important to understand the influence of children on purchase decisions of the family (Belch et al, 1985; Belch & Willis, 2002; Lee & Beatty, 2002; Chaudhary & Gupta, 2012; Wilson & Wood, 2004). Mc Neal has proposed that children be viewed as three markets in one:

- "The current market that spends money on their desires,
- A future market for most goods and services and
- A market of influential who cause many billions of dollars of purchases among their parents" (McNeal, 1987)

With this background the aim of the chapter is:

- To introduce two alternative theories used by marketing researchers and practitioners to explain how children develop as consumers and how they influence purchase decisions.
- To discuss the cornerstone elements of these two theories and the different perspectives to these theories brought forward by research done over the years.
- To analyze and highlight the importance of understanding the role of children as consumers in developing nations with special focus on India.
- To identify new research avenues to address the creative capacities of children when they influence purchase behavior especially in developing countries.

CONSUMER SOCIALIZATION THEORY

Research on children as consumers had started way back in 1960s but it was only in 1970s that it gained visibility in the marketing world. One of the first definitions of Consumer Socialization of children was given by Ward (1974) as "processes by which young people acquire skills, knowledge and attitudes relevant to their functioning as consumers in the market place". Over the years two major classes of influence have been identified for socialization process:

Figure 1. A conceptual framework of consumer socialization
Source: (Moschis & Churchill, 1978)

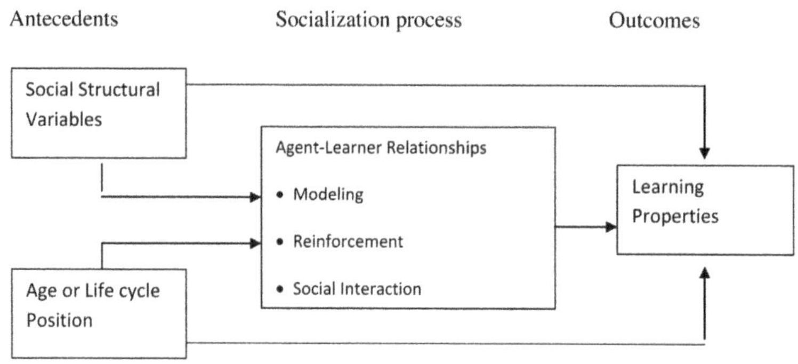

- Cognitive factors and environmental factors (Haynes et al, 1993).

Age related factors are classified as cognitive factors and environmental factors include agents like family, mass media, peers, culture etc.

A classic consumer socialization framework was proposed by Moschis and Churchill (1978). This framework has been widely used in marketing research since its proposal. The main elements included in the model are antecedents, socialization processes, and outcomes. Antecedents consist of social structural variables and age or life cycle position. Social structural variables include factors such as social class, family size, and family structure (Moschis & Churchill 1978). Family, mass media and peers are the three most studied consumer socialization agents. Among the three agents, family role has been found to be important and substantial.

Let us now try to understand the effect of different socialization agents.

Influence of Cognitive Factors (Age Related) on Consumer Socialization of Children

Researchers over the years have tried to explain the socialization process with change in age. One of the earliest theories was by Piaget. He developed the theory about childhood development and identified specific skills to specific age group. Sensori motor defines the age group from 0-2 years and Preoperational stage covers 2-7 years. As per the theory, the child is extremely self centered in Pre operational stage but begins to understand symbols. He starts to use symbols in a logical way in Concrete Operational stage (7-11 years) and also develops classification abilities. From 12 years to adulthood is the Formal Operations stage where he is able to do abstract thinking and apply it to real world. Ward (1974) also reinforced that children learning is influenced by stages in cognitive development and suggested that most useful framework for study of Consumer Socialization is an information processing view. On the basis of age difference in information processing Roedder (1981) defined three segments: Strategic, Cued and Limited. Strategic processors are typically older children who spontaneously employ storage and retrieval strategies. Younger children are Cued processors who also show storage and retrieval skills but only when prompted to do so. Limited processors are very young children who have not acquired efficient storage and retrieval skills. Ability of younger children to distinguish category boundaries is less as compared to older children (Roedder et al, 1992). Cognitive reactions to television advertising

Table 1. Stages in children's development as consumers

Characteristics	Perceptual Stage 3–7 Years	Analytical Stage 7–11 Years	Reflective Stage 11–16 Years
Knowledge structures			
Orientation	Concrete	Abstract	Abstract
Focus	Perceptual features	Functional/underlying features	Functional/underlying features
Complexity	Unidimensional Simple	Two or more dimensions Contingent (if-then)	Multidimensional Contingent (if-then)
Perspective	Egocentric (own perspective)	Dual perspectives (own+others)	Dual perspectives in social context
Decision-making and influence strategies			
Orientation	Expedient	Thoughtful	Strategic
Focus	Perceptual features	Functional/underlying features	Functional/underlying features
	Salient features	Relevant features	Relevant features
Complexity	Single attribute	Two or more attributes	Multiple attributes
	Limited repertoire of strategies	Expanded repertoire of strategies	Complete repertoire of strategies
Adaptive	Emerging	Moderate	Fully developed
Perspective	Egocentric	Dual perspectives	Dual perspectives in social context

Source: Roedder-John (2002)

were also linked to age. Children aged 10-11 years were found to develop a slightly more critical attitude towards advertising especially if they perceived the advertisement to be using untruthful ways to influence them (Uusitalo & Takala, 1993). In yet another study conceptual framework was used to divide children in various stages of socialization progress on the bases of age. The orientation in Perceptual stage (3-7 years) was described as simple, egocentric and expedient. Children develop the ability to analyze and discriminate on the basis of more than one dimension in analytical stage (7-11 years) In Reflective stage, children were found to be aware of other people's perspective and felt a need to confirm to group expectations (Roedder, 1999).

Influence of Socialization Agents

While age definitely affects the cognitive abilities of the children and that affects their socialization process, social factors also have a huge role to play in shaping the consumer socialization of children. Children of same age but in different settings would respond differently as Consumers. Researchers have identified family, peers, and media as important socializing agent. However recent research has also highlighted the importance of acknowledging the effect of cultural settings. In the following section we will try to understand the effect of different socialization agents:

Family as a Socialization Agent

Much research has been done to emphasize the importance of family in consumer socialization of children. Ward et al (1977) defined three alternative roles of the family in development of Consumer information processing skills:

1. "Direct impact on the development of general cognitive abilities and an indirect impact on development of consumer skills
2. Motivates children to apply general cognitive abilities in areas of consumer behavior
3. Teaches consumer skills which are not highly integrated with cognitive abilities."

Impact of family as a socialization agent can be studied and analyzed in three ways:

- Effect of family communication
- Effect of family demographics
- Role of mother/ father

Effect of Family Communication on Consumer Socialization

Using socio oriented and concept oriented as two dimensions of family communication four types of families were defined:

- Laissez faire (low socio orientation, low concept orientation),
- Protective (high socio orientation, low concept orientation),
- Plurastic (high concept orientation, low socio orientation) and
- Consensual (high socio orientation, high concept orientation) (McLeod & Chaffee, 1972)

Socio oriented parents emphasize harmonious relationships and encourage children to avoid any conflict. Children exposed to this type of communication usually submit to parents decisions.. They are not encouraged to ask questions or share their views especially when views are not the same as views of the parents/ elders. Parents with concept oriented communication emphasize individual ideas, beliefs and feelings. They encourage children to express ideas and to challenge others views. Family communication matrix has been the basis of studies which have identified the role of family communication on socialization of children (Figure 2). Moschis (1985) also conceptualized the family communication process and confirmed that parents appear to play an important role in consumer socialization of children (Moschis, 1985). Socio oriented families were found to encourage the children to evaluate their consumer behavior on the basis of perceived effect on others. Similarly, children from Plurastic families were found to have greater knowledge about consumer matters and were better able to distinguish exaggeration in advertisements (Moschis & Moore, 1979). Further studies on the effect of family communication on consumer socialization have shown that children from Plurastic families seem to be the most competent consumers

Figure 2. Family communication matrix

	Low Socio Orientation	High Socio Orientation
Low Concept Orientation	Laissez Faire	Protective
High Concept Orientation	Pluralistic	Consensual

and those from Laissez faire appear to be the least competent (Moschis et al, 1986). However, though studies have shown that family communication has a significant effect on youths cognition, Moschis et al (1986) suggest that these effects may not be carried to behavioral levels defining the youths participation in family consumer decisions (Moschis & Michell, 1986) The difference between different family patterns was reiterated in another study which highlighted that Plurastic encourage Consumer learning without emphasizing monitoring and control of consumption behavior and Protectives and Laissez faire deemphasize concept message (Carlson et al, 1990). The role of family communication in consumer socialization was reported as rather complex (Moschis et al, 1984). Importance of parental style was again emphasized in explaining children's exposure to online advertising (Wonsun Shin, 2010). There was a positive correlation between socio-oriented communication and restrictive mediation. At the same time restrictive mediation was found to be the second largest contributor to child materialism (Adib & El-Bassiouny, 2012). Family communication was synonymous with values and consumption skills sharing (Ayadi & Bree, 2010). Another research also suggests that concept-oriented family communication has no effect on youth's development of materialistic values, regardless of cultural background (Moschis et al, 2011). Parents restriction on television viewing also influences the socialization of children. Children who received more parental restriction regarding television viewing tended to be less conscious of brand names and style of clothing (Shim & Snyder, 1995). "Parents effect the consumer socialization of children when more anxious emotionally involved parents faced with the dilemma of dealing with conflict or engendering bad habits and wishing to limit their children's autonomy, may knowingly indulge their children's wishes" (Grossbart & Crosby, 1984).

Effect of Family Demographics on Consumer Socialization of Children

Children have been found to learn different consumer skills through different learning process at different ages from parents. Socio-economic status too has an effect on socialization of children as adolescents from higher socio-economic status socialize faster (Moschis & Churchill, 1978). Children of Parents with higher educational level see commercials as designed to induce purchases (Robertson & Rossiter, 1974). Parents decisions for children's snack food consumption was also influenced by situational factors. Children indicated that fewer limits were imposed on supermarket or self-purchased snacks (Marshall et al, 2007). Also, money education at home was linked to the number of children, the more the children, less money education happened (Shim & Snyder, 1995). Information from interpersonal sources was perceived as being more credible than information from commercial sources. Among the interpersonal sources, parents were regarded as the most reliable source of information (Fan & Lee, 2009). Family influence on socialization and decision making has also been found to be influenced by coalition patterns in the family. Three females within a family were found to be more influential than three males acting together. Female children had more influence in family decisions than male children (Lee & Collins, 2000). While gender of the child and number of children was not a determining factor on the decisions of the family to purchase any products as long as children were small (5-6 years), however gender difference plays a role and was also highlighted in another study which said that female adolescents are more likely to perform socially desirable consumer behavior than male adolescents. Knowledge of male adolescents appeared to be more than female adolescent about consumer matters (Moschis & Churchill, 1978; Isin & Alkibay, 2011).

Role of Mother/Father in Consumer Socialization of Children

Prominent role of mother in consumer socialization of children has been central in many studies. Mothers were identified as the main request target (Nash, 2009). Mothers were classified as Authoritarians, Permissives, Rigid, Controlling, Authoritative and Neglecting for a study conducted in United States. Compared to Authoritarians, Permissives had more consumer socialization goals, communicated more about consumption and were less restrictive. Authoritatives were more attuned to maturation levels and wanted to guide children development (Carlson & Grossbart, 1988). Mothers were primarily categorized as Plurastic or Consensual in a study conducted in Israel. Fathers were considered more agentic and classified as Protective (Bakir et al, 2006). Mothers employment status was also defined as a factor influencing consumer socialization of children. Children of full time employed mothers shopped for their clothing more often than children of mothers with part time/ no employment. This was in contrast to another study which found that better educated, more autonomous single mothers were found to be placing more of the burden for family decision making for grocery products on themselves and less influence to children (Ahuja & Stinson, 1993). Also mothers from higher income families perceived that their children expressed more interest in apparel shopping (Haynes et al, 1993). As per study conducted by Flouri (1999) mothers materialism level and communication style alone could reliably predict child's level of materialism (Flouri, 1999). Also intergenerational influence was mainly from mothers to daughters (Mandrik et al, 2005). The results suggest that nurturing mothers are more aware of advertising aimed at children and talk more to children regarding advertising and consumption than authoritarian mothers. Mothers who are nurturing and not authoritarian are more likely to yield to requests and favor more regulation than other parents (Wisenblit et al, 2013). The young women interviewed often trusted their mother to assist them gain the skills of shopping (Minahan & Huddleston, 2010). The influence of mothers interaction on consumer socialization of children was highlighted and mothers classified as Balancer, Nurturer, Diva, Protector, Struggler and Stoic in a study conducted in United States. Diva mothers saw media and marketplace influences as normal and did not see restrictions as a necessity. On the other hand Protector Mothers mistrust any potential influence on their children and exhibited strong negative attitudes about advertising and materialistic values of United States (Neeley & Coffey, 2007).

Father's role appeared to be very less than mother in Family communication pattern. However in a study conducted on single mother households, girls and black children were more positively affected by relations with fathers and father figures than were boys and white children. Divorced fathers were more influential in children's achievement than were married fathers (Coley, 1998). Mothers concept-oriented communication was positively linked to children's use of utilitarian, social, conspicuous decision making styles while mothers socio oriented communication was positively linked to children's use of undesirable decision making style and negatively to children's influence in family purchase decisions (Kim et al, 2009).

Influence of Media on Consumer Socialization of Children

Media is another socialization agent which influences children in becoming consumers. Children learn to use media to become aware of new products with age (Ward, 1974). It was found that children believe and like commercials less if they find the commercials using a forceful or a compelling tone. On the contrary if they feel that the advertisement is assisting them then they trust them (Robertson & Rossiter, 1974). As per Moschis and Churchill (1978) exposure to media alone is not sufficient for learning skills. Social processes condition adolescent's perception and interest in goods and services and that causes them to pay more attention to television programs and commercials (Moschis & Churchill, 1978). Advertising was found to have a marginal impact on preferences but little effect on final choice in a study involving children (4-8 years) for cereal products (Heslop & Ryan, 1980). Age also influences the way children understand commercials. While preschool children can tell the difference between a program and commercial, they are not always able to understand the difference in purpose of the two. Older children had higher level of awareness about commercials (Butter et al, 1981). Children aged 7-11 years were very receptive to commercials and had a positive attitude towards emotionally appealing advertisements. However it is only at 10-11 years that they develop a critical attitude towards commercials and tend to reject commercials directed at young adults. (Uusitalo & Takala, 1993). Television restrictions were less on older children. Also the younger children tend to ask more for the product they see in an advertisement compared to older children (Shim & Snyder, 1995). Age was found to be positively correlated with knowledge of persuasive intent at 7-8 years in another study (Childers, 2007). Teenagers purchase intentions were influenced positively by television celebrities and entertainers as role models (Makgosa, 2010). In order to help the child remember brand names visual cues were found to be effective. At the same time extensive visual cues were found to overtax young children processing abilities (Macklin, 1996). TV commercials and in-store experiences were the primary sources of new snack foods for Chinese children (Fan & Li, 2009). Given the varied and changing pattern of teen media consumption, television alone was no longer found to be the primary media influencer (Ghazali, 2011). The parents may think that they are sieving the information reaching the children, but study has proved that not only are children being exposed to adult oriented information but appear adept at processing that information also (Dotson & Hyatt, 2000). With the advent of internet and availability of multiple devices like tablets, mobile etc, the definition of media has changed for children. Children have far more access to media today than ever before and in the process the parental control over children's media use has become complicated. Children below a certain age may be able to manage the electronic devices but they lack the required cognitive and emotional skills and hence are vulnerable to the risks associated with media (Nikken & de Haan, 2015). There has been public concern over advertising to children. Negative effects of advertising were observed on children's food attitudes and choices leading to increase in obesity in children (Livingstone & Helsper, 2006). Similarly effect of ultra-thin models on ideal self-images was also studied. (Anschutz et al, 2012) In another study, early exposure to age appropriate programs designed around an educational curriculum is associated with cognitive and academic enhancement. In contrast exposure to pure entertainment and violent content in particular is associated with poorer cognitive development and lower academic achievements (Kirkorian et al, 2008) A model was proposed by Buttner et al (2014) to reduce the negative effects of advertising on children.

Influence of Peers in Consumer Socialization of Children

Influence of peers in Consumer Socialization of children is most probably one topic which has not been dealt in as much detail as other socialization agents. While peer influence is quite dominating in the early stages of consumer decisions, the influence is found to decline towards actual purchase suggesting that parents may mediate the effect of peer influence (Moschis & Mitchell, 1986). In a study done on children in the age group of 6-14 years it was found that sensitivity to peer group influence was highest by older age group and peer group influence was directly related to the conspicuousness of the product (Bachmann & John, 1993; Mandrik et al, 2005, Ghazali, 2011). Materialism in adolescents was also

Figure 3. Interventions for reducing the negative effects of advertising on children
Source: (Buttner et al., 2014)

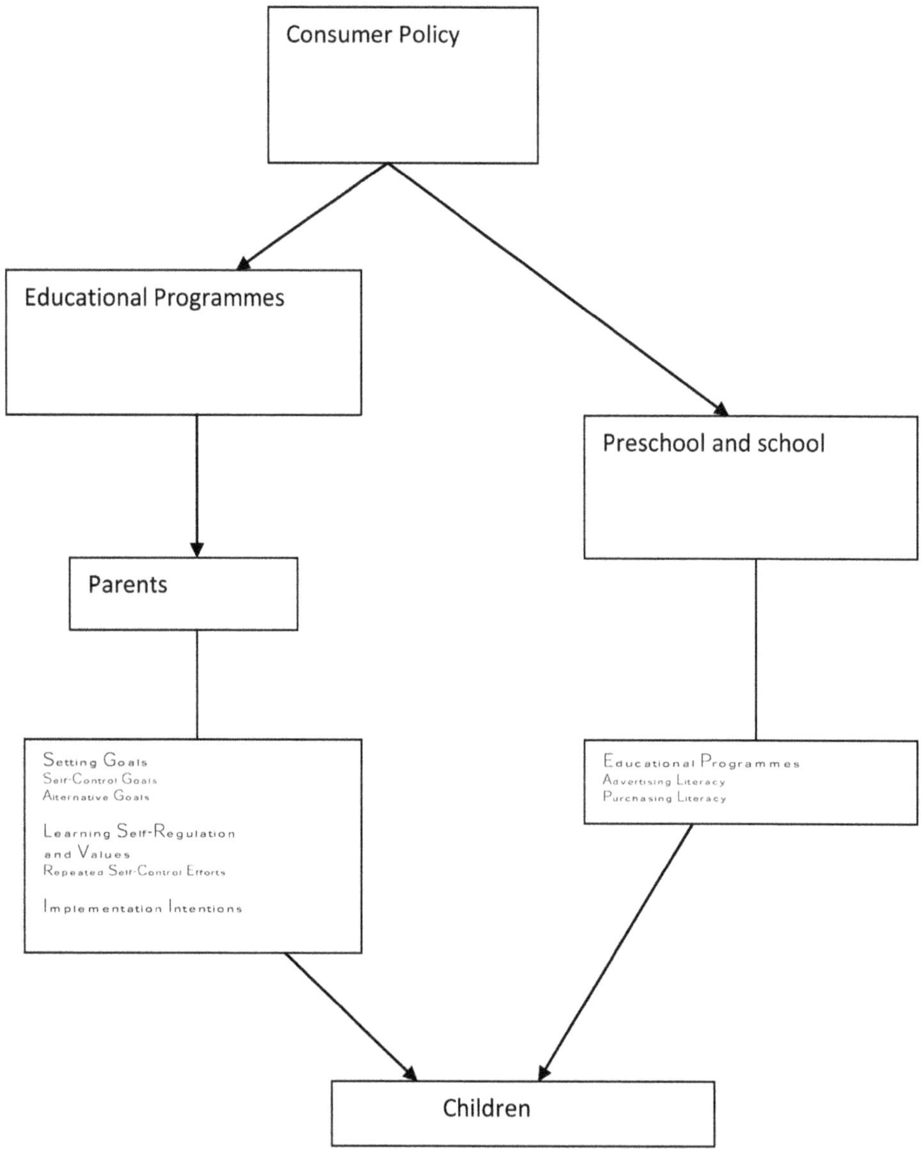

found to be related to peer influence (Flouri, 1999). Research suggest that the levels of peer influence were greater in normative stage than in informational situations (Opoku, 2012).

CHILDREN'S INFLUENCE IN FAMILY DECISIONS

Most of the research in the past has focused on the role of age and influence of various socialization agents (family, media, and peer) on consumer socialization of children. Market researchers and practitioners were in the forefront of children's consumer research, however academic researchers were comparatively slow to pick up on the cultural and monetary significance of children's place in consumption world (Cook, 2009). Recent research has highlighted the importance of adopting a reciprocal view of how parents and children may learn from each other in the socialization process (Ekstrom et al, 1987). The influence of children was found to be far larger than either the literature would lead one to suspect or than the families themselves declared. (Lee, 1994) Almost a decade later in another study in 2004, no significant difference was found between parents and children's views in influence perception of child (Wang et al, 2004). According to Wimalasiry (2004) the increase of the children influence on parents buying decisions in most of the developed countries is due to four factors;

- "First increase in number of working couples resulting in cash rich and time poor society,
- Second due to shift in family set up from joint to nuclear families,
- Third lesser number of children and
- Fourth repeated exposure to media."

All this has resulted in increase in the involvement of children in family decision making and hence an increase in their influence. Children and pre teenagers are segments definitely being targeted by marketers (Toomey & Francis, 2013). Another study highlighted that preadolescent children are not necessarily only in a learner role vis a vis their parents and may have a stronger influence in household decision making at an earlier age. The need to revaluate the traditional consumer socialization was again brought into focus (Dotson & Hyatt, 2000). Subsequently primary socialization was defined as basic understanding of consumer role and was most prominent during childhood while secondary socialization was defined as learning transmitted to a parent from child (Watne et al, 2011). Post 1990s child role in buying decision making has been emphasized time and again and explicitly acknowledged (Tomko, 2012; Martensen & Gronholdt, 2008; Kerrane et al, 2012; Wut & Chou, 2009).

It was observed that when families buy and consume food, parents were not the only participants and decision-makers. Children and parents did not always agree and it was proposed that research should include parents as well as children; and that food marketing should not only be directed at parents but also at children (Mikkelson & Norgaard, 2006). Accordingly, research should focus on deciphering the variety of consumption activities in which children are involved and on understanding the social and cultural conditions that make them adjust their participation by different degrees:

- "**First Degree:** A peripheral participation meaning that young children are mainly in a position of observers, when discovering the items brought home by their parents or older siblings, when accompanying their parents to shop in traditional markets and retail outlets, or even when observing shopping on-line at home.
- **Second Degree:** A more focused and active participation Meaning children now prescribe consumer items, which are legitimized by caregivers, peers or siblings.
- **Third Degree:** A central participation Meaning children now act as active and competent consumers, able to legitimately decide how to spend their own pocket money in some consumption areas that are culturally defined as specific spaces for children within a cultural community." (Marshall et al, 2007)

Majority of parents and children thought that children can influence their parents in deciding what to buy and what to eat (Suwandinata, 2011).

In order to understand influence of child on family purchase decisions, let us understand the effect of family demographics, family communication and type of product on child's influence. The chapter then discusses the different strategies adopted by children to increase their influence.

Family Demographics and Influence of Children on Purchase Decisions

Gender

Family demographics affect children's influence on purchase decisions. Female adolescents appeared to be more involved in consumer decisions than male adolescents and also with increasing age and money, adolescents acquired independence from parents in consumer decisions (Moschis & Mitchell, 1986). Female child had more influence on weekly purchases (Tomko, 2012). Gender, in another study, was found to be a significant discriminating variable predominantly for the youth sample. They felt that males have a stronger influence during the search and decision stages. However, parents felt that females played a more active role during the initiation phase (Beneke et al, 2011). Girls tend to be socialized differently than boys as parents suggested that they talk to girls more about purchase decisions than they do with boys (Neeley, 2005). Influence of female child in purchase decisions was more in some studies (Lee, 1994, Tomko, 2012).

Age of Child

Children's influence in family decision making increased with increase in age of the oldest child (Ahuja & Stinson, 1993; Ogden et al, 2012; Akinyele, 2010; Tomko, 2012). Older children had more influence on family weekly purchases (Tomko, 2012). Older children preferred to select more of their clothing for purchase (Haynes et al, 1993).

Number of Children

Number of children was not found to have any effect on the influence of the children (Isin & Alkibay, 2011; Akinyele, 2010). Though in another study children in smaller families were found to gain consumer capabilities earlier than do children in families with more children (Shim et al, 1995). First born children were found to have a greater influence in decision making process (Kerrane & Hogg, 2011). Children from small family were found to go co shopping more often than children from large family. Child of low or high education parents had the same influence in family decision making (Suwandinata, 2011).

Family Structure

Family structure was found to effect the influence of children as single parents tried reaching a consensus more often as compared with traditional two parent families (Geuens et al, 2003). Children's influence was found to be more in single parent families (Watne et al, 2011). Mothers and elder sons and fathers and elder daughters were found to work together to gain influence in the family decision. When mothers were employed outside the house then children had more decision power (Lee, 1994). In contrast, in another study, working situation of parents did not have a significant impact on adolescents influence in family decision making (Wang, 2007). In families where mother had a higher education, child's influence on weekly purchases was low (Tomko, 2012). Children either from employed or unemployed mothers had an equal influence in family decision making (Suwandinata, 2011).

Strategies Used by Children to Influence Purchase Decisions

Children cannot be taken lightly. They are an intelligent segment who is aware of their strengths and weaknesses. They employ various strategies to influence the decision making. Thus when they feel they deserve to have their way they utilize negative influence attempts and use positive influence attempts when they feel parent has a right to tell them (Williams & Burns, 2000; Marshall et al, 2007). Children tailor their influence strategies by incorporating the beliefs of their parents in their purchase requests (Kerrane et al, 2012). Use of trade off tactics was highlighted both as a rationale for parents ethical consumer decisions and as a disciplinarian tool with their children in relation to their non ethical demands (Carey et al, 2008). During the configuration and negotiation stages of decision-making process, the influence strategies adopted by children were found to play an important role (Lee & Collins, 2000; Thomson et al, 2007). They had lesser role in subdecisions – where to buy and how much to spend. Children exerted the highest influence in the initiation stage, followed by the final decision stage and the least influence is exerted in the search and evaluation stage (Chaudhary & Gupta, 2012). Child had much more influence in problem recognition, followed by final decision and least influence in information search stage (Wang et al, 2004). Children were found to have more influence in the choice making stage of decision making and parents still controlled the final decision (Wut & Chou, 2009; Desai T, 2008). Children were reported to exert influence on all decision stages in the family decision process but most on initiation and choice (Norgaard et al, 2007). Children adopted two strategies in terms of family socialization: a direct strategy placing demands on parents or a cooperative strategy helping parents (Pedersen et al, 2012). Children adopted a range of different strategies in wielding pester power . Boys were found to prefer silent treatment as an emotional strategy and fair play as competition strategy to influence parents (Fan & Li, 2009). Interestingly children were found to be less demanding and more persuasive in their parents approval (Wimalasiri, 2004).

Product Type and Its Effect on Influence of Children on Purchase Decisions

Child consumers in Turkey were found to purchase by themselves, make price comparisons, gave importance to brand and considered television advertising when making purchase decisions (Ozgen, 2003). Television advertising had an influence on the buying decisions of the teenagers (North & Kotze, 2001). In another research done in Brazil, results indicated that most parents allowed their children to make decisions regarding small purchases like ice cream, candies, snacks, however decisions were taken jointly or unilaterally by adults for computer games or electronics (Beyda, 2010). Kerrane highlighted that children's influence was increasing and they are exerting greater purchase influence across a wide range of products (Kerrane et al, 2012). Children's perceived influence was highest for products that related directly to the child (Ogden et al, 2012; Akinyele, 2010; Guneri et al, 2009; Lawler & Prothero, 2011). Children were found to have most influence on small and easy prepared meals and unhealthy food compared to healthy foods (Norgaard et al, 2007). Children played an important role in purchase decisions of food and personal hygiene products (Chickweche et al, 2012). Adolescents had most influence on products which were purchased for their own use (Wang, 2007). Even if small high-tech products were used by parents, children were found to be the decision makers for them. However, this was contrasted in another study which highlights that there is no significant difference in terms of children's influence between major and minor product decisions (Bao, 2001). For high risk products used by whole family, children of non-working mothers exerted marked influence on purchase (Isin & Alkibay, 2011). Children had maximum influence in the purchase of noisy goods, less influence for loud goods and the least influence in the purchase of quiet goods. Further quiet goods were defined as every day goods used by family, loud goods were expensive products used by family and noisy goods were goods used by children (Chaudhary & Gupta, 2012). The influencing power of children was dominating for products that could be connected to them (Polya, 2012). Extended discussion became more and more between parents and children as children's request moved from inexpensive to expensive products (Nash, 2009).

Family Communication and Its Effect on Influence of Child on Purchase Decisions

In consumption context a parent whose communication style is concept oriented tends to encourage child to develop an independent evaluation of consumption related issues and to express his/ her views about purchase decision. A concept-oriented parent actively encourages the child's inputs in consumption related discussions and activities (Wonsun shin, 2010). Concept oriented parents discussed with their children about companies collecting personal information on web (Youn, 2008). Family communication was found to be open for opinion between parents and children, however not everything was overt in family communication (Nargaard & Brunso, 2011). A Study also showed that Childs perceived influence was generally highest for Plurastic and Consensual parents (Bakir et al, 2006). Concept oriented parents perceived their children to have influence on family purchase decisions (Caruana & Vassallo, 2003). Parents of older children scored higher on the concept-oriented scale than did the parents of younger child (Neeley, 2005). Perception of influence is highest from plurastic and lowest from Protective parents (Caruana & Vassallo, 2003). Different forms of parental mediation were associated with different family communication patterns. Restrictive mediation was associated with socio-oriented family communication pattern (Wonsun Shin, 2010). Adolescents in concept-oriented families had greater influence in decision making than those in socio oriented (Wang, 2007). Parents with higher education levels and families with a higher household income engaged more frequently in concept oriented communication. Plurastic and consensual parents discussed with children about television commercials more often than laissez faire and protective parents (Chan & Mc Neal, 2003). Ekstrom et al proposed that childs influence differs under different circumstances and will also depend on his personal resources. They also proposed that children who are more involved in family decisions will experience greater satisfaction with decision outcome (Ekstrom et al, 1987).

"Though family is a resource exchange system, the resource theory assumes that family members are rational and thus family decision making cannot be explained fully by economic resources as affective and cognitive resources should be taken into account. Love for children encourages them to act in ways that go against the coping strategy of minimizing expenditure" (Wut & Chou, 2009; Hamilton & Catterall, 2006). Development of a children's model of influence, a model of family resocialisation has been mentioned as an area worthy of interest (Easterling et al, 1995). Further research has brought into focus, the need to understand, acknowledge that socialization process is bidirectional (Pedersen et al, 2012).

EXPLORING THE POSSIBILITY OF A UNIFIED THEORY TO EXPLAIN THE JOURNEY FROM CHILDREN LEARNING TO BE A CONSUMER TO CHILDREN PARTICIPATING IN PURCHASE DECISIONS

Research has been done in area of Consumer socialization and influence of child separately; however, to the best of authors knowledge no one has tried combining the two to propose a unified model. Children by influencing the family purchase decisions, in a way, educate/ reeducate the family members with their perspective. Thus children help in re-socialization of the family. If socialization is the process by which children learn the skills to become consumers then children's influence on family purchase decisions also helps the parents to learn/ re learn the skills to become consumers. The cycle in a way gets completed when children who learn socialization skills from parents also influence them and teach them.

A look at consumer socialization theory and reverse socialization theory reveals some close patterns. Role of Mother has been discussed in both the theories. Mother has been identified as an important socialization agent and comparatively role of father is limited. Mothers employment status effects the influence of the child also (Lee,1994; Isin & Alkibay, 2011). While age of child is an important factor in consumer socialization process (Roedder,1981; John, 1999), increase in age also increases the influence of child in family purchase decisions (Ahuja & Stinson, 1993). Family communication patterns have vastly been studied to examine the influence of family communication patterns on children's consumer socialization (Moschis & Moore, 1979; Moschis et al.,1984, 1986; Carlson et al., 1994; Mangleburg & Bristol, 1998; Hsieh et al., 2006; Carlson et al., 1990; Rose et al, 2002; Chan & McNeal, 2006). A few studies have been done to understand the effect of family communication patterns on influence of children on family decision making (Rose et al, 2002; Caruana & Vassallo, 2003). Accordingly the model (Socialization of children and re-socialization of parents: Relation to family variable) is a conceptual model to show how children who learn from parents, then teach parents and help in re-socialization of parents. The focus of the proposed model is how children influence family purchase decisions and how the end result is also re-socialization of parents (Sharma & Sonawaney, 2014). The model conceptualizes the influence of children only in relation to family variables and then integrates it with traditional consumer socialization model to explain both socialization and re-socialization. Conceptually this model proposes an integration of factors effecting socialization with factors affecting influence of the child. Theoretically it provides directions for future research.

RELEVANCE OF DEVELOPING NATIONS IN GLOBAL MARKETING SYSTEM AND THE NEED TO UNDERSTAND THE CHANGING ROLE OF CHILDREN AS CONSUMERS: SPECIAL FOCUS INDIA

Research in the western world started gaining grounds in this area in 1980s and 1990s but India was still far away from these studies. The closed economy, limited access to knowledge and different culture maybe did not cultivate a fertile ground for development of the area of research to understand child's influence on purchase decisions. The situation in India started changing in 1991. "A foreign exchange crisis in 1991 induced India to abandon decades of inward looking socialism and adopt economic reforms that have converted the once lumbering elephant into the latest Asian tiger" (Aiyar, 2011). This led or rather showed the path to other changes also. While economic reforms introduced the people to increased disposable income; technological changes made them more aware. Societal changes also ensured that role of children increased in family purchase decisions. India's population is projected to rise to700 million in2020 and is supported by strong economic growth. (unknown, 2012). India's middle class is expected to reach 41% of the population by 2025 and expected to control 59% of India's consumption power (Ablett et al, 2007). The Western countries have increasingly been defined as countries with aging population. India is an exception to this. India has a young population with 65% of its population below 35 years of age (Census 2011). A young economically empowered population can translate into an expanding consumer market. Spencer Stuart report has identified three major emerging markets in India- kids, youth and Urban Indian women. The report identifies that kids are influencers not only in product categories like confectionary and toys but also for products like car, electronics, refrigerators and air conditioners. The reason for the same have been identified as follows:

- "Higher degree of exposure to outside world has made children more clear of what they want
- The relative ease with which children are able to grasp technicalities and understand product features has made them an expert in the eyes of their parents
- "The relationship between parents and children has moved from hierarchical system to one driven by respect for children's views and abilities" Jacob Kurien
- The shift in role of kids in purchase decisions is identical across categories and cities
- Double income has boosted economic power of parents and they are ready to indulge children"

In the midst of all this, family an important socialization agent and an integral Institution of every Indian's life has survived but witnessed changes. Role of children in purchase decisions becomes a pertinent topic for researchers, marketers and policy makers.

A study conducted in India found that parents who resort to co viewing, explaining and teaching children about television advertisements could help them to regulate their buying response within family norms (Kapoor & Verma, 2005). Television has been a major source of educating children in India about fashion (Sharma, 2009). Like in the west, in India too children were found to respond differently to advertisements as the age increases. The study revealed that though television advertisements contribute significantly to Indian children's consumer socialization, the Indian children were not as easy a target as advertisers and critics believe (Kapoor & Verma, 2005). Exposure of children in age 11-16 years was more to internet in India than younger children (Desai, 2008) As compared to the West, India has been exposed to an absolutely different face of media in last two decades. Till two decades back India was dominated by two television channels both controlled by the Government. However in the last two decades the Indian population has been spoilt for choices in terms of number of channels available. With changing lifestyles, less time available with parents and availability of television channels 24*7, the exposure of children to media has increased multifold. In India also multiple media are accessed by children. In a study in India, it was observed that mean age at which children started watching television was 2.96 years and girls were found to spend more time watching television than boys (Raghav & Kumar, 2010). With increasing disposable income, it is also common to find urban households having separate television for children and parents. However it is internet, the newest form of media which is generating the greatest excitement among the youth. Teenage children in urban Indian households were significantly influenced by internet and this influence was found to be positively related to their role in family purchase decisions (Kaur & Medury, 2011).

While one study on Indian children showed that children had more impact on selection of children specific products than products for family use, another contrasted it by highlighting that children in India

Figure 4. Socialization of children and re-socialization of family: Relation to family variables

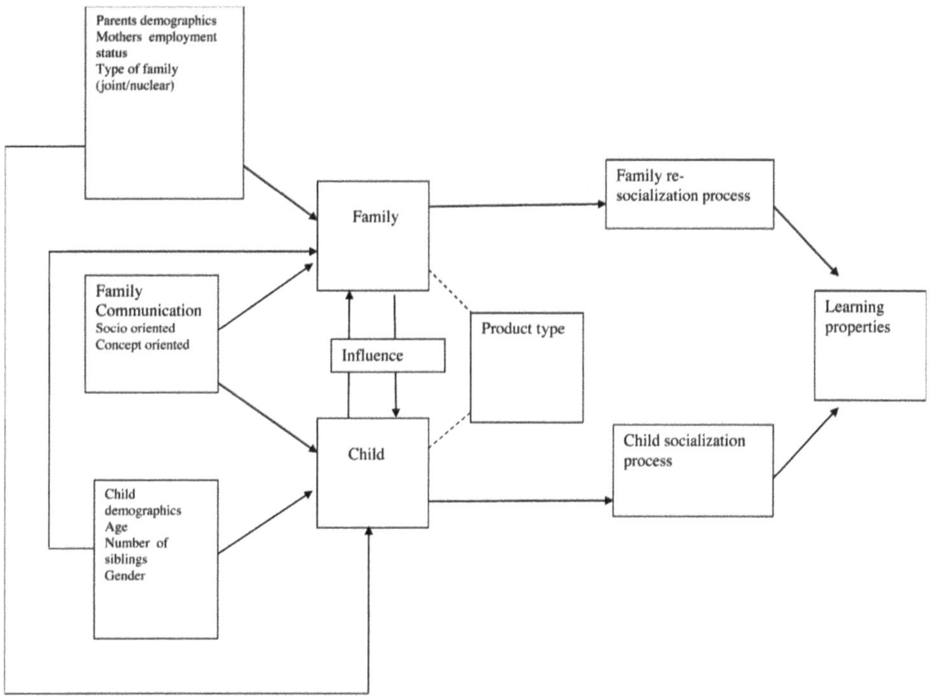

have an influence in various product categories used not only for direct consumption but also for family and household (Desai, 2008; Ali & Batra, 2011). Another study by the author found that Indian urban child had maximum influence on products used by children (ice cream, cycle, shoes, chocolate, child's hobby classes). On the other hand everyday products used by the family (dairy products, fruits and vegetables and bread) hold little interest for the child and that is accordingly reflected in their influence also. Thus children had least influence in everyday products used by the family (Sharma & Sonwaney, 2015). Interestingly it was the technical products used by the family (music system, mobile, play station, PC/laptop, car) for which both mother and child decided together. This product category invited equal influence from both mother and child. This may be explained by previous research where it has been indicated that parents believe that teenagers adopt easily to latest technology (Becker, 2005; Dobrow, 2006; Pechacek, 2007; Stone et al, 2001; Wilska, 2003). Parents have admitted to consulting their children for technological advice (Marsolen, 2013). Research has confirmed that Indian adolescents have a significant influence on the family decision making process (Kaur & Yedury, 2011).

Product Categories and Influence of Child

While two decades back in India, one could say with confidence that parents are more influential (in case of an argument the chances of parent winning the argument were more) but today children enjoy a different relationship with parents. Indian society differs vastly from the Western society in terms of family composition, family type, structure, norms, values, and behavior; it is important to understand children's influence in the purchase decision making in families in the Indian context (Jain & Bhatt, 2004). In Western developed countries, there exists a body of research in this field. But, studies specific to the

Indian environment are necessary given the size of market for children's products. Much of the research on consumer socialization and influence of children purchase decisions has been done in North America and Europe but it is the universality of research findings that should be examined (Cram, 1999) With the world becoming a global village the results of consumer socialization of children have also been tried in other cultures. Culture is defined as the sum total of learned beliefs, values and customs that serve to direct the consumer behavior of members of a particular society. Indian society too is driven by a set of core values. Geert Hoefstede matrix describes the effects of a society's culture on the values of its members and how they relate to behavior. The original four dimensions identified were individualism/ collectivism, uncertainty avoidance, power distance and masculinity/femininity. Power distance is the extent to which members of family accept and expect that power is distributed unequally. Cultures that endorse high power distance expect and accept that power relations are less democratic. The concept of individualism vs collectivism deals with how individuals live their lives socially. In a collective society social institutions or groups like family are given more priority than self. In a collective society individuals are more likely to value what is best for family over personal goals. On the other hand one's personal goals are more important than family goals in an individualistic society.

India's score on individual scale and power distance scale in comparison with the score of other western countries like United States of America and United Kingdom clearly reflects the vast cultural difference between these countries. With an individual score of 91 (U.S.A) and 89 (U.K) the society beliefs of these two countries are vastly different from India which has a score of 48. Family is a very important Institution in India and goals, wishes of the whole family are still higher on the priority list than individuals wishes and goals. The cultural difference between U.S.A and U.K and India is further reinforced by the score of Power distance. With a low score of 40(U.S.A) and 35 (U.K) the relationship in a group is more democratic. However with a huge power distance score of 77, Indian culture still believes in instructions/orders being passed from elders of the family to the younger members of the family. Younger members are expected to obey their orders and not question the leadership of elders. This was also obvious in studies done to compare Indian results with other cultures. In a study conducted one clear difference between Indian children and their western counterparts was related to strategic behavior. Indian children in third grade relied on different strategies or processes like repetition and rote rehearsal (Kurtz et al, 1988). In a study done on relatively urban, industrialized, literate and wealthy

Table 1.

Product Category	Products	Influence of Child
Technical products used by the family	Mobile PC/Laptop Music System Playstation Car	Both mother and child decide
Products used by the child	Cycle Chocolate Ice cream Childs spare time activity Shoes for child	Mostly child decides
Every day products used by the family	Fruits and vegetables Bread Dairy products	Mostly mother decides

Figure 5. Geert Hoefstede matrix score

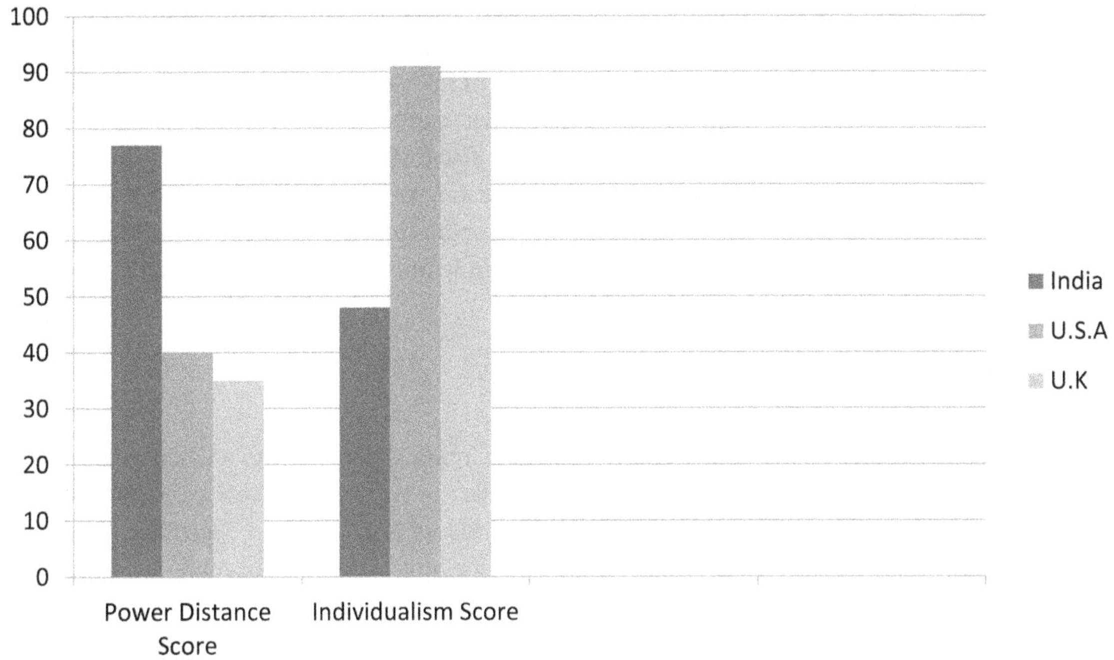

families of America, Britain and Japan, results showed some significant differences. Japanese children watched lesser television compared to American and British children. While Japanese families were more circumspect, and children were expected to learn through observation, trial and error, on the other hand American families were more open, expressive and children were expected to learn through purposive and expressive parental behavior (Ward et al, 1977; Rose, 1999). In another study done to examine the influence of parental style on consumer socialization in Australia, India and Greece, majority of the parents in India and Greece belonged to two parental styles-strict dependent and indulgent dependent. These styles exhibited higher levels of fostering dependence (Rose et al, 2002). Indian urban mothers were more socio oriented than concept oriented. The Indian culture is very different from the Western culture. Indian culture is dominated by collectivist attitude rather than individualistic attitude. The family bonding in India is still very high. Children in India may not have the purchasing power comparable to their Western counterparts, but they are still the center of the universe in the Indian family system, and they not only influence markets in terms of the parental decision-making to buy certain kinds of products, they are also future consumers" (Kaur & Singh, 2006). At the same time the younger generation is also influenced more by western culture. Also unlike other cultures, child is the responsibility of parents for a comparatively larger period of time. Decisions are still taken by family as a group rather than as an individual. In such a scenario one needs to examine the relevance of different concepts in Indian scenario.

FUTURE RESEARCH

The model suggested in the chapter is a theoretical model. Also the model has only considered the family variables. Integration of peer and media variables may lead to a comprehensive model integrating consumer socialization and reverse socialization. The role of media has specially become very important in the last decade. Technology has ensured that information is available at fingertips today for all. While this is a leap for mankind in bringing everyone on the same platform, specially where information and knowledge is concerned; it also treads the dangerous area of fake news and false information. Children are young with impressionable minds and future research must explore the effect of technology and media in shaping children as consumers. The future research may also test this model empirically. Finally more research should focus on the influence of culture. Most existing research is in western cultural context. More studies conducted in nonwestern parts of the world or comparative studies of two or more countries can further advance our knowledge in understanding role of children in family purchase decisions

CONCLUSION

Any study in marketing is relevant and useful if it can help, reinforce and/or provide new perspective to marketers, policy makers and researchers. The chapter reviewed two leading theories in understanding role of children as consumers-the consumer socialization theory and reverse socialization theory. The consumer socialization theory focuses on the learning process of children to become consumer. It focuses on cognitive factors and socialization agents. Thus it explains the making of child as a consumer through age and socialization agents like family, peers and media. Even among these socialization agents, family is considered the most important socialization agent. The consumer socialization theory has been subject of many researches (Ward, 1974; Carlson & Grossbart, 1988; Moschis & Churchill, 1978; Dotson & Hyatt, 2005; Moschis et al, 2011). but has been criticized for viewing socialization process as essentially one sided. It does not acknowledge children's role as source of influence. In contrast the reverse socialization theory indicates the influence of children on purchase decisions. In other words reverse socialization explains that role reversal takes place and parents take the learners position while learning from children.

The theoretical overview provided a premise to integrate consumer socialization theory and reverse socialization to understand how children and parents acquire learning properties to be a consumer. Based on the two theories a conceptual model was developed to understand and indicate the process of children and parents becoming consumers. It was proposed that family demographics, child demographics and family communication affect the socialization of children and reverse socialization of parents. This model integrated consumer socialization theory and reverse socialization theory to put forward a conceptual model to understand how parents and children acquire consumer skills. It thus filled the void or the question raised by researchers in questioning consumer socialization as a unidirectional process. As such it serves as a framework to the future research in area of understanding the making of children and parents as consumers. This model was bold and unique because on one hand it acknowledged relationships tested previously but it also ventured into those areas never explored before

For public policy makers the importance of this study cannot be overemphasized. The study clearly indicates that children play an important role in purchase decisions. Providing correct information to the child would play a crucial role in his/ her customer orientation. Products for which policy makers are seeking to deter or change children's views can be done by developing appeals which provide information to the child.

Further the chapter focused on the role of children as consumers in India. India has only recently become the focus of research in this area and hence compared to other parts of the world, research on this topic in India is limited. Hopefully this chapter will play an important role in the literature to understand role of children in family purchase decisions and encourage further discussions and debates.

REFERENCES

Adib, H., & El-Bassiouny, N. (2012). Materialism in young consumers. *Journal of Islamic Marketing*, *3*(3), 255–282. doi:10.1108/17590831211259745

Ahuja, R. D., & Stinson, K. M. (1993). Female-Headed Single Parent Families: An Exploratory Study of Children's Influence in Family Decision Making. *Advances in Consumer Research. Association for Consumer Research (U. S.)*, *20*(1), 469–474.

Aiyer, S. S. (2011). *The Elephant that Became a Tiger*. Center for Global Liberty and Prosperity (Development Policy Analysis). Retrieved from http://www.cato.org/publications/development-policy-analysis/elephant-became-tiger-20-years-economic-reform-india

Akinyele, S. T. (2010). The Influence Of Children On Family Purchasing Decisions In Ota, Nigeria. *Journal Of Contemporary Management Research*, *4*(2), 1–11.

Ali, A., & Batra, D. K. (2011). Children influence on parents buying decisions in Delhi (India). *European Journal of Business and Management*, *3*(11).

Anschutz, D. J., Engels, R. C., & Van Strien, T. (2012). Increased body satisfaction after exposure to thin ideal children's television in young girls showing thin ideal internalisation. *Psychology & Health*, *27*(5), 603–617. doi:10.1080/08870446.2011.613470 PMID:22512700

Ayodi, K., & Bree, J. (2010). An ethnography of transfer of food learning within the family. *Young Consumers*, *11*(1), 67–76. doi:10.1108/17473611011026028

Bachmann, G., & John, D. (1993). Children's Susceptibility to Peer Group Purchase Influence: An Exploratory Investigation. *Advances in Consumer Research. Association for Consumer Research (U. S.)*, *20*(1), 463–468.

Bakir, A., Rose, G. M., & Shoham, A. (2006). Family Communication Patterns: Mothers' and Fathers' Communication Style and Children's Perceived Influence in Family Decision Making. *Journal of International Consumer Marketing, 19*(2), 75-95. doi:10.1300/J046v19n02.05

Bao, Y. (2001). *Effect of Parental style and power on adolescents influence in family consumption decisions* (PhD thesis). Virginia Polytechnic Institute. Retrieved from http://www.google.co.in/url?sa=t&rct=j&q=&esrc=s&source=web&cd=1&ved=0CBsQFjAA&url=http%3A%2F%2Fwww.researchgate.net%2Fpublication%2F228362204_Effects_of_parental_style_and_power_on_adolescent's_influence_in_family_consumption_decisions%2Ffile%2Fd912f50f0ed6fb3d77.pdf&ei=1eK0U6nrHtKPuATTvoKIAw&usg=AFQjCNEaiQMvaFSeBq1glgcglmystbT5xw&sig2=2S8jpj7goktcGwVQwTOirg&bvm=bv.70138588,d.c2E

Becker, A. (2005). What a teen wants. *Broadcasting & Cable*, *135*, 16.

Belch, G. E., Belch, M. A., & Ceresino, G. (1985). Parental mid Teenage Child Influences in Family Decision Making. *Journal of Business Research, 13*(2), 163–176. doi:10.1016/0148-2963(85)90038-4

Belch, M. A., & Willis, L. A. (2002). Family decision at the turn of the century: Has the changing structure of households impacted the family decision-making process? *Journal of Consumer Behaviour, 2*(2), 111–124. doi:10.1002/cb.94

Beneke, Silverstone, Woods, & Schneider. (2011). The influence of the youth on their parents' purchasing decisions of high-technology products. *African Journal of Business Management, 5*(10), 3807–3812. doi:10.5897/AJBM10.359

Butter, E. J., Popovich, P. M., Stackhouse, R. H., & Garner, R. K. (1981). Discrimination of Television Programs and Commercials by Preschool Children. *Journal of Advertising Research, 21*(2), 53–56.

Büttner, O., Florack, A., & Serfas, B. (2014). A Dual-Step and Dual-Process Model of Advertising Effects: Implications for Reducing the Negative Impact of Advertising on Children's Consumption Behaviour. *Journal of Consumer Policy, 37*(2), 161–182. doi:10.100710603-013-9250-0

Carey, L., Shaw, D., & Shiu, E. (2008). The impact of ethical concerns on family consumer decision making. *International Journal of Consumer Studies, 32*(5), 553–560. doi:10.1111/j.1470-6431.2008.00687.x

Carlson, L., & Grossbart, S. (1988). Parental Style and Consumer Socialization of Children. *The Journal of Consumer Research, 15*(1), 77–94. doi:10.1086/209147

Carlson, L., Grossbart, S., & Tripp, C. (1990). An Investigation of Mothers' Communication Orientations and Patterns. *Advances in Consumer Research. Association for Consumer Research (U. S.), 17*(1), 804–812.

Carlson, L., Grossbart, S., & Walsh, A. (1990). Mothers' Communication Orientation and Consumer-Socialization Tendencies. *Journal of Advertising, 19*(3), 27–38. doi:10.1080/00913367.1990.10673190

Carlson, L., Walsh, A., Laczniak, R. N., & Grossbart, S. (1994). Family Communication Patterns and Marketplace Motivations, Attitudes, and Behaviors of Children and Mothers. *The Journal of Consumer Affairs, 28*(1), 25–53. doi:10.1111/j.1745-6606.1994.tb00813.x

Caruana, A., & Vassallo, R. (2003). Children's perception of their influence over purchases: The role of parental communication patterns. *Journal of Consumer Marketing, 20*(1), 55–66. doi:10.1108/07363760310456955

Chan, K., & McNeal, J. U. (2006). Rural Chinese children as consumers: Consumption experience and information sources. *Journal of Consumer Behavior: An International Review, 5*(3), 182–192. doi:10.1002/cb.170

Chankon, K., Yang, Z., & Hanjoon, L. (2009). Cultural differences in Consumer Socialisation: A Comparison of Chinese Canadian and Caucasian Canadian children. *Journal of Business Research, 62*(10), 955–962. doi:10.1016/j.jbusres.2008.08.005

Chaudhary, M., & Gupta, A. (2012). Children's influence in family buying process in India. *Young Consumers, 13*(2), 161–175. doi:10.1108/17473611211233512

Chikweche, Stanton, & Fletcher. (2012). Family purchase decision making at the bottom of the pyramid. *Journal of Consumer Marketing, 29*(3), 202 – 213.

Childers, C. (2007), Do looks really matter? An investigation of the impact of spokescharacter appearance on childrens purchasing influence Conference Papers. *International Communication Association, 2007 Annual Meeting*, 1.

Cram, F. (1999). Consumer Socialisation, Applied Psychology. *International Review (Steubenville, Ohio)*, *48*(3), 297–312.

Dobrow, L. (2006). Teen angel? Kinda. *Advertising Age*, *77*(1), 14.

Dotson, M. J., & Hyatt, E. M. (2000). A comparison of parents' and children's knowledge of brands and advertising slogans in the United States: Implications for consumer socialization. *Journal of Marketing Communications*, *6*(4), 219–230. doi:10.1080/135272600750036346

Dotson, M. J., & Hyatt, E. M. (2005). Major influence factors in children's consumer socialization. *Journal of Consumer Marketing*, *22*(1), 35–42. doi:10.1108/07363760510576536

Easterling, D., Miller, S., & Weinberger, N. (1995). Environmental consumerism: A process of children's socialization and families' resocialization. *Psychology and Marketing*, *12*(6), 531–550. doi:10.1002/mar.4220120606

Ekstrom, K. H., Tansuhaj, P. S., & Foxman, E. R. (1987). Children's Influence in Family Decisions and Consumer Socialization: A Reciprocal view. *Advances in Consumer Research. Association for Consumer Research (U. S.)*, *14*(1), 283–287.

Flouri, E. (1999). An Integrated Model of Consumer Materialism: Can Economic Socialization and Maternal Values Predict Materialistic Attitudes in Adolescents? *Journal of Socio-Economics*, *28*(6), 707–724. doi:10.1016/S1053-5357(99)00053-0

Geuens, M., De Pelsmacker, P., & Mast, G. (2003). How family structure affects parent—child communication about consumption. *International Journal of Advertising and Marketing to Children*, *4*(2), 57.

Grossbart, S. L., & Crosby, L. A. (1984). Understanding the Bases of Parental Concern and Reaction to Children's Food Advertising. *Journal of Marketing*, *48*(3), 79–92. doi:10.2307/1251331

Guneri, B., Yurt, O., Kaplan, M. D., & Delen, M. (2009). The influence of children on family purchasing decisions in Turkey. *Asian Journal of Marketing*, *2*(1), 20–32.

Hamilton, K., & Catterall, M. (2006). Consuming love in poor families: Childrens influence on consumption decisions. *Journal of Marketing Management*, *22*(9-10), 1031–1052. doi:10.1362/026725706778935655

Haynes, J. L., Burts, D. C., Dukes, A., & Cloud, R. (1993). Consumer Socialization of Preschoolers and Kindergartners as Related to Clothing Consumption. *Psychology and Marketing*, *10*(2), 151–166. doi:10.1002/mar.4220100207

Heslop, L. A., & Ryans, A. B. (1980). A Second Look at Children and the Advertising of Premiums. *The Journal of Consumer Research*, *6*(4), 414–420. doi:10.1086/208784

Hsieh, Y., Chiu, H., & Lin, C. (2006). Family communication and parental influence on children's brand attitudes. *Journal of Business Research, 59*(10/11), 1079–1086. doi:10.1016/j.jbusres.2006.09.016

Isin, F., & Alkibay, S. (2011). Influence of children on purchasing decisions of well-to-do families. *Young Consumers, 12*(1), 39–52. doi:10.1108/17473611111114777

Jain, P. C., & Bhatt, M. (2004). Consumer behaviour in Indian context. S. Chand Publication.

Jonathan, A., Aadarsh, B., Eric, B., Anupam, B., Diana, F., Ulrich, G., . . . Sumit, G. (2007). *The Bird of Gold: The Rise of India's Consumer Market.* McKinsey Global Institute. Retrieved from http://www.mckinsey.com/insights/asia-pacific/the_bird_of_gold

Kapoor, N., & Verma, D. S. (2005). Children's Understanding of TV Advertisements: Influence of Age, Sex and Parents. *Vision, 9*(1), 21-36.

Kaur, A., & Medury, Y. (2011). Impact of internet on teenagers influence on family purchases. *Young Consumers, 12*(1), 27–38. doi:10.1108/17473611111114768

Kaur & Singh. (2006). Children in family purchase decision making in India and the West: A Review. *Academy of Marketing Science Review, 8*, 1-30. Retrieved from http://www.amsreview.org/articles/kaur08-2006.pdf

Kerrane, B., & Hogg, M. (2011). How Best to Get their Own Way? Children's Influence Strategies within Families. *Advances in Consumer Research. Association for Consumer Research (U. S.), 39*, 366–373.

Kerrane, B., Hogg, M. K., & Bettany, S. M. (2012). Children's influence strategies in practice: Exploring the co-constructed nature of the child influence process in family consumption. *Journal of Marketing Management, 28*(7/8), 809–835. doi:10.1080/0267257X.2012.698633

Kirkorian, H. L., Wartella, E. A., & Anderson, D. R. (2008). Media and Young Children's Learning. *The Future of Children, 18*(1), 39–61. doi:10.1353/foc.0.0002 PMID:21338005

Kurtz, B. E., Borkowski, J. G., & Deshmukh, K. (1988). Metamemory and Learning in Maharashtrian Children: Influences from Home and School. *The Journal of Genetic Psychology, 149*(3), 363–376. doi:10.1080/00221325.1988.10532164

Lawlor, M.-A., & Andrea, P. (2011). Pester power- A battle of wills between children and their parents. *Journal of Marketing Management, 27*(5-6), 561–581. doi:10.1080/0267257X.2010.495281

Lee, C. K.-C., & Collins, B. A. (2000). Family decision making and coalition patterns. *European Journal of Marketing, 34*(9/10), 1181–1198. doi:10.1108/03090560010342584

Lee, K. C. C., & Beatty, S. E. (2002). Family structure and influence in family decision making. *Journal of Consumer Marketing, 19*(1), 24–41. doi:10.1108/07363760210414934

Lee. (1994). *Influence of children in family purchase decisions* (PhD thesis). University of Auckland. Retrieved from https://researchspace.auckland.ac.nz/handle/2292/1137

Levine, C. R. (1998). Children's socialization experiences and functioning in single mother households: The importance of fathers and other men. *Child Development, 69*(1), 219–230. doi:10.1111/j.1467-8624.1998.tb06144.x PMID:9499568

Livingstone, S., & Helsper, E. J. (2006). Does Advertising Literacy Mediate the Effects of Advertising on Children? A Critical Examination of Two Linked Research Literatures in Relation to Obesity and Food Choice. *Journal of Communication, 56*(3), 560–584. doi:10.1111/j.1460-2466.2006.00301.x

Macklin, M. (1996). Preschoolers' Learning of Brand Names from Visual Cues. *The Journal of Consumer Research, 23*(3), 251–261. doi:10.1086/209481

Mandrik, C. A., Fern, E. F., & Yeqing, B. (2005). Intergenerational influence: Roles of conformity to peers and communication effectiveness. *Psychology and Marketing, 22*(10), 813–832. doi:10.1002/mar.20087

Mangleburg, T. F., & Bristol, T. (1998). Socialization and Adolescents' Skepticism toward Advertising. *Journal of Advertising, 27*(3), 11–21. doi:10.1080/00913367.1998.10673559

Marshall, D., O'Donohoe, S., & Kline, S. (2007). Families, food, and pester power: Beyond the blame game? *Journal of Consumer Behaviour, 6*(4), 164–181. doi:10.1002/cb.217

Martensen, A., & Grønholdt, L. (2008). Children's influence on family decision making. *Innovative Marketing, 4*(4), 36–44.

McLeod, J. M., & O'Keefe, G. J. (1972). The Socialization Perspective and Communication Behavior. In F. G. Kline & P. J. Tichenor (Eds.), *Current Perspectives in Mass Communication Research* (pp. 121–168). Beverly Hills, CA: Sage Publications.

McNeal, J. U. (1987). *Children as consumers: Insights and implications*. New York, NY: Lexington Books.

Mikkelsen, M. R., & Nørgaard, M. K. (2006). Children's Influence on Family Decision-Making in Food Buying and Consumption. The National Institute of Public Health Denmark and MAPP- Centre for Research on Customer Relations in the Food Sector, Department of Marketing and Statistics, Aarhus School of Business Denmark.

Minahan, S., & Huddleston, P. (2010). Shopping with mum-mother and daughter socialization. *Young Consumers, 11*(3), 170–177. doi:10.1108/17473611011074241

Ming, W. T., & Ting-Jui, C. (2009). Children's influences on family decision making in Hong Kong. Young Consumers. *Insight and Ideas for Responsible Marketers, 10*(2), 146–156. doi:10.1108/17473610910964723

Monali, H., & McGuiggan, R. (2006). The relative Influence of Consumer Socialisation agents on Children and Adolescents: Examining the Past and Modeling the Future, European. *Advances in Consumer Research. Association for Consumer Research (U. S.), 7*, 119–124.

Moschis, Sim, Anil, Yamashita, & Bouzaglo. (2011). Family and television influences on materialism: a cross cultural life course approach. *Journal of Asia Business Studies, 5*(2).

Moschis, G. P. (1985). The Role of Family Communication in Consumer Socialization of Children and Adolescents. *The Journal of Consumer Research, 11*(4), 898–913. doi:10.1086/209025

Moschis, G. P., & Churchill, G. A. Jr. (1978). Consumer Socialization: A Theoretical and Empirical Analysis. *JMR, Journal of Marketing Research, 15*(4), 599–609. doi:10.2307/3150629

Moschis, G. P., & Mitchell, L. G. (1986). Television advertising and interpersonal influences on teenagers' participation in family consumer decision. *Advances in Consumer Research. Association for Consumer Research (U. S.)*, *13*(1), 181–186.

Moschis, G. P., & Moore, R. L. (1979). Family communication and consumer socialization. *Advances in Consumer Research. Association for Consumer Research (U. S.)*, *6*(1), 359–363.

Moschis, G. P., Moore, R. L., & Smith, R. B. (1984). The impact of family communication on adolescent consumer socialization. *Advances in Consumer Research. Association for Consumer Research (U. S.)*, *11*(1), 314–319.

Moschis, G. P., Prahato, A. E., & Mitchell, L. G. (1986). Family Communication Influences on the Development of Consumer Behavior: Some Additional Findings. *Advances in Consumer Research. Association for Consumer Research (U. S.)*, *13*(1), 365–369.

Nash, C. (2009). *Parent child purchase relationship* (PhD thesis). Dublin Institute of Technology. Retrieved from http://arrow.dit.ie/cgi/viewcontent.cgi?article=1025&context=busmas

Neeley, S. (2005). Influences on Consumer Socialisation. *Young Consumers*, *6*(2), 63–69. doi:10.1108/17473610510701115

Neeley, S. M., & Coffey, T. (2007). Understanding the "Four-Eyed, Four-Legged" Consumer: A Segmentation Analysis of U.S. Moms. *Journal of Marketing Theory and Practice*, *15*(3), 251–261. doi:10.2753/MTP1069-6679150305

Nikken, P., & de Haan, J. (2015). Guiding young children's internet use at home: Problems that parents experience in their parental mediation and the need for parenting support. *Cyberpsychology (Brno)*, 44–57. doi:10.5817/CP2015-1-3

Norgaard, M., & Brunso, K. (2007). Children's influence and participation in the family decision process during food buying. *Young Consumers*, *8*(3), 197–216. doi:10.1108/17473610710780945

Nørgaard, M., & Brunsø, K. (2011). Family conflicts and conflict resolution regarding food choices. *Journal of Consumer Behaviour*, *10*(3), 141–151. doi:10.1002/cb.361

North & Theuns. (2001). Parents and television advertisements as consumer socialization agents for adolescents: An exploratory study. *Journal of Family Ecology and Consumer Sciences, 29*, 91-99.

Ogden, Ogden, & Ramzy. (2012). *Perceptions of children's influence on Purchase decisions: A comparison between US and Egypt*. Retrieved from www.wbiconpro.com/516-Denise.pdf

Özgen, Ö. (2003). An analysis of child consumers in Turkey. *International Journal of Consumer Studies*, *27*(5), 366–380. doi:10.1046/j.1470-6431.2003.00306.x

Pechacek, A. (2007). I can't live without my … teens' top ten high-tech gadgets and web sites. *Young Adult Library Services*, *5*(2), 9–16.

Polya, E. (2012). *Purchase decision making process and roles within the family* (PhD thesis). Szent Istvan University. Retrieved from https://szie.hu//file/tti/archivum/Polya_E_Thesis.pdf

Raghav, P., & Kumar, A. (2010). The Influence of Television on Children and Adolescents in an Urban Slum. *Indian Journal of Community Medicine*, *35*(3), 447. doi:10.4103/0970-0218.69291 PMID:21031123

Rina, M. (2010). The influence of vicarious role models on purchase intentions of Botswana teenagers. *Young Consumers*, *11*(4), 307–319. doi:10.1108/17473611011093934

Robert, O. (2012). Young Saudi adults and peer group purchase influence; a preliminary investigation. *Young Consumers*, *13*(2), 176–187. doi:10.1108/17473611211233549

Robertson, T. S., & Rossiter, J. R. (1974). Children and Commercial Persuasion: An Attribution Theory Analysis. *The Journal of Consumer Research*, *1*(1), 13–20. doi:10.1086/208577

Roedder, D. L. (1981). Age Differences in Children's Responses to Television Advertising: An Information-Processing Approach. *The Journal of Consumer Research*, *8*(2), 144–153. doi:10.1086/208850

Roedder, J. D. (1999). Consumer Socialisation of children: A Retrospective look at twenty five years of research. *The Journal of Consumer Research*, *26*(3), 183–213. doi:10.1086/209559

Roedder & Lakshmi-Ratan. (1992). Age differences in Children's choice Behaviour: The Impact of Available Alternatives. *Journal of Marketing research, 26*, 216-26.

Roedder-John, D. (2002). Consumer socialization of children: a retrospective look at twenty-five years of research. In F. Hansen, J. Rasmussen, A. Martensen, & B. Tufte (Eds.), *Children: Consumption, Advertising and Media* (pp. 25–89). Copenhagen: Copenhagen Business School Press.

Rose, G. M. (1999). Consumer Socialisation, Parental Style and Developmental Time Tables in the United States and Japan. *Journal of Marketing*, *63*(3), 105–119. doi:10.2307/1251778

Rose, G. M., Boush, D., & Shoham, A. (2002). Family communication and children's purchasing influence: A cross-national examination. *Journal of Business Research*, *55*(11), 867–873. doi:10.1016/S0148-2963(01)00205-3

Scott, W. (1974). Consumer Socialisation: Initial Study results. *Advances in Consumer Research. Association for Consumer Research (U. S.)*, *I*, 120–125.

Sharma, A. (2009). Role and influence of children in buying children's apparel. *Indian Journal of Marketing*, *39*(7), 42–46.

Sharma, A. (2011). Role of family in consumer socialization of children: Literature Review.*Journal of Arts. Science and Commerce*, *2*(3), 161–167.

Sharma, A., & Sonwaney, V. (2014). Theoretical Modeling of Influence of children on Family Purcahse Decision Making. *Procedia: Social and Behavioral Sciences*, *133*, 38–46. doi:10.1016/j.sbspro.2014.04.167

Sharma, A., & Sonwaney, V. (2015). Exploring the role of family communication and brand awareness in understanding the influence of child on purchase decisions: Scale development and Validation, *Int. Journal of. Business Excellence*, *8*(6), 748–766. doi:10.1504/IJBEX.2015.072308

Sharma, R., & Dasgupta, P. (2009). Marketing to children: A planning framework. *Young Consumers*, *10*(3), 180–187. doi:10.1108/17473610910985991

Shim, S., & Snyder, L. (1995). Parents' Perception Regarding Children's Use of Clothing Evaluative Criteria: An Exploratory Study From the Consumer Socialization Process Perspective. *Advances in Consumer Research. Association for Consumer Research (U. S.)*, *22*(1), 628–632.

Stone, M., Stanton, H., Kirkham, J., & Pyne, W. (2001). The digerati: Generation Y finds its voice. Why cannot brands do the same? *Journal of Targeting, Measurement and Analysis for Marketing*, *10*(2), 158–167. doi:10.1057/palgrave.jt.5740042

Susanne, P., Alice, G., & Tino, B.-L. (2012). Family members' roles in healthy-eating socialization based on a healthy-eating intervention. Young Consumers. *Insight and Ideas for Responsible Marketers*, *13*(3), 208–223. doi:10.1108/17473611211261610

Suwandinata, H. (2011). *Children's influence on family decision making process in food buying and consumption* (PhD thesis). Retrieved from http://geb.uni-giessen.de/geb/volltexte/2012/8589/pdf/SuwandinataHanny_2012_01_19.pdf

Tanvi, D. (2008). *Children's influence on family purchase decision in India* (MA dissertation). University of Nottingham, Nottingham, UK.

The Changing face of India. (2012). *Citizen Today*, 8-9. Retrieved from http://www.ey.com/Publication/vwLUAssets/The_changing_face_of_India/$File/The_changing_face_of_India.pdf

Thomas, C. D. (2009). Knowing the child consumer: Historical and conceptual insights on qualitative children's consumer research. Young Consumers. *Insight and Ideas for Responsible Marketers*, *10*(4), 269–282. doi:10.1108/17473610911007111

Thomson, E. S., Laing, A. W., & McKee, L. (2007). Family purchase decision making: Exploring child influence behaviour. *Journal of Consumer Behaviour*, *6*(4), 182–202. doi:10.1002/cb.220

Tisser, B. T. (2010). Who teaches them to consume: A Study of Barzilian youngsters. *International Journal of Consumer Studies*, *34*(3), 298–304. doi:10.1111/j.1470-6431.2009.00857.x

Tomko Paul, R. (2012). *Understanding the factors affecting the influence of children on their parents total purchases* (PhD thesis). Capella University. Retrieved from http://media.proquest.com/media/pq/classic/doc/2662550201/fmt/ai/rep/NPDF?_s=xTqZvWcg%2FEYgxQjxIzJZcW9m7Y4%3D

Toomey Deborah, A., & Francis Alisha, L. (2013). Branded product placement and pre-teenaged consumers: Influence on brand preference and choice. Young Consumers. *Insight and Ideas for Responsible Marketers*, *14*(2), 180–192. doi:10.1108/17473611311325573

Uusitalo & Takala. (1993). Developmental Stage and Children's reaction to T.V advertising. *European Advances in Consumer Research*, *1*, 360-365.

Wang, D. (2007). *Adolescents perception of their influence in family decision making in China* (Dissertation in MA Marketing). University of Nottingham.

Wang, H., Hsieh, A.-T., Yeh, Y.-C., & Tsai, C.-W. (2004). Who is the decision maker: The parent or the child in group package tour? *Tourism Management*, *25*(2), 183–194. doi:10.1016/S0261-5177(03)00093-1

Ward, S., Wackman, D., & Wartella, E. (1977). The Development of Consumer Information- Processing Skills: Integrating Cognitive Development and Family Interaction Theoris. *Advances in Consumer Research. Association for Consumer Research (U. S.), 4*(1), 166–171.

Watne, Lobo, & Brennan.(2011). *Children as agents of Secondary Socialization for their parents, Young Consumers: Insight and Ideas for responsible marketers*. Doi:10.1108/17473611111185841

Williams, L. A., & Burns, A. C. (2000). Exploring the Dimensionality of Children's Direct Influence Attempts. *Advances in Consumer Research. Association for Consumer Research (U. S.), 27*(1), 64–71.

Wilska, T.-A. (2003). Mobile phone use as part of young people's consumption styles. *Journal of Consumer Policy, 26*(4), 441–463. doi:10.1023/A:1026331016172

Wilson, G., & Wood, K. (2004). The influence of children on parental purchases during supermarket shopping. *International Journal of Consumer Studies, 28*(4), 329–336. doi:10.1111/j.1470-6431.2004.00393.x

Wimalasiri, J. S. (2004). A cross-national study on children's purchasing behavior and parental response. *Journal of Consumer Marketing, 21*(4), 274–284. doi:10.1108/07363760410542183

Wisenblit, & Priluck, & Pirog. (2013). The influence of parental styles on childrens consumption. *Journal of Consumer Marketing, 30*(4), 320–327. doi:10.1108/JCM-02-2013-0465

Wonsun, S. (2010). *The role of Parental mediation in children's consumer socialization on the web* (PhD thesis). University of Minnesota. Retrieved from https://conservancy.umn.edu/bitstream/handle/11299/95674/Shin_umn_0130E_11299.pdf?sequence=1

Wonsun, S. (2010). Consumer Socialization Online: Antecedents And Consequences of Children's Skepticism Toward Online Advertising. *American Academy of Advertising Conference Proceedings, 115*. Retrieved from EBSCOhost

Ying, F., & Li, Y. (2009). Children's buying behavior in China: A study of their information sources. *Marketing Intelligence & Planning, 28*(2), 170–187. doi:10.1108/02634501011029673

Youn, S. (2008). Parental Influence and teen's attitude toward online privacy protection. *The Journal of Consumer Affairs, 42*(3), 362–388. doi:10.1111/j.1745-6606.2008.00113.x

Zaharah, G. (2011). The influence of Socialisation agents and demographic profiles on brand consciousness. *International Journal of Management and Marketing Research, 4*(1), 19–29.

KEY TERMS AND DEFINITIONS

Concept-Oriented Communication: A type of family communication that encourages children to ask questions and share their views with elders.

Consumer Socialization: It is the process by which children acquire necessary skills to become consumers.

Family Communication: It is the way in which information is shared among family members.

Reverse Socialization: It is the process by which children influence parents and help them relearn and reacquire skills to become consumers.

Socio-Oriented Communication: A type of family communication which encourages children to avoid conflict and discourages them from discussions/debates with elders.

Chapter 7
Celebrity Credibility Influence on Cosmetic Product Purchase Intention:
The Moderating Role of Ethnocentrism

Fatima Zohra Chekima
Universiti Malaysia Sabah, Malaysia

Brahim Chekima
Universiti Malaysia Sabah, Malaysia

ABSTRACT

One of the strategies that are used by companies to differentiate their cosmetic products is celebrity endorsement. Despite this popular advertising technique, researchers and advertisers have not agreed as to which celebrity source characteristics are most effective in influencing consumers' purchase intention. Another important factor that affects consumers' purchase intention is the consumer ethnocentrism level. Consumers in different countries have different preference over local and international products. Thus, the objective of this chapter is to examine the source credibility theory with the moderating role of ethnocentrism. The result suggests that celebrity endorsers' trustworthiness (TR), attractiveness (AT), and expertise (EX) had a significant positive influence on cosmetic product purchase intention (CPPI). The moderating role of ethnocentrism between AT, TR, and CPPI were examined and found to be significant. This indicates that AT and TR are stronger when consumers' ethnocentrism is high.

INTRODUCTION

Due to market globalization, more firms worldwide small or big, embrace international marketing as a business expansion approach that is achievable. There has been an overabundance of goods and services foreign or locally produced, available in the market. One of the industries is the cosmetic industry which has been growing and expanding around the world in both developing and developed countries. This phenomenon opens the doors for those interested in the business to promote their cosmetic products, the

DOI: 10.4018/978-1-5225-7906-9.ch007

continued growth and evolution of the cosmetic industry offer good opportunities (Ministry of Health, Malaysia, 2009). According to the U.S. Commercial Service (2014), Asia Pacific market value has increased to further than US$ 70billion, which makes it as the second highest after the Western European market. Asian cosmetics industry has become one of the fastest emerging markets.

Consumers' interest in cosmetics has been affected by heavy marketing, advertisements, and the growing affluence which increased their attraction to high-quality brands. According to the U.S. Commercial Service (2014), Malaysia's market for cosmetics and toiletries has a growth rate of 13% per year. In Malaysia, there are more than 60,000 kinds of cosmetics available in the local market (Ministry of Health, Malaysia, 2009). A global study found that TV advertising featuring celebrities is typically used in each country, even though there are great differences in preference between countries (Praet, 2001). Lately, the number of celebrities promoting the brand through different online environments is increasing (Wood & Burkhalter, 2014). According to Praet (2001), celebrity endorsement is noticeably more common in Asian countries than in Europe and United States (US). This was proved by a comparison of 6, 359 TV advertisements carried out cross-national from 25 countries, which the results showed that celebrity endorsements were used in the advertisements in Asia which was in South Korea and China, ranged from 61% to 25% respectively, while in European countries endorsers were used in less than 15% of advertisements.

In order to stand out of the chaos and give a matchless and important position in the minds of consumers, some companies enter deals with celebrities (Temperley & Tangen, 2006). These companies then hire these celebrities as endorsers or spokespersons to publicize and market the company's ideas, products, or services. In modern marketing, celebrity endorsement has become chart-topping (Choi & Rifon, 2007; McCracken, 1989). Moreover, according to O'Mahony and Meenaghan (1997), marketers believe that celebrities would be able to attract the attention of consumers towards the endorsed products and could transmit their image values to the product involved by virtue of their celebrity profile and engaging attributes therefore, marketers would invest high amount of asset to align the products with the well-known celebrities. Celebrity endorsements enjoy enduring fame as a way to improve marketing communications (Bergkvist & Zhou, 2016).

The underlying reason for using celebrity is that it would affect the consumer purchase intention through the phenomena that marketers think that the consumers attention towards the message could be drawn by celebrities' profile and attributes via rub-off effects would transmit the image values into a message communication (Farhat & Khan, 2011; Pringle & Binet, 2005; Pornpitakpan, 2004; O'Mahony & Meenaghan, 1997). In fact, companies in Malaysia are spending millions on celebrity endorsements and are expanding their budget on promotional activities (Freeman & Chen, 2015; Tan, 2011). McCracken (1989) proposed an example of meaning transfer process are celebrity endorsement. The meaning is allocated in the social and also the physical world established through the fundamental culture. Then by using fashion and advertising systems, consumer goods are transferred, and next towards the consumer' lives through the efforts of consumers. Therefore in this transfer, celebrity endorsement plays an important role.

Given the factors above, it can be said that the decision making in selecting a celebrity endorser is a challenging, uncertain and important decision. Choosing a celebrity that is recognized as credible could be a way in reducing the risk that could be faced, this is because many of the empirical evidence has revealed that a celebrity which is more persuasive will be a more credible source (Bannister, 1986; Lirtzman & Shuv-Ami, 1986; Friedman & Friedman, 1979; Fireworker & Friedman, 1977). Despite the popular advertising technique of using celebrity endorsement, market researchers and advertisers have not agreed as to which celebrity source characteristics are most effective in influencing consumers' purchase intention of the endorsed products or brands. This is because consumers in different countries have dissimilar preference over the characteristics of the endorser. Even though companies spend huge amount of money for the use of celebrity endorsement, it does not give assurance that it will succeed as a marketing tool (Wei & Li, 2013). Moreover, there is a limited research done to date on how consumers' purchase intention is influenced by celebrity endorsement and which characteristics are more important when choosing an endorser. This would be even more questionable in a multicultural country like Malaysia. The increased number of celebrity endorsement as a marketing tool in Malaysia has raised an interesting question on the effectiveness of celebrity endorsement on the Purchase Intention (Vien et al. 2017)

Despite the increasing trend of celebrity endorsement in Malaysia, there are limited information on how Malaysian consumers accept the cosmetic products being advertised by celebrities, mainly among the Malays, Chinese, and Indians ethnic groups. In other words, how do the multicultural Malaysians perceive advertisement by celebrities? Also, what are their behavior towards cosmetic products advertised by celebrities? Hence, the aim of this research is to examine the overall perceptions of Malays, Chinese and Indians consumers towards the celebrity endorsement of cosmetic products. This study also analyzes the consumers' perceptions towards the celebrity characteristics, and the influence of celebrity advertising towards consumers purchasing intention. The findings of this research have potential implications on the appropriate selection of celebrities for endorsement and also provide implications on multicultural marketing/advertising strategy in a cross-cultural setting as Malaysia. This research could also enhance the generalizability of the impact of advertising by celebrities in a developing country.

As organizations grow into international markets, there would be many crucial decisions to be taken which would have a significant impact on the performance globally. Some of the crucial decisions alternatives include the entry modes, promotion, marketing and advertising, production locations and others. Consumer product evaluations could be affected significantly through the selections of particular strategic alternatives. One of the important factors that affect consumers during decision making is the consumer ethnocentrism level. Based on Shimp and Sharma (1987), the ethnocentrism of consumers emphasizes on the rightness and morality in buying foreign products and the loyalty to locally produced goods. Furthermore, consumer ethnocentrism predictive ability of the buying intention varies from country to country (Balabanis, Diamantopoulos, Mueller, & Melewar, 2001). The basis of this theory could be traced to Sumner's (1906) basic concept of ethnocentrism that is "the interpretation of things which is one's own group as the main of everything and any others are evaluated based on it".

Generally, consumers have a higher quality view towards the local products as compared to foreign products in a developed country. Therefore, this would increase the encouragement of consumer ethnocentrism towards the acceptance of local products and rejection of foreign products (Ahmed & d'Astous, 2001). However, the opposite has been observed in developing countries such as in Turkey and Romania (Ger et al., 1993), China (Li, Fu, & Murray, 1997), and India (Batra et al., 2000). The consumers in these developing countries recognize the foreign products, especially those produced in more advanced countries, as having greater quality as compared to the local products. This is also the same on the ethnocentrism consumers which would perceive non-locally produced products as having better quality, particularly if the country of origin has a better image (Yagci, 2001). This situation has posed confusing effect and implication about ethnocentrism in marketing and consumer behavior studies (Isa et al. 2016; Wong et al. 2008).

According to Brodowsky (1998), individuals or consumers would have a positive view and assumption towards purchasing goods that are produced locally if the level of ethnocentrism is high. Pecotich and Rosenthal (2001) as well discovered that consumer's opinions in regards to the price and purchase intentions are directly affected by consumer ethnocentrism. Therefore, it is beneficial for researchers, marketers and advertisers to identify the level of ethnocentrism among consumers so that they can better appeal or meet customer needs and wants. In Malaysia, the government held campaigns off 'Buy Malaysian Products' to raise the public awareness regarding the quality of products and service offered in Malaysia is comparable with the international products.

The importance of ethnocentricity becomes a critical issue when one considers the increasing trend toward free trade and the high rate at which national economies are turning global. Over the years, consumer's feeling of foreign products is a subject of good interest. Therefore, marketers need to understand the user's ethnocentric tendencies to develop effective marketing and communication strategies within and beyond the borders of the country. Some studies have examined the factors related to the purchase of foreign products in the domestic market (Samiee et al., 2005; Klein 2002; Netemeyer et al., 1991; Shimp & Sharma, 1987). In general, through these studies it was found that consumer ethnocentrism was a significant influence on the willingness of consumers to purchase foreign products (Wang and Chen 2004); undeniably, it has been emphasized that ethnocentrism gives a stronger influence than the marketing strategy of buying decisions (Herche, 1994). While according to some studies in Malaysia, based on Nik-mat et al. (2015) and Hasimini et al. (2017), the level of ethnocentrism among Malaysian is high meanwhile as stated by Othman et al. (2008), the ethnocentrism of consumers in Malaysia is averagely low.

Furthermore, Wong et al. (2008), stated that though globalization proposes the world is becoming more alike, understated dissimilarities may have extensive consequences for practice, therefore, it is still the case that marketers need to comprehend this phenomenon within each market. Ethnocentrism dimensions might not be relevant globally, but it could be significant in some contexts, or at least the significance differs worldwide. Nevertheless, previous studies emphasized that more studies are necessary to examine the effect of consumers' ethnocentrism tendencies related with purchase intention due to the unpredictable results found earlier (Isa et al. 2016; Qing et al. 2012; Aneela et al. 2011; Wong et al. 2008). Moreover, according to some past research, the nationality of the endorser would have an impact on the purchase intention and the preference of local or international celebrity endorser difference between countries (Jerzyk et al. 2016; Ewa & Kamil, 2015; & Lin et al. 2015). Therefore, the authors included the ethnocentrism of consumers in the framework to determine which nationality is more preferred by the Malaysian consumers. This research is also supported by previous research suggestion to examine the role of consumer ethnocentrism in moderating the effectiveness of celebrity endorsers in international markets (Chao, Wuhrer & Werani, 2015).

UNDERPINNING THEORY

The Source Credibility Theory opposes that the value of a message could be affected by the endorser's recognition level of attractiveness, expertise, trustworthiness (Ohanian, 1991; McGuire, 1969). The degree that the resource is known as having significant experience or sufficient knowledge to not present a biased decision is referred to as credibility (Carroll, 2008; O'Mahony & Meenaghan, 1997). Research findings showed that source credibility is crucial to the success of celebrity endorsement (Wei & Li,

2013). According to Ohanian (1990), source credibility is usually utilized to attract attention to the positive characteristics of communicators which would influence the receiver's acknowledgment of the communication.

Researchers stated that the level of persuasion of a message mostly rests on the credibility of the source (Ohanian, 1991; Petty & Cacioppo, 1986; Sternthal et al., 1978). Studies have been carried out to examine the effectiveness of the endorser. These studies have recommended that consumers' brand recall and motivation to purchase could be increased through good endorsement efforts (Charbonneau and Garland, 2005; Till and Busler, 1998). In today's greatly crowded environment, celebrity endorsers uses their popularity not only to work to generate and retain attention, they also achieve a high rate of recall rates for marcom messages (O'Mahony & Meenaghan, 1997; Ohanian, 1991; Kamins et al., 1989; Friedman & Friedman, 1979).

In addition due to globalization, consumers now can easily switch between brands and products as compared to the past, since there are increased levels of competition and diversity in the cosmetics industry. Therefore, researchers of the theory of product differentiation (Baum & Mezias, 1992; Porter, 1991; Barney, 1991; Hannan et al., 1990) agree that firms may face less competition by distinguishing themselves from others. While the quality of services, brands and/or marketing campaigns associated with celebrities does not guarantee profit (Gitomer, 1998) recent studies have shown that celebrity endorsement leads to a favorable approach towards the credibility of the endorsed brand (Spry et al., 2011) and the endorsed product (Till et al., 2008). Moreover, it would be effective to use endorser from the credible source towards consumers which have an undesirable interpretation of the product (Daneshvary & Schwer, 2000). Therefore, the credible source can neutralize these opinions and have a positive outcome which is a greater message acceptance (Bryne et al., 2003).

On the other hand, source credibility could also cause negative impact although it has many positive effects. Marketers and advertisers should note that celebrities who endorse many products are seen as less credible as compared to those which endorse a specific product (Silvera & Austad, 2004). Based on Ohanian (1991) the researcher offered the following explanation for the insignificant effect of attractiveness and trustworthiness: "… in advertisements most celebrities are attractive, and as such, respondents have a mind set in which attractiveness is not a determinant factor in their brand-selection decisions. Further, with the widespread use of celebrities and athletes in paid commercials, the audience does not associate a high level of trustworthiness with individuals who get paid handsomely to promote a product." These descriptions seem to imply that respondents perceived the high attractiveness and low trustworthiness as being "common characteristics" among celebrities and thus they ignored these two aspects.

Moreover, according to some researchers, the findings of the effect of credibility on purchase intention is also unclear. In a study by Ohanian (1991), the impact of the celebrity spokespersons' perceived credibility on consumers' purchase intentions was analysed and found that a relationship exists between the expertise of the celebrity and intention to purchase. Conflicting to expectations the outcome of trustworthiness and attractiveness on buying intention couldn't be proved. This is in contrary with the result of Yoon et al., (1998) who proved that the three dimensions of endorser have average significance on respondent's purchase intention. Pornpitakpan (2004), also, found that all three components positively relate to purchase intention. Therefore, this could show that the components of source credibility may have different effects on the consumers' purchase intention, which will be important to study the importance and effect of all three components on consumer purchase intention of cosmetic products in Malaysia.

LITERATURE REVIEW AND RESEARCH HYPOTHESES

Attractiveness

According to McCroskey and McCain (1974), attractiveness is associated with how celebrity is perceived and the social values. Celebrity physical appearance, the resemblance to the receiver and personality are the factors included in social values (Choi, Lee, & Kim, 2005; Caballero & Solomon, 1984; Baker & Churchill, 1977; McGuire, 1958). Consumers may see celebrities as more attractive when they have much in common. Based on Bardia et al. (2011), celebrity physical attractiveness is interrelated to a person's earliest judgment passed on to next individual, that is driven by the characteristics and qualities of the celebrity endorser for example weight, height and facial beauty.

In order to increase the acknowledgment or consciousness towards a product or service, celebrity endorsement could be utilized as an important variable (Ranjbarian et al., 2010; Liu et al., 2007). Endorsers "which are considered attractive will be more likely to lead the consumer purchase intention" (Van Der Waldt et al., 2009). When endorsers are compared in terms of attractiveness factor, consumers are more influenced by attractive endorsers compared to less attractive ones (Kahle & Homer, 1985; Joseph, 1982). Therefore, effective messages can be created through an important factor which is attractiveness (Schlecht, 2003). Moreover, Chen and Huddleston (2009) pointed out that in a cluttered media environment, it is recognized that celebrities which are attractive have the 'stopping power' and are more attractive to consumers.

Therefore, physical attractiveness of celebrity could be utilized to enhance the effectiveness of an advertisement (Chan et al., 2013; Zahid et al., 2002; Till & Busler, 2000; Smith and Engel, 1968). Previous researchers found that physically unattractive endorsers are less favored compared to their physically attractive counterparts (Horai et al., 1974; Joseph, 1982). Furthermore, through celebrity endorser's attractiveness, a brand perception image can be significantly improved (Tantiseneepong et al., 2012; Bardia et al., 2011; Hakimi et al., 2011). If celebrities' physical attractiveness is congruent with the product endorsed, consumers develop a positive attitude towards the product and the advertisement evaluations (Kahle & Homer, 1985).

However, Baker and Churchill (1977) stated that although celebrity attractiveness could affect the consumers' evaluation, it may not necessarily affect their purchase intention. Though since many years ago, advertisers have frequently chose endorsers based on the physical attractiveness to affect the consumer attitude towards the product (Kahle & Homer, 1985; Chaiken, 1979). Moreover, according to some researchers (Kahle & Homer, 1985; Joseph, 1982) source attractiveness may only be effective if the product enhances the attractiveness of the user.

H1: There is a significant positive relationship between attractiveness and cosmetic product purchase intention.

Expertise

Expertise has been described by McCracken (1989) as "the perceived ability of the source to make valid assertions". In other words, the endorser is considered to be competent enough to deliver legal and precise information or deliberate on a particular subject (Hovland et al., 1953). An endorser that is more persuasive is found to have a higher level of expertise (Bardia et al., 2011; Aaker & Myers, 1987) and would create higher purchase intention (Chan et al., 2013; Erdogan, 1999; Ohanian 1991).

Research has shown that receiver's purchasing decision and perceived trustworthiness could be impacted by source expertise in the product or service (Smith et al., 2006). Likewise, Dean and Biswas (2001) state that endorsement persuasion in advertising functional and pricey brands, endorser's expertise emerges as the most effective construct. Thus, it is less effective to use conventional messages and advertorials transferred by the organization than to use a celebrity or athlete with relevant expertise as an endorser (Charbonneau & Garland, 2005). Besides, according to the results of the study by Chaovalit (2014), between credibility, there is an important link in terms of expertise and purchase intention.

Moreover, Speck, Schumann and Thompson (1988) discovered that celebrities which have expertise would develop higher remembrance of product information compared to non-celebrity; however, the distinction was not statistically significant. More particularly, favorable attitude towards the brand could be led through more solid facts on the product offering that is provided by the expertise of the celebrity (Magnini et al., 2008). These components of source expertise is critical in conceptualizing credibility and appeared to be persuasive in influencing consumers (Wu & Shaffer, 1987; Moore et al., 1988; Harmon and Coney, 1982; Sternthal, Phillips & Dholakia, 1978) also in impacting their behavior (McGinnies & Ward, 1980; Craig & John, 1978). Therefore according to Daneshvary and Schwer (2000), a most essential segment for endorsement to be effective is expertise as acknowledged.

Meanwhile based on the findings of Evans (1988), celebrities that endorse various products and services, which might be seen as outside their fields of expertise, will indirectly affect their perceived images and result in negative behavioral intentions. Moreover, Eisend and Langner (2010) reported a delayed positive outcome of expertise on the brand image and collaboration with attractiveness. This indicates that higher attractiveness level would be able to increase the favorable impact of expertise of celebrity.

H2: There is a significant positive relationship between expertise and cosmetic product purchase intention.

Trustworthiness

According to some researchers, trustworthiness is defined as the perceived enthusiasm of the celebrity to make legal declarations in the view of the consumer and provides information in a genuine, just, truthful, and honorable manner (Ohanian, 1990; McCracken, 1989; Nelson & Pearson, 1988; Hovland et al., 1953). As O'Mahony and Meenaghan (1997) mentioned, trust is the credibility of the source to create the basic features of the effects of changes in consumer attitude. Without trust, the other properties owned by the endorser cannot be effective in changing consumer attitudes (Miller and Basehart, 1969). Components of trust is important in the concept of credibility also has been proved to be effective in encouraging consumers (Moore, Hausknecht & Thamodaran 1988; Wu & Shaffer, 1987; Harmon & Coney, 1982; Sternthal, Phillips, & Dholakia, 1978) and the inspiration of attitude (McGinnies and Ward, 1980; Craig & John, 1978). This is in line with Atkin and Block (1983), which suggest that celebrities are accepted as more reliable than non-celebrity.

According to Wei and Li (2013), the findings of their study show that the source trustworthiness also affects consumers' behavioral intentions. Chao et al. (2015) also support the positive effect of trustworthiness on celebrity endorsement effectiveness. Therefore, celebrity trustworthiness is an important factor to advertisers. The most effective and suitable approach to make customers more self-assured regarding the product is through creating a level of trustworthiness (Hakimi et al., 2011; Ohanian, 1990). According to the study by Shimp (2003), a celebrity that has feature higher trustworthiness, relevance and honesty is more favorable by marketers. In addition, the good belief towards celebrities can have a good effect on the perception of customers' value and further affect their purchasing choice (Erdem & Swait, 2004).

Clearly, a positive relationship occurs among the trustworthiness, attraction and products associated with the strength of the argument; for instance, when strong product-related arguments mark the advertising copy, the effect of trustworthiness is less noticeable than it is for weak product-related arguments (Chan et al., 2013; Priester and Petty, 2003). According to Smith (1973), the messages that are shared by untrustworthy celebrity endorsers will be viewed questionably by consumers regardless of the celebrities' other qualities. Therefore, it is necessary that the endorser that is going to be chosen should be an individual whom consumers can relate to and is recognized as real, unbiased and honest (Temperley & Tangen, 2006).

On the other hand, according to the findings of Sertoglu et al. (2014), created spokespersons are perceived to be more trustworthy and having more expertise than celebrity endorsers whereas celebrity endorsers' attractiveness level is higher than of created spokespersons'. These results can be regarded as being inconsistent with the study of Atkin and Block (1983) who claimed that celebrity endorsers are perceived to be more trustworthy and expert. Moreover, the results seemed to strengthen the idea that created spokespersons could be more effective than celebrity endorsers as they allow for greater control, specific linkage to the product characteristics and can be associated with only one product or a brand (Tom et al., 1992).

H3: There is a significant positive relationship between trustworthiness and cosmetic product purchase intention.

Ethnocentrism

Accordingly, Luque-Martinez et al. (2000) mentioned that ethnocentrism symbolizes a worldwide tendency to perceive an individual's own group as the midpoint of the universe, hence blindly accepting those which are culturally similar and rejecting those individuals which are ethnically different. Ethnocentrism is a term consist of the words ''ethnic'' meaning group, while ''centrism'' which means focused (Usunier & Lee, 2005).

Consumers' behavior differentiates among those with strong and weak signs of ethnocentrism (Shimp & Sharma, 1987). For high ethnocentric consumers, national loyalty is seen as an important issue, as this influences these consumers to choose domestic products or services (Bruning, 1997). In contrast, low ethnocentric consumers prefer foreign products compared to domestic products (Kucukemiroglu, 1999), and have a lesser sense of belonging to the group. As the reflection of love for the country, a person is committed and always ready to sacrifice for the sake of the country (Druckman, 1994). Emotional attachment to the homeland guides the belief that the country is superior in most aspects (Karasawa, 2002).

Based on Luque-Martinez et al. (2000), the feelings of consumer concerning foreign products have been an issue of great concern. This interest has been reinforced because of the expanding internationalization of markets and greater globalization rivalry among products and services, also as a result of new "global scenario" that makes consumers feel more related with their traditional identities and ethnicity (Vida et al., 1996; Netemeyer et al., 1991).

Nevertheless, the response of ethnocentric consumer is not always in such an extreme means. Some consumers which are extremely ethnocentric would be having a lower concern for the information of the product regarding the country of origin (Gurhan-Canli & Maheswaran, 2000). This occurs in cases in which the observation of the product is related to the decent image of the country (level of industrialization, political situation, economic development, or admiration for the country), non-local products will be assessed highly (Yagci, 2001). Accordingly, a buyer might be ethnocentric concerning certain items for which domestic production is clearly better than that of foreign products, yet in the meantime he/she might not have a negative approach towards other products in which his/her nation is obviously lacking or is obviously far from offering the levels of quality that foreign countries provide.

H4a: Consumer ethnocentrism moderates the relationship between attractiveness and cosmetic product purchase intention.
H4b: Consumer ethnocentrism moderates the relationship between expertise and cosmetic product purchase intention.
H4c: Consumer ethnocentrism moderates the relationship between trustworthiness and cosmetic product purchase intention.

METHODOLOGY

Questionnaire

The objective of this study is to determine factors that motivate consumers to purchase cosmetic products in Malaysia using a cross-sectional survey. The questionnaire include respondents demographics, items pertaining to purchase intention of cosmetic products adapted from Ajzen (2015), attractiveness of celebrity endorsement adopted from McCracken (1989), expertise of celebrity endorsement adopted from McCracken (1989), trustworthiness of celebrity endorsement adopted from McCracken (1989) and questions concerning ethnocentrism of consumers adapted from Ramayah et al. (2011). All items were anchored on a 5-point Likert scale (1 = strongly disagree to 5 = strongly agree).

Figure 1. Research framework

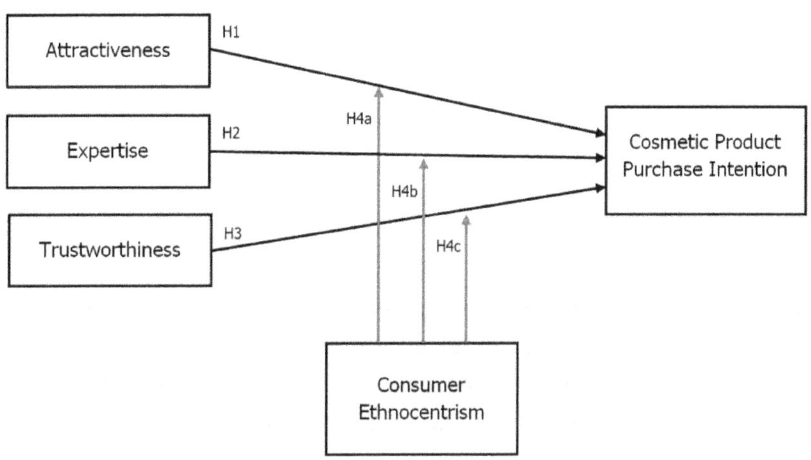

Sample and Data Collection

As this study is concerned with purchase intention of cosmetic products, a convenience sampling technique was employed to collect data from individuals who have the intention to buy the cosmetic product. A total of 250 questionnaires were distributed and 189 questionnaires (75.6%) were returned as completed. Respondents were sampled from several states in Malaysia and the participation of respondents in the study was on a voluntary basis.

To decide on the sample size of the respondents for this study, G*Power software was used to calculate the minimum sample size required based on statistical power (Faul et al. 2009). Since the model have 3 exogenous (predictors of organic food consumption), the effect size was set as medium (0.15) and power needed 0.95. The sample size required was 119. This study set out to collect data which was equal to or slightly larger than the required number. Given that the sample size exceeded 119, the power value in this study also exceeded 0.95. The minimum power required in marketing and behavioral science research is typically 0.8. It is also recommended for PLS-SEM to use "10 times" rule of thumb as the guide for estimating the minimum required sample size (Hair et al. 2011). This rule suggests that PLS- SEM only requires a sample size of 10 times the largest number of path or relationship in the structural model, which would call for a minimum sample size of 30 in our model (that is, 10 x 3 structural paths = 30 individuals). In both cases, it can safely conclude that a sample of 189 is deemed adequate/sufficient in this study.

Common Method Variance

Common method variance was examined since the data about the predictor and criterion variables were collected from a single source (respondent) (Podsakoff et al. 2003). Podsakoff and Todor (1985) also noted that: "Invariably, when self-reported measures obtained from the same sample are utilized in research, concern over same-source bias or general method variance arise" (p. 65). Several remedies have been employed to detect this problem including Harman's one-factor test. A factorial analysis without rotation in SPSS carried out and the result revealed that the first factor accounted for only 33.81% of the variance, much lower than the majority indicating method bias is not a serious issue in this study. As shown in Table (3), the construct correlation matrix shows that each of the inter-construct correlations was not more than 0.90 (Bagozzi et al. 1991), confirming that both tests indicate that common method bias is not a problem in this study.

ANALYSIS AND RESULTS

Profile of Respondents

Based on Table 1, it shows the respondents' demographic information. Based on the data collected, the majority of the respondents are female which represents 91.0% while male respondents were only 9.0%. Meanwhile, the age of the respondents was categorized into four groups which the first group consists of the age of 20-29 with 28.0% respondent, the second group comprises of the age 30-39 which have the

Table 1. Respondents' demographics information

Demographics		Frequency (N=189)	Percentage (%)
Gender	Male	17	9.0
	Female	172	91.0
Age	20-29	53	28.0
	30-39	69	36.5
	40-49	40	21.2
	50 and above	27	14.3
Academic qualification	Primary school or less	7	3.7
	High school	11	5.8
	Diploma, Pre-Uni or equivalent	41	21.7
	Bachelor Degree	90	47.6
	Master Degree	38	20.1
	Doctoral Degree	2	1.1
Annual income	MYR 50,000 and below	23	12.2
	MYR 50,001–100,000	56	29.6
	MYR 100,001–150,000	60	31.8
	MYR 150,001–200,000	32	16.9
	MYR 200,001 and above	18	9.5

highest respondents of 36.5%. Meanwhile, the last two groups are divided into the age of 40-49 and 50 and above which the respondents are 21.2% and 14.3% respectively. As for the academic qualification, this category is divided into six qualifications which the highest is bachelor degree (47.6%), second highest is diploma, pre-uni and equivalent (21.7%), the third is master degree with 20.1% and the last three categories are high school (5.8%), primary or less (3.7%) and lastly doctoral degree (1.1%). Regarding the annual income, most of the respondents have the income of MYR 100,001 – 150,000 with 31.8%, followed by MYR 50,001 – 100,000 (29.6%), next MYR 150,001 – 200,000 (16.9%), followed by MYR 50,000 and below (12.2%), and lastly MYR 200,001 and above (9.5%).

Model Assessment Using PLS-SEM

The proposed relationships (research model) were analyzed using the partial least squares technique (PLS-SEM) using SmartPLS 3.2.7 software (Ringle et al. 2015). PLS-SEM is a statistical technique that allows for simultaneous analysis of a large number of relationship in a conceptual model. Anderson and Gerbing (1988) recommended two-stage analytical procedures, firstly assessing the measurement model and followed by the assessment of structural model (testing the hypothesized relationship). A bootstrapping method (5,000 resamples) was employed to test the significance of the path coefficients and the loadings (Hair et al. 2014).

Assessment of the Measurement Model

The assessment of the measurement model involves an assessment of reliability and validity. Validity comprises of convergent validity and discriminant validity. Convergent validity is usually evaluated by examining indicator loadings, Average Variance Extracted (AVE) and Composite Reliability (CR) (Hair et al. 2011).

Convergent Validity

The outcome exhibited in Table 2 showing that all the loadings were higher than 0.4, the CR's were all above 0.7 and AVE scores were also greater than 0.5 as recommended by Hair et al. (2014). Hence, the measurement model's convergent validity is acceptable.

Discriminant Validity

After the convergent validity is established, the assessment of discriminant validity follows as it is imperative to determine whether every construct distinct from each other that indicate each construct measured the concept it intends to measure (Hair et al. 2014).

The Fornell and Larcker (1981) approach used to test the discriminant validity of the constructs by comparing the correlations among constructs and the square root of the AVE for that construct. According to Hair et al. (2011), each construct AVE's square root must be higher compared to other correlations amongst the construct and the other constructs. According to Table 3, it shows the AVEs' square roots for the constructs along the diagonal and the correlations among the constructs, indicating that the constructs established discriminant validity.

Assessment of the Structural Model

In the second stage of analysis, the structural models for organic food consumption were assessed. To assess the structural model, Hair et al. (2014) recommended looking at the beta, R^2 and the corresponding t-values through a bootstrapping with a resample of 5,000. Besides these regular indicators, Soto-Acosta et al. (2015) and Hair et al. (2014) suggested that researchers should also report effect sizes (f^2) and predictive relevance (Q^2).

The summary of the outcome of structural model analysis (hypothesis testing) is summarized in Table 4. The result indicate that attractiveness ($\beta = 0.361$, $p < 0.01$), expertise ($\beta = 0.205$, $p < 0.01$) and trustworthiness ($\beta = 0.434$, $p < 0.001$) were positively significant towards cosmetic products' purchase intention. Thus, H1, H2 and H3 were supported. Altogether, these factors explained 50.7% of the variance in cosmetic product purchase intention.

Next, the moderating effect or interaction of ethnocentrism was assessed. The interaction terms were created between attractiveness and ethnocentrism, expertise and ethnocentrism, and trustworthiness and ethnocentrism by mean centring the variables on reducing multicollinearity. After the moderator interactions included into the model, the R^2 increased to 0.572, showing a change of 6.5 percent. The results indicate that the interaction effect between attractiveness and ethnocentrism (H4a) ($\beta = 0.208$, $p< 0.05$) and between trustworthiness and ethnocentrism (H4c) ($\beta = 0.134$, $p< 0.05$) towards cosmetic product's purchase intention were significant. Thus, H4a and H4c have also been supported which indicate that

Table 2. Convergent validity of measurement model

Construct	Item	Loadings	CR	AVE
Attractiveness	AT1	0.725	0.854	0.541
	AT2	0.777		
	AT3	0.645		
	AT4	0.776		
	AT5	0.745		
Expertise	EXP1	0.877	0.889	0.619
	EXP2	0.593		
	EXP3	0.842		
	EXP4	0.818		
	EXP5	0.773		
Trustworthiness	TR1	0.657	0.863	0.513
	TR2	0.767		
	TR3	0.710		
	TR4	0.774		
	TR5	0.660		
	TR7	0.720		
Ethnocentrism	EC1	0.744	0.900	0.532
	EC3	0.825		
	EC4	0.769		
	EC5	0.680		
	EC6	0.692		
	EC8	0.778		
	EC9	0.665		
	EC10	0.666		
Cosmetic product purchase intention	CPPI1	0.719	0.901	0.568
	CPPI2	0.789		
	CPPI3	0.804		
	CPPI4	0.769		
	CPPI7	0.638		
	CPPI9	0.749		
	CPPI10	0.793		

the ethnocentrism found to strengthen the relationship between attractiveness and ethnocentrism also trustworthiness and ethnocentrism, while the moderating effect between expertise and ethnocentrism hypothesis H4b was not significant indicating no moderating effect observed. Dawson (2014) suggested plotting the interaction effect to observe how the interaction modifies the relationship between attractiveness and cosmetic product's purchase intention and trustworthiness and cosmetic product's purchase intention. The result is presented in Figure 2 and Figure 3. Based on the results, the relationship between

Table 3. Fornell-Larcker Criterion

	1	2	3	4	5
1. Attractiveness	**0.735**				
2. Cosmetic product purchasing intention	0.554	**0.754**			
3. Ethnocentrism	0.138	0.101	**0.729**		
4. Expertise	0.175	0.209	0.246	**0.787**	
5. Trustworthiness	0.413	0.591	0.114	0.107	**0.716**

Note: Diagonals (bolded) represent the square root of the average variance extracted while the off-diagonals are correlations among constructs. Diagonal elements should be larger than off-diagonal elements in order to establish discriminant validity

Table 4. Structural model analysis

Hypothesis	Relationship	Std. Beta	Std. Error	t-value	Decision	f^2	Q^2	R^2
H1	AT → CPPI	0.361	0.117	3.085**	Supported	0.276	0.243	0.507
H2	EXP → CPPI	0.205	0.065	3.153**	Supported	0.211		
H3	TR → CPPI	0.434	0.117	3.707***	Supported	0.303		
H4a	AT*EC → CPPI	0.208	0.101	2.059*	Supported	0.048		0.572
H4b	EXP*EC → CPPI	0.011	0.074	0.150	Not Supported	0.003		
H4c	TR*EC → CPPI	0.134	0.063	2.122*	Supported	0.067		

**p < 0.01, *p < 0.05

AT Attractiveness, EXP Expertise, TR Trustworthiness, EC Ethnocentrism, CPPI Cosmetic product purchase intention

Figure 2. Interaction plot of ethnocentrism on the relationship between AT and CPPI

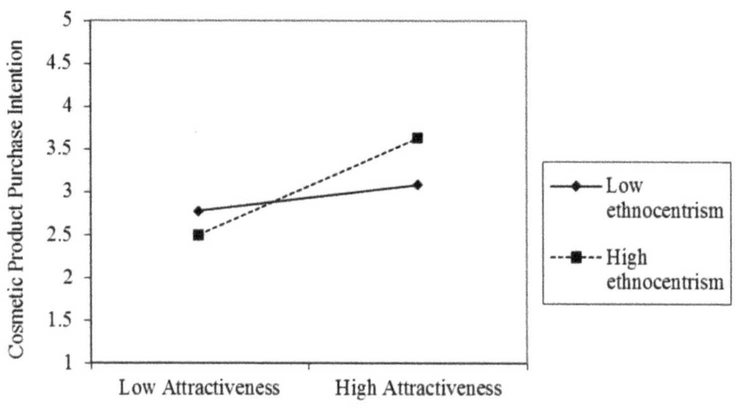

attractiveness and cosmetic product purchase intention is stronger when a consumer's ethnocentrism is high. Similarly, the relationship between trustworthiness and cosmetic product purchase intention is stronger when a consumer's ethnocentrism is high. The R^2 values are above the 0.35 value as suggested by Cohen (1988) indicating a substantial model and considered significant and meaningful for the purposes of interpretation (Hair et al. 2014).

Figure 3. Interaction plot of ethnocentrism on the relationship between TR and CPPI

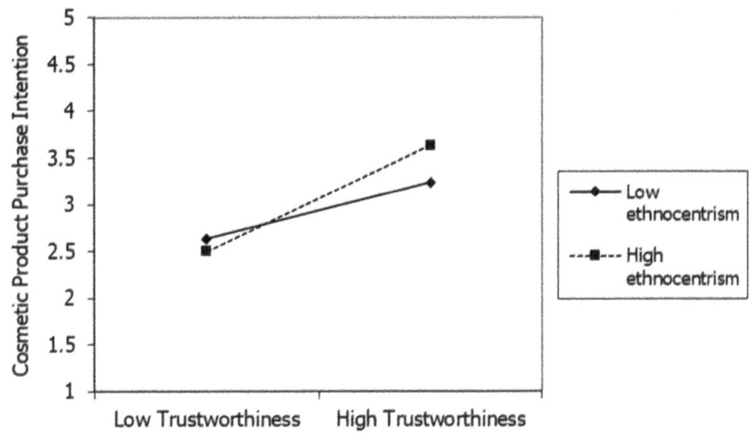

The effect size of all relationships was evaluated as emphasized by Hair et al. (2014) and Sullivan and Feinn (2012). It is suggested to observe the R^2 changes after a certain predictor is removed from the whole model and is measured only if the predictor causes a significant effect on the endogenous construct. Cohen (1988) has set a guideline to determine the effect size where values of 0.35, 0.15, and 0.02 indicate large, medium and small effect respectively. Therefore, based on Table 5, it is observed that all relationships produced significant effects where three indicated medium effects (attractiveness, expertise and trustworthiness) whereas two were small effects (AT*EC and TR*EC). The effect size f^2 between the direct hypotheses model and moderating model as recommended by Cohen (1988) was 0.151 which is classified as medium. The R^2 values exceeded 0.50 suggesting a significant medium effect which is sufficient for the explanatory purpose (Hair et al., 2014).

Moreover, blindfolding procedure was implemented to examine the model's predictive relevance. According to Hair et al. (2014), values of 0.35, 0.15 and 0.02 indicate that an exogenous construct has a large, medium or small predictive relevance for a specific endogenous construct. Referring to table 4, the predictive relevance (Q^2) value is 0.243 indicating a medium prediction capability of this research model.

DISCUSSION AND CONCLUSION

As the global market has been expanding, advertising has been widely used by marketers to differentiate their product from others. One of the advertising techniques chosen is using celebrity endorsers. Moreover, since the markets are expanding towards different countries, the consumer ethnocentrism is becoming an important factor to be given attention when expanding internationally. Therefore, this paper has investigated the effect of source credibility of celebrity endorsers towards purchase intention of cosmetics.

The finding of this study supports the hypothesis that endorsers' attractiveness assumed a considerable importance in deciding the purchase intention of cosmetics products. This finding is in line with Wang et al. (2017) and Chaovalit (2014), which stated that the purchase intention of consumers is influenced by the attractiveness of the celebrity endorser. When the celebrity endorser is attractive, consumers are more influenced and would encourage them to have a positive perception towards the product as compared to less attractive endorsers. This could be due to the individuals' daily life which almost every person would try to be attractive in order to be accepted easily by the society.

This research also confirmed the result that endorser's expertise could positively influence the purchase intention of cosmetic products. This outcome validates earlier research by Wang et al., (2017), Chaovalit (2014) and Chan et al. (2013). They also mentioned that celebrity endorser with expertise not only influences consumers to have the purchase intention, but it could also increase the purchase intention of consumers. This is explainable as an endorser with expertise generates a positive perception and attitude towards the products or services which could eventually influence the consumers' purchase intention (Wei and Li, 2013).

Trustworthiness of celebrity endorser also yields a positive relationship towards cosmetic products purchase intention which is in line with proceeding studies of Wang et al. (2017), Hakimi et al. (2011) and Ohanian (1990). Some consumers are willing to pay a higher amount of money to purchase products with trustworthy endorser instead of buying a product which has an unknown endorser or untrustworthy endorser. This is due to the increasing number of genuine and non-genuine cosmetic products in the market, consumers are not able to identify which is a good and genuine product and which is not. Therefore, the endorser could be one of the indicators to show that the product is authentic and could be used safely and feelings of trust among consumers towards the product.

The study revealed a significant impact of a consumer's ethnocentric attitude towards the endorsement effectiveness; ethnocentrism moderated the relationship between attractiveness (H4a), trustworthiness (H4c), and purchase intention of cosmetic products. Indirectly, the outcome suggests that consumer ethnocentrism increases the influence of attractiveness and trustworthiness of endorser, which will enhance consumers' purchase intention of cosmetic products. The result showed that the nationality of the celebrity endorser plays an important role in the minds of consumers and would affect their purchase intention of cosmetic products. Consumers in Malaysia would prefer to have endorser of local nationality, which is in line with the past research by Jerzyk et al. (2016), Ewa and Kamil (2015) and Lin et al. (2015). This happened in consumers with high ethnocentrism compared to lower ones, the higher the ethnocentrism level, the higher the preference to have a local nationality endorser. This means that consumers with already strong or high ethnocentric level will have a positive response towards a national celebrity endorser. However, consumers with low ethnocentric level will not show positive respond towards national celebrity endorser. It is also supported by Jerzyk et al. (2016), people with higher ethnocentrism have a positive attitude towards national endorser instead of the foreign endorser.

Based on the study in hand, it has employed the Theory of Source Credibility and has incorporated consumer ethnocentrism in Malaysia. This has improved the understanding of the factors that determine consumers' intention to purchase cosmetic products. The study offers a new forward motion towards the outcome of previous studies on the celebrity credibility, which is not much examined in the Malaysian context. Therefore, this study responded to the low number of research carried out in Malaysia as the majority of the studies in the aspect of Source Credibility Theory and Ethnocentrism were conducted in western countries (Suki, 2014).

The findings of the research can help marketers in selecting the celebrity endorser which is more suitable to reach the consumers in Malaysia. Based on the research, marketers should hire celebrities who are attractive, expert, and trustworthy also local nationality is more preferred by the Malaysian consumers. As stated by Wei and Li (2013) marketers should be cautious when choosing an appropriate celebrity endorser as there are risks involved and negative effects when the wrong endorser is chosen. The findings of this study are able to increase the literature and information on the Malaysian behavior in the use of celebrities, as these celebrities could act as encouragement to the consumers. Certainly, the outcome of this study shows the fact that Malaysian consumers' attitude towards the product and purchase intention are influenced by the celebrity endorsers' characteristics and also the nationality. A safer solution to increase and attract the purchase intention of consumers is by using a Malaysian celebrity who is credible as the endorser.

This could be an important message for part of local and foreign companies which are either expanding their business in Malaysia or starting a new cosmetic products business. The findings of this study can also help managers understand the mechanism of shaping ethnocentric attitudes in the local markets. A safer solution to increase and attract the purchase intention of consumers are by using a Malaysian celebrity as the endorser. Moreover, marketers would be able to have a more effective advertisement to reach the consumers based on their preference. Other than that, marketers could use this research as a reference framework when selecting appropriate endorsers. Doing so can help to maximize the impact of advertising efforts in order to generate positive behavioral intentions and eventually increase their sales as mentioned by the past research conducted by Sertoglu et al., (2014).

REFERENCES

Aaker, D. A., & Myers, J. G. (1987). *Advertising Management* (3rd ed.). Englewood Cliffs, NJ: Prentice-Hall, Inc.

Ahmed, S. A., & d'Astous, A. (2001). Canadian Consumers' Perceptions of Products Made in Newly Industrializing East Asian Countries. *International Journal of Commerce and Management.*, *11*(1), 54–81. doi:10.1108/eb047415

Atkin, C., & Block, M. (1983). Effectiveness of celebrity endorsers. *Journal of Advertising Research*, *23*(1), 57–61.

Baker, M., & Churchill, G. A. (1977). The Impact of Physically Attractive Models on Advertising Evaluations. *JMR, Journal of Marketing Research*, *14*(4), 538–555. doi:10.2307/3151194

Balabanis, G., Diamantopoulos, A., Mueller, R. D., & Melewar, T. C. (2001). The Impact of Nationalism, Patriotism and Internationalism on Consumer Ethnocentric Tendencies. *Journal of International Business Studies*, *32*(1), 157–175. doi:10.1057/palgrave.jibs.8490943

Bannister, B. D. (1986). Performance outcome feedback and attributional feedback: Interactive effects on recipient responses. *The Journal of Applied Psychology*, *71*(2), 203–210. doi:10.1037/0021-9010.71.2.203

Bardia, Y. H., Abed, A., & Majid, N. Z. (2011). Investigate the impact of celebrity endorsement on brand image. *European Journal of Scientific Research*, *58*(1), 116–132.

Batra, R., Ramaswamy, V., Alden, D. L., Steenkamp, J. B. E., & Ramachander, S. (2000). Effects of Brand Local and Non-local Origin on Consumer Attitudes in Developing Countries. *Journal of Consumer Psychology*, *9*(2), 83–95. doi:10.1207/S15327663JCP0902_3

Bergkvist, L., & Zhou, K. Q. (2016). Celebrity endorsements: A literature review and research agenda. *International Journal of Advertising*, *35*(4), 642–663. doi:10.1080/02650487.2015.1137537

Brodowsky, G. H. (1998). The effect of country of design and country of assembly on evaluative beliefs about automobiles and attitudes toward buying them: A comparison between low and high ethnocentric consumers. *Journal of International Consumer Marketing*, *10*(3), 85–113. doi:10.1300/J046v10n03_06

Bruning, E. R. (1997). Country of origin, national loyalty and product choice: The case of international air travel. *International Marketing Review*, *14*(1), 59–74. doi:10.1108/02651339710159215

Caballero, M., & Solomon, P. J. (1984). Effects of model attractiveness on sales response. *Journal of Advertising*, *13*(1), 17–23. doi:10.1080/00913367.1984.10672870

Chan, K., Ng, Y. L., & Luk, E. K. (2013). Impact of celebrity endorsement in advertising on brand image among Chinese adolescents. *Young Consumers*, *14*(2), 167–179. doi:10.1108/17473611311325564

Chao, P., Wuhrer, G., & Werani, T. (2015). Celebrity and Foreign Brand Name as Moderators of Country-of-Origin Effects. *International Journal of Advertising*, *24*(2), 173–192. doi:10.1080/02650487.2005.11072913

Charbonneau, J., & Garland, R. (2005). Talent, Looks or Brains? New Zealand Advertising Practitioners Views on Celebrity and Athlete Endorsers. *Marketing Bulletin*, *16*(3), 1–10.

Choi, S. M., Lee, W. N., & Kim, H. J. (2005). Lessons from the rich and famous: A cross-cultural comparison of celebrity endorsement in advertising. *Journal of Advertising*, *34*(2), 91–105. doi:10.1080/00913367.2005.10639190

Choi, S. M., & Rifon, N. J. (2007). Who is the celebrity in advertising? Understanding dimensions of celebrity images. *Journal of Popular Culture*, *40*(2), 304–324. doi:10.1111/j.1540-5931.2007.00380.x

Craig, C., & John, M. M. (1978). Assessing Communication Effects of Energy Conservation. *The Journal of Consumer Research*, *5*(2), 82–88. doi:10.1086/208718

Daneshvary, R., & Schwer, R. K. (2000). The Association Endorsement and Consumers' Intentions to Purchase. *Journal of Consumer Marketing*, *17*(3), 203–213. doi:10.1108/07363760010328987

Druckman, D. (1994). Nationalism, patriotism, and group loyalty: A social psychological perspective. *Mershon International Studies Review*, *38*(1), 43–68. doi:10.2307/222610

Erdem, T., & Swait, J. (2004). Brand credibility, brand consideration, and choice. *The Journal of Consumer Research*, *31*(1), 191–198. doi:10.1086/383434

Erdogan, B. Z. (1999). Celebrity Endorsement: A Literature Review. *Journal of Marketing Management*, *41*(3), 291–314. doi:10.1362/026725799784870379

Ewa, J., & Kamil, W. (2015). *The nationality and the type of celebrities endorsing products versus ethnocentric attitudes of Polish consumers*. Conference paper.

Farhat, R., & Mustafa Khan, B. (2011). Importance of Brand Personality to Customer Loyalty : A Conceptual Study. *New Media and Mass Communication*, *1*, 4–11.

Fireworker, R. B., & Friedman, H. H. (1977). The Effects of Endorsements on Product Evaluation. *Decision Sciences*, *8*(3), 576–583. doi:10.1111/j.1540-5915.1977.tb01104.x

Freeman, K. S., & Chen, C. C. 2015. *Wither the Impact of Celebrity Endorsement.* Paper presented at the International Conference on Communication, Media, Technology and Design, Dubai, UAE.

Friedman, H. H., & Friedman, L. (1979). Endorser effectiveness by product type. *Journal of Advertising Research, 19*(5), 63–71.

Ger, G., Belk, R. W., & Lascu, D. N. (1993). The development of consumer desire in marketizing and developing economies: The cases of Romania and Turkey. *Advances in Consumer Research. Association for Consumer Research (U. S.), 20*, 102–107.

Gurhan-Canli, Z., & Maheswaran, D. (2000). Determinants of country-of-origin evaluations. *The Journal of Consumer Research, 27*(1), 96–108. doi:10.1086/314311

Hakimi, B. Y., Abedniya, A., & Zaeim, M. N. (2011). Investigate the impact of celebrity endorsement on brand images. *European Journal of Scientific Research, 58*(1), 116–132.

Harmon, R. R., & Kenneth, A. C. (1982). The Persuasive Effects of Source Credibility in Buy and Lease Situations. *JMR, Journal of Marketing Research, 19*(2), 255–260. doi:10.2307/3151625

Herche, J. (1994). Ethnocentric Tendencies, Marketing Strategy and Import Purchase Behaviour. *International Marketing Review, 11*(3), 4–16. doi:10.1108/02651339410067012

Horai, J., Naccari, N., & Fatoullah, E. (1974). The effects of expertise and physical attractiveness upon opinion agreement and liking. *Sociometry, 37*(4), 601–606. doi:10.2307/2786431

Hovland, C. I., Janis, I. L., & Kelly, H. H. (1953). Communication and persuasion: Psychological studies in opinion change. *American Sociological Review, 19*(3), 355–357.

Jerzyk, E., Stefanska, M., Nestorowicz, R., & Rogala, A. (2016). *The influence of credibility and trust to form of communication message in the context of ethnocentrism.* Conference paper.

Joseph, W. B. (1982). The Credibility of Physically Attractive Communicators: A Review. *Journal of Advertising, 11*(3), 15–24. doi:10.1080/00913367.1982.10672807

Kahle, L. R., & Homer, P. (1985). Physical Attractiveness of the Celebrity Endorser: A Social Adaptation Perspective. *The Journal of Consumer Research, 11*(4), 954–961. doi:10.1086/209029

Karasawa, M. (2002). Patriotism, nationalism and internationalism among Japanese citizens: An etic-emic approach. *Political Psychology, 23*(4), 645–666. doi:10.1111/0162-895X.00302

Klein, J. G. (2002). Us versus Them, or Us versus Everyone? Delineating Consumer Aversion to Foreign Goods. *Journal of International Business Studies, 33*(2), 345–363. doi:10.1057/palgrave.jibs.8491020

Kucukemiroglu, O. (1999). Market segmentation by using consumer lifestyle dimensions and ethnocentrism: An empirical study. *European Journal of Marketing, 33*(5/6), 470–487. doi:10.1108/03090569910262053

Li, Z., Fu, S., & Murray, L. (1997). Country and product images: The perceptions of consumers in the people's republic of China. *Journal of International Consumer Marketing, 10*(2), 115–139.

Lin, C. Y., Chen, P. J., Wu, L. W., & Tseng, T. H. (2015). Does the Endorser's Nationality Matter? An Investigation of Young Taiwanese Consumers' Selecting Smartphone. *International Business Research*, *8*(11), 49. doi:10.5539/ibr.v8n11p49

Lirtzman, S. I., & Shuv-Ami, A. (1986). Credibility of source of communication on products' safety hazard. *Psychological Reports*, *58*(3), 707–718. doi:10.2466/pr0.1986.58.3.707 PMID:3726021

Liu, M. T., Huang, Y. Y., & Jiang, M. H. (2007). Relations among Attractiveness of Endorsers, Match-up, and Purchase Intention in Sport Marketing in China. *Journal of Consumer Marketing*, *24*(6), 358–365. doi:10.1108/07363760710822945

Luque-Martínez, T., Ibá˜nezz-Zapata, J. A., & del Barrio-García, S. (2000). Consumer ethnocentrism measurement. An assessment of the reliability and validity of the CETSCALE in Spain. *European Journal of Marketing*, *34*(11/12), 1353–1373. doi:10.1108/03090560010348498

Magnini, P. V., Honeycutt, E. D., & Cross, A. M. (2008). Understanding the use of celebrity endorsers for hospitality firms. *Journal of Vacation Marketing*, *14*(1), 57–69. doi:10.1177/1356766707084219

McCracken, G. (1989). Who is the Celebrity Endorser? Cultural Foundations of the Endorsement Process. *The Journal of Consumer Research*, *16*(3), 310–322. doi:10.1086/209217

McCroskey, J. C., & McCain, T. A. (1974). The measurement of interpersonal attraction. *Speech Monographs*, *41*(3), 261–266. doi:10.1080/03637757409375845

McGinnies, E., & Charles, D. W. (1980). Better Liked Than Right: Trustworthiness and Expertise as Factors in Credibility. *Personality and Social Psychology Bulletin*, *6*(3), 467–472. doi:10.1177/014616728063023

McGuire, W. J. (1958). Attitudes and Attitude Change. In Handbook of Social Psychology (Vol. 2). New York: Random House.

Miller, G. P., & Basehart, J. (1969). Source trustworthiness, opinionated statements, and response to persuasive communication. *Speech Monographs*, *36*(1), 1–7. doi:10.1080/03637756909375602

Moore, D. L., Hausknecht, D., & Thamodaran, K. (1988). Time Compression, Response Opportunity, and Persuasion. *The Journal of Consumer Research*, *13*, 12–24.

National Pharmaceutical Control Bureau. (2009). *Guidelines for Control of Cosmetics Products in Malaysia*. Malaysia Ministry of Health.

Nelson, P. E., & Pearson, J. C. (1988). Understanding and sharing. Dubuque, IA: W.C. Brown Publishers.

Netemeyer, R. G., Durvasula, S., & Lichtenstein, D. R. (1991). A cross-national assessment of the reliability and validity of the CETSCALE. *JMR, Journal of Marketing Research*, *28*(3), 320–327. doi:10.2307/3172867

Ohanian, R. (1990). Construction and Validation of A Scale to Measure Celebrity Endorser's Perceived Expertise, Trustworthiness, and Attractiveness. *Journal of Advertising*, *19*(3), 39–52. doi:10.1080/00913367.1990.10673191

Ohanian, R. (1991). The Impact of Celebrity Spokesperson's Perceived Image on Consumers' Intention to Purchase. *Journal of Advertising Research*, *31*(1), 46–52.

OMahony, S., & Meenaghan, T. (1997). The impact of celebrity endorsements on consumers. *Irish Marketing Review, 10*(2), 15-24.

Othman, M. N., Ong, F. S., & Wong, H. W. (2008). Demographic and lifestyle profiles of ethnocentric and non-ethnocentric urban Malaysian consumers. *Asian Journal of Business and Accounting, 1*(1), 5–26.

Pecotich, A., & Rosenthal, M. J. (2001). Country of Origin, Quality, Brand and Consumer Ethnocentrism. *Journal of Global Marketing, 15*(2), 31–60. doi:10.1300/J042v15n02_03

Pornpitakpan, C. (2004). The Effect of Celebrity Endorsers' Perceived Credibility on Product Purchase Intention. *Journal of International Consumer Marketing, 16*(2), 55–74. doi:10.1300/J046v16n02_04

Praet, C. L. C. (2001). Japanese advertising, the world's number one celebrity showcase? A crosscultural comparison of the frequency of celebrity appearances in TV advertising. In *Proceedings of the 2001 Special Asia-Pacific Conference of the American Academy of Advertising*. American Academy of Advertising.

Priester, J. R., & Petty, R. E. (2003). The influence of spokesperson trustworthiness on message elaboration, attitude strength, and advertising effectiveness. *Journal of Consumer Psychology, 13*(4), 408–421. doi:10.1207/S15327663JCP1304_08

Pringle, H., & Binet, L. (2005). How marketers can use celebrities to sell more efficiently. *Journal of Consumer Behaviour, 4*(3), 201–214. doi:10.1002/cb.2

Ranjbarian, B., Shekarchizade, Z., & Momeni, Z. (2010). Celebrity endorser influence on attitude toward advertisement and brands. *European Journal of Soil Science, 13*(3), 399–404.

Samiee, S., Shimp, T. A., & Sharma, S. (2005). Brand origin recognition accuracy: Its antecedents and consumers' cognitive limitations. *Journal of International Business Studies, 36*(4), 379–397. doi:10.1057/palgrave.jibs.8400145

Schlecht, C. (2003). Celebrities' Impact on Branding. Center on Global Brand Leadership, Columbia Business School.

Sertoglu, A., Catli, O., & Korkmaz, S. (2014). Examining the effect of endorser credibility on the consumers' buying intentions: An empirical study in Turkey. *International Review of Management and Marketing, 4*(1), 66–77.

Shimp, T. (2003). *Advertising, Promotion and Supplemental Aspects of Integrated Marketing Communication* (6th ed.). Fort Worth, TX: The Dryden Press.

Shimp, T. A., & Sharma, S. (1987). Consumer ethnocentrism construction and validation of the CETSCALE. *JMR, Journal of Marketing Research, 24*(3), 280–289. doi:10.2307/3151638

Smith, E. G., Meurs, L. V., & Neijens, P. C. (2006). Effects of Advertising Likeability: A 10 Year Perspective. *Journal of Advertising Research, 46*(1), 73–83. doi:10.2501/S0021849906060089

Smith, G. H., & Engel, E. (1968). Influence of a female model on perceived characteristics of an automobile. *The 76th Annual Convention of the American Psychological Associations Proceedings*, 681-682.

Speck, P. S., Schumann, D. W., & Thompson, C. (1988). Celebrity endorsements-scripts, schema and roles: Theoretical framework and preliminary tests. *Advances in Consumer Research. Association for Consumer Research (U. S.)*, *15*(1), 69–76.

Sternthal, B., Phillips, L. W., & Dholakia, R. (1978). The persuasive effect of source credibility: A situational analysis. *Public Opinion Quarterly*, *42*(3), 285–314. doi:10.1086/268454 PMID:10297222

Sumner, W. G. (1906). *Folkways: The Sociological Importance of Usages, Manners, Customs, Mores, and Morals*. New York, NY: Ginn and Company.

Tan, K. (2011). *Riding on the star power*. The Edge Malaysia.

Tantiseneepong, N., Gorton, M., & White, J. (2012). Evaluating responses to celebrity endorsements using projective techniques. *Qualitative Market Research*, *15*(1), 57–69. doi:10.1108/13522751211191991

Temperley, J., & Tangen, D. (2006). The Pinocchio factor in consumer attitudes towards celebrity endorsement: Celebrity endorsement, the Reebok brand, and an examination of a recent campaign. *Journal of Innovative Marketing*, *2*(3), 97–106.

Till, B. D., & Busler, M. (2000). The Match-up Hypothesis: Physical Attractiveness, Expertise, and the Role of Fit on Brand Attitude, Purchase Intentions, and Brand Beliefs. *Journal of Advertising*, *29*(3), 1–13. doi:10.1080/00913367.2000.10673613

U.S. Commercial Service Hong Kong. (2014). *Cosmetics and toiletries market overviews*. The U.S. Commercial Service.

Usunier, J. C., & Lee, J. A. (2005). *Marketing Across Cultures*. Harlow: Prentice Hall.

Van der Waldt, D., Van Loggerenberg, M., & Wehmeyer, L. (2009). Celebrity Endorsements versus Created Spokespersons in Advertising: A Survey among Students. *SAJEMS*, *12*(1), 110–114.

Vida, I., Damjan, J., & Fairhurst, A. (1996). Ethnocentric tendencies and consumer purchase behavior in Central and Eastern Europe: the case of Slovenia. *Proceedings of the Academy of Marketing Science: Multicultural Marketing Conference 1996*, 49-55.

Vien, C. V., Yun, C. T., & Fai, P. L. (2017). The Effect of Celebrity Endorsement on Brand Attitude and Purchase Intention. *Journal of Global Business and Social Entrepreneurship*, *1*(4), 141–150.

Wang, C. L., & Chen, Z. X. (2004). Consumer ethnocentrism and willingness to buy domestic products in a developing country setting: Testing moderating effects. *Journal of Consumer Marketing*, *21*(6), 391–400. doi:10.1108/07363760410558663

Wang, S. W., Kao, G. H. Y., & Ngamsiriudom, W. (2017). Consumers' attitude of endorser credibility, brand and intention with respect to celebrity endorsement of the airline sector. *Journal of Air Transport Management*, *60*, 10–17. doi:10.1016/j.jairtraman.2016.12.007

Wei, K. K., & Li, W. Y. (2013). Measuring the impact of celebrity endorsement on consumer behavioural intentions: A study of Malaysian consumers. *International Journal of Sports Marketing & Sponsorship*, *14*(3), 157–177.

Wong, C. Y., Polonsky, M. J., & Garma, R. (2008). The impact of consumer ethnocentrism and country of origin sub-components for high involvement products on young Chinese consumers' product assessments. *Asia Pacific Journal of Marketing and Logistics*, *20*(4), 455–478. doi:10.1108/13555850810909759

Wood, N. T., & Burkhalter, J. N. (2014). Tweet this, not that: A comparison between brand promotions in microblogging environments using celebrity and company-generated tweets. *Journal of Marketing Communications*, *20*(1-2), 129–146. doi:10.1080/13527266.2013.797784

Wu, C., & Shaffer, D. (1987). Susceptibility to Persuasive Appeals as a Function of Source Credibility and Prior Experience with the Attitude Object. *Journal of Personality and Social Psychology*, *52*(4), 677–688. doi:10.1037/0022-3514.52.4.677

Yagci, M. I. (2001). Evaluating the effects of country-of-origin and consumer ethnocentrism: A case of a transplant product. *Journal of International Consumer Marketing*, *13*(3), 63–85. doi:10.1300/J046v13n03_05

Zahid, M., Abdul, R., Jainthy, N., & Samsinar, M. S. (2002). Perceptions of advertising and celebrity endorsement in Malaysia. *Asia Pacific Management Review*, *7*(4), 535–554.

Chapter 8
The Effect of Celebrity Endorsements on Consumers' Buying Behavior in South West Nigeria

Stella Amara Aririguzoh
Covenant University, Nigeria

Emmanuel Mogaji
University of Greenwich, UK

Odion Oscar Odiboh
Covenant University, Nigeria

ABSTRACT

Advertisers engage celebrities to endorse their products. This chapter hinges on the meaning transfer theory of McCracken that says that celebrity image can be transferred to items that users buy. Using the survey method, this work examined if celebrity endorsements affect buying. Copies of the questionnaire were administered on 1,516 residents drawn from urban, suburban, and rural areas of Lagos and Ogun States, Nigeria. The Pearson correlation found positive relationships between celebrity endorsements and buyers' decisions. The tests show that celebrity endorsements influence the purchase decisions of the residents, and these buyers' avoidance of a product is more clearly influenced by celebrity endorsements. People buy products because of the celebrities that endorsed them. However, some respondents, especially those in the rural areas, were not as influenced into buying these products as are those from the urban and sub-urban areas. It is advised that advertisers pursue other avenues to draw patronage from this area.

DOI: 10.4018/978-1-5225-7906-9.ch008

BACKGROUND OF STUDY

Most celebrities are seen as famous, well known and successful individuals. Their glamour, fame, fortune, social network and lifestyles usually attract media attention. Piyush (2012) and Ranjbarian, Shekarchizade and Momeni (2010) say that the media make millions of people to constantly see their faces, hear their voices and read their names. Some scholars like Driessens (2013), Khatri (2006), Okorie and Agbaleke (2017) agree that celebrities shape their followers' opinions concerning anything through inspirational speeches, expression of talents, expertise, humanitarian advocacies and socially acceptable actions. Ranjbarian, Shekarchizade and Momeni (2010) write that people can become celebrities by ascription, achievement or attribution. Ascribed celebrities inherit family fame, royal flame and business names whilst other superstars achieve elevated status on account of their individual skills, winning of high laurels and accolades. Attributed celebrities achieve prominence by affiliation with famous personalities through regular co-appearances, consanguinity and professional personality management.

Most celebrities are associated with fame. Celebrity advertisements increase awareness and patronage of products. Evidence abounds that advertisers frequently use celebrities as credible sources to influence consumers' attitudes towards their brands and enhance their intention to purchase. McCracken (1989, p. 310) writes that a celebrity endorser is any individual who enjoys public recognition and who uses this recognition to market a consumer good by appearing with it in an advertisement. Atkin and Block (1983) note that these celebrities attract attention to the advertisement. Generally, they are individuals with attractive and likeable qualities and these are expected to be transferred to the products or services that they endorse. Much as celebrity advertisements promote brand awareness, strengthen brand image and help consumers' decision making, problems are aroused when the celebrity loses status due to moral, legal and controversial issues. As Sneha (2012, p.10) mentions, "when negative information is publicized about a celebrity, it not only influences the consumer's view of the celebrity but also the endorsed product."

Celebrity advertisements and endorsements have been studied by various scholars. Omenugha, Uzuegbunam and Ndolo's (2016) survey of some Nigerian youths show that these young people are exposed to celebrities in the media, love reading about, and watching them. Importantly, these celebrities influence their purchasing habits. Oyeniyi's (2014) study suggests that celebrity advertising affects sales of processed foods and soft drinks. Dumbili (2017) studied celebrity effect on alcohol and drinking behaviours of Nigerian youths. Uzuegbunam (2017) and Itiri (2015) looked at celebrity influence of youths' participation in the Nigerian general election. Nyarko, Asimah, Agbemava and Tsetse (2015) studied the influence of celebrity endorsement of *Fan Milk* on the buying behaviour of Ghanaian youths They find sales for this product increased. However, the endorsement could not compel everybody to buy *Fan Milk*.

Celebrities are not limited to a particular media of expression. The traditional media of television, radio, newspapers and magazines have captured their stardom. Newer celebrities have been captured through the new media of *YouTube*, *Facebook*, *Twitter* and several other online outlets. Traditional media celebrities include Bill Cosby, Mariam Makeba, Barak Obama and Pastor Daniel Kolawole Olukoya. New media celebrities are usually younger. Examples are Emmanuella of the Mark Angels Comedy and the Jalals; two *YouTube* sensations who are followed locally and globally by millions of people for their comics and pranks respectively. According to Akram, Muhammad, Raga and Sana (2017), celebrities cut across different fields of endeavour: politics, entertainment, sports, business, advocacy, religion and government. What Aririguzoh (2013) labels as the *communication imperative* or the command to communicate is actually what advertisers look for in celebrities. Celebrities are to communicate the advertised brands to their admirers and followers. Advertising professionals have cashed in on their popularity and mass followership to create awareness for some products and services. Belch and Belch (2012), Choi and Rifon (2007) and Odiboh (2002) point out that followership is a major element in advertising; but as McCracken (1989), Menon and Louis (2001) point out, celebrity status may not be permanent. Some lose followership occasioned by immoral conducts, criminal convictions, reduction in performance and outdated expertise while some others remain popular names even after death. What should a marketer do if his brand is suffering losses in a crisis situation? Amodu (2010) readily offers the deployment of public relations. Commercial organizations and prominent brands tend to use celebrities for specific communication roles. Odiboh, Olonode, Adesina, Yartey (2018) observe that some celebrities too are used by Non-Governmental Organizations or hired to support new technologies, for instance, e-transactions in communities.

In a growing economy like Nigeria, some advertisers have followed the norm of using famous people to advertise some products and services. Celebrity endorsement can create instant brand awareness, recall and patronage. Popular celebrity advertisements include Nollywood actress Ini Edo advertising *Glo* Telecommunications Network and footballer Kanu Nwankwo endorsing *Peak Milk.* Another celebrity like Pastor Enoch Adeboye - the General Overseer of the Redeemed Christian Church of God - has been seen in a Lagos State Government-sponsored advertisement asking people to pay their taxes so that the state can provide more social amenities. In Ghana celebrities too also endorse. Actress Jackie Appiah endorses the computer firm IPMC; singer Emmanuel Andrews (stage name, Samini), MTN; and professional footballer, John Mensah, *Jago Milk.* The legendary Ivorian football star, Didier Drogba became the Digital Bank Ambassador for Standard Chartered Bank in Africa.

As Nigeria's economy advances, the need for advertising continues to grow. Aggressive marketing communication strategies have been observed as brands aim to convince, capture, retain and recapture prospects through celebrity applications to products. Dzisah and Ocloo (2013) see advertising as part of marketing promotions. They add that advertisers use celebrities to positively influence the behaviour of the consumers towards purchasing what the company is offering. Professionals see these strategic windows as assured paths to attracting and encouraging increased patronage from customers. Amodu (2007) notes that even the banks are not left out in trying to attract customers. The marvel of celebrities is quickly spreading in Nigeria. This however poses a different challenge for brands in Nigeria where marketing managers have to take into consideration the country's multi-cultural nature; and how some consumers may examine the advertisement based on the celebrity that is endorsing the brand. Notably, the effect of celebrity advertisements on consumers' buying behaviour in Nigeria, an emerging market has received little scholarly attention. This is a gap this study aims to fill. This paper examined the effect of celebrity advertisements on the buying behaviour of consumers in the urban, suburban and rural areas in Lagos and Ogun States in south western Nigeria. Lagos is the media capital of Nigeria, housing most of the country's advertising agencies that engage the celebrities. Ogun State is proximate to Lagos, thereby benefiting from the spill over of product manufacturing and preponderant brand communication activities. Residents in the two states are exposed to different forms of celebrity advertisements.

STATEMENT OF THE PROBLEM

Advertising creates and maintains awareness about products and services through the mass media. Usually, it promotes specific goods and services to target consumers across rural, urban or suburban geo-boundaries. Urban centres are characterised by high flux of business activities and bubbly lifestyles. The urban places are in the metropolis. Rural areas are known to be sleepy in spite of the inhabiting population whose needs must be met. The rural areas are located outside the cities and towns but not included within the urban areas. Suburban areas are in between ruralscape and cityscape; inhabited by city workers and agro-cottage industry operators. The suburban areas are neither urban nor rural. Though each of these three locations have their media consumption peculiarities, access to advertisements of all sorts is guaranteed.

However, whilst celebrities may live with their metropolitan audiences, they remain distant from suburban and rural targets of endorsed advertisements. How would the advert messages influence buying behaviours across the demographic boundaries?

This research is expected to access the correlation between consumers buying behaviour and celebrity advertisements. Do celebrity advertisements have impact and actually influence the buying behaviours of consumers irrespective of their geographical locations? This is the major problem of investigation. Residents were selected from urban, suburban and rural areas in South western Nigeria. The selected urban areas are Victoria Island, Surulere and Ikeja while the rural communities are Ikotun, Iyesi, Egbeda, Atan and Ilugun, Abeokuta. The suburban regions are Oko Oba, Olorunsogo, Abeokuta and Ogba.

HYPOTHESES

Two hypotheses are formulated for this study:

Hypothesis 1

H_1: Celebrity endorsement has impact on the purchase decisions of urban, suburban and rural areas residents

Hypothesis 2

H_1: Residents avoidance of a product is more significantly influenced by celebrity endorsements

LITERATURE REVIEW

Nigerian brands have continued to use celebrities for advertisements. Zinkhan and Hong (1991) write that an advertisement's effectiveness is grounded in the interrelationship between a brand's perceived image and the consumer's self-image. Individuals derive meanings from an advertisement through culturally-accepted perception closely linked to the brand image held by the individual. Keller (1993, p.3) remarks that the perception about a brand is reflected by the brand's association in the memory of the individual. Fleck, Korchia and Roy (2012); Kamins and Gupta (1994); Lynch and Schuler (1994); Misra and Beatty (1990) confirm that companies select celebrities to endorse their brands in anticipation that these particular persons hopefully convey the right meaning and highlight the congruence between them and the brands. This further leads to the idea of congruence and its effect on advertisement effectiveness. Fleck, Korchia and Roy (2012) say that *congruence* has been used in several researches on brand extension, co-branding, sponsoring, and endorsement to assess the fit between a brand and another entity. Solomon (1996) shares the opinion that congruity is applied to advertising and consumer behaviour when addressing how outlooks are affected when a person, such as a celebrity, is linked to a brand or company. He lays emphasis on the congruence between the advertising cues and the brand. Heckler and Childers (1992) examine the congruence between visual and verbal elements in advertisements.

Advertisements are expected to create meanings in the minds of the consumers. Smith (2007) expects individuals to be actively engaged in the meaning-making process because meanings are individually constructed even though it is derived from a cultural boundary. Mick and Buhl (1992) add that personal history, nationality, the community, family, and the private self affect the meanings that consumers attach to advertisements. Williamson (1978) points out that the viewer/reader is an essential participant in the process of meaning transfer. He must successfully decode the message presented in the advertisement to make meaning out of it. In addition, Shimp (1993, p.11) suggests that advertisers aim to appeal to "customer's functional, symbolic and experiential needs through effective communications". Aririguzoh (2007) assumes that they are media literates. Maclnnis, Moorman and Jaworski (1991) and Tybout, Calder and Sternthal's (1981) studies report that advertising executional cues can influence communication effectiveness. However, they note that customers' processing of the message of the advertisement is a consequence of not only what they think about, but, also how they think about it. This explains why different individuals attach different meanings to the same advertisement.

Scholars like McCracken (1989); Erdogan, Baker and Tagg (2001) aver that a celebrity endorsement is not the same as a celebrity advertisement even though most people often use them interchangeably. However, they agree that a celebrity endorsement occurs when a famous name, signature or picture appears on a brand. The product is backed up with the authenticity of the personality. They are sometimes hired to speak about the brands at launches, and other events with large audiences. In celebrity advertisement, the celebrity appears in the advertisement and is seen using the product, commending its users or recommending it to potential users. Celebrity advertisements are used for competitive advantage and conversion of celebrity followers to brand admirers. Admiration is usually expected to translate to brand awareness and purchase. Aliede (2016) writes that celebrities may be associated with brand identity creation. Roozen and Claeys (2010) claim that celebrity advertisements attract positive effects for the target audience, brands, and the celebrity himself. Mogaji, Badejo and Charles (2018) share the view that sportswomen can also be brand ambassadors. As long as particular celebrities are shown in advertisements, they have the opportunities to attract more converts and increase their status value. Consumers grow confident since their heroes approve the products. Famous people sell products because their followers easily believe them and thus place the products on the top of their minds' ladder. Culture may be the rope tying the celebrities with their followers, especially if the product so endorsed has cultural significance in the eyes of consumers. Mogaji (2016) is of the opinion that this will enhance the perception of the brands that the celebrities are endorsing. Pil and Shavitt (1994) agree that advertising messages that reflect the dominant cultural norms are more persuasive than those that do not.

The credibility of the celebrity is crucial. Ohanian's (1990) source credibility model offers three credibility measures: expertise, trustworthiness, and attractiveness. Credibility refers to the 'extent to which the source is perceived as possessing expertise relevant to the communication topic and can be trusted to give an objective opinion on the subject'. The celebrity's credibility enhances consumers' attitude towards the advert and the brand. The studies of Erdogan, 1999), and Silvera and Benedikte (2004) provide evidence suggesting that companies employing celebrities in their advertising campaigns make significant profits.

THEORETICAL FRAMEWORK

The Meaning Transfer Theory of McCracken (1989) explains how effective celebrity endorsement influences the minds of the consumers through the transference of meanings. McCracken says that celebrities' effectiveness as endorsers rise from the cultural meanings consumers believe are bestowed on them. Celebrities transfer various meanings to the goods or services that they endorse. McCracken's postulations lie on three factors:

- The construction of celebrity image
- The movement of the celebrity image to the product
- The transfer of meaning from product to consumers

The celebrity is an icon known for specific things, for example, sports. A sportsman presence in an advertisement means that he is deliberately telling buyers that they should equate their value of him with the product. In other words, he is transferring the image he has built in his field of endeavour to the product that he is now endorsing. It is this transfer that creates consumer awareness and purchase. For example, if a sportsman endorses a brand of milk, he is directly telling the buyers and all his fans that buying and consuming this specific brand will make them to be like him: a successful sportsman. What they celebrity has actually done is to associate his personality traits to traits that the consumers may regard as important. Abdurrahaman, Owusu, Soladoye and Kalimuthu (2018, p. 417) point out that "celebrities, due to their relevance and popularity, therefore, are believed to have characteristically, the ability and power to influence buyers to swap their loyalties to the endorsed brands."

Celebrity endorsement is effective because the consumers associate the product with the endorser first, and then transfer this association to the product being endorsed. Advertisers try to create successful associations between the consumption of the product to the consumers' ideas of their own success stories. The consumers are made to feel that their purchasing the particular product endorsed by a celebrity make them to be connected to the endorsers. However, there is neither an automatic creation of meaning nor the automatic transformation of the consumer to exactly what the endorser is. It becomes the work of the advertiser to present the celebrity in such ways that align with the expectations of the consumers. The consumers must feel happy from using the product. It is not just enough to use celebrities in advertising. Kambitsis, Harahousou, Theodorakis and Chatzibeis (2002) add that these celebrities should be easily recognized and much admired. Thus, companies marketing their brands should pick celebrities that evoke the appropriate responses from the buyers.

METHOD OF STUDY

The survey research design is the method used to study a large number of people in their natural habitats, especially when an aggregation of their opinions on an issue is needed. It shows how the primary data is collected from the sample population and then analysed to draw a conclusion on the general population. The *probability sampling* technique allows the samples to be gathered in such a way that the individual elements in the population have equal chances of being selected. The sample locations are randomly chosen from Lagos and Ogun States. The locations are described as urban, suburban or rural. The urban areas of Victoria Island, Surulere and Ikeja are demarcated by streets. On each street are numbered houses. Individual elements are picked from individual houses. A similar fashion is followed for the suburban areas of Oko Oba, Olorunsogo, Abeokuta and Ogba. Some parts of the rural communities in Ikotun, Iyesi, Egbeda, Atan and Ilugun are not demarcated into clear cut streets. Samples were picked from different houses there. Each respondent was randomly chosen to guarantee every resident in a specified location an equal and independent chance of being included in the sample. The assumption is that the resultant sample is as close a representation of the whole population as possible. The total number of respondents for the study are drawn from the chosen areas as shown below:

- Urban: 501
- Suburban: 505
- Rural: *510*
- Total: *1,516* respondents

DATA PRESENTATION

Respondents from the rural, semi-urban and urban areas contributed 33.6%, 33.3% and 33.0% of the total respondents that were administered copies of the questionnaire. They are made up of 44.5% males and 55.5% females aged from 12 years and above. There are some respondents aged above 52 years. A few of them have no formal education or have basic education or secondary school education. Others have OND/NCE and university degrees. Others did not specify their educational status.

Irrespective of location, almost all the respondents know who is a celebrity. This may be because celebrities are famous, popular and regularly make appearances in the mass media or public events. The more they appear in these places, the more the public gets to know them. Some of them are already household names with their fans adoring them. Nevertheless, respondents from the rural areas do not know them as much as those in the urban and suburban areas do.

Table 1. Knowing who a celebrity is

Responses	Urban (%)	Suburban (%)	Rural (%)	Total (%)
Yes	31.9	32.1	30.4	**94.4**
No	1.2	1.2	3.2	**5.6**
Total	**33.0**	**33.3**	**33.6**	**100.0**

N = 1,516

Table 2. Knowing about celebrity advertisement

Responses	Urban (%)	Suburban (%)	Rural (%)	Total (%)
Yes	31.5	31.5	30.5	**93.5**
No	1.6	1.8	3.1	**6.5**
Total	**33.0**	**33.3**	**33.6**	**100.0**

N = 1,516

Almost all the respondents confirm that they know about celebrity advertisements. It is importantly to point out that the respondents in the urban and suburban areas know more of celebrity advertisements than those in the rural areas. Those in the rural areas know least. However, the gap is very small. This may be explained by the fact they celebrities may be urban based and more of their activities are carried out in these cosmopolitan areas.

Respondents further identify the first three classes of celebrities that they know. They are the actors, musicians and sportsmen. The most popular of the celebrities are those in the movie world. These may not be surprising since Nigeria's movie industry popularly called, *Nollywood*, churns out entertaining movies with speed. The actors and actress literarily charm their fans with their craft. The faces of actors and actresses adorn television and cinema screens. The second group of celebrities are musicians. Their sonorous and electrifying dance steps may have sent many respondents into dancing and imitating then. The sportsmen are also famous. Their physical fitness and prowess in competitive sports events for example, football, have endeared them to many. Nigeria has a lot of sports icons including Kanu Nwankwo. Nevertheless, there are also some distinguished celebrities in religion, for example, Pastor Daniel Olukoya; politics, for example, Dr Goodluck Jonathan; and literary circles such as Chimamanda Ngozi Adichie. It should be pointed out that respondents in the urban areas know of sports and religious celebrities most. Respondents from the suburban areas know movie and musical celebrities most. The respondents from the rural zones know of political celebrities and writers.

This data on this table (Table 4) establishes that most of the residents pay conscious attention to advertisements featuring celebrities. Whether they are living in urban, suburban and rural communities do not make any difference. It is most surprising that respondents from the rural and suburban locations

Table 3. Classes of celebrities

Responses	Urban (%)	Suburban (%)	Rural (%)	Total (%)
Movies	12.3	15.0	14.6	**42.0**
Musical	9.9	9.9	7.5	**27.3**
Sports	7.3	4.8	6.3	**18.5**
Religious	1.8	1.6	1.5	**4.9**
Political	1.4	1.2	2.0	**4.6**
Writers	0.3	0.7	1.4	**2.4**
Others	0	0.1	0.3	**0.4**
Total	**33.0**	**33.3**	**33.6**	**100.0**

N = 1,516

Table 4. Conscious paying of attention to celebrity advertisements

Responses	Urban (%)	Suburban (%)	Rural (%)	Total (%)
Yes	22.3	23.2	25.4	**70.9**
No	10.8	9.8	8.5	**29.1**
Total	**33.2**	**32.9**	**33.9**	**100.0**

N = 1,516

pay more attention to celebrity advertisements than those in the urban areas. However, the differences are almost insignificant. Residents in the urban areas live in cities where industrialization and paid employment are the norms. Those in the rural areas are people who value communal life and engage in subsistence living. There is little or no industrialization in their communities. The suburban residents have characteristics of the other two as most suburban areas are mixes of the industrialized cites and the rustic elements of rural life.

Respondents from these three different areas further confirm that they buy products because a celebrity has endorsed it. However, some interesting variations emerge. The respondents from the suburban areas appear most susceptible to buying products that have been so endorsed. They are followed by the respondents from the urban areas. But the respondents from the rural areas are least influenced in buying products because a celebrity has endorsed it. Rural dwellers may not be dazzled by the celebrity status of those endorsing products if they are *not one of their own.* Life in the rural areas are more based on personal relationships and face-to-face communication, not mass communication.

Table 5. Buying a product because of celebrity endorsement

Responses	Urban (%)	Suburban (%)	Rural (%)	Total (%)
Strongly Agree	4.4	5.1	4.6	**14.1**
Agree	9.3	9.1	8.6	**27.0**
Undecided	6.1	6.3	6.6	**19.0**
Disagree	10.5	9.8	9.7	**30.0**
Strongly Disagree	2.8	2.7	4.4	**10.0**
Total	**33.2**	**32.9**	**33.9**	**100.0**

N = 1,516

Table 6. Likelihood of buying a product endorsed by a celebrity

Responses	Urban (%)	Suburban (%)	Rural (%)	Total (%)
Strongly Agree	4.6	4.7	5.7	**15.0**
Agree	10.2	9.0	9.1	**28.3**
Undecided	6.8	6.5	7.1	**20.4**
Disagree	8.4	9.7	8.6	**26.8**
Strongly Disagree	3.1	3.4	3.1	**9.6**
Total	**33.0**	**33.3**	**33.6**	**100.0**

N = 1,516

It is interesting to find out an equal number of respondents from the urban and rural areas agreeing on the likelihood of their buying a product endorsed by a celebrity than one that is not so endorsed. However, a slightly lower number of respondents from the suburban areas also concur. A somewhat higher number of respondents from the rural communities disagree to this opinion. Similarly, some of the respondents from the urban and suburban areas also disagree. There are also some respondents from these three clusters who are undecided.

Overall, celebrity endorsement seems to have more positive impact on the respondents' purchase behaviour. However, the impact is more pronounced among residents in the suburban and urban areas than those resident in the rural areas. Respondents from the rural areas disagree that celebrity endorsements influence them in their decisions in buying a product. Some respondents from both the urban and suburban areas also disagree. It is important to notice the number of respondents who are undecided as to whether celebrity endorsements influence them in their decisions, especially those from the rural areas. Thus, it can be summarized that celebrity endorsement on products is more effective with residents in the urbanized and urbanizing areas than on those in the rural areas.

Celebrities endorsements may make products popular. However, the buyers reserve the right to which particular products that they want to purchase. Respondents who may be unfamiliar with a particular celebrity may refuse to buy a product that he is endorsing. It can be seen that a lesser number of respondents from the urban and suburban areas confirm that they may not buy a product if they are unfamiliar with the celebrity endorsing the product. More respondents from the rural areas agree that they will also not buy. More respondents from the suburban and urban than the rural areas disagreed on the opinion

Table 7. Positive impact of celebrity endorsement on a purchase decision

Responses	Urban (%)	Suburban (%)	Rural (%)	Total (%)
Strongly Agree	6.7	7.9	7.2	**21.8**
Agree	12.4	12.2	9.8	**34.4**
Undecided	6.7	4.9	8.0	**19.6**
Disagree	5.6	6.2	6.7	**18.5**
Strongly Disagree	1.7	2.0	1.9	**5.7**
Total	**33.0**	**33.3**	**33.6**	**100.0**

N= 1,516

Table 8. Not buying a product because of unfamiliarity with endorsing celebrity

Responses	Urban (%)	Suburban (%)	Rural (%)	Total (%)
Strongly Agree	3.0	1.6	4.8	**9.4**
Agree	4.5	5.8	4.9	**15.2**
Undecided	5.9	5.2	5.1	**16.2**
Disagree	14.6	13.7	13.7	**42.1**
Strongly Disagree	5.1	6.9	5.1	**17.2**
Total	**33.0**	**33.3**	**33.6**	**100.0**

N = 1,516

that they will buy a product if they are unfamiliar with the endorsing celebrity. Quite some number of respondents are indecisive. Thus, it can be drawn that residents in the rural areas will not buy products if the endorsing celebrities are not known to them.

More respondents from the rural areas claim that they may not buy a product because of the endorsing celebrity. This means that they are not influenced by the status of the celebrity into buying a product he has endorsed. His image does not influence them. However, the respondents in the cities, first and then the suburbs are not so disposed. They do not avoid buying a product because of the endorsing celebrity. It is possible that they actually buy the products because of the endorsement. This means that celebrity endorsements seem to have more impact on urban residents and least impact on the rural dwellers. It is important to point out that some respondents in the different locations were not decided as to whether they will or will not buy a product because of the celebrity who endorsed it.

Expectedly, most of the respondents from the rural areas agree that they will not buy some products if they do not know the celebrities endorsing them. They are closely followed by the respondents form the suburban areas. Those respondents from the urban cities trailed behind. This appears to follow the earlier findings where respondents from the rural areas do not seem to revel with celebrities. Nevertheless, the urban based respondents appear to glow in their knowledge of the acclaimed famous people. The urban and suburban based respondents disagree that they will not buy some products because of not their knowing the endorsing celebrities. The ruralites adhered to their pattern of not cheering the celebrities with buying products they have endorsed. Some other respondents are irresolute as to their buying some products because of not knowing the endorsing celebrity.

Table 9. Respondents not buying a product because of celebrity who endorsed it

Responses	Urban (%)	Suburban (%)	Rural (%)	Total (%)
Strongly Agree	2.6	3.1	3.8	**9.5**
Agree	4.3	4.6	4.8	**13.7**
Undecided	7.2	5.7	7.1	**20.0**
Disagree	14.6	15.0	13.9	**43.6**
Strongly Disagree	4.3	4.9	4.1	**13.3**
Total	**33.0**	**33.3**	**33.6**	**100.0**

N= 1,516

Table 10. Respondents not buying some products because of not knowing the endorsing celebrity

Responses	Urban (%)	Suburban (%)	Rural (%)	Total (%)
Strongly Agree	2.2	2.6	3.2	**8.1**
Agree	4.5	5.7	5.6	**15.8**
Undecided	5.7	4.6	5.5	**15.8**
Disagree	15.2	13.1	13.8	**42.1**
Strongly Disagree	5.3	7.3	5.5	**18.1**
Total	**33.0**	**33.3**	**33.6**	**100.0**

N= 1,516

TESTING THE HYPOTHESES

The hypotheses of the study are tested for acceptance or rejection using the Pearson Bivariate Two-Tailed Correlation tests. These tests compute the association between the independent and dependent variables. The independent variable is celebrity advertisements and the dependent variable is consumers' buying behaviour.

Hypothesis 1

H_i: Celebrity endorsements have impact on the purchase decisions of urban, suburban and rural areas residents.

A functional equation can be stated explicitly as follows:

$$Yce = a0 + a1Tbp + a2Tlb + a3Tep + U \ldots \quad (1)$$

where:

1 = Respondents buying a product because a celebrity has endorsed it
2 = Respondents more likely to buy a product that have been endorsed by a celebrity than one that is not so endorsed
3 = Overall, the presence of celebrity endorsement is positive when respondents are making a purchase decision to buy a product
U = Error term representing other factors not included in the model

At 0.01 level of significance, there are significant and positive relationships in the effect of celebrity endorsement and the buying behaviour of the residents in the urban, suburban and rural areas residents This means that respondents in the urban, suburban and rural areas buy a product because a celebrity has endorsed it. Hence, celebrity endorsements have positive influence on respondents purchasing behaviour.

Table 11. Correlation coefficients between celebrity advertisement and respondents buying the product

BUYING	LOCATION	1	2	3
1	Urban	1		
	Suburban	1		
	Rural	1		
2	Urban	.421**	1	
	Suburban	.499**	1	
	Rural	.421**	1	
3	Urban	.433**	.507**	1
	Suburban	.465**	.488**	1
	Rural	.399**	.385**	1

**Correlation is significant at the 0.01 level (2-tailed)

Respondents buy some products because celebrities endorsed them. There are also positive, but moderate and significant relationships among the urban (.421); sub-urban (.499); and rural (.421) respondents being more likely to buy products so endorsed by the celebrities than not buying the product. Respondents too are more likely to buy products that have been endorsed by celebrities than those not so endorsed. The likelihood is most pronounced among respondents from the urban areas (R= 0.507, P = 0.01), more among those in the suburban areas (.488) and least among those from the rural areas (.385). There are also positive and significant relationships from the urban (.433), semi-urban (.465) and rural (.399) areas on the overall positive effect of celebrity endorsement when they are making purchase decisions on buying a product. All the values are positive and significant. This means that celebrity advertising has a positive impact on the buying of the advertised products. This confirms Piyush's (p.5) observation "that brand communication messages delivered by celebrities and famous personalities generate a higher appeal, attention and recall than those executed by non-celebrities ". This is similar to the observation of Apejoye (2013, p.4) that "that celebrity endorsed advertisement does significantly impact on buyers' purchase intent. Nevertheless, it must be pointed out that the correlates for respondents from the rural areas are lower than those from the urban and suburban areas. Although these are positive relationships, they are weak. Celebrity advertisements impact is more pronounced in the urban and suburban areas than in the rural areas.

In accepting Hypothesis 1, it can be concluded that there are positive and significant correlations among all the variables that tested buyers' exposure to celebrity advertisement and their buying the same products that they are promoting. The relatively high correlation figures ranging from 0.385 - 0.507 indicate the various ways celebrity advertising has influenced the buying behaviour of the respondents. In other words, a firm and affirmative relationship exist between these celebrity advertisements and consumers purchasing behaviour. This means that the alternative hypothesis that states that celebrity endorsement has impact on the purchase decisions of urban, suburban and rural areas residents is accepted.

Hypothesis 2

H_1: Residents avoidance of a product is more significantly influenced by celebrity endorsements.

A functional equation can be stated explicitly as follows:

$$Ypd = a0 + a1Tab + a2Tnb + a3Tfc + U \ldots \quad (2)$$

where:

1 = Respondents avoiding buying a product because of the celebrity who endorsed it
2 = Respondents not buying some products because they do not know the celebrity endorsing it
3 = Respondents not buying a product if they are not familiar with the celebrity endorsing it
U = Error term representing other factors not included in the model

Running the Correlation Test (Table 12).

Positive and statistically significant relationships exist between respondents buying a product and the celebrity who endorsed it. This is highest among suburban respondents (.629) and least with the rural dwellers (.424). Respondents from the urban areas (.580) follow in a similar fashion. This means that

Table 12. Correlation coefficients between celebrity endorsements and respondents purchase decisions

DECISION	LOCATION	1	2	3
1	Urban	1		
	Suburban	1		
	Rural	.1		
2	Urban	580**	1	
	Suburban	.629**	.1*	
	Rural	.424**	1	
3	Urban	474**	.511**	1
	Suburban	.451**	. .530**	1
	Rural	.355**	.392**	1

**Correlation is significant at the 0.01 level (2-tailed)

respondents do not avoid buying products because of the celebrity who endorsed it. Will respondents not buy products because they do not know the celebrity that endorsed it? The correlates provide answers. Respondents from the urban (.474), suburban (.451) and rural areas (.355) say they will buy the products whether or not they know the celebrities endorsing them. They buy whether the celebrity is known or unknown to them. Respondents from the urban (.511), suburban (.530) and rural areas (.392) say that they will still buy the products whether or not they are familiar with the celebrity endorsing them. In other words, respondents will not waver in buying a product because of the celebrity who endorsed it; will still buy products whether or not they know the celebrity endorsing them; and even if the endorsing celebrity is unfamiliar to them.

In accepting Hypothesis 2, it can be seen that there are positive and significant correlations among all the variables that tested respondents purchasing products because of celebrity endorsements. Correlation values of .629. .580, .530 and others suggest that respondents buy products because of celebrity advertising even though they may not personally know these personalities. In other words, there is a clear and direct relationship between these celebrity advertisements and consumers purchasing behaviour. This confirms the findings of Jain and Roy (2016) that meanings are transferred to a brand through endorsement. It has been clearly established that irrespective of the location, the respondents are more significantly influenced by celebrity endorsements and will still prefer to buy the products that celebrities have endorsed. Drawing from these, the alternative hypothesis that states that residents in urban, suburban and rural areas buy products because of celebrity endorsements is upheld in this study.

DISCUSSION ON FINDINGS

It is interesting to find out that respondents from the three different locations know who a celebrity is and are very aware of advertisements featuring these famous people. However, those in the cities and their adjoining suburbs seem to know more of these renowned people and the advertisements where they feature than those in the rural areas. Possibly, the city dwellers recognize these talented people more than the rural residents because they are more exposed to the media, are media literate and may have even met some of these celebrities at different events. However, slightly more respondents from the country sides intentionally pay attention to advertisements where these successful people feature. This may possibly be explained by the fact that the celebrities have become household names and these respondents based in the rural areas see them as people to be envied, looked up to or to be imitated. Their stories of success may have challenged them to dare to believe and to persevere that their life situations can change dramatically. The city dwellers and their peripheral neighbours are already more familiar with the stars and may therefore not go out of their way to pay more attention to advertisements featuring them.

All the respondents regardless of their locations know the different classes of celebrities. These include the big names in the sports, movie and music industry. They also categorize the famous people in religion, politics and writing. Nonetheless, movie personalities are most popular with the suburban and rural dwellers than they are with the cosmopolitan residents. The rural dwellers may have more time to watch entertaining films than those in the urban settings who may be slaves to their jobs: rising up very early in the mornings to go to their different work places and returning late in the nights. But the respondents in the urban and suburban places know more of musical celebrities than their counterparts in the rural areas. They attend music festivals. It is also not uncommon for them to listen to music as they drive or commute to work. Music may have become a stress reliever for them. Urban residents also know more celebrity sportsmen and religious leaders. The rural respondents know more about political celebrities than those in the urban and semi-urban areas.

Interestingly, while respondents from the rural areas acknowledge knowing celebrities, yet they have not allowed these talented peoples' endorsement of products to influence their purchase behaviours. They do not buy products because celebrities have endorsed them. In fact, celebrity endorsements have not made appreciable impact on their purchase decisions to buy products. It may be that as much as they appreciate these celebrities, their economic conditions have not allowed them to buy the products the glamourous celebrities are used as models to advertise. They also do not buy some products even though they do not know or are unfamiliar with the celebrities endorsing them. Therefore, it will not be wise for the advertisers to focus much attention to buyers based in these types of locations.

Respondents from the suburban areas appear to be more influenced than their counterparts in the rural and urban areas in their buying decisions because of celebrity advertisements. They would more readily buy products validated by the stars when compared to the respondents from the urban and rural areas. It is therefore not surprising seeing them disagreeing on the likelihood of their buying a product that is not endorsed by a celebrity to one that is so endorsed. Most of them believe that celebrity endorsements have affirmatively swayed their purchasing the products they have validated. They also mostly disagree with three opinions: that they will not buy a product because of their unfamiliarity with the endorsing celebrity; not buying because they do not know the celebrity endorsing it; and not buying because of the particular endorsing celebrity. Much as it has been established that semi-urban residents are the most excited with celebrities, it is still recognized that they still buy products that these stars did not endorse and even those endorsed by personalities that these respondents are unaccustomed to.

Although most of the respondents from the urban areas agree that they buy products because of celebrity validations, yet quite a large chunk of residents still disagree to so doing. It is possible that as much as they admire these famous people, their economic situations have not allowed them to go out of their way to buy all that the celebrities have endorsed. Respondents from the urban areas are exactly like the rural respondents in saying that they would most likely buy a product endorsed by a celebrity than the one that is not. They confirm that celebrity endorsements have positive effect on their purchasing decisions. Neither the unfamiliarity of the endorsing celebrity nor their not knowing him discouraged them from buying the products. They also did not stop buying a product because of not knowing the endorsing celebrity. It can be seen that celebrity advertising impact on urban residents is neither as pronounced as it is with the suburban respondents but not as low as is found among the rural respondents.

CONCLUSION

Celebrities as famous people are courted by advertisers to endorse their products. This study establishes that celebrities influence their followers and admirers into buying the products that they endorse. Especially, it shows that celebrities' influence and fame permeate the three layers of the society: urban, suburban and rural. Residents in these three locations know who celebrities are and consciously pay attention to the products they advertise. They deliberately buy some products because celebrities have endorsed them. Nevertheless, celebrity endorsement seems to be less influential among the residents in the rural areas but more pronounced among those living in suburban and urban areas. In conclusion, celebrity endorsements have positive impact on the purchase decisions of residents irrespective of their location. Advertisers should consciously use celebrities in future advertising campaigns. However, they celebrities should be people that consumers see as carrying positive values that they can relate with. Where they target rural dwellers, product managers should look for faces and names that fit into the culture and lifestyles of these rural residents to achieve more impact.

SUGGESTIONS FOR FURTHER STUDIES

The following are recommended for further investigations in new studies:

- If celebrity advertisements work better than brand power on buyers purchase decisions.
- Identify the specific factors that advertisers consider in picking their brand ambassadors.
- Pin-point the specific variables that make residents in semi-urban areas to be more influenced by celebrity endorsements.
- The specific extent to which a celebrity's endorsement influence consumers' re-buy behavior.

REFERENCES

Abdurrahaman, D. T., Owusu, A., Soladoye, B. A., & Kalimuthu, K. R. (2018). Celebrity-brand endorsement: A study on its impacts on generation y-ers in Nigeria. *Asian Journal of Scientific Research, 11*(3), 415–427. doi:10.3923/ajsr.2018.415.427

Akram, S., Muhammad, N., Raga, M., & Sana, R. (2017). Factors influencing the effectiveness of celebrity endorsement in advertising. *British Journal of Marketing Studies, 5*(1), 1–16.

Aliede, J. E. (2016). Brand identity creation, sustenance and advertising in competitive marketing environment. *Kwararafa Journal of Contemporary Research, 2*(1), 27–45.

Amodu, L. O. (2007). An evaluation of the influence of customer relations on customer attraction to banks: A study of Prudent Bank. *International Journal of Communication*, (7): 390–396.

Amodu, L. O. (2010). Public relations: The art and social science of crisis management. In R. Akinfeleye (Ed.), *Mass communication: A book of readings* (pp. 110–124). Lagos: Department of Mass Communication, University of Lagos.

Apejoye, A. (2013). Influence of celebrity endorsement of advertisement on students' purchase intention. *Journal of Mass Communication and Journalism*, *3*(03). doi:10.4172/2165-7912.1000152

Aririguzoh, S. (2007). Media literacy and the role of English language in Nigeria. *International Journal of Communication*, (6): 144–160.

Aririguzoh, S. (2013). Human integration in globalization: The communication imperative. *Nigerian Journal of Social Sciences*, *9*(2), 118–141.

Atkin, C., & Block, M. (1983). Effectiveness of celebrity endorsers. *Journal of Advertising Research*, *23*, 57–61.

Belch, G. E., & Belch, M. A. (2012). *Advertising and promotion: An integrated marketing communications perspective*. New York: McGraw-Hill/Irwin.

Choi, S. M., & Rifon, N. J. (2007). Who is the celebrity in advertising? *Journal of Popular Culture*, *40*(2), 304–323. doi:10.1111/j.1540-5931.2007.00380.x

Driessens, O. (2013). The celebritization of society and culture: Understanding the structural dynamics of celebrity culture. *International Journal of Cultural Studies*, *16*(6), 641–657. doi:10.1177/1367877912459140

Dumbili, E. W. (2017). The influence of alcohol industry-sponsored "Gulder Ultimate Search" reality television series on the drinking behaviors of Nigerian youths. *Journal of Substance Use*, *22*(2), 159–167. doi:10.3109/14659891.2016.1166271

Dzisah, W. E., & Ocloo, C. E. (2013). Celebrity endorsement and consumer buying behaviour; enhancing the promotion function of marketing in the central business area of Accra, Ghana. *European Journal of Business and Management*, *5*(25), 197–208.

Erdogan, B. Z. (1999). Celebrity endorsement: A literature review. *Journal of Marketing Management*, *15*(4), 291–314. doi:10.1362/026725799784870379

Erdogan, B. Z., Baker, M. J., & Tagg, S. (2001). Selecting celebrity endorsers: The practitioner's perspective. *Journal of Advertising Research*, *41*(3), 39–48. doi:10.2501/JAR-41-3-39-48

Fleck, N., Korchia, M., & Roy, I. L. (2012). Celebrities in advertising: Looking for congruence or likability? *Psychology and Marketing*, *29*(9), 651–662. doi:10.1002/mar.20551

Heckler, S., & Childers, T. L. (1992). The role of expectancy and relevancy in memory for verbal and visual information: What is incongruency? *The Journal of Consumer Research*, *18*(4), 475–492. doi:10.1086/209275

Itiri, N. (2015). From entertainment to politics: Nigerian celebrities and the 2015 general elections. *VUNA Journal of History and International Relations*, *2*(2), 249–257.

Jain, V., & Roy, S. (2016). Understanding meaning transfer in celebrity endorsements: A qualitative exploration. *Qualitative Market Research*, *19*(3), 266–286. doi:10.1108/QMR-03-2015-0020

Kambitsis, C., Harahousou, Y., Theodorakis, N., & Chatzibeis, G. (2002). Sports advertising in print media: The case of 2000 Olympic Games. *Corporate Communications*, *7*(3), 155–161. doi:10.1108/13563280210436763

Kamins, M. A., & Gupta, K. (1994). Congruence between spokesperson and product type: A matchup hypothesis perspective. *Psychology and Marketing*, *11*(6), 569–586. doi:10.1002/mar.4220110605

Keller, K. L. (1993). Conceptualizing, measuring, and managing customer based: Brand equity. *Journal of Marketing*, *57*(1), 1–22. doi:10.2307/1252054

Khatri, P. (2006). Celebrity endorsement: A strategic promotion perspective. *Indian Media Studies Journal.*, *1*(1), 25–37.

Lynch, J. L., & Schuler, D. (1984). The matchup effect of spokesperson and product congruency: A schema theory interpretation. *Psychology and Marketing*, *11*(5), 417–445. doi:10.1002/mar.4220110502

Maclnnis, D. J., Moorman, C., & Jaworski, B. K. (1991). Enhancing and measuring consumers' motivation, opportunity, and ability to process brand information from ads. *Journal of Marketing*, *55*(4), 32–53. doi:10.2307/1251955

McCracken, G. (1989). Who is the celebrity endorser? Cultural foundations of the endorsement process. *The Journal of Consumer Research*, *16*(3), 310–321. doi:10.1086/209217

Menon, M. K., & Louis, E. B. (2001). *Celebrity advertising: An assessment of its relative effectiveness.* Retrieved from http://condor.depaul.edu/dweinste/celeb/celeb_adverts.html

Mick, D. G., & Buhl, M. C. (1992). A Meaning-based model of advertising experiences. *The Journal of Consumer Research*, *19*(3), 317–338. doi:10.1086/209305

Misra, S., & Beatty, S. E. (1990). Celebrity spokesperson and brand congruence. An assessment of recall and affect. *Journal of Business Research*, *21*(2), 159–173. doi:10.1016/0148-2963(90)90050-N

Mogaji, E. (2016). *Emotional appeals in UK banks' print advertisement* (Unpublished doctoral dissertation). University of Bedfordshire, Luton, UK.

Mogaji, E., Badejo, A., & Charles, S. (2018). Sportswomen as brand ambassadors: Prospect, challenges. *Project Report.* University of Greenwich. Retrieved from http://gala.gre.ac.uk/id/eprint/20955

Nyarko, I. K., Asimah, V., Agbemava, E., & Tsetse, E.K. (2015). The influence of celebrity endorsement on the buying behaviour of the Ghanaian youth: A study of *fan milk* Ghana ads. *International Journal of Business and Management Review, 3*(10), 83-98.

Odiboh, O., Olonode, A., Adesina, E., & Yartey, D. (2018). *Influence of e-communication and digital culture on Nigeria's indigenous socio-cultural systems: A focus on Abeokuta and Ota, Nigeria.* Paper presented at the fourth International *Conference* on Information Management (ICIM), London, UK.

Odiboh, O. O. (2002). *Integrated marketing communication.* Lagos: APCON.

Ohanian, R. (1990). Construction and validation of a scale to measure celebrity endorsers' perceived expertise, trustworthiness, and attractiveness. *Journal of Advertising*, *19*(3), 9–52. doi:10.1080/00913367.1990.10673191

Okorie, N., & Agbaleke, D. (2017). Celebrity endorsement influence on brand credibility: A critical review of previous studies. *Online Journal of Communication and Media Technologies.*, *7*(1), 15–20.

Omenugha, K. A., Uzuegbunam, C. E., & Ndolo, I. S. (2016). Celebrity culture, media and the Nigerian youth: Negotiating cultural identities in a globalised world. *Critical Arts*, *30*(2), 200–216. doi:10.1080/02560046.2016.1187791

Oyeniyi, O. (2014). Celebrity endorsements and product performance: A study of Nigerian consumer markets. *Management & Marketing Journal*, *15*(1), 41–51.

Pil, H. S., & Shavitt, S. (1994). Persuasion and culture: Advertising appeals in individualistic and collectivistic societies. *Journal of Experimental Social Psychology*, *30*(4), 326–350. doi:10.1006/jesp.1994.1016

Piyush, M. K. J. (2012). Celebrity endorsements and brand building. *Journal of Advertising*, 1-88. Retrieved from https://openpolicyontario.pbworks.com/f/Celebrity-Endorsements.Report1+%282%29.pdf

Pringle, H. (2015). *Stars in your ads: What evidence is there that celebrity sells*. Academic Press.

Ranjbarian, B., Shekarchizade, Z., & Momeni, Z. (2010). Celebrity endorser influence on attitude toward advertisements and brands. *European Journal of Soil Science*, *13*(3), 399–407.

Roozen, I., & Claeys, C. (2010). The relative effectiveness of celebrity endorsement for print advertisement. *Review of Business and Economic Literature*, *55*(1), 76–89.

Shimp, C. P. (1993). Observation and theory in behavior analysis. *Journal of the Experimental Analysis of Behavior*, *60*(2), 481–484. doi:10.1901/jeab.1993.60-481 PMID:16812715

Silvera, D. H., & Benedikte, A. (2004). Factors predicting the effectiveness of celebrity endorsement advertisements. *European Journal of Marketing*, *38*(11/12), 1509–1526. doi:10.1108/03090560410560218

Smith, J. A. (Ed.). (2007). *Qualitative Psychology: A Practical Guide to Research Methods* (2nd ed.). London: Sage Publications Ltd.

Sneha, K. (2012). *Does celebrity endorsements have an impact or influence the purchase intention or buying behaviour of the youth in India* (Unpublished master's thesis). University of Nottingham, Nottingham, UK.

Solomon, M. R. (1996). *Consumer Behavior: Buying, Having, and Being*. Prentice-Hall.

Uzuegbunam, C. E. (2017). Between media celebrities and the youth: Exploring the impact of emerging celebrity culture on the lifestyle of young Nigerians. *Mgbakoigba: Journal of African Studies*, *6*(2), 130–141.

Williamson, J. (1978). *Decoding advertisements: Ideology and meaning in advertising* (Vol. 13). London: Marion Boyars.

Zinkhan, G. M., & Hong, J. W. (1991). Self Concept and Advertising Effectiveness: A Conceptual Model of Congruency Conspicuousness, and Response Mode. In R. H. Holman & M. R. Solomon (Eds.), *Advances in Consumer Research* (Vol. 18, pp. 348–354). Provo, UT: Association for Consumer Research.

Chapter 9
Social Class and Consumer Behavior in Sub-Saharan Africa:
Implications for Cross-Cultural Marketing

Ayodele Oniku
University of Lagos, Nigeria

ABSTRACT

The development around social class evolvement in sub-Saharan African market dated back to pre-colonial era when traditional African institution operated on the basis of royalty, land ownership, subjugation of weak tribe, and superiority of strong and powerful tribes. The advent of slavery and migration of white settlers and traders (slaves and goods) further entrenched social class structure in the system. The advent of colonial rule greatly impacted social class system whereby new strata were created based on the new administrative system that colonial system introduced into sub-Saharan Africa. Largely, acquisition of formal education, salary and wage-collection jobs, business opportunities, Western religion, clothing styles, and new roles to the traditional chiefs opened doors for new social class strata. Social class has witnessed development and improvement that has further improved marketing system and consumer understanding in the society through design of products and services for the market.

INTRODUCTION

Social class measurement in behavioural marketing represents a fusion of socio-economic developments with different behaviours exhibited by consumers in market which invariably affect the buying decisions. In other words, social class is a function of economic power, lifestyles and societal values possesses by individual that influences his/her position in the social classification in terms of what he buys, uses or types of association he/she belongs to in the larger society. By and large, the social classification or level relies largely on the socio-economic power an individual controls and the level of societal values and prestige attached to each stratum of the social class.

In the early work of Myers, Stanton and Haug (1971), "social class is based upon the idea that a society …….constructs some ideal or optimum which is most highly regarded by members of the society

DOI: 10.4018/978-1-5225-7906-9.ch009

.... The more closely individuals or group conform with the ideal, the more they are respected and admired by others and the higher their position in the hierarchy of social levels. Higher societal levels or strata are said to carry more status in society than lower status; they are of higher social class" (Myers & Reynolds, 1967, p. 206). Thus, the basic operating powers that social class identification hinge on is socio-economic conformity, societal appraisal of hierarchy level and respect and status attributed to each hierarchy level and stratum. It further shows that social class mobility exists in that individual can aspire to move across the ladder rung as he/she increases the economic power he possesses which thrust certain respect and prestige on him. Thus, every society can be viewed in terms of social class because it defines the classification of skills, achievement, wealth, association, and other qualifications that set apart people within a system (Berkman, Lindquist & Sirgy, 1997).

In business and, largely marketing, social class is regarded as a basis to identify different consumers in market, and hence polarisation of market into different segments so that right products will be made available to the right consumers. American Marketing Association describes "social class as a national status hierarchy by which groups and individuals are distinguished in terms of esteem and prestige" (Peter & Olson, 1999, p. 317). The hierarchies for marketing decision recognition are entrenched in the following classes – upper, middle, working and lower class (Peter & Olson, 1999); the privileged/skill chooser, the semi-skilled chooser and disconnected chooser (Robenstine, 2001); the Peninsula People approach – upper class, upper-middle class, lower-middle class, upper-lower class and lower-lower class (Berkman *et al*, 1997).

Besides being a basis for market segmentation, social class levels further provide opportunities for marketing organisation in effective application of pricing, product, distribution and promotion decisions to meet the different requirements and needs of each stratum of social class. For instance, different good and services are available to meet social status needs, and products are equally available to propel or establish individual in desired social class status. Also, social class projects different lifestyles that individual or consumers in a society can aspire to experiment or exhibit; hence products and other marketing policies and strategies like promotion are tuned to help consumers identify and actualise chosen or aspired lifestyles. Social class reveals why consumer buys a particular goods or service at a particular time and what will be needed to fulfil the purpose. For instance, the yearning for a specific clothing style is a function of desired purpose or needs.

Importantly, social class is not really measured on individual economic power neither on consumption decisions but rather it is determined on the platform of household income or a family resources or economic power. The basis in turn shapes, largely, the type, volume and quality of consumption that can be attained e.g. education, leisure, accommodation, etc. This is further reflected in the fact that members of a household or family share the same characteristics which distinguish them from another families or households. So the level of income commands by a particular household will go a long way in determining the social class it belongs; and further reflected in the family members' lifestyle. Myers *et al.*, (1971) corroborate that expenditure on commodity groups like food; shelter and education really vary among different occupational groups which remains one of the potentials ways of determining social class. Peter and Olson (1999) further stress that social class of a family or household is affected by variables like social skills, status aspiration, community participation, family history, social acceptance; source of income, possessions, level of influence and association with others (Berkman *et al.*, 1997).

SOCIAL CLASS AND SUB SAHARAN AFRICA: PRE COLONIAL RULE AND COLONIAL ERA

Prior to colonialism and independence of many sub-Sahara African countries, the practice of social class was limited to ethnic and tribal belongingness. Africans displayed social class based on ethnic and tribal affiliation which proved superiority over each other (Kilson, 1958), thus individuals proved social class by the superiority attained by the tribe, ethnic or community they belong which conquered others through war. Consequently, exploits in terms of economic gains, enslavement and occupation of territories that came from war conquest trust superiority on tribes, ethnic groups and communities. Equally, male accepted dominance in the social structure naturally placed men in upper echelon of the social ladder while women – a wife leaned on the husband's social status and daughter leaned on the father's status to establish her social class (Little, 1946; Orock, 2007).

Furthermore, within the sub-Sahara African tribal or ethnic system, there were positions that distinguished certain people within the society and placed them on the upper rung of the social class ladder – royalty, chieftaincy title and family heritage. Thus, social class indicators were largely exhibited in terms size of cultivated farmland, number of slaves acquired, royalty status, chieftaincy status, number of wives acquired, size of livestock, etc. (Kilson, 1958; Little, 1953).

However, new identity for social structure and different definition of social class emerged among Africans in sub-Saharan region with advent of colonial government. The arrival of the Europeans and the different lifestyles, culture, consumption and behavioural patterns brought a change to Africans' orientations. The new life style among Africans has been variously tagged as new 'social categories' (Balaadier, 1954/55); 'imported oligarchy' (Jennings, 1956) because of the restructure in the social system alongside with new lifestyle that followed suit. In other words, the emergence of new social classifications led to permanent change in the face of social class structure in the traditional African society and it invariably birthed evolvement of new order in socio-economic classification – the people and the measurements.

Kilson (1958) accounts that colonial system used three potent tools that engineered new social classifications – *lingua franca,* education and western culture. The introduction of new languages in terms of English, French and Portuguese brings, firstly, an opportunity for group of Africans who learned the new language to communicate among themselves and the outside world which hitherto wasn't possible. Secondly, it provided basis for new political and social group. By and large, the new language brought about association with Europeans which elicited new opportunities in terms of labour-paying job and business connections with Europeans traders and Syrians traders across sub-Sahara African protectorates. Resultantly, ability to speak European language became a licence to attain a new social class in terms of opportunities that came with it, in Sierra-Leone and other West African countries, ability to speak English became a social condition far above cultural characteristic (Little, 1948). So many peasant Africans seized the opportunities to transform their lifestyles from subsistent farming to wage-paying job, mobility of labour to new cities, access to Europeans lifestyle (which they found more superior to African's) and dressing patterns that involuntarily came along with colonial service-offered jobs (Little, 1948, 1953).

According to a UN Report "among the factors that have operated to produce the different levels of social existence in contemporary West Africa, perhaps the most fundamental one has been the rise of a money and an exchange economy" (Kilson, 1958, p. 372). According to statistics, as of 1954 there were about 300,000 wage earners in Nigeria out of population of 31 million and Ghana (Gold coast) had 648,825 out of population of 4.1 million (Kilson, 1958).

Secondly, education was another tool that spurred change in the hitherto subsistent economy that permeated social classification and social class structure in different European colonies across sub-Saharan Africa. Acquisition of European/western education came with opportunity of belongingness or membership to a new society or class within the African system. People with education are evaluated as being superior than other members of the society, also, the ability to read newspaper and other books distinguished them from the larger illiterate members of the society who in turn regarded him as a 'social hybrid' (Little, 1948). It is noteworthy to understand that attainment of western education directly contributed to economic power of the person which on the larger scale elevated his socio-economic status.

On the third aspect, the combination of *lingua franca* and western/European education automatically behoved on persons the practice of western culture to fully attain and exhibit new symbol of social class. The symbols of the new social classification were firstly exhibited in practice of total departure from basic African life style; the newly educated Africans embraced western culture in all categories of education qualification and by levels that their incomes in wage-labour could provide. For instance, new life style were found in dressing styles, religion, leisure-time, games and club affiliations, and marital status. Also, the house furniture, enamel, drinking and style entertainment, religion affiliation, etc. were part of the symbols that distinguished Africans for their newly-found social class membership. Little (1948) reports that one of the hallmarks of new social status and classification is departure from consumption of white palm wine for European gin and whisky. Apparently, other illiterate members of the society held the educated people in high esteem and respect because of the newly-displayed lifestyle that were perceived superior to African lifestyle. The emergence of new social classes provided market for many imported items that found their ways into the hands of emerging African middle and working classes.

Nonetheless, another social classification and rung of new social structure was created among the enterprising farmers in the region. Largely, they are not literate but based on the fact that many of the farmers could equally afford a new life style in terms of food consumption, drinking and entertainment, furniture in homes, etc. The underpinning factor was that most of the African cash crops found lucrative markets in the international trading system which led to increase in the income of farmers. Equally, some other groups of people in agriculture-related activities e.g. produce buyers, experienced increase in their income as a result of the boom in cash crops. Thus, the emergence of another set of middle class among the illiterates but enterprising and wealthy indigenous Africans expanded the middle income class among the Africans. The distinct factor about the enterprising and rich farmers was they equally embraced western culture that changed their life style, but mostly in the areas of style of house construction, furnishing and insistence on western education for their children. Lloyds (1953) and Busia (1950) stress that cocoa farmers could own estate that worth as much as £50,000 and that out of estimated national income of Ghana (Gold coast) of £150 million over £50 million was attribute to cocoa farming . Other cash crops that elevated many illiterates African farmers to middle class strata were palm oil, palm kernel, ground nuts, etc.

Consequently, societal values and cultural beliefs experienced changes that were influenced by the western values and orientations that created new social class structure and classifications in sub-Sahara African system.

The advent of new socio-economic classifications among Africans in the region led to groupings of people into or evolvement of classes based on the level of education attainment or qualifications; position in the colonial administrative appointments; types of professions or specialisations; gender; spousal social status; etc. The above factors work in a way that each basis bequeaths certain status to people within the society, for instance, lawyers, teachers and medical doctors were seen and appraised more superior to native police; a cocoa farmer with more wealth and good association with European traders were seen more superior to local chiefs and any individual with traditional royal title but with no such association. In other words, society's perceptions and new value systems determine the ranking and classification of individual social status among the emerging middle class Africans.

According to Little (1948) members of the European community living within protectorates are accorded with superior lifestyles because they were all engaged in administrative and supervisory jobs, and importantly, they had education qualifications ranging from secondary education to a university degree. The position in jobs and educational qualifications automatically bequeathed to them higher salary and better lifestyle than the African workers in the same colonial administrative system. For instance, average European worker received a £400 or more per annum (Little, 1948).

The African middle class is further divided into two groups – the lower class and the upper class (Little, 1955). The lower class represents largely the African peasant and villagers who live subsistent on earnings from farming or small scale economic engagements. The group is characterised by dwelling in the villages with no urban experience. The group also covers "wage-labouring class" that their earning is comparable to peasants who live on subsistent economic engagements (Llyods, 1953).

On the other hand, there is upper class that is comprised of European entrepreneurs, senior colonial officials, District officers, business administrators who are prominently Europeans and Americans that live within the colonial protectorates (Kilson, 1958). In addition, the emerging African elites who are professionals in law field, medical, timber merchants, contractors, money lenders, etc. (Jennings, 1958). Besides educational attainment, according to Forde (1944) many Africans moved into the upper middle class as a result of "western notion of individual initiative and gain" (Kilson, 1958, p. 375). Perham (1931) furthers that among Africans in the elitist upper class are wealthy traders, transport contractors/owners, surveyors, newspapers owners, journalists, Bishops, archdeacons, etc. Many could afford to send their children to England for higher and university education and they build houses comparable to Europeans in terms of values, furnishings and other opulent taste.

SOCIAL CLASS AND CONTEMPORARY SUB-SAHARA AFRICAN NATIONS: POST-COLONIAL RULE

In recent time, the developing economies are undergoing different changes and developments in the market structures, especially in the areas of interaction between economic and technological environments which have entrenched consumer sophistication. For instance, improved income, improved standard of living, advancement in telecommunication system, improved literacy level, *etc.* have further stratified the African society into different social classes that leads to homogenisation of certain products or services to meet different emerging classes' needs. Thus, the new structural changes are not without consumer polarisation across the market. In other words, the implication of the emergence of different groups of consumers with varying needs and wants is found in the grouping of families or households with homogenous needs that differentiate them from another set of households and families. Also, consumer sophistication is witnessed in the new dimensions of demand for leisure and holiday, housing and shelter, automobile, children education, medical services, *etc.* The consumer sophistication further affects the shopping modes in terms of internet shopping (e-commerce), home delivery services, modern super market patronage, *etc.* By and large, the relationship between the emerging new market structures and consumer sophistication is emerging lifestyles among consumers which has become a reflection of new social classes that would influence business decisions.

Sub-Sahara African market is not excluded in the emergence of consumer sophistication, hence entrenchment of different social classes that are being influenced by different lifestyles that permeate market developments in recent time. For instance, family or household buying decisions and demand patterns are largely a function of social class' lifestyle because of the rapid changes and advancement in factors like income, occupation, possession, education, family background, political affinity, etc. Thus, social class and lifestyle cannot be under estimated and disconnected from the emerging demand patterns, and buying decisions.

Additionally, Sub-Sahara African market is experiencing a new dimension in emerging trends, for instance the choice of children education is a function of school geographical location (highbrow or low class residential area); family background; the social class membership of school founder or owner; parents' social class membership; school affiliation; the associated services in terms of student excursions (international or local); *etc*. Also, the choice of private medical services is equally a function of social class and this is further buttressed in the geographical location of certain private medical services in either highbrow or low income group areas to meet the need of the target market. The quality of services and charges are commensurate with the expected lifestyle in the geographical locations. Equally, the geographical location of emerging departmental shops and supermarkets in most sub-Sahara African economies reveals that social class factor influenced the decision on proximity to the target market. Likewise, other services and products like social gatherings, clothes, private estate, private cemetery, *etc.* are gradually experiencing decision strategy that recognises income, family background, education, *etc.* to define social class that form the target market and segmentation decisions.

FAMILY SYSTEM AND SOCIAL CLASS

One of the measures that determine social class status of individuals in any society is the economic power of the family. In the traditional African society, the status of a man in the larger society or community is a function of his family background, either by royal connection, economic wealth from flourishing enterprises or educational background. Family is described distinctively from household as a group of people who are related by blood, marriage and adoption. In other words, household comprises of people who are not biologically related but living together such as college roommates, unmarried couples, occupants of different rooms in the same building, etc. (Peter & Olson, 1999). Therefore the decision making process and purchasing behaviour would be different in a family united by marriage, blood and adoption than it will be found in a household. Family can be a set-up of parents with children, single parents, childless couples and smaller families. The importance of family set-up in behavioural discipline is that it provides a basis of analysis for business organisation on individual consumer's purchase decision and market behaviour.

Family is sub-divided into nuclear and extended systems. Nuclear family is usually made up of minimum of two persons i.e. one or more parents and one or more children living mostly together in a household. The extended family is made up of a nuclear family and additional relatives that are made up of grandparents under a household. In African setting the extended family grows beyond grandparents but with addition of cousins, nephews, uncles, aunts and step brothers living together in a household.

The influence of family on social class system is multi-dimensional in that family system affects individual's expression or exhibition of social class. Firstly, family linkage with social class structure is found in impact of economic power of head of the family, grand parents or family heritage on a member of the family in the community. The effect of this is that members of the family by birth-right assume certain social classification or status in the society. A woman married into such family also by virtue of marriage assumes certain social status and class in the community. The effect on consumption behaviours or patterns is that certain level of conspicuous consumption or affluence is displayed in buying decision. For instance, the house style or location in the community, education of the children, entertainment, dressing, *etc.* reflects affluence and ostentatious consumption. In African system, the influence of the family heritage on social class attained in the society by individual further reflects on marriage and ranking in the society.

Robertson (1984) discusses intergenerational reproduction class advantage in sociology, and the term encapsulates the linkage between family and social class structure in society. Impliedly, Intergenerational reproduction class advantage influences the attainment of certain social status by children through parents' decision to transfer certain wealth to children or facilitation of children entrepreneurial empowerment. It further goes to affect or influence pre-determined marital relationships between children in order to ensure that children marry to a family of certain or approved social class in society. Thus, parental influence becomes leverage for children to quickly and effortlessly attain or achieve certain social connections and business relationship in society. The larger effect on consumption patterns is that *status quo* is maintained within a family which invariably influences the affluent display, conspicuous consumption that portrays the family income, prestige and respect command in society. All these are pointers to social class identification in society.

In African system, special preferences are given to first son or first daughter or eldest brother or junior brother or sister. The privileged position entitles them, by birth right, blood relationship or family appendage, to receive from the wealth of the rich person in the family or share from the estate in death or while alive. Thus, the propensity to move across the ladder of social class can be easily enjoyed by the reason of family linkage which is not necessarily directly by birth. Hout and Rosen (2000) corroborate that many men (fathers) help fund their sons' enterprises and facilitate access to fund to start-up businesses.

The dynamism of extended family in African setting propagates sharing of wealth during lifetime and estate in death among family members beyond the biological children. Thus, many have experienced improved consumption patterns and attain a new social status by virtue of inheritance and influence of cousins, uncles, aunts and step-brother/sister.

Summarily, family system in African setting provides different opportunities to businesses, especially marketing opportunities, when compared to other part of the world. The demand patterns and buying behaviours that come along with different level of family linkages in social class structure is not always limited or inhibited by a nuclear family factor. Extended family system and larger family practice obtainable through polygamy system make demand patterns to be larger than expected. For instance, an influential man with about four (4) wives would display "equality or fairness" in sending all children to elite school locally or to study abroad. Likewise, the demand patterns for items like automobile, clothes, jewellery, *etc.* must reflect fairness and equality among the wives and their children in order to enjoy the existing social class status of the family. Impliedly, marketing approach in a polygamy-prone system like sub-Saharan Africa would definitely be different from what is practicable or advisable in a society where monogamy is the order of the day due to peculiarities of peoples' culture (Kaplan & Lancaster, 2002).

SOCIAL CLASS AND GENDER

The traditional African system allows men domination in the system and the resultant effect of this is that women are relegated to the background in the affairs of home management and society affairs at large. The early works on social class structure in sub-Saharan Africa attested to the fact that men were held superior to women folks (Little, 1948; Kilson, 1958). The implication of this is that it becomes difficult for a woman to aspire or qualify for any social class definition independently without a man providing a prop or as leverage. To a wife, she needs to lean on the husband social status classification to define her social class and for a daughter, she equally needs the father or her family background to define her social class or be ranked on any social class ladder in society.

The recent study in Cameroon, a central African nation, shows that western education has only changed the status quo of only few women who have access to formal education in the society from the traditional perception of women (Orock, 2007). The fact is that most of these women came from family where the fathers belong to a middle class or wealthy family, or the husband facilitated the women education. In other words, the government gender equality programme has only, largely, helped women who already have acquired formal education and are in formal employment while women in the rural areas and other who have no access to formal education still remains under the cloak of men hegemony. Orock (2007, p. 95) sums that “lack of attention paid to gender equality outside the sphere of ‘upper class’ Cameroonian women”, and it implies that aspiration of women to attain any upper level of social class ladder’s rung will be hindered and restricted without formal education or parental or husband’s leverage.

Impliedly, African society may not provide even playing ground for men and women to aspire to become a respectful and socially empowered person in the system. The social system tilts more opportunity towards men to do better than women in a typical sub-Sahara African system than women. Thus, men hegemony is witnessed in economic empowerment and advantaged social structure that might qualify them for higher level on social status classification, while women aspiration in society is dependent on men - husbands or fathers. The fewer the men who are at the upper level of the social class of society, the fewer the women and the larger the number of men on the upper level of social class ladder, the fewer the women relatively to their population African in society. For instance, many sub-Sahara African nations like Nigeria is witnessing Women pressure groups lobbying government to make it a constitutional mandate that a certain percentage of government political appointments be given to qualify women in society.

The implication of this to marketing strategies and policies is that organisations need to concentrate on men more when it comes to products and services that symbolise social classification status. Also, income and other variables being used to determine social class status of men may largely form the yardsticks to determine women disposable income or demand of products that satisfy or symbolise women social status in society. Studies have corroborated that purchase decision of many fulltime housewives and women not in working class is a function of households’ disposable incomes (Fry & Siller, 1970; McFadden, Luben & Khaw, 2009). Inevitably, the demand for product and service like education and people to fill certain professions in the society will be experience better performance in many sub-Sahara African markets when more men are the target market than women. Presently, school enrolment in certain part of African nations has larger population among male than females because of societal belief of men superiority/hegemony (Muhammed, 1977; Ayobade, 2012). The findings may not be unconnected to domination of men in certain highly rated professions like law, medicine, academic, engineering, *etc.* that many African societies embrace as symbol of upper social class attainment.

SOCIAL CLASS AND REFERENCE GROUP

Reference group is regarded as the group of people "whose perspective an individual assumes in forming values, beliefs, attitudes, opinions and overt behaviours" (Berkman *et al.*, 1996, p. 507). Reference groups operates in basic two ways to influence consumer buying decisions and purchase patterns – setting certain levels of aspirations and defining goods and services to satisfy such aspirations.

In colonial sub-Sahara African setting, the Europeans, Americans and other foreigners that dwelled across the colonies overtly presented their lifestyles and consumption patterns as a reference points for majority of Africans. Inevitably, the buying decision, consumption patterns in goods and services that spread across housing style/construction, entertainment, foods, dressing, enamel, music, *etc.* become yardsticks to determine social class structure among larger African citizens. In other words, despite the fact that many of the colonial administrators belonged to working class and middle class in their original countries, the Africans in the protectorate perceived the life styles, consumption patterns and buying decisions as superior styles over indigenous and traditional African system of living. Consequently, the only yardsticks to determine superiority among themselves was the ability and capacity to live like European, hence, European food, clothes, furniture, entertainment, *etc.* became social class structure definition.

According to Little (1948), Sierra Leoneans ranked the society into different reference groups that represented levels of social class ladder. Little stressed that the ranking in the protectorate followed suit: firstly, the Europeans community or groups (the white colonial administrators and traders); the Creole (they attended secondary education and dominated higher grades of government clerical staff; they wore European clothes and ate European foods. In fact they were mostly children of slaves from the USA and of Yoruba origin from Nigeria); followed by the literate native class (African who had been to school or who can speak English, succinctly, less educated and less wealthy Creole); followed by Literate class who had clerical job outside the colonial administrative system but with Syrians traders, and economic engagements like tailors, mechanics, and non-clerical staff of government departments; and lastly the illiterates in the society with no education and no link with modern lifestyles. Importantly, each group was further clearly differentiated by religious grouping, marital lifestyle and occupation.

Consequently, the groupings while representing reference groups in the economy, it equally leads to social class system that defined socio class structure in the system. The social orientations, values and beliefs of each reference group coupled with the consumption patterns and buying behaviours created different market for goods and services, or segmentation bases for products to be offered to different classes.

The influence of the fusion of social class and reference groups still persists in contemporary African system and it highly influences market behaviours of consumers' demand and producers' offerings alike in market. Children education, patronage of private health service and shopping in certain outlets reflect the fusion of reference groupings and social class among the consumers. Religious affiliations or denominations have brought many people together to seek common goods and services to satisfy their needs and collective interest of the groups e.g. the demand for education of children is witnessing the interplay of social class and reference group to determine products and market. For instance, many markets in sub-Sahara African society are witnessing the emergence of ownership of secondary school and universities being stratified on religious factor and the teaching standards or styles fully recognise the tenets and doctrines of each faith. Besides, the religious factor the social class factor comes into play in terms of amount of the school fees and quality of education offered. Parents not only look for educational centre that support their faith for children, they equally search for school fees affordability. The marketing practice is witnessed in selected private health centres and hotel services.

Also, it is noteworthy to understand that the communal-practice factor in African system permits a social class status of a member of the family to rub-off on the other members affiliated to the family. Mostly, the social class status of head of family undoubtedly has direct relationship with consumption pattern and life styles of the whole household. Typically, women married to a family with upper social class status in a society ultimately enjoy the new status in society. Equally, friendship and companionship with a member of family that commands a higher/upper social status in society to a large extent affects the consumption patterns and market behaviours of the companions because many capitalises on the association to improve on their social status and wellbeing – financial and social. African system allows communal system whereby close relationship, friendship and association can pave way to improve on wellbeing and finances which ultimately affect social class status. This further goes to determine market segmentation based on impacts and influence of social class status on reference grouping in society.

SOCIAL CLASS AND EDUCATION

The impact of education on socio-economic and socio-cultural development of sub-Sahara African countries goes beyond providing clerical staff for the colonial administrative system and consumer acculturation process it brought. In fact, education leads to emergence of polarisation of the society in terms of class system that became another means for indigenous Africans to become relevant in a society.

Education creates a socio-economic system that takes away Africans from subsistent peasant farming and created another means of livelihood via colonial administrative system whereby many Africans improved their living conditions. Importantly, lifestyles are affected, hence demand patterns and buying decisions attains new orders.

According to Berkman *et al.* (1996), there are five important keys that contribute to lifestyle – occupation, source of income, possessions, association with others and level of influence. Coincidentally, western education system introduced into the African community opens door for the attainment of the five indicators of life style.

Firstly, education provides a way to occupational mobility whereby people who had opportunity to get western education saw it as a key to get a better job than what ubiquitous peasant farming offered (Little, 1948; Little, 1955). In reality, the perception of African about education goes beyond enlightenment but also as a tool to bring a better food on the table, so many seek western education to change social class status; hence to improve the life style and living conditions. In contemporary sub-Saharan African the roles of education still majorly remains as a tool to get a labour-wage job that comes with good income that can sustain a particular desired lifestyle.

Education equally offers opportunity to improve possessions. Early studies on social class and African society reveal that as many numbers of Africans who got early education experienced improvement in their income because of the job that came along with possession of western education (Kilson, 1958; Lloyd, 1953). Importantly, one of the ways that early educated in Africans used to distinguish themselves among the larger populations was the acquisition of possessions that improved income in labour-wage jobs afforded them – house, clothes, bicycles, cars, *etc.* These items contributed to creation of new social class structure within the African settings. The trends remain in contemporary African society in that the upper class and the middle class of the society are largely dominated by educated people in the society either by virtue of the positions in the office, the types of occupation or entrepreneurial activities.

One of the significant features of social class structure in the system is that people of like mind, purpose and aspirations come under one umbrella to pursue common goals. One of the legacies left behind by the colonial government is western education that created educated elite of different levels with a unique way of attending to entertainment; recreational activities; and leisure. The important fact is that income is not the major determinant but the aspiration and common ground that social class provides for people of the same pursuit and ambition. Therefore, group of people come together as one under different names or clubs/associations and it invariably affects taste, demand patterns and buying behaviours in market.

Social class defines lifestyle based on the source of income among people in a society, and this has remained a veritable way to determine social class structure in society. The source of income is different from the level of income in the sense that level of income may not necessarily leads to attainment of a particular social class but a definite source of income may entitle individual to belong to a particular level of social class structure. People who share the same source of income mostly display the same of level of consumption patterns and lifestyles, and this is exemplified in sub-Sahara African system among the civil servants, wealthy business man, journalists, *etc.* The colonial era saw the rising of different social classes based on the sources of income of the people and how it affected their consumption pattern and buying decision. Lloyd (1953) accounts that wealthy farmers in the colonial African system uniformly spent part of their riches to send their children abroad to get higher and university education. This represents a consumption pattern and buying behaviour among people who share a particular source of income. In recent time, one of the symbols of wealthy business men and government contractors in Nigeria is the possession of private jet which represents a consumption pattern and buying behaviour.

Social class determines the level of influence people control in society. The connection of level of influence and social class is very significant in the daily activity of the African system because of the paternalistic system prevalence in the region. The political class are not the wealthiest in the society but they control coordinating power and exercise great influence in the affairs of the society and control of resources. At every level of the society, there are people who attain the status or belong to the influencing class either by virtue of traditional heritage, educational attainment, religious clout, political status, *etc.* They use the influence to change, direct or influence the behaviour patterns and attitudes of the people within their jurisdiction on certain issues which may affect business, consumption patterns and market behaviours. One of the importances of many religious and faith leaders is the influence they exercise over their members' buying decisions and consumption patterns in a typical sub-Sahara African country. For instance, the dressing style and fashion taste of many religion/faith members is directly typified after the religious leaders' style and taste.

SOCIAL CLASS AND PRIVATE EDUCATION

Undoubtedly, western education remains a great pivot in attainment of upper class status in a typical sub-Sahara African nation. The influence and effect impact all yardsticks to adjudge individual social status in society. The connection between social class and education in contemporary African society is the influence it has on income, association and occupation, and it spurs many parents to have special interest on their children qualitative education. Robenstine (2001) stress that privileged and skilled parents take time to collect information on schools aside from the ones within their proximity in order to decide on the children education than less-skilled/privileged parents. It is not accidental to see highly educated, wealthy and highly placed parents in the society deciding the choice of education in order to help the children to maintain or easily attain higher status in society. The system has furthered affected the attendance and enrolment of public schools, especially at primary education level which has been relegated to old fashioned and mostly patronise by parents or families on the lower level of the social class ladder who cannot afford private education for the children. Equally, the emergence of private universities and enrolment in many sub-Sahara African nations, where it is available, further deepens social class status differences in society because it is mostly affordable by children from upper class and middle class strata in the society. Likewise, the legacy of sending children abroad to elite school secondary schools and universities is still largely prevalent among children from upper echelon and upper middle class of sub-Sahara African society. All these represent the consumption pattern and buying behaviour that have accentuated upper class and middle class status among certain individuals in African society.

Contrarily, the development in the Europe showed how overtime, the educational system has been used to develop and create sustainable middle class. Pre 19th century, membership into elitist group used to be by nobility, hereditary and birth which automatically allowed handful of the population to have access to elitist position in the society. Likewise, the educational system was geared towards entrenching elitism in the society. According to Brezis (2011) recruitment and other form of economic empowerments in the society were accessed through family connections, patronage, and old-boys network.

Today, in order to entrench social cohesion which is strategic to execution and entrenchment of middle class development and sustainability, elite schools like OXBRIDGE in the UK; Grand Ecoles in France and Ivy Leagues in the USA are opened to individuals without nobility background through meritocracy on the basis of exam success. Invariably, the process has allowed mobility of individuals from poor background to elitist class in the society (Brezis, 2011). Impliedly, the process has secured expansion strategy for middle class in the society which automatically created large market for many consumer durables and more people have crossed into managerial position across industries and managerial enterprises in the systems.

SOCIAL CLASS AND OCCUPATION

Studies have generally shown that occupation is one of the major determinants of social class (Hughes & Perry-Jenkins, 1996; Millios, 2000; Tynes, 2001). The fact about occupation is that it relates the quality of labour to income and disposable income available to individuals. It further goes a long way to determine the consumption patterns of individuals or households. In many models and studies, social class structures are premised on categorisation of types or classes of labour possess by individuals. The "Peninsula People" model concludes that social class structure is based on a five hierarchy of Upper class, Upper-middle class, Lower-middle class, Upper-lower class and Lower-lower class (Berkman *et al.*, 1996). Equally, Gilbert and Kahl, (1993) itemise the social class structure under the classification of Capitalist, Upper-middle, Middle, Working, Working poor and Underclass. The significance of occupational categorisation is the ranking it provides in class membership. The contemporary sub-Saharan African society has clearly reinforced the categorisation in terms of respect and prestige that certain occupation command above other jobs.

Education has to a greater extent, since the colonial days, helps to entrench class membership in terms of the career built by people and the wage-earning labour of individuals. In other words, colonial era has institutionalised a system that occupation or career occupies a strategic means to determine social class structure in the society. The colonial era brought certain professions into limelight to the extent that engagement in such career automatically put individuals on a higher pedestal of social class structure – law, medicine, teaching, engineering, surveying, *etc.* (Kilson, 1956). The relevance of many of the professions was important because of the fact that Africans were needed to take over from colonial masters at attainment of independence, especially in British African colonies or protectorates.

In contemporary African society, certain occupations still remain relevant as qualification for upper and middle class positions in the society while some have lost the position they used to enjoy in colonial days as ticket to higher rung of the social class structure. Anecdotally, occupations like medicine; academic; accounting; banking; nursing; pharmacy; and engineering still enjoy the colonial days' status of higher and middle class status. On the other hand, profession like teaching, civil service, police, *etc.* may have lost the status over time. In many Africa societies they fall into what could be classify as lower middle class or upper lower class.

Interestingly, other professions have emerged or events in the society have made them to be classified as pedestals for middle class status across the region, for instance information technology engineering; military personnel; marketing/sales; *etc.* For instance, military was not previously adjudged to be occupation that could qualify individuals for a middle class status in colonial African society. However, the ascension of military personnel to political power through military *coups de'teat* and national administration have redefined the occupation as a ticket to upper rung of the social class structure in contemporary sub-Sahara African society. Many countries witnessed military coups from late 1960s till early 2000s and military officers handled national government administration and resources control of countries at different stage of development (Utomi, 1985).

By and large, the implication of occupation is the influence on buying behaviours and consumption patterns of people. The taste for foods, clothing, holiday, luxury items, cars, houses, *etc.* are affected in order to create balance between the occupations and class membership within the society. Occupation furthers gives direction to respect, prestige and dignity among individuals in society. Importantly, each class are associated with particular items or goods that symbolise the class membership and class structure. It isn't a mismatch that certain automobile, residential areas, club membership and style of dressing depict class membership.

SOCIAL CLASS AND MARRIAGE

The male hegemony in traditional African society gives room for men domination in nearly all facets of the social life; hence male equally assume the role of bread winner to entrench and affirm the hegemonic position. However, the relationship between social class and marriage goes beyond the traditional placement of men because of the dynamism that has permeated social system overtime as a result of social development like education, exposure and social programme like gender equality (Orock, 2007).

The fact remains that occupational rankings or classes among couples, especially the occupational and economic capacity of woman in a household, are major determinants to understanding the relationship that exist between social class and marriage. Hughes and Perry-Jenkins' (1996) study shows that decision, either joint or individual, on certain issues like good provider, care and nurturance of children, father involvement and financial necessity is a function of wife position as full-time house wife, working class and middle class. The household or family quality of decisions on family issues when there is a combination of middle class husband and wife is different from when it is a combination of working class partners. Likewise, the quality of decisions on family issues when it is a single bread winner (husband) is different from a situation when it is a combination of partners in working class or middle class in society.

Impliedly, the position of a spouse on social class structure will influence the buying decisions and patterns on family issue like child care. For instance, the decision of child education will reflect the position of the family bread winner(s) on the social class ladder. The position of good provider will be different with a single bread winner (husband) from working class partners. According to Rubin (1976) working class women tend to concentrate more on children care and nurturance than non-working who rely more on men's involvement; and middle class women rely on house-help to sort many house chores duties. Furthermore, with middle class and working class women, the responsible roles of husband is shaped differently with more involvement in certain areas of decision while men who is only the bread winners are mostly received as just bread winner while women do all other things Hughes and Perry-Jenkins (1996).

Importantly, the shape of market behaviours and buying decisions tend to change as marital relationship experiences change in who is responsible for family or household income. However, the experience in African society reveals that hegemonic nature of men in the society makes men to largely become the bread winner in many homes; wives and children automatically belongs to the class membership of the bread winner. For instance, if the bread winner belongs to either wealthy class, upper class or middle class the family most of the time exhibit the same class membership in buying decision and consumption patterns and vice versa.

SOCIAL CLASS STRUCTURE AND CLASSIFICATION IN SUB-SAHARAN AFRICA

One of the effects of the colonial system and rule is the change it brought to the face of social class structure and classification in the socio-economic setting of sub-Saharan Africa. The pre-colonial rule was more or less a feudal system where the kings and members of the royal family or founder of a community owns the land which was either put out on rent or slaves were made to cultivate depending on the status and relationship that existed between the ruling family and community dwellers. Thus, the practice of egalitarianism was a rare occurrence in the traditional African society, but the existence of handful upper/wealthy class and larger population of slaves of community dwellers who are forced or hired to cultivate land or leased the land and pay rent to the owners. The middle class is populated by handful of chiefs or selected few who played conspicuous traditional roles in implementing the King's decisions and maintaining law and orders in a community.

The colonial and post-colonial era came with new social structure systems that totally changed the system of socio-economic system and power in African society which led to emergence of many classes based on the opportunities that opened via western systems in terms of education, life style and economic engagements. Thus, many Africans experienced social class mobility through embracement of western life style and adoption of new social institutions that came with colonial system e.g. education; administrative occupation; technical jobs; *etc*.

The social class structures in sub-Saharan Africa may be defined in terms of different theories that guide emergence of social class structure in many societies based on the inter-relationship between economic and sociology. The Adam Smith's classical school theory postulates the existence of three classes in a social class – "the capitalists (owners of the means of production) who gain profit as income;

the workers who gain wages as income; and the land owner who gain rent as income (from the renting of their fields to the capitalist-farmers" (Milios, 2000). Classical theory, to a certain extent, defines the class structure and the economic power relationship between the upper echelon and ordinary man in a society. For instance, the capitalists represent the rich and wealthy in the society who created job opportunities for others to use their labour and earn wages and salary. The capitalists display opulence and conspicuous consumption to reflect their social status. They may further be classified as the government contractors and business men who own the technology, means of production and machineries that facilitate production of goods and services. The capitalist class, by and large, represents the upper class, the wealthy class and the super-rich in the social class structure. Equally, those who inherited large wealth, means of production and children of the wealthy who are already working in the family-owned wealth for continuity and entrenchment of family position in the society are categorised under capitalists.

The workers are the people employed to facilitate smooth operation of production system owned by the capitalists. They are characteristically known as the larger population of the society and the class may be further segmented into different classes depending on occupational status, income status and educational status. In other words, among the working class are classes like middle class, working class, the specialised workers, and the uneducated and unspecialised working class. Many factors are responsible for the polarisation in the group which include the level of education, the level of occupational specialisation or professional qualification and the income associated with specialisation.

The position of land-owners in contemporary African society is largely the government roles. Government is in the position to administer and regulate policies that guide allocation of lands for economic activities. Thus, in many African societies the ownership of land is vested in government and the allocation for economic engagements as well e.g. Nigeria. In actual sense, Nigeria still has cases where individual land-owners exist and they lease or sell to individual capitalists.

On the other hand, another classical theorist added a new scope to the operation of capitalists and the land-owners. According to Mill (1902) it is possible for some societies to have a situation where the social class structure has two classes in that there is merger of the land-owners and the capitalists as one class and the workers as another class in society (Milios, 2000). The operation of the fusion of capitalist and land-owner is a function of tradition and culture that is entrenched and found acceptable in society, and this may reflect old socialist practice. However, the merger of capitalists and land-owners give more power and control of resources in the hands of few in a society who occupy the upper-upper class, upper class and wealthy class in society

The contemporary sub-Sahara African market is not in many factors different from other markets around the world in terms of social class structure and socio-economic system. The operations of contemporary models like 'The Peninsula', Carman's scale, *etc.* have relevant in African market based on the effect of globalisation and advancement in technology which collectively have broken down the physical barriers in international markets. In other words, the symbols of social class and consumption patterns of a social class can be easily known and embraced based on the information from other foreign markets. For instance, the consumption of certain expensive wine, fashion labels, sport cars, *etc.* prevail among the same social class members in African market that can be compared with their counterparts in foreign markets.

However, the influence of culture affects assimilation, application and usage of certain products and services to portray social class differences in many markets, especially Africa. For instance, the way certain automobile products like Mercedes Benz Brands are embraced and used to exhibit upper class and middle class symbols may not find the same social application in Western Europe across the consumers. Likewise, the way foreign occupational training and university degrees are appreciated and evaluated to portray symbols of social class system in many African markets may be different from other international markets.

SOCIAL CLASS: EMERGENCE AND STRATEGIC ROLES OF MIDDLE CLASS

The roles of middle class are strategic to market development and, importantly, it is a driver to economic growth in every society. Succinctly, it is a major player in social class structure in that the position represents a parameter to determine volume of marketing activities in every market, more importantly it is a potential variable for attraction of foreign investment into retailing, manufacturing, services, etc. in international marketing activity. The size, given recognition and conspicuousness of middle class in national economy influence the performance, development and sustainability of major marketing activities like retailing, services, distribution and manufacturing activities. On a larger scale, ADB's (2010) reports stresses that the influence and importance of middle class in every economy is found in the areas of:

- Expanding markets for consumer durables
- Frugal innovation in economy
- Greater accountability in public service
- Economic growth

The implication of this is that the disparity witnessed in the volume of marketing activities across nations and markets is not unconnected the attention and strategic development devoted to the growth of middle class in the economic management.

Middle class represents the midway between the upper class and lower class of the society. The development and growth of middle class is well pronounced in a society where government has sound policy on social cohesion whereby mobility of citizenry across classes is uninhibited. According to ADB's (2010) report it "simply represents a range along the income continuum (a group that lies between the working class and the upper class)". Middle class is identified by the structure and patterns of the consumption style in a market, and this is notably recognised in the demand and spending of the class on education, electronics, automobile, mortgage, etc. Demographically, Easterly (2001) describes the middle class as the second, third, and fourth quintile of the distribution of per capital consumption expenditure (ADB, 2010). Middle class is further defined, based on the income available to consumer or per capital expenditure – absolute measures, of individuals with daily per capital expenditure of $2 - $4 or per capital expenditures of $6 - $10. By global middle class measurement, Kharas (2011, p. 3) reiterates middle class as "between the poor in Portugal/Italy and the rich in Luxembourg: $10 - $100 a day".

The story of middle class development across SSA is fraught with instability due to poor policy development in many countries. The development is primarily connected with the political instability which directly affected economic policy; emphatically the incursion of the military into governance in many SSAs has direct impact on the development of economic policy that would strengthen viable and strong middle class that is needed to stimulate marketing activities development. The movement of consumers across the social ladder and structure, hence economic empowerment of consumers is needed to stimulate sizeable proportion of the population to create viable environment for growth of marketing activities. Unfortunately, the development that characterises many SSA nations is the polarisation of the social class structure into two dominant classes of the rich - "Upper" class and the poor - "lower" class. The political class policy deliberately uses the national resources to empower their cronies and relatives on the larger society development, which invariably truncated the development and growth of middle class across the region.

Globally, the report on SSA on middle class development and the contribution of SSA's middle class to the global development is rated the least. According to statistics the report on SSA remains static while other global markets/regions experience growth between 2009 till date, and future projection into 2030. See Table 1.

From Table 1, the position of SSA is explicitly shown as a region with low and poor development of social cohesion policy; hence, the development of middle class may remain stagnated for over a long time. Two developments are imminent in SSA regarding middle class development; firstly, the region will remain a low level player in term of its contribution to the global middle class purchase volume. Secondly, the role of middle class in stimulating marketing system and activities within the region will remain "snail movement" and this will further worsen attractiveness of the region to international investments in certain areas of consumer durables. Equally the income elasticity associated with middle class demand patterns that influence and stimulate economic development will be elusive in the region. Strategically, market expansion that middle class is notably stimulated in every market may not be possible and it will further discourage business investors that rely on large and sizeable middle class in a market for investment. Ultimately, marketing activities in the areas of retailing, distribution, grocery, etc. will remain underdeveloped in many SSA markets due to poor policy on middle class development and growth.

SOCIAL CLASS AND MARKETING STRATEGIES IN AFRICA

The position and relevance of behavioural marketing practice in integrating social class divisions into society to the ultimate practice of producing goods and service that will ensure consumer satisfaction cannot be over-emphasised. The symbiotic relationship shows that while marketing practice pursues the

Table 1. The global middle class today and future: Size of the middle class, 2009 – 2030 (millions of people and global share)

	2009		2020		2030	
North America	338	18%	333	10%	322	7%
Europe	664	36%	703	22%	680	14%
Central & South America	181	10%	251	8%	313	6%
Asia Pacific	525	28%	1,740	54%	3,228	66%
Sub Saharan Africa	32	2%	57	2%	107	2%
Middle East and North Africa	105	6%	165	5%	234	5%
World	1,845	100%	3,249	100%	4,884	100%

Source: Kharas (2011) Brookings Institutions

goals of identification of appropriate segment and products that average consumer belongs to and products to satisfy them, social class structure provides the platform to achieve and actualise the marketing goals.

Product strategy of organisation demands that goods and services need to recognise the characteristics and peculiarities of the different types of consumers in market based on social class structure. The relevance of social class in product design is:

- To recognise different strata in a system based on disposable income affordability of consumers, and the way the lifestyle affect product features and functions
- To understand the peculiarity of households' consumption patterns that reflect family size, household income, marital style, family orientation, etc. All these factors determine categorisation of family as a social class
- To understand the interplay of societal culture, norms and values on consumption of certain goods and services that symbolise social class system and acceptability
- To entrench ostentatious consumption and conspicuous consumption that certain social classes permitted to portray and exhibit class differences and acceptability
- To determine what features and applications that products need to carry to clearly entrench social class differences among potentials consumers. This is important in both physical goods and services e.g. business class and first class seat on air flight
- To re-orientate society towards embracing and inculcating consumption patterns and buying decisions of certain products that portray social class identification and entrenchment
- To reduce the incidence of poor segmentation and non-identification of segments that promise sales potentials to organisations
- To create and project products that symbolise social class mobility among consumers as social class identification improves among consumers
- To identify life style, consumption patterns and buying behaviours as they change and differentiated across households, families and individuals, etc.

Furthermore, marketing communication strategies influence marketing policy on social class structure and consumer satisfaction. The use of advertising, sales promotion, personal selling and public relations has undertone of social class because the contents, message, picture and medium portrays social class identification in order to get the information to the right consumers.

The correlations between social class structure identification and business' marketing communication strategies are reflected in the objectives of:

- To integrate overt and subtle message of marketing communication that appeals to target market or social class. The contents of communication can be made in the language of a particular social class to appeal to the members in order to influence their buying decisions on products. The message mostly displayed in First class lounge in airports speak the language of the upper class and the many products advertisements on certain international magazines like Times International and The Economist mostly appeal to the upper and upper middle class members.
- To use pictures, symbols and other representations of status and respect to project products and services for consumers' understanding and acceptability. For instance, investment banking which largely focuses on the upper class, the super-rich and wealthy class of the society are mostly

projected through notable individuals in the society or the picture background of the promotion speaks of affluence and power e.g. furniture.

- To use marketing communication tools to portray and project cultural peculiarities of different markets that affect social class behaviour in order to aid and persuade consumer buying decisions. For instance, the same product can be projected to satisfy different social classes in different markets – automobile products.
- Using marketing communication elements to advance organisations' other marketing strategies that directly affect social class behaviour in order to differentiate products and services among consumers and stimulate interest for a product that matches pursued social class.
- Using marketing communication to project values that in a way that appeals and stimulates positive buying behaviour among the different social classes in a society e.g. the use of many consumer sales promotion tools appeal to lower class rung of the society than the upper class.
- Marketing communication equally works on injecting positive attitude towards a product among a class of consumers through the message contents and focus. For instance, advertising is popularly used for informative purpose that influence positive attitude among a class to embrace certain consumption patterns like health, education, *etc.* The marketing information to encourage breast feeding and use of breast pump is largely focussed on working class women in Nigeria. Equally, insurance product that has provision for investment on child education at elite university abroad is focussed on middle and working class segments of the society.

Equally, organisations' pricing policies can be strategically used to satisfy different social classes; hence products are made or featured to meet the needs of social class structure. The fact that income is a potential variable to entrench social class makes it plausible for pricing policy and strategy to become relevant to achieve it. Products like mobile telephone handsets reflects income or affordability of consumers, and anecdotally many consumers in sub-Sahara African market have embraced telephone handset to reflect social class membership in terms of the income available to consumers or disposable income. The system equally affects purchase decisions and buying patterns on acquisition of electronics' gadgets because many sub-Sahara African financial sectors are not deepened yet to embrace credit card system and instalmental purchase system. So many consumers rely on the disposable income to make choice.

Importantly, the application of marketing strategies to impact and influence social class members is a function of understanding the lifestyles, attitudes and values that each social class structure embrace. In other words, the more the organisation understands the disposition of social class to each variable the better for organisation to produce and offer right products to the right segment.

Traditionally, in sub-Sahara African system, the upper class which includes the wealthy class, super-rich and government contractors are known for life styles of opulence, conspicuous consumption, ostentatious life style, political god father, multiple chieftaincy titles, selective philanthropy, polygamy, large family, *etc.* (Ayobade, 2012; Kilson, 1958).

The middle class are identified for lifestyles of highly educated people with university degrees; dual citizenship for children; more of career building and less of entrepreneurship; monogamy with extra marital affairs; high standard for children upbringing; display of modernity in dressing, furnishing and residence apartment; private education for children; moderately religious; *etc.* (Little, 1948).

The working class shares some factors of lifestyle with the middle class but at lower level of affordability, thus, most of the lifestyles displayed by the middle class are repeated at working class but with lowered levels in terms of standard, affordability and accessibility, except with high level of religious beliefs and higher level of discipline and standard for children upbringing. While the middleclass members permit independence and freedom of opinion for children, the working class creates template that children must strictly follow and little room for flexibility and freedom.

The lower class of the society is known for certain lifestyles like illiteracy or low education; less-strict about child education; living in slum; polygamy; broke family; poor health standard; poor and unhealthy consumption patterns; patronage of upper class for free food and money; instrument of the political class for political agenda; highly religious especially traditional beliefs; etc.

WILL SUB-SAHARA AFRICAN YOUTHS REDEFINE OLD-AGE SOCIAL CLASS STRUCTURE?

Social class cohesion in sub-Saharan Africa has its peculiarity in that "the rich remain richer, and the poor remain poorer" because the upper class affiliation is a function of connection with the corridor of power. Most of the acclaimed rich and upper class members in many sub-Saharan Africa are cronies of the government of the day with the singular purpose of benefitting from the 'national cake' on the expense of the remaining citizens who are not well-connected. According to Gana (1985) larger majority of the African ruling classes have no faith in the system and the reason for this is that when they looted the treasury they keep the loots abroad, and mostly Europe and the USA. This is evident in the fact "that 80% to 90% of their accumulated surpluses (mostly loot from the public treasury) are kept not as investable funds in their national economies but in banks in the metropolitan centers" (Gana, 1985, p. 129). The work of Gana (1985) further reveals that the military tribunal trying former civilian politicians in the Rivers State of Nigeria identified a former civilian governor had 1.5 million pounds in his private bank account in London and that the former Congolese (old Zaire) President, Mobuto Sese Sekou was reputed to be the richest head of state in the world, with an estimated $6 million stacked away in Swiss banks in the 80s. Unabatedly, the trend still continues in contemporary Africa.

However, the new trends of increase in demand for university education; self-sponsored foreign degrees among youths; burgeoning enterprises ownership and high participation in SMEs among youths; youths' domination of digital marketing, social media and related ICT businesses; property ownership; youths' domination of entertainment industry; *etc.* signal that there might be a new definition for social class cohesions and the upward mobility may be more rapid and rampant among people from lower class background. In September, 2016 the founder of Facebook – Mark Zuckerberg, visited sub-Saharan Africa and Nigeria was on the list of the countries. Besides the official itinerary of the visit, the inspirational part in the visit was that more youths were re-energised that one could move from lowly level and become international acclaimed personality through sheer hardworking and spirit of innovation. Brown (1992) provides evidence of how tourism development in a local town in Gambia innovatively developed and managed by youths has changed the socio-economic status of many individuals in the system. In the same vein, Suriano (2011) states the Tanzanian experience on how the advent of Hip-Hop and Bongo flavour music pioneered by youths with modern innovation and technologies is affecting social class status of the youths in the industry. According to the author, at the earlier stage it was dominated by youths from rich families but the trend has changed with more youths irrespective of their background becoming musicians. Like Nollywood in Nigeria, many youths have developed career in the industry and the resultant effects is prominently noticed in the upward mobility in social class status and the immediate family in the societies.

The question of whether social class structure in many sub-Saharan Africa will remain two-extreme region is a function of time. The energy and vigour with which many youths have embraced many business and career opportunities to escape poverty line may soon redefine the structure of social class. With millions of US Dollars generated in entertainment industry and I.T- related sector and largely dominated by youths from low-class background, the question whether upper class is generational and exclusive right of political class may find a new answer.

CONCLUSION

The relevance of social class structure remains valid and indispensable to deepening marketing practice and strategies formulation in sub-Sahara African market. Importantly, the evolvement of certain factors and developments in the region have made social class structure and application of relevant models a *sine qua non* to behavioural analysts and business managers in order to enhance market practices and implementation of strategies in business. In recent time, the increase in population, changes and improvement in disposable income, globalisation effects, social status consciousness among the populace, increase and improvement in literacy rate; higher demand for university education among the citizenry, *etc.* have made recognition of social class imperative for a successful business operation. Equally, the need to create effective segmentation with right products for the right people makes social class as a premise to lay effective market strategy that generates good performance for businesses.

REFERENCES

Asian Development Bank. (2010). *The Rise of Asia's Middle Class.* Retrieved from www.adb.org/sites/

Ayobade, A. (2012). *Gender Differences and the influence of Socio-Cultural Factors in Accessing Formal Funds by Small-Scale Entrepreneurs* (PhD dissertation). Department of Sociology of the Faculty of Social Sciences, University of Lagos, Nigeria.

Barbeau, E. M., Leavy, S., & Balbach, E. D. (2004). Smoking, Social Class, and Gender: What Can Public Health Learn from the Tobacco Industry about Disparities in Smoking? *Tobacco Control, 13*(2), 115–120. doi:10.1136/tc.2003.006098 PMID:15175523

Belcher, J. C., & Crader, K. W. (1974). Social Class, Style of Life and Fertility in Preuto Rico. *Social Forces, 52*(4), 488–495. doi:10.1093f/52.4.488

Berkman, H. W., Lindquist, J. D., & Sirgy, M. J. (1996). *Consumer Behaviour.* NTC.

Brezis, E. S. (2011). *The Effects of Elite Recruitment on Social Cohesion and Economic Development.* Retrieved from www.oecd.org/development,pgd/

Brown, N. (1992). Beachboys as Culture Brokers in Bakau Town, The Gambia. *Community Development Journal: An International Forum, 27*(4), 361–370. doi:10.1093/oxfordjournals.cdj.a038626

Fry, J. N., & Siller, F. H. (1970). A Comparison of Housewife Decision Making in Two Social Classes. *JMR, Journal of Marketing Research, 7*(3), 333–337. doi:10.2307/3150291

Gana, A. T. (1985). The State in Africa: Yesterday, Today and Tomorrow. *International Political Science Review*, *6*(1), 115–132. doi:10.1177/019251218500600112

Hempel, D. J. (1974). Family Buying Decisions: A Cross Cultural Perspective. *JMR, Journal of Marketing Research*, *11*(3), 295–302. doi:10.2307/3151145

Hout, M., & Rosen, H. S. (2000). Self-employment, Family Background, and Race. *The Journal of Human Resources*, *35*(4), 670–692. doi:10.2307/146367

Hughes, R., & Perry-Jenkins, M. (1996). Social Class Issues in Family Life Education. *Family Relations*, *45*(2), 175–182. doi:10.2307/585288

Jennings, I. (1956, February). Approach to Self-Government. Corona, 61-62.

Jensen, R., & Peppard, D. M. (2007). Food-Buying Habits in Hanoi. *Journal of Social Issues in Southeast Asia*, *22*(2), 230–254. doi:10.1355/SJ22-2D

Kharas, H. (2011). *The Emerging Middle Class in Developing Countries*. Brookings Institution.

Kilson, M. L. Jr. (1958). Nationalism and Social Class in British West Africa. *The Journal of Politics*, *20*(2), 368–387. doi:10.2307/2127045

Little, K. (1953). The Study of Social Change in British West Africa. *Africa*, *23*(4), 274–301. doi:10.2307/1156180

Little, K. (1955). The African Elite in British West Africa. *Race and Relations in World Perspectives*, 267-288.

Little, K. L. (1948). Social Change and Social Class in the Sierra Leone Protectorate. *American Journal of Sociology*, *54*(1), 10–21. doi:10.1086/220263

Lloyd, P.C. (1953, January). Cocoa, Politics and the Yoruba Middle Class. *West Africa*, 39.

Llyod, P. C. (1953, October). New Economic Classes in Western Nigeria. *African Affairs*, 327–334. doi:10.1093/oxfordjournals.afraf.a094171

McFadden, E., Luben, R., & Khaw, K. (2009). Different Measures of Social Class in Women and Mortality. *European Journal of Epidemiology*, *24*(5), 231–236. doi:10.100710654-009-9332-0 PMID:19322666

Milios, J. (2000). Social Classes in Classical and Marxist Political Economy. *American Journal of Economics and Sociology*, *59*(2), 283–302. doi:10.1111/1536-7150.00027

Muhammed, S. I. (1997). *Some Possibilities in Closing Gender Disparities in Education. The Nigerian Academy of Education in Collaboration with the Chris Ogunbanjo Foundation Akoka*. Jas Publishers.

Myers, J. H., Stanton, R. R., & Haug, F. A. (1971). Correlates of Buying Behaviour: Social Class Vs. Income. *Journal of Marketing*, *35*(4), 8–15. doi:10.2307/1250451

Orock, R. T. E. (2007). Gender Equality: Whose Agenda? Observation from Cameroon. *Development in Practice*, *17*(1), 93–97. doi:10.1080/09614520601092220

Peter, P. J., & Olson, J. C. (1999). Consumer Behaviour and Marketing Strategy. Irwin/McGraw-Hill.

Robenstine, C. (2001). Social Class and the Politics of School Choice. *Journal of Thought*, *36*(1), 55–65.

Robinson, R. (1984). Forecasting and Small Business: A study of the strategic planning Process. *Journal of Small Business Management*, *22*(2), 19–27.

Schaninger, C. M. (1981). Social Class versus Income Revisited: An Empirical Investigation. *JMR, Journal of Marketing Research*, *18*(2), 192–208. doi:10.2307/3150954

Suriano, M. (2011). Hip-Hop and Bongo Flavour in Contemporary Tanzania: Youths' Experiences, Agency, Aspirations and Contradictions. *Africa Development. Afrique et Developpement*, *36*(3/4), 113–126.

Tynes, S. R. (2001). Bringing Social Class Home: The Social Class Genealogy and Poverty Lunch Projects. *Teaching Sociology*, *29*(3), 286–298. doi:10.2307/1319188

Utomi, P. (1985). Legitimacy and Governance: One More Year of Military Rule in Nigeria. *A Journal of Opinion*, *14*, 39-42.

KEY TERMS AND DEFINITIONS

African Religions: Traditional African religious practices that involve idolatry and the tenets are totally different from Christianity.

African Society: A collection of people united by tradition, norms, values and culture that emphasize idolatry, polygamy, extended family practice, peasant farming, victims of slavery, low economic potentials, etc.

Chieftaincy: A family traditional and heritage title that determines the privileged class of the holder and offspring or family members in the society.

Indigenous Africans: Class of people that dwell on sub-Saharan Africa who have their roots in Africa and live within the system and another group who were returned slaves and live within the African communities.

Individual/Family Land Owners: A practice whereby a community land belongs to a particular family who in turn sells the land to others as a source of income earnings.

Military Coup D'état: Popular military intervention across the sub-Sahara African nations that promote military men to political class and public administrators.

Political Class: Class of Africans who by virtue of their business or profession developed a closed relationship with colonial government or military ruling class and become part of the ruling class.

Western Education: A replacement to primitive African style of learning that emphasizes formal method of classroom education for all and sundry and is based on communication in writing, reading, and numeric.

Chapter 10
Place Consumption:
Interrogating the Relationship Between Nation Brand and City Brand

Sanya Ojo
University of East London, UK

ABSTRACT

This chapter investigates the influence of country of origin's reputation on the notion of place brand and vice versa. Employing a case study methodology, cases of Lagos (Nigeria) and Dubai (UAE) are examined to generate a model of place brand/branding. This model highlights the flow of causality between a nation brand and a city brand. Four themes are highlighted as matters of interest to focus on when recommending a way forward for Lagos city to generate and improve its global reputation in order to increase the footfalls of visitors and expats.

INTRODUCTION

In the crowded and complex global marketplace, people loosely assess cities mostly through a few simple clichés. For examples, Tokyo is modernity, Paris is love, New York is energy, Washington is power, Milano is fashion, Lagos is lawlessness, Rio and Las Vegas are fun, and Barcelona is culture (Ozer, 2016). Typecasts and cliché could dominate perceptions of some cities as external audiences are indisposed to process vast amounts of information about a city and its nation's history, culture, society. Accordingly, an effective branding should be able to break down negative stereotypes and clichés that are usually ascribed to places/nations.

From this standpoint, this chapter explores the concept of place brand through the interrogation of the relationships between nation brand and place brand to contribute a better understanding of city brand/branding. Most of the literatures on brand marketing assume the flow of causality from nation (country) brand to place (city) brand. In essence, the status, prestige, and standing of a country are presumed to rub off on the city brand, for instance, cities like London, Paris, and New York do well on most brand indicators because of the international standings of their respective countries on the world stage.

DOI: 10.4018/978-1-5225-7906-9.ch010

However, from this study's perspective, city brands do not necessarily have to align with nation brands to be effective and successful. Whilst it is likely a city's reputation is impacted by the reputation of its country, the Reputation Institute (2017) research demonstrates that sometimes the cities reputations do not correspond to that of their countries. Hence, there seem to be instances when a city's brand will be more successful than that of its constituent country and may, in fact, propel the nation brand to higher levels such that the flow of causality is from the city's brand to the nation brand rather than the opposite. This reverse relationship is interrogated using a case study of two different cities, Dubai (UAE) and Lagos (Nigeria). The branding activities of both cities are evaluated and a model of city brand is formulated to guide the attention of academics, policymakers, and practitioners in the direction of a strategically oriented approach to city branding.

Brand Consumption

The practice of branding nations and places is growing in intensity since nations and places are competing fiercely in the global marketplace. Miletsky and Smith (2009: 2) contend that "brand is the sum total of all user experiences with a particular product or services, building both reputation and future expectations of benefit". Many cities, regions, and countries invested huge resources in producing brands to attract bigger investments and recognition. According to Kearn and Philo (1993: 11): "Places become to be consumed, advertised and marketed much as any product". Though a relatively new concept, place brand/branding has been assessed as important to consumers and investors who make their economic decisions based on countries' images. Successful place branding helps to reinforce positive images and reduces the effect of negative images and can be effective in differentiation strategies. Thus, branding has a huge impact on cities/countries' competitiveness since effective branding can confer a competitive advantage to a place or nation especially in the developing parts of the world (Mihailovich, 2006). Place branding not only applies to cities, regions, and countries but also applies lower down the spatial scale (Ashworth & Voogt, 1994) to places such as shopping destinations and leisure parks. However, this study focus is on cities, and place brand/city brand will be used interchangeably. In addition, contiguous terms such as nation brand, country brand, and country reputation will be applied interchangeably for ease of presentation/analysis.

To achieve its objectives, some pertinent questions needed investigation; such as what effects do a country's reputation and attributes have on a city's brand/branding outcomes? Can a city's brand be isolated from the negative reputation/image of the country within which it is situated? Under what conditions can a city's brand thrive irrespective of its country's poor reputation/image in the world? Two cities, Dubai and Lagos, were selected to generate a model of place/city brand. The paper is arranged into six sections including contextual and research settings; conceptual framework; methodology; findings; discussion; conclusions and policy implications.

CONTEXTUAL AND RESEARCH SETTINGS

Given the absence of rigorous academic research on interactions between nation and city brands, this study analysed two cities, one in the Middle-East (Dubai) and the other in West Africa (Lagos). The cities were selected because they typify good examples of the causality flows from place brand to nation brand and from nation brand to place brand. For instance, Dubai demonstrates the positive impact of a place brand on the image of its country (UAE) (Balakrishnan, 2008), whereas, Lagos branding exemplifies the difficulties attached to a place brand triggered by a weak nation brand (Anholt, 2007). Furthermore, their selection is consistent with other comparative two-city case studies, which are common in marketing papers (e.g. Graf, 2009; Botz-Bornstein, 2012).

Essentially, both cities are similar in some respects, for instance, both are large cities and have substantial political influence in their regions. They both have port locations, which are central to trade and of significant economic importance to their respective countries. Just as Dubai's entire existence as a city depended on financial markets (Botz-Bornstein, 2012), so also is Lagos the commercial nerve centre of Nigeria (Ekundayo, 2013). One key factor in the place marketing efforts of these two cities seems to be the degree of political autonomy or independence of their national governments (although the UAE and Nigeria operate different political systems). Yet, there are differentiating factors such as the composition of their population mix; whereas Dubai total population (about 94%) is foreign (Botz-Bornstein, 2012) Lagosians are mainly Nigerians. Whilst Lagos is governed by democratically elected government, Dubai is ruled by a royal family. Undoubtedly, many other factors differentiate the cities and render difficult any attempt to draw strong causal claims about the impact of place branding practices on rates of achieving positive global visibility. In effect, the application of this comparative case study will lead to a modest but nevertheless important goal of underlining the conditions in which a place branding/rebranding may achieve success by circumventing the country of origin's reputation risk. Although firm conclusions are not drawn about the efficacy of the policies adopted in each city-setting, the comparison only assists to direct attention to important issues around countries' 'reputation capital' as either facilitating or incapacitating place brand/branding.

Furthermore, two contrasting views of cities (relational and territorial) are adopted in this paper. Relational approach sees cities as open and unbounded, influenced by globalisation and social processes that facilitate their distinct characteristics. The territorial approach, on the other hand, sees cities as closed, more grounded and exhibiting trends that are confined to that particular geographical unit (Jonas, 2012). However, both perspectives are relevant in this paper as they offer balanced accounts of the city/place, for instance, Bulkeley (2005) argues that scalar boundaries are fluid and contested and networks are bounded as well. On the one hand, the relational approach manifests in the current trends of Nigerians (investors, tourists, expats, business persons, labourers, etc.) going to Dubai regularly (Arnold, 2012; Babatunde, 2016). Yet, the territoriality of Dubai (UAE) is noticeable in the recent bilateral anti-corruption agreements between Nigeria and UAE to curb corrupt Nigerian officials who were attracted to Dubai as a destination of choice to hide their loots (*Vanguard Newspaper*, 2017).

CONCEPTUAL BACKGROUND

This paper conceives that the country of origin (COO) effect influences different types of legitimacy that help or hinder place brand/branding. Therefore, in this section, aside from concepts around brand/branding, notions such as soft power, reputation capital are analysed towards the formulation of a place brand model. The COO effect acts as a cognitive cue that shapes consumers' products/services evaluations and choices and possesses symbolic and emotional meaning to customers (Verlegh & Steenkamp, 1999). Such symbolic/reputation and emotional nuances transform COO into an 'image' attribute, which is a considerable determinant of consumer preferences (Lefkoff-Hagius & Mason, 1993).

Nation Brand/Branding

Nation brand concept relates to the application of branding and marketing communications methods for reshaping the perception of a country to the international audiences. Related to product branding, nation branding uses all types of procedures, technology, and media. According to Dinnie (2015: 15), nation branding is "the unique, multi-dimensional blend of elements that provide the nation with culturally grounded differentiation and relevance for all of its target audiences". Equally, Kerr and Wiseman (2013: 354) describe nation branding as "the application of corporate marketing concepts and techniques to countries, in the interests of enhancing their reputation in international relations". Active repositioning of a nation through branding can produce a competitive advantage over others (Gilmore, 2002) and bestows benefits in many areas (e.g. investments). The notion of nation branding attempts to minimise the identity-image gap by identifying prejudices and misperceptions. Additionally, nation branding enables countries to dismantle and counter the negative forces that could hinder their economic development or damage their reputation in the international arena. Thus, the operating mechanism of nation branding is considerably associated with questions of territory, economic power, ideologies, politics or religion (Kaneva, 2011).

Connected to the concept of nation brand are terms such as 'brand state' and 'brand equity', which are derived from the analysis and application of brand image and brand identity. Brand state denotes the way a nation completely shows and represents itself to the world (Anholt, 2006). The term also signifies the consistent and comprehensive structure that governs a realistic, competitive, and credible strategic vision for a nation. This vision is reinforced, enriched, and sustained by every act of exchange/communication between the nation and others (Anholt, 1998). Whereas, a nation's brand equity is a mixture of components incorporating the markets' opinions of its economic/political fundamentals and perception of its image. According to Farquhar (1989), brand equity is the 'added value' a product is endowed with, and a strong brand image could be built and maintained by leveraging brand equity.

Nation branding is becoming popular for countries as an image enhancing device for the creation of more favourable conditions for foreign direct investments, tourism, trade and political relations with other countries. Similarly, governments are turning to nation branding and marketing strategies to conceal issues generated by poor policies (Anholt, 2010). Essentially, Nation branding is typified by its 'soft' power approach (Nye, 2004; De Grazia, 2005), as compare to the 'hard' power approach epitomised by military or economic resources, which is usually attractive in the projection of national interest in international diplomacy. As a result, nation branding "is perceived as a rhetorical and functional equivalent to national identity" and operate as a form of proactive management and control, a national discourse for a global context (Aronczyk, 2008: 49).

However, some researchers argue against the notion of nation branding, for example, Gudjonsson (2005) rejects the idea of nation branding, arguing that although governments can use branding techniques, nations cannot be branded. Likewise, De Chernatony (2001) contends that there is no such thing as a 'brand', but in reality, what exists is a spectrum of brand interpretations. Unlike product branding, it is more difficult to transform a country and satisfy audiences unless there is a considerable intervention arrangement (Marazza, 2007). For instance, it is easier to change a product's package or flavour than to construct a new airport or highway. Nevertheless, it may be difficult to add a mountain or alter a country's weather, but with technological advancement, some seemingly tough innovative projects have been created. For instance, the man-made beaches in Orlando (US) and Birmingham (UK) and the artificial Palm Islands in Dubai (UAE). In addition, Anholt (2006: 2) reiterates that in relation to the nation-state; "in most countries, there are many other bodies, agencies, ministries, special interest groups, non-governmental organisations (NGOs) and companies all promoting their version of the country too". Invariably, it is difficult to congregate the different consumption intentions and decisions of diverse customers who are spread over several regions to create a congruent and coherent value chain in a nation branding.

Place Brand/Branding

There is no generally accepted definition of place branding (Kavaratzis & Ashworth, 2005; Anholt, 2010) since the concept attracts inputs from several academic disciplines (Sayer, 2010; Sevin, 2014). For example, from the marketing perspective, place branding has been described "as the practice of applying brand strategy and other marketing techniques and disciplines to the economic, political and cultural development of cities, regions and countries" (Ashworth & Kavaratzis, 2007: 521). Van Ham (2010: 136) defines it from the political standpoint; arguing that "place branding can be considered an effort to manage, if not necessarily wield, the social power of a geographical location by using strategies developed in the commercial sector". Meanwhile, Zenker and Braun's (2010: 3) psychological perspective describes a place brand as "a network of associations in the consumers' mind based on the visual, verbal and behavioural expression of a place". In essence, the categorisation of place branding rather becomes a complex process (Sevin, 2014).

In their findings, Foroudi *et al.* (2016) show that the main indicators to recognising and favouring a place brand consist of the national culture and infrastructure. The former includes country's name, country's brand, country attributes, social changes, geography and environment, people, culture (history, language, etc.). The latter includes security, economic condition, technological advancement, tourism development goals, place marketing and promotional strategy. In addition, the researchers identify five key moderators of the outcomes of place branding as political perception, social media and news, place awareness, place association and tourism experience.

From a place marketing perspective place brand is an umbrella brand covering the city brand and destination brand. The idea of the city brand as a destination brand has been explored from a varied range of perspectives, for example, from the image formation process (Gunn, 1972; Gartener, 1993) to the diverse external and internal factors that can influence this information-making process (Baloglu & McClery, 1999). Consequently, image is an important element of destination/place branding (e.g. Blain *et al.*, 2005), for instance, according to Frost (2004), the image individuals have of a country reveals a lot about how they perceive it as a tourist destination, a place to invest or a source of consumer goods. Peoples' perception of a place determines their expectations and is an important success factor in place/destination marketing (e.g. Leisen, 2001). A number of factors such as war, natural disaster, health-related issues, crisis, etc. harm a place/destination's image in people's perception (Romila, 2008).

Some studies' results, taking a tourism perspective, indicate that visitors' choices of destinations are based on the degree to which they generate favourable images (Gartener, 1989; Woodside & Lyonski, 1989). Destination images are thus the means by which prospective tourists determine a destination's potential for satisfaction (Pearce, 1982). Nonetheless, Turok (2009: 26) contends that "the branding of cities is infinitely more difficult than for commercial products because of their complex and contradictory qualities". Authors such as Olins (1999) and Drenttel (2004) oppose the application of traditional branding techniques/principles to sell places and countries. For instance, they both claimed that a place (city/country) should not be sold like a common commodity.

Branding Strategy: Nation Brand vs. City Brand

The relationship between a country brand/branding and a city brand/branding has been explored in the literature and sometimes, it appeared that country branding, city branding and region branding processes are integral parts that cannot be separated in some instances (Herstein, 2012).

However, the factors that influence the image of a country are different from the factors that affect a city and region, and as Peirce and Ritchie (2007) observe, the national stories may present a number of challenges, including a negative image and low consumer demand to a city brand. In this regard, the work of branding a country is different from that of branding a city or region (Caldwell & Freire, 2004). Sahin and Baloglu's (2014) study highlights the difference in branding a country versus branding a city. The authors believe that country branding should be segmented because branding country destinations (particularly the big countries) as a whole is similar to firms attempting to sell all their products to everyone without segmenting the market and developing customised products and offers for each segment. City branding can be regarded as product customisation for certain segments. Thus, Sahin and Baloglu (2014: 243) argue: "It is harder to convince consumers with many broad appeals such as in the case of country branding, than with specific and salient ones in the case of city branding. It is practically impossible or very hard at best to enjoy a whole country adequately in one trip and the communication of many broad appeals can get lost in their own clutter". Herstein (2012) also argues that city branding appears to be a much more involved process than country/region branding, and it is difficult for cities to become individual objects of attraction in their own right since they lack the ability to identify themselves with well-known core competencies, mainly human assets such as politicians, mayors, artists, and celebrities (Gilmore, 2002).

Consequently, the strategy of city branding has to be defined carefully, given that it can create more disadvantages than advantages by confusing the brands of countries, states, communities, and cities, and this confusion has happened many times (Sahin & Baloglu, 2014). For instance, sending diverse messages to different stakeholders can generate a lack of coordination among institutions, or promotional activities for the brand of a country or a state can cause confusion in a city's branding strategy (Gómez *et al.*, 2016). Sahin and Baloglu (2014) contend that brand confusion might develop because of potential conflicts between national and sub-brands such as states, territories, and cities. In some cases, especially in small countries (e.g. Luxembourg) where there are one or two major cities, city branding could be easily executed. In large countries, however, such as Nigeria, it is much more challenging to coordinate a seamless branding strategy.

It is the case that the name of a country is a built-in label that can add value to or subtract value from a product (or city) in the same manner that a brand does (e.g. Gómez *et al.*, 2016). Like brands, cities satisfy functional, symbolic and emotional needs (Rainisto, 2003) and the attributes that satisfy those needs need to be orchestrated into the city's unique proposition (Ashworth & Voogd, 1990). Invariably, branding a city as a destination somewhat isolates the city from sources of negative perceptions of a country. Problems, such as insecurity, political/military conflict, issues of underdevelopment and poverty that cause negative perceptions of certain regions within a country may exist. A developed and popular city far removed from these kinds of problems that may be constantly connected to the country can "avoid these negative influences when it markets itself alone rather than as part of that country or region" (Sahin & Baloglu, 2014: 243). For instance, the 'Boko Haram' terrorists' activities in Nigeria occur mainly in the Northern-East part of Nigeria and Lagos seems immune. Likewise, Dubai has been immune from incidences of terrorism/conflicts distressing parts of the Middle-East region.

Reputation Capital

Klewes and Wreschniok (2009: 3) contend that "reputation can best be understood as the sum of the expectations that the public places on the future behaviour of an agent or institution based on the public's direct or indirect experiences". A key aspect of the idea of reputation is the concept of reputational capital, which proposes that organisations can gradually accumulate and then mobilise their intangible assets over time to improve their reputation with various audiences (Jackson, 2004; Klewes & Wreschniok, 2009). Jackson (2004: 104) explains reputational capital: "The trick is to move from establishing reputation and credibility to building reputational capital". Jackson (2004) further argues that it takes time to build trust such that reputational capital is built and sustained over a long period, and that an organisation's reputational capital increases as it pursues pathways of fundamental virtue that cuts across all of its stakeholders over time. In connecting to place brand, Van Ham (2010: 136) asserts that "States used place branding to affect, even modify their reputation to similar means and processes to commercial brands". Nevertheless, according to Schultz *et al.* (2006), because reputation is derived from actions and behaviours of several stakeholders, it is hard to isolate one variable that influences perceptions to a greater degree than others across all stakeholders.

The importance of reputation capital is detectible in the recently instituted reputation ranking survey of world's reputable countries. The Reputation Institute (2013) has been conducting annual surveys on reputation and admiration of countries and cities to establish the connection between a favourable image and economic outcomes. In the surveys, which employs 23000 consumer ratings in the G8 countries, 100 cities are selected based on some values categorised into three classes; advanced economy, appealing environment, and effective government. Developed from these factors are; the beauty of the urban environment, the safety, the cultural and gastronomic heritage together with the standard of living. For example, in 2017, the Reputation Institute's RepTrak study ranked UAE 27th and Nigeria 52nd in the world (Trad, 2017), and on the cities' league table, Dubai was ranked the 36th most reputable city in the world (Bobley, 2017), but Lagos was not on the list.

Soft Power

The term 'soft power' derives from the concept expounded by Nye (2004) to examine the reputational and ideological power of nation-states. It focuses on getting others to want a preferred outcome by co-option rather than coercion. Closely linked with brand state, soft power resources are the assets that produce attraction that mostly leads to acquiescence (Ojo, 2017). Its variables are ordered into three major groups: global image, global integrity, and global integration (Ernst & Young, 2012). Global image is a measure of a country's global popularity and admiration, particularly that of its culture. Global integrity measures how much a country observes ethical or moral codes, and Global integration measures the interconnectedness of a country with the rest of the world (Ernst & Young, 2012). Gilboa (2008: 55) argues that: "soft power is a nation's values, cultures and policies for the development of politics, economics, and cultures". A country's soft power is governed by the attractiveness of its culture, values, and policies to others. Soft power works when it influences how these outsiders behave; for instance, China's introduction of the 'Belt and Road Initiative' as an investment vehicle in a number of countries is an attempt to increase its influence on the world stage (Wo-lap, 2016).

The recognition of the influence of soft power facilitates an annual survey of national soft power index dubbed the Soft Power 30, which is now used as a benchmark by governments around the world. This index gauges top thirty countries using six sub-indices, which are: Government (e.g. political values, good governance), Culture (e.g. music, sports, tourism), Global Engagement (e.g. diplomatic resources, engaging with international audiences), Education (e.g. global scholarship, foreign students), Digital (the extent to which technology is embraced and the digital world is engaged, and the use of digital diplomacy through social media platforms), and Enterprise (e.g. capacity for innovation, and ability to foster enterprise and commerce).

However, the concept of soft power has been described as delusional (Mattern, 2005), an unclear attraction (Hall, 2010), and too 'soft' to achieve national interests (Ferguson, 2009). Likewise, Matsuda (2007) argued that soft power should be applied on the bases of bilateral cultural exchange and not just in unilateral cultural imperialism. Furthermore, Mattern (2005) argues that any piece of art (e.g. literature, films, music and cultural diplomacy) has a 'representational force' behind it, which depict a country. Inherently, the concept of soft power is infused with a big paradox since its 'power' is actually wielded by the receiving party through its response and reaction rather than the possessor. Nonetheless, due to its distinctive quality, a nation's soft power over another is not easily exploited to an advantage in any methodical approach (Blechman, 2004), and it can take many generations to build.

METHODOLOGY

A case-based qualitative approach is employed in this study to explore a complex experience in a real-life context (Ghauri & Grønhaug, 2005). The embedded case study is deemed suitable because the research theme is underdeveloped and needs theory building (Eisenhardt, 1989). As a critical case, this study investigates the relationships between a country's reputation and city brand using two cities, Dubai and Lagos, as exemplars. Thus, it presents new knowledge that can be used to develop or revise the existing theory (Flyvbjerg, 2006) on the flow of causality between the concepts of nation brand and city brand, particularly given the received view that a city's brand is driven by a country's image/reputation. In other words, the study considers nation brand from a reversed perspective; rather than looking at how a country's image/reputation affects perceptions of city, it examines how a city image affects a country's image.

Since the scholarly objective is to obtain the greatest possible amount of information on a given phenomenon, i.e., nation brand/city brand relationship, an atypical as well as critical case can be more apposite (e.g., the choice of Dubai/Lagos), as opposed to a representative case. According to Flyvbjerg (2006: 229), "this is because the typical or average case is often not the richest in information. Atypical or extreme cases often reveal more information because they activate more actors and more basic mechanisms in the situation studied". Hence, a critical case like Dubai/Lagos is a suitable selection, having strategic importance in relation to understanding and theorising about the halo effect of city brand on nation brand. Although there are limitations in the application of a single case study, instrumental characteristics that develop from repetitive processes or otherwise documented patterns support the theorising (Welch *et al.*, 2010).

Contextual Justification

Dubai and Lagos are disparate and are only linked by the interest of the researcher for the topic under investigation. Each city struggles to position itself in the most attractive possible manner, using the generally established tools of city narratives, tourism branding, event branding, smart city branding, etc. The selection of the Dubai and Lagos can be rationalised by four points. First, the two-city case illustrates the prominence of both cities in their regions and their growing reputations vis-à-vis their respective countries (UAE/Nigeria). Dubai provides evidence on how city brand can positively affect the nation brand (Balakrishnan, 2008). Second, the data illustrates a proactive dimension of branding as the rising brand image of Lagos (compared to Nigeria's image) demonstrates (e.g. The Economist, 2015). Moreover, the data indicates succeeding Lagos governments have been proactive in managing and improving the city's image exclusively and independent of Nigeria's global reputation. Third, this case is one of the exceptional examples of using cities in emerging economies as comparable units in place brand research. Fourth, the choice of cities follows a purposive sampling technique (Cresswell & Plano, 2011). This requires the identification and selection of information-rich cases to methodically determine and evaluate the similarities and dissimilarities among entities when variation and complexity are detected. The above-mentioned rationalisations have theoretical relevance and can be applied to the city/place reputation 'pull logic' of nation brand. The case showcases the capacity of cities to enhance the image of their countries through developmental programs and growth oriented policies. This spill-over effect is similar to White's (2012) findings that the halo effects of a country's products generates a positive assessment of the country.

Data Collection and Analysis

The research design is processual and builds on an exploratory and descriptive strategy (Halinen *et al.*, 2013). The study documents and analyses the branding strategies of Dubai and Lagos, their related dynamics, and lessons for Lagos brand managers. It employs insights from the nation brand and place/city brand research streams that produce a collectively constructed embedded case study (Salmi, 2011). The systematic search flow (SSF) was the method used for the literature review. According to Ferenhof and Fernandes (2016: 551), the systematic review is "a method of scientific investigation with a rigorous and explicit process to identify, select, collect data, analyse, and describe the relevant contributions to research". There are three distinct phases in this method, including; description of the research protocol, analysis of the data, and the synthesis. This method was selected because of its effectiveness in showing the procedures employed at each stage of the systematic review production, in order to process, analyse, and produce the synthesis with consistency in creating scientific knowledge (Chang *et al.*, 2018).

The iterative search and retrieval procedure commenced by developing a set of search concepts related to the theme of the study (the relationship between nation and city branding), thus relating to different ways of conceptualising the causal relationship between a country's brand and a city's brand. Locational terms (e.g. city, destination, region, place, metropolis, Dubai, Lagos, UAE, Nigeria, etc.), as well as brand/branding phrases (selling, communicating, marketing, promoting, making, regeneration, transformation, etc.) were then (in different combinations) used as entries (abstracts and keywords) in searching the following major online databases: Google Scholar, Business Source Premier, Sage, Elsevier, Springer Link, Academic Source, and open sources including local, regional, international media, practitioners' reports and internet-based sources.

For the stage of standardising the selection of articles, sequential filters were applied for interpreting summaries and interpreting articles (e.g. Lucarelli & Berg, 2011). Articles dealing with Dubai and Lagos separately or jointly and representative of the researched theme were selected. In addition, articles that offer an integrated insight (i.e. multidisciplinary/multidimensional) in their analyses or in the metrics used, and which are directly related to the theme of city branding, were also harvested. Following this stage of the literature review, a conceptual framework development was done by determining the key trends in city branding research that aim to deliver the causality of direction between nation brand and city brand. Analysis of the data was iterative in shifting between data and evolving categories and concepts (Alvesson & Skoldberg, 2000), which are revealed in the next section.

A Case of Two Cities

City of Dubai

Dubai is part of the seven monarchies that made up the UAE, others are Abu Dhabi, Ajman, Fujairah, Ras al-Khaimah, Sharjah, and Umm al-Quwain. Nevertheless, Dubai and Abu Dhabi are best known internationally among UAE's states. Some of Dubai's symbolic infrastructure developments such as the Burj Al Arab, the Palm Jumeira, and the Burj Khalifa (the world's tallest building) are recognised around the world and have attracted a multitude of visitors to the UAE. Thanks to Dubai and Abu Dhabi, the UAE appears to do well on some key nation-brand indicators (Brand Finance, 2014). For example, tourism, investment/migration, culture/heritage, people, governance, and export are thriving (see Anholt, 2006). On tourism, the UAE's authorities have skilfully used tourism to capture global imagination such that there is significant visitors' interest in the country and its man-made tourist attractions (Balakrishnan, 2008). For instance, in 2014, over 13 million people visited the UAE (DIT, 2015) largely driven by Dubai's high global visibility generated by its tourism industry and reputation as a business and international transport hub. On investment/migration, Dubai, has been able to attract foreign direct investments (FDI) to the UAE through incentives such as zero tax, trade free zones, and favourable property-ownership laws (PwC, 2015). For example, the UAE is ranked 2nd globally in drawing and receiving FDIs by the United Nations Conference on Trade and Development (UNCTAD) 2014 report (Wam, 2014). In 2014-15, Davos' World Economic Forum (World Competitiveness Report) ranked the country 12th in the world in terms of overall economic competitiveness (Wam, 2014). Additionally, the UAE is ranked 9th out of 181 nations for investments in tourism by the World Travel and Tourism Council report in 2013 (Wam, 2014). The biennial Dubai air show has become a mega deal-making forum that further boosted Dubai reputation on the world stage (Hotten, 2017). Furthermore, the majority of Dubai's residents are expatriates (Dubai Statistics Center, 2016), for instance, out of the estimated population of 9.3 million people, only 950,000 are Emiratis (AOHR-UK, 2014).

On culture/heritage, Dubai is fast becoming a cultural hotspot on the heels, for instance, the recent launching of Dubai Opera, the spectacular Etihad Museum, as well as the flourishing arts district Al Quoz (Golf in Dubai, 2017). On governance, there is a mixed review. Whilst most Emiratis are contented with the political situation, some expats and most migrants' workers grapple with draconian and repressive laws and practices (Hari, 2009). On export, it could be argued that Dubai's brand of liberal Islamic practices, for example, tolerant dress codes for foreigners, availability of alcohol in pubs and clubs (Emirates247, 2016), is adopted by liberal Moslem nations in the region (e.g. Qatar, Bahrain). On the whole, the Dubai has built a globally resonant brand image that has transited from the shadows of often negative regional associations (Coombe, 2010).

Yet, the perception of Dubai as an 'oasis of fun' is not without criticism, for instance, there were reports of human rights abuse of immigrant workers (Law, 2015) and some instances of visitors and expats falling foul of Dubai's considerably harsh social laws (Lumley, 2017).

City of Lagos

Lagos State is one of the thirty-six States in the Federal Republic of Nigeria, and Lagos is the premier city in the State. The city's landscape is dominated by its system of islands, sandbars, and lagoons. Lagos city's four main islands of Lagos, Iddo, Ikoyi, and Victoria, are connected to each other and to the mainland by a number of bridges (Encyclopædia Britannica, 2017). With a population of about twenty million, Lagos is the economic capital of Nigeria; produces about $90 billion a year in goods and services, making its economy bigger than that of most African countries (The Economist, 2015). If the city is a country, it would be the seventh largest economy in Africa (Sandys, 2016).

The long-term objective of the Lagos State government is to become the number one tourists' destination in Nigeria and create brand awareness to further showcase the potentials of the city to the international audiences. Realising that strong marketing communication is needed to achieve this objective, successive governments embarked on a number of projects and programmes across all sectors that would be of interest to the international audiences and generate the socio-economic development of the State. For instance, the present government is upgrading the quality of the city's environment, improve its security and transportation system. Particularly, there is an on-going citywide landscaping involving planting of trees, shrubs, grassing and paving along major roads, which themselves are under rehabilitation (Omidire, 2016). On security, the government and the organised private sectors continue to donate vehicles, communication gadgets and other equipment to assist the police and enhance the security profile of Lagos (Encyclopædia Britannica, 2017). For instance, the government donated security equipment valued at N4.765 billion to the State Police Command in 2015 (Ogbonnikan, 2017). Infrastructure developments are also prioritised as investments in transportation, power and water supply are ongoing. An example is the regeneration of the city through its historical physical features such as the National Arts Theatre and the surrounding areas (Amakihe, 2016). The government also focuses on marketing Lagos as a cultural hub through implementing projects such as the "One Lagos" programme launched as part of the Lagos@50 celebrations (Sandys, 2016).

The concerted efforts of the Lagos State government to rebrand the city could be viewed against the backdrop of similar attempts (past and present) by the Nigerian governments, some State governments, and the organised private sector in the country. For example, in the past, the Nigerian governments embarked on branding/rebranding programs including the Image Project (also known as the Heart of Africa Project) towards improving Nigeria's internal and external images (Nworah, 2007). Another re/branding exercise was the "Nigeria: Good People, Great Nation" campaign, which is an attempt to re-orientate Nigerians towards self-belief and change the perception of the country both locally and internationally (Ochu, 2009). Other place/destination image projects include the Cross River State Tinapa Holiday and Business Resort initiated in 2007 as a way of boosting business and tourism in the Cross River state of Nigeria (Nze, 2010); the Abuja Carnival, modelled after the Rio de Janeiro Carnival in Brazil, staged to celebrate 30 years of the Federal Capital Territory (informationng.com, 2016). The organised private sector involvement is witnessed in the internationally acclaimed film industry – 'Nollywood'. Nigerians' Nollywood is the world's second-largest film industry after Bollywood and it is mainly located in Lagos. The industry has given rise to a potpourri of creative and innovative young filmmakers from across Nigeria and is much engrained in the cultural fabric of Nigerians (Sandys, 2016). This is noteworthy as culture and heritage (e.g. films and movies) are significant assets of nation branding (Anholt, 2007). Communication apparatus like films act as a cultural medium that articulates and propagates people's past and present realities as well as their aspirations. Clearly, Nigeria's soft power may potentially be sourced from attributes such as its cultural exports (Nollywood, music, dress, food and other indigenous products), its political and iconic personalities. For example, Nigeria's entertainment industry, particularly its film and music industry, permeates the airwaves on the African continent and beyond. Nigeria boasts of internationally renowned artists who have made their mark in their respective music genres (Akwagyiram, 2016).

However, Nigeria image (and Lagos by extension) has suffered from reports of terrorism, ethno-religious violence, kidnapping, fraud/internet scams, and environmental degradations (Agunbiade & Ayotunde 2011; Owuamanam *et al.,* 2012). Nworah (2006) also listed image damaging problems such as bribery and corruption, unemployment, poor infrastructural development, poor work ethics, organisational irresponsibility, etc. These are compounded by the generally poor image of the African continent in the global arena (Wanjiru, 2006; Abimbola, 2006). According to Egwemi (2010), images of African countries are fettered by factors including the prejudices of the global system towards them, weak and corrupt governance structure, infrastructural deficiency, etc., thus, Africa's tourism potential remains unfulfilled (Osei and Gbadamosi, 2011). Consequently, the rebranding exercises in Nigeria were variously condemned as ineffective and constituent a wastage of resources (e.g. Agbese 2009; Egwemi 2010).

FINDINGS: CITY BRANDING – MATTERS ARISING

In assessing both Dubai and Lagos current positions, some potential problematic issues come into focus, which must be resolved in order to formulate an effective brand, particularly for Lagos. First, national identity is extremely hard to separate from place brand. For example, it could be very difficult for outsiders to dissociate the Lagos brand from their perceived image of Nigeria, and it may be difficult to isolate a distinctive Lagos characteristics from the general African common traits. The challenge is for Lagos to promote its distinctive uniqueness separate from the common Nigerian attributes. Likewise, whatever the achievements of the Dubai brand, the city will still be seen from the Arabian perspective with its associated connotations (e.g. autocracy).

Second, a major challenge in city branding is how to convey a distinct message or image to diverse audiences in various countries. It is nearly unfeasible to create a simple image or core message for a city that can be used by different industry sectors (e.g. Fan, 2006). For instance, it is difficult to develop an advertisement for Lagos/Dubai that could possibly help to sell various services such as tourism, property, cultural commodities (music, films, cuisine, dress, etc.). Thus, the problem in city/place branding is attempting to be one thing to all audiences on all occasions. The message/image has to be pertinent and plausible to connect well with the audience. According to Fan (2006), an image that thrills in one culture or in a situation may not have the same effect in another. In general, it is nearly impracticable to control and coordinate the autonomous stakeholders under a single brand management structure (Giannopoulos *et al.*, 2011). Besides, it is often problematic to ascribe single meaning to the tourism destination products by the different markets and market segments involved (Fyall and Leask, 2007). In essence, an attempt to be one thing to all audiences or all things to all audiences reduces the impact of a message. According to Anholt (2010: 5) "the tiniest village is infinitely more complex, more diverse and less unified than the largest corporation, because of the different reasons why people are there".

Third, the time dimension of the place brand is also a factor. Several of the stereotypes and cultural undertones about Lagos (or Dubai) are historically rooted and cannot be easily forgotten by people in the face of some marketing promotions. For instance, the many preconceptions and stereotypes with regards to corruption, safety issues, weak governance, and poor infrastructures in Lagos/Nigeria could be a source of concern for many potential consumers (e.g. visitors). Similarly, the presumption of human rights and workers (immigrants) abuses in Dubai (e.g. Roth, 2017) could be difficult to shake off. Invariably, an understanding of the customer's existing perception of a place becomes imperative.

Fourth, aside from the external international audiences, the internal audience also plays an important role in the process of place branding. Studies (e.g. Erisman, 1983; Nworah, 2006) have indicated the powerful effects tourism has on cultures and local societies, for instance, Turner and Ash (1975: 197) consider tourism as "the enemy of authenticity and cultural identity". The concept of social carrying capacity; defined by Boniface and Cooper (2005: 33) as "a measure of the ability of the host community to tolerate tourism" is relevant here. The natives (internal audience) could be left feeling alienated if the country is branded in a way that seems 'foreign' to them. In some instances, a domestic audience may even find the depiction of their country to foreigners impertinent and distasteful. For example, the government's demolition of thousands of homes in parts of Lagos to create a modern mega city did not go down well with the locals (Kazeem, 2017). Correspondingly, in a survey by Zaidan and Kovacs (2017) the majority of Emiratis (62.6%) believed that development in Dubai serves the tourists' needs primarily rather than the local residents. Mueller and Schade (2012: 82) emphasise that "due to the number of mostly independently organised internal target groups of places with often diverging goals the problems of finding, communicating and keeping the brand promise is accepted to be a far more complex task compared to the branding of products".

Table 1 shows a compilation of benchmark performance across some major indices between the two cities.

Table 1. Comparative indicators between Dubai and Lagos

INDICATOR	DUBAI/UAE	LAGOS/NIGERIA
Population Density	400 people/km^2	7941 people/km^2
Unemployment Rate	0.4%	21%
Gross Domestic Product (GDP)	$82.1 billion	$30 billion
Median Age of Population	27 years	17.9 years
Number of Airports	2	1
Global Cities Index (measures global engagement of cities across five dimensions: business activity, human capital, information exchange, cultural experience and political engagement)	2.3	0.84
Level of Corruption (the effectiveness of law enforcement and transparency of making business)	6.8	2.4
Murder Rate (per 100,000 inhabitants)	2.99	12.2
Average Minimum Temperature	22.3°C	22.6°C
Average Salary	$3323	$200
Maximum Income Tax	1%	25%
Ethnic Groups	9	8
Economist Intelligence Unit (EIU) Hot Spots (survey of 120 countries)	23rd	119th
Globalisation and World Cities (survey of 307 countries)	10th	97th

Sources: Versus.com, 2018; JLL.com, 2015

DISCUSSION: FORMULATING AN INTEGRAL MODEL OF PLACE BRAND

The model represented in Figure 1 is an attempt to capture the factors influencing city/place brand/branding by highlighting the features of the country of origin, which intermingle with national culture and infrastructure. National culture and infrastructure are extracted from the template drawn by Foroudi *et al.* (2016). The country of origin aspects of soft power and reputation capital combined strategically with items on national culture and infrastructure scales to shape successful place/city branding and effective place brand.

However, Figure 2 shows the flow of causality between a nation brand and a place brand. To use the case cities' example, Dubai fits well with Figure 2B as the city's brand, well recognised around the world, appears to confer reputational capital on its country (UAE). Whereas, Figure 2A sums up the reality of Nigeria's reputation effect on the difficult task of branding Lagos. Still, a third path is represented in 2C which refers to both city and nation brands impacting each other correspondingly. Megacities such as London, New York, Tokyo, Hong Kong, etc. are good examples of this situation.

On the one hand, countries' international reputation is critical to the progress, prosperity, and good management of places/cities within their territories. In fact, a city's status will be significantly enhanced if its country has good reputation or image. On the other hand, a robust city's image could bestow reputation capital to its country. For instance, the London brand contributes higher reputation to the image

Figure 1. An integrative model of city brand
Source: Research Analysis

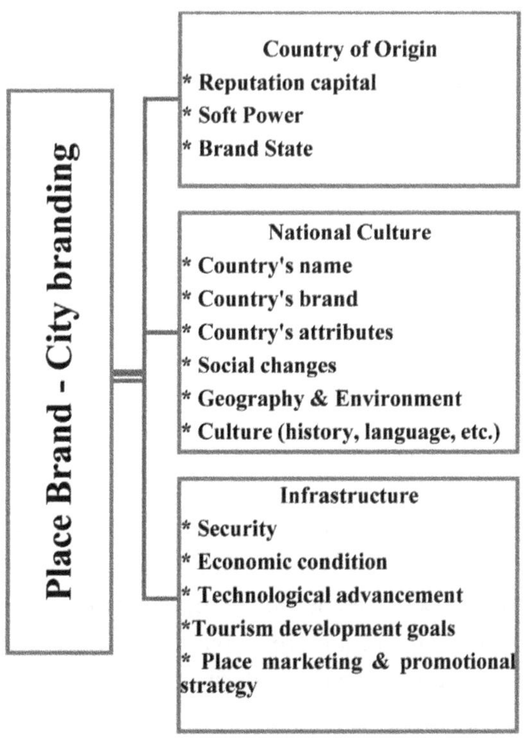

Figure 2. Nation brand/place brand flow of causation
Source: Research Analysis

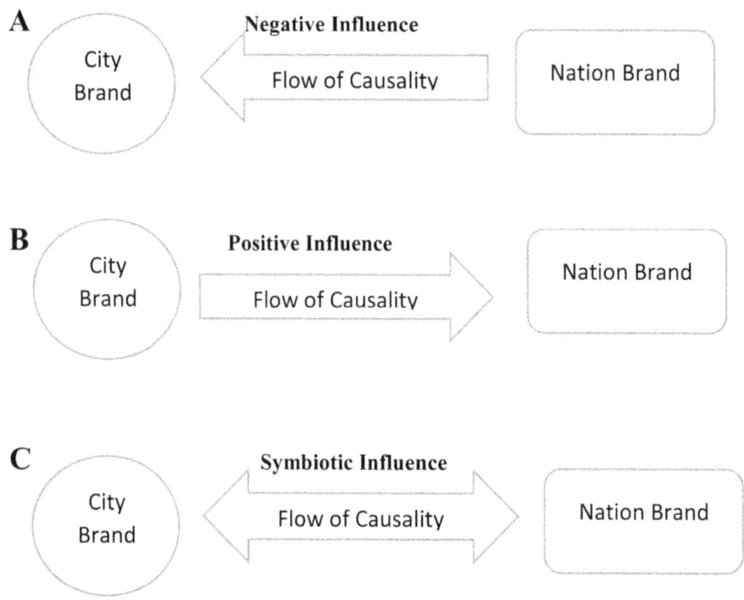

of the UK than cities like Manchester or Glasgow. Yet, a city's brand/branding can be encumbered by the negative image of its country similar to Anholt's (2007) contention that, aside from their own badly defined images, individual countries can suffer from the potentially negative image of the continent in which they are embedded. For instance, the brand image of Africa tends to be dominated, albeit unfairly, by generalised perceptions of famine and disaster rather than differentiated images of individual countries in the continent each with its own unique identity and phases of development (Osei and Gbadamosi, 2008). One could easily imagine the difficulties of brand/rebranding cities in Africa or similar region with poor reputation/image.

There are examples of places/cities that have a higher reputation than their own countries. For example, the allure of places/locations like the Greek Islands (e.g. Corfu, Crete, Mykonos, Rhodes, Hydra, Patmos, etc.) is far greater than the Greece mainland itself. The fascination of the Islands has helped Greece (and possibly Turkey) to attract international tourists. Certainly, many tourists going to Hawaii (USA), Tuvalu (Tuvalu), Easter Island (Chile), Bora Bora or Tahiti (French Polynesia) all in the Polynesian Islands are swayed by those places individual attributes rather than that of their countries of origin.

Just like Dubai, a city like Lagos can become an 'oasis' of fun and destination of choice for international tourists if its rebranding exercise is carefully managed. Lagos generates higher internally generated revenues than any other State in Nigeria (ThisDaylive.com, 2017) and this could be prudently used to provide infrastructural necessities and improve the national cultural architecture. As Keller (2008: 48) argues, "the power of a brand lies in what resides in the minds of the customers", therefore a successful Lagos branding campaign will help creates a more favourable image among the international audience and this could have a positive impact on Nigeria's international image.

CONCLUSION AND POLICY IMPLICATIONS

The two-city case of Dubai and Lagos provides an exploratory platform to link city/place branding and strategic planning, and the imperativeness of understanding those current and potential links within the national context. Whereas Dubai's brand could be seen as contributing to the rising profile of UAE on the world stage, Lagos brand's success could only be based on strategic isolation from Nigeria's poor reputation. Though the two cities are classified as emerging world cities the differences between them are wide (see Table 1).

The combination of factors (COO, National Culture, & Infrastructure) illustrated in Figure 1 is germane for effective city branding; particularly when driven by clear objectives, clear decision making, and good communication processes (Moulanen & Rainsto, 2009). Nevertheless, a country or a city with a negative image underpinned by crime, war, poverty, disease, or corruption will have a poor reputation and unable to attract many tourists, foreign investors, trading partners or even consumers for locally produced products (Anholt, 2007). Invariably, a positive image enables a nation/city to achieve a more advantageous position in global economic and political competition, and attracts tourists and investors (Lee and Yoon, 2010).

The Lagos State governments set a vision of making Lagos an attractive destination for tourists and to raise enough revenue to improve its infrastructure. Yet, attracting positive recognition is difficult in an over-crowded and deregulated global marketplace underpinned by the supposedly 'attention economy' (Aronczyk, 2008). The international market environment is structured such that "a wealth of information creates a poverty of attention" (Davenport & Beck, 2001: 11) in it. Indeed, cities, like countries, compete in the global marketplace such that acquiring and maintaining a good reputation is turning to be the cost of entry into that marketplace. In essence, the application of the concept of place branding as a communications strategy in the Lagos' practical initiatives to organise and manage its projected global image needs careful handling. For a city like Lagos to enhance its status, it has to create a constantly harmonised steady flow of effective and relevant ideas, products, and policies (Anholt, 2013).

The implication is that Lagos should focus more on developing multi-dimensional marketing elements to improve its global image. For example, the branding and image of a city "and the successful transference of this image to its exports - is just as important as what they actually produce and sell" (True, 2006: 74). Dubai should also continue to improve on its marketing strategies so that its core competencies do not become core rigidity (). It is incumbent on cities like Lagos (same applies to Dubai) to regularly appraise and examine the international perception of themselves and develop a strategy for its management. One of the approaches mentioned by Anholt (2013) is to engage in a cultural relationship, which is a more effective way of branding a nation/city. The cultural relationship activity entails the process of educating others to get to know a city/place better, thus, increasing and celebrating its complexity instead of reducing it. In effect, engagement is more productive than promotion, and cities that consistently practised cultural relations tend to engender conducive socio-economic environment.

An important implication of this study is the prospect for cities to create effective brands irrespective of the reputation (strong or weak) of their countries of origin. Thus, the reverse relationship between nation brand and city brand has the potential to expand the theoretical framework of city/place brand. Another implication is the need for Lagos brand managers to allocate resources for fostering long-term relationships with investors and other target audiences, and its media strategy needs to be balanced by face-to-face contacts. In echoing Anholt (1998), city branding should be regarded as a long-term project and immediate result should not be anticipated. It is essential that Lagos brand managers create differentiation in their communication to the international community in order to gain a competitive advantage in the competitive global marketplace. Two important tools that can help a city manage its international standing are brand image and brand identity. Hence, it is necessary to regularly check that these two are harmonised in order to flag potential problems and forestall reputation mishaps (Davies & Chun, 2002).

Since the current spate of rebranding activities of the Lagos State governments may not be successful or effective given the reputation of Nigeria on the world stage. It behoves on Lagos State authorities to devise a solitary system in their branding/rebranding strategy. If successful, the Lagos brand could rub off on Nigeria in at least two major areas. First, it could generate a competitive race by other States and cities in Nigeria as they will also want to improve their own internally generated revenues through increased in local and international tourists' visits. According to Boisen *et al*. (2011: 136), a "coherent, strong and attractive place brand will help promote economic development" and is likely to support spatial-transformations (Ashworth, 2011). Second, the Nigeria brand will be positively enhanced as international entities come to link Lagos with Nigeria.

This study contributes by highlighting the reverse relationship between nation brand and city brand and the likelihood of cities (e.g. Lagos/Mexico City) located in regions/countries (e.g. Nigeria/Mexico) with reputation/image problems to independently and strategically formulate a positive image for themselves. However, gaps (e.g. the formulated model is too generic, few number of cases, depth of analysis, and methodology) in the study provide avenue for further research in this area of study.

REFERENCES

Abimbola, T. (2006). Market access for developing economies: Branding in Africa. *Place Branding and Public Diplomacy*, *2*(2), 108–117. doi:10.1057/palgrave.pb.5990049

Agbese, D. (2009). *Rebranding Nigeria: An Appraisal*. Available at: http://www.newswatchngr.com/index.php?option=com_content&task=view&id=1232&Itemid=1

Agunbiade, O. M., & Ayotunde, T. (2011). Spirituality in Cybercrime (Yahoo Yahoo) Activities among Youths in South West Nigeria. In *Youth Culture and Net Culture: Online Social Practices* (pp. 357–380). IGI Global.

Akwagyiram, A. (2016). *Nigeria's music scene becomes a cultural export*. Available at: https://www.reuters.com/article/us-nigeria-music/nigerias-music-scene-becomes-a-cultural-export-idUSKCN0ZN124

Alvesson, M., & Skoldberg, K. (2000). *Reflexive Methodology: New Vistas for Qualitative Research*. London: Sage.

Amakihe, E. (2016). Branding Lagos through regeneration of historical physical features. *Journal of Urban Regeneration & Renewal*, *10*(1), 50-57.

Anholt, S. (1998). Nation-Brands of the Twenty-First Century. *Journal of Brand Management*, *5*(6), 395–406. doi:10.1057/bm.1998.30

Anholt, S. (2006). The Anholt-GMI City Brands Index: How the world sees the world's cities. *Place Branding*, *2*(1), 18–31. doi:10.1057/palgrave.pb.5990042

Anholt, S. (2007). *Competitive Identity: The New Brand Management for Nations, Cities and Regions*. London: Palgrave Macmillan. doi:10.1057/9780230627727

Anholt, S. (2010). *Places: Identity, Image and Reputation*. London: Palgrave Macmillan.

Anholt, S. (2013). Beyond the Nation Brand: The Role of Image and Identity in International Relations, Exchange. *The Journal of Public Diplomacy*, *12*(1), 6–12.

AOHR-UK. (2014). *Forced Disappearance and Torture in the United Arab Emirates*. Available at: http://aohr.org.uk/images/releases/forced-disappearance-torture-in-UAE.pdf

Arnold, T. (2012). *Dubai property draws Nigerians*. Available at: https://www.thenational.ae/business/property/dubai-property-draws-nigerians-1.394019

Aronczyk, M. (2008). "Living the Brand": Nationality, Globality and the Identity Strategies of Nation Branding Consultants. *International Journal of Communication*, *2*, 41–65.

Ashworth, G. J. (2011). Should we brand places? *Journal of Town and City Management*, *1*(3), 248–252.

Ashworth, G. J., & Kavaratzis, M. (2007). Beyond the logo: Brand management for cities. *Journal of Brand Management*, *16*(8), 520–531. doi:10.1057/palgrave.bm.2550133

Ashworth, G. J., & Voogd, H. (1990). *Selling the City: Marketing Approaches in Public Sector Urban Planning*. London: Belhaven Press.

Ashworth, G. J., & Voogt, H. (1994). Marketing and place promotion. In S. V. Ward & J. R. Gold (Eds.), *Place Promotion, the Use of Publicity and Marketing to Sell Towns and Regions* (pp. 39–52). Chichester, UK: John Wiley.

Babatunde, J. (2016). *Why Nigerians still visit Dubai-Obinwa*. Available at: https://www.vanguardngr.com/2016/11/nigerians-still-visit-dubai-obinwa/

Balakrishnan, M. S. (2008). Dubai – a star in the east: A case study in strategic destination branding. *Journal of Place Management and Development*, *1*(1), 62–91. doi:10.1108/17538330810865345

Baloglu, S., & McCleary, K. W. (1999). A Model of destination image formation. *Annals of Tourism Research*, *26*(4), 868–879. doi:10.1016/S0160-7383(99)00030-4

Blain, C., Stuart, E. L., & Brent, J. R. (2005). Destination Branding: Insights and Practices from Destination Management Organizations. *Journal of Travel Research*, *43*(4), 328–338. doi:10.1177/0047287505274646

Blechman, B. M. (2004). Book review, "Soft power: The means to success in world politics." *Political Science Quarterly*, 680–681. doi:10.1002/j.1538-165X.2004.tb01291.x

Bobley, G. (2017). *The 2017 Reputation Survey Reveals That Dubai Is the Most Reputable City in the GCC*. Available at: https://me.popsugar.com/love/2017-Reputation-Survey-44106521

Boisen, M., Terlouw, K., & Van Gorp, B. (2011). The selective nature of place branding and the layering of spatial identities. *Journal of Place Management and Development*, *4*(2), 135–147. doi:10.1108/17538331111153151

Boniface, B., & Cooper, C. (2005). *Worldwide destinations: The geography of travel and tourism*. Elsevier.

Botz-Bornstein, T. (2012). A Tale of Two Cities: Hong Kong and Dubai Celebration of Disappearance and the Pretension of Becoming. *Transcience*, *3*(2), 1–16.

Brand Finance. (2014). *Nation Brands: The Annual Report on Nation Brands*. Available at: http://brandfinance.com/images/upload/brand_finance_nation_brands_report_2014_final_edition.pdf

Bulkeley, H. (2005). Reconfiguring environmental governance: Towards a politics of scales and networks. *Political Geography*, *24*(8), 875–902. doi:10.1016/j.polgeo.2005.07.002

Caldwell, N., & Freire, J. (2004). The differences between branding a country, a region and a city: Applying the Brand Box Model. *Journal of Brand Management*, *12*(1), 50–59. doi:10.1057/palgrave.bm.2540201

Chang, D. L., Sabatini-Marques, J., da Costa, E. M., Selig, P. M., & Yigitcanlar, T. (2018). Knowledge-based, smart and sustainable cities: A provocation for a conceptual framework. *Journal of Open Innovation: Technology, Market, and Complexity*, *4*(5), 1–17.

Coombe, W. D. (2010). *Branding Dubai: Global Perceptions of a 21st Century Emirate*. American University of Beirut.

Cresswell, J. W., & Plano, C. V. L. (2011). *Designing and Conducting mixed method research* (2nd ed.). Thousand Oaks, CA: Sage.

Davenport, T., & Beck, J. (2001). *The Attention Economy: Understanding the New Currency of Business*. Boston: Harvard Business School Press.

Davies, G., & Chun, R. (2002). Gaps between the Internal and External Perceptions of the Corporate Brand. *Corporate Reputation Review*, *5*(2/3), 143–159.

De Chernatony, L. (1999). Brand management through narrowing the gap between brand identity and brand reputation. *Journal of Marketing Management*, *15*(1-3), 157–179. doi:10.1362/026725799784870432

De Chernatony, L. (2001). *From Brand Vision to Brand Evaluation*. Oxford, UK: Butterworth Heinemann.

De Chernatony, L., & Harris, F. (2001). Corporate branding and corporate brand performance. *European Journal of Marketing*, *35*(3/4), 441–456. doi:10.1108/03090560110382101

De Grazia, V. (2005). *Irresistible Empire: America's Advance through Twentieth-Century Europe*. Cambridge, MA: Belknap Press.

Dinnie, K. (2015). *Nation branding: Concepts, Issues, Practice*. London: Routledge.

DIT. (2015). *Doing business in the United Arab Emirates: UAE trade and export guide*. Available at: https://www.gov.uk/government/publications/exporting-to-the-united-arab-emirates/exporting-to-the-united-arab-emirates

Drenttel, W. (2004). *My Country Is Not A Brand*. Available at: https://designobserver.com/feature/my-country-is-not-a-brand/2707

Dubai Statistics Center. (2016). *Expatriates living in Dubai*. Available at: https://www.dsc.gov.ae/Report/Gross%20Domestic%20Product%20at%20Current%20Prices%202015-2014.pdf

Egwemi, V. (2010). Managing Nigeria's Image Crisis: Akunyili's Rebranding Programme to the Rescue (?) Current Research. *Journal of Economic Theory*, *2*(3), 131–135.

Eisenhardt, K. M. (1989). Building theories from case study research. *Academy of Management Review*, *14*(4), 532–550. doi:10.5465/amr.1989.4308385

Ekundayo, J. M. (2013). *Out of Africa: Fashola-Reinventing Servant Leadership to Engender Nigeria's Transformation*. Bloomington, IN: Author House.

Emirate247. (2016). *Dubai's hotel industry soaring high*. Available at: http://www.emirates247.com/news/dubai-s-hotel-industry-soaring-high-2016-04-28-1.628595

Encyclopædia Britannica. (2017). *Lagos: Nigeria*. Available at: https://www.britannica.com/place/Lagos-Nigeria

Erisman, H. M. (1983). Tourism and cultural dependency in the West Indies. *Annals of Tourism Research*, *10*(3), 337–361. doi:10.1016/0160-7383(83)90061-0

Ernst and Young. (2012). *Rapid-growth markets soft power index*. Available at: http://www.ey.com/Publication/vwLUAssets/Rapid

Fan, Y. (2006). Branding the Nation: What is being Branded? *Journal of Vacation Marketing*, *12*(1), 5–14. doi:10.1177/1356766706056633

Farquhar, P. H. (1989). Managing Brand Equity. *Marketing Research*, *1*(3), 24–33.

Ferenhof, H., & Fernandes, R. (2016). Desmistificando a revisão de literatura como base para a redação científica: Método SSF. *Revista ACB*, *21*, 550–563.

Ferguson, N. (2009). Think Again: Power. *Foreign Policy*. Available at: http://foreignpolicy.com/2009/11/03/think-again-power/

Flyvbjerg, B. (2006). Five misunderstandings about case-study research. *Qualitative Inquiry*, *12*(2), 219–245. doi:10.1177/1077800405284363

Foroudi, P., Gupta, S., Kitchen, P., Foroudi, M. M., & Nguyen, B. (2016). A framework of place branding, place image, and place reputation: Antecedents and moderators. *Qualitative Market Research*, *19*(2), 241–264. doi:10.1108/QMR-02-2016-0020

Frost, R. (2004). *Mapping a Country's Future*. Available at: http://www.brandchannel.com/features_effect.asp?pf_id=206

Fyall, A., & Leask, A. (2007). Destination marketing: Future issues-Strategic challenges. *Tourism and Hospitality Research*, *7*(1), 50–63. doi:10.1057/palgrave.thr.6050029

Gartner, W. C. (1989). Tourism image: Attribute measurement of state tourism products using multidimensional calling techniques. *Journal of Travel Research*, *28*(2), 15–19. doi:10.1177/004728758902800205

Gartner, W. C. (1993). Image formation process. *Journal of Travel & Tourism Marketing*, *2*(2), 191–215.

Ghauri, P., & Gronhaug, K. (2010). *Research Methods in Business Studies: A Practical Guide* (4th ed.). London: FT-Pearson.

Giannopoulos, A. A., Piha, P. L., & Avlonitis, G. J. (2011). An International Conference on the Future of Nation Branding, Tourism and International Investments in a Globalized World & Cultural Diplomacy in the Global Economy: A Forum for Young Leaders (CDEC). Berlin, Germany.

Gilboa, E. (2008). Searching for a theory of public diplomacy. *The Annals of the American Academy of Political and Social Science*, *616*(1), 55–77. doi:10.1177/0002716207312142

Gilmore, F. (2002). A country - can it be repositioned? Spain - the successful story of country branding. *Journal of Brand Management*, *9*(4/5), 281–293. doi:10.1057/palgrave.bm.2540078

Golf in Dubai. (2017). *Dubai Heritage and Culture*. Available at: https://www.golfindubai.com/visit-dubai/culture

Gómez, M., Fernández, A. C., Molina, A., & Aranda, E. (2016). City branding in European capitals: An analysis from the visitor perspective. *Journal of Destination Marketing & Management*, *7*, 190–201. doi:10.1016/j.jdmm.2016.11.001

Graf, A. (2009). Marketing a city-state: Hamburg and Singapore in comparison. In A. Graf & C. B. Huat (Eds.), *Port Cities in Asia and Europe* (pp. 176–189). New York: Routledge.

Gudjonsson, H. (2005). Nation branding. *Place Branding*, *1*(3), 283–298. doi:10.1057/palgrave.pb.5990029

Gunn, C. A. (1972). *Vacationscape. Designing Tourist Regions, Taylor and Francis*. Washington, DC: University of Texas.

Halinen, A., Törnroos, J. Å., & Elo, M. (2013). Network process analysis: An event-based approach to study business network dynamics. *Industrial Marketing Management*, *42*(8), 1213–1222. doi:10.1016/j.indmarman.2013.05.001

Hall, T. (2010). An Unclear Attraction: A Critical Examination of Soft Power as an Analytical Category. *The Chinese Journal of International Politics*, *3*(2), 189–211. doi:10.1093/cjip/poq005

Hari, J. (2009). *The dark side of Dubai*. Available at: http://www.independent.co.uk/voices/commentators/johann-hari/the-dark-side-of-dubai-1664368.html#

Herstein, R. (2012). The thin line between country, city and region branding. *Journal of Vacation Marketing*, *18*(2), 147–155. doi:10.1177/1356766711435976

Hotten, R. (2017). *Dubai Airshow: Airbus seals order with US firm Indigo*. Available at: http://www.bbc.co.uk/news/business-41994142

Informationng.com. (2016). *The Abuja Carnival*. Available at: https://www.informationng.com/2016/12/abuja-carnival-records-poor-turnout.html

Jackson, K. T. (2004). *Building Reputational Capital: Strategies for Integrity and Fair Play That Improve the Bottom Line*. Oxford, UK: Oxford University Press.

JLL.com. (2015). *Globalisation and Competition: The New World of Cities*. Available at: http://www.jll.com/Research/jll-new-world-of-cities-globalisation-and-competition-2015.pdf

Jonas, A. E. G. (2012). Region and Place: Regionalism in question. *Progress in Human Geography, 36*(2), 263–272. doi:10.1177/0309132510394118

Kaneva, N. (2011). Nation Branding: Toward an Agenda for Critical Research. *International Journal of Communication, 5*, 117–141.

Kavaratzis, M., & Ashworth, G. J. (2005). City branding: An effective assertion of identity or a transitory marketing trick? *Tijdschrift voor Economische en Sociale Geografie, 96*(5), 506–514. doi:10.1111/j.1467-9663.2005.00482.x

Kazeem, Y. (2017). *Lagos wants to be a modern mega city so it's forcing thousands of slum dwellers from their homes*. Available at: https://qz.com/936761/lagos-wants-to-be-a-modern-mega-city-so-its-forcing-thousands-of-slum-dwellers-from-their-homes/

Kearns, G., & Philo, C. (Eds.). (1993). *Selling Places. The City as Cultural Capital, Past and Present*. Oxford, UK: Pergamon Press.

Keller, K. L. (1993). Conceptualizing, Measuring and Managing Customer-Based Brand Equity. *Journal of Marketing, 57*(1), 1–22. doi:10.2307/1252054

Keller, K. L. (2008). *Strategic Brand Management: Building, Measuring, and Managing Brand Equity* (3rd ed.). Upper Saddle River, NJ: Pearson Prentice Hall.

Kerr, G. (2006). From Destination Brand to Location Brand. *Journal of Brand Management, 13*(4/5), 276–283. doi:10.1057/palgrave.bm.2540271

Kerr, P., & Wiseman, G. (2013). *Diplomacy in a Globalizing World: Theories and Practice*. New York: Oxford University Press.

Klewes, J., & Wreschniok, R. (2009). Introduction. In J. Klewes & R. Wreshniok (Eds.), *Reputation Capital: Building and Maintaining Trust in the 21st Century* (pp. 1–6). London: Springer. doi:10.1007/978-3-642-01630-1_1

Law, B. (2015). *United Arab Emirates: Revealing the dark face of the Gulf state where human rights abuses are a daily occurrence*. Available at: http://www.independent.co.uk/news/world/middle-east/united-arab-emirates-revealing-the-dark-face-of-the-gulf-state-where-human-rights-abuses-are-a-daily-a6683741.html

Lee, S., & Yoon, Y. (2010). The return on investment (ROI) of international public relations: A country-level analysis. *Public Relations Review, 36*(1), 15–20. doi:10.1016/j.pubrev.2009.08.011

Lefkoff-Hagius, R., & Mason, C. H. (1993). Characteristic, beneficial, and image attributes in consumer judgments of similarity and preference. *The Journal of Consumer Research, 20*(1), 100–110. doi:10.1086/209336

Leisen, B. (2001). Image segmentation: The case of a tourism destination. *Journal of Services Marketing, 15*(1), 49–66. doi:10.1108/08876040110381517

Lucarelli, A., & Berg, P. O. (2011). City branding: A state-of-the-art review of the research domain. *Journal of Place Management and Development, 4*(1), 9–27. doi:10.1108/17538331111117133

Lumley, S. (2017). *Stay clear of Dubai, urge family of 'hip touch' Brit*. Available at: https://www.metro.news/stay-clear-of-dubai-urge-family-of-hip-touch-brit/774818/

Marazza, A. (2007). *A country brand is more than just a logo. Eight golden rules for branding a destination*. Available at: http://www.landor.com/index.cfm

Matsuda, T. (2007). *Soft Power and its perils: US Cultural Policy in Early Postwar Japan and Permanent Dependency*. Stanford University Press.

Mattern, J.B. (2005). Why 'Soft Power' Isn't So Soft: Representational Force and the Sociolinguistic Construction of Attraction in World Politics. *Millenium – Journal of International Studies, 33*(3), 583-612.

Mihailovich, P. (2006). Kinship branding: A concept of holism and evolution for the nation brand. *Place Branding*, *2*(3), 229–247. doi:10.1057/palgrave.pb.5990060

Miletsky, J., & Smith, G. L. (2009). *Perspectives on Branding*. Boston: Course Technology.

Moilanen, T., & Rainisto, S. (2009). *How to Brand Nations, Cities, & Destinations*. Basingstoke, UK: Palgrave. doi:10.1057/9780230584594

Mueller, A., & Schade, M. (2012). Symbols and place identity: A semiotic approach to internal place branding – case study Bremen (Germany). *Journal of Place Management and Development*, *5*(1), 81–92. doi:10.1108/17538331211209068

Nworah, U. (2006). *Rebranding Nigeria Critical Perspectives on The Heart Of Africa Image Project*. Available at: http://www.nigerialinks.com/pdf/RebrandingNigeria.pdf

Nworah, U. (2007). Branding Nigeria's Cities. In Advertising News (vol. 2). Lagos: APCON Publications.

Nye, J. (2004). *Soft Power: The Means to Success in World Politics*. New York: Perseus Books.

Nze, V. (2010, March 12). Tinapa - Cross River's Gift to Tourism. *Daily Champion*.

Ocho, C. (2009). *With 'Good People, Great Nation*. Country Rebrands. Available at http://allafrica.com/stories/200903180560.html

Ogbonnikan, F. (2017). *RRS: Rebranding for a Safer Lagos*. Available at: https://www.thisdaylive.com/index.php/2017/03/31/rrs-rebranding-for-a-safer-lagos/

Ojo, S. (2017). Examining the Impact of Symbolic Capital in Ethnic and Diaspora Entrepreneurship. In S. Ojo (Ed.), *Diaspora and Transnational Entrepreneurship in the Global Contexts* (pp. 66–89). Hershey, PA: IGI Global. doi:10.4018/978-1-5225-1991-1.ch004

Olins, W. (1999). *Trading Identities*. London: The Foreign Policy Centre.

Omidire, D. (2016). *Lagos State Unveils Urban Development Projects for Megacity Initiative*. Available at: https://estateintel.com/lagos-state-unveils-urban-development-projects-for-megacity-initiative/

Osei, C., & Gbadamosi, A. (2011). Re-branding Africa. *Marketing Intelligence & Planning*, *29*(3), 284–304. doi:10.1108/02634501111129257

Owuamanam, J., Alechenu, J. & Onuba, I. (2012). *Bombings threatening our economy*. Academic Press.

Ozer, S. U. (2016). The Role of Culture in City Branding. In A. Bayraktar & C. Uslay (Eds.), *Strategic Place Branding Methodologies and Theory for Tourist Attraction* (pp. 227–244). Hershey, PA: IGI Global.

Pearce, P. L. (1982). Perceived changes in holiday destinations. *Annals of Tourism Research*, *9*(2), 145–164. doi:10.1016/0160-7383(82)90044-5

Peirce, S., & Ritchie, B. W. (2007). National Capital Branding: A Comparative Case Study of Canberra, Australia and Wellington, New Zealand. *Journal of Travel & Tourism Marketing*, *22*(3-4), 67–78. doi:10.1300/J073v22n03_06

PwC. (2015). *Doing Business in the UAE A tax and legal guide*. Available at: https://www.pwc.com/m1/en/tax/documents/doing-business-guides/doing-business-guide-uae.pdf

Reputation Institute. (2013, October 17). *City RepTrak Study* (Press Release). Author.

Reputation Institute. (2017). *2017 Global Reptrak® - Most Reputable Companies in The World*. Available at: https://www.reputationinstitute.com/resources/registered/pdf-resources/2017-global-reptrak-most-reputable-companies-in.aspx

Romila, C. (2008). *Tourism Marketing and Crisis Management. Global Media.*

Roth, K. (2017). *United Arab Emirates: Events of 2016*. Available at: https://www.hrw.org/world-report/2017/country-chapters/united-arab-emirates

Sahin, S., & Baloglu, S. (2014). City branding: Investigating a brand advocacy model for distinct segments. *Journal of Hospitality Marketing & Management*, *23*(3/4), 239–265. doi:10.1080/19368623.2013.779562

Salmi, A. (2011). International research teams and collective case studies: an abductive approach. In R. Piekkari & C. Welch (Eds.), *Rethinking the Case Study in International Business and Management Research* (pp. 431–452). Cheltenham, UK: Edward Elgar. doi:10.4337/9780857933461.00033

Sandys, A. (2016). *Place branding: Lagos, Nigeria*. Available at: http://www.transformmagazine.net/articles/2016/place-branding-lagos-nigeria/

Sanusi. (n.d.). Available at: http://www.punchng.com/news/bombings-threatening-our-economy sanusi/

Sayer, A. (2010). *Method in Social Science: A Realist Approach*. London: Routledge.

Schultz, M., Moritsen, J., & Gabrielsen, G. (2006). Sticky reputation: Analyzing a ranking system. *Corporate Reputation Review*, *4*(1), 24–41. doi:10.1057/palgrave.crr.1540130

Sevin, E. (2014). Understanding cities through city brands: City branding as a social and semantic network. *Cities (London, England)*, *38*, 47–56. doi:10.1016/j.cities.2014.01.003

The Economist. (2015). *Learning from Lagos*. Available at: https://www.economist.com/news/middle-east-and-africa/21656701-nigerias-commercial-capital-crowded-noisy-violentand-model-rest

ThisDaylive.com. (2017). *Lagos Generates More IGR than 30 States Combined*. Available at: https://www.thisdaylive.com/index.php/2017/05/30/lagos-generates-more-igr-than-30-states-combined/

Trad, N. G. (2017). *2017 Country Reputation Ranking: Leaders, Highlights and Trends.* Available at: http://placebrandobserver.com/country-reputation-ranking-reptrak-2017/

True, J. (2006). Globalisation and Identity. In *Globalisation and Identity* (p. 74). South Melbourne: Oxford University Press.

Turner, L., & Ash, J. (1975). *The golden hordes: International tourism and the pleasure periphery.* London: Constable & Robinson Limited.

Turok, I. (2009). The Distinctive City: Pitfalls in the Pursuit of Differential Advantage. *Environment & Planning A, 41*(1), 13–30. doi:10.1068/a37379

Van Ham, P. (2010). *Social Power in International Politics.* Abingdon, UK: Routledge. doi:10.4324/9780203857847

Vanguard Newspaper. (2017). *Buhari signs 9 agreements with UAE to strengthen FG's anti-corruption campaign.* Available at: https://www.vanguardngr.com/2017/08/buhari-signs-9-agreements-uae-strengthen-fgs-anti-corruption-campaign/

Verlegh, P., & Steenkamp, J. (1999). A review and meta-analysis of country-of-origin research. *Journal of Economic Psychology, 20*(5), 521–546. doi:10.1016/S0167-4870(99)00023-9

Versus.com. (2018). *Dubai city versus Lagos.* Available at: https://versus.com/en/dubai-city-vs-lagos

Wam. (2014). *UAE ranks among most developed countries.* Available at: http://www.emirates247.com/news/emirates/uae-ranks-among-most-developed-countries-2014-12-06-1.572337

Wanjiru, E. (2006). Branding African countries: A prospect for the future. *Place Branding and Public Diplomacy, 2*(1), 84–95. doi:10.1057/palgrave.pb.5990047

Welch, C., Piekkari, R., Plakoyiannaki, E., & Paavilainen-Mäntymäki, E. (2010). Theorising from case studies: Towards a pluralist future for international business research. *Journal of International Business Studies, 42*(5), 740–762. doi:10.1057/jibs.2010.55

White, C. (2012). Brands and national image: An exploration of inverse country-of-origin effect. *Place Branding and Public Diplomacy, 8*(2), 110–118. doi:10.1057/pb.2012.6

Wo-lap, W. L. (2016). *Getting lost in 'One Belt, One Road'.* Available at: http://www.ejinsight.com/20160412-getting-lost-one-belt-one-road/

Woodside, A. G., & Lysonski, S. (1989). A General Model of Traveler Destination Choice. *Journal of Travel Research, 27*(Spring), 8–14. doi:10.1177/004728758902700402

Zaidan, E., & Kovacs, J. F. (2017). Resident Attitudes towards Tourists and Tourism Growth: A Case Study from the Middle East, Dubai in United Arab Emirates. *European Journal of Sustainable Development, 6*(1), 291–307. doi:10.14207/ejsd.2017.v6n1p291

Zenker, S., & Braun, E. (2010). The Place Brand Centre – A Conceptual Approach for the Brand Management of Places. In *EMAC (European Marketing Academy), 39th European Marketing Academy Conference.* Brussels: EMAC.

Chapter 11
Facilitating Consumers' Adoption of E-Government in South Africa:
Supply Side-Driven Virtuous Cycles

Richard Shambare
University of Venda, South Africa

ABSTRACT

This chapter examines the diffusion and adoption of electronic governance systems (e-government) in South Africa. The purpose of the chapter is to determine how the supply side in South Africa has facilitated consumers' adoption of e-government. To achieve this objective, an extensive review of the literature encapsulating e-government, South African public services, information communication technologies (ICTs), and commerce was conducted. Findings revealed interesting results. First among many was that e-government is viewed by the government as a panacea to a plethora of socio-economic problems facing the country. It was further revealed that e-government initiatives at the municipality level are quite instrumental in driving the e-government agenda in South Africa. Of note, municipalities have rolled out various e-government programs. As a result, the country's overall e-government rankings were observed to have significantly improved in the recent past. The chapter concludes by highlighting several opportunities through which e-government could be further strengthened.

1. INTRODUCTION

The use of ICTs in the provision of public goods and services, commonly known as electronic government (e-government or e-gov), is a fast developing phenomenon. e-Government is simply leveraging on the power of the Internet to provide public services on-demand, i.e., 24 hours–7 days a week (Heeks, 2006). For instance, e-government allows for ratepayers to view and settle bills online on a municipality website, among other features, anytime and from anywhere (e-Tshwane, 2018). Although the e-government hype is rapidly diffusing in different parts of the world, it is not as widely received in developing countries.

DOI: 10.4018/978-1-5225-7906-9.ch011

In Africa, for example, most countries are observed to be lagging behind on the various e-gov indices such as e-government development index (EGDI) and the e-participation index (EPI). With the diffusion of these new innovations, it is clear that consumers' uptake of e-government is sporadic. As illustrated in past studies (c.f., Mosekwa, 2018; Mutula & Mostert, 2010; Shambare, 2016), adoption rates are, on the whole, quite low.

Specifically, Shambare (2016) identified some barriers and constraints inhibiting the rapid uptake of e-government in developing countries. Some of the barriers identified amounted to consumers' attitudinal issues and structural features. Citizens' behavioural and attitudinal factors such as risk, trust, and illiteracy accounted for most of the consumer constraints. On the other hand, structural barriers consisted of poor infrastructure, limited availability of Internet connection, high Internet data costs, and apathy from governments to establish e-government portals. While the above-mentioned constraints are characteristic of the state of e-government in most developing countries, South Africa, in the last three to five years, has reversed this trend, as increasingly more consumers are resorting to e-government.

The latest United Nations e-Government 2018 survey sheds new light and points towards a positive rebound for South Africa. In the period up until 2014, South Africa's e-Participation global ranking declined from 83rd position in 2012 to 97th position in 2014 (United Nations, 2018). However, today, its global ranking stands at an impressive 39th position, which even surpasses Mauritius – the highest ranked African country in terms of e-government. According to United Nations (2018:33), e-participation refers to the practice of striving for the "digital inclusion" of all citizens within a country. In other words, e-participation, as a government programme, strives for total ICT-coverage. This means connecting those unconnected to the Internet; and not leaving anyone unconnected to the use of information and communication technologies to broaden and deepen civic participation by enabling citizens to connect with one another and with their elected representatives (McIntosh, 2004).

Clearly, the South African case study is an impressive one. It, therefore, was opportune for this chapter to examine the e-participation ambitions of the South African government. More importantly, the strategies employed to help citizens overcome barriers associated with e-government adoption are worthy of investigation. In doing so, the chapter seeks to highlight the many consumer behaviour lessons learnt from the South African e-government case study. Chief among these is that supply-side interventions including branding and advertising are crucial steps in promoting adoption of innovations. Naturally, such intervention is dependent on service providers' comprehension of consumers' needs. It is against this background that this chapter examines some of the supply-side considerations in the consumers' adoption of e-government in South Africa.

The rest of the chapter is structured as follows: Section 2 examines the e-government agenda in South Africa. It focuses on the various e-government initiatives, scope and the various e-gov indicators. Section 3 provides an analysis of the supply-side of e-government programmes in South Africa. Therein, the different strategies employed by government and public sector organisations are discussed. Then in Section 4, some suggestions and opportunities of e-government initiatives are discussed. Lastly, Section 5 provides some concluding remarks.

2. E-GOVERNMENT IN SOUTH AFRICA

Beginning in 1994, at the dawn of democracy, the South African government committed to redressing past injustices of the apartheid era. Embedded within this agenda, the South African government prioritised two programmes: (1) enhancing the dignity of all South Africans through improved service delivery and the unrestricted access to quality public goods and services to all citizens; and (2) leapfrogging South Africa into the information age. e-Government, therefore, presented itself as a solution that potentially could address both these challenges simultaneously. Consequently, the government sought to provide strategic direction for the movement towards information and communication technologies (ICTs) by promulgating the Green Paper on e-Commerce and the White Paper on Science and Technology in 2000. The latter documents, thereby, can be deemed to have provided the foundations for the National e-Government Framework (Western Cape, 2001) as well as subsequent e-government programmes in the country (Shambare, 2016).

The apartheid history and the impending growth of the knowledge economy in the late 20th century increased pressure for the South African government to adopt e-government systems. The government, thus, needed to find a lasting solution to unite the country and resolve these problems. Hence, e-government was identified the e-government route as a form of governance designed to restore and maintain citizens' dignity (South Africa, 1997). Consequently, e-government in South Africa was catapulted by public sector organisations (PSOs). These PSOs introduced a wide variety of e-government initiatives ranging from telephone call centres to websites to electronic tax (e-tax) (Komba & Ngulube, 2012; Mutula & Mostert, 2010; Shambare, 2016).

2.1. Defining E-Government Within the South African Context

As an academic discipline, e-government is still developing (Belanger & Carter, 2008; Heeks, 2006), and as such, is prone to having a multiplicity of definitions on what constitutes e-government (Rorissa, Demissie, & Pardo, 2011). For instance, Heeks (2006) defines e-government as the utilisation of ICTs by PSOs. On the other hand, Layne and Lee (2001:13) define "e-government as government's use of technology, particularly web-based Internet applications to improve access to and deliver government information and services to citizens, business partners, employees, organisations, and government entities." From studying these two definitions, the variations in the definitions become clear. Although it is tempting to restrict e-government to the use of technology by PSOs or government (Akakandelwa, 2011; Heeks, 2006), such as definition fails to fully acknowledge the extent and bounds of e-government.

For this reason, this chapter proposes a holistic definition that encompasses various other factors including environmental issues and desired outcomes as integral aspects of e-government. Consequently, e-government is conceptualised as the reinvention and reorganisation of government and reformulation of the government-to-citizen interaction in a manner than not only increases citizens' participation in governance, but also empowers them (Dlamini, Ngobeni, & Mutanga, 2010; Hornung et al., 2007; Western Cape, 2001). Technology, therefore, is one of many components of e-government. For example, the implementation of e-government programmes such as e-tax requires reorganisation of revenue authorities beyond just publishing an e-tax website. The revenue office would need to design of new communications channels, new data submission forms, and even new tax regulations to support the e-tax system. In addition, strong technical support systems and project management infrastructure are necessary for the viability of e-government systems (Mazengera & Mavetera, 2006). The reorganisation of PSOs is illustrated in Figure 1, which demonstrates that the e-government evolution takes place in three distinct stages – the Old Government, New Government, and the e-Government Phases.

Prior to the advent of information technology (IT), in the Old Government phase, government-citizen interactions were limited to citizens completing paper-based applications (e.g., passport application

Figure 1. The evolution of E-Government

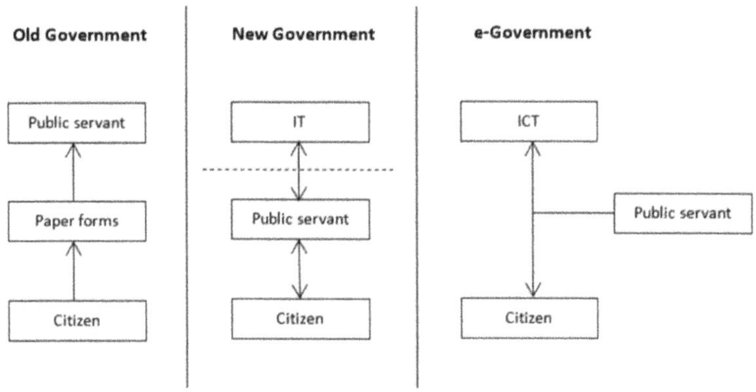

forms). Thereafter, public servants would manually process the forms. With the advent of IT, in the New Government phase, citizens still interacted with public servants within government offices. The government employees, in turn, would utilise IT systems to process forms. However, in the e-Government phase, citizens actively interact with the government directly using ICT-driven self-service platforms Public servants, if needed, only serve as support mechanisms. From the foregoing, therefore, e-government is defined to mean:

1. All attempts by government or any PSO to leverage their activities through the application of a variety of technological innovations (e.g., email, fax, Internet, SMS, social media, and telephone).
2. The use of these technological innovations to improve the efficiency of PSOs and government in as far as the provision and delivery of public goods and services.
3. The expansion of government and public goods as well their provisions beyond the traditional working hours and physical buildings.
4. A reorganisation and, to a certain extent, reinvention of government to become more responsive to citizens', businesses' and other constituents' needs.

2.1.1. Benefits of E-Government

e-Government promises a multitude of benefits to both citizens and PSOs. Past studies reveal that e-government consistently improves quality of life and reduces costs and time for service delivery, thereby improving governance (Koh & Prybutok, 2003; Mazengera & Mavetera, 2006; Reynolds & Regio, 2001; United Nations, 2014). In particular, the development and implementation of e-government programmes can be associated with the following benefits:

1. **Delivering of Integrated Public Services:** More than just offering services online instead of in-line, governments can provide value-added and integrated services.
2. **Bridging the Digital Divide:** Governments can promote the access to new technologies as well as provide computer literacy education. This applies mostly to developing countries.
3. **Promoting Government-Customer Relationships:** Rather than providing services in a uniform way to all citizens, governments can utilise new technologies to customise and personalise services.

4. **Reduced Corruption and Increased Transparency:** Since e-government allows for stronger institutional capacity on the part of the government (Koh & Prybutok, 2003; United Nations, 2014), services become more enhanced and more easily accessible. With this, there is increased transparency and reduced incidents of corruption (Shambare, 2012).
5. **Fostering Economic Development**: Governments can help businesses to move online and assist them to use online tools. It also helps to develop local skills and increase employment prospects.
6. **Creating a More Participative Form of Government**: Ultimately, e-government can lead to direct democracy. For instance, at the local level, municipalities can support online debates, discussion forums and Internet voting to inform decision-making processes.

Authors such as Hornung et al. (2007) assert that there is a compounding effect of benefits of e-government, which gradually and progressively build up over time (see Figure 2). In other words, e-government enables PSOs to become more effective; which, over time, develops centres of excellence. Ultimately, it is these centres of excellence that drive efficiencies in the production of public goods and services. Increased efficiency, naturally, promotes open and transparent administrative processes, which in time progress to accountability. Eventually, as more individuals use e-government and participate in civic duties and governance, the highest benefits in the form of e-Democracy become realised (Dlamini et al, 2010).

Figure 2 demonstrates that the overall benefits of e-government accrue and realisable to the entire society, and not necessarily only to the individual citizens that utilise them. This line of thought is supported by the South African government that acknowledges e-government as a catalyst for poverty alleviation, wealth creation and the improvement of the standard and the quality of life (South Africa, 1997; Western Cape, 2001).

2.1.2. Approaches to E-Government

There are two major practical approaches to e-government – online and offline e-government. Figure 3 summarises the different approaches to e-government. The type of technology that mediates e-government services distinguishes the e-government approaches (Dlamini et al, 2010).

Figure 2. The cumulative accrual of E-Government benefits

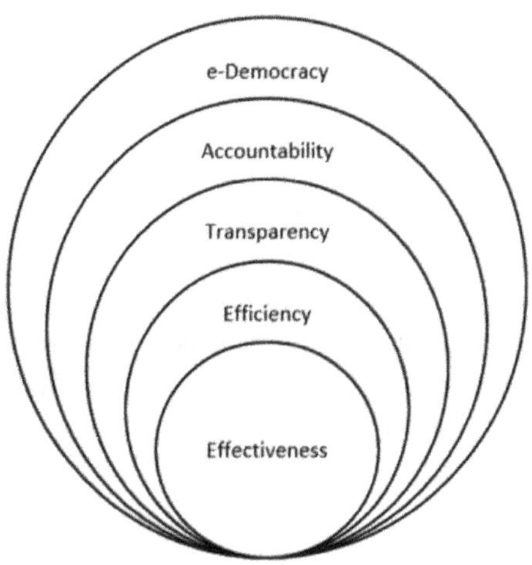

Figure 3. Approaches to E-Government

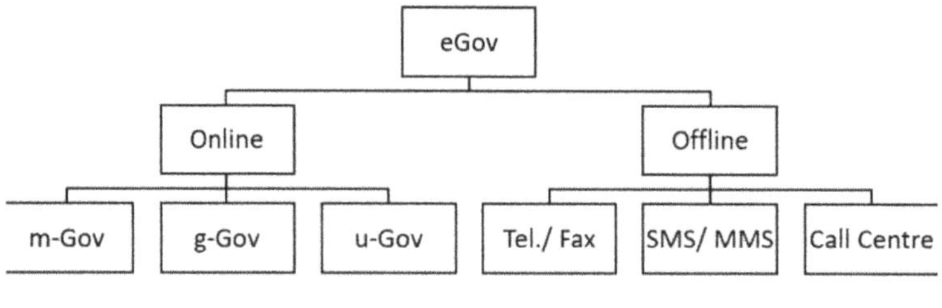

Online e-government services refer to those services that rely on the Internet and Web-based technologies, including the use of mobile phones in mobile government (m-gov), Global Positioning Satellites (GPS) applications for e-government (g-gov) and ubiquitous government (u-gov). Offline e-government services utilise technologies that do not rely on the Internet, such as telephones, faxes, and short message services (SMS).

2.2. The Scope Of E-Government in South Africa

Although the South African government and many PSOs began using ICTs to interact with their employees, businesses, and the public, it was only in 2000 when the government provided a comprehensive national e-government agenda. In the same year, the Green Paper on e-Commerce and the White Paper on Science and Technology provided the foundations for the National e-Government Framework (Western Cape, 2001).

The growth of the knowledge economy in the late 20th century increased pressure for the government to adopt e-government systems. The rise of the information age further coincided with the birth of the 'new democratic South Africa,' in 1994. The new South African government was concerned with two major problems:

1. The urgent need to redress the injustices of apartheid policies that institutionalised disparity in service delivery. These policies meant that only a privileged few enjoyed unrestricted access to quality public goods and services while the majority largely lacked access to public goods and services. The government needed to find a lasting solution to unite the country and resolve the service delivery problem. Hence, e-government was identified as a driver of the principles of Batho Pele – a form of governance designed to restore and maintain human dignity (South Africa, 1997).
2. The country was lagging in terms of socio-economic development, and in particular ICT usage. At the turn of the 21st century it became clear that the knowledge economy was fast replacing the production economy (Heeks, 2006). Increased use of ICTs was fuelling globalisation. In this context, the government became interested in the power of technology and its ability to improve the standard and quality of life of citizens.

At a macro level, developing e-government was seen as a win-win situation – a method for reducing the technology gap (Shambare, 2014), which ultimately would make South Africa an attractive investment destination. More importantly, e-government was viewed as a mechanism to abolish the pluralism in service delivery and to restore human dignity (South Africa, 1997). As a result, South Africa committed to increasing its investment in e-government programmes. But, to successfully roll out e-government to all citizens, the South African government relied on principles of equity, fairness, respect, and morality. To this end, e-government in the country was largely informed by the principles of Batho Pele, which loosely translates to mean " considering people first" in English.

2.2.1. The Principles of Batho Pele as the Framework for E-Government in South Africa

Batho Pele is a Sotho phrase. Batho Pele has its roots in the collective African philosophies of *Ubuntu* or *Unhu* that seek to espouse "good or ideal morals" and behaviour (Gelfand, 1970). According to this philosophy, a person fully becomes mature and 'complete' by making his or her needs subservient to those of others (Gelfand, 1970). By extension, a government can only be a true government of the people by serving its constituents. Consequently, the new government regarded unconditional service delivery to all South Africans, regardless of colour or race, as a prerequisite to citizenship, and an imperative to building a strong democratic society (South Africa, 1997).

Unlike the apartheid regime, whose policies were biased towards the white minority population and big businesses; the new government needed to embark on plans to extend equitable service delivery to all South Africans. The Batho Pele, as a political ideology, was adopted as a means to restore dignity and humanity to a divided country (Kaisara & Pather, 2011). Former President Nelson Mandela's Administration, in October 1997, introduced eight principles to guide the implementation of Batho Pele:

1. **Consultation:** From time to time, government should conduct consultations with its 'customers' – citizens, businesses, and other constituents. Consultation serves two primary purposes:
    a. It affords government the opportunity to interact with its customers and determine the types of products and services required by the latter, and
    b. It provides feedback on the quality of services the government provides. Tools such as customer surveys, interviews with individual users and consultation with various representative groups are some of the ways the government intends to practice this principle.
2. **Setting Service Standards:** Benchmarking against international standards should be undertaken constantly to ensure the country remains competitive. Standards must be in place for citizens to evaluate how far service provision goes towards meeting their needs.
3. **Increasing Access:** Government intends to address the inequalities created by apartheid by increasing access to public services. To achieve this objective, gateways, multi-purpose centres and call centres have been erected around the country.
4. **Ensuring Courtesy:** This principle emphasizes treating citizens with consideration and respect. An open, honest and transparent community with citizens is desired to instil confidence amongst citizens in public services.
5. **Providing Information:** Information must be readily available where it is needed, and alternative plans made should this option fail. The information should be as comprehensive as possible.
6. **Openness and Transparency:** Public office bearers should be accountable to the citizens on their resource utilisation and structures of governance. This principle is intended to also encourage citizen participation in governance.

7. **Redress:** This principle promotes the quick identification of substandard performances and improving them to required standards. Citizens are encouraged to air their grievances as this will allow for public servants to improve services.
8. **Value for Money:** The government notes that some of the improvements that could be effected do not require any substantial investments on their part, rather they have a potential to reduce costs. Public servants could save costs and time by giving the correct information timeously.

Overall, the Batho Pele initiative seeks to enhance the quality and accessibility of government services by improving efficiency and accountability to the recipients of public goods and services (Kaisara & Pather, 2011). In other words, it is intended to reinvent government along the lines of commercial businesses, which "cannot afford to ignore the needs of customers" and which survives only by putting "customers first" (South Africa, 1997:13).

2.2.2. E-Government Indicators in South Africa

This commitment is evident in the improving country e-gov indicators. Table 1 provides a summary of these indices, between the years 2014 and 2018.

The major indices in terms of e-government are the EGDI and EPI indices. EGDI is a composite index that measures "the readiness and capacity of [a country's] institutions to use ICTs to deliver public services" (United Nations, 2018:xx). The constituent indices of the EGDI are the telecommunications infrastructure, the human capital index, and the national online presence. The EPI, on the other hand, measures the extent to which consumers are connected to ICTs (McIntosh, 2004). Both the EGDI and EPI range from 0 to 1; with a zero indicating very little investment in e-government infrastructure and 1 signifying total commitment. Global country rankings, are, therefore, determined from these indices. A country with the highest levels of indices, naturally, is ranked the highest. That with the second highest, is in turn ranked, number 2, and so on until the lowest rank of 193rd as calculated from the 193 countries participating in the United Nations bi-annual e-government survey. It is important to note that 14 of the 16 lowest ranked countries in terms of EGDI are in Africa. Suffice to say, as technology advances and the digital divide widens, most African countries are further declining in e-government rankings. And for South Africa to improve its rankings amidst this widespread decline in South Africa is commendable.

Table 1. South Africa's e-government indicators

e-Gov Indicator	2014	2016	2018	% Change (2018 vs. 2014)
Global rank	93	76	68	26.9%
SADC rank	2	2	2	-
EGDI (global)	.4869	.5546	.6618	35.9%
EGDI (SADC)	**.3726**	**.3988**	**.4443**	**19.2%**
E-participation rank (global)	97	76	39	59.8%
E-participation Index	.3333	.5593	.8483	154.5%
E-participation Index (SADC)	**.2549**	**.2915**	**.3697**	**45.0%**

From Table 1, it is obvious that South Africa has made considerable advances in both the EGDI and EPI indicators. Its EGDI index increased by close to 36 per cent from .4869 in 2014 to .6618 in 2018. In the same period, EPI also increased by 155 per cent; from .3333 to .8483. Overall, South Africa's improvement in the rankings was 25 notches from 93rd to 68th position, a 27 per cent increase. It is also instructive to learn that improvements in both EPI and EGDI, as shown by the significant spearman correlations in Table 2, have had a positive effect on South Africa's ranking.

Studying Tables 1 and 2 is, therefore, instructive to analyse the e-government supply-side, particularly those that have had a facilitating effect on e-government adoption in the recent past.

3. AN ANALYSIS OF THE SUPPLY SIDE OF E-GOVERNMENT IN SOUTH AFRICA: FACILITATING CONDITIONS OF ADOPTION

Beginning in 1994, at the dawn of democracy, the South African government committed to redressing past injustices of the apartheid era. Embedded within this agenda, the South African government prioritised enhancing the dignity of all South Africans through improved service delivery and the unrestricted access to quality public goods and services to all citizens. But, to efficiently and effectively provide public services in a rapidly globalising world demanded the use of e-government, which required South Africa to leapfrog its technology into the information age. e-Government, therefore, presented itself as a solution that potentially could address both the segregation and the service delivery challenges simultaneously. Consequently, the government provided strategic direction for the movement towards information and communication technologies (ICTs) by promulgating the Green Paper on e-Commerce and the White Paper on Science and Technology in 2000. These policy documents, thereby, served as the foundations for the National e-Government Framework (Western Cape, 2001) as well as subsequent e-government programmes in the country (Shambare, 2016).

The apartheid baggage and the impending growth of the knowledge economy in the late 20th century increased pressure for the South African government to adopt e-government systems. The government, thus, needed to find a lasting solution to unite the country and resolve these problems. Hence, e-government was identified the e-government route as a form of governance designed to restore and maintain citizens' dignity (South Africa, 1997). Consequently, public sector organisations (PSOs) introduced a wide variety of e-government initiatives ranging from telephone call centres to websites to electronic tax (e-tax) (Komba & Ngulube, 2012; Mutula & Mostert, 2010; Shambare, 2016). With the slow diffusion of these new innovations, it became clear that consumers' uptake of e-government was sporadic. As illustrated in past studies (c.f., Mosekwa, 2018; Mutula & Mostert, 2010; Shambare, 2016), adoption

Table 2. Spearman correlation of e-government indicators

Indicator	1	2	3
1. Global rank	1		
2. EGDI	-1.000*	1	
3. EPI	-1.000*	-1.000*	1

*p < .01

rates were, on the whole, quite low. The adoption of e-government in South Africa was sporadic across the population spectrum. While some communities were characterised by high levels of adoption, other communities hardly knew of the e-government concept.

Shambare (2016) specifically identified barriers and constraints inhibiting the uptake of e-government. Two such identified constraints were consumer attitudes and structural barriers. Consumers' perceived risk, disposition of trust, and illiteracy accounted for most of the consumer constraints. On the other hand, structural barriers consisted of poor infrastructure, limited availability of Internet connections, high Internet data costs, and apathy (and at times lack of capacity) of government departments to establish e-government portals. Within the last three to five years empirical evidence, as depicted in Table 1, suggests that e-government adoption trends in South Africa are improving. This is primarily due to the fact that the South African government acknowledged that the vast majority of its citizens that lacked access to ICTs had a negative effect on socio-economic development (Western Cape, 2001). Consequently, revisiting its commitment to e-government was regarded as a developmental vehicle. The most notable intervention has been the call for local governments to leverage service delivery through comprehensive and coordinated e-government services such as the creation of websites and mobile apps.

The remainder of this section continues with an examination of the strategies employed by the South African government to promote and facilitate the adoption of e-government.

3.1. The Reduction of E-Government Structural Barriers

Structural barriers refer to those factors related to e-government architecture and ICT infrastructure that limit consumers' access and utilisation of e-government. South Africa, similar to numerous other developing countries, experiences e-government structural barriers (United Nations, 2018). Some of the most cited barriers include poor and antiquated telecommunications infrastructure, limited Internet connectivity, high costs of Internet data, high levels of consumer illiteracy, high costs of computer hardware, lack of consultation and corruption. It goes without saying that the presence of structural barriers is inversely related to consumers' adoption of e-government services.

In the case of South Africa, the ICT infrastructure, in comparison to the rest of the developing world (see Tables 1 and 2), is quite good. Despite this, however, it could still benefit from general improvements so as to catch up with the rapid advancements in the global telecommunications industry. In tackling e-gov structural barriers, the South African government embarked on a two-pronged approach, which involved: (1) the reversing of technological poverty and (2) increasing government-to-citizen consultation on e-government programmes. On the one hand, the government sought to reverse technological poverty by increasing consumers' access to the Internet. On the other hand, the South African government quickly realised that despite all its good intentions, the success of e-government programmes depends on consumers' buy-in (Heeks, 2006). Besides, e-government initiatives are meant to improve citizens' quality of life, and not to diminish it.

3.1.1. Structural Barriers and Technological Poverty

Within the last few decades in South Africa, Internet access, in particular, and usage of technology, in general, was sporadic and limited. Despite the presence of a well-developed ICT infrastructure, consumers' access to ICT was mostly limited first by apartheid policies and subsequently by high costs associated with technology. Up until 1994, the distribution of ICT infrastructure was skewed according to racial profile. The areas which predominantly catered for the white population had the best ICT infrastructure. In contrast, townships and rural areas, where the black majority lived, lacked such infrastructure. Since 1994, the democratic South African government has committed to balancing the availability of ICT infrastructure, among other disparities.

However, in post-apartheid South Africa, a combination of poverty and exorbitant costs associated with connecting to the Internet (i.e., the price of purchasing ICT hardware and software as well as the Internet data costs) impedes the vast majority of the population from becoming digital citizens. Authors such as Shambare (2014) explain that such a phenomenon is the result of the vicious cycle of technological poverty. Shambare (2014:543) specifically defines technological poverty as the lack of access to technology. As Figure 4 summarises, technological poverty is a function of the Vicious Cycle of Technology Affordability-Non Adoption (V-CAN) (Shambare, 2014). Technologically poor consumers are too poor to afford technology; and because they do not use technology, they are technologically poor.

As in all forms of poverty (e.g., in the case of 'economic' poverty), technological poverty suffers from vicious cycles – the interconnection or a causal chain of unfavourable factors leading to an unfavourable position. Naturally, vicious cycles have an amplifying effect on the prevalence of poverty; and without government intervention, consumers' state of poverty will almost remain permanent. Given the ongoing technological advancements and without government intervention, technological poverty, as demonstrated in Figure 4 in most developing countries will almost always persist. Therefore, without government, breaking the claws of V-CAN cycles is quite difficult. It is for this reason that many governments take interest in promoting consumers' access to and adoption of technology by promoting technology virtuous cycles. In South Africa, e-gov virtuous cycles manifest at local government level-driven e-government (Kaisara & Pather, 2011; Maumbe, & Klaas, 2009; South Africa, 1997; Western Cape, 2001).

Figure 4. Technological poverty

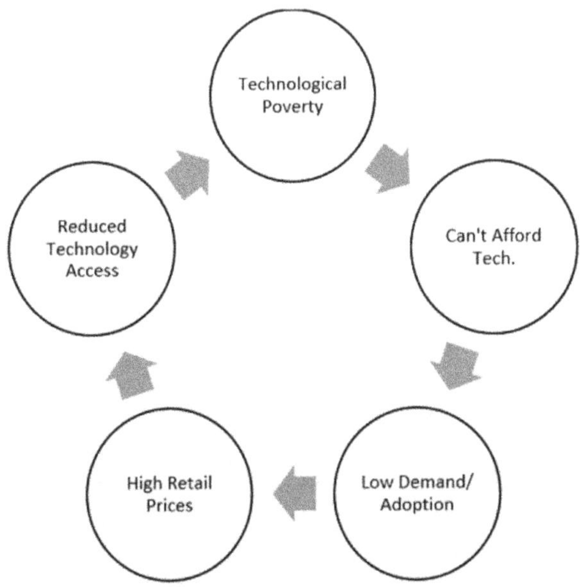

3.1.2. Reversing Technological Poverty With E-Gov Virtuous Cycles in South Africa

South Africa operates on a three-tiered system of governance, which consists of the local, provincial, and national governments. There are nine provinces, which are further sub-divided into 52 municipalities. Each municipality is an autonomous local governing body charged with the delivery of basic services for consumers such as utilities (water and electricity), schools, libraries healthcare, and emergency rescue services. Since municipalities are closest to and interact with consumers more regularly, any meaningful e-government initiative ought to reside within this level of government. It is for this reason that e-gov virtuous cycles, in South Africa, have been concentrated at the municipal level of government.

Unlike vicious cycles that perpetuate a detrimental poverty position, virtuous cycles are remarkably different in that they result in positive outcomes. Free Wi-Fi programmes are an example of these virtuous cycles. Figure 5, below, shows that municipalities are at the core of this virtuous cycle, which begins with the provision of free Wi-Fi. Because of the free Wi-Fi, consumers' Internet connectivity familiarity will naturally increase. With increased familiarity, consumers tend to visit more websites, which opens up the door to other functionalities of the Internet. From this, consumers develop confidence and self-efficacy from using the Internet. Heightened levels of confidence triggers demand for the Internet, which in turn increases demand for free Wi-Fi. This cycle repeats itself several times until consumers become fully-fledged digital citizens.

3.1.2.1. Free Wi-Fi

Free Wi-Fi has numerous other benefits other than just creating digital citizens. The provision of free Wi-Fi services by municipalities such as the City of Tshwane's TshwiFi service is a strategy aimed at encouraging consumers' use of both the Internet and e-government services. On TshwiFi services, residents have a daily quota of 500MB of free Internet access. Furthermore, all City of Tshwane websites

Figure 5. The E-Gov virtuous cycle

and online services are accessible free of charge. To encourage widespread coverage of the free Internet service, TshwiFi hotspots are strategically placed at high-traffic locations across the city, at bus stations, train station, municipal offices, and at schools. At these locations, there is usually large billboards advertising free Wi-Fi zone such as the one indicated in Figure 6.

It must also be noted that schools, in South Africa, are historically important catalysts for Internet adoption – both fixed-line and mobile Wi-Fi (Shambare, 2016; Shambare & Mvula, 2011), it is, therefore, quite strategic to have free Internet services housed at schools for a number of reasons. The first one being that population density tends to be high at schools, thus, the reach of the free Wi-Fi is greatly extended. The second reason, having free Wi-Fi hotspots at schools, naturally, converts schools into community centres where people gather around. Another benefit is that schools become safer. Opportunistic and petty acts of deviance such as substance abuse and vandalism would be reduced due to the increase in prying eyes of community members. A fourth reason is that children greatly influence family decision-making. So, by exposing children to free Internet services, plays a dual effect – marketing e-government to the children, as end users, themselves. On the other hand, school children inadvertently acts as 'mouthpieces' and advertising agents for e-government. By so doing, school learners become catalysts for e-government adoption. This, they achieve by seeking all the relevant information, which they would pass over to their parents, guardians, and the community at large.

Government-sponsored free Internet services, thus, go a long way into promoting the adoption of e-government, as they significantly reduce the cost of accessing the Internet. This is consistent with the observations that Internet access plays a critical role in the adoption of services such as e-commerce and e-government. Evidence from South Africa, as summarised in Table 1, therefore, confirms the positive relationship between Internet familiarity, awareness, and adoption.

3.1.2.2. Other E-Government Services Provided by South African Municipalities

In the effort to further deepen e-government services, municipalities use various services. From a supply-side point of view, these services are intended to encourage consumers to use e-government products. Municipalities use various combinations of e-government products; these range from websites to mobile apps to social media platforms. Table 3 provides a summary of these services provided by the various

Figure 6. The E-Gov virtuous cycle

municipalities in the country. Therein, it is encouraging to learn the supply-side of e-government is committed. Some of the milestones of municipalities include:

- All municipalities have fully functioning websites
- A number of these websites are transaction-enabled. Consumer can process transactions such as paying rates and taxes on the websites.
- A majority of the municipalities have active and running social media platforms from which they use to disseminate information.
- Mobile applications (or apps) are increasingly becoming popular. Because the majority of consumers use mobile phones, mobile apps are proving to be quite popular.

Overall, the above-mentioned products, as applied by municipalities are indicative of the supply side's commitment towards e-government.

3.1.2.3. Reduced Internet Data Tariffs

High data costs was another barrier identified that limits the number of South African consumers utilising the Internet. Since the majority (about 85 per cent) of the population use their mobile phones to connect to the Internet, they rely on the Big-Four mobile network providers (Vodacom, MTN, Cell C, and Telkom) for connectivity. Although data costs have reduced drastically, they still are considerably high. Mobile service providers have been accused of operating a cartel that maintains exorbitant prices. For instance, in a comparative analysis of the cost of data, Mochiko (2017) found that 1 Gigabyte of data in South Africa costs as much as US$1. Comparatively, in Mozambique, 1 Gigabyte costs $2.27 and in Tanzania it is $2.39. It is against this background that the South African Competition Commission has taken a keen interest in reviewing the competition in the sector. Furthermore, the government is working on plans to increase competition so as to bring down the costs of mobile data. President Ramaphosa outlined summarised government's policy position by alluding that, "We will finalise our engagements with the telecommunications industry and other stakeholders to ensure that the allocation of spectrum

Table 3. Content analysis of municipalities' e-government initiatives

Province	# of Municipalities	Municipalities With Websites	Municipal Websites That Are Transaction-Enabled	Social Media Presence					Municipalities With Mobile Apps
				Facebook	Twitter	Linked-In	YouTube	Flickr	
Eastern Cape	8	8	2	8	8	8	8	8	3
Free State	5	5	0	4	4	4	4	4	1
Gauteng	5	5	3	5	5	5	5	5	3
KwaZulu Natal	11	11	1	9	9	9	9	9	2
Limpopo	5	5	0	4	4	4	4	4	0
Mpumalanga	3	3	0	2	2	2	2	2	0
Northern Cape	5	5	0	5	5	5	5	5	1
North West	4	4	0	4	4	4	4	4	1
Western Cape	6	6	1	6	6	6	6	6	3

reduces barriers to entry, promotes competition, and reduces the cost to consumers" (Ramaphosa, 2018 as cited by Mybroadband, 2018). It, therefore, goes without saying that the recent reduction in data costs had a positive effect on the number of consumers accessing the Internet. Despite this, further reductions will definitively promote e-government adoption.

3.2. Strategies to Reduce Behavioural Barriers to E-Government Adoption

In his study on the adoption of e-government systems in South Africa, Shambare (2016) found that trust and risk were among the major barriers to consumers' uptake of new e-government innovations (Belanger & Carter, 2008). The perceived trust and risk issues mostly arose from a combination of the lack of awareness and limited experience in the use of Internet technologies on the part of consumers. As a means to increase awareness of Internet technologies in general, and e-government initiatives, in general, a vast number of government agencies and municipalities embarked on promotional campaigns. The purpose of these campaigns are twofold. First, to promote awareness of the e-government initiative. In this regard, the product features as well as its functionalities and benefits would be shared with the general public. Second, to conscientise consumers on the security of e-government services. A vignette of an example of such an advertisement is that of the South African Revenue Service (SARS) illustrated in Figure 7.

Figure 7, above, highlights two important features of the SARS e-tax – its purpose and benfits (i.e, Why eFile?) and security features. Several marketing campaigns of e-government initiatives are also featured on television and radio.

3.2.1. Enhancing Government-to-Citizens Consultations

In all e-government initiatives, existing and new, consultation and communication among stakeholders is critical. Of these, consumers' buy-in is of utmost importance. Consumers need to get all the information about the 'new product' – its features, advantages, and benefits. Securing consumers' approval and

Figure 7. SARS e-filing advertisement

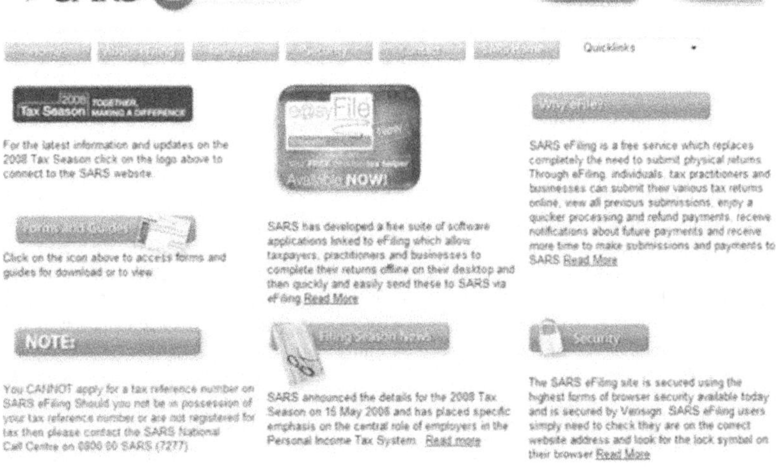

buy-in often is associated with high levels of diffusion and adoption. Where consumer buy-in is limited, the acceptance of an innovation tends to be depressed. So, by all means possible, the supply-side ought to provide as much information about the proposed new initiative. Over and above this, the new product ought to be sufficiently marketed. Without such consultation, consumers are less likely to buy into the new product.

A case in point of a South African e-government project that collapsed due to the lack of consultation is the electronic toll (e-Toll). The e-Toll system was introduced in 2014 in Gauteng Province as part of a scheme to help fund for road improvements and maintenance. However, owing to poor consultation, the e-Toll project has largely been a failure. Government has suffered several bruising court experiences with citizens and civic organisations, who are fighting for the total removal of the e-Toll system. One of the leading civic organisation championing the fight against e-Toll is the Organisation Undoing Tax Abuse (OUTA). OUTA's opposition to e-Tax is well known. In the following case study, OUTA outlines its justification for opposing e-Tolls.

Box 1. Case studies

WHY WE OPPOSE E-TOLLING?

SANRAL's proposed plans to apply an electronic tolling (e-Toll) process to Gauteng Freeways has been labelled by OUTA is irrational, unreasonable and impractical. It was most certainly not planned with the best intentions for the public in mind. This became more evident as OUTA's supporters engaged rather intensively since 2010 with SANRAL, after learning about their plans to "toll" the Gauteng motorists through a most elaborate system of gantries, systems and strategies. The more we engaged, the more we realised that this plan of SANRAL's did not attract the necessary levels of engagement and planning that a process of this magnitude required. We also learned that SANRAL had taken on something far more complex than they could handle and that it was fraught with inefficiencies, was extremely costly and they ignored far simpler methods, which exist within Government policy to collect revenue for this project.

REASONS AND GROUNDS ON WHY WE OPPOSE THE TOLLING OF GFIP ROADS

- **E-Tolling of GFIP Is Irrational and Unreasonable:** Tolling Gauteng's freeways is an unnecessary waste of billions of SA Tax payer's money. We do realise the need to pay for the freeway improvements, but we expect to do so through efficient means to collect these "taxes". Raising funds for costly (road upgrade) projects of this nature, should be done with the least negative impact on the pockets of the public, whilst achieving the goal of funding the infrastructure. As such, if existing or new funding mechanisms are available, these should be considered and used, unless of course a valid reason is provided and is acceptable to society, i.e. the people who ultimately pay.

The installation of an elaborate and complex toll gantries, electronic tags in every vehicle and the revenue collection system for this specific project, means that users will pay not only for the expense of the road construction but additionally, they must suffer the heavy and unnecessary burden of this specific toll collection system. It is estimated that the electronic tolling processes planned by SANRAL will cost R1,7 billion per annum (based on the tender awarded by SANRAL to ETC for this work, at R8,4bn for the first five year period, excluding set up costs) just to operate and administer. The road construction capital costs of R18 billion (i.e., excluding other costs related to e-Tolls), if paid over 20 years with interest, amounts to approximately R1,67 billion per annum (or R40,7 billion over 20 years), including maintenance. e-Tolling in Gauteng was planned to raise over R95 billion (i.e. 236% of the required amount) and will be a burden to the road user – an utter and unnecessary waste of the road-users money.

- **Poor Planning and Incorrect Information When Deciding to E-Toll:** In the High Court papers files by SANRAL and the Department of Transport, initial estimates of the e-Tolling revenue collection process were R395 million per annum. These were the figures presented to the Minister of Transport (Min Jeff Radebe) at the time of the decision to toll. This was done with no formal calculation and in the end, the tender was awarded at R1,7bn per annum (or R8,4bn for 5 years), some 330% higher.
- **Lack of Consultation and Transparency:** While SANRAL will have us believe that they did all they could to be consultative in this decision, the simple truth is they failed and fell far short of what would be expected in a matter of this magnitude. This was demonstrated by the outrage and surprise that virtually all citizens expressed when the gantries went up, and not only the individual road user, but also business and large fleet organisations were shocked by the extent and implications of the SANRAL e-Toll plans. Our legal challenge has shown that SANRAL did the *bare minimum* to expose and engage with society on their elaborate plan to toll the Gauteng freeway upgrade. From one advert placed in six newspapers in October 2007 to over 3,5 million licensed vehicles/ motorists in Gauteng, SANRAL received only 28 responses to their request for submissions (one was a petition with 55 signatories).

Adapted from: https://www.outa.co.za/about-outa/why-we-oppose-e-tolling/

Discussion Questions:

1. Why is consultation important in e-government projects?
2. To what extent do you think extensive consultation would have changed the outcome of the e-Toll programme in South Africa?

To avoid the undesirable outcomes of lack of consultation, government has changed its modus operandi in as far as rolling out of new programmes. Extensive consultation is carried out so as to allow consumers to comment and have their inputs considered in new initiatives. For instance, the Department of Telecommunications and Postal Services in May 2017 rolled out nationwide public consultation conferences on its planned e-strategy and e-government programmes (South Africa, 2017), which it feels will form the basis for developing the fourth industrial revolution. The efforts to involve the public in e-government programmes should be considered to be a positive step in the right direction towards enhanced e-government.

4. FURTHER OPPORTUNITIES FOR E-GOVERNMENT IN SOUTH AFRICA

In discussing the e-government opportunities in South Africa, the point of departure is recognising three critical imperatives related to e-government in the current South African socio-political landscape. These are the presence of world-class ICT infrastructure, high levels of ICT adoption, and service delivery challenges across the various government levels, from local to provincial to national departments.

Firstly, with respect to ICTs, South Africa has a well-developed infrastructure that is, to a certain degree, comparable to developed countries. High speed broad band Internet, fixed-line telephones, and mobile phone services are among some of the capabilities of the sector.

Secondly, the adoption of technological innovations including mobile phones by South Africans is among the highest in Sub-Saharan Africa, and even in the world. Furthermore, consumers' acceptance of innovations, including the Internet, mobile phones, and web-based applications such as email and social media, is rapidly growing. To date, with a mobile penetration rate in excess of 138 per cent, South Africa has one of the fastest growing mobile industries in the African continent (World Wide Worx, 2015).

Thirdly, service delivery constraints are a major challenge facing the South African government. In a study on the prevalence of service delivery protests, Grant (2014) demonstrates that service delivery

Figure 8. Fertile environment for E-Government implementation

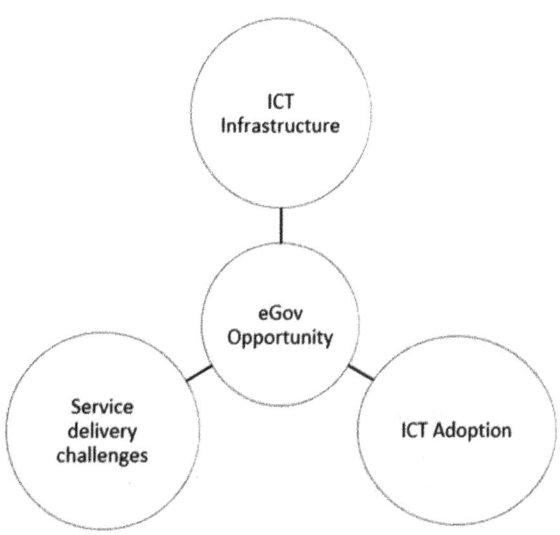

protests in the last few years are increasing. Data also suggests that the number of these demonstrations is likely to keep increasing in the foreseeable future.

The success of any new ICT programme including e-government depends on primarily two factors: (1) widespread acceptance of the innovation from both the supply and the demand side, and (2) existence of facilitating conditions with which both the service providers and users or beneficiaries of the initiatives are compelled or at least encouraged to migrate to the computerised system. Evidence, thus far, points to a massive improvement to the state of e-government in South Africa. From this perspective, it is posited that the current state of affairs in South Africa is a fertile environment for developing a thriving e-government programme. These opportunities for e-government to develop are outlined in more detail below.

4.1. ICT Infrastructure

With respect to ICT, South Africa has a well-developed infrastructure. The 2011 Census survey revealed that 89 per cent of the 14.5 million households in the country have access to mobile phones, whilst 75 per cent of households have access to a television set and 68 per cent have access to a radio (Statistics South Africa, 2012). However, penetration of radio was much higher, reaching nearly 90 per cent of the population. The Census further showed that only 35 per cent of households have dedicated access to the Internet and only 15 per cent have access to a landline telephone. Overall, the ICT sector in South Africa is characterised by an exponential growth of the mobile sector, with a penetration rate of about 136 per cent.

The ability of South Africa to compete in the global economy is dependent, to a large extent, on the state of its ICT sector and in particular the country's ability to facilitate and grow the sector to meet its citizens' needs for affordable, accessible high speed Internet access. The rapid deployment of fast and affordable broadband infrastructure remains a powerful lever to create an internationally competitive knowledge economy, improve productivity and expand access to new markets. E-government is regarded as an important facilitator for ICT development. This is particularly applicable in emerging markets where government and government services are a key input for ICT demand and supply. In South Africa, e-government initiatives are aimed at delivery of more services to citizens in an efficient and effective manner (South Africa, 1997; 2000).

The provincial governments have their own portals, the best functioning of which are the Gauteng Provincial Government and the Western Cape Provincial Government. The South African e-Government programme also extends to local government level, the best examples of which are programmes of the metropolitan municipalities of Cape Town, Johannesburg, Ekurhuleni, Tshwane and eThekwini. Thirteen metropolitan areas have adopted online-payment systems to facilitate payment of traffic fines. Users can pay directly online or use kiosks at large retail chains around the country. Above all, municipalities are increasingly looking towards mobile apps to leverage their e-government positioning.

4.2. Diffusion of ICT in South Africa

Uptake of technological innovations including mobile phones by South Africans is among the highest in Sub-Saharan Africa, and even in the world. Furthermore, the numbers of South Africans who are relying on technological innovations including the Internet, mobile phones, and web-based applications such as email and social media, is rapidly growing. To date, with a mobile penetration rate in excess of 138 per cent, South Africa has one of the fastest growing mobile industries in the African continent and indeed, the world. The latest data from the United Nation's (2018) survey does confirm South Africa's commitment to promoting e-government.

Having said this, however, high data costs still seem to be depressing rapid diffusion of e-government products, as these products still are quite expensive for certain groups of consumers. At close to US$7 per gigabyte of data, the Internet still remains out of reach for many South Africans. Furthermore, increasing consultation and reducing corruption will most likely have a positive effect on the diffusion of ICTs in South Africa (Rogers, 1995).

4.3. Service Delivery Challenges in South Africa

Service delivery constraints continue to be a major challenge facing the South African government. This problem permeates from local municipalities all the way to the national government. At the local level, ratepayers consistently complain about incorrect and inaccurate billing. Often these result in a myriad of problems, including service delivery protests, which usually result in property losses. At a national level, departments such as the licencing department, home affairs, and the social services have numerous challenges of their own.

5. CONCLUSION

This purpose of this chapter was to examine the e-government supply-side in South Africa with a view to determine how it has facilitated consumers' adoption of e-government. Consequently, an extensive review of the literature was conducted. This revealed interesting results. First among many was that e-government is viewed by the government as a panacea to a plethora of socio-economic problems facing the country. One of these is the aftermath of apartheid. Since the country is emerging from apartheid, a political policy that fragmented service delivery along racial lines, the vast majority of South Africans did not have access to basic service delivery. As such, the South African government views e-government to be the vehicle through which it will realise its vision of creating an equal and prosperous democratic society.

It was very encouraging that there is evidence to suggest that the South African government is keeping true to its work and is making concerted efforts at developing e-government in the country. The chapter discovered that e-government, particularly at the local government or municipality level, is quite active. Virtuous cycles including the provision of free Wi-Fi services and efforts to reduce the cost of accessing the Internet are bearing positive fruits. However, Internet data costs still remain quite high. In spite of this, both ICT usage and e-government services are increasingly becoming a familiar fixture in South Africa. Over the last three years, in particular, the country made considerable improvements in its e-government. It recorded improvements in all its e-government indices. Of note, its global rankings climbed by 25 notches, from position 93 to 68 in the United Nations 2018 e-government survey. In addition, its EGDI and EPI scores showed impressive improvements.

Notwithstanding this investment in e-government and ICT, the biggest challenge in South Africa's e-government agenda remains high Internet data cost. The average cost of mobile data is approximately three times that of other countries in Africa. Since mobile phones are the preferred devices of connecting to the Internet, the cost of data bundles still remains a major concern. Having said this, the chapter recommends that government and other PSOs should continue increasing e-government awareness, introducing many variations of e-government such as m-government and offline e-government, and enhancing PPPs to improve infrastructure, particularly in rural areas. While the above-mentioned recommendations more directed to South Africa, these are very much applicable to other developing countries that seek to increase their digital footprint.

REFERENCES

Akakandelwa, A. (2011). An Exploratory Survey of the SADC e-government Web Sites. *Library Review*, *60*(5), 421–431. doi:10.1108/00242531111135317

Belanger, F., & Carter, L. (2008). Trust and Risk in e-government adoption. *The Journal of Strategic Information Systems*, 17.

Dlamini, I. Z., Ngobeni, S. J., & Mutanga, M. B. (2010). South African Egov: Secure E-Services. *Proceedings of eChalleges e-2010 Conference and Exhibition*, 1-8.

e-Tshwane. (2018). *e-Tshwane*. Available at: https://www.e-tshwane.co.za/eTshwane/

Gelfand, M. (1970). Unhu – The personality of the Shona. *Studies in Comparative Religion*, *4*(1).

Grant, L. (2014). *Research shows sharp increase in service delivery protests*. Retrieved from http://mg.co.za/article/2014-02-12-research-shows-sharp-increase-in-service-delivery-protests

Heeks, D. (2006). *Implementing and managing e-Government*. London: Sage.

Hornung, H., Cecília, M., & Baranauskas, C. (2007). Interaction Design in eGov systems: challenges for a developing country. *Anais do XXVII Congreso da SBC*.

Kaisara, G., & Pather, S. (2011). The e-Government Evaluation Challenge: A South African Batho Pele-aligned Service Quality Approach. *Government Information Quarterly*, *28*(2), 211–221. doi:10.1016/j.giq.2010.07.008

Koh, C., & Prybutok, V. (2003). The three ring model and development of an instrument for measuring dimensions of e-government functions. *Journal of Computer Information Systems*, *43*(3), 34–39.

Komba, M. M., & Ngulube, P. (2012). Factors for e-government adoption: Lessons from selected African countries. *Mousaion*, *30*(2), 24–32.

Layne, K., & Lee, J. (2001). Developing fully functional E-government: A four stage model. *Government Information Quarterly*, *18*(2), 122–136. doi:10.1016/S0740-624X(01)00066-1

Maumbe, B., & Klaas, N. (2009). Crafting an E-Government Development Model for South Africa: A Strategic New Direction for the Western Cape Province. *International Conference on Information Management. CONF-IRM 2009 Proceedings*.

Mazengera, B. & Mavetera, N. (2006). Factors Contributing To Successful E-Government Implementation in Southern African Development Community (SADC) Countries. *Innovation and Knowledge Management: A Global Competitive Advantage.*

McIntosh, A. (2004). Characterizing E-Participation in Policy-Making. *Proceedings of the 37th Hawaii International Conference on System Sciences.* 10.1109/HICSS.2004.1265300

Mochiko, T. (2017). *SA's big data rip-off: The #DataMustFall campaign failed to convince SA's biggest phone companies to reduce prices.* Available at: https://www.businesslive.co.za/fm/fm-fox/digital/2017-05-05-sas-big-data-rip-off/

Mosekwa, K. (2018). *The influence of disposition of trust on the adoption of SARS electronic tax filing in the city of Tshwane* (MTech dissertation). Business School, Tshwane University of Technology.

Mutula, S. M., & Mostert, J. (2010). Challenges and opportunities of e-government in South Africa. *The Electronic Library, 28*(1), 38–53. doi:10.1108/02640471011023360

Mybroadband. (2018). *High mobile data prices – operators respond.* Available at: https://mybroadband.co.za/news/cellular/249519-high-mobile-data-prices-operators-respond.html

Reynolds, M., & Regio, M. (2001). *E-government as a Catalyst in the Information Age.* Microsoft E-Government Initiatives.

Rogers, E. M. (1995). *Diffusion of innovations: Modifications and model of telecommunications.* New York: Free Press.

Rorissa, A., Demissie, D., & Pardo, T. (2011). Benchmarking e-government: A comparison of frameworks for computing e-government index and ranking. *Government Information Quarterly, 28*(3), 354–362. doi:10.1016/j.giq.2010.09.006

Shambare, R. (2012). A cold drink for my brother in uniform: Applying the theory of planned behaviour to explain corruption in South Africa. *Proceedings of the 6th Iinternational Business Conference.*

Shambare, R. (2014). The adoption of WhatsApp: Breaking the vicious cycle of technological poverty in South Africa. *Journal of Economics and Behavioral Studies, 6*(7), 542–550.

Shambare, R. (2016). Consumer Adoption of E-government in South Africa: Barriers, Solutions, and Implications. In A. Gbadamosi (Ed.), Consumerism and Buying Behavior in Developing Nations. Academic Press. doi:10.4018/978-1-5225-0282-1.ch009

Shambare, R., & Mvula, A. (2011). South African students' perceptions of Facebook: Some implications for instructors. *African Journal of Business Management, 5*(26), 10567–10564.

South Africa. (1997). *Batho Pele — 'People first'.* White paper on transforming public service delivery, Notice 1459 of 1997. Government of South Africa, Department of Public Service and Administration. Pretoria: Government Printer.

South Africa. (2000). *A Green Paper on electronic commerce for South Africa.* Author.

South Africa. (2017). *Telecommunications and Postal Services consults on e-strategy, e-government and ICT SMME support strategies, 8 to 9 May*. Available at: https://www.gov.za/speeches/dtps-consult-nationally-e-strategy-e-government-and-ict-smme-support-strategies-5-may-2017

Statistics South Africa. (2015). *Publications*. Available at: http://www.statssa.gov.za/?s=census+2011&sitem=publications

United Nations. (2014). *United Nations e-government survey 2014*. Available from: http://unpan3.un.org/egovkb/Portals/egovkb/Documents/un/2014-Survey/E-Gov_Complete_Survey-2014.pdf

United Nations. (2018). *United Nations e-Government Survey 2018*. Available from: https://publicadministration.un.org/egovkb/en-us/Reports/UN-E-Government-Survey-2018

Western Cape. (2001). *The Cape Online E-government Programme*. Provincial Government of the Western Cape. Available from: https://www.westerncape.gov.za/text/2014/October/capeonline_strategy_aug2001.pdf

World Wide Worx. (2015). *South African Social Media Landscape 2015*. Available at: http://www.worldwideworx.com/wp-content/uploads/2014/11/Exec-Summary-Social-Media-2015.pdf

KEY TERMS AND DEFINITIONS

Adoption: Refers to consumers' decision to use or utilize a technological innovation (in this case e-government services) in order to improve their life or work.

Batho Pele: A South African political ideology that seeks to uphold traditional African values, beliefs, and practices in government. Batho Pele was introduced by the new democratic government of South Africa as a vehicle to promote the participation of all citizens in governance structures. Batho Pele is a derivate of the Ubuntu Philosophy.

Disposition to Trust: Also known as DoT, refers to consumers' personality disposition. It refers to individuals' propensity to trust other people. DoT is composed of two concepts: faith in humanity and a trusting attitude. Faith in humanity is the general assumption that all people are good-natured and dependable. From this point of view, there is no reason not to trust anyone. On the other hand, a trusting attitude assumes that if one deals with other people as if they are well meaning and reliable, then these people will act in a manner that promotes trustworthiness.

E-Government: Refers to a system in which citizens and various other stakeholders interact and transact with the government remotely by means of information communication technologies such as telephone, e-mail, and the internet.

M-Government: A variation of e-government which relies on mobile telephony for government-to-citizens interactions.

Public-Private Partnership: Also known as PPP, is a synergistic arrangement through which government (or public sector entities) partner with the private sector in order to pool resources, expertise, and skills in order to efficiently provide high standard public goods and services. Examples of PPP projects include major infrastructure projects such as the construction of roads, hospitals, schools, and wi-fi projects.

Technological Poverty: A condition through which a consumer lack access to or has limited access to ICTs and technology, in general.

Trust of Government: Consumers' perceptions and confidence in the ability and integrity of government departments to provide efficient online services via e-government platforms.

Ubuntu: Refers to an African philosophy that seeks to promote harmonious relations and interaction among people. This philosophy suggests that a person can only truly and fully exist if he or she co-exists with others in his or her community. In other words, this means that one should always have a strong sense of consideration for others.

Chapter 12
The Impact of Human Values and Knowledge on Green Products Purchase Intention

Brahim Chekima
Universiti Malaysia Sabah, Malaysia

Khalifa Chekima
Universiti Malaysia Sabah, Malaysia

ABSTRACT

Marketing managers keenly seek to understand the green market. However, insufficient information on how to foster consumers' green behavior is slowing the growth of green markets and becoming a barrier for firms when communicating strategies for effectively promoting green products. Therefore, this chapter attempts to examine the impact of environmental knowledge and cultural values on consumers' green purchase intentions. A survey was administered and a total of 200 valid questionnaires were obtained. Structural equation modeling (SEM) technique was used to assess the model. The finding shows that cultural values significantly related to green product purchase intention. The results also indicate environmental knowledge is not a significant factor influencing buying intention of green products. The discussions and implications of these findings are further elaborated.

INTRODUCTION

Rapid economic development, technological advances, unsustainable consumption and the increasing global population can no longer be separated from the negative impacts on the environment. This has led to major environmental degradation and disasters faced today. Drastic changes in climate, water and air pollutants, damage to flora and fauna, ozone layer depletion, acid rain and deforestation are among the so often occurring negative environmental disasters and events. Ecological destruction continues unabated due to human activities and economic growth (Selles, 2013). the An effective way of reducing this consequence on the environment would be through the green consumption at an individual's level (Yadav & Pathak, 2017). According to Sreen et al. (2018), companies have started concentrating

DOI: 10.4018/978-1-5225-7906-9.ch012

on 'Sustainability' as a business aim by embracing strategies of green marketing to encourage green product purchase to potential as well as current customers. This gives an opportunity for marketers to venture into a new category of green products to increase and maximize profits while expanding their market share but in the meantime, they face a big challenge to develop and communicate strategies effectively to arouse intentions to buy green products and ensure optimal sales. Godelnik (2012) states that although consumers' spending increases, including for green products, "green glass ceiling" still unbreakable and its market share is still very small. The author further clarifies based on the company's market report by Mintel, that despite that millions of people around the world have adopted an alternative to the traditional use (sustainable consumption) in 2012; this shift seems to still represent a minor share of overall economic activity. In the following year, Gleim et al., (2013) estimated the market share for green products is less than 4% worldwide.

Accordingly, numerous investigations have been carried out over the last 20 years to identify and understand the factors that promote pro-environment behavior among consumers (Suki, 2015; Wu et al., 2015; Thongplew et al., 2013), however, most have addresses marketing strategies rather than consumer behavior. Without an in-depth understanding of consumer behavior for this product category, this seems to be among the greatest barrier to sustainable consumption (Tseng and Hung, 2013) and also difficult to devise effective marketing strategies. Thus, based on mentioned the alarming condition of the environment, very small market share of green products as well as previous research findings, the main objective of this study is to investigate the factors motivating consumers' intention to purchase green products. Based on an extensive review of the literature and to the best of author's knowledge, only a few studies focused on the impact of cultural values on green products purchase intentions. This study focuses on purchase intentions rather than behavioral, for intentions has broader implications and often will have a positive impact on individual actions (Schlosser et al., 2006; Pierre et al., 2005; Ajzen & Driver, 1992).

This study brings new insight to understand the role of the culture on green purchase intentions, as for the last few years cultural components have been recognized worldwide to influence individual's behavior in the market (Sreen et al. 2018; Wang et al. 2017; Kim et al., 2002; Yaveroglu & Donthu 2002; Steenkamp et al., 1999). Culture has a strong influence on consumers' behaviors (Schiffman & Kanuk, 2010) and the fundamental determinant of a person's desires and behavior (Kotler, 2003). Strizhakova and Coulter (2013) further suggest investigating individuals' cultural backgrounds because it can aid to motivate or encourage pro-environment behavioral in general and forming green purchasing intentions in particular. It is explainable that culture is dynamic and plays an important role in shaping attitude and behavior in various aspects of the individuals. Soyez (2013) in his study found that the main drivers of eco-friendly are attitude and norms, which the latter includes individuals' cultural values. Besides that, although environmental advertising is widely practiced to communicate green products to consumers and has been firmly established as a fairly common practice in the 2000s (Peattie & Crane, 2005), however in academic, little research has focused to investigate on its awareness, perception and effectiveness to form a positive attitude and encourage consumers' intentions to buy green products.

By investigating the mentioned factors, this research contributes to the understanding of the motivational drivers of consumer purchasing intention and substantiates the body of knowledge in green marketing, which upholds sustainable development and cleaner production. The findings of this research are also anticipated to provide a useful reference for the managerial use (producers and retailers) to further develop appropriate marketing strategies to communicate and promote green products effectively. The findings of this study could be generalized with care to some extent with most South East Asian countries (Singapore, Indonesia, Thailand, Philippines, Brunei, China as well as India) with which Malaysia shares multiple cultural, geographic, economic and political aspects.

The paper proceeds with a literature review presenting a summary of research findings surrounding variables such as green purchasing intentions, environmental knowledge, man-nature orientation and long-term orientation. Following are the methodology, the findings, and discussions. Finally, implications and future research suggestions proposed.

LITERATURE REVIEW

Green Purchase Intention

Scholars by navigating the buying process found one of the pillars that make the process of buying a whole to be a purchase intention. Newberry et al., (2003) observed that purchasing intentions is a frequent tool engaged in predicting purchase behavior while O'Keefe (2002) affirms that behavioral intentions are the most suitable aspect for predicting actions of individuals under many conditions including the green market. In general connotation, Spears and Singh (2004) together with Peter and Olson (2008) agree that the purchase intentions is a consciously decided plan to make an effort to buy a particular product or service. Aligned with that definition, Nik Abdul Rashid (2009) defines green purchase intentions as the probability and willingness of individuals in their purchase consideration to give preference to green products compared to conventional products. The green purchase intention is described as a distinct kind of environmentally friendly behavior that individuals perform to express their concern to the environment. Furthermore, green purchasing intentions was confirmed as a proxy for the actual green purchasing behavior (Ramayah et al., 2010) and an accurate measure of future sales compared to other sales forecasting tools (Armstrong et al., 2000). Thus, since purchase intentions finally lead to purchase behavior, Follows and Jobber (2000) has recommended it as a main predictive component.

Environmental Knowledge

Previous studies examining the behavior of pro-environment has indicated that consumer behaviors and intentions are associated with several motivators/factors, among which was the environmental knowledge. Chan, 2001 along with Haron et al., (2005) refers to environmental knowledge as an individual ability to understand and evaluate the impact of the ecosystem on the society as well as the amount of information he or she has regarding environmental issues. Earlier, Vining and Ebreo (1990) claims that consumer knowledge about environment been acknowledged as an important motivator for environmentally friendly behavior. Werner and Alvensleben (2011) states that knowledge creates a positive influence on a person' viewing habits of buying and using eco-friendly products. Environmental knowledge itself involves relationships leading to environmental features or effects, joint responsibilities required for sustainable development, what people know about the environment, and appreciation of 'whole systems' (Mostafa, 2007). By employing the Theory of Planned Behavior, researchers established that the more knowledgeable the consumers are about the environment, the more they know about the effects of the human actions towards the environment, and the more we expect them to purchase green products (Rahbar and Abdul Wahid, 2011; Nik Abdul Rashid, 2009; Mostafa, 2007; Laroche et al., 1996).

Reviewing past findings, Wang and Hazen (2016) and Schahn and Holzer, (1990) proposes that knowledge relating to environmental matters is an influencing factor for the environmental responsible behavior. This is supported by several studies that have endeavored by explaining how students joining environmental courses showed an increase in responsible environmental behavior (Jaus, 1984; Jordan et al., 1986; Ramsey and Rickson 1976; Ramsey, 1993). This is evident in the study of Bradley et al., (1999) which describes that students possess positive environmental attitudes in the environmental course was more likely to demonstrate encouraging environmental attitudes once the course is over. In the same study, Bradley et al., (1999) further confirms that environmental attitudes will improve in parallel with increased knowledge. Amyx et al., (1994) also confirms that consumers with sufficient knowledge on environmental issues are more willing to pay an additional price to purchase environmentally friendly products as a result of positive attitude. Loroche et al., (2001) have validated that eco-literacy also known as environmental knowledge, is significantly correlated with attitudes and environmental behavior. Similarly, another study by Rahbar and Abdul Wahid (2011) of the environmental volunteers in Penang, Malaysia, found that individuals with more ecological knowledge tend to positively influence his/her green purchase intentions and behavior or vice versa. In fact, a lack of knowledge or information has been identified as an important barrier to act pro-environment (Kennedy et al., 2009). A meta-analysis of previous studies has also shown that people who have greater knowledge on environmental issues and how to address them were more willing to engage pro-environment behavior compared to those who do not have or lacking in this knowledge (Hines, Hungerford, Tomer, 1986-1987). As environmental knowledge appears to be a necessary motivator for ecological behavior, a close examination of consumers' environmental knowledge toward green purchase intentions seems worthwhile. Thus, this leads to the following hypothesis:

Hypothesis 1: Green purchase intention is positively influenced by environmental knowledge.

Man-Nature Orientation

Cultural orientation through an understanding of the values will help us understand the motivation of individuals and will illuminate the many elements of individual behavior alone and in social settings, in and across cultures (Schwartz, 1994; Schwartz & Sagiv, 1995). Among the objectives of this study were to investigate the influence of culture on green purchasing behavior. Different cultural value orientations were discussed by some social theorists over the past few decades (Schwartz, 1992; Triandis 1989; Hofstede, 1980, 2001; Rokeach, 1979; Kluckhohn & Strodbeck 1961; Kluckhohn 1956). Values are considered as principles that guide the formation of attitudes to act (Rokeach, 1973). Man-nature orientation dimension is examined in this study which was developed in the 1940s and 1950s that found in the Value Orientation Theory, developed in the 1940s and 1950s by Florence Kluckhohn and Fred Strodtbeck (Kluckhohn & Strodtbeck, 1961).

Man-nature orientation (MNO) is defined as the friendly conducts of humans toward nature, because of the love of nature and the vigor of protecting nature behavior (Churchill, 1979). In addition, Chan (2001) referred to man-nature orientation "as the relationship between human beings and the natural environment". Fundamentally, this cultural value is concerned with the relationship rooted between man and nature as well as the attitude of the former towards the surrounding environment. Man-nature orientation considers how human dominates, lives harmoniously with nature or subjugated to nature (Samovar et al., 1981). Chan (2001) put forward that man-nature orientation operates at the level of affective which can stimulate norms, where all consumer behavior rests. The researchers, based on several previous studies, found that norms occasionally change and are ambiguous; however, the impact is greater in guiding the practice of everyday life through intentions and behavior (Chung et al., 2012; O'Neal, 2007; Kalafatis et al., 1999; Ajzen, 1991).

To date, there is a lack of empirical studies that investigated the relation between man-nature orientation and purchase intention despite having theories and prospects that proposed cultural values as motivator an influencer on intention and behavior. Man-nature orientation has been examined in clothing fashions and impulsive buying, confirming its positive role in facilitating buying behavior (Rajagopal, 2011; Kacen and Lee, 2002). Likewise, man-nature orientation associated positively with consumer ecological attitude on environmentally friendly buying behavior (Sabrina, 2007). This is desirable in terms of psychology, in which usually attitudes influence thoughts (the reasoning function) and feelings (emotional function) that ultimately affect consumer behavior include buying intentions (Hoyer and MacInnis, 2004). Hoyer and MacInnis (2004) recommend cultural orientation values along with consumers' beliefs to be included in future research when examining the factors of purchase intentions. This argument is further amplified by Fletcher and Crawford (2013) who states that marketing can be targeted of cultural universals, although the way these universals reflected in each culture is likely to differ. Based on the reviewed literature, this study aims to contribute to the very few studies to measures man-nature orientation values towards green purchase intentions. Thus, this becomes the basis of hypothesis two in this study which is stated as:

Hypothesis 2: Green purchase intention is positively influenced by man-nature orientation.

Long-Term Orientation

Long-term orientation is among the dimensions of cultural orientation that deals with time - past, present and future. Long-term orientation "stands for the fostering of virtues oriented towards future rewards, in particular perseverance and thrift" (Hofstede, 2001). In another word, it relates to how much society values long-standing compared to short-term values and tradition. This is an additional dimension to Hofstede's' initial four national culture dimensions, uncovered by Bond (1987) and later proposed by Hofstede (1991) as the long- versus short-term orientation as it has been proven to be an important, independent dimension, particularly in Asian cultures. According to Bearden et al., (2006), long-term orientation is a prominent facet of national cultural values and of itself influences consumers' decision-making process, however, research on its impact is lacking.

Base on the pertinent review of the literature, this is among the earliest research that attempts to incorporate and investigate the influence of long-term orientation values on purchase intentions of green products. While Hofstede argues that his cultural dimensions should not be measured at the individual or organizational level (Minkov and Hofstede, 2011), this study adopted the Cultural Values Scale (CVSCALE) proposed by Yoo et al., (2011) to capture Hofstede's long-term orientation at the individual level. It was developed as an extension of Hofstede (1991) cultural scale values that were initially designed to measure the cultural values at the national level. Bearden et al., (2006) further explain that long-term orientation will influence individuals' level of ethical values in which defined as the extent to which one considers accepted norms of right and wrong in his/her decisions. Thus, it would be expected that those who plan for future success would be less likely to engage in unethical behavior (conventional purchasing behavior) because such behavior if discovered holds harmful long-term consequences as this will have an impact on environment deterioration. Hence, the long-term oriented person will more likely to plan ahead before making a purchase and are less tempted by immediate desires or quick outcome derive from their purchase. This is supported by Gul (2013) which found that long-term orientation was a good predictor of environmental attitude formation in Turkey, an emerging market with collectivist culture between the East and the West. Consequently, it is expected that long-term oriented person will lead to positive green purchase intentions and thus the next hypothesis is stated as:

Hypothesis 3: Green purchase intention is positively influenced by long-term orientation.

The research model included pro-environmental motivational factors and its impact on green purchasing intentions. The hypotheses have been formulated based on aforementioned research studies to define the research framework shown in Figure 1. The research framework was developed using structural equation modeling.

METHODOLOGY

Sample and Data Collection

This study conducted self-administered questionnaire surveys to collect the research data. Since green products are relatively new products category in Malaysia, they are primarily available at large Supermarkets and malls in the major and most populous states such as Kuala Lumpur, Selangor and Sabah. This study thus targeted both male and female customers at the age of 18 and 65 who have purchasing power and active in shopping (Salzman, 2012) at supermarkets. The sample was selected by convenience, as there was no available access to sampling frames, databases or records to select individuals randomly. Additionally, to ensure participants were qualified to answer the survey questions and meaningful data collected, a screening question that asked participants if they aware of or and had previously purchased green products was asked. As an incentive for completing the survey, a token was given to all respondents. In total, 200 valid questionnaires were obtained which is considered sufficient and acceptable for Partial Least Square Structural Equation Modelling (PLS-SEM) (Hair et al., 2017).

Figure 1. Research Framework

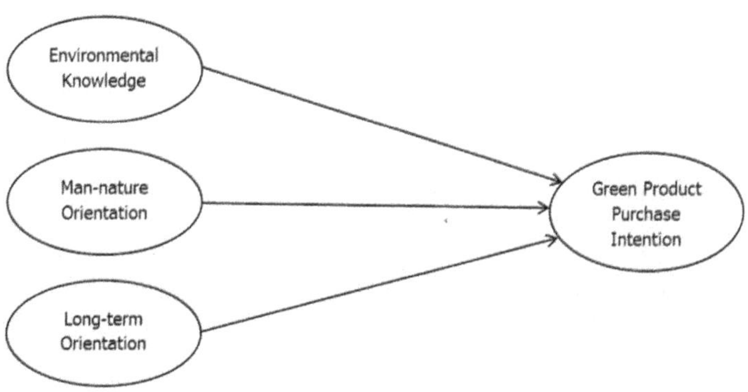

Measurement Instruments

Previous studies have been reviewed to ensure a comprehensive list of measures has been included. The initial instrument consists of 25 items were pre-tested on a sample of 30 subjects. The pretest was developed and administered in a series of meetings and interviews with post-graduate students and senior academics to review and evaluate the relevance of the constructs to suit the purpose/objectives of this study as well as correcting, refining and enhancing the instruments scales. Based on the comments, feedback and suggestions, two items were dropped and some minor wording changes were made to the final version.

The first section gathers demographic information on the respondents, the second section includes the independent variables consists of green purchase intentions adapted from Mostafa (2006) and Chan (2001), environmental knowledge adapted from Haron et al., (2005) and Tanner and Kastn(2003), man-nature orientation developed by Chan (2001) and six items of long-term orientation values were measured based on the work of Yoo et al., (2011). All items were measured using a five-point Likert-type scale, ranging from 1 to 5, where 1 denotes "strongly disagree or highly unlikely", and 5 represents "strongly agree or highly likely" (Malhotra and Birks, 2007).

FINDINGS

Respondents Profile

The demographic profile of respondents includes, gender, age, educational level, employment and yearly income level is presented in Table 1.

Just over half the sample (56%) was female with a majority having tertiary education. Most respondents are between 20 and 29 and 30 and 39 years old, with two most common annual income categories between MYR 50,001 – 100,000 (33.5%) and MYR 100,001 – 150,000 (41.0%).

Table 1. Demographic profiles of respondents

Demographics		Frequency (N=200)	Percentage (%)
Gender	Male	88	44.0
	Female	112	56.0
Age (Years)	20-29	73	36.5
	30-39	80	40.0
	40-49	34	17.0
	51-65	13	6.5
Highest academic qualification	Secondary school or lower	11	5.5
	Pre-University or equivalent	49	24.5
	Bachelor Degree	119	59.5
	Post-Graduate	21	10.5
Yearly Income	MYR 50,000 and below	28	14.0
	MYR 50,001 – 100,000	67	33.5
	MYR 100,001 – 150,000	82	41.0
	MYR 150,001 – 200,000	10	5.0
	MYR 200,001 and above	6	3.0
	Missing	7	3.5

This study used structural equation modeling (SEM) to examine the proposed model. SmartPLS 2.0 software (Ringle et al., 2005) was used to examine the relationships among the constructs of the research model by conducting partial least squares (PLS) analysis. Partial Least Squares (PLS) assesses the psychometric properties of the measurement model and estimates the parameters of the structural model. PLS analysis was preferred as the methodological choice as it allows us to simultaneously evaluate both the measurement and structural model (Chin, 1998) as well as maximizes the variance explained of the dependent variables (Hair et al., 2017). As suggested by Anderson and Gerbing (1988), the data analysis began with measurement model to determine whether all indicator variables appropriately reflect their underlying constructs and whether the measurement model has acceptable fit to the data then followed by an assessment of structural model.

Assessment of the Measurement Model

As suggested by Hair et al. (2010), reflective measurement model assessment in the PLS analysis includes composite reliability (CR) to evaluate internal consistency among items for each construct, item loading, and average extracted variance (AVE) to assess convergent validity.

As shown in Table 3, the item loadings are greater than 0.70 (Hair et al., 2013), while the average variance extracted (AVE) which reflects the overall amount of variance in the indicators accounted for by the latent construct, were all greater than the cut-off value of 0.50 (Chen, 2014; Hair et al., 2012). The results of composite reliability (CR) for constructs were confirmed satisfactory with values above cut-off value 0.70 (see Table 2) (Hair et al., 2017). Therefore, this indicates that convergent validity established.

Discriminant Validity

Discriminant validity is the extent to which items measure distinct concepts and is indicated by the low correlations between the measure of interest and the measures of other constructs (Cheung and Lee, 2010). Discriminant validity can be examined by comparing the ratio between the square root of AVE and correlations (Fornell and Larcker, 1981). As shown in Table 3, the diagonal elements of the matrix, which represents the square root of the AVEs, are higher than the corresponding inter-construct correlations indicating adequate discriminant validity (Hair et al., 2011).

The Structural Model and Path Analysis

After the constructs were confirmed to be reliable and valid, we proceeded with the path analysis to test hypotheses. Table 4 shows the structural model parameter estimates. The overall model explained a significant variance of ($R^2 = 0.517$) 51.7% in green purchasing intention via latent variables; considered significant and meaningful for the purposes of interpretation (Hair et al., 2014). In social science research, the interpretations of R^2 of 0.75 is considered substantial, 0.50 is moderate, and 0.25 is weak (Wong, 2013).

Table 4 shows the structural model parameter estimates. Man-nature orientation is positively significant ($\beta = 0.387$, $p < 0.01$) towards green purchase intentions and so do long-term orientation ($\beta = 0.\ 144$, $p < 0.01$), whereas environmental knowledge is not a significant predictor of green purchase intentions (β

Table 2. Convergent validity of measurement model

Construct	Item	Convergent Validity		
		Loadings	AVE	Composite Reliability
Environmental Knowledge	EK1	0.866	0.674	0.953
	EK10	0.805		
	EK2	0.694		
	EK3	0.768		
	EK4	0.870		
	EK5	0.836		
	EK6	0.803		
	EK7	0.822		
	EK8	0.847		
	EK9	0.877		
Green Product Purchase Intention	GPIG1	0.892	0.766	0.942
	GPIG2	0.881		
	GPIG3	0.877		
	GPIG4	0.824		
	GPIG5	0.901		
Man-Nature Orientation	MNO1	0.922	0.703	0.904
	MNO2	0.876		
	MNO3	0.792		
	MNO4	0.754		
Long-Term Orientation	LTO1	0.887	0.735	0.943
	LTO2	0.845		
	LTO3	0.867		
	LTO4	0.877		
	LTO5	0.847		
	LTO6	0.816		

Table 3. Fornell-Larcker criterion

Latent Variables	1	2	3	4	5
1. Environmental Knowledge	**0.820**				
2. Green Product Purchase Intention	0. 002	**0.875**			
3. Long-term Orientation	0.791	0.379	**0.857**		
4. Man-nature Orientation	0.677	0.758	0.085	**0.838**	

Note: Diagonals (in bold) represent square roots of average variance extracted (AVE) while the other entries represent the squared correlations

Table 4. Summary of the structural model

Hypotheses	Hypotheses Paths	Path Coefficients	T-Values	Results
H1	EK > Green Product Purchase Intention	0.055	1. 625	Not supported
H2	MNO > Green Product Purchase Intention	0.387	6.442**	Supported
H3	LTO > Green Product Purchase Intention	0.144	3.155**	Supported

Note: EK; Environmental Knowledge, MNO; Man-Nature Orientation, LTO; Long Term Orientation,
**p< 0.01, *p< 0.05

= 0.055, p > 0.05). Thus, H2 and H3 were supported whereas H1 was not. In overall, it was found that cultural value of man-nature orientation is the strongest predictor of green purchase intentions follows by cultural value of long-term orientation.

DISCUSSIONS

Sustainable consumption and development have attracted the attention of both practitioners and academic researchers. Identifying and understanding how various factors affect the intention of green purchasing is topical in green consumer behavior discipline. Accordingly, the current study was to explain consumers' green purchase intention motivational drivers.

The result in Table 4 shows that environmental knowledge did not significantly influence green purchase intention. Therefore, this finding questions the assertion that the more knowledgeable the consumers are about a subject, the more they know about the effects of the human actions towards it, the more we expect them to walk the right action and vice-versa. The possible explanation for the yielded result of this study is supported by Tanner and Kast (2003) and Schahn and Holzer (1990) who found the action-related knowledge to be positively related to green food purchases and environmental action, whereas the factual knowledge was not a predictor of the latter. The questions in this study were adopted from surveys administered based on factual knowledge. Moreover, Smith-Sebasto and Fortner (1994) quoted claiming that "when the relationship between environmental knowledge and behaviors/intention appears to be stronger, it is knowledge about ecological behaviors (i. e knowledge about what and how something can be done) rather than factual knowledge about the environment that is related to ecological behavior.

As for cultural influence, man-nature orientation was posited to be positively related green purchase intentions. This study found that the statistical result supported the hypothesis. This is consistent with previous studies (Sreen et al. 2018; Rehman and Dost, 2013; Chan, 2001). This finding indicates that man-nature orientation is a constant part of individuals' life, which shapes people's eco-friendly behavior subsequently leads to positive green products purchase intention. In other words, man-nature orientation values allow or and increases consumers interest and desire for green products as a mean for expressing their wish to protect the environment and live harmoniously with nature. Man-nature orientation is perceived as an important attribute as Schiffman & Kanuk (2007), Kotler (2003) and Schiffman and Kanuk (1994) stated that culture has a strong influence on consumers' behaviors that occur so "natural" and "automatic" and a fundamental determinant of a person's desires and behavior. It can be reasoned that man-nature orientation is a constant value of individuals' lifestyle, which leads to and shapes pro-environmental behavior which successively forms intentions to buy green products when faced with options in the decision-making process. In some sense, man-nature orientation values will evoke consumers' desire and intentions to buy green products as a mean to preserve the environment and maintain living harmoniously with nature as demonstrated by respondents in this study. This may be because Asians in general (including Malaysians) perceive themselves as living in harmony with nature compared to Westerners who see themselves as separate from nature (de Mooij, 2004), causing them to adhere to the values of man-nature orientation that have influenced their purchase intentions of green product.

The cultural dimension of long-term orientation was also hypothesized to be positively related to green purchase intentions. This study found that the hypothesis was supported and underpinned previous studies (Chekima et al., 2017; Gul, 2013; Samarasinghe, 2012; Beardon et al., 2006) which found that long-term orientation is a prominent cultural facet and influence consumers' purchase decision making as well as a good predictors for environmental attitude formation. Then in line with the long-term orientations' facets such as thrift and persistence to ensure future rewards, the respondents in this study displayed a positive relation long-term orientation towards green purchase intentions since green consumption perceived to save money and conserve the environment, in the long run, to guarantee a better living for all. In addition to our recommendations based on theory, it also makes sense since environmentally sensitive and protective behavior can mostly be observed in the long-term rather than within the time period the behavior carried out. The results support the works of Sarigollu (2009) which theorize that long-term oriented people are more likely to develop values and attitudes pertaining to the protection of the natural environment.

Implications

From theoretical perspectives, this study is the first to develop a model that explain drivers of consumers' green purchasing behavior by integrating and examined various major aspects; namely, individuals' possess knowledge on environment and cultural values (man-nature orientation and long-term orientation) in a single framework. The findings of this study bring new insights and interesting findings where it has identified and confirmed that cultural values play a significant role in green consumer behavior. This research provides a basis and paves the way to future researchers to explore in depth with reference to other cultural values or additional predictors that could promote pro-environmental activities and purchase intentions in Malaysia as well as other countries.

Developing such model is important to fill an information gap that exists between academics (as evidenced by an insufficient number of research and innovation of consumers green purchasing behavior) and practitioners (as evident by widespread of green products). Thus, the understanding of the green purchase determinant and the value of attachment, they give to the environment provides useful insights to practitioners and contribute immensely to the body of knowledge simultaneously to sustainable consumption as well as sustainable development.

In terms of research, this study provides further evidence of the usefulness and validation of using CVSCALE developed by Yoo and colleagues to measure the influence of culture at the individual level. Applications of cultural values are increasing in cross-cultural studies (Prasongsukarn, 2009). This is due to the increasing globalization of markets with which facilitate products crossing the border; making cultural context as important and interesting to be studied to understand the consumer behavior (Patterson et al., 2006). However, the existing literature of cross-cultural business rather chaotic due to the cultural valuation methods in using a conflicting scale and lack of a universally accepted scale. It is understood that by measuring the cultural values and not equate it with the national culture, researchers can avoid the ecological fallacy, which occurs when the ecological or country-level relationships are construed as if they apply to individuals (see Hofstede 1980). Thus, adoption of CVSCALE is recommended and can benefit multi-cultural business practitioners and cross-cultural researchers, which this scale connects cultural values to individual behaviors and attitudes.

Based on the results of the partial least square (PLS) technique in testing hypotheses in this study, man-nature orientation values exerted the most significant influence on green purchase intentions, followed by long-term orientation. Cultural values of both man-nature orientation and long-term orientation provide a stronger effect and therefore more useful profile of green consumption. The research findings provide managerial implications for green marketers. The results offer consumer segments (based on cultural values) for green products in green marketing. Understanding how different consumer orientations and value responses vary green purchase intentions enables green marketers to develop customized strategies to align consumer segment, thereby increasing the effectiveness and efficiency of green sales activities.

As evident in this study that the influence of culture is dynamic, which functions to give reasons, therefore it is recommended for marketers to promote individuals toward green products through advertising based on cultural reasoning will help to induce their intentions to purchase green products. This can be carried out by applying or instilling certain elements of the man-nature orientation and long-term orientation in advertising, will enable marketers to reflect those values through demonstration of how green product can maintain and protect the environment, save money that benefits in the long run and reminds of the responsibility to act accordingly through environmentally friendly behaviour because we are part of nature to keep it and not vice versa. Marketers can engage and reflect certain cultural values effectively through environmental advertising at the same time providing environmental advertising a competitive advantage over normal advertising that can affect consumers' cognitive-emotional functioning (information processing, perception and attitude) and exert strong intentions to acquire green products. Besides that, a systematic educational program and proper societal and social marketing approach, marketers along with government can utilize these cultural values to increase individual's' environmental awareness and stimulate intention to buy green products that assist to achieve and accelerate sustainable national and ecology development.

As confirmed in this study, surprisingly environmental knowledge has been found to have a negative relationship towards green purchase intention. Hence it is strongly suggested for green marketers to promote their green products based on cause-related marketing method rather than viral marketing method. Coddington (1990) quoted that "the seeds that are sown under the right approach to environmental marketing are the seeds of environmental education". Also, the government should introduce an environmental subject in the formal curriculum in schools and higher institutions to enhance citizens' specific knowledge concerning the environment to foster green buying behavior.

LIMITATIONS AND FUTURE DIRECTIONS

As with all research, this study also has certain limitations highlight the need for further research. Firstly, although the result of this study has further proven the usefulness of the CVSCALE in measuring Hofstede's cultural dimension, the cultural assessment method for individual-level is rather chaotic in the business literature due to the lack of universally accepted scales. Future research needs to keep validating these measures on pro-environmental behavior using a larger sample, demographically diverse samples and samples from other countries, as well as employing other dimensions based on CVSCALE (etc. collectivism, individualism, feminism and masculinity). A convenient start will be to replicate current study to see whether similar findings may be made when culture is measured at the individual level. Such similarities or differences between individual-level and national-level of Hofstede's' cultural dimensions will provide insights into psychological, sociological and business managerial differences of the same construct.

Secondly, it would be interesting to extend this research by emphasizing on a particular green product. It can be implemented with a special focus on the electric and electronic appliance, automobiles, environmentally friendly cleaning products, food and agriculture. This is crucial as different organic food product could be determined by distinct factors (Liobikiene and Bernatoniene, 2016; Padel and Foster, 2005).

Despite these limitations, the study makes several contributions to the field of consumer buying behavior and green marketing.

REFERENCES

Amyx, D. A., DeJong, P. F., Lin, Chakraborty, G., & Wiener, J.L. (1994). Influencers of purchase intentions for ecologically safe products: an exploratory study. In *AMA Winter Educators' Conference Proceedings*. American Marketing Association.

Anderson, J. C., & Gerbing, D. W. (1988). Structural equation modeling in practice: A review of a recommended two-step approach. *Psychological Bulletin*, *103*(3), 411–423. doi:10.1037/0033-2909.103.3.411

Armstrong, J. S., Morwitz, V. G., & Kumar, V. (2000). Sales forecasts for existing consumer products and services: Do purchase intentions contribute to accuracy? *International Journal of Forecasting*, *16*(3), 383–397. doi:10.1016/S0169-2070(00)00058-3

Bearden, W. O., Money, R. B., & Nevins, J. L. (2006). A Measure of Long-Term Orientation: Development and Validation. *Journal of the Academy of Marketing Science*, *34*(3), 456–467. doi:10.1177/0092070306286706

Bond, M. H. (1987). Chinese Values and the Search for Culture-Free Dimensions of Culture. *Journal of Cross-Cultural Psychology*, *18*(2), 143–164. doi:10.1177/0022002187018002002

Bradley, J. C., Waliczek, T., & Zajicek, J. (1999). Relationship between environmental knowledge and environmental attitude of high school students. *The Journal of Environmental Education*, *30*(3), 17–21. doi:10.1080/00958969909601873

Chan, R., & Lau, L. (2001). Explaining green purchasing behavior: A cross-cultural study on American and Chinese consumers. *Journal of International Marketing*, *14*(2/3), 9–40.

Cheung, S. F., Chan, D. K. S., & Wong, Z. S. Y. (1999). Re-examining the Theory of Planned Behavior in Understanding Wastepaper Recycling. *Environment and Behavior*, *31*(5), 587–612. doi:10.1177/00139169921972254

Chung, J. E., Stoel, L., Xu, Y., & Ren, J. (2012). Predicting Chinese consumers' purchase intentions for imported soy-based dietary supplements. *British Food Journal*, *114*(1), 143–161. doi:10.1108/00070701211197419

De Mooij, M. (2004). *Consumer Behaviour and Culture: Consequences for Global Marketing*. Sage.

Fletcher, R., & Crawford, H. (2013). *International marketing: an Asia Pacific perspective, 6th*. Frenchs Forest, NSW: Pearson Australia.

Follows, S. B., & Jobber, D. (2000). Environmentally responsible purchase behaviour: A test of a consumer model. *European Journal of Marketing*, *34*(5/6), 723–746. doi:10.1108/03090560010322009

Fornell, C., & Larcker, D. F. (1981). Evaluating structural equation models with unobservable variables and measurement error. *JMR, Journal of Marketing Research*, *18*(1), 39–50. doi:10.2307/3151312

Gleim, M. R., Smith, J., Andrews, D., & Cronin, J. J. Jr. (2013). Against the green: A multi-method examination of the barriers to green consumption. *Journal of Retailing*, *89*(1), 44–61. doi:10.1016/j.jretai.2012.10.001

Godelnik, R. (2012, December 28). *2012: Four Trends in Sustainable Consumption*. Retrieved from http://www.triplepundit.com/2012/12/sustainable-consumption-trends/

Gul, M. C. (2013). Long-term Orientation, Perceived Consumer Effectiveness, and Environmentally Conscious Consumer Behavior: The Case of Turkey. *International Journal of Marketing Studies.*, *5*(5), 23–31. doi:10.5539/ijms.v5n5p24

Hair, J. F., Black, W. C., Babin, B. J., & Anderson, R. E. (2010). *Multivariate Data Analysis*. Upper Saddle River, NJ: Prentice-Hall.

Hair, J. F., Sarstedt, M., Ringle, C. M., & Mena, J. A. (2012). An assessment of the use of partial least squares structural equation modeling in marketing research. *Journal of the Academy of Marketing Science*, *40*(3), 414–433. doi:10.100711747-011-0261-6

Haron, S. A., Paim, L., & Yahaya, N. (2005). Towards sustainable consumption: An examination of environmental knowledge among Malaysians. *International Journal of Consumer Studies*, *29*(5), 426–436. doi:10.1111/j.1470-6431.2005.00460.x

Hines, J. M., Hungerford, H. R., & Tomera, A. N. (1986/87). Analysis and synthesis of research on responsible environmental behaviour: A meta-analysis. *The Journal of Environmental Education*, *18*(2), 1–8. doi:10.1080/00958964.1987.9943482

Hofstede, G. (1980). *Culture's Consequences: International differences in work-related values*. Beverly Hill, CA: Sage.

Hofstede, G. (2001). *Culture's consequences: Comparing values, behaviors, institutions, and organizations across nations* (2nd ed.). Thousand Oaks, CA: Sage Publications, Inc.

Hoyer, W., & MacInnis, D. (2004). *Consumer behavior* (3rd ed.). Boston, MA: Houghton Mifflin Company.

Jaus, H. H. (1984). The development and retention of environmental attitudes in elementary school children. *The Journal of Environmental Education*, *15*(3), 33–36. doi:10.1080/00958964.1984.9942679

Jordan, J. R., Hungerford, H. R., & Tomera, A. N. (1986). Effects of two residential environmental workshops on high school students. *The Journal of Environmental Education*, *18*(1), 15–22. doi:10.1080/00958964.1986.9942726

Kacen, J. J., & Lee, J. A. (2002). The Influence of Culture on Consumer Impulsive Buying Behavior. *Journal of Consumer Psychology*, *12*(2), 163–176. doi:10.1207/S15327663JCP1202_08

Kalafatis, S. P., Pollard, M., East, R., & Tsogas, M. H. (1999). Green marketing and Ajzen's theory of planned behavior: A cross-market examination. *Journal of Consumer Marketing*, *16*(5), 441–460. doi:10.1108/07363769910289550

Kennedy, E. H., Beckley, T. M., McFarlane, B. L., & Nadeau, S. (2009). Why we don't walk the talk: Understanding the environmental values/behaviour gap in Canada. *Human Ecology Review*, *16*(2), 151–160.

Kim, Y., & Choi, S. M. (2005). Antecedents of green purchase behaviour: An examination of collectivism, environmental concern, and PCE. *Advances in Consumer Research. Association for Consumer Research (U. S.)*, *32*, 592–599.

Kluckhohn, F. R., & Strodtbeck, F. L. (1961). *Variations in value orientations*. Evanston, IL: Row, Peterson.

Kluckhohn, C. (1956). *Toward a Comparison of Value Emphasis in Different Cultures*. In L. D. White (Ed.), *The State of Social Sciences* (pp. 116–132). Chicago: The University of Chicago Press.

Laroche, M., Bergeron, J., & Barbaro-Forleo, G. (2001). Targeting consumer who are willing to pay more for environmentally friendly products. *Journal of Consumer Marketing*, *18*(6), 503–520. doi:10.1108/EUM0000000006155

Malhotra, N., & Birks, D. (2007). *Marketing Research: an Applied Approach*. Harlow: Prentice Hall.

Minkov, M., & Hofstede, G. (2011). The evolution of Hofstede's doctrine. *Cross Cultural Management*, *18*(1), 10–20. doi:10.1108/13527601111104269

Mostafa, M. M. (2007). Antecedents of Egyptian consumers' green purchase intentions: A hierarchical multivariate regression model. *Journal of International Consumer Marketing*, *19*(2), 97–126. doi:10.1300/J046v19n02_06

Newberry, C. R., Klemz, B. R., & Boshoff, C. (2003). Managerial implications of predicting purchase behavior from purchase intentions: A retail patronage case study. *Journal of Services Marketing*, *17*(6), 609–620. doi:10.1108/08876040310495636

Nik Abdul Rashid, N. R. (2009). Awareness of eco-label in Malaysia green marketing initiative. *International Journal of Business and Management*, *4*, 132–141.

O'Neal, P. W. (Ed.). (2007). *Motivation of Health Behavior*. New York: Nova Science Publishers Inc.

Patterson, P. G., Cowley, E., & Prasongsukarn, K. (2006). Service failure recovery: The moderating impact of individual-level cultural value orientation on perceptions of justice. *International Journal of Research in Marketing*, *23*(3), 263–277. doi:10.1016/j.ijresmar.2006.02.004

Peattie, K., & Crane, A. (2005). Green marketing: Legend, myth, farce or prophesy? *Qualitative Market Research*, *8*(4), 357–370. doi:10.1108/13522750510619733

Peter, J. P., & Olson, J. C. (2008). *Consumer behaviour and marketing strategy* (8th ed.). New York, NY: McGraw-Hill Education.

Pierre, C., Morwitz, V. G., & Reinartz, W. J. (2005). Do intentionss really predict behavior? Self-generated validity effects in survey research. *Journal of Marketing*, *69*(2), 1–14. doi:10.1509/jmkg.69.2.1.60755

Prasongsukarn. (2009). Validating the Cultural Value scale (CVSCALE) a Case Study of Thailand. *ABAC Journal, 29*(2), 1–13.

Rahbar, E., & Abdul Wahid, N. (2011). Investigation of green marketing tools' effect on consumers' purchase behavior. *Business Strategy Series*, *12*(2), 73–83. doi:10.1108/17515631111114877

Rajagopal, D. (2011). Consumer culture and purchase intentions toward fashion apparel in Mexico. *Journal of Database Marketing and Customer Strategy Management.*, *18*(4), 286–307. doi:10.1057/dbm.2011.33

Ramayah, T., Jason, L. W. C., & Mohamad, O. (2010). Green Product Purchase Intentions: Some Insights from a Developing Country. *Resources, Conservation and Recycling*, *54*(12), 1419–1427. doi:10.1016/j.resconrec.2010.06.007

Ramsey, C. E., & Rickson, R. E. (1976). Environmental knowledge and attitudes. *The Journal of Environmental Education*, *8*(1), 10–18. doi:10.1080/00958964.1976.9941552

Ramsey, J. M. (1993). The effects of issue investigation and action training on eighth-grade students' environmental behavior. *The Journal of Environmental Education*, *2*(3), 31–36. doi:10.1080/00958964.1993.9943501

Ringle, C. M., Wende, S., & Will, A. (2005). *SmartPLS 2.0 (M3) beta.* Retrieved from http://www.smartpls.de

Rokeach, M. (1973). *The Nature of Human Values.* New York: Free Press.

Sabrina, O. S. (2007). *Predicting environmentally purchase behaviour: a test of the value-attitude-behavior hierarchy.* The 2nd Indonesian Business Management Conference, Jakarta, Indonesia.

Samarasinghe, R. (2012). The Influence of Cultural Values and Environmental Attitudes on Green Consumer Behaviour. *International Journal of Behavioral Science.*, *7*, 83–98.

Sarigollu, E. (2009). A Cross-Country Exploration of Environmental Attitudes. *Environment and Behavior*, *41*(3), 365–386. doi:10.1177/0013916507313920

Schahn, J., & Holzer, E. (1990). Studies of individual environmental concern: The role of knowledge, gender, and background variables. *Environment and Behavior*, *22*(6), 767–786. doi:10.1177/0013916590226003

Schiffman, L., & Kanuk, L. L. (2010). Consumer Behavior (10th ed.). Pearson Education, Inc.

Schwartz, J., & Miller, T. (1991). The earth's best friends. *American Demographics*, *13*, 26–35.

Schwartz, S. H. (1994). Are there universal aspects in the structure and contents of human values? *The Journal of Social Issues*, *50*(4), 19–45. doi:10.1111/j.1540-4560.1994.tb01196.x

Schwartz, S. H., & Sagiv, L. (1995). Identifying culture-specifics in the content and structure of values. *Journal of Cross-Cultural Psychology*, *26*(1), 92–116. doi:10.1177/0022022195261007

Selles, H. (2013). The relative impact of countries on global natural resource consumption and ecological degradation. *International Journal of Sustainable Development and World Ecology*, *20*(2), 97–108. doi:10.1080/13504509.2013.780190

Steenkamp, J. B. E. M., Hofstede, F. T., & Wedel, M. A. (1999). Cross-national investigation into the individual and national cultural antecedents of consumer innovativeness. *Journal of Marketing*, *63*(2), 155–169. doi:10.2307/1251945

Straughan, R. D., & Roberts, J. A. (1999). Environmental segmentation alternatives: A look at green consumer behavior in the new millennium. *Journal of Consumer Marketing*, *16*(6), 558–575. doi:10.1108/07363769910297506

Strizhakova, Y., & Coulter, R. (2013). The "green" side of materialism in emerging BRIC and developed markets: The moderating role of global cultural identity. *International Journal of Research in Marketing*, *30*(1), 69–82. doi:10.1016/j.ijresmar.2012.08.003

Suki, N.M. (2015). *Customer environmental satisfaction and loyalty in the consumption of green products*. Academic Press.

Tan, B. C., & Lau, T. C. (2010). The Influencing Factors of Green Purchase Behaviour: *An Exploratory Study. International Conference on Marketing (ICMAR2010).*

Tanner, C., & Kast, S. W. (2003). Promoting sustainable consumption: Determinants of green purchase by Swiss consumers. *Psychology and Marketing*, *20*(10), 883–902. doi:10.1002/mar.10101

Thongplew, N., Spaargaren, G., & Koppen, V. C. S. A. (2013). Greening consumption at the retail outlet: The case of the Thai appliance industry. *International Journal of Sustainable Development and World Ecology*, *21*(2), 99–110. doi:10.1080/13504509.2013.867551

Triandis, H. C. (1993). The contingency model in cross-cultural perspective. In M. M. Chemers & R. Ayman (Eds.), *Leadership theory and research: Perspectives and directions* (pp. 167–188). San Diego, CA: Academic Press.

Vining, J., & Ebreo, A. (1992). Predicting recycling behaviour from global and specific environmental attitudes and changes in recycling opportunities. *Journal of Applied Social Psychology*, *22*(20), 1580–1607. doi:10.1111/j.1559-1816.1992.tb01758.x

Werner, J., & Alvensleben, R. V. (2011). Consumer Attitudes towards Organic Food in Germany (F.R.). *Symposium on Horticultural Economics, 8*, 155.

Wong, K. K. K. (2013). Partial least squares structural equation modeling (PLS-SEM) techniques using SmartPLS. *Marketing Bulletin*, *24*, 1–23.

Wu, J. H., Wu, C. W., Lee, C. T., & Lee, H. J. (2015). Green purchase intentions: An exploratory study of the Taiwanese electric motorcycle market. *Journal of Business Research*, *68*(4), 829–833. doi:10.1016/j.jbusres.2014.11.036

Yaveroglu, I. S., & Donthu, J. (2002). Cultural influences on the diffusion of products. *Journal of International Consumer Marketing*, *14*(4), 49–36. doi:10.1300/J046v14n04_04

Yoo, B., Donthu, B., & Lenartowicz, T. (2011). Measuring Hofstede's Five Dimensions of Cultural Values at the Individual Level: Development and Validation of CVSCALE. *Journal of International Consumer Marketing*, *23*(3/4), 193–210.

KEY TERMS AND DEFINITIONS

Environmental Knowledge: Environmental knowledge is the amount of information individuals have concerning environmental issues and their ability to understand and evaluate its impact on society and the environment.

Green Purchasing Intention: Green purchase intention stands for a willingness and distinct kind of environmentally friendly behavior by individuals to give preference to green products compared to conventional products to express their concern to the environment.

Long-Term Orientation: Long-term orientation is a cultural orientation that deals with time—past, present, and future—to foster virtues oriented towards future rewards, in particular perseverance and thrift.

Man-Nature Orientation: Man-nature orientation is referred as the friendly behavior or relationship between human beings and the natural environment because of the love of nature and the passion to protect it.

Structural Equation Modeling: Structural equation modeling (SEM) as a second-generation technique, is a statistical technique for building and testing simultaneous modeling of relationships among multiple variables.

Chapter 13
Expanding Research Agenda for Sustainable Consumption and Social Institutions:
A Case of South Africa

Neha Purushottam
University of South Africa, South Africa

ABSTRACT

Sustainable development is part of the developmental agenda for developed and developing countries both. For developing countries, growth is critical but resource consuming. Therefore, it is important to ensure equitable growth in these countries without degradation of natural and social environment and resources. Sustainable consumption and production both are part of Sustainable Development Goal 12. Mostly countries focus on the production rather than on the consumption, which needs to be changed. South Africa faces challenges of under-consumption in lower income classes and over-consumption in affluent and aspiring middle classes. Examination of institutional actors highlights the gap, which can be filled by social institutions. Social institutions are active and growing in South Africa and were identified suitable to promote sustainable consumption through cooperation, collaboration, and partnerships. This chapter attempts to expand the research agenda to examine the role and potential of social institutions in facilitating sustainable consumption in a developing country like South Africa.

INTRODUCTION

Food, water and energy security forms the basis of a resilient economy, but as a water-scarce country with little arable land and a dependence on coal-fired power and oil imports, South Africa's economy is testing the limits of its resources constraints. (p4, Von Bormann, and Gulati, 2014).

South Africa is one of the two largest economies of Africa and together with Nigeria "*account for 50% of the continent's GDP in* 2017" (p11, Euromonitor, 2018). South Africa is witnessing growth in

DOI: 10.4018/978-1-5225-7906-9.ch013

population and affluence. However, South Africa has highest level of inequality in the world with "*consumption expenditure Gini coefficient 0.63 in 2015*" (p60, The World Bank, 2018). It is one of the nine African economies which are consuming resources beyond their capacity (United Nations Economic Commission for Africa, 2009). It is almost unique country in Africa in the sense that it is democratic, has strong judiciary, advanced baking system and good infrastructure but also has high number of low income households with unemployment around *27%* (p23, Euromonitor International, 2018). The report also highlights an interesting point that South Africa has poor youth and rich population of 65 plus age group. Interestingly this inequality between rich and poor in South Africa is growing (Sulla and Zikhali, 2018). South Africa, like any other developing countries is continuously under international pressure to ensure that its economic growth is equitable and the growth is decoupled with degradation of natural and social environment and resources does not happen (UNEP, 2014). South Africa is facing complex and contradictory sustainability problems; therefore there is an urgent need for more integrative and comprehensive approaches to ensure progress towards sustainability goals. For developing country like South Africa finding a balance between economic growth and sustainable development is a must.

In African cities growing middle class is attracted to "western consumption patterns such as private car ownership, increased meat consumption, and emergence of low-density detached housing developments in sub-urban areas" (p4, UN Economic and Social Council, 2009). Same is true for South African consumers who are identified price conscious but aspirational with affinity towards brands (Euromonitor International, 2018). Adding challenge to this situation is issue of urbanization which affects consumption and in Africa the growth of urbanization is the highest in the world at "*3.5 percent per year*" (UN Economic and Social Council, 2009). In developing countries like South Africa, growing aspirational middle class and urbanization along with inequality and materialistic tendencies is a critical challenge to the sustainable development (UN DESA, 2013; Staniškis, 2012; Assadourian, 2010; Dauvergne, 2010; UN Economic and Social Council, 2009). Like many African countries, South Africa witnesses hyper or over-consumption among affluent class and under-consumption among poor (Spangenberg, 2014; Zhao & Schroeder, 2010; UN Economic and Social Council, 2009). In the country, the growing affluence among middle and higher income class is contributing to the materialistic and wasteful consumption, unhealthy lifestyle and aspiration for holistic well-being (Schaefer & Crane 2005; Staniškis, 2012, World Economic Forum, 2013). At the other side of it, is the population of poor which do not have sufficient access to resources, lacks food security and struggle for basic necessities (Dauvergne, 2010; UN Economic and Social Council, 2009). The unsustainability of consumption creates more pressure on poor by restricting their '*ecological spaces*' (p8, UN Economic and Social Council, 2009). Therefore, for South Africa, it is absolutely essential to make sure to achieve equity in consumption across classes (affluent and poor) and geographies (urban and rural) and to ensure inclusive growth.

Growing unsustainability of consumption in the country is a threat to sustainable consumption goals and needs an urgent attention. Investing in sustainable consumption may help South Africa in finding this balance (Cohen, 2005). However, the efforts to address sustainable consumption are far behind than the efforts to address issues of sustainable production. Progress towards sustainable consumption also get affected by it being a new concept, absence of clear definition, lack of clear boundaries of the concept, limited awareness about the issues covered under the concept etc. (UN economic and social council, 2009). The discussion so far clearly indicates that South Africa has to invest in its economic growth while ensuring sustainable development which makes investing in sustainable consumption a necessity (Cohen, 2005).

On this background, this chapter examines the possibilities for social institutions in facilitating sustainable consumption. In the process it highlights pertinent research enquiries to expand the research agenda in South African context. The first section provides historical background of sustainability, production and consumption. In this section importance of focusing on sustainable consumption is instituted. The next section covers brief discussion on the theoretical aspects of consumption. This section attempts to present various dimensions of consumption without understanding which it is difficult to direct it. The third section explores nuances of definitions and scope of sustainable consumption and attempts to understand it at micro and macro levels. The fourth section examines approaches to sustainable consumption to present appropriateness of 'reconfiguration' perspective for developing countries like South Africa. In the following section, this chapter reviews the efforts of various institutional actors like consumers, businesses, government, education institutions and media through reviewing their role and limitations. The next section expands on the importance, possibilities and difficulties of social institutions in promoting sustainable consumption. The seventh section explores prospects for social institutions in South African context by highlighting major research enquiry and thus adds to the research agenda set for developing countries. The last section concludes with recognizing that social organizations have major role to play in promoting sustainable consumption in South Africa. However, it also comprehends that social organizations will able to attain their goals through cooperation and alliances with other institutional actors in the current multi-polar world.

SUSTAINABILITY, PRODUCTION AND CONSUMPTIUON: UNDERSTANDING INTER-LINKAGES

Growing unsustainability is the most critical issue to manage as it contributes to the shortage of resources like water, energy, food etc.; dampens quality of life by pollution and unmanaged waste and creates issues for the wellbeing of whole biosphere and ecosystem (Peattie and Collins 2009; ölander and Thøgersen 1995; Etzioni 1998; Fisk 1973). The slow realisation of grave danger has contributed in sustainability becoming priority agenda for the national plans (Barber, 2003). In the process, sustainable development and sustainability emerged as a solution to ensure equitable sustenance of quality of life (Lozano, 2008).

Sustainability in its simplistic form is defined as "capacity to maintain" (Starik and Kanashiro, 2013), "capacity to support for long term" (p1, Sutton, 2004) a balance in economic, environmental and social aspects of life (Goodland, 1995). A detailed account of history and timeline of sustainability is given elsewhere (Turner, 2008; Filho, 2000 and Goodland, 1995). In brief, it seems that long back, the existence of term was mostly used in addressing issues related to human and environmental interactions in sixties and seventies (Sutton, 2004). The term sustainability and debate associated with it came to forefront with "*The Limits to Growth*" publication in 1972 (Turner, 2008; Goodland, 1995). This publication brought the world's attention to the challenges of growing population and finite capacity of earth's ecosystem w.r.t. providing resources, pollution management and waste disposal (Staniškis, 2012; Turner, 2008). Moreover, systems view of growth believes humans, other non-human living beings, environment, societal systems and technology affect each other as they all are part of a bigger system (Turner, 2008). The Brundtland Report published by World Commission on Environment and Development in 1987 has contributed to propagating these issues (Filho, 2000). This report provides one of the most widely used definitions of sustainable development by adding dimensions of inter-generational and intra-generational equity to the definitions of sustainability (Sutton, 2004; Belz and Peattie, 2012). Over a period of time, various aspects were added in the definitions of sustainability which added flexibility to the concept and expanded its scope of use (Geels et al., 2015; Lozano, 2008; Parris and Kates, 2003).

Sustainable development intends to (a) sustain nature, life support, and community and (b) develop humans, economy and society (Parris and Kates, 2003). In this regard, sustainable consumption and production (SCP) are considered strategic interventions to minimise and mitigate negative impacts caused by production and consumption (UN economic and social council, 2009). They are part of Sustainable development goal (SDG) 12 under development agenda for 2030 (Gulati and Naudé, 2017). Sustainable production initiatives focused on resource and supply chain inefficiencies, cleaner production processes and eco-innovations (Staniškis, 2012). While sustainable consumption efforts focused on the issues related to the growth in population, income and materialistic consumption tendencies (Dauvergne, 2010). Unsustainability of consumption was mainly noticed in three product categories-food and drink, housing, and transportation (Peattie and Collins, 2009). The seriousness about unsustainability of current consumption can be understood by the facts that (a) the ratio of consumption to renewal captivity is high as current consumption is "30% larger than nature's capacity to regenerate" (p1015, Staniškis, 2012); (b) the rate of consumption has gone up as "humans today extract and use around 50% more natural resources than only 30 years ago"; (c) presence of inequality in per capita consumption as "people in rich countries consume up to 10 times more natural resources than those in the poorest countries" (p3, Giljum, Hinterberger, Bruckner, Burger, Frühmann, Lutter, ... & Warhurst, 2009); and the most complex one is (d) the growth of unsustainable consumption in developing economies. Besides the seriousness of this issue, it is interesting to note that during initial years, sustainable consumption remained at the periphery of sustainable development talks. The situation was due to the facts that consumption was considered sovereign, essential for economic growth and firms being the primary source of the problem (Cohen, 2005). In nineties, it was realised that simultaneous addressing of consumption with production is critical (Barber, 2003; Stevens, 2010) for the sustainable future. The world realised importance of sustainable consumption when developing countries (India and China were at the forefront in raising it) brought attention to the fact that developed countries are the main contributors to the unsustainability by associating materialistic consumption in developed countries to growing pollution, garbage and depletion of resources (Cohen, 2005). The way economic development has progressed in 'north' (often termed as 'west' contributed to the growth of affluence which contributed to the materialistic unsustainable consumption (Assadourian, 2010). When the purpose of consumption shifted from fulfilling needs to a communicator of image, status and position, it became materialistic in nature and added to unsustainability (Kilbourne and Pickett, 2008). Adding to this, were the issue of the outsourcing of ecological costs by developed countries to the developing countries which has globalized the problem (Spangenberg, 2010) and has also contributed to the delay in focusing on consumption. It is important to note that in developing countries consumers have little say over weaker environmental policies and where policy makers are satisfied to keep these "costs at a safe distance – in terms of time and space" (p 90, Shrivastava, 2014). This indicates that geopolitical fairness w.r.t. sustainability cost and benefit is a big contributor to the complexity of sustainable consumption scenario (Prothero et al 2011).

Discussions on sustainable production are beyond the scope of this chapter as it intends to focus only on the issues related to sustainable consumption. Sustainable consumption has strong prospects in addressing sustainability concerns as it can direct production and the whole economic system towards sustainability (Staniškis, 2012). The unsustainability in consumption is important for countries to focus on as consumption with growing affluence and consumerism depletes resources and contributes to environmental degradation. Therefore, there is no doubt that consumption and sustainability in consumption are important to ensure a successful journey towards sustainable development (Peattie and Collins, 2009).

UNDERSTANDING CONSUMPTION

Consumption is "the process by which goods, services or ideas are used and transformed" and "value" is created for the consumers (p5, Babin and Harris, 2012). It is also important to understand that consumption is a 'process' not an event of '*purchase*' and therefore consumption also includes usage and post usage activities (Peattie and Collins, 2009) like replacement, alternate usage, renting, recycling, disposing etc. (Protero et al, 2011).

In literature, consumption is examined from different theoretical perspectives and each one of them focuses on different aspects of consumption. From economic perspective, consumption creates "utilitarian functional value" (p 278, Connolly and Prothero, 2003) and under this perspective, the role of consumption is limited to functional and physical value creation. From psychological, social and cultural perspectives, consumers use consumption to communicate about self, their achievement and their good life (Connolly and Prothero, 2003; Schaefer and Crane 2005). Consumption in its hedonistic form is a mean by which consumers express their status, structure their societal relationships and position themselves in the hierarchies of society (Peattie and Collins, 2009; Schaefer and Crane 2005; McCracken (1998) in Dolan, 2002). Consumption is also contextual with its roots in social, cultural and historical settings and is used as a socio-cultural differentiator (Dolan, 2002). From cultural perspective, at individual level, consumption provides value in terms of self-worth, identity, happiness, approval (Assadourian, 2010) and is used as a mean to build relations; while at macro level consumption indicates social interdependencies (Dolan, 2002). Interestingly, from political perspective, consumption is "relative and hierarchical" (p 17, Shah et al., 2012). It is interesting to note that from economic and psychological perspectives, consumption is more individualistic (Schaefer and Crane 2005). In these theoretical perspectives, consumer is independent in his thinking and therefore, his behaviour can be influenced by manipulating psychological and/or marketing variables (Hargreaves, 2011). From sociological, cultural, political and anthropological perspectives, consumption is a set of socio-cultural activities or practices (Spaargaren, 2002). Consumer sociologists contributed to the development of "theory of practice" and indicated that consumer is a "socially conditioned actor, a social self, embedded in normative and institutional contexts and considered a bearer of practices" (p 129, Warde, 2015).

On the basis of review above, it can be summarised that (a) consumption is a multifaceted holistic process, (b) consumption has both individualistic and socio-cultural components which determine its nature, scale, scope and value derived from it, (c) consumption creates utilitarian, psychological, socio-cultural and communication values and (d) understanding consumption as a social process and practice, acknowledges dynamism and complexity in it.

SUSTAINABLE CONSUMPTION: DEFINITIONS AND SCOPE

In 1994, during the Oslo Symposium, sustainable consumption was defined as "the use of goods and services that respond to basic needs and bring a better quality of life, while minimizing the use of natural resources, toxic materials and emissions of waste and pollutants over the life cycle, so as not to jeopardise the needs of future generations". - Oslo Roundtable on Sustainable Production and Consumption (1994).

As discussed earlier, the basic purpose of consumption is to satisfy needs by creating value. Dolan (2002) identified that from individualistic perspective, sustainable consumption is consumption not exceeding basic needs with consideration for the environment. However, the domain of needs is dynamic in nature and is growing in scope, diversity and complexity with time (Briceno and Stagl, 2006), economic development, globalization, technological progression and societal changes (Witt, 2001). As a result, the scope of sustainable consumption is also growing (Staniškis, 2012). Initially, sustainable consumption was defined as consumption which focuses on sensible and efficient use of resources (Fisk, 1973). Later it was realized that sustainable consumption is not limited to utilization of resources but covers waste disposal and pollution management as well (Peattie and Collins, 2009). Moreover, a process view made it easier to see how usage and disposal can contribute to sustainability. Sustainable consumption occurs away from consumerism and materialism tendencies (Peattie and Collins, 2009).

At macro level, sustainable consumption is defined as consumption which creates value in terms of utility, equity (ecological and social) and waste reduction (Seth, Sethia and Srinivas, 2011). This definition is based on the triple bottom line definition of sustainability which covers economic, environmental and social aspects across the dimensions of time (Lozano, 2008). Ensuring availability and quality of resources for future generations' vis-à-vis satisfying needs of current generation is also part of its scope (World Economic Forum, 2013; Reisch, 2001).

It is important to note that sustainable consumption is not limited to the absence of over-consumption but its definition includes absence of under-consumption as well (Spangenberg, 2014). Sustainable consumption also ensures equal sharing of ecological costs and benefits w.r.t. higher, middle and lower income classes of society (Peattie and Collins, 2009), developed, developing and underdeveloped countries and present and future generations (Seyfang and Paavola, 2008). As per these researchers, it is also important to ensure social equitability during ecological value creation; otherwise such situation may contribute to the emergence of environmental social inequality. Under this view, sustainable consumption is not about equating economic value against combined social and environmental values but equal value creation w.r.t. each of these three dimensions (Staniškis, 2012). These aspects of sustainable consumption are very significant in the context of developing countries like South Africa where disparities of income and unequal distribution of wealth are common characteristics (World Economic Forum, 2013). The advocate of approaches based on consumption believes that they provide a more comprehensive set of causes and a wider range of solutions (Gulati and Naudé, 2017).

THEORETICAL DOMAIN OF APPROACHES TO ACHIEVE SUSTAINABLE CONSUMPTION

Approaches to achieve sustainable consumption vary with respect to orientation, intensity and scope. Researchers identified two different theoretical perspectives on how to achieve sustainable consumption. Approaches based on these perspective are termed as weak and strong sustainable consumption (O'Rourke and Lollo, 2015; Lorek and Fuchs, 2013). Weak sustainable consumption perspective is mostly focused on improving efficiency through IPAT (impact, population, affluence and technology) by curbing population growth and affluence; while promoting growth of technology (O'Rourke and Lollo, 2015). In this perspective, technological solution and product innovations are used to improve efficiency in usage of natural resources (Lorek and Fuchs, 2013). The strong sustainable perspective believes that there is a limit to what efficiency improvements can do and therefore, strongly focuses on curbing the resource consumption and working on social innovations (Lorek and Fuchs, 2013). The strong perspective is system based and believes in power of social and political processes to address unsustainability in consumption by changing both levels and patterns (O'Rourke and Lollo, 2015).

On the basis of focus, degree and scope of their orientation, the theoretical domain of sustainable consumption is categorized under 'Reformist', 'Revolutionary' or 'Reconfiguration' categories (p2, Geels et al., 2015). 'Reformist' orientation display similarity with the weak sustainable consumption perspective. Under 'Reformist' orientation, efforts are limited to the use of eco-labels and other marketing tactics in directing consumption towards green products; under 'Revolutionary' orientation efforts are more radical and structural in nature (Geels et al., 2015). A middle way was termed as reconfiguration orientation where multiple actors like consumers, businesses, civil society, media etc engage in collaborative transitionary approaches like 'Social practice theory' and 'multi-level perspective-*MLP'* (Geels et al., 2015). For more information on critical analysis of these domains and approaches a reading of paper by Geels et al. (2015) is recommended.

Priorities w.r.t. sustainability challenges vary among developed and developing countries (Seyfang and Paavola, 2008) and therefore sustainable consumption is addressed differently in these contexts (Gadgil and Guha, 1994). In the developed countries, sustainable consumption issues are more focused around quality of life and started as an upper middle class phenomenon and were led initially by science and innovations; while in developing countries the issues were focused around necessities of life and hence were mainly poor class movement focusing on equity, resources shortage, employment, depletion of land, pollution, survival etc. and were led by ideological and social activists (Gadgil and Guha, 1994). Involvement of poor class in the developing country context is understandable as poor are affected more by environmental degradation (Spangenberg, 2014). In these countries, resources are stressed due to population growth, increasing urbanization and growing materialistic tendencies (Euromonitor international, June 2018). The severity of unsustainability of growth can be understood by the fact that "the per capita "material footprint" of developing countries grew from 5 metric tons in 2000 to 9 metric tons in 2017, representing a significant improvement in the material standard of living" (p10, United Nation, 2018*)*. Interestingly, this report also indicates that this footprint is double or more for developed countries and also that to certain extent the lifestyle in developed countries is being supported by the materials extracted from developing countries. These historical differences resulted in the different priorities of sustainable consumption in developed and developing countries. It is important to highlight that simultaneous presence of over-consumption and under-consumption is one of the most difficult challenges for developing countries which rely on resource utilization and economic growth for the development.

It is interesting that equity of consumption in developing countries was covered under strong sustainable consumption perspective developed by O'Rourke and Lollo (2015). Prima facie, it seems that 'Reconfiguration' perspective and approaches covered under this perspective like social practice theory and MLA will be more suitable for South African context because of (a) their non-radical nature which improves chances of acceptability among institutions, policymakers and consumers, (b) their ability to addresses multiple aspects of practice by distributing agency across (Sahakian and Wilhite, 2014), (b) their ability to avoid 'rebound effect' (Sahakian and Wilhite, 2014) through continuous interactions between systems and agency (Geels et al., 2015) which improves their chances of success and (c) their inherent flexibility in these approaches.

INSTITUTIONAL ACTORS: EFFORTS AND CHALLENGES

The efforts towards sustainable consumption can be categorized as per the institutional actors namely consumers, business, government, educational institutions and media (Refer Table 1). These efforts range from ensuring equity in consumption, reduction in consumption to efficient consumption (Belz and Peattie, 2012; Schaefer and Crane 2005).

In institutional actors analysis, government, businesses and consumers emerged as major actors while media and education were identified still exploring their true potential. Literature is skewed in focusing on role of governments, businesses and consumers. Interestingly, these major actors have different primary orientations than sustainable consumption which are inherent in their nature; they are rigid and lack energy of social change which indicates to explore new actors for concurrent handling of over-consumption and under-consumption (Brown, 1991).

Table 1. Institutional interventions: Efforts and limitations

Actors	Efforts	Limitations
Consumers	• To promote sustainable choices, to motivate eco-labelled products purchase (Black and Cherrier, 2010) • To maintain the level of consumption, • To limit the consumption • To recycle and manage waste (Peattie and Collins, 2009)	• Considering sustainability a macro issue and leaving it for government and businesses to solve • Scope of influence is limited. • do not see maintenance, post usage and disposal as parts of sustainable consumption (Belz and Peattie, 2012) • Unawareness among masses about how to contribute (Connoly and Protehro, 2003), • At this level it is micro solution to macro problem (Dolan, 2002).
Business	• Initiatives (like investment in eco-efficiency, pollution prevention and cleaner production) are focused towards sustainable production (Varey, 2011). • Promote SC by providing sustainable products, by educating consumers about sustainable options, usage and disposal (Seyfang and Paavola, 2008). • Tries to direct consumers towards sustainable lifestyle by contributing in building social infrastructure	• Businesses is inherently profit driven and played major role in driving materialism through promotion and by contributing in product obsolescence (Assadourian, 2010) • Businesses fall short on building social infrastructure and often need support of other actors (Belz and Peattie, 2012). • Social and regulatory checks needed.
Government	• Facilitate the process by enabling policies and infrastructure (Schaefer and Crane 2005). • Strong hold on rewards (subsidies and rebate) and penalties (taxes and regulations) (Akenji, 2014; Stevens, 2010). • Ability to make sustainable practices attractive	• Sustainable consumption issues are still not the priority for many (Schaefer and Crane 2005) • Moreover, in developing countries consumption is needed to grow to sustain the growth. This makes it difficult to trust blindly on governments to give priorities to initiatives to curb hyper or over-consumption (Akenji, 2014).
Educational Institutions	• By sensitizing society about sustainability issues through tuition and research (Assadourian, 2010). • By opting for green campuses and trying to make their processes environmentally efficient (van Weenen, 2000 and Comm and Mathaisel, 2005).	• Business or government ownerships may influence their interests. • Limited scope.
Media	• Facilitates acceptance of sustainable lifestyle (Assadourian, 2010). • creates awareness about issues, options and promotes such movements	• Business or government ownerships may influence their interests. • Limited resources.

EXPANDING ON SUSTAINABLE CONSUMPTION AND SOCIAL INSTITUTION

Social institutions are well known actors in the area of sustainability and there is a need to explore their potential w.r.t. sustainable consumption. Non-profit organizations (NPO), non-governmental organizations (NGO), civil society organizations (Selsky and Parker, 2005), religious organizations, associations, networks, cross sectoral partnerships, social movement (Brown, 1991), community- based organizations (Middlemiss, 2011) and tradition based organizations (Assadourian, 2010) all can fit under the umbrella definition of social institutions. For the purposes of this chapter, social institutions are institutions which do not have business and government ownership.

Effective social institutions have orientation, capabilities, networks and resources to pursue their aims. Their affiliations with the citizens and their ability to facilitate multi-dimensional, multi-sectoral or multi-institutional relationships both at horizontal and vertical levels make them a strong actor for transformation towards sustainable consumption (Selsky and Parker, 2005; Brown, 1991). These researchers believed social institutions have ability to address diverse consumption challenges of hyper/over-consumption and under-consumption in the developing country context. However, their orientation, value systems, relationships, networks, collaborative nature and interdependencies might affect progress (Briceno and Stagl, 2006; Dolan, 2002). Various social institutions contribute to the journey towards sustainable consumption in their unique ways.

Civil societies are created by concerned 'citizen consumers' who create a advocating or activist group for joint corrective actions in this regard (Forno and Graziano, 2014). Civil societies have capacity to enable trickle down of policies from top to bottom, support grass-root innovations and to decentralize the power of relations (Dolan, 2002). These societies have successful record in promoting sustainable consumption (Assadourian, 2010) but their scope has been limited and often could benefit from partnerships. Advocacy and political activism is often associated traits with such organizations. However, this is changing as they are moving from activism to strategic partnerships (Hartman, Hofman and Stafford, 1999). Even in South African context such partnership is strongly recommended by Hamann and Acutt (2003) who suggested that these organizations should opt for power-based and rights-based strategies to ensure fairness, efficiency and effectiveness in the partnerships. Modern civil society organizations are integrating with other organizations (at inter-sectoral, inter-institutional and inter-geographical levels), collaborating, coordinating projects and handling multiple partners which makes them perfect candidate to provide a central and effective platform for the change towards sustainable consumption. To propagate sustainable consumption in South Africa active participation of civil society is critical especially in the historical country context.

Since the consumption has socio-cultural dimension it can be directed through social institutions with religious orientations (Assadourian, 2010; Narayanan, 2010). They can help to revive traditional and communal sustainable consumption practices (often related to culture) which have lost their place with the spread of westernized consumer culture and bring them back to mainstream consumer lifestyle (Assadourian, 2010; Narayanan, 2010). However, more exploration is needed in this area to understand the impact of religious organizations in promoting sustainable consumption. Literature indicates that the community- based organizations can also be very effective as they influence consumption through communal practices. Prime facie, there is strong potential for religious and communal organizations to contribute considering that Africa is mainly a community based society.

The role of NGOs in addressing sustainability challenges is well documented. However, NGOs fall short to understand sustainable consumption and thus remain focused to narrow scope and they are reliant on the donors (Lorek and Spangenberg, 2014). However, these organizations have ability to acquire new knowledge regarding sustainable consumption and may choose collaborative partnerships which in turn make them effective and efficient in their role (Lorek and Spangenberg, 2014; Lorek and Fuchs, 2013).

The review so far indicates that the unsustainability of consumption is becoming dire and it demands partnerships among many institutions (Scott, martin and Schouten, 2014; Akenji, 2014; Staniškis, 2012; Selsky and Parker, 2005; Brown, 1991). These institutions will need to come out of their silos and work in unity. Interestingly unavailability of clear boundaries of sustainable consumption and multiplicity of approaches contributes to the challenges of implementation which creates conducive case for cooperation and collaborations (Spangenberg, 2010; Hartman, Hofman and Stafford, 1999). Bottom-up practical solutions or scale up grassroots innovations were identified accelerator of progress towards sustainable consumption (Akenji, 2014). These efforts can be accelerated by using power relation between social groupings and between cultural value systems (Dolan, 2002). world is As the world is becoming multi-polar, dynamic and complex partnership among governmental, business, sociological, anthropological, cultural institutions is needed to establish equitable, effective and efficient sustainable consumption practices (Geels et al., 2015; Warde, 2015; Assadourian, 2010; Spangenberg, 2010; Connoly and Protehro, 2003 and Dolan, 2002).

POSSIBILITIES FOR SOCIAL INSTITUTIONS IN PROPAGATING SUSTAINABLE CONSUMPTION IN SOUTH AFRICA: SETTING A RESEARCH AGENDA

The uniqueness of South African context is charted clearly in earlier sections. The sustainable consumption challenges are different in South Africa than developed countries as social aspects of sustainability needs are more severe (UN Economic and Social Council, 2009). Social institutions are important part of social and economic landscape in South Africa. In *March 2016*, number of registered organization was *1,53,677* and the average growth rate of registered social institutions was *80%* during 2011-2016 (p13, Department of social development, 2015). The limitations of western oriented growth and development model in developing country context (Shrivastava, 2014) indicate that the South Africa should look for sustainable consumption models and strategies suitable for African and developing country context. This suggests bright prospect for social organizations in South Africa which have fair understanding of the context, experience and orientation to lead the way towards sustainable consumption. Urban consumer social groups are well connected, skilled, and resourceful which give them power to voice these issues (Assadourian 2014).

Based on the discussions so far a research agenda can be prepared covering following themes:

- Country specific issues like contingencies, priorities, history, culture etc. are important determinant of sustainable consumption (Assadourian, 2010; Dolan, 2002). An enquiry into how contextual issues like Food-energy-water nexus (Von Bormann, and Gulati, 2014), post-apartheid issues affects sustainable consumption in South Africa can be deemed necessary.
- With the progression of communication technology, social media has contributed in propagating social movement (Miller, 2017). In South Africa, internet based activism 'fee-must-fall' was able to display power potential of social media (Thomas, 2015). Therefore, how social media can promote sustainable consumption in developing countries South Africa is a pertinent research enquiry.

- Baumgart, Collins and Turner (2002) identified that community-based sustainability initiatives in South Africa can be an effective "rural development strategy" for nature conservation and eco-tourism. Therefore, the enquiries like how communities can contribute in promoting sustainable consumption in the areas like food, energy and water and how effective they can be? Such enquiries may help in identifying if transferability of skills among social institutions is possible across spectrum of sustainable consumption or not?
- The efforts towards sustainable consumption need *"innovation and options beyond the constraints of the current dispensation and structure of the economy"*. (p28, Gulati and Naudé, 2017). Therefore, an enquiry into possible social innovations for sustainable consumption can contribute to solution landscape.
- Sharing economy is a becoming part of South African lifestyle (Euromonitor International, 2017) and a deeper probe is needed to understand the way sharing economy can help in promoting sustainable consumption.
- In case of sustainable consumption "*leapfrog*" is using innovations to avoid doing same mistakes which were done by developed countries while chasing economic growth (Ekins and Lemaire, 2012). Technology or socially driven leapfrogging can improve quality of life and ensures equity of growth (Hubacek, Guan and Barua, 2007). There is an urgent need to explore the avenue of possible leapfrogging and models in South Africa.
- South Africa is young, diverse and multicultural country and Youth in Africa prefer collective action to individual actions and is positive towards NGOs and other social institutions (UNESCO, 2001). Therefore, an exploration of the preference of South African youth for social organizations and their influence on youth can be a prized enquiry.
- In South African with growing sustainability concerns market for standardization and eco-label is growing (Hughes, McEwan and Bek, 2015) and there is a need to examine the way social institutions can promote process of standardization and labelling. Moreover, role of social institution in building faith in such standardization can be an interesting enquiry (Schaefer and Crane, 2005).
- It would be interesting to know the way South African consumers make sustainability choices in conflicting environment of developing county context. To make such complex sustainable consumption choices need awareness and infrastructure (Prothero et al 2011). Therefore, it would be pertinent to explore the role social institutions plays in creating awareness and facilitating infrastructure for sustainable consumption?
- Simultaneous presence of under and over consumption can be addressed with 'quality in limit' for affluent class and 'sufficiency with quality' for the poor classes (Spangenberg, 2014). Therefore, exploration in social institutions experience in addressing issues of over and under consumption can be an interesting exercise.
- Often civil society is linked to political aspects, activism and radical approaches which are aligned with 'revolutionary' orientation (Geels et al., 2015). However, examination of these organizations through 'reconfiguration' perspective w.r.t. cooperation, collaboration partnership with business and government (Hartman, Hofman and Stafford, 1999) can be a valuable sociological enquiry.
- It has emerged from the review that social institutions in South Africa mainly focused on issues of equity and social justice. However, there is a need to look at inefficient use of resources and wastage and its impact on sustainable consumption.

CONCLUSION

The objective of this chapter was to highlight the role and potential of social institutions in a developing country like South Africa. The discussions clearly establish the potential of social organizations in promoting sustainable consumption in South Africa. This chapter is mainly based on review of literature therefore the contribution is through (a) identifying gaps in the literature in the area of social institutions and sustainable consumption in developing countries context and (b) expanding research agenda for the matters and possible contribution of social organizations in stimulating sustainable consumption. This chapter recognizes that South Africa is a complex African country with simultaneous presence of under and over-consumption and social institutions like NGOs, civil society and community based organization can be significant to handle these challenges. It also suggests that modern social organizations prefer cooperation, collaboration and partnership with other institutions in place of conventional activism. This chapter concludes by expanding research agenda in the area of social institutions and sustainable consumption by presenting emerging research themes and by appealing to future researchers to advance the agenda ahead.

REFERENCES

Akenji, L. (2014). Consumer scapegoatism and limits to green consumerism. *Journal of Cleaner Production*, *63*, 13–23. doi:10.1016/j.jclepro.2013.05.022

Assadourian, E. (2010). Transforming cultures: From consumerism to sustainability. *Journal of Macromarketing*, *30*(2), 186–191. doi:10.1177/0276146710361932

Babin, B. & Harris, E. (2009). *CB3*. Cengage Learning.

Badruddin, S. T. (2015). Role of NGOs in the protection of environment. *Journal of Environmental Research and Development*, *9*(3), 705–712.

Barber, J. (2003). Production, consumption and the world summit on sustainable development. *Environment, Development and Sustainability*, *5*(1-2), 63–93. doi:10.1023/A:1025319915498

Belz, F., & Peattie, K. (2012). *Sustainability Marketing* (2nd ed.). John Wiley & Sons Ltd.

Black, I., & Cherrier, H. (2010). Anti-consumption as part of living a sustainable lifestyle: Daily practices, contextual motivations and subjective values. *Journal of Consumer Behaviour*, *9*(6), 437–453. doi:10.1002/cb.337

Briceno, T., & Stagl, S. (2006). The role of social processes for sustainable consumption. *Journal of Cleaner Production*, *14*(17), 1541–1551. doi:10.1016/j.jclepro.2006.01.027

Brown, L. D. (1991). Bridging organizations and sustainable development. *Human Relations*, *44*(8), 807–831. doi:10.1177/001872679104400804

Cohen, M. J. (2005). Sustainable consumption in national context: an introduction to the symposium. *Sustainability: Science, Practice, &. Policy*, *1*(1), 22–28.

Comm, C. L., & Mathaisel, D. (2005). A case study in applying lean sustainability concepts to universities. *International Journal of Sustainability in Higher Education, 6*(2), 134 – 146.

Connolly, J., & Prothero, A. (2008). Green Consumption Life-politics, risk and contradictions. *Journal of Consumer Culture, 8*(1), 117–145. doi:10.1177/1469540507086422

Dauvergne, P. (2010). The problem of consumption. *Global Environmental Politics, 10*(2), 1–10. doi:10.1162/glep.2010.10.2.1

Department of Social Development South Africa. (2015). *State of South African NPO Register 2014-2015.* Author.

Dolan, P. (2002). The Sustainability of "Sustainable Consumption. *Journal of Macromarketing, 22*(2), 170–181. doi:10.1177/0276146702238220

Ekins, P., & Lemaire, X. (2012). *Sustainable Consumption and Production for Poverty Alleviation. United Nations Environment Programme.* Retrieved July 1, 2015 from www.unep.org/pdf/SCP_Poverty_full_final.pdf

Etzioni, A. (1998). Voluntary Simplicity: Characterization, Select Psychological Implications, and Societal Consequences. *Journal of Economic Psychology, 19*, 619–643.

Euromonitor. (2017, September). *Consumer lifestyles in South Africa.* London: Euromonitor.

Euromonitor International. (2013, August). *How BRICS consumers behave.* London: Euromonitor.

Euromonitor International. (2018, March). *Shifting market frontiers: Africa rising.* London: Euromonitor.

Filho, W. L. (2000). Dealing with misconceptions on the concept of sustainability. *International Journal of Sustainability in Higher Education, 1*(1), 9–19. doi:10.1108/1467630010307066

Fisk, G. (1973). Criteria for a Theory of Responsible Consumption. *Journal of Marketing, 37*(2), 24–31. doi:10.2307/1250047

Forno, F., & Graziano, P. R. (2014). Sustainable community movement organisations. *Journal of Consumer Culture, 14*(2), 139–157. doi:10.1177/1469540514526225

Geels, F. W., McMeekin, A., Mylan, J., & Southerton, D. (2015). A critical appraisal of Sustainable Consumption and Production research: The reformist, revolutionary and reconfiguration positions. *Global Environmental Change, 34*, 1–12. doi:10.1016/j.gloenvcha.2015.04.013

Goodland, R. (1995). The concept of environmental sustainability. *Annual Review of Ecology and Systematics, 26*(1), 1–24. doi:10.1146/annurev.es.26.110195.000245

Gulati, M., & Naudé, L. (2017). *Chewing over consumption based carbon emissions accounting.* WWF-SA. Retrieved on July 7th, 2018 from www.wwf.org.za/report/consumption_based_carbon_accounting

Hamann, R., & Acutt, N. (2003). How should civil society (and the government) respond to 'corporate social responsibility'? A critique of business motivations and the potential for partnerships. *Development Southern Africa, 20*(2), 255–270. doi:10.1080/03768350302956

Hargreaves, T. (2011). Practice-ing behaviour change: Applying social practice theory to pro-environmental behaviour change. *Journal of Consumer Culture*, *11*(1), 79–99. doi:10.1177/1469540510390500

Hartman, C. L., Hofman, P. S., & Stafford, E. R. (1999). Partnerships: A path to sustainability. *Business Strategy and the Environment*, *8*(5), 255–266. doi:10.1002/(SICI)1099-0836(199909/10)8:5<255::AID-BSE214>3.0.CO;2-O

Hubacek, K., Guan, D., & Barua, A. (2007). Changing lifestyles and consumption patterns in developing countries: A scenario analysis for China and India. *Futures*, *39*(9), 1084–1096. doi:10.1016/j.futures.2007.03.010

Hughes, A., McEwan, C., & Bek, D. (2015). Mobilizing the ethical consumer in South Africa. *Geoforum*, *67*, 148–157. doi:10.1016/j.geoforum.2015.07.011

Jones, P., Clarke-Hill, C., Comfort, D., & Hillier, D. (2008). Marketing and sustainability. *Marketing Intelligence & Planning*, *26*(2), 123–130. doi:10.1108/02634500810860584

Kilbourne, W., & Pickett, G. (2008). How materialism affects environmental beliefs, concern, and environmentally responsible behavior. *Journal of Business Research*, *61*(9), 885–893. doi:10.1016/j.jbusres.2007.09.016

Lorek, S., & Fuchs, D. (2013). Strong sustainable consumption governance–precondition for a degrowth path? *Journal of Cleaner Production*, *38*, 36–43. doi:10.1016/j.jclepro.2011.08.008

Lorek, S., & Spangenberg, J. H. (2014). Sustainable consumption within a sustainable economy–beyond green growth and green economies. *Journal of Cleaner Production*, *63*, 33–44. doi:10.1016/j.jclepro.2013.08.045

Lozano, R. (2008). Envisioning sustainability three-dimensionally. *Journal of Cleaner Production*, *16*(17), 1838–1846. doi:10.1016/j.jclepro.2008.02.008

Middlemiss, L. (2011). The power of community: How community-based organizations stimulate sustainable lifestyles among participants. *Society & Natural Resources*, *24*(11), 1157–1173. doi:10.1080/08941920.2010.518582

Miller, V. (2017). Phatic culture and the status quo: Reconsidering the purpose of social media activism. *Convergence*, *23*(3), 251–269. doi:10.1177/1354856515592512

Narayanan, Y. (2010). Sustainable consumption as a means to self-realization: A Hindu perspective on when enough is enough. *Sustainable Development*, *18*(5), 252–259. doi:10.1002d.476

O'Rourke, D., & Lollo, N. (2015). Transforming Consumption: From Decoupling, to Behavior, to Systems Change for Sustainable Consumption. *Annual Review of Environment and Resources*, *40*(1), 233–259. doi:10.1146/annurev-environ-102014-021224

Ölander, F., & Thøgersen, J. (1995). Understanding of consumer behaviour as a prerequisite for environmental protection. *Journal of Consumer Policy*, *18*(4), 345–385. doi:10.1007/BF01024160

Oslo Roundtable on Sustainable Production and Consumption. (1994). Symposium: *Sustainable Consumption*. Retrieved on December 7th, 2015 from http://www.iisd.ca/consume/oslo004.html

Parris, T. M., & Kates, R. W. (2003). Characterizing and measuring sustainable development. *Annual Review of Environment and Resources*, *28*(1), 559–586. doi:10.1146/annurev.energy.28.050302.105551

Peattie, K. (2001). Golden goose or wild goose? The hunt for the green consumer. *Business Strategy and the Environment*, *10*(4), 187–199. doi:10.1002/bse.292

Peattie, K., & Collins, A. (2009). Guest editorial: Perspectives on sustainable consumption. *International Journal of Consumer Studies*, *33*(2), 107–112. doi:10.1111/j.1470-6431.2009.00758.x

Prothero, A., Dobscha, S., Freund, J., Kilbourne, W. E., Luchs, M. G., Ozanne, L. K., & Thøgersen, J. (2011). Sustainable consumption: Opportunities for consumer research and public policy. *Journal of Public Policy & Marketing*, *30*(1), 31–38. doi:10.1509/jppm.30.1.31

Reisch, L. (2001). Time and Wealth: The role of time and temporalities for sustainable patterns of consumption. *Time & Society*, *10*(2-3), 367–385. doi:10.1177/0961463X01010002012

Sahakian, M., & Wilhite, H. (2014). Making practice theory practicable: Towards more sustainable forms of consumption. *Journal of Consumer Culture*, *14*(1), 25–44. doi:10.1177/1469540513505607

Schaefer, A., & Crane, A. (2005). Addressing sustainability and consumption. *Journal of Macromarketing*, *25*(1), 76–92. doi:10.1177/0276146705274987

Scott, K., Martin, D. M., & Schouten, J. W. (2014). Marketing and the New Materialism. *Journal of Macromarketing*, *34*(3), 282–290. doi:10.1177/0276146714532471

Selsky, J. W., & Parker, B. (2005). Cross-sector partnerships to address social issues: Challenges to theory and practice. *Journal of Management*, *31*(6), 849–873. doi:10.1177/0149206305279601

Seyfang, G., & Paavola, J. (2008). Inequality and sustainable consumption: Bridging the gaps. *Local Environment*, *13*(8), 669–684. doi:10.1080/13549830802475559

Shah, D. V., Friedland, L. A., Wells, C., Kim, Y. M., & Rojas, H. (2012). Communication, Consumers, and Citizens Revisiting the Politics of Consumption. *The Annals of the American Academy of Political and Social Science*, *644*(1), 6–19. doi:10.1177/0002716212456349

Sheth, J. N., Sethia, N. K., & Srinivas, S. (2011). Mindful consumption: A customer-centric approach to sustainability. *Journal of the Academy of Marketing Science*, *39*(1), 21–39. doi:10.100711747-010-0216-3

Shrivastava, A. (2014). The Earth, not the sky, is the limit: India and 'The Great Transition' to an ecological world. *Futures*, *56*, 87–93. doi:10.1016/j.futures.2013.10.013

Spangenberg, J. H. (2002). Environmental space and the prism of sustainability: Frameworks for indicators measuring sustainable development. *Ecological Indicators*, *2*(3), 295–309. doi:10.1016/S1470-160X(02)00065-1

Spangenberg, J. H. (2010). World civilisations at crossroads: Towards an expansionist or a sustainable future—lessons from history. *Futures*, *42*(6), 565–573. doi:10.1016/j.futures.2010.01.007

Spangenberg, J. H. (2014). Institutional change for strong sustainable consumption: sustainable consumption and the degrowth economy. *Sustainability: Science, Practice, & Policy*, *10*(1), 62–77.

Staniškis, J. K. (2012). Sustainable consumption and production: How to make it possible. *Clean Technologies and Environmental Policy, 14*(6), 1015–1022. doi:10.100710098-012-0535-9

Starik, M., & Kanashiro, P. (2013). Toward a theory of sustainability management: Uncovering and integrating the nearly obvious. *Organization & Environment, 26*(1), 7–30. doi:10.1177/1086026612474958

Stevens, C. (2010). Linking sustainable consumption and production: The government role. *Natural Resources Forum, 34*(1), 16–23. doi:10.1111/j.1477-8947.2010.01273.x

Sulla, V., & Zikhali, P. (2018, March). *Overcoming Poverty and Inequality in South Africa: An Assessment of Drivers, Constraints and Opportunities.* Washington, DC: The World Bank Group. Retrieved on July, 25th, 2018 from http://documents.worldbank.org/curated/en/530481521735906534/pdf/124521-REV-OUO-South-Africa-Poverty-and-Inequality-Assessment-Report-2018-FINAL-WEB.pdf

Sutton, P. (2004). What is sustainability. *Eingana, The Journal of the Victorian Association for Environmental Education*, 1-7.

The World Bank. (2015). *World Development Indicators database: Gross domestic product 2014, PPP.* Retrieved from December 6th, 2015 databank.worldbank.org/data/download/GDP_PPP.pdf

Thomas, S. (2015). *#FeesMustFall: how SA students are using social to subvert traditional media.* Retrieved 19th August 2018 from https://memeburn.com/2015/10/feesmustfall-how-sas-students-are-using-social-to-subvert-traditional-media-narratives/

Turner, G. M. (2008). A comparison of the Limits to Growth with 30 years of reality. *Global Environmental Change, 18*(3), 397–411. doi:10.1016/j.gloenvcha.2008.05.001

UN DESA. (2013). *Report of the World Social Situation 2013: Inequality Matters.* Retrieved December 1, 2015 from www.un.org/esa/socdev/documents/reports/InequalityMatters.pdf

UN DESA, Population Division. (2015). *World Population Prospects: The 2015 Revision, Key Findings and Advance Tables.* Working Paper No. ESA/P/WP.24. Retrieved December 1, 2015 from esa.un.org/unpd/wpp/publications/files/key_findings_wpp_2015.pdf

UN Economic and Social Council. (2009). *Africa Review Report on Sustainable Consumption and Production.* Retrieved March 15, 2018 from https://sustainabledevelopment.un.org/content/documents/AfricanReviewReport-on-SustainableConsumptionSummary.pdf

UNEP. (2014). *United Nations Environment Programme Annual Report.* Retrieved January 31st, 2015 from http://www.unep.org/annualreport/2014/en/index.html

UNESCO. (2001). *Youth, sustainable consumption patterns and lifestyles.* Retrieved July 31st, 2018 from http://unesdoc.unesco.org/images/0012/001242/124238e.pdf

van Weenen, H. (2000). Towards a vision of a sustainable university. *International Journal of Sustainability in Higher Education, 1*(1), 20–34. doi:10.1108/1467 630010307075

Varey, R. J. (2011). A sustainable society logic for marketing. *Social Business, 1*(1), 69–83. doi:10.1362/204440811X570563

Von Bormann, T., & Gulati, M. (2014). *The food energy water nexus: Understanding South Africa's most urgent sustainability challenge*. WWF-SA. Retrieved on July 7th, 2018 from http://awsassets.wwf.org.za/downloads/wwf_few_report_3.pdf

Warde, A. (2005). Consumption and theories of practice. *Journal of Consumer Culture*, *5*(2), 131–153. doi:10.1177/1469540505053090

Warde, A. (2015). The Sociology of Consumption: Its Recent Development. *Annual Review of Sociology*, *41*(1), 117–134. doi:10.1146/annurev-soc-071913-043208

Witt, U. (2001). Learning to consume–A theory of wants and the growth of demand. *Journal of Evolutionary Economics*, *11*(1), 23–36. doi:10.1007/PL00003851

World Economic Forum. (2013). *Sustainable Consumption: Stakeholder Perspectives*. Retrieved on February, 25th, 2014 from http://www3.weforum.org/docs/WEF_ENV_SustainableConsumption_Book_2013.pdf

Zhao, W., & Schroeder, P. (2010). Sustainable consumption and production: Trends, challenges and options for the Asia-Pacific region. *Natural Resources Forum*, *34*(1), 4–15. doi:10.1111/j.1477-8947.2010.01275.x

KEY TERMS AND DEFINITIONS

Consumption: It is a dynamic, socio-cultural, multifaceted process that covers the act of needing, searching, obtaining, utilizing, and disposing, through which value is created and consumers' needs are satisfied.

Social Institutions: An organization without business and government ownership consisting group of people striving for some social, religious, spiritual, community, environmental goals.

South Africa: An African emerging market economy with around 56 million people, South Africa is complex due to its political history, young democracy, and inequality of wealth and income.

Sustainable Consumption (at Macro Level): It is a complex and dynamic concept that ensures equity of consumption; absence of hyper/over-consumption and under-consumption; minimization of ecological cost and its equal distribution in society now and in future.

Sustainable Consumption (at Micro Level/Individual Level): Consumption process that is incurred to satisfy needs, which improves quality of life, which incur minimal environment cost, which does not compromise with social equity.

Chapter 14
Marketing Solar Energy in Ghana:
A Relational Perspective

John Kuada
Aalborg University, Denmark

Esther Mensah
Premier Resource Consulting, Ghana

Andreea I. Bujac
Aalborg University, Denmark

Jeanne S. Bentzen
Aalborg University, Denmark

ABSTRACT

This chapter reports the results of an exploratory qualitative investigation into buying behaviors and growth challenges within the solar energy industry in Ghana. It is premised on the understanding that African firms may experience "liabilities of localness" when marketing renewable energy products developed in the West. That is, customers doubt their capabilities to produce and install these products. Thus, market-driven growth of the solar energy sector in Ghana requires firm-level capability development through institutional support that promotes effective cross-border inter-firm collaborations as well as trust-building relationships with local customers. The results of the study confirm these observations. They show that Ghanaian consumers tend to evaluate the capabilities of foreign solar energy providers as superior to those of local firms. However, collaborations between local and foreign firms have enhanced their credibility. Firms rely mainly on word-of-mouth recommendations to attract new customers and see customer price consciousness as a major growth constraint.

DOI: 10.4018/978-1-5225-7906-9.ch014

INTRODUCTION

Renewable energy technologies are increasingly recognised as central pillars in the development of sustainable energy sources in most Sub-Sahara African (SSA) countries (Ikejemba et al., 2017). They are also essential to the attainment of UN Sustainable Development Goals (SDGs) which aim at ending poverty, protecting the planet, and ensuring prosperity for all by 2030. Solar photovoltaic (PV) energy, in particular, has been seen by various stakeholders (governments, policy-makers, energy planning agencies and donors) as having a huge potential on the sub-continent thanks to the abundant solar radiation that is available (Mas'ud, et al., 2016). The understanding is that PV technology allows for the decentralization of energy supplies, even to remote rural populations in off-grid areas. This awareness has generated some amount of academic interest with recent contributions from such scholars as Ondraczek (2013) as well as Hansen, Pedersen and Nygaard (2015) who studied renewable energy projects in Kenya and Tanzania, and Amankwah-Amoah (2014 and 2016) who studied developments of the energy sector in Ghana, Nigeria, South Africa, and Kenya. Similarly, Ikejemba et al. (2017) studied the management of renewable energy projects nine countries (Nigeria, Ghana, Kenya, Gabon, South Africa, Tanzania, Mozambique, Ethiopia and Malawi.). In spite of its immense potentials and the increase in the number of government and donor-funded solar energy diffusion projects, these studies have concluded that the solar energy industry is growing at a snail pace in Sub-Sahara African countries compared to other parts of the world.

The present study is in line with the growing literature on the development of renewable energy sector in Africa. It notes, however, that academic interest has, so far, emphasized macro issues such as government policies (Ikejemba et al., 2017), implementation failures (Mas'ud, et al., 2016), and technology development (Amankwah-Amoah, 2016). Although these studies provide relevant policy prescriptions, they do not provide insights into consumers' decision making processes and marketing efforts required to stimulate the diffusion of the technology. It has generally been acknowledged in marketing literature that customers tend to be apprehensive of making purchase decision with respect to unfamiliar products (Peter Ramaseshan and Nayar, 2002). Thus, since the renewable energy sector in SSA is at an embryonic stage and potential customers are unfamiliar with solar energy products, one can argue that effective marketing strategies are required to stimulate solar PV adoption by consumers. In other words, marketing is one of the key strategic challenges of new entrants into the solar energy sector. However, the manner in which firms decide on their strategic marketing processes and priorities in Africa has so far received very little attention (Chelariu et al., 2002; Winston & Dadzie, 2002; Gbadamosi, 2013; Boso, Debrah, and Amankwah-Amoah, 2018). Against this backdrop, the present chapter differentiates itself from previous studies by focusing on marketing dimensions of solar energy sector development. It reports the results of an exploratory qualitative investigation into the marketing ecosystem that firms selling solar energy products are in the process of creating in Ghana and how this system influences the growth of the sector.

Several factors justify the choice of Ghana for this study. First, Ghana is the second largest economy in West Africa and it is generally regarded as the "gateway to West Africa" (Amankwah-Amoah, 2016). In 2012, Ghana's GDP grew by 8.2% and was one of the highest in West Africa. The country was also ranked the fourth investment destination in Africa by the African Business Panel survey of 2011 (Kuada, 2015). But, since then growth has declined steadily and was barely 3.3% in 2016 – partly due to unstable power supplies (African Development Bank Group, 2017). The government seeks to address the problem by increasing the share of renewable energy in the country's total energy consumption from its current level of 0.18% to 10% by 2020 – with solar energy contributing the bulk of the increase. Second, the country is endowed with abundant solar radiation necessary for energy generation. Available data show that the average solar radiation is about 5kWh/m2 per day with an average of 6 hours of sunshine per day (Mas'ud, et al., 2016). Third, Ghana's energy policies tend to influence policies in other West African countries (Amankwah-Amoah, 2016). Thus, understanding the growth process of the solar industry in Ghana can have policy and strategy implications in its neighbouring countries. In that way, West African countries can hopefully enhance their contributions to addressing global climate change challenges through reduced dependence on inefficient energy sources.

In terms of structure, the chapter continues with a discussion of some major determinants of marketing strategies in emerging economies. These discussions are then pulled together into a conceptual model that should guide the empirical part of the investigation. This is followed by presentation of the study context and data collection methods. The results are presented using a thematic approach and respondents' statements as illustrative evidence. Subsequently, the results are discussed and implications are drawn with reference to previous related studies.

THEORETICAL BACKGROUND AND CONCEPTUAL MODEL

A general understanding presented in management literature is that managers respond to and develop marketing strategies on the basis of their perceptions of environmental constituencies and trends that shape the market opportunity spaces within which their firms compete. Following Homburg, Artz, and Wieseke (2012) the environmental characteristics include institutional variables, industry structures and configurations, demand patterns, as well as consumer attitudes and behaviours which combine to impact marketing strategies and market performance. Others argue that firms formulate strategies to take advantages of opportunities and navigate constraints using existing firm-level resources or leveraging new resources through interactions with actors within or outside the operational environments (Kuada, 2016). Following Teece (2007), firms that have the capacity to sense, select, and shape opportunities, and synchronise their strategic moves and resources in pursuit of these opportunities tend to do better than their counterparts. This section of the chapter outlines some of the key variables that have been identified in the literature to impact the adoption of solar-energy products in emerging economies such as Ghana.

Institutional Characteristics

As noted above, effective marketing strategies require firms to consistently consider how changes in their ambient institutional environment can impact their core businesses and the activities of their partners. Economists describe institutions as structures and mechanisms that reproduce and convey norms, rules, conventions, and habits that govern and shape economic life (North, 1990). Leaning on this perspective, Scott (2004) classifies institutions in terms of their regulative, normative, and cultural-cognitive characteristics. The regulative characteristics are reflected in rules and policies that proscribe or prescribe managerial behaviours. With regard to the renewable energy sector, previous studies have suggested that government institutions can play an important role in its development through the formulation of growth enabling policies, and by enhancing public awareness of the potential of such energy sources (Ondraczek, 2013; Amankwah-Amoah, 2016). Furthermore, the government can institute financing systems which favour diffusion RE technology – e.g. by providing temporary tax exemptions for the purchase of solar PV equipment (Ikejemba et al., 2017).

Apart from specific government policies, development of the renewable energy sector may be promoted through norms, values, beliefs and assumptions that define the accepted moral and ethical behaviours of actors within the industry. These institutional characteristics combine to define networks of relationships within societies and industries. They also help to contain the socially undesirable consequences of unguarded market systems, levelling the playing field for all stakeholders (Kuada, 2015).

Distinctions are usually drawn between formal and informal institutions. Formal institutions essentially play regulatory roles in societies and businesses (e.g. policies, laws and regulations). The informal institutions include tribal rules, norms, values and beliefs (Boso, Debrah, & Amankwah-Amoah, 2018). As can be expected, both types of institutions have differential impacts on marketing activities. Previous studies have shown that in countries where formal institutions are poorly developed, there is a difficulty in enforcing contracts and property rights in courts. This compels firms to engage in arm's-length, spot-market types of transactions rather than entering into long-lasting contractual relationships (Fafchamps, 1996). In such countries, informal institutions become prominent in managing relationship within the transactional space within which vendors and buyers operate (Arnold and Quelch, 1998). For example, firms operating in these environments may consider it advantageous to use local community leaders (or local opinion leaders) to disseminate information about products and services, and thus product endorsements by local kings, chiefs, and priests tend to become normal marketing practices (Acquah, 2012).

Both formal and informal institutions have been found to have profound impacts on marketing practices in Africa (Tesar & Kuada, 2013). The formal institutions tend to view marketing functions and intermediaries as standing between consumers and the producers, draining the economic system of vitality. As a result, market-related policies tend to be rigidly regulatory and prohibitive, offering no inducement for the private sector to undertake investments in marketing facilities that could improve the coordination of activities within the national marketing systems (Abbott, 1987). Previous studies have shown that African countries that demonstrate greater openness to local and foreign business participation within the renewable energy sector experience faster growth than those with rigid rules and regulations (Ondraczek, 2013; Hansen, Pedersen, & Nygaard, 2015).

Despite their propensity to regulate, the formal institutions have been found to be weak and lack capacity to enforce their rules in some African countries (Nandone & Kuada, 2016). This creates operational uncertainty that firms must deal with individually or jointly. Thus, firms operating in such environments have been advised to focus not only on their individual strategies, but also to be collectively proactive about diagnosing and shaping their external environments (Marquis & Raynard, 2015), which they can do collectively through networks of horizontal and vertical relations. Such collective mobilisation of resources and strategies can, in fact, help grow markets for new products more rapidly than individual initiatives on their own.

Industry Characteristics

Past studies have suggested that growth in industries is linked to the process of technological development. This is also true of the solar-energy industry as it is one of the fastest growing industries in the world, mainly due to innovations and manufacturing of solar-energy products, which have contributed to overall cost reductions. The structural dynamics generated by this growth has some impact on the marketing of solar products in emerging economies (Ernst et. al., 2015). The conventional thinking is that technologies appropriate for low-income emerging economies are small-scale, labour-intensive, easy to use and repair, and harmless to the environment (Schumacher, 1973). This implies that some technologies developed in the West must be adapted to fit the specific features and conditions of specific emerging economies. In the case of the solar-energy industry, this may entail simplifying the solar technology through modularized design to enable a low-cost production and delivery (Amankwah-Amoah, 2016; Amankwah-Amoah & Sarpong, 2016). It may also entail either loose or close-knit collaborations with other firms (both horizontally and vertically) in order to speed up the local knowledge absorption process and the leveraging of scarce resources. Innovative business models and marketing practices may also be developed. Collaborations are also required to ensure that intermediate products or services transferred between stages along the value chain are of appropriate quality. Information exchange and knowledge sharing along the chain can be critical as well.

Building on the above arguments, it has been suggested that learning capabilities characterise firms that operate within emerging industries. Learning and knowledge transfers that may occur in one firm tend to migrate beyond the boundaries of the firm through the process of inter-firm mobility of the labour force and/or create spin-off of new firms (Kuada & Hansen, 2006). According to Pérez-Nordtvedt, Kedia, Datta, and Rasheed (2008), participants in a learning process choose the type of knowledge to acquire and the mode of this acquisition on the basis of four factors: comprehension, usefulness, speed, and cost of acquisition. Comprehension here refers to the extent to which the new knowledge transferred is fully understood by the recipient; usefulness is viewed as the extent to which such knowledge is assessed to be relevant and salient to organizational success; speed is seen in terms of how rapidly (the recipient) acquires the new knowledge; and cost refers to the costs and resources associated with the knowledge transfer.

The attractiveness of knowledge source to a recipient firm is also important to knowledge transfer outcomes (Spencer, 2000). Attractiveness may relate to the type of knowledge required as well as the credibility of the source. Previous studies have suggested that managers in developing country firms tend to evaluate knowledge from partners in developed countries as relatively more attractive and superior to those from other firms simply because these firms are located in higher technology frontiers (Kuada, 2003; Kuada & Hansen, 2006). As firms learn how to overcome specific competitive challenges, they develop potentially valuable capabilities that give them important advantages and therefore impact their performance.

Market Characteristics

The marketing literature informs that consumers' willingness to buy a new product depends on a set of product attributes, economic considerations and marketing services - all of which combine to define their beliefs, feelings and behavioural intentions toward the product. Building on this understanding, several studies have listed the following key determinants of any product evaluation and purchase decisions: (1) the incremental benefit offered by the product relative to the product that currently serves that need, (2) the perceived ease-of-use of the product, (3) the ability and willingness to pay for the product, and (4) the availability and access of the product (Sheth & Sisodia, 2012). The first two characteristics relate to the nature of the product, the next relates to the cost of acquiring the product, while the last relates to the marketing efforts required to make the product available to the customer. Selling new technologies such as solar-energy products in Africa is quite challenging because most customers are price-sensitive and do not have skills required to use products with complicated functionalities. Furthermore, as repair services are not readily available in these countries the products must be robust for them to be attractive to ordinary customers. Early adopters are sensitive about these product attributes and their degree of satisfaction can be an indicator of the speed of the product's market penetration (Gbadamosi, 2013). In other words, early adopters' word-of-mouth recommendations are important in persuading potential customers to adopt the product (Talukdar, Sudhir, & Ainslie, 2002; Peter, Ramaseshan & Nayar, 2002).

Leaning on the product life cycle theory, it has also been argued that the relative level of satisfaction and familiarity of early adopters depends partly on the number of years that the new product introduction in a given country lags behind its introduction in the country-of-origin (COO). A product that has been in the market for several years is more likely to have many of its initial deficiencies addressed and would have moved along the experience curve for many manufacturers, leading to a more appealing price-value proposition in other countries. At comparable stages of the diffusion process, adopters in lag countries are thus likely to be more satisfied with their product than those in countries-of-origin (Ganesh & Kumar, 1996).

Another source of product evaluation is the stereotypical image associated with countries-of-origin of products (Iacob, Kuada & Lawson, 2014). Past research has shown that consumers have a significant propensity to hold biased perceptions (positively or negatively) of products from specific countries (Shimp & Sharma, 1987). One source of bias stems from the level of economic development of the countries of origin of products under consideration. Products manufactured in advanced Western countries tend to be viewed as being of better quality than those from developing or less developed countries (Saffu & Scott, 2009). Similarly, services offered by technical staff from Western countries tend to be viewed as being more reliable and trustworthy than those by developing country personnel.

Firm Characteristics

The discussions above indicate that successful introduction of new products into emerging market contexts requires some new firm level capabilities other than those needed in the developed countries (Ernst, et. al., 2015). For example, due to infrastructure deficiency and institutional voids, firms often need to build entire business ecosystems from scratch (Seelos & Mair, 2007). This may mean some degree of adaptation of the products and services intended to be introduced, creation of new marketing routines and/or refinement of existing routines (Heirati, & O'Cass, 2016). These adaptations require top management ability to keep the firms agile enough for them to be able to sense and shape opportunities and threats and to maintain high levels of competitiveness through enhancing, combining, and reconfiguring their resources. Teece (2007) explains this agility in terms of three clusters of activities and adjustments: (1) identification and assessment of an opportunity (sensing); (2) mobilisation of resources to address an opportunity and to capture value from doing so (seizing); and (3) continued renewal (transforming). Sensing is seen as an entrepreneurial set of capabilities that involves exploring technological opportunities, probing markets, and listening to customers. Seizing capabilities include designing business models to satisfy customers. It also includes securing access to the necessary human resources – e.g. through collaborations and networks of relationships. The transformation of capabilities is needed periodically to soften the rigidities that develop over time through the adoption of standard operating procedures.

Again, institutional weaknesses in the emerging markets also require firms to develop capabilities to influence both the industries in which they operate and government policies in the country of operation (Chen, Li, & Liu, 2015). It has also been suggested that where institutions are weak, managers will need to cultivate social ties with business and political institutions to create an enabling environment for the growth of new sectors (Marquis & Raynard, 2015).

Marketing Strategies

The four-set characteristics discussed above will inform a firm's marketing strategy formulation. Several scholars see marketing strategy formulation as an integrative process of applying the collective knowledge, skills, and resources of a firm to the market-related needs of customers (Prahalad, & Hart, 2002; Kuada, 2016). This process has proved challenging for many firms operating in SSA countries, partly because of institutional weaknesses and infrastructural deficiencies discussed earlier, combined with 'leapfrogging' trends by consumers in some of these countries– especially with respect to information and communication technologies that produce new market dynamics. It means that the transfer of strategies that have previously proved successful in the Western economies may not enjoy similar degrees of success in SSA. Firms must, therefore, base their marketing strategies on market intelligence pertaining to current and future customer needs (Kohli & Jaworski, 1990; Narver & Slater, 1990). However, market knowledge acquisition is constrained by poor quality of published data, lower disclosure requirements for businesses and consumers' unfamiliarity with research procedures. Thus, instead of adopting a traditional planning-based approach to marketing strategy development (Kuada, 2016), such development tends to be more improvisational, with a greater propensity to be spontaneous and intuitive (Boso, Debrah, & Amankwah-Amoah, 2018).

With respect to solar-energy products, a pilot investigation conducted by the present authors reveal that many firms sell the same products to both consumers and business customers – i.e. engage in what Quelch (1987) labels dual marketing. The advantages of dual marketing include avoidance of dependency on either consumers or a limited number of organizational customers, as well as an ability to shift resources as changing growth rates alter the relative attractiveness of the two markets. But, a key challenge that marketers face in adopting a dual marketing strategy is to determine the manner in which their firms' marketing efforts can be organized and directed at both markets to simultaneously exploit their idiosyncrasies and stimulate synergy between the marketing efforts for both markets (Biemans, 2001).

Market Performance

The intended effect of a firm's marketing strategy is to improve its marketplace performance. Furthermore, a firm's marketing resources and capabilities result in positional advantages that define its market performance and, ultimately, its financial performance. Similarly, Kaplan & Norton (1992) suggest that the implementation of marketing strategy is more successful if it is reflected in performance measures.

Performance is usually measured either objectively or subjectively. Objective measures may be in terms of financial measures (e.g. sales volume, turnover, profit, and returns on marketing investments), competitive market measures (e.g. market share, relative growth rate), or consumer behaviour measures (e.g. penetration rate and degrees of satisfaction). Examples of subjective measures include reports from salespersons themselves (i.e. self-reports). Although many scholars show preference for objective measures, a study by Homburg, Artz, & Wieseke (2012) found that comprehensive market performance analysis is not always necessary. Firms that do not follow a differentiation strategy or operate in environments with low levels of marketing complexity and dynamism do not benefit in any significant manner from elaborate performance analyses. Furthermore, the breadth of performance measures has no performance effects in terms of market knowledge acquisition from the operational environment. This indicates that subjective assessments that stimulate management decisions can be equally fine, especially for smaller entrepreneurial firms.

CONCEPTUAL MODEL

The discussions above provide concepts that can guide the empirical data collection and analysis in this study. Although there is an emerging consensus among researchers that the external environment complements a firm's internal capabilities research has not made satisfactory progress in establishing a meaningful link between the external environment and firm-specific capabilities. In the current study market-focused learning capability emerges as an important link between a firm's external environment and marketing strategy. Firms that perceive their industry environment as turbulent make efforts to gain as much insight as they can into their environmental characteristics (including institutions, industry, customers and competitors). These insights may be obtained through relational arrangements with key actors within the operational environments. The market-focused learning enables them to develop marketing strategies that deliver superior solutions to their target market segments. These relationships are schematically illustrated in Figure 1 (see Figure 1). The model shows that institutional characteristics such as rules, norms and values combine with industry characteristics, market characteristics and firm characteristics to influence marketing strategies which, in turn, influence market performance of firms. The model should guide the empirical investigation into the marketing ecosystem that vendors of solar-energy products in Ghana are in the process of creating and the manner in which the relationships they have developed influence the buying decision processes of their customers and the overall growth of the industry.

METHODOLOGY

Given the limited prior empirical research on the subject the study uses a multi-case method to examine the processes by which some of the leading firms within the solar-energy sector market their products in Ghana. In order to identify and select appropriate participants for the study, the authors consulted the Ghana Energy Commission's database for a list of solar-energy firms in the country at the time of the data collection. The commission classifies the firms in two categories: (1) Independent Power Producers

Figure 1. Conceptual Model

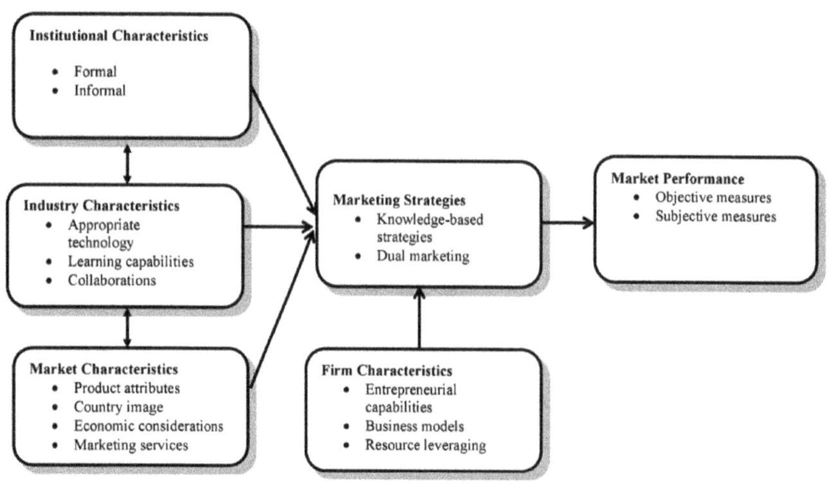

(IPPs) – i.e. firms that were licensed to operate their own solar power plants to generate and sell power to the National Grid, and (2) Solar Installation Firms - i.e. firms that install solar systems for customers. The database showed that the IPPs numbered 59 while the solar installation firms numbered 105. But some of the IPPs were also engaged in installations and were therefore on both lists. The researchers decided to target the IPPs that did installation at the same time since these firms were relatively large and had a longer operational history. They were therefore likely to provide comprehensive information about the industry. The researchers identified 25 of these firms and contacted all of them by email and followed this up with telephone calls after two weeks. These initial contacts produced no positive responses – most of them declined participation due to pressure of work. The researchers therefore decided to adopt a snowball (or chain–referral) sampling approach in the belief that referrals could encourage participation. This approach has justification in research (see Goodman, 1961; Heckathorn, 1997; Yin, 2003) and has been used by other researchers such as Etemad-Sajadi (2015) in similar exploratory investigations. These efforts resulted in the selection of the twelve firms which participated in the study. The researchers decided to interview twelve current and potential users of solar energy at the same time in order to maintain some balance in the targeted participants. The interviews were conducted between May and June 2017 and lasted between 1 and 1½ hours each. The interview transcripts were written within 24 hours after each interview in order to reduce the incidence of memory decay (in situations where the respondents disallowed taping the interviews). The respondents were then requested to read through the transcripts to make sure that their experiences were fully captured in the transcripts.

The data were then analysed using Ritchie and Spencer's (1994) thematic approach, which entails a 'comprehensive data treatment'. This involves incorporating, analysing, and inspecting all the data collected in order to capture their richness. Table 1 provides an overview of the twelve firms included in the study, noting their countries of origin, ownership types and nature of business.

Table 1. List of solar-energy firms interviewed

Name	Country of Origin	Ownership	Profile and Nature of Business
Ada Solar Energy Limited	2 Danes and a Nigerian	Joint venture(JV)	rooftop installations and solar power plant development
Barefoot Power African Limited	Australia	Subsidiary of a multinational company	
DENG	Denmark	Wholly owned foreign company	rooftop installations and distribution of solar components
Strategic Power Solutions (SPS)	Ghana	Wholly owned local company	solar panel manufacturing, rooftop installations and solar power plant development
DC Solar	Ghana	Wholly owned local company	rooftop installations and solar power plant development
AB Solar	Ghana	Wholly owned local company	Solar power plant development
Tino Solutions	Ghana	Wholly owned local company	rooftop installations and solar component distribution
Suka Wind &Solar Energy Limited	Ghana	Wholly owned local company	rooftop installations and solar component distribution
WindSol Energy	Ghana	Wholly owned local company	rooftop installations and solar component distribution
AekoSolar	Ghana	Wholly owned local company	rooftop installations
Sylprin Company	Ghana	Wholly owned local company	rooftop installations
Green Solar Africa (GSA)	Ghana/Sierra Leone	Joint venture	rooftop installations

The authors also interviewed twelve customers (six customers who were using solar energy for their businesses as well as in their private homes and six customers who were not using solar energy at the time of data collection). The aim of the customer interviews was to understand the reasons for adoption and non-adoption of the solar products and the experiences of the adopters. The customers were also selected using the snow-ball process. The first three business customers were recommended to the authors by AekoSolar. The other three came from similar recommendations from other solar-energy firms. The customers include Icy-Cup, a yoghurt producing and retailing company with 13 outlets, RayBen Diagnostics, a medical laboratory for clinical diagnostic, and ABB Hairdressing Saloon. The list also included a micro-finance firm, a printing press and a student hostel company.

In order to gain insight into perspectives of institutions on the solar-energy sector, the researchers also interviewed five institutions - the Ghana Energy Commission, SNV Netherlands Development Agency, The Kwame Nkrumah University of Science and Technology Energy Center, Danish International Development Agency and Kumasi Institute of Technology Energy and Environment.

FINDINGS

General Profile of Firms

The results reveal that the following four main categories of firms are currently active in the solar sector in Ghana: (i) manufacturers of solar components such as panels, (ii) producers of solar energy that feed into the national energy grid, (iii) installation service providers, and (iv) distributors of solar components. Although some of the firms are engaged in multiple activities, the most dominant service currently provided within the industry is the installation of rooftop solar panels. In terms of ownership, there were two wholly owned foreign firms (DENG, and Barefoot Power); two Joint ventures (JVs) between Ghanaians and foreign partners (Chinese-SPS JV, and Green Solar Africa); and eight wholly owned Ghanaian firms. Eight of the twelve firms interviewed were start-ups in the solar sector. Four of them have had other businesses prior to entering the solar-energy sector (Tino Solutions was in ICT consultancy, Sylprin was in fire prevention, AB Solar was in the distribution of consumables, printing and glasses, while SPS was in the marketing of holographic materials). They therefore brought some prior knowledge to the sector and this appeared to have enhanced their absorptive capacities.

Overview of the Solar-Energy Market

The leading firms within the industry engage in dual marketing. For example, firms such as Green Solar Africa (GSA), WindSol Energy, Suka and SPS act as agents for foreign solar firms by implementing solar installations for foreign firms which secure contracts from Ghanaian customers. They also sell solar components such as panels to DC solar and DENG. DENG furthermore supplies components to firms such as AekoSolar. Similarly, Tino Solutions undertakes solar power installations to both businesses and household users. AB solar sells the power it generates from its 60-MegaWatt Solar Power Plant to the Ghana Government through the National grid and engages in installations to households. In other words, the evidence suggests a nework of collaborative relationships among the local firms.

Market Growth Determinants and Prospects

Government policies were cited as among the factors that have motivated the establishment of firms such as AB Solar and Ada Solar. In 2011 the Renewable Energy Law (Act 832) was passed. This provided the legal framework for private participation in power supply as a strategy for attaining the goal of increasing the share of renewables in the nation's energy consumption to 10% by 2020. Around the same time the government launched "National Rooftop Campaign" that encouraged the installation of solar-energy systems for households. These policy initiatives drew business as well as public attention to solar energy as an alternative to hydropower and thermal energy sources.

The general sentiment expressed by the respondents during the interviews is that the growth prospects within the industry are fairly good. Firms experience increasing demand for solar installations, which they attribute to three factors: the erratic power supplies, the rising utility bills in Ghana, and the falling prices of solar technologies. Small business owners in the country – e.g. private clinics, hotels, restaurants and bakeries – are turning to solar energy as an alternative energy source, seeing it as more reliable and relatively less expensive in the long run. For example, the owner of Rayben (a diagnostic centre) now uses 80% solar, 10% grid and 10% diesel generator as sources of energy. The same holds true for owners of fuel and gas stations that depend on electricity to run their businesses. But while solar energy is relatively cheap in the long run, the upfront cost has been a huge deterrent for many household users. The average installation cost for rooftop solar energy is about US$ 4,000, an amount equal to about a third of a university lecturer's annual salary. Small businesses may have to invest about US$ 100,000 in installations in order to cover their energy needs. In spite of these relatively high levels of investment, there is a general understanding among the small businesses that such investments are wise economic decisions. The respondent from DC Solar informed that *"I think gradually people are coming to understand that there is a lot of benefit you can get from solar. Once you are able to pay for the full cost you are assured you can get an uninterrupted power.........Business looks positive for now and the future"*.

Also, the respondent at WindSol informed as follows:

It used to take about four months to convince a potential customer to accept an offer, now if you are lucky you can close a deal in a month. This is how we measure the market, it is improving. And so we are very hopeful about the sector.

The shorter time frame for convincing potential customers to accept a solar solution for their energy needs is taken as evidence of a growing demand.

Current government energy tax policies have also been cited as favouring the growth of the renewable energy sector. According to the CEO of DENG *"high tariffs have kindled the interest in solar"*. Similarly, Group CEO of Suka argued that *"Ghana has one of the highest electricity tariffs in Africa and so there are organizations and hotels that have decided that they do not want energy from conventional sources.......some are turning to renewables, others will want to use diesel generator."*

One of the household users interviewed (a university professor) has this to say:

I couldn't stand the constant power outage which was destroying my household appliances and making life difficult for my family. I initially installed solar as a backup to energy from the central grid. But now I want to go off the grid and use my solar power throughout because compared to the grid it is constant, affordable and reliable.

Marketing Efforts and Industry Development

As expected, the marketing efforts required to serve potential customers include offering good quality and affordable solutions to the energy needs of households and small businesses, providing good and trustworthy delivery and after-sales services, and financial arrangements to those who may not immediately be able to afford the upfront investment. Most firms currently depend on various forms of collaborative arrangements with foreign business partners to be able to fulfil their marketing promises. The few manufacturers of solar products (including panels) rely entirely on foreign technology suppliers in order to establish their factories and train their staff. For example, the Marketing Manager of SPS explained their approach and experience as follows:

Our production system was set up by an Italian firm. They came over to do the whole matching phase and calibration. Then experts from Japan spent a week to train our people. Now our workers have acquired knowledge and skills to operate the machines on their own. ....Our team is confident on how to assemble and manufacture. Periodically, too, we have a Japanese company called MPC, they provide us with some cutting machines. So we have an exchange programme with them every six months – we send our people there or they send their people to train our staff.

The business development manager of DC solar also acknowledges the importance of collaborations with foreign partners. He describes their collaborations as follows:

...Sometimes people tend to trust foreigners than Ghanaians but at the end of the day it's the local business that really does the implementation...these foreign guys have the leverage. They have been in the business for a very long time and they do get business in Ghana. So we form partnership with them. They get the contract and we implement it together....sometimes we do not even have to finance it, we will act as sub-contractors, install everything and we just get our cut. There is also an advantage of credibility. You know that when you have done work with established foreign firms, it enhances your credibility....

Likewise, the Director of Operations for GSA also informs that "When foreign firms get contracts they need someone that is actually on the ground here to implement the project. That's how we get some of our business. These firms have been coming back to us to implement.... There is a company in America that contacted us last month..... Others have seen what we do and are impressed so when they get the contract they want us to implement it for them".

These statements indicate that an increasing number of foreign firms use partnership arrangements as entry modes in Ghana. Ghanaian firms appear to experience liabilities of localness, whereby Ghanaian customers tend to trust foreign firms a lot more than the local firms – although the local firms have the technical competences to do the installations. This observation gains additional credence from the experiences of two customers. The first is the co-founder of RayBen Diagnostics who brought a solar firm from Germany to install their solar system for their laboratory. The second is the manager of Icy-Cup who flew a UK solar firm into Ghana because his firm did not believe that local firms had the capacity to meet their needs effectively.

Institutional actors that have been following the industry trends (e.g. fellows at the Kwame Nkrumah University of Science and Technology Energy Center, and Kumasi Institute of Technology Energy and Environment) tend to think that the distrust that customers have about local firms is temporary. As individual firms build their reputations and demonstrate their skills in service delivery, word-of-mouth recommendations will lead to a general acknowledgement of the local capabilities within the industry. They also agree that in the interim, there is the need for technology and knowledge transfer from foreign firms to their local counterparts.

Interview results indicate some elaborate arrangements between some firms for technology and knowledge transfer with view to upgrading the process and functional capabilities of the Ghanaian firms. For example, Tino Solutions expanded into solar installations after importing inverters from Victron of the Netherlands as a power backup system in 2008 for its ICT customers. Since 2012, Victron has been visiting Tino Solutions in Ghana annually to train its network of local distributors and solar engineers on how to install the products. Similarly, DC Solar stated that it learns about quality standards and new emerging trends as well as new solar technologies from working alongside its partners, especially during joint executions of projects. The business development manager explains the arrangements and benefits as follows:

You get to learn how the foreign firms do their things, the new things, new trends. ...In terms of technology, there are lots of transfers. Once we are collaborating we are always in the trend of what is really new in the industry. I would say that is some of the advantages.

There is also evidence of collaboration among the Ghanaian firms themselves. The results indicate that social ties play an important role in these relationships. For example, the Technical Support Officer of WindSol Energy had worked in DENG for more than five years and remains in regular professional contacts with his former colleagues. The owner of AekoSolar also has a personal relationship with the owner of DENG, and this facilitates their business interactions as well. He explains their relationship in the following words:

Fred Bosteen [the CEO of DENG] is an old Danish guy who has been in this country for a long time. I am a dealer for DENG. Fred is a friend of mine, I have known him for a long time .. If I get a job and I need panels badly, then I order from them. They will bring it to me and after doing the job I pay them. Usually they give me 30 days of credit and we have worked like that for five years and it works well.

As noted above, installation cost is another important variable that customers consider in their decision to adopt solar-energy systems. For most potential customers, getting loans to finance the installations is not a viable option. Here are samples of their responses to the question about getting loans: *"No, it won't be a good idea, too expensive". "We have no collateral to secure the loan plus they charge very high interest rates". "I don't deal with banks in my business because the interest rates are too high and the charges are outrageous".*

Vendors therefore need to factor finance into their marketing mix strategies. Some have adopted relatively bold solutions. For example, WindSol Energy has opened a microfinance organization to give a medium to long term lower interest financing to their customers. Others are considering different models of financing, including lease arrangements, especially for business customers or credits for individuals in permanent and averagely paid jobs. But none of these considerations have actually been implemented.

With respect to promotion, the firms rely on word-of-mouth recommendations rather than advertising using conventional channels and the social media. It appears the current capacity level of the firms fits the growth of the industry, and there has been no need to scale up the levels of promotion as of now.

DISCUSSIONS

The results of the study indicate that some of the characteristics outlined in the conceptual model (Figure 1) influence marketing efforts of firms in the Ghanaian solar industry. One of the recurrent themes in previous studies is that institutional support in the form of policies which promote the development of strong entrepreneurial culture, openness to foreign investors and effective interfirm collaborations is necessary for the growth of the renewable energy sector in SSA (Ondraczek, 2013; Amankwah-Amoah, 2016). Additionally, institutionally-sponsored initiatives that raise potential consumers' awareness of the available renewable energy technologies are also deemed important (Amankwah-Amoah, & Sarpong, 2016; Mas'ud, et al., 2016). The evidence from the study suggests that institutional rules such as the Renewable Energy Law (Act 832) and promotional campaigns have created a motivating environment for the entry of private firms in the industry. Initially, some consumers and business customers were apprehensive about the skills and capabilities of the local firms to satisfactorily carry out installations. For this reason, some customers have preferred to contract with foreign firms to deliver the services or to supervise the local firms in the service delivery processes. But as time passes, the reputation of local firms appears to grow gradually based on the customers' experiences of service deliveries. The results also reveal some degree of local and cross-border inter-firm collaboration at both vertical and horizontal levels. These collaborations have facilitated knowledge sharing and joint delivery of services and have produced positive effects on reputation building on the part of Ghanaian firms that have experienced liabilities of localness. They have also enabled local firms to adapt their solar solutions to meet local customer needs and resource characteristics. The authors of this study have not been informed of any situation in which a partner has performed actions that resulted in negative outcomes for a Ghanaian firm. This suggests that, so far, there has been an implicit trust between the collaborative partners. The results are, therefore, consistent with arguments in previous studies that social network ties do facilitate inter-firm knowledge dissemination, and where trust exists between people in relations, they are willing to share new knowledge (Anderson & Narus, 1990; Gulati, 1995).

The results have also shown that Quelch's (1987) concept of dual marketing aptly captures aspects of the marketing efforts within the industry. That is, some of the firms sell the same products to both households and business customers. The need for autonomy appears to be a key motivational factor that influences Ghanaian small business owners' decision to acquire solar PV technology – it provides them freedom from the unreliable services of the national electricity firms. On the whole, both market segments appear to be similar on nearly all fronts apart from volumes and investment costs. Thus, from a strategic marketing perspective, business customers can simply be viewed as "consumers at work". It means firms target both segments with similar marketing efforts.

In general, both consumers and business customers tend to be price conscious. Although the business owners are willing to pay the upfront costs of the installations (seeing them as investments), potential consumers of solar home systems are less inclined to do so. Seen from a societal perspective, this implies that upfront costs necessary for Ghana to switch to solar energy become burden on individual consumers. This partly accounts for the slow pace of diffusion of the technology. The general understanding among researchers is that given that renewable energy systems are still in the first phase of the product life-cycle government policies are required to stimulate adoption (Ondraczek, 2013). Fortunately, the cost of the PV technology is declining rapidly due, in part, to significant technological breakthroughs. Furthermore, some global players (e.g. Hanwha-Solar-One, Trina Solar, Yingli Green Energy, and JA Solar) are reported to introduce business models that allow them to sell solar products at affordable prices in developing countries (Amankwah-Amoah, 2014). These developments will hopefully reduce the cost of PV technologies offered to consumers in SSA to a level that renders government subsidies unnecessary.

IMPLICATIONS

The study also highlight the potential benefits in adopting a decentralised approach to addressing Ghana's energy problem and fulfilling government objectives of increasing renewable energy's share of the nation's total energy consumption. This is consistent with findings from previous studies that have drawn attention to the weaknesses of a centralised energy distribution strategy (Ikejemba et al, 2017). For example, Kumi (2017) has argued that the existing centralised energy supply systems are plagued by poor management, high levels of distribution losses, and non-payment of bills. These factors have hampered the ability of the centralised power companies to make significant investments to improve the sector. With declining costs and technological improvements in electricity storage and control systems, it can be argued that liberalisation of Ghana's energy sector will become a more cost-effective, timely and reliable approach to meet the energy needs of consumers. Studies elsewhere have shown that the idea of providing consumers in developing countries with electricity through grid extension alone is becoming obsolete (Mas'ud, et al., 2016). Markets for both mini-grids and stand-alone systems are evolving rapidly and Ghana must not lose out of this emerging trend.

As noted above, previous studies have also highlighted the role that decentralized energy supply systems can play in the attainment of UN Sustainable Development Goals (Amankwah-Amoah, & Sarpong, 2016). For example, access to energy in rural communities in SSA will open up a plethora of opportunities for local entrepreneurs to establish microenterprises that run off of electricity (including, processing, retailing and repair services). It will also stimulate growth and productivity within the agri-business sector. Therefore, marketing efforts must not only exploit the existing demand but also expand the size of the market by bringing large numbers of non-users into the consumption space. To this end, marketing efforts must be "democratized" through institutional policies and support programmes that can ensure the affordability of renewable energy technologies, particularly to rural consumers who will be less able to pay the relatively large upfront installation costs (Sinha and Sheth, 2018). In this regard, the possibilities of developing microcredit schemes must be explored. One possibility is to design Pay-As-You-Consume (PAYC) business models, with the support of mobile pay systems that are becoming popular in the country.

Furthermore the emerging collaborative network of firms within the industry also carries potentials for these firms to collectively shape the future development of the industry. Building on experiences elsewhere, the firms can formalize these relationships into industry association that can inform policy makers about the challenges and opportunities within the industry and the manner in which the institutional environment can help stimulate the growth process (Marquis & Raynard, 2015).

LIMITATIONS AND FURTHER RESEARCH

The study presented in this chapter had some limitations, and these can guide future research efforts. First, data for the present study have been collected only in the major cities in Ghana. Further research is needed to explore the extent of adoption of solar PV energy in rural parts of the country. Second, the focus of this study has been on solar electricity installations. It therefore excludes other solar based products such as water heaters, air conditioners, and refrigeration systems etc., all of which contribute to reduction in conventional energy usage. A wider product range must be considered in future studies. Third, there is a dearth of knowledge about how households that adopt solar products use them or the extent to which actual use patterns match up with the ones in other developing countries (Stojanovski, Ognen, Thurber, Mark and Wolak, 2017). This is another area requiring future research attention. Finally, research is also required to help firms within the industry to develop affordable financial models that can grow the market.

SUMMARY AND CONCLUSION

This study adds to the limited knowledge of the renewable energy sector in Ghana. The results reveal that the industry has a promising future. Demand is increasing and the number of firms operating within the industry is growing. But the current capacity is far below the national expectations. Stimulating the market remains an important challenge for the country to harness the full potential of the abundant solar energy it has. The study also draws attention to factors that influence the growth of the industry, including institutional arrangements as well as firm level and market characteristics. It shows, in concert with previous studies that reduction of investment costs, increase in reliability, and dissemination of market information are crucial for the growth of the industry. In addition to this, it notes that collaborative arrangements among lead firms and foreign partners help build local firm capabilities and reputation and allow them to deliver solar-energy solutions to the growing market segment of businesses and households. Finally, the study also draws attention to some of the constraints to growth and suggests possible solutions.

REFERENCES

Abbott, J. C. (1987). *Agricultural Marketing Enterprises for the Developing World.* Cambridge, UK: Cambridge University Press.

Acquaah, M. (2012). Social networking relationships, firm-specific managerial experience and firm performance in a transition economy: A comparative analysis of family owned and nonfamily firms. *Strategic Management Journal, 33*(10), 1215–1228.

African Development Bank Group. (2017). *African Economic Outlook – Entrepreneurship and Industrialization.* Abidjan: AfDB Publication. Retrieved from https://www.afdb.org/fileadmin/uploads/afdb/Documents/Publications/AEO_2017_Report_Full_English.pdf

Amankwah-Amoah, J. (2014). Solar energy in sub-Saharan Africa: The challenges and opportunities of technological leapfrogging. *Thunderbird International Business Review, 57*(1), 15–31.

Amankwah-Amoah, J. (2016). The evolution of science, technology and innovation policies: A review of the Ghanaian experience. *Technological Forecasting and Social Change, 110*, 134–142.

Amankwah-Amoah, J., & Sarpong, D. (2016). Historical pathways to a green economy: The evolution and scaling-up of solar PV in Ghana, 1980–2010. *Technological Forecasting and Social Change*, *102*, 90–101.

Anderson, J. C., & Narus, J. A. (1990). A model of distributor firm and manufacturer firm working partnerships. *Journal of Marketing*, *54*, 42–58.

Arnold, D. J., & Quelch, J. A. (1998). New strategies in emerging markets. *Sloan Management Review*, *40*(1), 7–20.

Baurzhan, S., & Jenkins, G. P. (2016). Off-grid solar PV: Is it an affordable or appropriate solution for rural electrification in Sub-Saharan African countries? *Renewable & Sustainable Energy Reviews*, *601*, 405–1418.

Biemans, W. (2001). Designing a Dual Marketing Program. *European Management Journal*, *19*(6), 670–677.

Boso, N., Debrah, Y. A., & Amankwah-Amoah, J. (2018). International marketing strategies of emerging market firms: Nature, boundary conditions, antecedents, and outcomes. *International Marketing Review*, *35*(2), 202–214.

Chelariu, C., Ouattarra, A., & Dadzie, K. (2002). Market Orientation in Ivory Coast: Measurement Validity and Organizational Antecedents in a sub-Saharan African Economy. *Journal of Business and Industrial Marketing*, *17*(6), 456–470.

Chen, H., & Li, Y., & Liu, Yi. (2015). Dual capabilities and organizational learning in new product market performance. *Industrial Marketing Management*, *46*, 204–213.

Ernst, H., Kahle, H. N., Dubiel, A., Prabhu, J., & Subramaniam, M. (2015). The Antecedents and Consequences of Affordable Value Innovations for Emerging Markets. *Journal of Product Innovation Management*, *32*, 65–79.

Etemad-Sajadi, R. (2015). The impact of service tradability on the choice of entry mode: The case of computer-related service firms. *Total Quality Management Journal*, *27*(1), 79–93.

Fafchamps, M. (1996). The Enforcement of Commercial Contracts in Ghana. *World Development*, *24*(3), 427–448.

Ganesh, J., & Kumar, V. (1996). Capturing the cross-national learning effect: An analysis of an industrial technology diffusion. *Journal of the Academy of Marketing Science*, *24*, 328–337.

Gbadamosi, A. (2013). Consumer involvement and marketing in Africa: Some directions for future research. *International Journal of Consumer Studies*, *37*, 234–242.

Goodman, L. A. (1961). Snowball Sampling. *Annals of Mathematical Statistics*, *32*(1), 148–170.

Gulati, R. (1995). Does Familiarity Breed Trust? The Implications of Repeated Ties for Contractual Choices in Alliances. *Academy of Management Journal*, *38*, 85–112.

Hansen, U. E., Pedersen, M. B., & Nygaard, I. (2015). Review of solar PV policies, interventions and diffusion in East Africa. *Renewable & Sustainable Energy Reviews*, *46*, 236–248.

Heckathorn, D. D. (1997). Respondent-Driven Sampling: A New Approach to the Study of Hidden Populations. *Social Problems*, *44*(2), 174–199.

Heirati, N., & O'Cass, A. (2016). Supporting new product commercialization through managerial social ties and market knowledge development in an emerging economy. *Asia Pacific Journal of Management*, *33*, 411–433.

Homburg, C., Artz, M., & Wieseke, J. (2012). Marketing Performance Measurement Systems: Does Comprehensiveness Really Improve Performance? *Journal of Marketing*, *76*(3), 56–77.

Iacob, A., Kuada, J., & Lawson, L. (2014). Relationships between brand perception, ideology and consumer ethnocentrism in post-communist Romania. *Journal of Euromarketing*, *23*, 85–110.

Ikejemba, E. C., Mpuan, P. B., Schuur, P. C., & Van Hillegersberg, J. (2017). The empirical reality & sustainable management failures of renewable energy projects in Sub-Saharan Africa (part 1 of 2). *Renewable Energy*, *102*, 234–240.

Kaplan, R. S., & Norton, D. P. (1992). The Balanced Scorecard: Measures That Drive Performance. *Harvard Business Review*, *70*(1), 71–79. PMID:10119714

Kohli, A., & Jaworski, B. (1990). Market orientation: The construct, research propositions and managerial implications. *Journal of Marketing*, *54*, 1–18.

Kuada, J. (2003). *Culture and Technological Transformation in the South: Transfer or Local Innovation?* Copenhagen: Samfundslitteratur.

Kuada, J. (2015). *Private Enterprise-Led Economic Development in Sub-Saharan Africa: The Human Side of Growth*. London: Palgrave Macmillan.

Kuada, J. (2016). *Marketing Decisions and Strategies – An International Perspective*. London: Adonis & Abbey Publishers.

Kuada, J., & Hansen, M. W. (2006). Theories of cross-border linkages. In M. W. Hansen & H. Schaumburg-Müller (Eds.), *Transnational Corporations and Local Firms in Developing Countries – Linkages and Upgrading* (pp. 29–60). Copenhagen: Copenhagen Business School Press.

Kumi, E. N. (2017). *The electricity situation in Ghana: Challenges and opportunities. CGD Policy Paper.* Center for Global Development. Retrieved from https://www.cgdev.org/ publication/

Marquis, C., & Raynard, M. (2015). Institutional strategies in emerging markets. *The Academy of Management Annals*, *9*(1), 291–335.

Mas'ud, A. A., Wirba, A. V., Muhammad-Sukki, F., Albarracín, R., Abu-Bakar, S. H., Munir, A. B., & Bani, N. A. (2016). A review on the recent progress made on solar photovoltaic in selected countries of sub-Saharan Africa. *Renewable & Sustainable Energy Reviews*, *62*, 441–452.

Mensah, E. (2017). *Cross-border Inter-firm Networks and the Growth of Ghana's Solar Power Sector* (Unpublished MSc Thesis). International Business Centre, Aalborg University.

Nandonde, F. A., & Kuada, J. (2016). Modern food retailing buying behaviour in Africa: The case of Tanzania. *British Food Journal*, *118*(5), 1163–1178.

Narver, J. C., & Slater, S. (1990). The effect of market orientation on business profitability. *Journal of Marketing*, *54*, 20–35.

North, D. C. (1990). *Institutions, Institutional Change, and Economic Performance*. Cambridge, UK: Cambridge University Press.

Ondraczek, J. (2013). The sun rises in the east (of Africa): A comparison of the development and status of solar energy markets in Kenya and Tanzania. *Energy Policy*, *56*, 407–417.

Pérez-Nordtvedt, L., Kedia, B. L., Datta, D. K., & Rasheed, A. A. (2008). Effectiveness and efficiency of cross-border knowledge transfer: An empirical examination. *Journal of Management Studies*, *45*(4), 714–744.

Peter, R., Ramaseshan, B., & Nayar, C. V. (2002). Conceptual model for marketing solar based technology to developing countries. *Renewable Energy*, *25*, 511–524.

Prahalad, C. K., & Hart, S. L. (2002). The fortune at the bottom of the pyramid. *Strategy Business*, *26*, 54–67.

Quelch, J. A. (1987). Why not exploit dual marketing? *Business Horizons*, *30*(1), 52–60.

Ritchie, J., & Spencer, L. (1994). Qualitative data analysis for applied policy research. In A. Bryman & R. Burgess (Eds.), *Analyzing Qualitative Data* (pp. 173–194). London: Sage.

Saffu, K., & Scott, D. (2009). Developing country perceptions of high- and low-involvement products manufactured in other countries. *International Journal of Emerging Markets*, *4*(2), 185–199.

Schumacher, E. F. (1973). *Small is Beautiful: Economics as if People Mattered*. London, UK: Blond and Briggs.

Scott, W. R. (2004). Institutional theory. In G. Ritzer (Ed.), *Encyclopaedia of Social Theory* (pp. 408–414). Thousand Oaks, CA: Sage.

Seelos, C., & Mair, J. (2007). Profitable business models and market creation in the context of deep poverty: A strategic view. *The Academy of Management Perspectives*, *21*, 49–63.

Sheth, J. N., & Sisodia, R. S. (2012). *The 4 A's of marketing: Creating value for customers, companies, and society*. Routledge.

Shimp, T., & Sharma, S. (1987). Consumer ethnocentrism: Construction and validation of the CETSCALE. *JMR, Journal of Marketing Research*, *23*, 280–289.

Sinha, M., & Sheth, J. (2018). Growing the pie in emerging markets: Marketing strategies for increasing the ratio of non-users to users. *Journal of Business Research*, *86*, 217–224.

Spencer, J. W. (2000). Knowledge flows in the global innovation system: Do U.S. firms share more scientific knowledge than their Japanese rivals? *Journal of International Business Studies*, *31*(3), 521–530.

Stojanovski, O., Thurber, M., & Wolak, F. (2017). Rural energy access through solar home systems: Use patterns and opportunities for improvement. *Energy for Sustainable Development*, *37*, 33–50.

Talukdar, D., Sudhir, K., & Ainslie, A. (2002). Investigating new product diffusion across products and countries. *Marketing Science*, *21*(1), 97–114.

Teece, D. J. (2007). Explicating dynamic capabilities: The nature and micro foundations of (sustainable) enterprise performance. *Strategic Management Journal*, *28*(13), 1319–1350.

Tesar, G., & Kuada, J. (Eds.). (2013). *Marketing Management and Strategy: An African Casebook.* London: Routledge.

Winston, E., & Dadzie, K. (2002). Market orientation of Nigerian and Kenyan firms: The role of top managers. *Journal of Business and Industrial Marketing*, *17*(6), 471–480.

Yin, R. K. (2003). *Case Study Research Design and Methods.* London: Sage Publications.

Chapter 15
Market Relational Mediation Practices:
Exploring Nigerian Immigrant Entrepreneurs' Responses to Consumer Needs in Ghana

Thomas Antwi Bosiakoh
Macquarie University, Australia

Vera Williams Tetteh
Macquarie University, Australia

Christian T. Djamgbah
Macquarie University, Australia

Phyllis Antwi Bosiakoh
S. Antonio Da Padova Village, Australia

ABSTRACT

The importance of developing societies in the global marketplace is never in doubt as they constitute a vital consumer base for products and services from developed countries. Yet, there is a general paucity of research on consumption behavior in developing societies. This chapter draws on Nigerian immigrants' informal entrepreneurship in Ghana to explore how these entrepreneurs respond to consumer demands and needs and the specific clientele attraction strategies they deploy to sustain and expand their businesses. The chapter argues that understanding the entrepreneurs' responses to consumer needs and their customer attraction strategies contributes to a better understanding of these businesses in their current forms, scope, and their future prospects. Ultimately, the chapter sheds light on what shapes consumption practices that make the existence of these businesses in the developing world possible and their relevance for the global marketplace and the globalization discourse.

DOI: 10.4018/978-1-5225-7906-9.ch015

INTRODUCTION AND BACKGROUND

This chapter focuses on Nigerian immigrant business owners in Ghana. It explores their perspectives and responses to consumer needs and demands and attraction strategies they adopt with the view to show how these work in the context of a developing country. The country of focus is Ghana. Also known as the Gold Coast in the colonial times, Ghana played host to diverse groups of immigrants, and continues to do so from within Africa and other parts of the world outside Africa (Jahoda, 1961; Peil, 1974; Boahen, 1977; DeCorse, 2001; Adepoju, 2003). The ten major international immigrant groups in Ghana are of Nigerian, Togolese, Burkinabe, English, Chinese, Indians, Lebanese, Malian, Ivorian and Liberian origins. About a decade ago, Twum-Baah's (2005) work profiled the volume and characteristics of international migrants in Ghana to reveal that, Ghana's immigration figures are dominated by people of Nigerian origin. Arhin's (1979) classical work and others (e.g. Amenumey, 2008; Anquandah, 1985; Davies, 1966; Kobo, 2010; and Massing, 2000 etc.) show historical origin and activities of Nigerians and other immigrant groups such as Malian and Burkinabe in Ghana. Antwi Bosiakoh and Williams Tetteh (2018) provide an overview of the driving factors and information about why Nigerian immigrants venture to Ghana, and are entrepreneurial in Ghana.

Recent studies on Nigerian migration across the world highlight how Ghana ranks high in terms of destination preference for Nigerian immigrants. Five-percent of the estimated 5.2 million Nigerians living in other countries (Orozco & Mills, 2007) is known to be resident in Ghana (Mberu & Pongou, 2010; Olatuyi, Awoyinka & Adeniyi, 2013; Orozco & Mills, 2007). Also, Ghana is the third top destination of Nigerian migrants in the global south, following Sudan and Cameroon, and the fifth destination on a global scale (Olatuyi et. al., 2013).

Regardless of their origin countries, migrants in various parts of the world are known to be entrepreneurial as some venture into business development in their new contexts (see for example Kalitanyi & Visser, 2010; Rath 2000). Nigerian immigrants also create their own jobs through establishing businesses in destination countries including Ghana. Their entrepreneurial pursuit and successes are often measured by standards including their provision of jobs within the new contexts (Antwi Bosiakoh, 2017b; Eades, 1994; Hill, 1970). To date, scholarly focus on Nigerian immigrants' business creation/operational activities in Ghana, have omitted, or at best shed very little light on the strategies deployed to attract clientele and address customer demands. Given that clientele attraction strategies and customer demand responses are core components of both business development, maintenance and also business expansion processes, this chapter fills that gap by investigating these two domains. The chapter contends that understanding Nigerian immigrants' clientele attraction strategies and how they address consumer demands provide a valuable contribution to knowledge. This argument is based on two points. The first point is that, this knowledge contributes to a better understanding about these businesses in their current forms and scope as well as the prospects they hold for the future. The second point is that, by understanding these activities, we gain deeper insights into what shapes the consumption practices that make the existence of these businesses in the developing world possible, as well as their relevance in the global marketplace and the globalisation discourse. The study is guided by two research questions, namely 1) How do contemporary Nigerian immigrant entrepreneurs (operating in a developing country, Ghana) seek to understand and respond to consumer needs? and 2) What strategies do the entrepreneurs deploy to attract clientele-base to sustain and expand their businesses?

The chapter is organized as follows: The introduction is followed by discussions on the notion of relational mediation in business with a focus on responses to customer needs, and clientele attraction strategies. Next, a description of the methods employed for the collection of data and analysis is presented, followed by presentation of the findings. The final section is the discussion/conclusion with recommendations for future research.

RELATIONAL MEDIATION IN BUSINESS OPERATIONS

Relational mediation is a time tested marketing technique (Palmatier, Burke Jarvis, Bechkoff, & Kardes, 2009). Used in this chapter, the notion of relational mediation encapsulates the strategies and practices deployed by entrepreneurs and businesses to *connect* or *engage* effectively with clients (Palmatier, Dant, Grewal & Evans, 2006). Clients include fellow business operators both in their market of operation and elsewhere, including suppliers. Relational mediation thus entails diverse market relationships, approaches to responding to the needs of consumer and consumer attraction strategies. These practices and strategies are embedded in different aspects of the entrepreneurial and or business operation processes. Particularly, they are embedded in the interactions with customers and fellow business operatives directly and indirectly, for the creation of convivial and trustful relationships and the protection of business interests. They also make up a part of what Granovetter (1985) refers to as *relational embeddedness* in economic rationality and the undergirding principle in interpersonal relations including normative expectations, reciprocity transactions and the quest for mutual approval. The concept further highlights the 'network of social relations with customers, suppliers, banks, competitors, and, not to be ignored law enforcers' (Kloosterman, 2010, p. 27). Relational mediation involves a three-dimensional management approach as follows: (a) market relationships, (b) responding to the needs of consumers, and (c) implementing consumer attraction strategies (Figure 1).

Figure 1 shows the three dimensions to the relational mediation notion in business operations. In line with the purposes of this chapter on Nigerian immigrants' informal entrepreneurs in Ghana, and the scope in this chapter, the focus is on two of the dimensions, namely: a) *response to consumer needs or customer demands*, and b) *clientele attraction.* These are discussed respectively.

Responding to Consumer Needs or Customer Demands

In any business environment, customers are the focus. However, according to Child, Dennis, Gokey, et. al. (1997), businesses are increasingly shifting from practices of just *getting* consumers/customers to

Figure 1. Three dimensions of relational mediation in business

keeping consumers/customers. But these are not exclusive practices as the process of 'keeping' consumers/customers also entails 'getting' consumers/customers. As such, central to the success of most business operations in contemporary times is the need not only to understand consumer needs or customer demands, both current and in the future (Day (2000; Carraher, Parnell & Spillan, 2009) but also to display a responsiveness to these needs and demands (Carraher, et. al, 2009). As Carraher, et. al. (2009: 243) point out, understanding the needs and demands of consumers/customers is intelligence and this should be central when forming and maintaining relationships for a sturdy and competitive advantage. Day (2000: 25) succinctly highlights this imperative for businesses to understand consumer needs and customer demands as an aim for businesses:

[they] pursue this objective by developing a deep understanding of their [consumer/customer] needs and changing requirements, then tailoring their offering to these needs as closely as possible and giving continuing incentives for the [consumer/]customer to concentrate most of their purchases with them. (p. 25)

Similarly, Du, Jiao and Tseng (2003) recognize the significance of integrating consumer/customer preferences in business operations, particularly in product or service specifications, or what they term as the 'patterns for customization and personalization' (p. 387). Additionally, customer relationship management (CRM) has emerged as one of the key strategies businesses use to respond to customer demands (Josiassen, Assaf, & Cvelbar, 2014; Keramati et al., 2010; Navimipour & Soltani, 2016). CRM is shown to be 'a technology-based management tool for developing and leveraging customer knowledge to nurture, maintain and strengthen profitable relationships with customers' (Foss et al., 2008, p. 69). This strategy forms an important part of businesses' responsive attitudes to consumer needs or customer demands, and underlies businesses' continued investment in new marketing and customer attraction strategies. Desouza, et al. (2008) place these more broadly into consumer/customer-driven innovation with an emphasis on how to leverage benefits, both actual and assumed and how to fill consumer/customer maintenance gaps.

In sum, these processes are geared towards a deeper understanding of consumers/customers to provide appropriate responses to their sentiments. They are a part of the broader understanding of 'consumer behaviour' (Du, et. al., 2003) offering useful insight into consumer/customer influences on businesses and their agency in consumption process and practices, more generally at the demand side of the demand-supply relations in business.

Employing Clientele Attraction Strategies

Most businesses including Nigerian immigrant entrepreneurships in Ghana employ several marketing strategies to win and keep clients. *Clientele attraction* is one of the marketing strategies businesses or entrepreneurs employ to grow their consumer/customer bases. Day (2000) refers to clientele attraction strategies in broad terms as 'managing market relationship'. Grönroos (2001) particularly points out that attraction constitutes offering something special or interesting other than what competitors offer, and can be based on product quality, prices, locations, or promotion. This conceptualization aligns with what Johnson and Scholes (1984) call the '4 Ps' – *price*, *product*, *place*, and *promotion*.

More recently, scholarship on clientele attraction propose six strategies by which consumers/customers are attracted (Bolton et al., 2007). The first strategy is the *co-create value* strategy. This is linked to shareholder wealth whereby businesses tend to focus on providing convenience to consumer/customers during the buying process (Berry, Seiders, & Grewal, 2002). This strategy works on the idea that when consumers/customers experience outstanding service, they tend to come back and the businesses or entrepreneurs reap profits. The second is the *customised pricing for profitability* strategy. This works on the basis of segmenting consumer needs or customer demands by offering effective customised prices. The third is *service excellence* which addresses the need for consistency in service delivery across the business chain. The fourth relates to *customer perception of service value*. This entails how businesses/entrepreneurs create awareness and assure consumers/customers of quality of products. The fifth strategy is termed *service recovery* and works on the assumption that businesses, like all human interactional fields, are fraught with problems and there is need for resolution and recovery. Thus this strategy revolves around the resolution of customer complaints in swift and prompt manner to win back clientele confidence. The final strategy is called *servicescape*, entailing the maintenance of both physical structures as well as the ambience within the business transaction environment. In relation to the latter, Morin et al. (2007) note that the presence of music in a service environment portrays a quality servicescape which offers a competitive advantage over competitors with no music.

These clientele attraction strategies, located at the supply side of the demand-supply relations in business, have diverse implications for business operation and help in understanding how Nigerian immigrants' informal entrepreneurs in Ghana attract clients. As business marketing scholarship suggests, the success of any business, including those of Nigerian immigrants in Ghana, depends on how well these attraction strategies are integrated for a functional marketing whole (Johnson & Scholes, 1984; Kotey & Meredith, 1997; Bolton et al., 2007).

METHODS

This is a multi-site study that explored Nigerian immigrant entrepreneur's understanding of the consumer needs or customer demands and supplier responses. A 7-month qualitative fieldwork was conducted in Ghana from January to July 2015 (Antwi Bosiakoh, 2017b). The fieldwork was conducted in localities in Accra, Kumasi and Ashaiman. Accra and Kumasi are the biggest cities in Ghana and are in the south and middle belts of the country, respectively. Ashaiman, is in the southern part of the country and is an emerging sub-urban settlement. Both Accra, and Kumasi are the nerve-centres of economic activities in Ghana and play host to the largest number of immigrants in Ghana. In the 2010 Population and Housing Census of Ghana, there were 600,049 foreign nationals (Ghana Statistical Services (GSS) 2013). Out of this number, eighty-six percent were from Africa, with sixty-eight percent from the regional bloc-the Economic Community of West African States (ECOWAS) (p. 206). A fifth (20.24%) of the total non-Ghanaian nationals were found in the Greater Accra region and 16.7% in the Ashanti region. A fifth (21%) of the ECOWAS nationals from Nigeria were concentrated in the Greater Accra region and close to 15% in the Ashanti region. Ashaiman on its part has become attractive to new immigrants because of the presence of other migrants, both internal and international.

The data were gathered through the use of face-to-face in-depth interviews and observational tools across the three research sites. Each interview lasted for close to one hour and observation fieldnotes were also collected. In total, 41 Nigerian immigrant entrepreneurs were interviewed and observed as per the three research sites: Accra (n= 17), Kumasi (n= 14) and Ashaiman (n= 10) (Figure 2).

The interviews were all conducted in English and audio recorded for transcription. Before the start of each interview, a consent statement was read out and respondents assured of confidentiality. Further

Figure 2. Business locations of the entrepreneurs

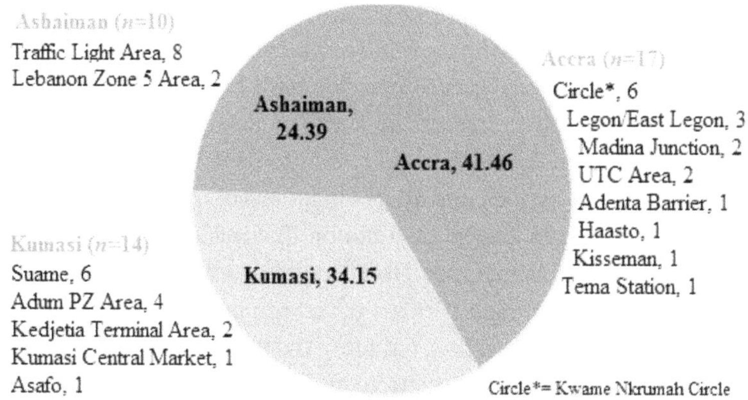

to the interviews, the businesses were observed, and field notes were taken. Most of the entrepreneurs also encouraged photos of their business to be taken. However due to adherence to ethical concerns and anonymity, these were only used for analysis purposes and are not provided with the study in this chapter. Pseudonyms are also used for the participants.

The recorded interviews with the 41 participants were transcribed following which thematic analysis (Braun & Clarke, 2006; Clarke & Braun, 2017) process was deployed to generate codes and thematic identification. As Patton (2002) advises, coded data allows for easy analysis and discussion, and in this chapter, thematic analysis allowed coding, identification and interpretation of the data and 'not simply summariz[ing] the data content' (Clarke & Braun, 2017, p. 297). Response to customer needs and clientele attraction are the two themes that formed the basis for organising and reporting the subsequent sections of the chapter on consumer demand or customer needs and clientele attraction as understood by Nigerian immigrant entrepreneurs in the context of Ghana.

CONSUMER PREFERENCES/PRACTICES AND NEEDS

The analyses of the data revealed that Nigerian immigrant entrepreneurs in Ghana showed a great depth of perspectives about their integration of diverse consumer needs into their operations in a way that suggests not only their responsiveness to these needs (Carraher, et. al, 2009) but also, and more importantly, the significant roles of consumption practices in the making/existence and sustenance of these businesses. Hence this section focuses on consumer preferences and practices, or the broader notion of consumer behaviour in the operation of Nigerian informal entrepreneurial activities in Ghana.

Majority of the Nigerian immigrant informal entrepreneurial activities that were recorded for this study showed business activities that involved phone and IT-related accessories, food-related activities and auto mobile spare parts trading activities (Antwi Bosiakoh, 2017a; 2017b). Table 1 also provides a summary of the participants' entrepreneurial activities.

The participants reflected on how as trading entrepreneurs, their specific focus needed to align with what their clients want and indeed how they demand to be treated. A number of entrepreneurs in this study shared these sentiments in diverse ways. For example, one participant who operates a CD/Electri-

Table 1. Participants' informal entrepreneurial activities

A	CD/Electricals/Phone accessories – retailers/wholesaler	15
B	Automotive spare parts dealer	6
C	Nigerian restaurant	3
D	Nigerian foodstuff/produce	3
E	Laundry	2
F	Watches – wholesaler/retailer	2
G	Sachet water vendor	1
H	Tailoring and shoemaking material vendor	1
I	Chemical store	1
J	Scrap dealer	1
K	Glass and photo framer/vendor	1
L	Metal fabricator	1
M	Second-hand bag/luggage repairer and seller	1
N	Event management	1
O	Industrial materials/hardware dealer	1
P	TVs, TV stands & tables vendor	1
Total		**41**

cals and Phone accessories shop at Lebanon Zone 5 area in Ashaiman noted that 'customers generally like to be welcomed and be treated well' (Chibueze). Similarly, many entrepreneurs constantly made a mention of 'treating customers well' as a strategy for attracting and retaining customers. Recognizing this as essential, some entrepreneurs consciously invest enormous efforts to 'build good relations' with their customers, or as some of them expressed it, they tried 'to be good to the customers'. Embedded in these narratives on 'treating customers well', 'build[ing] good relations', and trying 'to be good to the customers' is the idea that when customers have problems and they discuss them with you, the entrepreneur, you must endeavour to help them. The following is a dialogue illustrating how the entrepreneurs attempt to treat customers well by building good relations or being good to them in that sense:

Researcher: *What do you do to attract your customers?*
Achebe: *I treat my customers well.*
Researcher: *How?*
Achebe: *For instance, if someone buys a remote control from me and comes to complain that it isn't working, I apologise and change it for them. That way next time when they want to buy something, the person would come to buy from me.*

According to Achebe, treating customers well ensures that they continue to come to you whenever they need something. For some entrepreneurs, treating customers well also meant 'giving them good (reduced) price', (Bolton et al., 2007) 'interacting with them with smiling face', 'sometimes allowing very good and reliable customers to take goods on credit when they need it', and listening to customers. Bakasi understands this strategy well and explains how it applies in his business:

The way I attend to them ...the way I treat them ... the way I speak to them, etc. These things make them come back. You know it is because of them that is why I am here so I must treat them very well so that tomorrow they will come back.

This entrepreneur's recognition that the customers form the whole basis of their business is particularly edifying and directs thinking to the nexus between the need for businesses to understand consumer/ customers' needs as an objective (Day, 2000: 25) and businesses' responsiveness to these needs (Day, 2000; Carraher, et. al., 2009). On her part, Chimamanda who operates a laundry in Accra, acknowledges that customers have a far more structuring impact on her business. She points out that as a business person, she listens carefully to customers and incorporates customer suggestions into her business strategies. This is a typical instance of what is identified in the literature as co-creation (Bolton et al., 2007).

Similar to Chimamanda's approach to incorporating customer's ideas into her business, Chetachukwu, a phone accessories shop owner, also told of how she listens to find out what customers need or ask for and tries to incorporate them into the portfolio of items in his business. He explains that by so doing, he 'moves [his business] with the changing needs of the customers'. Therefore, for these entrepreneurs, in listening to customers (Chimamanda) and acting on what customers say (Chetachukwu), they appear to operationalise what Udoka, another entrepreneur succinctly referred to as 'knowing what the market really wants' and 'being as creative as possible to capitalise on it'. Jibola, operator of wholesaling and retailing watch shops, metaphorically likened this situation and his own business operations to the operation of a fuel pump station, emphasizing the need of businesses to reflect customer consumption inclines:

Well, I believe this business is like a petrol station. If you don't have petrol, nobody will come to your station. If you have it and other stations don't have, even if you are far off, everybody will drive to buy from you.

In a similar vein, Obinna, an auto-spare parts trader, noted his business is first, a response to what customers want: '... if you don't have the goods..., the ones that the customers want, they will not come in the first place for you to treat them well'. Therefore, the arguments by Jibola and Obinna call for a reconsideration of the place of 'treating the customer well' strategy in the operation of these immigrant's informal businesses in Ghana. In line with this, some entrepreneurs noted that treating customers well is important, but as a business person the first thing is to have what the customers need as this is what will bring them to the business in the first place. Obinna concedes, however, that business people need more than this to sustain customers coming to the business. He identifies the need for character and a positive attitude of treating them well (Berry, Seiders, & Grewal, 2002), especially if other businesses also have what the customers need. Nnamdi, for instance, operates a Nigerian restaurant and knows there are other Nigerian restaurants located at where he operates. So, abiding by Obinna's admonition, he has subscribed to a digital satellite television that broadcasts general entertainment programmes, including movies, lifestyle and culture, sports, documentaries, news and commerce, children, music, religion, among others. Additionally, Nnamdi has a betting game right inside his restaurant which he says responds to some other needs of his customers. Emerging from these accounts by the entrepreneurs is the view that, their businesses respond to consumption preference regimes of customers. Here is a direct association between consumption behaviour and businesses' response attempts which are conceptually embedded in co-creation (Bolton et al., 2007; Berry, Seiders, & Grewal, 2002).

A key dimension to how some Nigerian informal entrepreneurs in Ghana respond to the needs of their customers is to offer 'quality goods'. This relates to what Du, Jiao and Tseng (2003: 387) recognize as the attempt to integrate customer quality specifications and preferences in business operations in product or service offering. Chetachukwu offers important insight into this situation: 'I give them [the customers] the right goods … the original ones', and explains further that as a result, his customers 'trust what they buy' from him. He continues that even though there are instances where his prices are a bit higher than what others offer, when the customers try his goods, 'they keep coming back. They get to know the quality and it is the quality of the goods that sustains this business'. For these entrepreneurs, this builds trust in their business and creates good customer perception of service value (Bolton et al., 2007). Obike is another such entrepreneur. He believes the 'quality' of items he offers is his way of responding to what customers want. His business involves going to Nigeria on a weekly/fortnight basis to bring Nigerian foodstuffs to Ghana for retail. He emphasizes on the time he takes to ensure that his goods are properly preserved to maintain freshness.

[I] take time to preserve the vegetables well so when they [customers] come and they see it as exactly as what is in Nigeria, they are happy and patronise it. That is why our goods come every week and always fresh.

This process in his particular business operation ensures service excellence and consistency in product offering.

CLIENTELE ATTRACTIONS STRATEGIES

The Nigerian immigrant entrepreneurs of focus in this study show a keen understanding of their clientele as evidenced in their use of specific clientele attraction strategies for running their businesses successfully. The examples they provided are mainly promotional and advertisement strategies which can be seen as conventional or technology mediated. Promotion and advertisement strategies are a vital part of the overall marketing mix. They are needed for the promotion of visibility for businesses and for the stimulation of sales and business growth (Belch & Belch, 2007). The entrepreneurs deploy such strategies to attract and maintain customers, promote their businesses, win consumer loyalty and the support of customers and their networks within the general society. The promotional and advertisement techniques that they reveal in their interviews are topicalised and discussed next under the two subsections: conventional strategies and technology-mediated promotions.

Conventional Strategies

In most developing countries including Ghana, the context of this study, traditional methods of advertising including hand-painted artwork and wooden signs (see Djossa, 2018) continue to be the main strategy employed by the informal economy to draw clientele attention. In this study, five conventional methods of advertising and promotion are deployed by the entrepreneurs, namely word of mouth, face-to-face interactions between the entrepreneurs and prospective customers in the vicinity of the shop or at social gatherings signage, flyers/brochures/business cards, TV/radio, and on-site item display strategies. Arguments in favour of such traditional methods of advertising outline their advantages over *online* methods and point out how they will continue to be of relevance regardless of the strengths of online methods (Hanekom & Scriven, 2002; Markham, Gatlin-Watts & Bounds, 2001). In line with this notion, some scholars observe that online advertising methods are best used to supplement conventional methods (Karimova, 2011; Markham, et. al., 2001) and they are 'no substitute' to conventional strategies (Bonello, 2000, [cf. Hanekom & Scriven, 2002, p. 55]).

For those with small-scale business types such as sachet water vending or Nigerian foodstuff/produce selling, word of mouth was the most prominent approach. For example, Adamma, a small-scale sachet water vendor explained that her approach to promoting her business has been to talk to people about her 'ice-cold water'. Her strategy involved talking to anyone, including those who happen to walk past her container shop and owners of cars that are parked near her shop. She also had a good relationship with the several girls who retail her water for discounts – 'I come to their level' to 'promote my water'. Another participant, this time a Phone and IT Accessories seller described his word of mouth strategy as follows:

I go around telling people ... I use word of mouth to tell [people] what I do. (Ezediugwu)

Among them, the one with the most strategies was in the Events Management business and his strategies included radio and television appearances. In this business, the respondent reiterated that they do promotion on the radio and television' and 'sometimes the promotion is verbal through conversation with people to introduce the business and ask them to give it a try' (Kelechi). Kelechi further explained that his verbal approach is at its best during social gatherings. He identified the church and association meetings as places where he attended to distribute business flyers and also engage in conversation with people. Similarly, and to promote her Nigerian foodstuff/produce business Oluchi said she attended almost every Nigerian social event in Kumasi and sometimes outside of Kumasi. At each event, her approach has been to 'tell people about her business'.

The second conventional approach is the use of signage. Most entrepreneurs placed standing wooden or metal board in front of or near their businesses. In some cases, the signboard was fixed to the upper frontage of the business/shop. Typically, on the signboard, an arrow pointed to the business/shop. These signs usually have the basic details of the business – the name, products or services offered and phone number(s). Like the word-of-mouth strategy, signboard advertising was often combined with other strategies.

[I] have signboard, flyers, and business cards that [I] give to people and ask them to share with their friends. (Obike)

Several other participants also spoke about placing billboards with business details at strategic locations. Of them also mentioned using flyers, brochures, and business cards to promote their businesses. The following are quotes of the entrepreneurs on the deployment of these strategies:

I have business cards and flyers ... (Kelechi)

I have brochures and flyers that I distribute to people to promote my business. (Onyekachi)

[I] always give my business cards to customers. (Oladele)

I have business cards to direct people to my business. (Udoka)

Further to these testaments, advertisement was also done through networks or friends. For example, one participant, pointed out that being aware of the ethnic nature of his business – the fact that he provides Nigerian-specific menus in his restaurant, the promotional strategy involved taking business cards and flyers to social programmes (church and association meetings where he meets friends and ethnic people) for distribution. The friends are expected to give out his business cards/flyers to their own friends, and so on and so forth. According to this restaurateur, this strategy works well as he often receives calls from people he never knows asking for directions to his restaurant.

Some entrepreneurs also promoted their businesses on Radio FM stations, in newspapers and on televisions. Onyekachi is one such business person. His advertisements are interesting for one reason – the fact that even though his business is in Accra, he not only advertises on Accra-based FM radios but also on the Tema-based Adom FM station, and together with the newspaper and television advertisements, the visibility of Onyekachi's business extends beyond Accra to far-off places wherever these advertising media reach. Similarly, Eze, advertises his auto spare parts business not only on the Ashaiman-based Sena Radio, but also on one of Accra's top FM stations, Joy FM and Adom FM in Tema.

Another participant's CD/Electrical/Phone Accessories business is promoted on television in a different way. As movie/music CDs and electrical accessories merchant, Chibueze noted that the music and movie CDs are not his personal products. The owners are the producers and so it was their role to advertise and promote their products on radio and television.

...these are not my personal goods. They belong to some other people and I am selling them. I am therefore here just to sell them. (Chibueze)

So to utilize such 'free promotion' Chibueze has located his business at a 'good' place for customers to find him. Thus after the customers have seen or heard about the movies or songs on TV and radio, his business would then be easy to be found by the customers. Therefore, for Chibueze, the location of one's business is equally important to any conventional business promotion or advertising strategy.

Others such as Achebe who is in the same business line as Chibueze said that in addition to locating his business at a 'good place', playing some of the music on large sound-speakers forms and important part of the promotion strategy.

I think it is the music I play that advertises for me. When people hear it, they come and buy. That is how I promote my business. (Achebe)

Location is also temporal, that is, it is connected to duration of the business being in operation. Osita argued that his business had been located at the Ashaiman Traffic Light Area for a long time and many customers know him. In this way, location is connected to duration of stay which together promote the business. Other entrepreneurs noted this important feature of business location and how this also links to the display of goods for advertising the business as follows:

In this place ... when we display our goods, people passing around see them and patronise us. (Osuofia)

Perhaps a more direct location-specific advertisement/promotion is provided by Nwafor:

I am located where people know these things are sold ... that when they come around they can get all their phone accessories. That is the place I am located so people come around and enter shops asking about one product or the other and if we have, we sell to them. (Nwafor)

Technology-Mediated Strategies

Besides the conventional strategies discussed above, technology mediated strategies in the current digital age play a huge role in how the entrepreneurs of focus in this study promoted their businesses. The internet provides an important space where these entrepreneurs regardless of their developing world context situation, keep abreast with trends in the present digital age. Some entrepreneurs in developing countries including most of the ones under focus for this chapter, deploy technology-mediated business promotion strategies. These are online-based social media platforms as advertisement mediums. The three most notable strategies the Nigerian immigrant entrepreneurs mentioned in their interviews are the use of internet advertising, Facebook advertisements, and WhatsApp. Below are two exemplary descriptions about the use of these technology-mediated advertisement techniques for business promotion.

Nigerians in Kumasi here have a forum – the Nigerian Youth Association (NYA) with a Facebook account and I am one of the admins, so anything that happens here I post it for them to see. When we make order from Nigeria for vegetables, we get them posted there. So yes, I advertise on Facebook, etc. (Nnamdi)

We have marketers of advertising companies coming into our office to help us with advertisement. We are thus on the OLX Ghana online platform ... we also have electronic signboards to promote the business. (Chimamanda)

Nnamdi and Chimamanda's descriptions are part of the broad episodes of how some entrepreneurs utilise web-based tools to achieve positive, fast and efficient business advertising goals. Nnamdi's Facebook posts and Chimamanda's presence on the OXL Ghana online platform provide visibility for their businesses to thousands of people logging onto those platforms on daily basis. Additionally, Nnamdi's experience shows elements of a positive digital-age instrumentality through his effective use of Facebook as an advertising tool. And Chimamanda employs the services of professional marketing managers to help with her business advertisement on the OXL Ghana online platform, other entrepreneurs use 'business photos' as their WhatsApp profile pictures. This way, friends and customers who have the business number and are also on WhatsApp see this photo and 'thus maintain the business presence on the phones of these friends and customers'. In Figure 3, we provide several narrative voices of the entrepreneurs on how their businesses draw on the internet, WhatsApp and Facebook.

As shown in Figure 3, several entrepreneurs use web and technology-based tools not only to attract their customers but also to facilitate business transactions with suppliers and their customers. For example, the use of WhatsApp facilitated communication with suppliers and customers, for sending and receiving product orders, as well as for promoting business. For immigrant entrepreneurs involved in largely informal entrepreneurial activities, the deployment of these advertising and operational strategies appears interesting from a mixed embedded point of view. This is particularly so in reference to the existence of the *permissive environment* of internet and mobile services platforms, and the ways in which this environment interacts with the endowed *social capital* characteristic of the entrepreneurs. According to Internet World Statistics[1], Ghana with a population of about 29 million, has a total internet penetration

Figure 3. Internet, Facebook and WhatsApp usage in the operations of the entrepreneurs' businesses

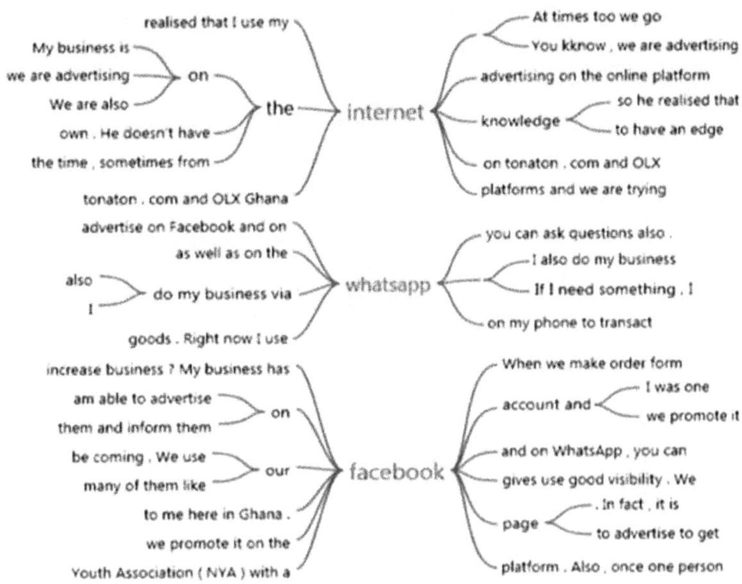

of 34.3% (Internet World Statistics, 2018). Additionally, there is a high mobile voice subscriber base, 132% as at April 2016 (National Communication Authority [NCA], 2016). This internet penetration and mobile voice subscription base allow the entrepreneurs to deploy various internet/technology-mediated strategies for their business operation and advertising. For example, the high mobile voice subscribers base suggests potential mobile money services accounts that can be registered and operated. This context of internet penetration and mobile subscriber base serve well, the interest of the entrepreneurs, many of whom (82.9%)[2] have high social capital in the form of education – secondary level of schooling or better – which they draw on for their businesses.

DISCUSSION AND CONCLUSION

This chapter has explored consumer behaviour in a developing nation from the perspectives of Nigerian immigrant entrepreneurs in Ghana. The chapter has provided insights about the entrepreneurs' understanding of their customers/consumers' needs and demands, and their business' responses to these in the context of their operations in Ghana. Drawing on two aspects of the notion of relational mediation in business operations, namely, responding to consumer needs or customer demand, and clientele attraction strategies, the chapter shows what the participants do to keep their businesses thriving. Earlier studies have stressed that in the developing country contexts where there is an absence of professional marketing agents, certain key components of advertising and promotion may not be present for businesses (Ahmad & Saber, 2015). While there is ongoing debate about the ability of some enterprises to pursue comprehensive marketing strategies because of the absence of professional marketing managers (Law & Ng, 2011; Yolal, Emeksiz, & Cetinel, 2009), the interviews with the Nigerian immigrant entrepreneurs within this study exemplify comprehensive understanding of customer demands and promotional and advertising practices. They utilise these strategies profitably without resorting to professional marketing managers. Our participants have shared experiences that show how they use both traditional approaches and contemporary available tools in the current digital age to meet customer demands and consumer needs. Previous studies have also shown how operation in informal economies reflects mixed-embededness (Antwi Bosiakoh & Williams Tetteh, 2018; Kloosterman, 2010). This chapter finds this to be the case for the participants in the study who are mostly part of the informal economy, and outside the formal sector. In this sector, actors/operators often tend to be vulnerable and face difficulties keeping the business enterprises viable and relevant to the niche markets made up mostly of ethnic consumers and mainstream clientele. They put in tremendous effort to build their clientele base for the diverse enterprises they operate. The narratives from the entrepreneurs show their keen recognition of all these expectations and challenges and it is in these expectation/challenge contexts that they have embedded their businesses.

In conclusion and more significantly, the chapter contributes to a better understanding of businesses in the developing world context in their current forms and provides nuanced insights into how they hold together and prospects for the future. Also, the study holds potential for more studies on consumerism in the developing world, particularly those engineered by immigrants and these can be comparative with the study in this chapter. This chapter has implications for the need to focus on different immigrant groups to help understand the ways in which the different groups of immigrant business operatives respond to consumer needs and demands. Finally, the chapter makes contribution to knowledge about structures and consumption practices that make the existence of such businesses in the developing world possible as well as their relevance in the global market-place in the present digital age. Going into the future, this study paves the way and hold potential for a more in-depth and comprehensive study about consumer behaviour towards immigrant businesses in Ghana and in the broader developing world context.

REFERENCES

Adepoju, A. (2003). Migration in West Africa. *Development*, *46*(3), 37–41. doi:10.1177/10116370030463006

Ahmad, S. Z., & Saber, H. (2015). Understanding marketing strategies with particular reference to small- and medium-sized hotel businesses in the United Arab Emirates. *Tourism and Hospitality Research, 15*(2), 115–129. doi:10.1177/1467358414567799

Amenumey, D. E. K. (2008). *Ghana: A Concise History from Pre-Colonial Times to the 20th Century.* Accra: Woeli Publishing Services.

Anquandah, J. (1985). *Ethnoarchaeological Clues to Ghana's Great Past and – A Greater Future? University of Ghana Monographs and papers in African Archaeology, No. 2.* Department of Archaeology, University of Ghana.

Antwi Bosiakoh, T. (2017a). Nigerian Immigrant Entrepreneurs in Contemporary Ghana: Insights on Locational/Sectoral Niches and Inter-Generational (Dis) Continuities. *Urban Forum*, *28*(2), 143-163.

Antwi Bosiakoh, T. (2017b). *Mixed embeddedness and Nigerian immigrants' informal entrepreneurship in Ghana* (PhD thesis). Macquarie University, Sydney, Australia.

Antwi Bosiakoh, T., & Williams Tetteh, V. (2018). Nigerian immigrant women's entrepreneurial embeddedness in Ghana, West Africa. *International Journal of Gender and Entrepreneurship*, IJGE-05-2018-0043. doi:10.1108/IJGE-05-2018-0043

Arhin, K. (1979). *West African Traders in Ghana in the Nineteenth and Twentieth Centuries*. London: Longman.

Belch, G. E., & Belch, M. A. (2007). Advertising and Promotion (7th ed.). McGraw Hill/Irwin.

Berry, L. L., Seiders, K., & Grewal, D. (2002). Understanding service convenience. *Journal of Marketing*, *66*(3), 1–17. doi:10.1509/jmkg.66.3.1.18505

Boahen, A. A. (1977). Ghana before the coming of the Europeans. *Ghana Social Science Journal*, *4*(2), 93–106.

Bolton, R. N., Grewal, D., & Levy, M. (2007). Six strategies for competing through service: An agenda for future research. *Journal of Retailing*, *83*(1), 1–4. doi:10.1016/j.jretai.2006.11.001

Braun, V., & Clarke, V. (2006). Using thematic analysis in psychology. *Qualitative Research in Psychology*, *3*(2), 77–101. doi:10.1191/1478088706qp063oa

Carraher, S., Parnell, J. A., & Spillan, J. E. (2009). Customer service-orientation of small retail business owners in Austria, the Czech Republic, Hungary, Latvia, Slovakia, and Slovenia. *Baltic Journal of Management*, *4*(3), 251–268. doi:10.1108/17465260910990975

Child, P., Dennis, R. J., Gokey, T. C., McGuire, T. I., Sherman, M., & Singer, M. (1997). Can Marketing Regain the Personal Touch? *The McKinsey Quarterly*, *3*, 112–125.

Clarke, V., & Braun, V. (2017). Thematic analysis. *The Journal of Positive Psychology*, *12*(3), 297–298. doi:10.1080/17439760.2016.1262613

Davies, O. (1966). *The Invasion of Ghana from the Sahara in the Early Iron Age. Volta Basin Research Project Publication No. 18*. Reprint from Actes Du V Congres PanAfricain De Pre-Histoire Et De L'etde Du Quarternaire.

Day, G. S. (2000). Managing market relationships. *Journal of the Academy of Marketing Science*, *28*(1), 24–30. doi:10.1177/0092070300281003

DeCorse, C. R. (2001). *An Archaeology of Elmina: Africans and Europeans on the Gold Coast, 1400-1900*. Smithsonian Institute Press.

Djossa, C. A. (2018). *Celebrating Ghana's amazing handpainted barbershop signs: These vibrant artworks advertised the freshest styles and sleekest cuts*. Retrieved from: https://www.atlasobscura.com/articles/ghana-artists-paintings-wooden-signs

Du, X., Jiao, J., & Tseng, M. M. (2003). Identifying customer need patterns for customization and personalization. *Integrated Manufacturing Systems*, *14*(5), 387–396. doi:10.1108/09576060310477799

Eades, J. S. (1994). *Strangers and Traders: Yoruba Migrants, Markets and the State in Northern Ghana*. Trenton, NJ: Africa World Press Incorporated.

Foss, B., Stone, M., & Ekinci, Y. (2008). What makes for CRM system success—Or failure? *Journal of Database Marketing & Customer Strategy Management*, *15*(2), 68–78. doi:10.1057/dbm.2008.5

Ghana Statistical Service (GSS). (2013). *2010 Population and Housing Census: National Report*. Accra: Ghana Statistical Service.

Granovetter, M. (1985). Economic action and social structure: The problem of embeddedness. *American Journal of Sociology*, *91*(3), 481–510. doi:10.1086/228311

Gro¨nroos, C. (2001). *Service Management and Marketing: A Customer Relationship Management Approach*. Chichester, UK: Wiley.

Hanekom, J., & Scriven, C. (2002). Traditional and online advertising: An explanation of current and future trends. *Communication*, *28*(1), 49–59.

Harvey, M. E., & Brand, R. R. (1974). The spatial allocation of migrants in Accra, Ghana. *Geographical Review*, *64*(1), 1–30. doi:10.2307/213792

Hill, P. (1970). The Occupations of Migrants in Ghana. Anthropological Papers, No. 42: Ann Arbor, MI: Museum of Anthropology, University of Michigan.

Internet World Statistics. (2018). *Internet Users Statistics for Africa*. Retrieved from http://www.internetworldstats.com/stats1.htm#africa

Jahoda, G. (1961). *White man: A study of the attitudes of Africans to Europeans in Ghana before independence*. Oxford University Press.

Johnson, G., & Scholes, K. (1984). *Exploring Corporate Strategy*. London: Prentice-Hall International.

Josiassen, A., Assaf, A. G., & Cvelbar, L. K. (2014). CRM and the bottom line: Do all CRM dimensions affect firm performance? *International Journal of Hospitality Management*, *36*, 130–136. doi:10.1016/j.ijhm.2013.08.005

Kalitanyi, V., & Visser, K. (2010). African immigrants in South Africa: Job takers or job creators? *South African Journal of Economic and Management Sciences*, *13*(4), 376–390. doi:10.4102ajems.v13i4.91

Karimova, G. Z. (2011). Interactivity and Advertising Communication. *Journal of Media and Communication Studies*, *3*(5), 160–169.

Keramati, A., Mehrabi, H., & Mojir, N. (2010). A process-oriented perspective on customer relationship management and organizational performance: An empirical investigation. *Industrial Marketing Management*, *39*(7), 1170–1185. doi:10.1016/j.indmarman.2010.02.001

Kloosterman, R. C. (2010). Matching opportunities with resources: A framework for analyzing (migrant) entrepreneurship from a mixed embeddedness perceptive. *Entrepreneurship and Regional Development*, *22*(1), 25–45. doi:10.1080/08985620903220488

Kobo, O. (2010). 'We are citizens too': The politics of citizenship in independent Ghana. *The Journal of Modern African Studies*, *48*(1), 67–94. doi:10.1017/S0022278X0999022X

Kotey, B., & Meredith, G. G. (1997). Relationships among owner/manager personal values, business strategies, and enterprise performance. *Journal of Small Business Management*, *35*(2), 37–64.

Law, R., & Ng, C. (2011). Marketing strategies for small hotels: The case of Cheung Chau in Hong Kong. *Asia Pacific Journal of Tourism Research, 16*(1), 21–38. doi:10.1080/10941665.2011.539389

Markham, S., Gatlin-Watts, R., & Bounds, W. (2001). Internet advertising vs. traditional advertising: The current situation. *Journal of Promotion Management, 6*(1-2), 3–17. doi:10.1300/J057v06n01_02

Massing, A. W. (2000). The Wangara, an Old Soninke Diaspora in West Africa? *Cahiers d'Etudes Africaines, 40*(158), 281–308. doi:10.4000/etudesafricaines.175

Mberu, B. U., & Pongou, R. (2010). *Nigeria: multiple forms of mobility in Africa's demographic giant.* Retrieved from http://www.migrationpolicy.org/article/nigeria-multipleforms-mobility-africas-demographic-giant

Morin, S., Dubé, L., & Chebat, J.-C. (2007). The role of pleasant music in servicescapes: A test of the dual model of environmental perception. *Journal of Retailing, 83*(1), 115–130. doi:10.1016/j.jretai.2006.10.006

Navimipour, N. J., & Soltani, Z. (2016). The impact of cost, technology acceptance and employees' satisfaction on the effectiveness of the electronic customer relationship management systems. *Computers in Human Behavior, 55*, 1052–1066. doi:10.1016/j.chb.2015.10.036

NCA. (2016). *Industry information telecom subscriptions for April, 2016.* Accra: National Communication Authority.

Olatuyi, A., Awoyinka, Y., & Adeniyi, A. (2013). *Nigerian diasporas in the South: Harnessing the potential for national development.* Research Report No. ACPOBS/2013/PUB06. ACP Observatory on Migration and International Organization for Migration.

Orozco, M., & Mills, M. (2007). *Remittances, competition and fair financial access opportunities in Nigeria.* Washington, DC: USAID.

Palmatier, R. W., Dant, R. P., Grewal, D., & Evans, K. R. (2006). Factors Influencing the Effectiveness of Relationship Marketing: A Meta-Analysis. *Journal of Marketing, 70*(October), 136–153. doi:10.1509/jmkg.70.4.136

Palmatier, R. W., Jarvis, C. B., Bechkoff, J. R., & Kardes, F. R. (2009). The Role of Customer Gratitude in Relationship Marketing. *Journal of Marketing, 73*(September), 1–18. doi:10.1509/jmkg.73.5.1

Patton, M. (2002). *Qualitative Research and Evaluation Methods* (3rd ed.). Thousand Oaks, CA: Sage.

Peil, M. (1974). Ghana's aliens. *The International Migration Review, 8*(3), 367–381. doi:10.1177/019791837400800303

Rath, J. (2000). *Immigrant business: The economic political, and social environment.* New York, NY: St. Martin's Press. doi:10.1057/9781403905338

Twum-Baah, K. A. (2005). Volume and characteristics of international Ghanaian migration. In T. Manuh (Ed.), *At home in the world? International migration and development in contemporary Ghana and West Africa* (pp. 55–77). Accra: Sub-Saharan Publishers.

Yolal, M., Emeksiz, M., & Cetinel, F. (2009). Marketing of SMHEs in Turkey: A comparative analysis. *Journal of Hospitality Marketing & Management, 18*(4), 372–385. doi:10.1080/19368620902799577

ENDNOTES

1 Internet World Stats – http://www.internetworldstats.com/stats1.htm#africa Accessed 1/7/2016 at 11:05am.

2 The breakdown is as follows: Secondary level (41.4%); Post-secondary including 'O' level and diploma (12.2%); and Tertiary (29.3%).

Chapter 16
Consumerism and Entrepreneurial Opportunity:
The Case of MMM

Adedayo Abinusawa
University of East London, UK

ABSTRACT

Despite significant research on consumerism, little is known about its impact on entrepreneurial opportunity production. Where existing literature focuses on describing consumerism, this chapter investigates how consumerism can influence the production of entrepreneurial opportunity for some. The case study of Mavrodi Mundial Movement (MMM) is examined from secondary data sources (such as articles, journals, magazines, etc.) to obtain historical information. The analysis shows that by understanding consumerism, the individuals behind MMM were able to produce and exploit an entrepreneurial opportunity in different markets.

INTRODUCTION

Consumerism, according to Wright and Rogers (2015), is the belief that personal well-being, to a large extent, depends on higher levels of consumption. This statement builds on Goodwin et al.'s (2008) argument that to say that some people have consumerist values or attitudes means that they always want to consume more, and that they find meaning and satisfaction in life, to a large extent, through the purchase of new consumer goods. This belief has inspired social movements seeking to increase the rights and power of buyers in relation to sellers (Kotler, 1971). There have been three key waves of anti-consumerism in modern times: the first emphasises value for money, information and labelling; the second stresses investigative anti-corporate work; the third focuses on global issues (New & Ramsay, 1997). These have been driven by the long history of organisations incorporating emancipatory ideals into marketing campaigns, often with limited transformative outcomes (Gbadamosi et al., 2018; Johnston & Taylor, 2008).

Entrepreneurs (i.e. entrepreneurial individuals and firms) can have transformative impact. Acs et al. (2013) illustrate this point in their paper on 'the social value of productive entrepreneurship'. They

DOI: 10.4018/978-1-5225-7906-9.ch016

showed that enterprises have had a profound impact on the world. Entrepreneurs can impact consumerism because where the market is not in equilibrium, profit opportunities exist, and entrepreneurs discover and act on these profit opportunities to equilibrate the market (Holcombe, 2003). By understanding consumerism, and societal concerns, entrepreneurs can produce better entrepreneurial opportunities. For example, Barksdale & Darden (1972) show that as public concern regarding consumer issues increases, the consumer forms definite opinions about business policies and practices, the consumerism movement, and government legislation. Hence, where consumer demand and market deficiencies exist, the entrepreneur, if s/he is to be successful, must fill in for them (Burg, Podoynitsyna, Beck, & Lommelen, 2012; Leibenstein, 1968). However, little is known about the linkages between consumerism and entrepreneurial opportunity. It is this gap in knowledge that this chapter aims to address.

THEORITICAL BACKGROUND

The Concept of Consumerism

Consumerism, the notion that personal well-being to a large extent depends on higher levels of consumption, has eroded pervasive value systems that were well established before the eighteenth century in various societies around the world (Stearns, 2006). None of these societies provided a fertile ground for consumerism, as widespread consumerism did not exist, particularly as some of them were quite hostile to any potential consumerism (Day & Aaker, 1970; Stearns, 2006; Trentmann, 2004). Businesses have long sought to address the negative impacts of consumerism by developing products and marketing practices that combine short and long term consumer values (Kotler, 1971); however, where consumerism leads to overconsumption and unacceptable levels of inappropriate social behaviour, it is detrimental to both business and society (Yani-de-Soriano & Slater, 2009). Consumerism is strongly associated with wealth and inequality. For instance, Schor (2002) describes consumerism as an unusually large increase in the dominant norm of consumer aspiration. She suggests that the previously dominant norm of comfort has been replaced by a norm of affluence or luxury. In structural terms, this can be described as a shift to a situation in which the upper 20% of the income and wealth distribution (whose consumer patterns are roughly synonymous with affluence and luxury) become a widespread emulative target throughout the society (Schor, 2002). In fact, this indicates that majority of society has shifted from being content with little, to being discontent with much. As affluence increases, it breeds consumerism and impatience thereby undermining wellbeing (Offer, 2006). Therefore, despite widespread recognition of the relationship between diet, exercise and heart disease, the flow of food, the immediacy of pleasure, and associations between appetite and health override latent concerns about the negative impacts of dietary excesses on long-term health and chronic illness (Wilson, 2010). Consequently, although individual prosperity and consumerism may be encouraged, there is a sense that this prosperity will be curtailed in the presence of social calamity, because if things were going well for an individual, it is of little consolation if the person's family, friends, and community are in crises (Jackson, 2010).

The concept of consumerism has multiple meanings, many of which are heavily value-laden (Shaw & Aldrigde, 2003). Many scholars follow the illustrations outlined by Peter Drucker (1969) and Philip Kotler (1971), who focused on the opportunity consumerism provided for marketing (Buskirk & Rothe, 1970; Jolibert & Baumgartner, 1981; Yani-de-Soriano & Slater, 2009). They suggest two main opposing theories about the role of the consumer in the market place of a free enterprise system. One theory suggests that the consumer is king. Birmingham (1969) argues that the consumer is at least as much a sovereign as Queen Elizabeth II of England, as it is their monetary choice in the market that decides the success or failure of producers. An opposing argument suggests that the consumer is a pawn (Buskirk & Rothe, 1970). This view is based on the idea that research conducted by skilled behavioural scientists, have been used to deceive the consumer to the extent that s/he is incapable of intelligent selection (Buskirk & Rothe, 1970). Hence, their monetary influence is illogical and cannot impact production of goods and or services in the marketplace.

Drucker (1969) and Kotler (1971) both took a marketing approach, where the consumer is viewed as the dominant force since their purchase determines market success for competing firms (Buskirk & Rothe, 1970). Unlike other researchers (Johnston & Taylor, 2008), Drucker (1969) and Kotler (1971) do not describe marketing as a means to deceive the consumer, but as an effective engine of economic development, particularly in its ability to support development of sustainable products and services that address socio-economic challenges (Drucker, 1958; Kotler, 2011). Therefore, the understanding of consumerism need not be limited to over-consumption but can also support the development and sustainability of positive value systems in society. In essence, good consumerism can be prescribed. Adams & DeBont (2007) illustrate this point by showing that there is a new type of consumer, one that is reflexive and informed, with highly specified information needs and perceptions, as well as highly developed skills and tactics for acquiring information. They suggest that individuals must be assisted by firms to develop skills for reflexive consumerism. This depiction of consumerism is underpinned by the idea that an individual's prosperity and the prosperity of those around him/her are intertwined (Jackson, 2010).

In as much as a shift towards more sustainable consumption patterns are required (Tanner & Sybille, 2003), many firms struggle to identify new business opportunities aligned to consumer movements typical of consumerism (Prothero et al., 2011; Sanne, 2002). These opportunities include those associated with addressing sustainability challenges that pervade our societies (Prothero et al., 2011; Sanne, 2002) – for example, diet and health challenges (Wilson, 2010). Redefining consumerism could encompass the belief that personal wellbeing depends to a large extent on consumption that benefits the individual and his/her society. Consumerism, defined this way, deviates from the suggestion that consumption is detrimental to business and society, and leads to overconsumption and unacceptable levels of inappropriate social behaviour (Yani-de-Soriano & Slater, 2009). The redefinition of consumerism can be driven by socially conscious entrepreneurs and innovators who might be keen to play a role in addressing serious social problems while enhancing social wealth (Zahra, Rawhouser, Bhawe, Neubaum, & Hayton, 2008); thereby reducing the potential tension between social, profit (Marshall, 2011), and entrepreneurial opportunity objectives.

The Concept of Entrepreneurial Opportunity

In his book *Entrepreneurial Opportunity Recognition through Social Networks*, Robert Singh (2000) defined entrepreneurial opportunity as a feasible, profit-seeking, potential venture that provides an innovative new product or service to the market, improves on an existing product/service, or imitates a profitable product/service in a less-than-saturated market. Singh shows that for an opportunity to exist and be a construct capable of examination, it must be identifiable before the venture is founded and success is gained. In essence, an entrepreneur's personality traits, social networks, and prior knowledge are antecedents of entrepreneurial alertness to business opportunities (Ardichvili, Cardozo, & Ray, 2003). To produce entrepreneurial opportunity (see Figure 1), it proceeds through several stages, including conceptualization of an opportunity idea by an entrepreneur, objectification of that idea, and enactment of the opportunity into a new venture (Wood & Mckinley, 2010). However, not all opportunity ideas survive this full process, as between the conceptualization stage and the objectification stage, some ideas are abandoned due to inadequate objectification, and some objectified opportunities are abandoned due to insufficient resource support, between the objectification stage and the enactment stage (Wood & Mckinley, 2010).

Some research on individual aspects of entrepreneurial opportunity production includes work on conceptualisation of an opportunity idea (DeKoning & Muzyka, 1999; Shane, 2000), opportunity objectification (Giones, Zhou, Miralles, & Katzy, 2013), objectified opportunity and opportunity abandonment (Weick, 1995), opportunity enactment (Alvarez & Barney, 2014), consensus among knowledgeable peers, entrepreneur's social ties, and entrepreneur's reputation (Shane & Cable, 2002; Tocher, Oswald, & Hall, 2015). Vasilchenko & Morrish (2011) support this view by showing that established and newly formed social networks can be instrumental in the exploration (opportunity seeking) of entrepreneurial opportunities, as they potentially lead to collaborative cooperation and form part of an entrepreneur's broader business network that facilitates exploitation (advantage seeking) of business opportunities culminated by successful entry into new markets. Although the effect of exploration and exploitation cannot be fully captured through their direct effects on profit performance, strategic learning plays a mediating role in enabling the dissemination, interpretation, and implementation of both exploration and exploitation strategies (Siren, Kohtamaki, & Kuckertz, 2012). To better understand how entrepreneurial opportunity emerges, Suddaby, Bruton, & Si (2015) identified two key themes. The first theme is the unique role of imprinting, or the profound influence of social and historical context in constraining the perceptual apparatus of entrepreneurs and delimiting the range of opportunities for innovation available to them. Second, their analysis offers insight into the counterbalancing role of reflexivity, operating at both individual and collective levels of analysis, in generating the ability of entrepreneurs to overcome the constraints of imprinting. A better understanding of how social challenges and consumerism affect processes such as entrepreneurial opportunity production would therefore be useful in theory and practice. Therefore, the next section investigates the role of consumerism in the emergence of entrepreneurial opportunity.

Figure 1. The production of entrepreneurial opportunity
(Adapted from Wood and McKinley, 2010)

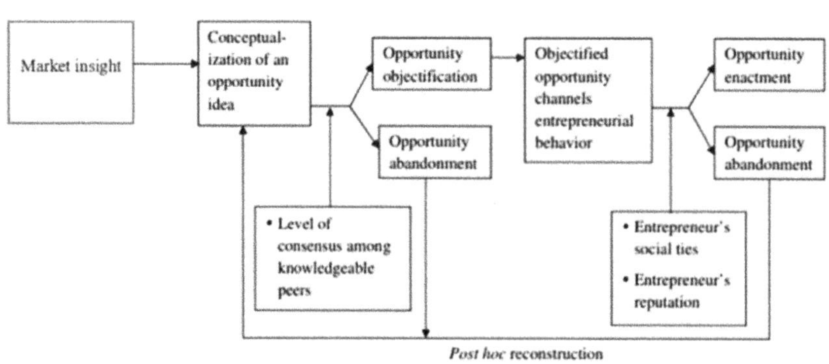

Consumerism and Entrepreneurial Opportunity

Several studies have proposed to draw on consumerism for entrepreneurial opportunity (Drayton, 2002; Hockerts & Wüstenhagen, 2010; Thompson, Kiefer, & York, 2011; Zahra et al., 2008). Relevant studies include Hockerts & Wüstenhagen's (2010) analysis of the interplay between incumbents and new entrants, and how it is their compounded impact that promotes the sustainable transformation of industries; and Zahra et al.'s (2008) explanation of the forces contributing to the formation and rapid internationalization of social ventures, where they suggest that social entrepreneurship has emerged as an important topic because social entrepreneurs play a role in addressing serious social problems on a worldwide scale while enhancing social wealth. Sustainable entrepreneurship has also been identified by Thompson et al. (2011) as a means of developing strategies to meet sustainable laws and goals through activities such as urban planning and transportation, local and individual lifestyles, and ethical consumerism. In his work on 'The citizen sector: Becoming as entrepreneurial and competitive as business', Drayton (2002) argues that the rapid emergence of a strongly entrepreneurial and competitive citizen sector will have profound impacts on the rest of society as:

1. Business and society will end their divorce, and as they learn to talk and the social side closes today's huge productivity gap, they will converge;
2. Government will face growing competition in operations, which will force it to continue surrendering market share or to learn to compete;
3. The spread of social entrepreneurship will greatly strengthen democracy;
4. The dynamics of globalization will change dramatically as citizen groups and the constituencies they mobilize rapidly become key actors;
5. The world's squalor gap will begin to close because as the productivity of the social sector increases, much more than the salaries of its workers will improve.

Given his observations, Drayton (2002) stated that "literacy, health, environmental safety, and all the other areas that have suffered will catch up. The much berated imbalance of consumerism of today is not caused (as the name implies) by misplaced values but by the fact that for these centuries the products of business have become steadily less expensive relative to social goods. Close the business / social gap and consumerism will simply fade away." (Drayton, 2002, p. 91)

Creating products that address social challenges is a huge obstacle for firms, especially those that create sustaining innovations (that make good products better in the eyes of an incumbent's existing customers. E.g. the fifth blade in a razor, the clearer TV picture, better mobile phone reception (Christensen, Raynor, & McDonald, 2015)). These improvements can be incremental advances or major breakthroughs, but they all enable firms to sell more products to their most profitable customers (Christensen et al., 2015).

In as much as consumerism and entrepreneurial opportunity production have been explicitly acknowledged by the proponents of consumerism-driven entrepreneurial opportunity emergence, the linkage between these concepts and the factors that influence the negative exploitation of consumerism have received limited attention in existing literature (see Abela (2006)).

This gap provides an opportunity to better examine the drivers of entrepreneurial opportunity production from consumerism that could potentially address the unethical use of the understanding of consumerism for entrepreneurial opportunity production (Boyles, 2001). This issue is addressed in this chapter by adopting the conceptualisation of entrepreneurial opportunity as *identifying market failures as opportunities* (Thompson et al., 2011). By conceptualising entrepreneurial opportunity as *identifying market failures as market opportunities*, a consumerism-entrepreneurial opportunity framework is used that focuses on identifying the role of consumerism in entrepreneurial opportunity production. This conceptualisation positions entrepreneurial opportunity as a means of creating value from market failure and consumerism as an influencing factor in producing entrepreneurial opportunity (see Figure 2).

Research Methodology

This study explores how consumerism influences entrepreneurial opportunity production. Focus is placed on an emerging market firm through an in-depth investigation of the role consumerism plays in the emergence of entrepreneurial opportunity. A qualitative approach was deemed appropriate for this study, more specifically a single case study design to understand the role consumerism plays in emergence of entrepreneurial opportunity. Following Eisenhardt (1989), the research question (how can consumerism influence entrepreneurial opportunity?) was defined. The rationale for selecting a single case rather than a multiple case design follows Yin's (2009) suggestion that the single case can represent the critical test of a significant theory. The case study was selected before the research was initiated.

Case Selection

The specified selection criteria for the case study is summarised in Table 1 and described as follows. Following Yin (2009), a critical case study was selected using the following criteria: First, the company must have a prior history of creating an entrepreneurial opportunity from products that have become less expensive compared to social goods (Drayton, 2002). Second, the company must have operations in emerging markets including Africa. "The rise of the new middle classes in emerging markets has been the subject of significant media, political, and business attention in recent years. Attention to the new middle classes is closely tied to the contemporary imperative for growth. It is argued that to maintain the current scale of production, an ever greater scale of consumption is required, and future demand

Figure 2. Market failure, entrepreneurial opportunity, and consumerism cycle

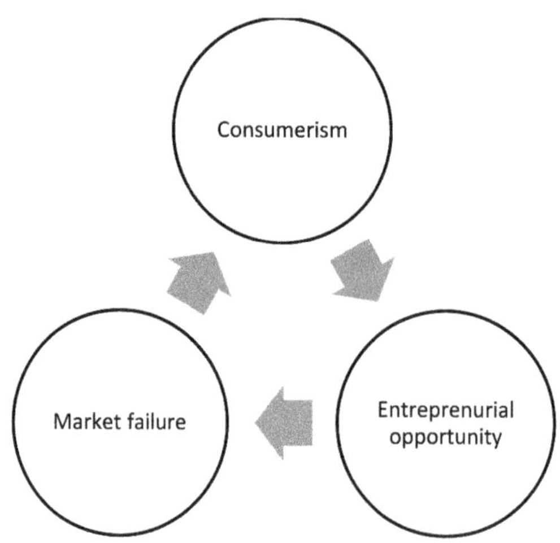

Table 1. Summary of case study

Company Name	Product	Governance Structure	Operating Areas (Include)
MMM Global (MMM)	Financial social network	Private	Argentina, Australia, Bangladesh, Brazil, Cambodia, China, Colombia, Eastern Africa, Hong Kong, India, Indonesia, Japan, Korea, Kuwait, Malaysia, Mexico, Peru, Philippines, Singapore, Africa (Ghana, Kenya, Nigeria, South Africa, Uganda, Zimbabwe), Spain, Thailand, Turkey, USA, Venezuela, and Vietnam.

rests with the new middle classes in emerging markets" (Kravets & Sandikci, 2014, p.125). The selected case study has operations in African countries including Ghana, Kenya, Nigeria, South Africa, Uganda, and Zimbabwe.

Case Study

"Th[ese] MMM people are very useless, they just came to dupe us". These were the words of an MMM social network user, reported in the November 4, 2017 Vanguard newspaper article, *Many Nigerians weep as MMM announces Restart*. Nigerians lost about $51 million when MMM collapsed in March 2018. At its peak, MMM had around three million users in Nigeria, but in December 2016, after a rumoured slowdown following increased scrutiny from the government, it briefly suspended operations that was restarted in 2017. Beyond Nigeria, MMM established operations in other African countries, including Ghana, Kenya, and Zimbabwe. In some countries, its operations were based on bitcoin rather than cash. Before its international expansion, MMM ran a Russian operation where it allowed (individual) investors to buy its shares (i.e. Mavros) that could be resold at MMM offices for a profit. Beyond Russia, it positioned itself as a mutual aid fund, and financial social network, and promised to pay participants 30% return on investment every thirty days. The social network is designed to connect communities of people over the internet and offline through events employing a brokerage model, where it brings financial aid seekers and providers together and facilitates transactions.

MMM (www.mmmglobal.online) was established in 1989 by Sergei Mavrodi, his brother Vyacheslav Mavrodi, and Olga Melnikova. As of 2011, it (according to its website) had a presence in 107 countries and had worked with more than 138 million participants. In March 2018, when Sergei Mavrodi died, MMM had defrauded millions across the world.

Data Collection and Analysis

Following Yin (2009), data was collected from documentation and archival records. This satisfies the rationale for using multiple sources of evidence (i.e. triangulation) as Yin (2009) suggests that with data triangulation, the potential problems of construct validity is addressed because multiple sources of evidence essentially provide multiple measures of the same phenomenon. Data was collected from a variety of documents and archival records, including written reports of events, formal studies of the same case being studied, news clippings and other articles appearing in the mass media and in community newspapers, and secondary data (such as data previously collected from questionnaires about MMM).

A case study protocol was established to increase the reliability of the case study research and was used to guide the investigation in carrying out the data collection from the single case study (Yin, 2009).

Data collection relied heavily on information from secondary individual reports (written reports of events, formal studies of the same case being studied, news clippings and other articles appearing in the mass media and in community newspapers), and a protocol was used to extract data from documents to ensure consistency and keep the investigation targeted on the case study topic. Case study questions (i.e. the specific questions that the case study investigator must keep in mind in collecting data, and the potential sources of information for answering each question (Yin, 2009)) were used as reminders to the investigator, regarding the information that needed to be collected and why. Their main purpose was to keep the investigator on track as data collection proceeded (Yin, 2009).

Data analysis was structured along two steps involving: (1) developing a case description, and (2) explanation building. A descriptive framework for organising the case study came from the literature review (Figure 2), which revealed gaps in literature on how consumerism could influence entrepreneurial opportunity. An initial case description was used to organise the case study after data was extracted from secondary material. A key aspect of this process was developing a chronology of events from the establishment of the organisation being examined to exploitation of entrepreneurial opportunity in the marketplace. The use of written reports was mainly important to ensure that multiple perspectives of the phenomena under investigation were captured. Upon completion of the chronology of events, an explanation is built by stipulating a presumed set of causal links about how consumerism can affect entrepreneurial opportunity production. This second step was an analytic technique, and a type of pattern matching (used to code data) in which the explanation reflects a theoretically significant proposition in which the causal links reflect critical insights into theory (Glaser & Strauss, 1967; Yin, 2009), particularly in the areas of consumerism and entrepreneurial opportunity. For this chapter, the single case study is focused on the impact of consumerism on entrepreneurial opportunity. The key proposition is that, because products of business have become less expensive relative to social goods, a certain type of consumerism and entrepreneurial opportunity will be produced. For example, as Thompson et al. (2011) suggest, market failures can be identified as opportunities, for some, which implies that businesses will produce new entrepreneurial opportunity from market failure, and this opportunity will be idiosyncratic to each business. The explanation building process from Yin (2009) is followed, to (1) make the initial theoretical proposition, (2) compare the findings of the single case study against the proposition, and (3) revise the proposition (where necessary). Manual coding was used to organise textual data into themes (Basit, 2003), and investigate the causal links between consumerism and entrepreneurial opportunity.

Findings

MMM describes itself as a community of ordinary people, selflessly helping each other, a kind of the global fund of mutual aid. It thrives in emerging markets and/or climates where participants have no clear idea what a legitimate investment fund product looks like.

[MMM] provides a platform that helps millions of participants worldwide free. The money is then transferred to them given by their own goodwill towards others who needed help in the past. Technically one must provide help to a needy before he can receive help with a promise of 30% of whatever amount you provided as help to others after 30 days. This sounded very juicy and lucrative for millions of poor and average Nigerians that could barely afford 3 square meals a day. Some people including some organisations invested public monies in the scheme. - Formal study of the same case (Elias at al., 2017).

Investment in [MMM] schemes have positive and significant impacts on depreciation in income levels, poor access to quality housing and poor educational standards. - Formal study of the same case (Elias at al., 2017).

Let [Mavrodi] go, he didn't kill anyone. They should put in jail those who caused this chaos.- MMM participant in Hees (2018) commented in late 1994 when Mavrodi was arrested for tax evasion in connection with MMM.

MMM is fraudulent because it uses the contributions of new investors to pay the old ones... Those who partake in such schemes would reap initially while later, it would fail because it is not sustainable. - Expert opinion (Eniola, 2016).

No profit is being created, and the people that are going to pay for all your profit right now are the people that are going to get stuck when MMM finally crashes.- Expert opinion (Hegarty, 2016).

There were structural weaknesses in Nigeria and the other countries where MMM successfully operated. In Nigeria, experts said recession pushed the people to MMM.

Owing to the fact that salaries are not paid and the hardship in the country, I decided to invest a little amount of money and gain little. - MMM participant (Eniola, 2016).

I started a small business at the Federal University of Technology in Akure. The strike on the campus also crippled sales. A close friend of mine asked me to join MMM in order to make ends meet.- MMM participant (Eniola, 2016).

[MMM] schemes are a coping strategy for economic recession.- Formal study of the same case (Jack & Ibekwe, 2018).

There were many MMM global offices where people could buy MMM shares, but few where they could be re-sold. Unfortunately, this troubling signal was not immediately obvious to investors as the financial regulation in countries where MMM operated were underdeveloped, and where laws did exist, they either did not prohibit MMM from operating or MMM found a way to circumvent them. Even when governments began to crack down on bank accounts linked to MMM, its operators circumvented the banks and required participants to use cryptocurrency (bitcoin). MMM uses the bitcoin infrastructure in its transactions and regulates the transaction process. Some regulators have attempted to shutdown MMM operations, but others don't seem to know how, or if they had the regulatory authority to do so, because users claim to willingly participate in providing aid to other users.

The attention of the Securities and Exchange Commission, Nigeria ("SEC") has been drawn to the activities of an online investment scheme tagged 'MMM Federal Republic of Nigeria (nigeria.mmm.net). The platform has embarked on an aggressive online media campaign to lure the investing public to participate in what it called "mutual aid financial network" with a monthly investment return of 30%. The Commission hereby notifies the investing public that the operation of this investment scheme has no tangible business model hence it's a PONZI SCHEME where returns are paid from other people's invested sum. Also, its operation is not registered by the Commission. The general public is hereby advised to distance themselves from this online scheme. Please note that anyone that subscribe to this illegal activity does so at his/her own risk. - Financial services regulator (SEC, 2016).

I will tell you that MMM has empowered me financially... It's like a charity organization where you provide and get help. If you help someone, you get twice what you give. - MMM user (Adepoju, 2016).

The participants in MMM programmes lacked trust in government institutions which influenced their decisions to participate in its programmes. People should ideally trust the government relatively more than other institutions. However, where trust in government is lacking, it can create a climate where people may be unable to clearly differentiate between a potentially fraudulent investment scheme and a regulated but un-reliable financial institution.

Ordinarily with my experience with the failed wonder banks, I should be the one advising people not to put in for MMM but with the way it started, it was too nice to shun. - MMM user (Eniola, 2016).

To begin a transaction, an MMM user declares the willingness to give help, after which their account is credited with MMM shares. The user shares grow from the moment of deposit, and the rate of growth (calculated daily at 00:00 hours GMT) may be slow or rapid, depending on user activity. To promote the website and make participation more attractive, MMM encourages users to be involved in development of the MMM platform. As a result, it also enables users (through the MMM extra service) to earn money from daily tasks posted on their personal office (space on the MMM website). The users who performed tasks were rewarded with shares. However, to access tasks, participants were required to purchase a special MMM share (i.e. Mavro-Extra), after which they were able to access MMM Extra, which lists current web-tasks. Instructions and recommendations (via screenshots, for example) were provided to help with task completion. MMM users could request help at any time, but only after confirmation of user shares. This means users had to make a bitcoin transfer before they could participate in the MMM system. Where a user received a request for help, if they failed to complete it within 36 hours, they were removed from the MMM system.

All participants should consider themselves as a donor when they put the money into the MMM system, so they never expect to lose the money in the future. - MMM platform manager (Purba, 2017).

MMM states on its website that money received from MMM cannot be considered as a yield and that nobody promises or guarantees to pay it. The company promotes a referral and guider bonus to encourage user participation. For the referral scheme, existing users are rewarded from deposits of the new participants invited, which means that by inviting new members into the community, users made an additional contribution to its development. However, MMM states nobody coerces the members of the community into inviting new participants, although it states while participants understand that the MMM network cannot exist without development and participants' encouragement in the form of referral bonuses, which motivates many people to take an active position in referrals. A guider can create their own structure and get a bonus from each donation of every user in their structure. Therefore, a guider structure can have its own leader whose rank is higher than those of newer users who join the structure. Guider bonuses are credited in the same way as referrals but depend on their level within the community.

However, guiders are only able to access new money deposited, which is available for withdrawal after a confirmation of the help they have provided.

So far, it has been weeks of testimonies. I enrolled five people in the scheme and settled my debt effortlessly. - MMM user (Eniola, 2016).

Friends' recommendation, expected benefits, current economic situations, ease of obtaining funds and the get rich quick syndrome were the most influencing factors on [MMM] scheme participation... The demographic characteristic of the respondents (location, age, gender, marital status, employment status and educational level) have statistically significant influence on [MMM] scheme participation. - Formal study of the same case (Obamuyi et al., 2018).

Using the observations described above, the next section will compare the findings of the case study against the proposition: market failures can be identified as opportunities and can revise the proposition (if necessary).

Consumerism and Entrepreneurial Opportunity Production

Consumerism and Entrepreneurial Opportunity Production

The documents and formal studies of the same case examined in this report clearly demonstrated that users of MMM believed that their personal well-being, to a large extent, depended on higher levels of consumption of MMM products and that by participating in the referral scheme, they would be rewarded from deposits of the new participants invited.

When you register on MMM and refer people to it, even if you are not investing, you earn 10% of the amount the person invests. - 3rd party report (Onyeji, 2016)

There is Guider's Bonus comprising of four levels - +5%, 3%, 1% and 0,25%. You may take this bonus out two weeks after your referral has provided help and got his Mavro confirmed. It works like Referral Bonus. Guider's bonus is paid only for 'new' money. There is also bonus for Testimonial video. Bonus for the video in a Letter of happiness is 5 per cent of the amount of received help. After receiving help you have to send a Letter of happiness. If you attach a video to it, you will get a bonus. The bonus is credited for each Letter of happiness - 3rd party report (Umoru et al. 2016).

Moreover, an additional 10% accrues to individuals for referrals to the scheme to the tune of whatever amount the person was able to provide as help. - Formal study of the same case (Elias at al., 2017).

I pay on your behalf to those accounts and then inform the owners of your payment; I also send proof. After this process, I continue to monitor. This of course is why people like me get 5 percent referral bonus. I have 13 participants under me. - MMM user (Odunsi, 2017).

The statements show that MMM did not hesitate to take advantage of consumerism (e.g. MMM guiders are only able to access new money deposited, which is available for withdrawal after a confirmation of the help they have provided) and governed its system a way that incentivised participation (e.g. Order for providing help comes to you in your Personal Office. If you do not complete it within 36 hours, you will be removed from the System – MMM website) and encouraged consumption of its product.

In spite of the bitter experience that millions of Nigerians have had since the foremost Ponzi scheme in the country, MMM, pulled a break on its operation last December, similar schemes are springing up and many Nigerians are investing in them.... Operators of MMM later claimed the suspension was because its system was experiencing heavy workload... The scheme however resumed operations... millions of investors not able to access payment and few new ones joining since then. - 3rd party report (Onyeji, 2017).

Even with this minor setback, I still strongly have confidence in MMM. The government and the press will amplify this but we all know that MMM is not going anywhere... This is a temporary measure to save the system and saving the system is saving our money. Our money is safe. By January, the system will be back and it will be stronger... The abrupt action of MMM has brought lot of fears and panic already which could even in itself crash the system. Guiders will have to come up with a plan to put the mind of Nigerians at ease. I don't know how they will do that but it has to be done. We need a constructive counter move from MMM against the enormous negativity going on via social media right now or else my one million naira and those of my friends will be gone. – MMM users (Adepoju, 2016).

In addition to consumerism, market failure played a key role in enabling MMM to flourish.

High-risk customers such as politically exposed persons could exploit the non-face-to-face feature of MMM by using the identity of low-risk customers (e.g. pensioners) to open MMM accounts. The Bitcoin funding option may present a higher money laundering risk than Bank wire, MasterCard, Visa Debit and Interac. . - Formal study of the same case (Esoimeme & Sasegbon, 2018).

Ponzi schemes [such as MMM] are a coping strategy for economic recession... Until the economic downturn is adequately addressed and the economy revamped, Ponzi schemes would continue to thrive. - Formal study of the same case (Jack & Ibekwe, 2018).

DISCUSSION AND CONCLUSION

This study shows that businesses can leverage consumerism in producing entrepreneurial opportunity. It was observed that entrepreneurs actively attempt to produce opportunities in environments that exhibited market failure (e.g. regulation of industrial activity). The effect is evident in the case of MMM where (1) users, who were seeking to improve their consumption ability, participated in MMM programmes, but were unable to distinguish between legal and illegal financial schemes, and (2) the company capitalised on lax regulation and distrust for government as well as existing financial institutions to position MMM as a legitimate alternative. It was observed that where market deficiencies exist, for the entrepreneur to succeed, s/he fills in for the deficiencies. This study further shows that new business opportunities are recognised, where entrepreneurs can find relationships between changes in technology, demographics, markets, government policies, and other factors, to identify ideas for new products or services (Baron, 2006; Baron & Ensley, 2006). Government's lack of adequate regulation can encourage consumerism and the production of entrepreneurial opportunity. For instance, the MMM case illustrates that the business flourished in areas where financial regulation was extremely underdeveloped.

This study's main contribution relates to the production of entrepreneurial opportunity from consumerism. This study complements prior studies on consumerism, entrepreneurial opportunity, and market failure by providing insight into the logic underlying the production of entrepreneurial opportunity from consumerism. The findings are consistent with those of Kotler (1971), p. 55, which states that:

consumerism actually should be, must be, and I hope will be, the opportunity for marketing... the alert company will see consumerism as a new basis for achieving a differential competitive advantage in the marketplace. A concern for consumer well-being can be turned into a profitable opportunity in at least two ways: through the introduction of needed new products and through the adoption of a companywide consumerism orientation.

Next to its contributions, this study has two main limitations: (1) the focus was on a single case study. Although this research provides insight into the relationship between consumerism and entrepreneurial opportunity, it remains unclear whether the findings can be generalizable to other studies; and (2) the study relied on qualitative data to examine the impact of consumerism on entrepreneurial opportunity. Eisenhardt & Graebner (2007) points out that case studies from qualitative research can be used as the basis to test results of the research using quantitative data. Hence, it will be encouraging for future research to use quantitative data in examining the impact of consumerism on entrepreneurial opportunity production.

REFERENCES

Abela, A. (2006). Marketing and consumerism: A response to O'Shaughnessy and O'Shaughnessy. *European Journal of Marketing*, *40*(1/2), 5–16. doi:10.1108/03090560610637284

Acs, Z., Boardman, M., & McNeely, C. (2013). The Social Value of Productive Entrepreneurship. *Small Business Economics*, *40*(3), 785–796. doi:10.100711187-011-9396-6

Adams, S., & DeBont, A. (2007). Information Rx: Prescribing Good Consumerism and Responsible Citizenship. *Health Care Analysis*, *15*(4), 273–290. doi:10.100710728-007-0061-9 PMID:17972056

Adepoju, P. (2016, December 15). *The meteoric rise of one of the world's largest Ponzi schemes in Nigeria*. Cable News Network.

Alvarez, S., & Barney, J. B. (2014). *Toward a Creation Theory of Entrepreneurship*. Working Paper, Fisher College of Business.

Ardichvili, A., Cardozo, R., & Ray, S. (2003). A theory of entrepreneurial opportunity identification and development. *Journal of Business Venturing*, *18*(1), 105–123. doi:10.1016/S0883-9026(01)00068-4

Barksdale, H. C., & Darden, W. R. (1972). Consumer Attitudes toward Marketing and Consumerism. *Journal of Marketing*, *36*(4), 28–35. doi:10.2307/1250423

Baron, R. (2006). Opportunity Recognition as Pattern Recognition: How Entrepreneurs " Connect the Dots " to Identify New Business Opportunities. *The Academy of Management Perspectives*, *20*(1), 104–119. doi:10.5465/amp.2006.19873412

Baron, R., & Ensley, M. (2006). Opportunity Recognition as the Detection of Meaningful Patterns: Evidence from Comparisons of Novice and Experienced Entrepreneurs. *Management Science*, *52*(9), 1331–1344. doi:10.1287/mnsc.1060.0538

Basit, T. (2003). Manual or electronic? The role of coding in qualitative data analysis. *Educational Research*, *45*(2), 143–154. doi:10.1080/0013188032000133548

Birmingham, R. (1969). The Consumer as King: The Economics of Precarious Sovereignty. *Case Western Reserve Law Review*, *20*(2), 354–377.

Boyles, D. R. (2001). *The Exploiting Business.* Educational Policy Studies Faculty Publication.

Burg, E., Podoynitsyna, K., Beck, L., & Lommelen, T. (2012). Directive Deficiencies: How Resource Constraints Direct Opportunity Identification in SMEs. *Journal of Product Innovation Management*, *29*(6), 1000–1011. doi:10.1111/j.1540-5885.2012.00976.x

Buskirk, R., & Rothe, J. (1970). Consumerism--An Interpretation. *Journal of Marketing*, *34*(4), 61–65. doi:10.2307/1250713

Christensen, C. M., Raynor, M. E., & McDonald, R. (2015). What is disruptive innovation? *Harvard Business Review*, *93*(12), 44–53. PMID:17183796

Day, G., & Aaker, D. (1970). A guide to consumerism. *Journal of Marketing*, *34*(3), 12–19. doi:10.2307/1249814

DeKoning, A. J., & Muzyka, D. F. (1999). *Conceptualizing Opportunity Recognition as a Socio-Cognitive Process.* SSE/EFI Working Paper Series in Business Administration No 1999:13.

Drayton, W. (2002). The citizen sector: Becoming as entreprenurial and competitive as business. *California Management Review*, *44*(3), 120–133. doi:10.2307/41166136

Drucker, P. (1958). Marketing and Economic Development. *Journal of Marketing*, *22*(3), 252–259. doi:10.2307/1247116

Drucker, P. (1969). *Consumerism in Marketing, A speech to the National Association of Manufacturers.* New York: Association of Manufacturers.

Eisenhardt, K. M., & Graebner, M. E. (2007). Theory building from cases: Opportunities and challenges. *Academy of Management Journal*, *50*(1), 25–32. doi:10.5465/amj.2007.24160888

Eisenhardt, M. (1989). Building Theories from Case Study Research. *Academy of Management Review*, *14*(4), 532–550. doi:10.5465/amr.1989.4308385

Elias, I. A., Etim, E. O., Etukafia, N. I., Akpanuko, E. E., & Ntiedo, B. E. (2017). Synopsis of Nigerian Economy and the Growth of Ponzi Schemes. *Global Journal of Management and Business Research: B Economics and Commerce, 17*(3), 2249–4588.

Eniola, T. (2016, December 1). Ponzi palava: Nigerians count losses, blame recession for MMM woes. *The Punch Newspaper*.

Esoimeme, E. E., & Sasegbon, D. (2018). The money laundering risks and vulnerabilities associated with MMM Nigeria. *Journal of Money Laundering Control*, *21*(1), 112–119. doi:10.1108/JMLC-01-2017-0002

Gbadamosi, A., Fletcher, K.-A., Emmanuel-Stephen, C., & Olutola, I. (2018). Consumerism and consumer protection: A focus on young consumers. In A. Gbadamosi (Ed.), *Young Consumer Behaviour: A Research Companion* (pp. 391–413). London: Routledge, Taylor & Francis Group.

Giones, F., Zhou, Z., Miralles, F., & Katzy, B. (2013, June). From Ideas to Opportunities: Exploring the Construction of Technology-Based Entrepreneurial Opportunities. *Technology Innovation Management Review*, 13–20.

Glaser, B. G., & Strauss, A. L. (1967). The discovery of grounded theory. *International Journal of Qualitative Methods*, *5*, 1–10.

Goodwin, N., Nelson, J. A., Ackerman, F., & Weisskopf, T. (2008). Consumption and the Consumer Society. Global Development and Environment Institute.

Hees, S. (2018, April 25). Russia's greatest Ponzi mastermind is dead, but his legacy lives on in the crypto world. *Quartz*.

Hegarty, S. (2016, December 1). *Nigeria's MMM Ponzi scheme: Will investors get their money?* BBC World Service.

Hockerts, K., & Wüstenhagen, R. (2010). Greening Goliaths versus emerging Davids - Theorizing about the role of incumbents and new entrants in sustainable entrepreneurship. *Journal of Business Venturing*, *25*(5), 481–492. doi:10.1016/j.jbusvent.2009.07.005

Holcombe, R. (2003). The origins of entrepreneurial opportunities. *The Review of Austrian Economics*, *16*(1), 25–43. doi:10.1023/A:1022953123111

Jack, J., & Ibekwe, C. C. (2018). Ponzi Schemes : An Analysis on Coping with Economic Recession in Nigeria. *The Nigerian Journal of Sociology and Anthropology*, *16*(1), 72–90.

Jackson, T. (2010). *Prosperity without Growth: Economics for a Finite Planet*. London: Earthscan.

Johnston, J., & Taylor, J. (2008). *Feminist Consumerism and Fat Activists: A Comparative Study of Grassroots Activism and the Dove Real Beauty Campaign*. The University of Chicago Press.

Jolibert, A. J. P., & Baumgartner, G. (1981). Toward a Definition of the Consumerist Segment in France. *The Journal of Consumer Research*, *8*(1), 114. doi:10.1086/208847

Kotler, P. (1971). What consumerism means for marketers. *Harvard Business Review*, *50*(3), 48–57.

Kotler, P. (2011). Reinventing Marketing to Manage the Environmental Imperative. *Journal of Marketing*, *75*(4), 132–135. doi:10.1509/jmkg.75.4.132

Kravets, O., & Sandikci, O. (2014). Competently Ordinary : New Middle Class Consumers in the Emerging. *Journal of Marketing*, *78*(4), 125–140. doi:10.1509/jm.12.0190

Leibenstein, H. (1968). Entrepreneurship and Development. *The American Economic Review*, *58*(2), 72–83.

Marshall, S. (2011). Conceptualizing the International For-Profit Social Entrepreneur. *Journal of Business Ethics*, *98*(2), 183–198. doi:10.100710551-010-0545-7

New, S., & Ramsay, J. (1997). A critical appraisal of aspects of the lean chain approach. *European Journal of Purchasing and Supply Management*, *3*(2), 93–102. doi:10.1016/S0969-7012(96)00019-6

Obamuyi, T. M., Iriobe, G. O., Afolabi, T. S., Akinbobola, A. D., Elumaro, A. J., Faloye, B. A., ... Oni, A. O. (2018). Factors Influencing Ponzi Scheme Participation In Nigeria. *Advances in Social Sciences Research Journal*, *5*(5), 429–444. doi:10.14738/assrj.55.4547

Odunsi, W. (2017, January 1). MMM: Anxiety among participants as January 13 draws close. *Daily Post.*

Offer, A. (2006). *The Challenge of affluence.* New York: Oxford University Press.

Onyeji, E. (2016, December 1). 7 trending Ponzi schemes in Nigeria in 2016. *Premium Times.*

Onyeji, E. (2017, March 30). MMM, other Ponzi schemes thrive in Nigeria, despite past woes. *Premium Times.*

Prothero, A., Dobscha, S., Freund, J., William, E., Luchs, M., & Ozanne, L. (2011). Sustainable Consumption : Opportunities for Consumer Research and Public Policy. *Journal of Public Policy & Marketing*, *30*(1), 31–38. doi:10.1509/jppm.30.1.31

Purba, D. (2017). The Economics Perspective of The Practice of MMM- Indonesia. *AFEBI Islamic Finance and Economic Review*, *2*(1), 75–91.

Sanne, C. (2002). Willing consumers—or locked-in? Policies for a sustainable consumption. *Ecological Economics*, *42*(1–2), 273–287. doi:10.1016/S0921-8009(02)00086-1

Schor, J. (2002). Understanding the New Consumerism: Inequality, Emulation and the Erosium of Well Being. *PSW Paper*, *2*(April), 1–13.

SEC. (2016). *Public Alert on the Activities of "MMM Federal Republic of Nigeria" (Nigeria.mmm.net).* Securities & Exchange Commission.

Shane, S. (2000). Prior Knowledge and the Discovery of Entrepreneurial Opportunities. *Organization Science*, *11*(4), 448–469. doi:10.1287/orsc.11.4.448.14602

Shane, S., & Cable, D. (2002). Network Ties, Reputation, and the Financing of New Ventures. *Management Science*, *48*(3), 364–381. doi:10.1287/mnsc.48.3.364.7731

Shaw, I., & Aldrigde, A. (2003). Consumerism, Health and Social Order. *Social Policy and Society*, *2*(1), 35–43. doi:10.1017/S147474640300109X

Singh, R. (2000). *Entrepreneurial Opportunity Recognition through Social Networks*. Psychology Press.

Siren, C., Kohtamaki, M., & Kuckertz, A. (2012). Exploration and exploitation strategies, profit performance, and the mediating role of strategic learning: Escaping the exploitation trap. *Strategic Entrepreneurship Journal*, *6*(6), 18–41. doi:10.1002ej.1126

Stearns, P. N. (2006). Consumerism in world history: The global transformation of desire (2nd ed.; Vol. 1). Routledge. doi:10.4324/9780203969885

Suddaby, R., Bruton, G. D., & Si, S. X. (2015). Entrepreneurship through a qualitative lens: Insights on the construction and/or discovery of entrepreneurial opportunity. *Journal of Business Venturing*, *30*(1), 1–10. doi:10.1016/j.jbusvent.2014.09.003

Tanner, C., & Sybille, W. K. (2003). Promoting Sustainable Consumption: Determinants of Green Purchases by Swiss Consumers. *Psychology and Marketing*, *20*(10), 883–902. doi:10.1002/mar.10101

Thompson, N., Kiefer, K., & York, J. (2011). Distinctions not dichotomies: Exploring social, sustainable, and environmental entrepreneurship. In *Social and Sustainable Entrepreneurship* (pp. 205–233). Emerald Group Publishing Limited. doi:10.1108/S1074-7540(2011)0000013012

Tocher, N., Oswald, S., & Hall, D. (2015). Proposing social resources as the fundamental catalyst toward opportunity creation. *Strategic Entrepreneurship Journal*, *9*(9), 119–135. doi:10.1002ej.1195

Trentmann, F. (2004). Beyond consumerism: New historical perspectives on consumption. *Journal of Contemporary History*, *39*(3), 373–401. doi:10.1177/0022009404044446

Umoru, H., Komolafe, B., Ovuakporie, E., Agbakwuru, J., & Asomba, I. (2016). *MMM: How it affects the banks – Bankers.* Vanguard Media Limited.

Vasilchenko, E., & Morrish, S. (2011). The Role of Entrepreneurial Networks in the Exploration and Exploitation of Internationalization Opportunities by Information and Communication Technology Firms. *Journal of International Marketing*, *19*(4), 88–105. doi:10.1509/jim.10.0134

Weick, K. (1995). Sensemaking in Organizations. *Administrative Science Quarterly*, *23*(6), 62–83.

Wilson, C. (2010). Eating, eating is always there: Food, consumerism and cardiovascular disease. Some evidence from Kerala, south India. *Anthropology & Medicine*, *17*(3), 261–275. doi:10.1080/13648470.2010.526699 PMID:21153961

Wood, M., & Mckinley, W. (2010). The production of entreprenurial opportunity: A constructivist perspective. *Strategic Entrepreneurship Journal*, *4*(1), 66–84. doi:10.1002ej.83

Wright, E., & Rogers, J. (2015). *American Society: How it really works* (2nd ed.). Norton Sociology.

Yani-de-Soriano, M., & Slater, S. (2009). Revisiting Drucker's theory: Has consumerism led to the overuse of marketing? *Journal of Management History*, *15*(4), 452–466. doi:10.1108/17511340910987347

Yin, R. K. (2009). *Case Study Research: Design and Methods. Essential guide to qualitative methods in organizational research* (Vol. 5). London: Sage Publications, Inc.

Zahra, S., Rawhouser, H., Bhawe, N., Neubaum, D., & Hayton, J. (2008). Globalisation of Social Entrepreneurship Opportunities. *Strategic Entrepreneurship Journal*, *2*(2), 117–131. doi:10.1002ej.43

Compilation of References

Aaker, D. A., & Myers, J. G. (1987). *Advertising Management* (3rd ed.). Englewood Cliffs, NJ: Prentice-Hall, Inc.

Aaker, J. L. (1997). Dimensions of Brand Personality. *JMR, Journal of Marketing Research*, *34*(August), 347–356. doi:10.2307/3151897

Aaker, J., & Fournier, S. (1995). A Brand as a Character, A Partner and a Person: Three Perspectives on the Question of Brand Personality. *Advances in Consumer Research. Association for Consumer Research (U. S.)*, *22*.

Abbad, M., Abbad, R., & Saleh, M. (2011). Limitations of e-commerce in developing countries: Jordan case. *Education, Business and Society*, *4*(4), 280–291. doi:10.1108/17537981111190060

Abbott, J. C. (1987). *Agricultural Marketing Enterprises for the Developing World*. Cambridge, UK: Cambridge University Press.

Abdurrahaman, D. T., Owusu, A., Soladoye, B. A., & Kalimuthu, K. R. (2018). Celebrity-brand endorsement: A study on its impacts on generation y-ers in Nigeria. *Asian Journal of Scientific Research*, *11*(3), 415–427. doi:10.3923/ajsr.2018.415.427

Abela, A. (2006). Marketing and consumerism: A response to O'Shaughnessy and O'Shaughnessy. *European Journal of Marketing*, *40*(1/2), 5–16. doi:10.1108/03090560610637284

Abimbola, T. (2006). Market access for developing economies: Branding in Africa. *Place Branding and Public Diplomacy*, *2*(2), 108–117. doi:10.1057/palgrave.pb.5990049

Acikdilli, G., Ziemnowicz, C., & Bahhouth, V. (2018). Consumer Ethnocentrism in Turkey: Ours are Better than Theirs. *Journal of International Consumer Marketing*, *30*(1), 45–57. doi:10.1080/08961530.2017.1361882

Acquaah, M. (2012). Social networking relationships, firm-specific managerial experience and firm performance in a transition economy: A comparative analysis of family owned and nonfamily firms. *Strategic Management Journal*, *33*(10), 1215–1228.

Acs, Z., Boardman, M., & McNeely, C. (2013). The Social Value of Productive Entrepreneurship. *Small Business Economics*, *40*(3), 785–796. doi:10.100711187-011-9396-6

Adams, S., & DeBont, A. (2007). Information Rx: Prescribing Good Consumerism and Responsible Citizenship. *Health Care Analysis*, *15*(4), 273–290. doi:10.100710728-007-0061-9 PMID:17972056

Adcock, D., Bradfield, R., Halborg, A., & Ross, C. (2001). *Marketing Principles and Practice* (4th ed.). Essex, UK: Pearson Education Limited.

Adepoju, P. (2016, December 15). *The meteoric rise of one of the world's largest Ponzi schemes in Nigeria*. Cable News Network.

Adepoju, A. (2003). Migration in West Africa. *Development*, *46*(3), 37–41. doi:10.1177/10116370030463006

Adib, H., & El-Bassiouny, N. (2012). Materialism in young consumers. *Journal of Islamic Marketing*, *3*(3), 255–282. doi:10.1108/17590831211259745

Adler, A. (1935). The fundamental views of individual psychology. *International Journal of Individual Psychology*, *1*, 5–8.

Adnan, H. (2014). An Analysis of the Factors Affecting Online Purchasing Behavior of Pakistani Consumers. *International Journal of Marketing Studies*, *6*(5), 133–148.

African Development Bank Group. (2017). *African Economic Outlook – Entrepreneurship and Industrialization*. Abidjan: AfDB Publication. Retrieved from https://www.afdb.org/fileadmin/uploads/afdb/Documents/Publications/AEO_2017_Report_Full_English.pdf

Agbese, D. (2009). *Rebranding Nigeria: An Appraisal*. Available at: http://www.newswatchngr.com/index.php?option=com_content&task=view&id=1232&Itemid=1

Agunbiade, O. M., & Ayotunde, T. (2011). Spirituality in Cybercrime (Yahoo Yahoo) Activities among Youths in South West Nigeria. In *Youth Culture and Net Culture: Online Social Practices* (pp. 357–380). IGI Global.

Ahmad, S. Z., & Saber, H. (2015). Understanding marketing strategies with particular reference to small-and medium-sized hotel businesses in the United Arab Emirates. *Tourism and Hospitality Research*, *15*(2), 115–129. doi:10.1177/1467358414567799

Ahmed, S. A., & d'Astous, A. (2001). Canadian Consumers' Perceptions of Products Made in Newly Industrializing East Asian Countries. *International Journal of Commerce and Management.*, *11*(1), 54–81. doi:10.1108/eb047415

Ahmed, S. A., & d'Astous, A. (2008). Antecedents, Moderators, and Dimensions of Country-of-Origin Evaluations. *International Marketing Review*, *25*(1), 75–106. doi:10.1108/02651330810851890

Ahmed, Z. U., Ismail, I., Sadiq, M., Sohail Tabsh, I., & Alias, H. (2010). Malaysian consumers' credit card usage behavior. *Asia Pacific Journal of Marketing and Logistics*, *22*(4), 528–544. doi:10.1108/13555851011090547

Ahmed, Z. U., Johnson, J. P., Yang, X., Fatt, C. K., Teng, H. S., & Boon, L. S. (2004). Does country of origin matter for low-involvement products. *International Marketing Review*, *21*(1), 102–120. doi:10.1108/02651330410522925

Ahuja, R. D., & Stinson, K. M. (1993). Female-Headed Single Parent Families: An Exploratory Study of Children's Influence in Family Decision Making. *Advances in Consumer Research. Association for Consumer Research (U. S.)*, *20*(1), 469–474.

Aiyer, S. S. (2011). *The Elephant that Became a Tiger*. Center for Global Liberty and Prosperity (Development Policy Analysis). Retrieved from http://www.cato.org/publications/development-policy-analysis/elephant-became-tiger-20-years-economic-reform-india

Akakandelwa, A. (2011). An Exploratory Survey of the SADC e-government Web Sites. *Library Review*, *60*(5), 421–431. doi:10.1108/00242531111135317

Akamp, M., & Müller, M. (2013). Supplier management in developing countries. *Journal of Cleaner Production*, *56*, 54-62.

Akenji, L. (2014). Consumer scapegoatism and limits to green consumerism. *Journal of Cleaner Production*, *63*, 13–23. doi:10.1016/j.jclepro.2013.05.022

Akinyele, S. T. (2010). The Influence Of Children On Family Purchasing Decisions In Ota, Nigeria. *Journal Of Contemporary Management Research*, *4*(2), 1–11.

Akram, S., Muhammad, N., Raga, M., & Sana, R. (2017). Factors influencing the effectiveness of celebrity endorsement in advertising. *British Journal of Marketing Studies*, *5*(1), 1–16.

Akwagyiram, A. (2016). *Nigeria's music scene becomes a cultural export*. Available at: https://www.reuters.com/article/us-nigeria-music/nigerias-music-scene-becomes-a-cultural-export-idUSKCN0ZN124

Alfadl, A. A., Izham, M., Ibrahim, M., & Hassali, M. A. A. (2013). Scale development on consumer behavior toward counterfeit drugs in a developing country: A quantitative study exploiting the tools of an evolving paradigm. *BMC Public Health*, *13*(829), 1–9. PMID:24020730

Ali, A., & Batra, D. K. (2011). Children influence on parents buying decisions in Delhi (India). *European Journal of Business and Management*, *3*(11).

Aliede, J. E. (2016). Brand identity creation, sustenance and advertising in competitive marketing environment. *Kwararafa Journal of Contemporary Research*, *2*(1), 27–45.

Al-Khatib, J. A., Stanton, A. D., & Rawwas, M. Y. A. (2005). Ethical segmentation of consumers in developing countries: A comparative analysis. *International Marketing Review*, *22*(2), 225–246. doi:10.1108/02651330510593287

Altintas, M. H., & Tokol, T. (2007). Cultural openness and consumer ethnocentrism: An empirical analysis of Turkish consumers. *Marketing Intelligence & Planning*, *25*(4), 308–325. doi:10.1108/02634500710754565

Alvarez, S., & Barney, J. B. (2014). *Toward a Creation Theory of Entrepreneurship.* Working Paper, Fisher College of Business.

Alvesson, M., & Skoldberg, K. (2000). *Reflexive Methodology: New Vistas for Qualitative Research*. London: Sage.

Amakihe, E. (2016). Branding Lagos through regeneration of historical physical features. *Journal of Urban Regeneration & Renewal*, *10*(1), 50-57.

Amankwah-Amoah, J. (2014). Solar energy in sub-Saharan Africa: The challenges and opportunities of technological leapfrogging. *Thunderbird International Business Review*, *57*(1), 15–31.

Amankwah-Amoah, J. (2016). The evolution of science, technology and innovation policies: A review of the Ghanaian experience. *Technological Forecasting and Social Change*, *110*, 134–142.

Amankwah-Amoah, J., & Sarpong, D. (2016). Historical pathways to a green economy: The evolution and scaling-up of solar PV in Ghana, 1980–2010. *Technological Forecasting and Social Change*, *102*, 90–101.

Amendolagine, V., Boly, A., Coniglio, N. D., Prota, F, & Seric, A. (2013). FDI and Local Linkages in Developing Countries: Evidence from Sub-Saharan Africa. *World Development, 50*, 41–56.

Amenumey, D. E. K. (2008). *Ghana: A Concise History from Pre-Colonial Times to the 20th Century*. Accra: Woeli Publishing Services.

Amodu, L. O. (2007). An evaluation of the influence of customer relations on customer attraction to banks: A study of Prudent Bank. *International Journal of Communication*, (7): 390–396.

Amodu, L. O. (2010). Public relations: The art and social science of crisis management. In R. Akinfeleye (Ed.), *Mass communication: A book of readings* (pp. 110–124). Lagos: Department of Mass Communication, University of Lagos.

Ampuero, O., & Vila, N. (2006). Consumer perceptions of product packaging. *Journal of Consumer Marketing*, *23*(2), 100–112. doi:10.1108/07363760610655032

Amyx, D. A., DeJong, P. F., Lin, Chakraborty, G., & Wiener, J.L. (1994). Influencers of purchase intentions for ecologically safe products: an exploratory study. In *AMA Winter Educators' Conference Proceedings*. American Marketing Association.

Anamika, S. (2012). *Indian celebrity endorsed perfumes*. Retrieved July 19, 2015, from http://anamikas.hubpages.com/hub/Indian-Celebrity-endorced-Perfumes-Shilpa-Shetty-Amitabh-Bachchan

Anderson, J. C., & Gerbing, D. W. (1988). Structural equation modeling in practice: A review of a recommended two-step approach. *Psychological Bulletin*, *103*(3), 411–423. doi:10.1037/0033-2909.103.3.411

Anderson, J. C., & Narus, J. A. (1990). A model of distributor firm and manufacturer firm working partnerships. *Journal of Marketing*, *54*, 42–58.

Andrews, J., Lin, C.-T., Levy, A., & Lo, S. (2014). Consumer Research Needs from the Food and Drug Administration on Front-of-Package Nutritional Labeling. *Journal of Public Policy & Marketing*, *33*(1), 10–16. doi:10.1509/jppm.33.1.10

Anholt, S. (1998). Nation-Brands of the Twenty-First Century. *Journal of Brand Management*, *5*(6), 395–406. doi:10.1057/bm.1998.30

Anholt, S. (2006). The Anholt-GMI City Brands Index: How the world sees the world's cities. *Place Branding*, *2*(1), 18–31. doi:10.1057/palgrave.pb.5990042

Anholt, S. (2007). *Competitive Identity: The New Brand Management for Nations, Cities and Regions*. London: Palgrave Macmillan. doi:10.1057/9780230627727

Anholt, S. (2010). *Places: Identity, Image and Reputation*. London: Palgrave Macmillan.

Anholt, S. (2013). Beyond the Nation Brand: The Role of Image and Identity in International Relations, Exchange. *The Journal of Public Diplomacy*, *12*(1), 6–12.

Anquandah, J. (1985). *Ethnoarchaeological Clues to Ghana's Great Past and – A Greater Future? University of Ghana Monographs and papers in African Archaeology, No. 2*. Department of Archaeology, University of Ghana.

Anschutz, D. J., Engels, R. C., & Van Strien, T. (2012). Increased body satisfaction after exposure to thin ideal children's television in young girls showing thin ideal internalisation. *Psychology & Health*, *27*(5), 603–617. doi:10.1080/08870446.2011.613470 PMID:22512700

Antwi Bosiakoh, T. (2017a). Nigerian Immigrant Entrepreneurs in Contemporary Ghana: Insights on Locational/Sectoral Niches and Inter-Generational (Dis) Continuities. *Urban Forum*, *28*(2), 143-163.

Antwi Bosiakoh, T. (2017b). *Mixed embeddedness and Nigerian immigrants' informal entrepreneurship in Ghana* (PhD thesis). Macquarie University, Sydney, Australia.

Antwi Bosiakoh, T., & Williams Tetteh, V. (2018). Nigerian immigrant women's entrepreneurial embeddedness in Ghana, West Africa. *International Journal of Gender and Entrepreneurship*, IJGE-05-2018-0043. doi:10.1108/IJGE-05-2018-0043

AOHR-UK. (2014). *Forced Disappearance and Torture in the United Arab Emirates*. Available at: http://aohr.org.uk/images/releases/forced-disappearance-torture-in-UAE.pdf

Apejoye, A. (2013). Influence of celebrity endorsement of advertisement on students' purchase intention. *Journal of Mass Communication and Journalism*, *3*(03). doi:10.4172/2165-7912.1000152

Ardichvili, A., Cardozo, R., & Ray, S. (2003). A theory of entrepreneurial opportunity identification and development. *Journal of Business Venturing*, *18*(1), 105–123. doi:10.1016/S0883-9026(01)00068-4

Arhin, K. (1979). *West African Traders in Ghana in the Nineteenth and Twentieth Centuries*. London: Longman.

Aririguzoh, S. (2007). Media literacy and the role of English language in Nigeria. *International Journal of Communication*, (6): 144–160.

Aririguzoh, S. (2013). Human integration in globalization: The communication imperative. *Nigerian Journal of Social Sciences*, *9*(2), 118–141.

Armstrong, G., & Kotler, P. (2000). *Marketing: An Introduction* (5th ed.). Upper Saddle River, NJ: Prentice-Hall Inc.

Armstrong, J. S., Morwitz, V. G., & Kumar, V. (2000). Sales forecasts for existing consumer products and services: Do purchase intentions contribute to accuracy? *International Journal of Forecasting*, *16*(3), 383–397. doi:10.1016/S0169-2070(00)00058-3

Arnold, T. (2012). *Dubai property draws Nigerians*. Available at: https://www.thenational.ae/business/property/dubai-property-draws-nigerians-1.394019

Arnold, D. J., & Quelch, J. A. (1998). New strategies in emerging markets. *Sloan Management Review*, *40*(1), 7–20.

Aronczyk, M. (2008). "Living the Brand": Nationality, Globality and the Identity Strategies of Nation Branding Consultants. *International Journal of Communication*, *2*, 41–65.

Ashworth, G. J. (2011). Should we brand places? *Journal of Town and City Management*, *1*(3), 248–252.

Ashworth, G. J., & Kavaratzis, M. (2007). Beyond the logo: Brand management for cities. *Journal of Brand Management*, *16*(8), 520–531. doi:10.1057/palgrave.bm.2550133

Ashworth, G. J., & Voogd, H. (1990). *Selling the City: Marketing Approaches in Public Sector Urban Planning*. London: Belhaven Press.

Ashworth, G. J., & Voogt, H. (1994). Marketing and place promotion. In S. V. Ward & J. R. Gold (Eds.), *Place Promotion, the Use of Publicity and Marketing to Sell Towns and Regions* (pp. 39–52). Chichester, UK: John Wiley.

Asian Development Bank. (2010). *The Rise of Asia's Middle Class*. Retrieved from www.adb.org/sites/

Assadourian, E. (2010). Transforming cultures: From consumerism to sustainability. *Journal of Macromarketing*, *30*(2), 186–191. doi:10.1177/0276146710361932

Atkin, C., & Block, M. (1983). Effectiveness of celebrity endorsers. *Journal of Advertising Research*, *23*(1), 57–61.

Ayobade, A. (2012). *Gender Differences and the influence of Socio-Cultural Factors in Accessing Formal Funds by Small-Scale Entrepreneurs* (PhD dissertation). Department of Sociology of the Faculty of Social Sciences, University of Lagos, Nigeria.

Ayodi, K., & Bree, J. (2010). An ethnography of transfer of food learning within the family. *Young Consumers*, *11*(1), 67–76. doi:10.1108/17473611011026028

Babatunde, J. (2016). *Why Nigerians still visit Dubai-Obinwa*. Available at: https://www.vanguardngr.com/2016/11/nigerians-still-visit-dubai-obinwa/

Babin, B. & Harris, E. (2009). *CB3*. Cengage Learning.

Bachmann, G., & John, D. (1993). Children's Susceptibility to Peer Group Purchase Influence: An Exploratory Investigation. *Advances in Consumer Research. Association for Consumer Research (U. S.)*, *20*(1), 463–468.

Badruddin, S. T. (2015). Role of NGOs in the protection of environment. *Journal of Environmental Research and Development*, *9*(3), 705–712.

Bailey, W., & Gutierrez de Pineres, S. (1997). Country of Origin Attitudes in Mexico: The Malinchismo Effect. *Journal of International Consumer Marketing*, 9.

Baker, M. J., & Michie, J. (1995). *Product country images: perceptions of Asian cars*. University of Strathclyde, Department of Marketing, Working Paper Series 95.

Baker, M., & Churchill, G. A. (1977). The Impact of Physically Attractive Models on Advertising Evaluations. *JMR, Journal of Marketing Research*, *14*(4), 538–555. doi:10.2307/3151194

Bakir, A., Rose, G. M., & Shoham, A. (2006). Family Communication Patterns: Mothers' and Fathers' Communication Style and Children's Perceived Influence in Family Decision Making. *Journal of International Consumer Marketing*, *19*(2), 75-95. doi:10.1300/J046v19n02.05

Balabanis, G., & Diamantopoulos, A. (2004). Domestic Country Bias, Country-of-Origin Effects, and Consumer Ethnocentrism: A Multidimensional Unfolding Approach. *Journal of the Academy of Marketing Science*, *32*(1), 80–95. doi:10.1177/0092070303257644

Balabanis, G., Diamantopoulos, A., Mueller, R. D., & Melewar, T. C. (2001). The Impact of Nationalism, Patriotism and Internationalization on Consumer Ethnocentric Tendencies. *Journal of International Business Studies*, *22*(1), 157–175. doi:10.1057/palgrave.jibs.8490943

Balabanis, G., & Siamagka, N. T. (2017). Inconsistencies in the behavioural effects of consumer ethnocentrism. *International Marketing Review*, *34*(2), 166–182. doi:10.1108/IMR-03-2015-0057

Balakrishnan, M. S. (2008). Dubai – a star in the east: A case study in strategic destination branding. *Journal of Place Management and Development*, *1*(1), 62–91. doi:10.1108/17538330810865345

Baloglu, S., & McCleary, K. W. (1999). A Model of destination image formation. *Annals of Tourism Research*, *26*(4), 868–879. doi:10.1016/S0160-7383(99)00030-4

Bannister, B. D. (1986). Performance outcome feedback and attributional feedback: Interactive effects on recipient responses. *The Journal of Applied Psychology*, *71*(2), 203–210. doi:10.1037/0021-9010.71.2.203

Bannister, J. P., & Saunders, J. A. (1978). UK Consumers' Attitudes towards Imports: The Measurement of National Stereotype Image. *European Journal of Marketing*, *12*(8), 562–570. doi:10.1108/EUM0000000004982

Banyan Botanicals. (2015). *Ayurvedic Herbs*. Retrieved from www.banyanbotanicals.com

Bao, Y. (2001). *Effect of Parental style and power on adolescents influence in family consumption decisions* (PhD thesis). Virginia Polytechnic Institute. Retrieved from http://www.google.co.in/url?sa=t&rct=j&q=&esrc=s&source=web&cd=1&ved=0CBsQFjAA&url=http%3A%2F%2Fwww.researchgate.net%2Fpublication%2F228362204_Effects_of_parental_style_and_power_on_adolescent's_influence_in_family_consumption_decisions%2Ffile%2Fd912f50f0ed6fb3d77.pdf&ei=1eK0U6nrHtKPuATTvoKIAw&usg=AFQjCNEaiQMvaFSeBq1glgcglmystbT5xw&sig2=2S8jpj7goktcGwVQwTOirg&bvm=bv.70138588,d.c2E

Barat, S. (2014). Religion in Consumer Society: Brands, Consumers and Markets. *Journal of Consumer Marketing*, *31*(3), 228–230.

Barbeau, E. M., Leavy, S., & Balbach, E. D. (2004). Smoking, Social Class, and Gender: What Can Public Health Learn from the Tobacco Industry about Disparities in Smoking? *Tobacco Control*, *13*(2), 115–120. doi:10.1136/tc.2003.006098 PMID:15175523

Barber, J. (2003). Production, consumption and the world summit on sustainable development. *Environment, Development and Sustainability*, *5*(1-2), 63–93. doi:10.1023/A:1025319915498

Bardia, Y. H., Abed, A., & Majid, N. Z. (2011). Investigate the impact of celebrity endorsement on brand image. *European Journal of Scientific Research*, *58*(1), 116–132.

Barksdale, H. C., & Darden, W. R. (1972). Consumer Attitudes toward Marketing and Consumerism. *Journal of Marketing*, *36*(4), 28–35. doi:10.2307/1250423

Baron, R. (2006). Opportunity Recognition as Pattern Recognition: How Entrepreneurs " Connect the Dots " to Identify New Business Opportunities. *The Academy of Management Perspectives*, *20*(1), 104–119. doi:10.5465/amp.2006.19873412

Baron, R., & Ensley, M. (2006). Opportunity Recognition as the Detection of Meaningful Patterns: Evidence from Comparisons of Novice and Experienced Entrepreneurs. *Management Science*, *52*(9), 1331–1344. doi:10.1287/mnsc.1060.0538

Bartlett, F. C. (1932). *Remembering*. London: Cambridge University Press.

Basit, T. (2003). Manual or electronic? The role of coding in qualitative data analysis. *Educational Research*, *45*(2), 143–154. doi:10.1080/0013188032000133548

Batra, R., Ramaswamy, V., Alden, D. L., Steenkamp, J. B. E., & Ramachander, S. (2000). Effects of Brand Local and Non-local Origin on Consumer Attitudes in Developing Countries. *Journal of Consumer Psychology*, *9*(2), 83–95. doi:10.1207/S15327663JCP0902_3

Baurzhan, S., & Jenkins, G. P. (2016). Off-grid solar PV: Is it an affordable or appropriate solution for rural electrification in Sub-Saharan African countries? *Renewable & Sustainable Energy Reviews*, *601*, 405–1418.

BBC News UK. (2005). *Unilever parts with perfume names.* Retrieved July 19, 2015, from http://news.bbc.co.uk/1/hi/business/4566831.stm

Bearden, W. O., Money, R. B., & Nevins, J. L. (2006). A Measure of Long-Term Orientation: Development and Validation. *Journal of the Academy of Marketing Science*, *34*(3), 456–467. doi:10.1177/0092070306286706

Bear, M. F., Connors, B. W., & Paradisco, M. A. (1996). *Neuroscience: Exploring the Brain.* London: Williams & Wilkins.

Becker, A. (2005). What a teen wants. *Broadcasting & Cable*, *135*, 16.

Beer Statistics. (2017). *Beer Statistics 2017 edition.* The Brewers of Europe, December 2017.

Béjot, N., & Doittau, B. (2004). Advertising to children in France. *Young Consumers*, *5*(3), 69–72. doi:10.1108/17473610410814274

Belanger, F., & Carter, L. (2008). Trust and Risk in e-government adoption. *The Journal of Strategic Information Systems*, 17.

Belch, G. E., & Belch, M. A. (2007). Advertising and Promotion (7th ed.). McGraw Hill/Irwin.

Belcher, J. C., & Crader, K. W. (1974). Social Class, Style of Life and Fertility in Preuto Rico. *Social Forces*, *52*(4), 488–495. doi:10.1093f/52.4.488

Belch, G. E., & Belch, M. A. (2012). *Advertising and promotion: An integrated marketing communications perspective.* New York: McGraw-Hill/Irwin.

Belch, G. E., Belch, M. A., & Ceresino, G. (1985). Parental mid Teenage Child Influences in Family Decision Making. *Journal of Business Research*, *13*(2), 163–176. doi:10.1016/0148-2963(85)90038-4

Belch, M. A., & Willis, L. A. (2002). Family decision at the turn of the century: Has the changing structure of households impacted the family decision-making process? *Journal of Consumer Behaviour*, *2*(2), 111–124. doi:10.1002/cb.94

Bello, K. B., Suleiman, J. B. A., & Danjuma, I. (2012). Perspectives on Consumerism and Consumer Protection Act in Nigeria. *European Journal of Business and Management*, *4*(10), 72–78.

Belz, F., & Peattie, K. (2012). *Sustainability Marketing* (2nd ed.). John Wiley & Sons Ltd.

Beneke, Silverstone, Woods, & Schneider. (2011). The influence of the youth on their parents' purchasing decisions of high-technology products. *African Journal of Business Management*, *5*(10), 3807–3812. doi:10.5897/AJBM10.359

Berger, J. (2013). Contagious: Why things catch on. New York: Simon & Schuster.

Bergkvist, L., & Zhou, K. Q. (2016). Celebrity endorsements: A literature review and research agenda. *International Journal of Advertising*, *35*(4), 642–663. doi:10.1080/02650487.2015.1137537

Berry, L. L., Seiders, K., & Grewal, D. (2002). Understanding service convenience. *Journal of Marketing*, *66*(3), 1–17. doi:10.1509/jmkg.66.3.1.18505

Bhattacharya, P. (2011). The Body Shop gets closer to mass market in India. *GCI Magazine*, *9*(3), 10–13.

Bianchi, C., & Saleh, A. (2010). On importer trust and commitment: A comparative study of two developing countries. *International Marketing Review*, *27*(1), 55–86.

Biemans, W. (2001). Designing a Dual Marketing Program. *European Management Journal*, *19*(6), 670–677.

Bilkey, W. J., & Nes, E. (1982). Country-of-origin effects on product evaluations. *Journal of International Business Studies*, *13*(1), 89–99. doi:10.1057/palgrave.jibs.8490539

Birmingham, R. (1969). The Consumer as King: The Economics of Precarious Sovereignty. *Case Western Reserve Law Review*, *20*(2), 354–377.

Black, I., & Cherrier, H. (2010). Anti-consumption as part of living a sustainable lifestyle: Daily practices, contextual motivations and subjective values. *Journal of Consumer Behaviour*, *9*(6), 437–453. doi:10.1002/cb.337

Blain, C., Stuart, E. L., & Brent, J. R. (2005). Destination Branding: Insights and Practices from Destination Management Organizations. *Journal of Travel Research*, *43*(4), 328–338. doi:10.1177/0047287505274646

Blechman, B. M. (2004). Book review, "Soft power: The means to success in world politics." *Political Science Quarterly*, 680–681. doi:10.1002/j.1538-165X.2004.tb01291.x

Blythe, J. (2001). Essentials of Marketing (2nd ed.). Pearson Education Limited.

Boahen, A. A. (1977). Ghana before the coming of the Europeans. *Ghana Social Science Journal*, *4*(2), 93–106.

Bobley, G. (2017). *The 2017 Reputation Survey Reveals That Dubai Is the Most Reputable City in the GCC.* Available at: https://me.popsugar.com/love/2017-Reputation-Survey-44106521

Boisen, M., Terlouw, K., & Van Gorp, B. (2011). The selective nature of place branding and the layering of spatial identities. *Journal of Place Management and Development*, *4*(2), 135–147. doi:10.1108/17538331111153151

Bolton, R. N., Grewal, D., & Levy, M. (2007). Six strategies for competing through service: An agenda for future research. *Journal of Retailing*, *83*(1), 1–4. doi:10.1016/j.jretai.2006.11.001

Bond, M. H. (1987). Chinese Values and the Search for Culture-Free Dimensions of Culture. *Journal of Cross-Cultural Psychology*, *18*(2), 143–164. doi:10.1177/0022002187018002002

Boniface, B., & Cooper, C. (2005). *Worldwide destinations: The geography of travel and tourism*. Elsevier.

Bonnefond, C., & Clément, M. (2014). Social-Class and Body Weight among Chinese Urban Adults: The Role of the Middle Classes in the Nutrition Transition. *Social Science & Medicine*, *112*, 22–29. doi:10.1016/j.socscimed.2014.04.021 PMID:24788113

Booth, D. A., & Freeman, R. P. J. (2014). Mind-reading versus Neuromarketing: How Does a Product make an impact on the Consumer? *Journal of Consumer Marketing*, *31*(3), 177–189. doi:10.1108/JCM-08-2013-0674

Boso, N., Debrah, Y. A., & Amankwah-Amoah, J. (2018). International marketing strategies of emerging market firms: Nature, boundary conditions, antecedents, and outcomes. *International Marketing Review*, *35*(2), 202–214.

Bostock, J., & Riley, B. (1855). *Pliny the Elder, Historia Naturalis* (ca. 77 AD). Retrieved July 19, 2015, from www.scentedpages.com/pdf/historia_naturalis.pdf

Botz-Bornstein, T. (2012). A Tale of Two Cities: Hong Kong and Dubai Celebration of Disappearance and the Pretension of Becoming. *Transcience*, *3*(2), 1–16.

Boyd, H. W. Jr, Ray, M. L., & Strong, E. C. (1972). An Attitudinal Framework for Advertising Strategy. *Journal of Marketing*, *36*(April), 27–33. doi:10.2307/1250974

Boyd, W. B. Jr, Walker, O. C. Jr, Mullins, J., & Larréché, J. C. (2002). 'Marketing Management', A strategic Decision-making Approach', New York: McGraw-Hill. *Higher Education*, 122.

Boyles, D. R. (2001). *The Exploiting Business*. Educational Policy Studies Faculty Publication.

Bradley, J. C., Waliczek, T., & Zajicek, J. (1999). Relationship between environmental knowledge and environmental attitude of high school students. *The Journal of Environmental Education*, *30*(3), 17–21. doi:10.1080/00958969909601873

Brand Finance. (2014). *Nation Brands: The Annual Report on Nation Brands*. Available at: http://brandfinance.com/images/upload/brand_finance_nation_brands_report_2014_final_edition.pdf

Braun, V., & Clarke, V. (2006). Using thematic analysis in psychology. *Qualitative Research in Psychology*, *3*(2), 77–101. doi:10.1191/1478088706qp063oa

Brewer, W. F., & Nakamura, G. V. (1984). The nature and functions of schema. In *Centre for the Study of Reading Technical Report, No. (325)*. University of Illinois.

Brezis, E. S. (2011). *The Effects of Elite Recruitment on Social Cohesion and Economic Development*. Retrieved from www.oecd.org/development,pgd/

Briceno, T., & Stagl, S. (2006). The role of social processes for sustainable consumption. *Journal of Cleaner Production*, *14*(17), 1541–1551. doi:10.1016/j.jclepro.2006.01.027

British American Tobacco targeting African Children with cigarettes. (n.d.). In *YouTube*. Retrieved from: http://www.youtube.com/watch?v=ldbRXAOiwWs

Brodowsky, G. H. (1998). The effect of country of design and country of assembly on evaluative beliefs about automobiles and attitudes toward buying them: A comparison between low and high ethnocentric consumers. *Journal of International Consumer Marketing*, *10*(3), 85–113. doi:10.1300/J046v10n03_06

Brown, L. D. (1991). Bridging organizations and sustainable development. *Human Relations*, *44*(8), 807–831. doi:10.1177/001872679104400804

Brown, N. (1992). Beachboys as Culture Brokers in Bakau Town, The Gambia. *Community Development Journal: An International Forum, 27*(4), 361–370. doi:10.1093/oxfordjournals.cdj.a038626

Brown, S. (1998). *Postmodern Marketing 2: Telling Tales*. London: ITP.

Bruning, E. R. (1997). Country of origin, national loyalty and product choice: The case of international air travel. *International Marketing Review, 14*(1), 59–74. doi:10.1108/02651339710159215

Brunk, M. (1973). The Anatomy of Consumerism. *Journal of Advertising, 2*(1), 9–46. doi:10.1080/00913367.1973.10672477

Bulkeley, H. (2005). Reconfiguring environmental governance: Towards a politics of scales and networks. *Political Geography, 24*(8), 875–902. doi:10.1016/j.polgeo.2005.07.002

Burg, E., Podoynitsyna, K., Beck, L., & Lommelen, T. (2012). Directive Deficiencies: How Resource Constraints Direct Opportunity Identification in SMEs. *Journal of Product Innovation Management, 29*(6), 1000–1011. doi:10.1111/j.1540-5885.2012.00976.x

Burt, S., & Gabbott, M. (1995). The elderly consumer and non-food purchase behaviour. *European Journal of Marketing, 29*(2), 43–57. doi:10.1108/03090569510080941

Business Standard. (2012). *Deo-drama hots up for men*. Retrieved July 19, 2015, from, http://www.business-standard.com/india/news/deo-drama-hotsfor-men/472713/

Buskirk, R., & Rothe, J. (1970). Consumerism--An Interpretation. *Journal of Marketing, 34*(4), 61–65. doi:10.2307/1250713

Butler, M. J. (2013). Operationalising Interdisciplinary research – a model of Co-Production in Organisational Cognitive Neuroscience. *Frontiers of Human Neuroscience, 7*, 720. Retrieved on 4/06/2015 from: www.ncbbi.nlm.nih.gov/pmcparticles/PMC3893564/

Butler, M. J. (2008). Neuromarketing and the Perception of Knowledge. *Journal of Consumer Behaviour, 7*(4-5), 415–419. doi:10.1002/cb.260

Butter, E. J., Popovich, P. M., Stackhouse, R. H., & Garner, R. K. (1981). Discrimination of Television Programs and Commercials by Preschool Children. *Journal of Advertising Research, 21*(2), 53–56.

Büttner, O., Florack, A., & Serfas, B. (2014). A Dual-Step and Dual-Process Model of Advertising Effects: Implications for Reducing the Negative Impact of Advertising on Children's Consumption Behaviour. *Journal of Consumer Policy, 37*(2), 161–182. doi:10.100710603-013-9250-0

Caballero, M., & Solomon, P. J. (1984). Effects of model attractiveness on sales response. *Journal of Advertising, 13*(1), 17–23. doi:10.1080/00913367.1984.10672870

Caldwell, N., & Freire, J. (2004). The differences between branding a country, a region and a city: Applying the Brand Box Model. *Journal of Brand Management, 12*(1), 50–59. doi:10.1057/palgrave.bm.2540201

Carey, L., Shaw, D., & Shiu, E. (2008). The impact of ethical concerns on family consumer decision making. *International Journal of Consumer Studies, 32*(5), 553–560. doi:10.1111/j.1470-6431.2008.00687.x

Carlson, L., & Grossbart, S. (1988). Parental Style and Consumer Socialization of Children. *The Journal of Consumer Research, 15*(1), 77–94. doi:10.1086/209147

Carlson, L., Grossbart, S., & Tripp, C. (1990). An Investigation of Mothers' Communication Orientations and Patterns. *Advances in Consumer Research. Association for Consumer Research (U. S.), 17*(1), 804–812.

Carlson, L., Grossbart, S., & Walsh, A. (1990). Mothers' Communication Orientation and Consumer-Socialization Tendencies. *Journal of Advertising*, *19*(3), 27–38. doi:10.1080/00913367.1990.10673190

Carlson, L., Walsh, A., Laczniak, R. N., & Grossbart, S. (1994). Family Communication Patterns and Marketplace Motivations, Attitudes, and Behaviors of Children and Mothers. *The Journal of Consumer Affairs*, *28*(1), 25–53. doi:10.1111/j.1745-6606.1994.tb00813.x

Carraher, S., Parnell, J. A., & Spillan, J. E. (2009). Customer service-orientation of small retail business owners in Austria, the Czech Republic, Hungary, Latvia, Slovakia, and Slovenia. *Baltic Journal of Management*, *4*(3), 251–268. doi:10.1108/17465260910990975

Caruana, A., & Vassallo, R. (2003). Children's perception of their influence over purchases: The role of parental communication patterns. *Journal of Consumer Marketing*, *20*(1), 55–66. doi:10.1108/07363760310456955

Casanova, J. (2001). Religion, the New Millennium, and Globalization. *Sociology of Religion*, *62*(4), 415-441.

Cassim, S. (2005). Advertising to Children in South Africa. *Young Consumers. Quarter*, *2*, 51–55.

Cassim, S., & Langton, R. (1996). Current issues in the regulation of deceptive advertising: Some consequences for South Africa. *South African Journal of Business Management*, *27*(1), 82.

Catholic Forums. (2015). *Is wearing perfumes wrong?* Retrieved July 19, 2015, http://forums.catholic.com/

Celsi, R. L., & Olson, J. C. (1988). The role of Involvement in Attention and comprehension Processes. *The Journal of Consumer Research*, *15*(September), 210–224. doi:10.1086/209158

Census India. (2011). *2011 Census Data*. Retrieved July 19, 2015, from, http://censusindia.gov.in/

Chambor. (2011). *Corporate Overview*. Retrieved July 19, 2015, from www.chambor.com

Chang, D. L., Sabatini-Marques, J., da Costa, E. M., Selig, P. M., & Yigitcanlar, T. (2018). Knowledge-based, smart and sustainable cities: A provocation for a conceptual framework. *Journal of Open Innovation: Technology, Market, and Complexity*, *4*(5), 1–17.

Chan, K. (2006). Consumer socialization of Chinese children in schools: Analysis of consumption values in textbooks. *Journal of Consumer Marketing*, *23*(3), 125–132. doi:10.1108/07363760610663286

Chan, K., & McNeal, J. U. (2006). Rural Chinese children as consumers: Consumption experience and information sources. *Journal of Consumer Behavior: An International Review*, *5*(3), 182–192. doi:10.1002/cb.170

Chan, K., Ng, Y. L., & Luk, E. K. (2013). Impact of celebrity endorsement in advertising on brand image among Chinese adolescents. *Young Consumers*, *14*(2), 167–179. doi:10.1108/17473611311325564

Chankon, K., Yang, Z., & Hanjoon, L. (2009). Cultural differences in Consumer Socialisation: A Comparison of Chinese Canadian and Caucasian Canadian children. *Journal of Business Research*, *62*(10), 955–962. doi:10.1016/j.jbusres.2008.08.005

Chan, R., & Lau, L. (2001). Explaining green purchasing behavior: A cross-cultural study on American and Chinese consumers. *Journal of International Marketing*, *14*(2/3), 9–40.

Chao, P., Wuhrer, G., & Werani, T. (2015). Celebrity and Foreign Brand Name as Moderators of Country-of-Origin Effects. *International Journal of Advertising*, *24*(2), 173–192. doi:10.1080/02650487.2005.11072913

Charbonneau, J., & Garland, R. (2005). Talent, Looks or Brains? New Zealand Advertising Practitioners Views on Celebrity and Athlete Endorsers. *Marketing Bulletin*, *16*(3), 1–10.

Chari, M. D. R., & Dixit, J. (2014). Business groups and entrepreneurship in developing countries after reforms. *Journal of Business Research*. doi:10.1016/j.jbusres.2014.12.006

Chaudhary, M., & Gupta, A. (2012). Children's influence in family buying process in India. *Young Consumers*, *13*(2), 161–175. doi:10.1108/17473611211233512

Chelariu, C., Ouattarra, A., & Dadzie, K. (2002). Market Orientation in Ivory Coast: Measurement Validity and Organizational Antecedents in a sub-Saharan African Economy. *Journal of Business and Industrial Marketing*, *17*(6), 456–470.

Cheng, H., & Patwardhan, P. (2010). One region, two worlds? Cultural values in Chinese and Indian TV commercials. *Asian Journal of Communication*, *20*(1), 69–89. doi:10.1080/01292980903440863

Chen, H., & Li, Y., & Liu, Yi. (2015). Dual capabilities and organizational learning in new product market performance. *Industrial Marketing Management*, *46*, 204–213.

Chen, T. B., & Chai, L. T. (2010). Attitude towards the Environment and Green Products: Consumers' Perspective. *Management Science and Engineering*, *4*(2), 27–39.

Cheung, S. F., Chan, D. K. S., & Wong, Z. S. Y. (1999). Re-examining the Theory of Planned Behavior in Understanding Wastepaper Recycling. *Environment and Behavior*, *31*(5), 587–612. doi:10.1177/00139169921972254

Chikweche, Stanton, & Fletcher. (2012). Family purchase decision making at the bottom of the pyramid. *Journal of Consumer Marketing, 29*(3), 202 – 213.

Childers, C. (2007), Do looks really matter? An investigation of the impact of spokescharacter appearance on childrens purchasing influence Conference Papers. *International Communication Association, 2007 Annual Meeting*, 1.

Child, P., Dennis, R. J., Gokey, T. C., McGuire, T. I., Sherman, M., & Singer, M. (1997). Can Marketing Regain the Personal Touch? *The McKinsey Quarterly*, *3*, 112–125.

Chironga, M., Leke, A., Lund, S., & van Wamelen, A. (2011). Cracking the next growth market: Africa. *Harvard Business Review*, *89*(5), 117–122. PMID:21510523

Chiu, W., Lee, K., & And Won, D. (2014). Consumer Behavior Toward Counterfeit Sporting Goods. *Social Behavior and Personality*, *42*(4), 615–624. doi:10.2224bp.2014.42.4.615

Choi, S. M., Lee, W. N., & Kim, H. J. (2005). Lessons from the rich and famous: A cross-cultural comparison of celebrity endorsement in advertising. *Journal of Advertising*, *34*(2), 91–105. doi:10.1080/00913367.2005.10639190

Choi, S. M., & Rifon, N. J. (2007). Who is the celebrity in advertising? Understanding dimensions of celebrity images. *Journal of Popular Culture*, *40*(2), 304–324. doi:10.1111/j.1540-5931.2007.00380.x

Christensen, C. M., Raynor, M. E., & McDonald, R. (2015). What is disruptive innovation? *Harvard Business Review*, *93*(12), 44–53. PMID:17183796

Chryssochoidis, G., Krystallis, A., & Perreas, P. (2007). Ethnocentric Beliefs and Country-of-Origin (COO) Effect. *European Journal of Marketing*, *41*(11/12), 1518–1544. doi:10.1108/03090560710821288

Chung, J. E., Stoel, L., Xu, Y., & Ren, J. (2012). Predicting Chinese consumers' purchase intentions for imported soy-based dietary supplements. *British Food Journal*, *114*(1), 143–161. doi:10.1108/00070701211197419

Clarke, B. (2005). Children get Media Smart in the UK. *Young Consumers*, *6*(4), 29–34. doi:10.1108/17473610510680894

Clarke, V., & Braun, V. (2017). Thematic analysis. *The Journal of Positive Psychology*, *12*(3), 297–298. doi:10.1080/17439760.2016.1262613

Cohen, M. J. (2005). Sustainable consumption in national context: an introduction to the symposium. *Sustainability: Science, Practice, &. Policy*, *1*(1), 22–28.

Coleman, R. P. (1983). The continuing significance of Social class in Marketing. *The Journal of Consumer Research*, *10*(December), 265–280. doi:10.1086/208966

Combes, J., Ebeke, C. H., Etoundi, S. M. N., & Yogo, T. U. (2014). Are Remittances And Foreign Aid A Hedge Against Food Price Shocks In Developing Countries? World Development, 54, 81–98.

Comm, C. L., & Mathaisel, D. (2005). A case study in applying lean sustainability concepts to universities. *International Journal of Sustainability in Higher Education, 6*(2), 134 – 146.

Connolly, J., & Prothero, A. (2008). Green Consumption Life-politics, risk and contradictions. *Journal of Consumer Culture*, *8*(1), 117–145. doi:10.1177/1469540507086422

Consumer Protection Act. (2009). *I know my rights. Do you know Yours*. The Department of Trade and Industry, Republic of South Africa. Retrieved on 20/06/2015 from http://www.consumer_protection_pocketguide.pdf

Consumers International. (2011). *A guide to developing consumer protection law. Open Society Initiative for Southern Africa (OSISA)*. Consumers International, May. ISBN No.

Consumers International. (2015). *Consumer Rights*. Retrieved on 13/06/2015 from http://www.consumersinternational.org/who-we-are/consumer-rights

Coombe, W. D. (2010). *Branding Dubai: Global Perceptions of a 21st Century Emirate*. American University of Beirut.

Corner, P. D. (2009). Insights from an Eastern Spiritual Tradition. *Journal of Business Ethics*, *85*(3), 377–389. doi:10.100710551-008-9776-2

Craig, C., & John, M. M. (1978). Assessing Communication Effects of Energy Conservation. *The Journal of Consumer Research*, *5*(2), 82–88. doi:10.1086/208718

Cram, F. (1999). Consumer Socialisation, Applied Psychology. *International Review (Steubenville, Ohio)*, *48*(3), 297–312.

CREAT India. (2007). *Consumer Education*. Retrieved July 19, 2015, from http://www.creatindia.org/consumer-education-%20clubs-reading-material.pdf

Cresswell, J. W., & Plano, C. V. L. (2011). *Designing and Conducting mixed method research* (2nd ed.). Thousand Oaks, CA: Sage.

Crotty, J., Driffield, N., & Jones, C. (2016). Regulation as Country-Specific (Dis-) Advantage: Smoking Bans and the Location of Foreign Direct Investment in the Tobacco Industry. *British Journal of Management*, *27*(3), 464–478. doi:10.1111/1467-8551.12161

CTCR. (2007). *Tobacco Papers*. The Centre for Tobacco Control Research. Scotland, UK: University of Strathclyde. Available online at: http://www.tobaccopapers.com/

Cui, G., Lui, H.-K., Chan, T.-S., & Joy, A. (2012). Decomposition of cross-country differences in consumer attitudes toward marketing. *Journal of Consumer Marketing*, *29*(3), 214–224. doi:10.1108/07363761211221747

Cui, T.-S., & Cui, G. (2004). Consumer attitudes toward marketing in a transitional economy: A replication and extension. *Journal of Consumer Marketing*, *21*(1), 10–26. doi:10.1108/07363760410513932

Czinkota, R. M., & Ronkainen, A. I. (2011). *Global business: Positioning ventures ahead*. London: Routledge.

Dahlen, M., Lange, F., & Smith, T. (2010). *Marketing Communications: A Brand Narrative Approach*. Chichester, UK: Wiley & Sons Ltd.

Daley, P. (2013). Rescuing African bodies: Celebrities, consumerism and neoliberal humanitarianism. *Review of African Political Economy*, *40*(137), 375–393. doi:10.1080/03056244.2013.816944

Daneshvary, R., & Schwer, R. K. (2000). The Association Endorsement and Consumers' Intentions to Purchase. *Journal of Consumer Marketing*, *17*(3), 203–213. doi:10.1108/07363760010328987

Dangerfield, B. C. (2003). *The pursuit of understanding: Modelling dynamic behaviour in disease, life and love*. Inaugural Lecture: Professor Brian Dangerfield, 12 November 2003, University of Salford. Retrieved August 19, 2018 from http://usir.salford.ac.uk/17837/

Darley, W. K., & Johnson, D. M. (1993). Cross-National Comparison of Consumer Attitudes Towards Consumerism in Four Developing Countries. *The Journal of Consumer Affairs*, *27*(1), 37–54. doi:10.1111/j.1745-6606.1993.tb00736.x

Dauvergne, P. (2010). The problem of consumption. *Global Environmental Politics*, *10*(2), 1–10. doi:10.1162/glep.2010.10.2.1

Davenport, T., & Beck, J. (2001). *The Attention Economy: Understanding the New Currency of Business*. Boston: Harvard Business School Press.

Davies, G., & Chun, R. (2002). Gaps between the Internal and External Perceptions of the Corporate Brand. *Corporate Reputation Review*, *5*(2/3), 143–159.

Davies, M. A. P., & Wright, L. T. (1993). The Importance of Labelling Examined in Food Marketing. *European Journal of Marketing*, *28*(2), 57–67. doi:10.1108/03090569410055283

Davies, O. (1966). *The Invasion of Ghana from the Sahara in the Early Iron Age. Volta Basin Research Project Publication No. 18*. Reprint from Actes Du V Congres PanAfricain De Pre-Histoire Et De L'etde Du Quarternaire.

Day, E., Stafford, M. R., & Camacho, A. (1995). Opportunities for involvement research: A scale-development. *Journal of Advertising*, *24*(3), 69–75. doi:10.1080/00913367.1995.10673484

Day, G. S. (2000). Managing market relationships. *Journal of the Academy of Marketing Science*, *28*(1), 24–30. doi:10.1177/0092070300281003

Day, G., & Aaker, D. (1970). A guide to consumerism. *Journal of Marketing*, *34*(3), 12–19. doi:10.2307/1249814

De Chernatony, L. (1999). Brand management through narrowing the gap between brand identity and brand reputation. *Journal of Marketing Management*, *15*(1-3), 157–179. doi:10.1362/026725799784870432

De Chernatony, L. (2001). *From Brand Vision to Brand Evaluation*. Oxford, UK: Butterworth Heinemann.

De Chernatony, L., & Harris, F. (2001). Corporate branding and corporate brand performance. *European Journal of Marketing*, *35*(3/4), 441–456. doi:10.1108/03090560110382101

De Grazia, V. (2005). *Irresistible Empire: America's Advance through Twentieth-Century Europe*. Cambridge, MA: Belknap Press.

De Mooij, M. (2004). *Consumer Behaviour and Culture: Consequences for Global Marketing*. Sage.

De Mooij, M. (2010). *Global Marketing and Advertising: Understanding Cultural Paradoxes*. Thousand Oaks, CA: SAGE Puplications.

de Mooij, M. (2011). *Consumer Behaviour and Culture* (2nd ed.). London: Sage.

DeCorse, C. R. (2001). *An Archaeology of Elmina: Africans and Europeans on the Gold Coast, 1400-1900*. Smithsonian Institute Press.

DeKoning, A. J., & Muzyka, D. F. (1999). *Conceptualizing Opportunity Recognition as a Socio-Cognitive Process*. SSE/EFI Working Paper Series in Business Administration No 1999:13.

Deliya, M. M., & Parmar, J. B. (2012). Role of packaging on consumer buying behavior – Patan district. *Global Journal of Management and Business Research, 12*(10), 48–69.

Deming, D. M., Briefel, R. R., & Reidy, K. C. (2014). Infant Feeding Practices and Food Consumption Pattern of Children participating in WIC. *Journal of Nutrition Education and Behavior, 46*(3), s29–s37. doi:10.1016/j.jneb.2014.02.020 PMID:24809994

Department of Social Development South Africa. (2015). *State of South African NPO Register 2014-2015*. Author.

Dike, O., & Onah, J. (2014). Evaluating Consumers' Protective Measures Against unethical Marketing of Medical Drugs in Nigeria. *International Journal of Business and Management Invention, 3*(1), 14–21.

Ding, Q. (2017). Chinese products for Chinese people? Consumer ethnocentrism in China. *International Journal of Retail & Distribution Management, 45*(5), 550–564. doi:10.1108/IJRDM-11-2016-0212

Dinnie, K. (2015). *Nation branding: Concepts, Issues, Practice*. London: Routledge.

DIT. (2015). *Doing business in the United Arab Emirates: UAE trade and export guide*. Available at: https://www.gov.uk/government/publications/exporting-to-the-united-arab-emirates/exporting-to-the-united-arab-emirates

Djossa, C. A. (2018). *Celebrating Ghana's amazing handpainted barbershop signs: These vibrant artworks advertised the freshest styles and sleekest cuts*. Retrieved from: https://www.atlasobscura.com/articles/ghana-artists-paintings-wooden-signs

Dlamini, I. Z., Ngobeni, S. J., & Mutanga, M. B. (2010). South African Egov: Secure E-Services. *Proceedings of eChalleges e-2010 Conference and Exhibition*, 1-8.

Dmitrovic, T., Vida, I., & Reardon, J. (2009). Purchase behavior in favor of domestic products in the West Balkans. *International Business Review, 18*(5), 523–535. doi:10.1016/j.ibusrev.2009.05.003

Dobrow, L. (2006). Teen angel? Kinda. *Advertising Age, 77*(1), 14.

DoH. (2008a). *NHS Stop Smoking Services & Nicotine Replacement Therapy*. Department of Health, UK. Available online at: http://www.dh.gov.uk/en/Policyandguidance/Healthandsocialcaretopics/Tobacco/Tobaccogeneralinformation/DH_4002192

DoH. (2008b). *Reducing exposure to second hand smoke*. Department of Health, UK. Available online at: http://www.dh.gov.uk/en/Policyandguidance/Healthandsocialcaretopics/Tobacco/Tobaccogeneralinformation/DH_4080093

Dolan, P. (2002). The Sustainability of "Sustainable Consumption. *Journal of Macromarketing, 22*(2), 170–181. doi:10.1177/0276146702238220

Donoghue, S., & de Klerk, H. M. (2009). The right to be heard and to be understood: A conceptual framework for consumer protection in emerging economies. *International Journal of Consumer Studies, 33*(4), 456–467. doi:10.1111/j.1470-6431.2009.00773.x

Dotson, M. J., & Hyatt, E. M. (2000). A comparison of parents' and children's knowledge of brands and advertising slogans in the United States: Implications for consumer socialization. *Journal of Marketing Communications, 6*(4), 219–230. doi:10.1080/135272600750036346

Dotson, M. J., & Hyatt, E. M. (2005). Major influence factors in children's consumer socialization. *Journal of Consumer Marketing*, *22*(1), 35–42. doi:10.1108/07363760510576536

Dowouna-Hammond, M. C., Atuguba, D. R., & Nabila, D. L. (2006). *Legal and Policy Framework for Consumer Protection in Ghana*. Accra: Friedrich Ebert Foundation, Ghana.

Drayton, W. (2002). The citizen sector: Becoming as entreprenurial and competitive as business. *California Management Review*, *44*(3), 120–133. doi:10.2307/41166136

Drenttel, W. (2004). *My Country Is Not A Brand*. Available at: https://designobserver.com/feature/my-country-is-not-a-brand/2707

Dresden, B., & Barnard, J. (2003). Legal and regulatory controls on advertising and marketing to children in the United Kingdom. *Young Consumers*, *5*(1), 77–83.

Driessens, O. (2013). The celebritization of society and culture: Understanding the structural dynamics of celebrity culture. *International Journal of Cultural Studies*, *16*(6), 641–657. doi:10.1177/1367877912459140

Drucker, P. (1958). Marketing and Economic Development. *Journal of Marketing*, *22*(3), 252–259. doi:10.2307/1247116

Drucker, P. (1969). *Consumerism in Marketing, A speech to the National Association of Manufacturers*. New York: Association of Manufacturers.

Druckman, D. (1994). Nationalism, patriotism, and group loyalty: A social psychological perspective. *Mershon International Studies Review*, *38*(1), 43–68. doi:10.2307/222610

Du Plessis, E. (2011). *The Branded Mind* (1st ed.). London, UK: Kogan Page Limited.

Dubai Statistics Center. (2016). *Expatriates living in Dubai*. Available at: https://www.dsc.gov.ae/Report/Gross%20Domestic%20Product%20at%20Current%20Prices%202015-2014.pdf

Dubois, N., & Janmohamed, S. (2011). *The rise of the young Muslim consumer*. Retrieved July 19, 2015, from http://sparksheet.com/branding-halal-the-rise-of-the-young-muslim-consumer/

Dumbili, E. W. (2017). The influence of alcohol industry-sponsored "Gulder Ultimate Search" reality television series on the drinking behaviors of Nigerian youths. *Journal of Substance Use*, *22*(2), 159–167. doi:10.3109/14659891.2016.1166271

Durvasula, S., & Lysonski, S. (2008). A double-edged sword: Understanding vanity across cultures. *Journal of Consumer Marketing*, *25*(4), 230–244. doi:10.1108/07363760810882425

Durvasula, S., & Lysonski, S. (2010). Money, money, money – how do attitudes toward money impact vanity and materialism? – The case of young Chinese consumers. *Journal of Consumer Marketing*, *27*(2), 169–179. doi:10.1108/07363761011027268

Du, X., Jiao, J., & Tseng, M. M. (2003). Identifying customer need patterns for customization and personalization. *Integrated Manufacturing Systems*, *14*(5), 387–396. doi:10.1108/09576060310477799

Dzisah, W. E., & Ocloo, C. E. (2013). Celebrity endorsement and consumer buying behaviour; enhancing the promotion function of marketing in the central business area of Accra, Ghana. *European Journal of Business and Management*, *5*(25), 197–208.

Eades, J. S. (1994). *Strangers and Traders: Yoruba Migrants, Markets and the State in Northern Ghana*. Trenton, NJ: Africa World Press Incorporated.

Easterling, D., Miller, S., & Weinberger, N. (1995). Environmental consumerism: A process of children's socialization and families' resocialization. *Psychology and Marketing*, *12*(6), 531–550. doi:10.1002/mar.4220120606

East, R. (1997). *Consumer Behaviour: Advances and Applications in Marketing Hertfordshire*. Prentice Hall.

East, R. (1997). *Consumer Behaviour: Advances and Applications in Marketing*. Hertfordshire: Prentice Hall.

Edwards, P. (2013). *Neuroscience and Reductionism: Some Realist Reflections*. Birmingham Business School. Discussion Paper Series, 2013 – 2008.

Egwemi, V. (2010). Managing Nigeria's Image Crisis: Akunyili's Rebranding Programme to the Rescue (?) Current Research. *Journal of Economic Theory*, *2*(3), 131–135.

Eisenhardt, K. M. (1989). Building theories from case study research. *Academy of Management Review*, *14*(4), 532–550. doi:10.5465/amr.1989.4308385

Eisenhardt, K. M., & Graebner, M. E. (2007). Theory building from cases: Opportunities and challenges. *Academy of Management Journal*, *50*(1), 25–32. doi:10.5465/amj.2007.24160888

Ekins, P., & Lemaire, X. (2012). *Sustainable Consumption and Production for Poverty Alleviation. United Nations Environment Programme*. Retrieved July 1, 2015 from www.unep.org/pdf/SCP_Poverty_full_final.pdf

Ekstrom, K. H., Tansuhaj, P. S., & Foxman, E. R. (1987). Children's Influence in Family Decisions and Consumer Socialization: A Reciprocal view. *Advances in Consumer Research. Association for Consumer Research (U. S.)*, *14*(1), 283–287.

Ekundayo, J. M. (2013). *Out of Africa: Fashola-Reinventing Servant Leadership to Engender Nigeria's Transformation*. Bloomington, IN: Author House.

Elias, I. A., Etim, E. O., Etukafia, N. I., Akpanuko, E. E., & Ntiedo, B. E. (2017). Synopsis of Nigerian Economy and the Growth of Ponzi Schemes. *Global Journal of Management and Business Research: B Economics and Commerce*, *17*(3), 2249–4588.

Ellison, S., & Sidel, R. (2003). *Procter & Gamble Nears Deal To Buy Wella for $5.9 Billion*. Retrieved July 19, 2015, from www.wsj.com

Emirate247. (2016). *Dubai's hotel industry soaring high*. Available at: http://www.emirates247.com/news/dubai-s-hotel-industry-soaring-high-2016-04-28-1.628595

Emirates247. (2015). *Muslims can spray on alcohol based perfumes*. Retrieved July 19, 2015, from http://www.emirates247.com

Encyclopædia Britannica. (2017). *Lagos: Nigeria*. Available at: https://www.britannica.com/place/Lagos-Nigeria

Engel, J. F., Blackwell, R. D., & Miniard, P. W. (1995). *Consumer Behavior* (8th ed.; pp. 364–365). Orlando, FL: The Dryden Press.

Engen, T. (1982). *The perception of odors*. New York, NY: Academic Press.

Eniola, T. (2016, December 1). Ponzi palava: Nigerians count losses, blame recession for MMM woes. *The Punch Newspaper*.

Erdem, T., & Swait, J. (2004). Brand credibility, brand consideration, and choice. *The Journal of Consumer Research*, *31*(1), 191–198. doi:10.1086/383434

Erdogan, B. Z. (1999). Celebrity Endorsement: A Literature Review. *Journal of Marketing Management*, *41*(3), 291–314. doi:10.1362/026725799784870379

Erdogan, B. Z., Baker, M. J., & Tagg, S. (2001). Selecting celebrity endorsers: The practitioner's perspective. *Journal of Advertising Research, 41*(3), 39–48. doi:10.2501/JAR-41-3-39-48

Erdogan, B. Z., & Uzkurt, C. (2010). Effects of ethnocentric tendency on consumers' perception of product attitudes for foreign and domestic products. *Cross Cultural Management, 17*(4), 393–406. doi:10.1108/13527601011086595

Erisman, H. M. (1983). Tourism and cultural dependency in the West Indies. *Annals of Tourism Research, 10*(3), 337–361. doi:10.1016/0160-7383(83)90061-0

Ernst and Young. (2012). *Rapid-growth markets soft power index*. Available at: http://www.ey.com/Publication/vwLU-Assets/Rapid

Ernst, H., Kahle, H. N., Dubiel, A., Prabhu, J., & Subramaniam, M. (2015). The Antecedents and Consequences of Affordable Value Innovations for Emerging Markets. *Journal of Product Innovation Management, 32*, 65–79.

Escalas, J. E., & Bettman, J. R. (2005). Self-construal, reference groups and brand meaning. *The Journal of Consumer Research, 32*(3), 378–389. doi:10.1086/497549

Esoimeme, E. E., & Sasegbon, D. (2018). The money laundering risks and vulnerabilities associated with MMM Nigeria. *Journal of Money Laundering Control, 21*(1), 112–119. doi:10.1108/JMLC-01-2017-0002

Etemad-Sajadi, R. (2015). The impact of service tradability on the choice of entry mode: The case of computer-related service firms. *Total Quality Management Journal, 27*(1), 79–93.

e-Tshwane. (2018). *e-Tshwane*. Available at: https://www.e-tshwane.co.za/eTshwane/

Etzel, M. J., & Walker, B. J. (1974). Advertising Strategy for Foreign Products. *Journal of Advertising Research, 14*, 41–44.

Etzioni, A. (1998). Voluntary Simplicity: Characterization, Select Psychological Implications, and Societal Consequences. *Journal of Economic Psychology, 19*, 619–643.

Euromonitor International. (2013, August). *How BRICS consumers behave*. London: Euromonitor.

Euromonitor International. (2018, March). *Shifting market frontiers: Africa rising*. London: Euromonitor.

Euromonitor. (2017, September). *Consumer lifestyles in South Africa*. London: Euromonitor.

Evanschitzky, H., Wangenheim, F. V., Woisetschla, D., & Blut, M. (2008). Consumer ethnocentrism in the German market. *International Marketing Review, 25*, 7–32. doi:10.1108/02651330810851863

Ewa, J., & Kamil, W. (2015). *The nationality and the type of celebrities endorsing products versus ethnocentric attitudes of Polish consumers*. Conference paper.

Eze, A. G. (2012). Consumer Rights as Constitutional Rights: A comparative analysis of some selected jurisdictions. *Nnamdi Azikiwe University Journal of International Law and Jurisprudence*, 184 – 196.

Fafchamps, M. (1996). The Enforcement of Commercial Contracts in Ghana. *World Development, 24*(3), 427–448.

Fan, Y. (2006). Branding the Nation: What is being Branded? *Journal of Vacation Marketing, 12*(1), 5–14. doi:10.1177/1356766706056633

Farhat, R., & Mustafa Khan, B. (2011). Importance of Brand Personality to Customer Loyalty : A Conceptual Study. *New Media and Mass Communication, 1*, 4–11.

Farquhar, P. H. (1989). Managing Brand Equity. *Marketing Research, 1*(3), 24–33.

Fatusia, A. O., & Hindin, M. J. (2010). Adolescents and youth in developing countries: Health and development issues in context. *Journal of Adolescence*, *33*(4), 499–508. doi:10.1016/j.adolescence.2010.05.019 PMID:20598362

Ferenhof, H., & Fernandes, R. (2016). Desmistificando a revisão de literatura como base para a redação científica: Método SSF. *Revista ACB*, *21*, 550–563.

Ferguson, N. (2009). Think Again: Power. *Foreign Policy*. Available at: http://foreignpolicy.com/2009/11/03/think-again-power/

Festervand, T. A., Lumpkin, J. R., & Lundstrom, W. J. (1985). Consumers' Perceptions of Imports: An Update and Extension. *Akron Business and Economic Review*, *16*, 31–33.

Festervand, T. A., & Sokoya, S. K. (1994). Consumer Ethnocentrism in a Developing Economy: A Preliminary Investigation. *The International Executive*, *36*(1), 95–105. doi:10.1002/tie.5060360107

Festinger, L. (1957). *A Theory of Cognitive Dissonance*. Stanford, CA: Stanford University Press.

Filho, W. L. (2000). Dealing with misconceptions on the concept of sustainability. *International Journal of Sustainability in Higher Education*, *1*(1), 9–19. doi:10.1108/1467630010307066

Fireworker, R. B., & Friedman, H. H. (1977). The Effects of Endorsements on Product Evaluation. *Decision Sciences*, *8*(3), 576–583. doi:10.1111/j.1540-5915.1977.tb01104.x

Fisher, C. E., Chin, L., & Klitzman, R. (2010). Defining Neuromarketing: Practices and Professional Challenges. *Harvard Review of Psychiatry*, *18*(4), 230–237. doi:10.3109/10673229.2010.496623 PMID:20597593

Fisk, G. (1973). Criteria for a Theory of Responsible Consumption. *Journal of Marketing*, *37*(2), 24–31. doi:10.2307/1250047

Fleck, N., Korchia, M., & Roy, I. L. (2012). Celebrities in advertising: Looking for congruence or likability? *Psychology and Marketing*, *29*(9), 651–662. doi:10.1002/mar.20551

Fletcher, R., & Crawford, H. (2013). *International marketing: an Asia Pacific perspective, 6th*. Frenchs Forest, NSW: Pearson Australia.

Flouri, E. (1999). An Integrated Model of Consumer Materialism: Can Economic Socialization and Maternal Values Predict Materialistic Attitudes in Adolescents? *Journal of Socio-Economics*, *28*(6), 707–724. doi:10.1016/S1053-5357(99)00053-0

Flyvbjerg, B. (2006). Five misunderstandings about case-study research. *Qualitative Inquiry*, *12*(2), 219–245. doi:10.1177/1077800405284363

Follows, S. B., & Jobber, D. (2000). Environmentally responsible purchase behaviour: A test of a consumer model. *European Journal of Marketing*, *34*(5/6), 723–746. doi:10.1108/03090560010322009

Fornell, C., & Larcker, D. F. (1981). Evaluating structural equation models with unobservable variables and measurement error. *JMR, Journal of Marketing Research*, *18*(1), 39–50. doi:10.2307/3151312

Forno, F., & Graziano, P. R. (2014). Sustainable community movement organisations. *Journal of Consumer Culture*, *14*(2), 139–157. doi:10.1177/1469540514526225

Foroudi, P., Gupta, S., Kitchen, P., Foroudi, M. M., & Nguyen, B. (2016). A framework of place branding, place image, and place reputation: Antecedents and moderators. *Qualitative Market Research*, *19*(2), 241–264. doi:10.1108/QMR-02-2016-0020

Foss, B., Stone, M., & Ekinci, Y. (2008). What makes for CRM system success—Or failure? *Journal of Database Marketing & Customer Strategy Management*, *15*(2), 68–78. doi:10.1057/dbm.2008.5

Foxall, G. R., & Goldsmith, R. E. (1994). *Consumer Psychology for marketing*. London: Routledge.

Freeman, K. S., & Chen, C. C. 2015. *Wither the Impact of Celebrity Endorsement.* Paper presented at the International Conference on Communication, Media, Technology and Design, Dubai, UAE.

Friedman, H. H., & Friedman, L. (1979). Endorser effectiveness by product type. *Journal of Advertising Research, 19*(5), 63–71.

Friedman, P., Dyke, L. S., & Murphy, S. A. (2009). Expatriate Adjustment from the Inside Out: An Ethnographic Account. *International Journal of Human Resource Management, 20*(2), 252–268. doi:10.1080/09585190802670524

Frost, R. (2004). *Mapping a Country's Future.* Available at: http://www.brandchannel.com/features_effect.asp?pf_id=206

Fry, J. N., & Siller, F. H. (1970). A Comparison of Housewife Decision Making in Two Social Classes. *JMR, Journal of Marketing Research, 7*(3), 333–337. doi:10.2307/3150291

Fyall, A., & Leask, A. (2007). Destination marketing: Future issues-Strategic challenges. *Tourism and Hospitality Research, 7*(1), 50–63. doi:10.1057/palgrave.thr.6050029

Gana, A. T. (1985). The State in Africa: Yesterday, Today and Tomorrow. *International Political Science Review, 6*(1), 115–132. doi:10.1177/019251218500600112

Ganesh, J., & Kumar, V. (1996). Capturing the cross-national learning effect: An analysis of an industrial technology diffusion. *Journal of the Academy of Marketing Science, 24*, 328–337.

Gartner, W. C. (1989). Tourism image: Attribute measurement of state tourism products using multidimensional calling techniques. *Journal of Travel Research, 28*(2), 15–19. doi:10.1177/004728758902800205

Gartner, W. C. (1993). Image formation process. *Journal of Travel & Tourism Marketing, 2*(2), 191–215.

Gaurdian. (2015). *Procter & Gamble sells 43 of its beauty brands to Coty for $15bn.* Retrieved July 19, 2015, from www.theguardian.com

Gbadamosi, A. (2018a). The Changing Landscape of Young Consumer Behaviour. In Young Consumer Behaviour: A Research Companion. Oxfordshire, UK: Routledge.

Gbadamosi, A. (2018b). The Changing Landscape of Young Consumer Behaviour. In Young Consumer Behaviour: A Research Companion (pp. 3-22). Oxfordshire, UK: Routledge.

Gbadamosi, A. (Ed.). (2016). Handbook of Research on Consumerism and Buying Behaviour in Developing Nations. Hershey, PA: IGI Global.

Gbadamosi, A. (Ed.). (2018a). Young Consumer Behaviour: A Research Companion. Oxfordshire, UK: Routledge.

Gbadamosi, A., Fletcher, K., Emmanuel Stephen, C., & Olutola, I. C. (2018). Consumerism and Consumer Protection: A Focus on Young Consumers. In Young Consumer Behaviour: A Research Companion (pp. 391-413). Oxfordshire, UK: Routledge.

Gbadamosi, A., Fletcher, K., Emmanuel Stephen, C., & Olutola, I. C. (2018). Consumerism and Consumer Protection: A Focus on Young Consumers. In Young Consumer Behaviour: A Research Companion. Routledge.

Gbadamosi, A. (2009). Cognitive dissonance: The implicit explication in low-income consumers' shopping behaviour for 'low-involvement' grocery products. *International Journal of Retail & Distribution Management, 37*(12), 1077–1095. doi:10.1108/09590550911005038

Gbadamosi, A. (2010). Regulating child-related advertising in Nigeria. *Young Consumers*, *11*(3), 204–214. doi:10.1108/17473611011074278

Gbadamosi, A. (2012a). Exploring Children, Family, and Consumption Behaviour: Empirical Evidence from Nigeria. *Thunderbird International Business Review*, *54*(4), 591–605. doi:10.1002/tie.21486

Gbadamosi, A. (2012b). Acculturation: An Exploratory Study of Clothing Consumption among Black African Women in London (UK). *Journal of Fashion Marketing and Management*, *16*(1), 5–20. doi:10.1108/13612021211203005

Gbadamosi, A. (2013). Consumer Involvement and Marketing in Africa: Some Directions for Future Research. *International Journal of Consumer Studies*, *37*(2), 234–242. doi:10.1111/j.1470-6431.2012.01096.x

Gbadamosi, A. (2013). Consumer involvement and marketing in Africa: Some directions for future research. *International Journal of Consumer Studies*, *37*, 234–242.

Gbadamosi, A. (2015a). Family Consumption Systems in Africa: A Focus on Children. In S. Nwankwo & K. Ibeh (Eds.), *Routledge Companion to Business in Africa* (pp. 146–159). Oxfordshire, UK: Routledge.

Gbadamosi, A. (2015b). Exploring the Growing Link of Ethnic Entrepreneurship, Markets, and Pentecostalism in London (UK): An Empirical study. *Society and Business Review*, *10*(2), 150–169. doi:10.1108/SBR-11-2014-0053

Gbadamosi, A. (2015c). Brand Personification and Symbolic Consumption among Ethnic Teenage Consumers: An Empirical study. *Journal of Brand Management*, *22*(9), 737–759. doi:10.1057/bm.2015.40

Gbadamosi, A. (2018b). The Anatomy of International Students' Acculturation in UK Universities. *Industry and Higher Education*, *32*(2), 129–138. doi:10.1177/0950422218760335

Gbadamosi, A. (2018d). Women Entrepreneurship, Religiosity, and Value-co-creation with Ethnic Consumers: Revisiting the Paradox. *Journal of Strategic Marketing*. doi:10.1080/0965254X.2017.1344293

Gbadamosi, A., Fletcher, K.-A., Emmanuel-Stephen, C., & Olutola, I. (2018). Consumerism and consumer protection: A focus on young consumers. In A. Gbadamosi (Ed.), *Young Consumer Behaviour: A Research Companion* (pp. 391–413). London: Routledge, Taylor & Francis Group.

Gbadamosi, A., Hinson, R., Eddy, T. K., & Ingunjiri, I. (2012). Children's attitudinal reactions to TV advertisements: The African experience. *International Journal of Market Research*, *54*(4), 543–566. doi:10.2501/IJMR-54-4-543-566

Geels, F. W., McMeekin, A., Mylan, J., & Southerton, D. (2015). A critical appraisal of Sustainable Consumption and Production research: The reformist, revolutionary and reconfiguration positions. *Global Environmental Change*, *34*, 1–12. doi:10.1016/j.gloenvcha.2015.04.013

Gelfand, M. (1970). Unhu – The personality of the Shona. *Studies in Comparative Religion*, *4*(1).

Ger, G., Belk, R. W., & Lascu, D. N. (1993). The development of consumer desire in marketizing and developing economies: The cases of Romania and Turkey. *Advances in Consumer Research. Association for Consumer Research (U. S.)*, *20*, 102–107.

Geuens, M., De Pelsmacker, P., & Mast, G. (2003). How family structure affects parent—child communication about consumption. *International Journal of Advertising and Marketing to Children*, *4*(2), 57.

Ghalandari, K., & Norouzi, A. (2012). The Effect of Country of Origin on Purchase Intention: The Role of Product Knowledge. *Research Journal of Applied Sciences, Engineering and Technology*, *4*, 1166–1171.

Ghana Statistical Service (GSS). (2013). *2010 Population and Housing Census: National Report*. Accra: Ghana Statistical Service.

Ghauri, P., & Gronhaug, K. (2010). *Research Methods in Business Studies: A Practical Guide* (4th ed.). London: FT-Pearson.

Giannopoulos, A. A., Piha, P. L., & Avlonitis, G. J. (2011). An International Conference on the Future of Nation Branding, Tourism and International Investments in a Globalized World & Cultural Diplomacy in the Global Economy: A Forum for Young Leaders (CDEC). Berlin, Germany.

Gilbert, D. C., & Jackaria, N. (2002). The efficacy of sales promotions in UK supermarkets: A consumer view. *International Journal of Retail & Distribution Management*, *30*(6), 315–322. doi:10.1108/09590550210429522

Gilboa, E. (2008). Searching for a theory of public diplomacy. *The Annals of the American Academy of Political and Social Science*, *616*(1), 55–77. doi:10.1177/0002716207312142

Gilmore, F. (2002). A country - can it be repositioned? Spain - the successful story of country branding. *Journal of Brand Management*, *9*(4/5), 281–293. doi:10.1057/palgrave.bm.2540078

Giones, F., Zhou, Z., Miralles, F., & Katzy, B. (2013, June). From Ideas to Opportunities: Exploring the Construction of Technology-Based Entrepreneurial Opportunities. *Technology Innovation Management Review*, 13–20.

Glaser, B. G., & Strauss, A. L. (1967). The discovery of grounded theory. *International Journal of Qualitative Methods*, *5*, 1–10.

Gleim, M. R., Smith, J., Andrews, D., & Cronin, J. J. Jr. (2013). Against the green: A multi-method examination of the barriers to green consumption. *Journal of Retailing*, *89*(1), 44–61. doi:10.1016/j.jretai.2012.10.001

Glimcher, P. (2003). *Decisions, Uncertainty and the Brain: The Science of Neuroeconomics*. London: MIT Press.

Global Outlook. (2012). *India targeted by international perfume giants*. Retrieved July 19, 2015, from www.researchandmarkets.com

Godelnik, R. (2012, December 28). *2012: Four Trends in Sustainable Consumption*. Retrieved from http://www.triplepundit.com/2012/12/sustainable-consumption-trends/

Goldstein, S. B., & Keller, S. R. (2015). US College Students' Lay Theories of Culture Shock. *International Journal of Intercultural Relations*, *47*, 187–194. doi:10.1016/j.ijintrel.2015.05.010

Golf in Dubai. (2017). *Dubai Heritage and Culture*. Available at: https://www.golfindubai.com/visit-dubai/culture

Gómez, M., Fernández, A. C., Molina, A., & Aranda, E. (2016). City branding in European capitals: An analysis from the visitor perspective. *Journal of Destination Marketing & Management*, *7*, 190–201. doi:10.1016/j.jdmm.2016.11.001

Good, L. K., & Huddleston, P. (1995). Ethnocentrism of Polish and Russian consumers: Are feelings and intentions related? *International Marketing Review*, *12*(5), 35–48. doi:10.1108/02651339510103047

Goodland, R. (1995). The concept of environmental sustainability. *Annual Review of Ecology and Systematics*, *26*(1), 1–24. doi:10.1146/annurev.es.26.110195.000245

Goodman, L. A. (1961). Snowball Sampling. *Annals of Mathematical Statistics*, *32*(1), 148–170.

Goodwin, N., Nelson, J. A., Ackerman, F., & Weisskopf, T. (2008). Consumption and the Consumer Society. Global Development and Environment Institute.

Graf, A. (2009). Marketing a city-state: Hamburg and Singapore in comparison. In A. Graf & C. B. Huat (Eds.), *Port Cities in Asia and Europe* (pp. 176–189). New York: Routledge.

Granovetter, M. (1985). Economic action and social structure: The problem of embeddedness. *American Journal of Sociology*, *91*(3), 481–510. doi:10.1086/228311

Grant, L. (2014). *Research shows sharp increase in service delivery protests*. Retrieved from http://mg.co.za/article/2014-02-12-research-shows-sharp-increase-in-service-delivery-protests

Granzin, K. L., & Olsen, J. E. (1998). Americans' choice of domestic over foreign products: A matter of helping behavior? *Journal of Business Research*, *43*(1), 39–54. doi:10.1016/S0148-2963(97)00101-X

Greendex. (2015). *Third annual survey*. Retrieved July 19, 2015, from http://environment.nationalgeographic.com/environment/greendex/

Green, K. C., & Armstrong, J. S. (2012). Evidence on the effects of mandatory disclaimers in advertising. *Journal of Public Policy & Marketing*, *31*(2), 293–304. doi:10.1509/jppm.12.053

Gro¨nroos, C. (2001). *Service Management and Marketing: A Customer Relationship Management Approach*. Chichester, UK: Wiley.

Grønhaug, K., & Kleppe, I. A. (2010). The Sociological Basis of Marketing. In Marketing Theory: A Student Text. London: Sage Publication Ltd. doi:10.4135/9781446280096.n7

Grossbart, S. L., & Crosby, L. A. (1984). Understanding the Bases of Parental Concern and Reaction to Children's Food Advertising. *Journal of Marketing*, *48*(3), 79–92. doi:10.2307/1251331

Gudjonsson, H. (2005). Nation branding. *Place Branding*, *1*(3), 283–298. doi:10.1057/palgrave.pb.5990029

Gulati, M., & Naudé, L. (2017). *Chewing over consumption based carbon emissions accounting*. WWF-SA. Retrieved on July 7th, 2018 from www.wwf.org.za/report/consumption_based_carbon_accounting

Gulati, R. (1995). Does Familiarity Breed Trust? The Implications of Repeated Ties for Contractual Choices in Alliances. *Academy of Management Journal*, *38*, 85–112.

Gul, M. C. (2013). Long-term Orientation, Perceived Consumer Effectiveness, and Environmentally Conscious Consumer Behavior: The Case of Turkey. *International Journal of Marketing Studies.*, *5*(5), 23–31. doi:10.5539/ijms.v5n5p24

Guneri, B., Yurt, O., Kaplan, M. D., & Delen, M. (2009). The influence of children on family purchasing decisions in Turkey. *Asian Journal of Marketing*, *2*(1), 20–32.

Gunn, C. A. (1972). *Vacationscape. Designing Tourist Regions, Taylor and Francis*. Washington, DC: University of Texas.

Gürhan-Canli, Z., & Maheswaran, D. (2000). Cultural Variations in Country-of-Origin Effects. *JMR, Journal of Marketing Research*, *37*(3), 309–317. doi:10.1509/jmkr.37.3.309.18778

Gurhan-Canli, Z., & Maheswaran, D. (2000). Determinants of country-of-origin evaluations. *The Journal of Consumer Research*, *27*(1), 96–108. doi:10.1086/314311

Guthrie, M., Kim, H., & Jung, J. (2008). The effects of facial image and cosmetic usage on perceptions of brand personality. *Journal of Fashion Marketing and Management*, *12*(2), 164–181. doi:10.1108/13612020810874863

Haffar, M., Al-Hyari, K., Muhammed, A., & Al-Weshah, G. (2012). Religious beliefs and consumer behaviour: From loyalty to boycotts. *Journal of Islamic Marketing*, *3*(2), 155–174. doi:10.1108/17590831211232564

Hair, J. F., Black, W. C., Babin, B. J., & Anderson, R. E. (2010). *Multivariate Data Analysis*. Upper Saddle River, NJ: Prentice-Hall.

Hair, J. F., Sarstedt, M., Ringle, C. M., & Mena, J. A. (2012). An assessment of the use of partial least squares structural equation modeling in marketing research. *Journal of the Academy of Marketing Science*, *40*(3), 414–433. doi:10.100711747-011-0261-6

Hakimi, B. Y., Abedniya, A., & Zaeim, M. N. (2011). Investigate the impact of celebrity endorsement on brand images. *European Journal of Scientific Research, 58*(1), 116–132.

Halinen, A., Törnroos, J. Å., & Elo, M. (2013). Network process analysis: An event-based approach to study business network dynamics. *Industrial Marketing Management, 42*(8), 1213–1222. doi:10.1016/j.indmarman.2013.05.001

Halliru, M. (2012). The development of consumerism in Nigeria: Prospects and challenges. *International Journal of Arts and Commerce, 1*(4), 274–285.

Hall, T. (2010). An Unclear Attraction: A Critical Examination of Soft Power as an Analytical Category. *The Chinese Journal of International Politics, 3*(2), 189–211. doi:10.1093/cjip/poq005

Hamann, R., & Acutt, N. (2003). How should civil society (and the government) respond to 'corporate social responsibility'? A critique of business motivations and the potential for partnerships. *Development Southern Africa, 20*(2), 255–270. doi:10.1080/03768350302956

Hamidizadeh, M. R., Alavije, M. R. K., & Rezaee, M. (2014). The Effect of Perceived Business Ethics on Brand Personality Dimensions & Creation of Brand Equity in Developing Countries. *Central European Business Review, 3*(3), 46–53. doi:10.18267/j.cebr.93

Hamilton, K., & Catterall, M. (2006). Consuming love in poor families: Childrens influence on consumption decisions. *Journal of Marketing Management, 22*(9-10), 1031–1052. doi:10.1362/026725706778935655

Hamin, & Elliott, G. (2006). A less-developed country perspective of consumer ethnocentrism and "country of origin" effects: Indonesian evidence. *Asia Pacific Journal of Marketing and Logistics, 18*(2), 79–92. doi:10.1108/13555850610658246

Hammerl, M., Dorner, F., Foscht, T., & Brandstätter, M. (2016). Attribution of symbolic brand meaning: The interplay of consumers, brands and reference groups. *Journal of Consumer Marketing, 33*(1), 32–40. doi:10.1108/JCM-12-2014-1243

Han, C. M., & Terpstra, V. (1988). Country-of-origin effects for uni-national and bi-national products. *Journal of International Business Studies, 19*(2), 235–256. doi:10.1057/palgrave.jibs.8490379

Hanekom, J., & Scriven, C. (2002). Traditional and online advertising: An explanation of current and future trends. *Communication, 28*(1), 49–59.

Hansen, U. E., Pedersen, M. B., & Nygaard, I. (2015). Review of solar PV policies, interventions and diffusion in East Africa. *Renewable & Sustainable Energy Reviews, 46*, 236–248.

Hargreaves, T. (2011). Practice-ing behaviour change: Applying social practice theory to pro-environmental behaviour change. *Journal of Consumer Culture, 11*(1), 79–99. doi:10.1177/1469540510390500

Hari, J. (2009). *The dark side of Dubai.* Available at: http://www.independent.co.uk/voices/commentators/johann-hari/the-dark-side-of-dubai-1664368.html#

Harmon-Jones, E., & Harmon-Jones, C. (2008). Action-Based Model of Dissonance: A Review of Behavioral, Anterior Cingulate, and Prefrontal Cortical Mechanisms. *Social and Personality Psychology Compass, 2/3*(3), 1518–1538. doi:10.1111/j.1751-9004.2008.00110.x

Harmon, R. R., & Kenneth, A. C. (1982). The Persuasive Effects of Source Credibility in Buy and Lease Situations. *JMR, Journal of Marketing Research, 19*(2), 255–260. doi:10.2307/3151625

Haron, S. A., Paim, L., & Yahaya, N. (2005). Towards sustainable consumption: An examination of environmental knowledge among Malaysians. *International Journal of Consumer Studies, 29*(5), 426–436. doi:10.1111/j.1470-6431.2005.00460.x

Harrison, R., Shaw, D., & Newholm, T. (2005). *The Ethical Consumer.* London: Sage Publication.

Hartman, C. L., Hofman, P. S., & Stafford, E. R. (1999). Partnerships: A path to sustainability. *Business Strategy and the Environment*, *8*(5), 255–266. doi:10.1002/(SICI)1099-0836(199909/10)8:5<255::AID-BSE214>3.0.CO;2-O

Harvey, J., Carter, S., & Mudimu, G. (2000). A comparison of work values and motives among Zimbabwean and British managers. *Personnel Review*, *29*(6), 723–742. doi:10.1108/00483480010296933

Harvey, M. E., & Brand, R. R. (1974). The spatial allocation of migrants in Accra, Ghana. *Geographical Review*, *64*(1), 1–30. doi:10.2307/213792

Hastings, G., & Aitken, P. (1995). Tobacco advertising and children's smoking: A review of the evidence. *European Journal of Marketing*, *29*(11), 6–17. doi:10.1108/03090569510100678

Haub, C. (2012). *World Population Data Sheet, 2012: Population Reference Bureau (PRB)*. Retrieved from http://www.prb.org/Publications/Datasheets/2012/world-population-data-sheet.aspx

Hawkins, D. I., Best, R. J., & Coney, K. A. (2001). *Consumer Behavior: Building Marketing Strategy* (8th ed.). New York: McGraw-Hill Company Inc.

Haynes, J. L., Burts, D. C., Dukes, A., & Cloud, R. (1993). Consumer Socialization of Preschoolers and Kindergartners as Related to Clothing Consumption. *Psychology and Marketing*, *10*(2), 151–166. doi:10.1002/mar.4220100207

Heckathorn, D. D. (1997). Respondent-Driven Sampling: A New Approach to the Study of Hidden Populations. *Social Problems*, *44*(2), 174–199.

Heckler, S., & Childers, T. L. (1992). The role of expectancy and relevancy in memory for verbal and visual information: What is incongruency? *The Journal of Consumer Research*, *18*(4), 475–492. doi:10.1086/209275

Heeks, D. (2006). *Implementing and managing e-Government*. London: Sage.

Hees, S. (2018, April 25). Russia's greatest Ponzi mastermind is dead, but his legacy lives on in the crypto world. *Quartz*.

Hegarty, S. (2016, December 1). *Nigeria's MMM Ponzi scheme: Will investors get their money?* BBC World Service.

Heirati, N., & O'Cass, A. (2016). Supporting new product commercialization through managerial social ties and market knowledge development in an emerging economy. *Asia Pacific Journal of Management*, *33*, 411–433.

Hello. (2010). *Perfume or eau de toilette? What's the difference?* Retrieved July 19, 2015, www.hellomagazine.com

Hempel, D. J. (1974). Family Buying Decisions: A Cross Cultural Perspective. *JMR, Journal of Marketing Research*, *11*(3), 295–302. doi:10.2307/3151145

Herche, J. (1994). Ethnocentric Tendencies, Marketing Strategy and Import Purchase Behaviour. *International Marketing Review*, *11*(3), 4–16. doi:10.1108/02651339410067012

Herstein, R. (2012). The thin line between country, city and region branding. *Journal of Vacation Marketing*, *18*(2), 147–155. doi:10.1177/1356766711435976

Heslop, L. A., & Ryans, A. B. (1980). A Second Look at Children and the Advertising of Premiums. *The Journal of Consumer Research*, *6*(4), 414–420. doi:10.1086/208784

Hibbert, S., Hogg, G., & Quinn, T. (2006). Consumer response to social entrepreneurship. *International Journal of Nonprofit and Voluntary Sector Marketing*, *7*(3), 288–301. doi:10.1002/nvsm.186

Hill, P. (1970). The Occupations of Migrants in Ghana. Anthropological Papers, No. 42: Ann Arbor, MI: Museum of Anthropology, University of Michigan.

Hinduism. (2015). *The heart of Hinduism.* Retrieved July 19, 2015, from http://hinduism.iskcon.org/lifestyle/808.htm

Hines, J. M., Hungerford, H. R., & Tomera, A. N. (1986/87). Analysis and synthesis of research on responsible environmental behaviour: A meta-analysis. *The Journal of Environmental Education, 18*(2), 1–8. doi:10.1080/00958964.1987.9943482

Hockerts, K., & Wüstenhagen, R. (2010). Greening Goliaths versus emerging Davids - Theorizing about the role of incumbents and new entrants in sustainable entrepreneurship. *Journal of Business Venturing, 25*(5), 481–492. doi:10.1016/j.jbusvent.2009.07.005

Hoek, J., & Dewhirst, T. (2012). The Meaning of "Light" and "Ultralight" Cigarettes: A Commentary on Smith, Stutts, and Zank. *Journal of Public Policy & Marketing, 31*(2), 223–231. doi:10.1509/jppm.11.142

Hofer, P., & Bieri, J. (2005). Advertising to children in Switzerland. *Young Consumers, 6*(3), 80–81. doi:10.1108/17473610510701232

Hofstede, G. (1980). *Culture's Consequences: International Differences in Work-Related Values.* Beverley Hills, CA: Sage.

Hofstede, G. (1980). *Culture's Consequences: International differences in work-related values.* Beverly Hill, CA: Sage.

Hofstede, G. (1984). The cultural relativity of the quality of life concept. *Academy of Management Review, 9*(3), 389–398. doi:10.5465/amr.1984.4279653

Hofstede, G. (2001). *Culture's consequences: Comparing values, behaviors, institutions, and organizations across nations* (2nd ed.). Thousand Oaks, CA: Sage Publications, Inc.

Hofstede, G., & Bond, M. H. (1988). The Confucius connection: From cultural roots to economic growth. *Organizational Dynamics, 16*(4), 4–21. doi:10.1016/0090-2616(88)90009-5

Holcombe, R. (2003). The origins of entrepreneurial opportunities. *The Review of Austrian Economics, 16*(1), 25–43. doi:10.1023/A:1022953123111

Homburg, C., Artz, M., & Wieseke, J. (2012). Marketing Performance Measurement Systems: Does Comprehensiveness Really Improve Performance? *Journal of Marketing, 76*(3), 56–77.

Hooper, B. (2000, December). Globalisation and Resistance in Post-Mao China: The Case of Foreign Consumer Products. *Asian Studies Review, 24*(4), 439–470. doi:10.1080/10357820008713286

Horai, J., Naccari, N., & Fatoullah, E. (1974). The effects of expertise and physical attractiveness upon opinion agreement and liking. *Sociometry, 37*(4), 601–606. doi:10.2307/2786431

Hornung, H., Cecília, M., & Baranauskas, C. (2007). Interaction Design in eGov systems: challenges for a developing country. *Anais do XXVII Congreso da SBC.*

Hotten, R. (2017). *Dubai Airshow: Airbus seals order with US firm Indigo.* Available at: http://www.bbc.co.uk/news/business-41994142

Hout, M., & Rosen, H. S. (2000). Self-employment, Family Background, and Race. *The Journal of Human Resources, 35*(4), 670–692. doi:10.2307/146367

Hovland, C. I., Janis, I. L., & Kelly, H. H. (1953). Communication and persuasion: Psychological studies in opinion change. *American Sociological Review, 19*(3), 355–357.

Howard, J. A., & Sheth, J. N. (1968). A Theory of Buyer Behaviour. In H. H. Kassarijan & S. T. Robertson (Eds.), *Perspectives in consumer Bahavior* (pp. 467–468). Glenview, IL: Scot, Foresman & Co.

Howard, J. A., & Sheth, J. N. (1969). *Theory of Buyer Behavior*. New York: Wiley.

Hoyer, W., & MacInnis, D. (2004). *Consumer behavior* (3rd ed.). Boston, MA: Houghton Mifflin Company.

Hsieh, Y., Chiu, H., & Lin, C. (2006). Family communication and parental influence on children's brand attitudes. *Journal of Business Research*, *59*(10/11), 1079–1086. doi:10.1016/j.jbusres.2006.09.016

Hsu, J. L., & Nien, H. P. (2008). Who are ethnocentric? Examining consumer ethnocentrism in Chinese societies. *Journal of Consumer Behaviour*, *7*(6), 436–447. doi:10.1002/cb.262

Huang, Y.-A., Phau, I., & Lin, C. (2010). Consumer animosity, economic hardship, and normative influence: How do they affect consumers' purchase intention? *European Journal of Marketing*, *44*(7/8), 909–937. doi:10.1108/03090561011047463

Hubacek, K., Guan, D., & Barua, A. (2007). Changing lifestyles and consumption patterns in developing countries: A scenario analysis for China and India. *Futures*, *39*(9), 1084–1096. doi:10.1016/j.futures.2007.03.010

Hubert, M. (2010). Does Neuroeconomics give new impetus to Economic and Consumer research? *Journal of Economic Psychology*, *31*(5), 812–817. doi:10.1016/j.joep.2010.03.009

Hubert, M., & Kenning, P. (2008). A current Overview of Consumer Neuroscience. *Journal of Consumer Behaviour*, *7*(4-5), 272–292. doi:10.1002/cb.251

Huddleston, P., Good, L. K., & Stoel, L. (2001). Consumer ethnocentrism, product necessity and Polish consumers' perceptions of quality. *International Journal of Retail & Distribution Management*, *29*(5), 236–246. doi:10.1108/09590550110390896

Hughes, A., McEwan, C., & Bek, D. (2015). Mobilizing the ethical consumer in South Africa. *Geoforum*, *67*, 148–157. doi:10.1016/j.geoforum.2015.07.011

Hughes, R., & Perry-Jenkins, M. (1996). Social Class Issues in Family Life Education. *Family Relations*, *45*(2), 175–182. doi:10.2307/585288

Hu, X., Li, L., Xie, C., & Zhou, J. (2008). The effects of country-of-origin on Chinese consumers' wine purchasing behaviour. *Journal of Technology Management in China*, *3*(3), 292–306. doi:10.1108/17468770810916195

Iacob, A., Kuada, J., & Lawson, L. (2014). Relationships between brand perception, ideology and consumer ethnocentrism in post-communist Romania. *Journal of Euromarketing*, *23*, 85–110.

Ikejemba, E. C., Mpuan, P. B., Schuur, P. C., & Van Hillegersberg, J. (2017). The empirical reality & sustainable management failures of renewable energy projects in Sub-Saharan Africa (part 1 of 2). *Renewable Energy*, *102*, 234–240.

IMF. (2018). *Regional Economic Outlook: Sub-Saharan Africa*. Retrieved from https://www.imf.org/en/Publications/REO/SSA/Issues/2018/04/30/sreo0518

Informationng.com. (2016). *The Abuja Carnival*. Available at: https://www.informationng.com/2016/12/abuja-carnival-records-poor-turnout.html

Insch, G. S., & McBride, J. B. (2004). The impact of country-of-origin cues on consumer perceptions of product quality: A binational test of the decomposed country-of-origin construct. *Journal of Business Research*, *57*(3), 256–265. doi:10.1016/S0148-2963(02)00323-5

Internet World Statistics. (2018). *Internet Users Statistics for Africa*. Retrieved from http://www.internetworldstats.com/stats1.htm#africa

Isin, F., & Alkibay, S. (2011). Influence of children on purchasing decisions of well-to-do families. *Young Consumers*, *12*(1), 39–52. doi:10.1108/17473611111114777

Itiri, N. (2015). From entertainment to politics: Nigerian celebrities and the 2015 general elections. *VUNA Journal of History and International Relations*, *2*(2), 249–257.

Jack, J., & Ibekwe, C. C. (2018). Ponzi Schemes : An Analysis on Coping with Economic Recession in Nigeria. *The Nigerian Journal of Sociology and Anthropology*, *16*(1), 72–90.

Jackson, K. T. (2004). *Building Reputational Capital: Strategies for Integrity and Fair Play That Improve the Bottom Line*. Oxford, UK: Oxford University Press.

Jackson, T. (2010). *Prosperity without Growth: Economics for a Finite Planet*. London: Earthscan.

Jaffe, E. D., & Nebenzahl, I. D. (1996). *National Image & Competitive Advantage: The Theory and Practice of Country-of-Origin Effect*. Copenhagen Business School Press.

Jaffrey, M. (1992). *The Madhur Jaffrey Cookbook: Over 650 Indian, Vegetarian and Eastern Recipes*. Tiger Books.

Jahoda, G. (1961). *White man: A study of the attitudes of Africans to Europeans in Ghana before independence*. Oxford University Press.

Jain, P. C., & Bhatt, M. (2004). Consumer behaviour in Indian context. S. Chand Publication.

Jain, V., & Roy, S. (2016). Understanding meaning transfer in celebrity endorsements: A qualitative exploration. *Qualitative Market Research*, *19*(3), 266–286. doi:10.1108/QMR-03-2015-0020

Jainworld. (2015). *Cruelty free cosmetics*. Retrieved July 19, 2015, http://jainworld.com/jainfood/crueltyfree.asp

Jaus, H. H. (1984). The development and retention of environmental attitudes in elementary school children. *The Journal of Environmental Education*, *15*(3), 33–36. doi:10.1080/00958964.1984.9942679

Javalgi, R. G., Khare, V. P., Cross, A. C., & Scherer, R. F. (2005). An Application of the Consumer Ethnocentrism Model to French Consumers. *International Business Review*, *14*, 325–344.

Javor, A., Koller, M., Lee, N., Chamberlain, L., & Ransmayr, G. (2013). Neuromarketing and Consumer Neuroscience: Contributions to neurology. *BMC Neurology*, *13*(1), 1–12. doi:10.1186/1471-2377-13-13 PMID:23383650

Jennings, I. (1956, February). Approach to Self-Government. Corona, 61-62.

Jensen, R., & Peppard, D. M. (2007). Food-Buying Habits in Hanoi. *Journal of Social Issues in Southeast Asia*, *22*(2), 230–254. doi:10.1355/SJ22-2D

Jerzyk, E., Stefanska, M., Nestorowicz, R., & Rogala, A. (2016). *The influence of credibility and trust to form of communication message in the context of ethnocentrism*. Conference paper.

JLL.com. (2015). *Globalisation and Competition: The New World of Cities*. Available at: http://www.jll.com/Research/jll-new-world-of-cities-globalisation-and-competition-2015.pdf

Jobber, D., & Fahy, J. (2003). Foundations of Marketing. London: McGraw-Hill Education (UK) Limited.

Johnson, G., & Scholes, K. (1984). *Exploring Corporate Strategy*. London: Prentice-Hall International.

Johnston, J., & Taylor, J. (2008). *Feminist Consumerism and Fat Activists: A Comparative Study of Grassroots Activism and the Dove Real Beauty Campaign*. The University of Chicago Press.

Jolibert, A. J. P., & Baumgartner, G. (1981). Toward a Definition of the Consumerist Segment in France. *The Journal of Consumer Research*, *8*(1), 114. doi:10.1086/208847

Jonas, A. E. G. (2012). Region and Place: Regionalism in question. *Progress in Human Geography*, *36*(2), 263–272. doi:10.1177/0309132510394118

Jonathan, A., Aadarsh, B., Eric, B., Anupam, B., Diana, F., Ulrich, G., . . . Sumit, G. (2007). *The Bird of Gold: The Rise of India's Consumer Market.* McKinsey Global Institute. Retrieved from http://www.mckinsey.com/insights/asia-pacific/the_bird_of_gold

Jones, M. L. (1986). Management development: An African focus. *Management Education and Development*, *17*(3), 202–216. doi:10.1177/135050768601700306

Jones, P., Clarke-Hill, C., Comfort, D., & Hillier, D. (2008). Marketing and sustainability. *Marketing Intelligence & Planning*, *26*(2), 123–130. doi:10.1108/02634500810860584

Jordan, J. R., Hungerford, H. R., & Tomera, A. N. (1986). Effects of two residential environmental workshops on high school students. *The Journal of Environmental Education*, *18*(1), 15–22. doi:10.1080/00958964.1986.9942726

José, A., & Cobas, J. A. (1987). Ethnic Enclaves and Middleman Minorities: Alternative Strategies of Immigrant Adaptation? *Sociological Perspectives*, *30*(2), 143–161. doi:10.2307/1388996 PMID:12315137

Joseph, W. B. (1982). The Credibility of Physically Attractive Communicators: A Review. *Journal of Advertising*, *11*(3), 15–24. doi:10.1080/00913367.1982.10672807

Josiassen, A., Assaf, A. G., & Cvelbar, L. K. (2014). CRM and the bottom line: Do all CRM dimensions affect firm performance? *International Journal of Hospitality Management*, *36*, 130–136. doi:10.1016/j.ijhm.2013.08.005

Josiassen, A., & Harzing, A. W. (2008). Descending from the Ivory Tower: Reflections on the Relevance and Future of Country-of-Origin Research. *European Management Review*, *5*(4), 264–270. doi:10.1057/emr.2008.19

Kacen, J. J., & Lee, J. A. (2002). The Influence of Culture on Consumer Impulsive Buying Behavior. *Journal of Consumer Psychology*, *12*(2), 163–176. doi:10.1207/S15327663JCP1202_08

Kahle, L. R., & Homer, P. (1985). Physical Attractiveness of the Celebrity Endorser: A Social Adaptation Perspective. *The Journal of Consumer Research*, *11*(4), 954–961. doi:10.1086/209029

Kahneman, D., & Snell, J. (1992). Predicting a Changing Taste: Do people know what they will like? *Journal of Behavioral Decision Making*, *5*(3), 187–200. doi:10.1002/bdm.3960050304

Kaisara, G., & Pather, S. (2011). The e-Government Evaluation Challenge: A South African Batho Pele-aligned Service Quality Approach. *Government Information Quarterly*, *28*(2), 211–221. doi:10.1016/j.giq.2010.07.008

Kalafatis, S. P., Pollard, M., East, R., & Tsogas, M. H. (1999). Green marketing and Ajzen's theory of planned behavior: A cross-market examination. *Journal of Consumer Marketing*, *16*(5), 441–460. doi:10.1108/07363769910289550

Kalitanyi, V., & Visser, K. (2010). African immigrants in South Africa: Job takers or job creators? *South African Journal of Economic and Management Sciences*, *13*(4), 376–390. doi:10.4102ajems.v13i4.91

Kambitsis, C., Yvonne, H., Nicholas, T., & Giannis, C. (2002). Sports advertising in print media: The case of 2000 Olympic games. *Corporate Communications*, *7*(3), 155–161. doi:10.1108/13563280210436763

Kamins, M. A., & Gupta, K. (1994). Congruence between spokesperson and product type: A matchup hypothesis perspective. *Psychology and Marketing*, *11*(6), 569–586. doi:10.1002/mar.4220110605

Kaneva, N. (2011). Nation Branding: Toward an Agenda for Critical Research. *International Journal of Communication*, *5*, 117–141.

Kapito, J. (2000). *For a strong and binding framework.* Convention on tobacco Control (FCTC) at the Public Hearing of the World Health Organization. Retrieved from: http://www.who.int/tobacco/framework/public_hearings/tobacco_control_advocate_consumer_association.pdf

Kaplan, R. S., & Norton, D. P. (1992). The Balanced Scorecard: Measures That Drive Performance. *Harvard Business Review, 70*(1), 71–79. PMID:10119714

Kapoor, N., & Verma, D. S. (2005). Children's Understanding of TV Advertisements: Influence of Age, Sex and Parents. *Vision, 9*(1), 21-36.

Karasawa, M. (2002). Patriotism, nationalism and internationalism among Japanese citizens: An etic-emic approach. *Political Psychology, 23*(4), 645–666. doi:10.1111/0162-895X.00302

Karimova, G. Z. (2011). Interactivity and Advertising Communication. *Journal of Media and Communication Studies, 3*(5), 160–169.

Karmarkar, U. R. (2011). *Note on Neuromarketing.* Harvard Business School.

Kassarjian, H. H. (1971). Personality and Consumer Behaviour A review. *JMR, Journal of Marketing Research, 8*(November), 409–419. doi:10.2307/3150229

Kathuria, L. M., & Gill, P. (2013). Purchase of branded commodity food products: Empirical evidence from India. *British Food Journal, 115*(9), 1255–1280. doi:10.1108/BFJ-08-2011-0209

Kaur & Singh. (2006). Children in family purchase decision making in India and the West: A Review. *Academy of Marketing Science Review, 8*, 1-30. Retrieved from http://www.amsreview.org/articles/kaur08-2006.pdf

Kaur, A., & Medury, Y. (2011). Impact of internet on teenagers influence on family purchases. *Young Consumers, 12*(1), 27–38. doi:10.1108/17473611111114768

Kavaratzis, M., & Ashworth, G. J. (2005). City branding: An effective assertion of identity or a transitory marketing trick? *Tijdschrift voor Economische en Sociale Geografie, 96*(5), 506–514. doi:10.1111/j.1467-9663.2005.00482.x

Kaynak, E., & Kara, A. (2002). Consumer perceptions of foreign products: An analysis of product-country images and ethnocentris. *European Journal of Marketing, 36*(7/8), 928–949. doi:10.1108/03090560210430881

Kaynak, E., Kucukemiroglu, O., & Hyder, A. S. (2000). Consumers' country-of-origin (COO) perceptions of imported products in a homogenous less-developed country. *European Journal of Marketing, 34*(9/10), 1221–1241. doi:10.1108/03090560010342610

Kaynak, E., Kucukemiroglu, O., & Odahasi, Y. (1992). Consumer Complaint Handling in an Advanced Developing Economy: An Empirical Investigation. *Journal of Business Ethics, 11*(11), 813–829. doi:10.1007/BF00872359

Kazeem, Y. (2017). *Lagos wants to be a modern mega city so it's forcing thousands of slum dwellers from their homes.* Available at: https://qz.com/936761/lagos-wants-to-be-a-modern-mega-city-so-its-forcing-thousands-of-slum-dwellers-from-their-homes/

Kearns, G., & Philo, C. (Eds.). (1993). *Selling Places. The City as Cultural Capital, Past and Present.* Oxford, UK: Pergamon Press.

Keller, K. L. (1993). Conceptualizing, measuring, and managing customer based: Brand equity. *Journal of Marketing, 57*(1), 1–22. doi:10.2307/1252054

Keller, K. L. (2008). *Strategic Brand Management: Building, Measuring, and Managing Brand Equity* (3rd ed.). Upper Saddle River, NJ: Pearson Prentice Hall.

Kennedy, E. H., Beckley, T. M., McFarlane, B. L., & Nadeau, S. (2009). Why we don't walk the talk: Understanding the environmental values/behaviour gap in Canada. *Human Ecology Review*, *16*(2), 151–160.

Keramati, A., Mehrabi, H., & Mojir, N. (2010). A process-oriented perspective on customer relationship management and organizational performance: An empirical investigation. *Industrial Marketing Management*, *39*(7), 1170–1185. doi:10.1016/j.indmarman.2010.02.001

Kerrane, B., & Hogg, M. (2011). How Best to Get their Own Way? Children's Influence Strategies within Families. *Advances in Consumer Research. Association for Consumer Research (U. S.)*, *39*, 366–373.

Kerrane, B., Hogg, M. K., & Bettany, S. M. (2012). Children's influence strategies in practice: Exploring the co-constructed nature of the child influence process in family consumption. *Journal of Marketing Management*, *28*(7/8), 809–835. doi:10.1080/0267257X.2012.698633

Kerr, G. (2006). From Destination Brand to Location Brand. *Journal of Brand Management*, *13*(4/5), 276–283. doi:10.1057/palgrave.bm.2540271

Kerr, P., & Wiseman, G. (2013). *Diplomacy in a Globalizing World: Theories and Practice*. New York: Oxford University Press.

Keya Seth Aromatherapy. (2012). *About us*. Retrieved July 19, 2015, from www.keyaaromatherapy.com

Keya Seth. (2015). *Keya Seth's Aromotherapy Company*. Retrieved Oct 29, 2015, from http://keyaseth.in/about.html

Khan, H., Bamber, D., & Quazi, A. (2012). Relevant or redundant: Elite consumers' perception of foreign-made products in an emerging market. *Journal of Marketing Management*, *28*(9-10), 1190–1216. doi:10.1080/0267257X.2011.635153

Kharas, H. (2011). *The Emerging Middle Class in Developing Countries*. Brookings Institution.

Khatri, P. (2006). Celebrity endorsement: A strategic promotion perspective. *Indian Media Studies Journal.*, *1*(1), 25–37.

Khraim, H. S. (2010). Cosmetics Buying Behavior of Young UAE Female Consumers: The Influence of Demographics. *Skyline Business Journal, 6*(1).

Kilbourne, W., & Pickett, G. (2008). How materialism affects environmental beliefs, concern, and environmentally responsible behavior. *Journal of Business Research*, *61*(9), 885–893. doi:10.1016/j.jbusres.2007.09.016

Kilson, M. L. Jr. (1958). Nationalism and Social Class in British West Africa. *The Journal of Politics*, *20*(2), 368–387. doi:10.2307/2127045

Kimmel, A. J. (2010). The Psychological Basis of Marketing. In M. J. Baker & M. Saren (Eds.), *Marketing Theory: A Student Text* (pp. 121–144). London: Sage Publication Ltd. doi:10.4135/9781446280096.n6

Kim, Y., & Choi, S. M. (2005). Antecedents of green purchase behaviour: An examination of collectivism, environmental concern, and PCE. *Advances in Consumer Research. Association for Consumer Research (U. S.)*, *32*, 592–599.

Kinra, N. (2006). The effect of country of origin on foreign brand names in the Indian market. *Marketing Intelligence & Planning*, *24*(1), 15–30. doi:10.1108/02634500610641534

Kirkorian, H. L., Wartella, E. A., & Anderson, D. R. (2008). Media and Young Children's Learning. *The Future of Children*, *18*(1), 39–61. doi:10.1353/foc.0.0002 PMID:21338005

Kirkpatrick, E. L., Cowls, M., & Tough, R. (1934). The Life cycle of the Farm Family in Relation to Its Standard of Living (Research Bulletin No. 121). Madison, WI: University of Wisconsin Agricultural Experiment Station.

Klein, J. G. (2002). Us versus Them, or Us versus Everyone? Delineating Consumer Aversion to Foreign Goods. *Journal of International Business Studies*, *33*(2), 345–363. doi:10.1057/palgrave.jibs.8491020

Klein, J. G., Ettenson, R., & Krishnan, B. C. (2006). Extending the construct of consumer ethnocentrism: When foreign products are preferred. *International Marketing Review*, *23*(3), 304–321. doi:10.1108/02651330610670460

Klewes, J., & Wreschniok, R. (2009). Introduction. In J. Klewes & R. Wreshniok (Eds.), *Reputation Capital: Building and Maintaining Trust in the 21st Century* (pp. 1–6). London: Springer. doi:10.1007/978-3-642-01630-1_1

Kloosterman, R. C. (2010). Matching opportunities with resources: A framework for analyzing (migrant) entrepreneurship from a mixed embeddedness perceptive. *Entrepreneurship and Regional Development*, *22*(1), 25–45. doi:10.1080/08985620903220488

Kluckhohn, C. (1956). *Toward a Comparison of Value Emphasis in Different Cultures.* In L. D. White (Ed.), *The State of Social Sciences* (pp. 116–132). Chicago: The University of Chicago Press.

Kluckhohn, F. R., & Strodtbeck, F. L. (1961). *Variations in value orientations.* Evanston, IL: Row, Peterson.

Knight, G. A., & Calantone, R. J. (2000). A flexible model of consumer country-oforigin perceptions A cross-cultural investigation. *International Marketing Review*, *17*, 127–145. doi:10.1108/02651330010322615

Kobo, O. (2010). 'We are citizens too': The politics of citizenship in independent Ghana. *The Journal of Modern African Studies*, *48*(1), 67–94. doi:10.1017/S0022278X0999022X

Koch, C. (2004). *Quest for Consciousness: A Neurobiological Approach.* Englewood, CO: Roberts & Company Publishers.

Koester, J. V. (2003). Legal briefing: Advertising to children in the USA. *Young Consumers*, *4*(1), 65–71. doi:10.1108/17473610310813735

Koh, C., & Prybutok, V. (2003). The three ring model and development of an instrument for measuring dimensions of e-government functions. *Journal of Computer Information Systems*, *43*(3), 34–39.

Koh, L. P., & Lee, T. M. (2012). Sensible consumerism for environmental sustainability. *Biological Conservation*, *151*(1), 3–6. doi:10.1016/j.biocon.2011.10.029

Kohli, A., & Jaworski, B. (1990). Market orientation: The construct, research propositions and managerial implications. *Journal of Marketing*, *54*, 1–18.

Komba, M. M., & Ngulube, P. (2012). Factors for e-government adoption: Lessons from selected African countries. *Mousaion*, *30*(2), 24–32.

Kotey, B., & Meredith, G. G. (1997). Relationships among owner/manager personal values, business strategies, and enterprise performance. *Journal of Small Business Management*, *35*(2), 37–64.

Kotler, P. (1971). What consumerism means for marketers. *Harvard Business Review*, *50*(3), 48–57.

Kotler, P. (2011). Reinventing Marketing to Manage the Environmental Imperative. *Journal of Marketing*, *75*(4), 132–135. doi:10.1509/jmkg.75.4.132

Kotler, P., & Armstrong, G. (2016). *Principles of Marketing* (16th ed.). Essex, UK: Pearson Education Limited, Inc.

Kraidy, M. M. (2003). Glocalisation. *Journal of International Communication*, *9*(2), 29–49. doi:10.1080/13216597.2003.9751953

Kravets, O., & Sandikci, O. (2014). Competently Ordinary : New Middle Class Consumers in the Emerging. *Journal of Marketing*, *78*(4), 125–140. doi:10.1509/jm.12.0190

Krugman, H. E. (1965). The Impact of Television Advertising: Learning without Involvement. *Public Opinion Quarterly*, *29*(Fall), 349–356. doi:10.1086/267335

Kuada, J. (2003). *Culture and Technological Transformation in the South: Transfer or Local Innovation?* Copenhagen: Samfundslitteratur.

Kuada, J. (2015). *Private Enterprise-Led Economic Development in Sub-Saharan Africa: The Human Side of Growth*. London: Palgrave Macmillan.

Kuada, J. (2016). *Marketing Decisions and Strategies – An International Perspective*. London: Adonis & Abbey Publishers.

Kuada, J., & Hansen, M. W. (2006). Theories of cross-border linkages. In M. W. Hansen & H. Schaumburg-Müller (Eds.), *Transnational Corporations and Local Firms in Developing Countries – Linkages and Upgrading* (pp. 29–60). Copenhagen: Copenhagen Business School Press.

Kucukemiroglu, O. (1999). Market segmentation by using consumer lifestyle dimensions and ethnocentrism: An empirical study. *European Journal of Marketing*, *33*(5/6), 470–487. doi:10.1108/03090569910262053

Kumi, E. N. (2017). *The electricity situation in Ghana: Challenges and opportunities. CGD Policy Paper.* Center for Global Development. Retrieved from https://www.cgdev.org/ publication/

Kurtz, B. E., Borkowski, J. G., & Deshmukh, K. (1988). Metamemory and Learning in Maharashtrian Children: Influences from Home and School. *The Journal of Genetic Psychology*, *149*(3), 363–376. doi:10.1080/00221325.1988.10532164

Lamb, C. W. Jr, Hair, J. F. Jr, & McDaniel, C. (1999). *Essentials of Marketing*. South-Western College Publishing.

Lancaster, G., & Reynolds, P. (2002). *Marketing: the one semester introduction*. Oxford, UK: Butterworth-Heinemann.

Laroche, M., Bergeron, J., & Barbaro-Forleo, G. (2001). Targeting consumer who are willing to pay more for environmentally friendly products. *Journal of Consumer Marketing*, *18*(6), 503–520. doi:10.1108/EUM0000000006155

Law, B. (2015). *United Arab Emirates: Revealing the dark face of the Gulf state where human rights abuses are a daily occurrence*. Available at: http://www.independent.co.uk/news/world/middle-east/united-arab-emirates-revealing-the-dark-face-of-the-gulf-state-where-human-rights-abuses-are-a-daily-a6683741.html

Lawlor, M.-A., & Andrea, P. (2011). Pester power- A battle of wills between children and their parents. *Journal of Marketing Management*, *27*(5-6), 561–581. doi:10.1080/0267257X.2010.495281

Law, R., & Ng, C. (2011). Marketing strategies for small hotels: The case of Cheung Chau in Hong Kong. *Asia Pacific Journal of Tourism Research*, *16*(1), 21–38. doi:10.1080/10941665.2011.539389

Layne, K., & Lee, J. (2001). Developing fully functional E-government: A four stage model. *Government Information Quarterly*, *18*(2), 122–136. doi:10.1016/S0740-624X(01)00066-1

Le Guay, P. (2003). The regulation of advertising to children in Australia. *Young Consumers*, *4*(2), 63–67. doi:10.1108/17473610310813834

Lee. (1994). *Influence of children in family purchase decisions* (PhD thesis). University of Auckland. Retrieved from https://researchspace.auckland.ac.nz/handle/2292/1137

Lee, C. K.-C., & Collins, B. A. (2000). Family decision making and coalition patterns. *European Journal of Marketing*, *34*(9/10), 1181–1198. doi:10.1108/03090560010342584

Lee, D., & Ganesh, G. (1999). Effects of partitioned country image in the context of brand image and familiarity: A categorization theory perspective. *International Marketing Review*, *16*(1), 18–41. doi:10.1108/02651339910257610

Lee, K. C. C., & Beatty, S. E. (2002). Family structure and influence in family decision making. *Journal of Consumer Marketing*, *19*(1), 24–41. doi:10.1108/07363760210414934

Lee, N., Broderick, A. J., & Chamberlain, L. (2007). What is "Neuromarketing"? A discussion and agenda for future research. *International Journal of Psychophysiology*, *63*(2), 199–204. doi:10.1016/j.ijpsycho.2006.03.007 PMID:16769143

Lee, N., Butler, M., & Senior, C. (2010). The Brain in Business: Neuromarketing and Organisational Cognitive neuroscience. *Journal of Marketing*, *49*, 129–131. doi:10.100712642-010-0033-8

Lee, S., & Yoon, Y. (2010). The return on investment (ROI) of international public relations: A country-level analysis. *Public Relations Review*, *36*(1), 15–20. doi:10.1016/j.pubrev.2009.08.011

Lefkoff-Hagius, R., & Mason, C. H. (1993). Characteristic, beneficial, and image attributes in consumer judgments of similarity and preference. *The Journal of Consumer Research*, *20*(1), 100–110. doi:10.1086/209336

Leibenstein, H. (1968). Entrepreneurship and Development. *The American Economic Review*, *58*(2), 72–83.

Leisen, B. (2001). Image segmentation: The case of a tourism destination. *Journal of Services Marketing*, *15*(1), 49–66. doi:10.1108/08876040110381517

Lenartowicz, T., & Roth, K. (2001). Does subculture within a country matter? A cross-culture chapter of motivational domains and business performance in Brazil. *Journal of International Business Studies*, *32*(2), 305–325. doi:10.1057/palgrave.jibs.8490954

Levine, C. R. (1998). Children's socialization experiences and functioning in single mother households: The importance of fathers and other men. *Child Development*, *69*(1), 219–230. doi:10.1111/j.1467-8624.1998.tb06144.x PMID:9499568

Levitt, T. (1983, May). The globalization of markets. *Harvard Business Review*, 92–102.

Lewis, D., & Briader, D. (2005). Market Researchers make increasing use of Brain Imaging. *Advances in Clinical Neuroscience & Rehabilitation: ACNR*, *5*(3), 35.

Lin, C. Y., Chen, P. J., Wu, L. W., & Tseng, T. H. (2015). Does the Endorser's Nationality Matter? An Investigation of Young Taiwanese Consumers' Selecting Smartphone. *International Business Research*, *8*(11), 49. doi:10.5539/ibr.v8n11p49

Lindebaum, D., & Zundel, M. (2013). Not quite a revolution: Scrutinizing Organisational Cognitive Neuroscience in Leadership Studies. *Human Relations*, *66*, 857–877. doi:10.1177/0018726713482151

Lindsey-Mullikin, J. (2003). Beyond Reference Pricing: Understanding Consumers' Encounters with Unexpected prices. *Journal of Product and Brand Management*, *12*(3), 140–153. doi:10.1108/10610420310476906

Lirtzman, S. I., & Shuv-Ami, A. (1986). Credibility of source of communication on products' safety hazard. *Psychological Reports*, *58*(3), 707–718. doi:10.2466/pr0.1986.58.3.707 PMID:3726021

Little, K. (1955). The African Elite in British West Africa. *Race and Relations in World Perspectives*, 267-288.

Little, K. (1953). The Study of Social Change in British West Africa. *Africa*, *23*(4), 274–301. doi:10.2307/1156180

Little, K. L. (1948). Social Change and Social Class in the Sierra Leone Protectorate. *American Journal of Sociology*, *54*(1), 10–21. doi:10.1086/220263

Liu, M. T., Huang, Y. Y., & Jiang, M. H. (2007). Relations among Attractiveness of Endorsers, Match-up, and Purchase Intention in Sport Marketing in China. *Journal of Consumer Marketing*, *24*(6), 358–365. doi:10.1108/07363760710822945

Livingstone, S., & Helsper, E. J. (2006). Does Advertising Literacy Mediate the Effects of Advertising on Children? A Critical Examination of Two Linked Research Literatures in Relation to Obesity and Food Choice. *Journal of Communication, 56*(3), 560–584. doi:10.1111/j.1460-2466.2006.00301.x

Li, Z., Fu, S., & Murray, L. (1997). Country and product images: The perceptions of consumers in the people's republic of China. *Journal of International Consumer Marketing, 10*(2), 115–139.

Lloyd, P.C. (1953, January). Cocoa, Politics and the Yoruba Middle Class. *West Africa*, 39.

Llyod, P. C. (1953, October). New Economic Classes in Western Nigeria. *African Affairs*, 327–334. doi:10.1093/oxfordjournals.afraf.a094171

Lorek, S., & Fuchs, D. (2013). Strong sustainable consumption governance–precondition for a degrowth path? *Journal of Cleaner Production, 38*, 36–43. doi:10.1016/j.jclepro.2011.08.008

Lorek, S., & Spangenberg, J. H. (2014). Sustainable consumption within a sustainable economy–beyond green growth and green economies. *Journal of Cleaner Production, 63*, 33–44. doi:10.1016/j.jclepro.2013.08.045

Lowe, H. D. (1965, Fall). Doing Business in Developing Countries. *Business Horizon*, 25-33.

Lozano, R. (2008). Envisioning sustainability three-dimensionally. *Journal of Cleaner Production, 16*(17), 1838–1846. doi:10.1016/j.jclepro.2008.02.008

Lu Wang, C., & Xiong Chen, Z. X. (2004). Consumer ethnocentrism and willingness to buy domestic products in a developing country setting: Testing moderating effects. *Journal of Consumer Marketing, 21*(6), 391–400. doi:10.1108/07363760410558663

Lucarelli, A., & Berg, P. O. (2011). City branding: A state-of-the-art review of the research domain. *Journal of Place Management and Development, 4*(1), 9–27. doi:10.1108/17538331111117133

Luedicke, M. K. (2011). Consumer acculturation theory: (crossing) conceptual boundaries. *Consumption Markets & Culture, 14*(3), 223–244. doi:10.1080/10253866.2011.574824

Lumley, S. (2017). *Stay clear of Dubai, urge family of 'hip touch' Brit.* Available at: https://www.metro.news/stay-clear-of-dubai-urge-family-of-hip-touch-brit/774818/

Luque-Martínez, T., Ibá˜nezz-Zapata, J. A., & del Barrio-García, S. (2000). Consumer ethnocentrism measurement. An assessment of the reliability and validity of the CETSCALE in Spain. *European Journal of Marketing, 34*(11/12), 1353–1373. doi:10.1108/03090560010348498

Lutz, R. (1985). *Affective and cognitive Antecedents nof Attitude Toward the Ad: a conceptual Framework. In Psychological Processes and Advertising Effects: Theory, Research and Application* (pp. 45–63). Lawrence Erlbaum.

Lynch, J. L., & Schuler, D. (1984). The matchup effect of spokesperson and product congruency: A schema theory interpretation. *Psychology and Marketing, 11*(5), 417–445. doi:10.1002/mar.4220110502

Lysonski, S., & Durvasula, S. (2013). Nigeria in transition: Acculturation to global consumer culture. *Journal of Consumer Marketing, 30*(6), 493–508. doi:10.1108/JCM-07-2013-0626

Lysonski, S., Durvasula, S., & Zotos, Y. (1996). Consumer decision-making styles: A multi-country investigation. *European Journal of Marketing, 30*(12), 10–12. doi:10.1108/03090569610153273

Lysonski, S., Durvasula, S., & Zotos, Y. (2004). The Metamorphosis of Greek Consumers' Sentiments Toward Marketing and Consumerism. *Journal of Euromarketing, 13*(4), 5–29. doi:10.1300/J037v13n04_02

Macklin, M. (1996). Preschoolers' Learning of Brand Names from Visual Cues. *The Journal of Consumer Research, 23*(3), 251–261. doi:10.1086/209481

Maclnnis, D. J., Moorman, C., & Jaworski, B. K. (1991). Enhancing and measuring consumers' motivation, opportunity, and ability to process brand information from ads. *Journal of Marketing, 55*(4), 32–53. doi:10.2307/1251955

Madichie, N. O., & Yamoah, F. A. (n.d.). Country Image and Consumer Food Quality Perception: A Developing Country Perspective. *The Consortium Journal, 10*(2), 89-100.

Madichie, N. (2010). The Nigerian movie industry "Nollywood"-a nearly perfect marketing case study. *Marketing Intelligence & Planning, 28*(5), 625–649. doi:10.1108/02634501011066537

Madichie, N., & Opute, A. P. (2016). Consumer Protection in Sub-Saharan Africa: An Exploration of "Big Tobacco" Marketing Practices. In A. Gbadamosi (Ed.), *Handbook of Research on Consumerism and Buying Behavior in Developing Nations* (pp. 311–333). IGI Global. doi:10.4018/978-1-5225-0282-1.ch014

Magnini, P. V., Honeycutt, E. D., & Cross, A. M. (2008). Understanding the use of celebrity endorsers for hospitality firms. *Journal of Vacation Marketing, 14*(1), 57–69. doi:10.1177/1356766707084219

Maher, J. K., Lord, J. B., Hughner, R. S., & Childs, N. M. (2006). Food advertising on children's television. *Young Consumers, 7*(4), 41–52. doi:10.1108/17473610610717964

Maheshwari, V., Vandewalle, I., & Bamber, D. (2011). Place branding's role in sustainable development. *Journal of Place Management and Development, 4*(2), 198–213. doi:10.1108/17538331111153188

Maklan, S., & Knox, S. (1997). Reinventing the brand: Bridging the gap between customer and brand value. *Journal of Product and Brand Management, 6*(2), 119–129. doi:10.1108/10610429710175655

Malhotra, N., & Birks, D. (2007). *Marketing Research: an Applied Approach*. Harlow: Prentice Hall.

Mandrik, C. A., Fern, E. F., & Yeqing, B. (2005). Intergenerational influence: Roles of conformity to peers and communication effectiveness. *Psychology and Marketing, 22*(10), 813–832. doi:10.1002/mar.20087

Mangleburg, T. F., & Bristol, T. (1998). Socialization and Adolescents' Skepticism toward Advertising. *Journal of Advertising, 27*(3), 11–21. doi:10.1080/00913367.1998.10673559

Marazza, A. (2007). *A country brand is more than just a logo. Eight golden rules for branding a destination*. Available at: http://www.landor.com/index.cfm

Markham, S., Gatlin-Watts, R., & Bounds, W. (2001). Internet advertising vs. traditional advertising: The current situation. *Journal of Promotion Management, 6*(1-2), 3–17. doi:10.1300/J057v06n01_02

Marquis, C., & Raynard, M. (2015). Institutional strategies in emerging markets. *The Academy of Management Annals, 9*(1), 291–335.

Marquis, M. (2004). Strategies for influencing parental decisions on food purchasing. *Journal of Consumer Marketing, 21*(2), 134–143. doi:10.1108/07363760410525696

Marshall, D., O'Donohoe, S., & Kline, S. (2007). Families, food, and pester power: Beyond the blame game? *Journal of Consumer Behaviour, 6*(4), 164–181. doi:10.1002/cb.217

Marshall, S. (2011). Conceptualizing the International For-Profit Social Entrepreneur. *Journal of Business Ethics, 98*(2), 183–198. doi:10.100710551-010-0545-7

Martensen, A., & Grønholdt, L. (2008). Children's influence on family decision making. *Innovative Marketing, 4*(4), 36–44.

Martinez, P. (2012). *The Consumer Mind: Brand Perception and the Implication for Marketers* (1st ed.). London, UK: Kogan Page Limited.

Mas'ud, A. A., Wirba, A. V., Muhammad-Sukki, F., Albarracín, R., Abu-Bakar, S. H., Munir, A. B., & Bani, N. A. (2016). A review on the recent progress made on solar photovoltaic in selected countries of sub-Saharan Africa. *Renewable & Sustainable Energy Reviews*, *62*, 441–452.

Maslow, A. (1943). A Theory of Human Motivation: The basic needs. *Psychological Review*, *50*(4), 370–396. doi:10.1037/h0054346

Massing, A. W. (2000). The Wangara, an Old Soninke Diaspora in West Africa? *Cahiers d'Etudes Africaines*, *40*(158), 281–308. doi:10.4000/etudesafricaines.175

Matsuda, T. (2007). *Soft Power and its perils: US Cultural Policy in Early Postwar Japan and Permanent Dependency*. Stanford University Press.

Mattern, J.B. (2005). Why 'Soft Power' Isn't So Soft: Representational Force and the Sociolinguistic Construction of Attraction in World Politics. *Millenium – Journal of International Studies, 33*(3), 583-612.

Maumbe, B., & Klaas, N. (2009). Crafting an E-Government Development Model for South Africa: A Strategic New Direction for the Western Cape Province. *International Conference on Information Management. CONF-IRM 2009 Proceedings*.

Mazengera, B. & Mavetera, N. (2006). Factors Contributing To Successful E-Government Implementation in Southern African Development Community (SADC) Countries. *Innovation and Knowledge Management: A Global Competitive Advantage.*

Mberu, B. U., & Pongou, R. (2010). *Nigeria: multiple forms of mobility in Africa's demographic giant*. Retrieved from http://www.migrationpolicy.org/article/nigeria-multipleforms-mobility-africas-demographic-giant

McClure, S. M., Li, J., Tomlin, D., Cypert, K. S., Montague, L. M., & Montague, P. R. (2004). Neural correlates of Behavioral preferences for culturally familiar drinks. *Neuron, 44*(3), 379–387. doi:10.1016/j.neuron.2004.09.019

McCracken, G. (1989). Who is the Celebrity Endorser? Cultural Foundations of the Endorsement Process. *The Journal of Consumer Research*, *16*(3), 310–322. doi:10.1086/209217

McCroskey, J. C., & McCain, T. A. (1974). The measurement of interpersonal attraction. *Speech Monographs*, *41*(3), 261–266. doi:10.1080/03637757409375845

McFadden, E., Luben, R., & Khaw, K. (2009). Different Measures of Social Class in Women and Mortality. *European Journal of Epidemiology*, *24*(5), 231–236. doi:10.100710654-009-9332-0 PMID:19322666

McGinnies, E., & Charles, D. W. (1980). Better Liked Than Right: Trustworthiness and Expertise as Factors in Credibility. *Personality and Social Psychology Bulletin*, *6*(3), 467–472. doi:10.1177/014616728063023

McGuire, W. J. (1958). Attitudes and Attitude Change. In Handbook of Social Psychology (Vol. 2). New York: Random House.

McHugh, J. (2012). *Sandalwood and Carrion: Smell in Indian Religion and Culture*. Oxford University Press. doi:10.1093/acprof:oso/9780199916306.001.0001

McIntosh, A. (2004). Characterizing E-Participation in Policy-Making. *Proceedings of the 37th Hawaii International Conference on System Sciences*. 10.1109/HICSS.2004.1265300

McLain, S., & Sternquist, B. (1991). Ethnocentric Consumers: Do They Buy American? *Journal of International Consumer Marketing*, *4*(1-2), 39–57. doi:10.1300/J046v04n01_03

Mcleay, F. J., & Oglethorpe, D. (2013). Social marketing, parental purchasing decisions, and unhealthy food in developing countries: A Nigerian typology. *Journal of Consumer Behaviour*, *12*(3), 232–242. doi:10.1002/cb.1426

McLeod, J. M., & O'Keefe, G. J. (1972). The Socialization Perspective and Communication Behavior. In F. G. Kline & P. J. Tichenor (Eds.), *Current Perspectives in Mass Communication Research* (pp. 121–168). Beverly Hills, CA: Sage Publications.

McMahon, C. (1996). Indian attars. *International Journal of Aromatherapy*, *7*(4), 10–13. doi:10.1016/S0962-4562(96)80023-3

McNeal, J. U. (1987). *Children as consumers: Insights and implications*. New York, NY: Lexington Books.

McRoberts, O. M (1999). Understanding The "New" Black Pentecostal Activism: Lessons From Ecumenical Urban Ministries in Boston. *Sociology of Religion, 60*(1), 47-70.

Meggs, W. J., Dunn, K. A., Bloch, R. M., Goodman, P. E., & Davidoff, A. L. (1996). Prevalence and nature of allergy and chemical sensitivity in a general population. *Archives of Environmental Health*, *51*(4), 275–282. doi:10.1080/00039896.1996.9936026 PMID:8757407

Menon, M. K., & Louis, E. B. (2001). *Celebrity advertising: An assessment of its relative effectiveness*. Retrieved from http://condor.depaul.edu/dweinste/celeb/celeb_adverts.html

Mensah, E. (2017). *Cross-border Inter-firm Networks and the Growth of Ghana's Solar Power Sector* (Unpublished MSc Thesis). International Business Centre, Aalborg University.

Meschi, E., & Vivarelli, M. (2009). Trade and Income Inequality in Developing Countries. World Development, 37(2), 287–302.

Mick, D. G., & Buhl, M. C. (1992). A Meaning-based model of advertising experiences. *The Journal of Consumer Research*, *19*(3), 317–338. doi:10.1086/209305

Middlemiss, L. (2011). The power of community: How community-based organizations stimulate sustainable lifestyles among participants. *Society & Natural Resources*, *24*(11), 1157–1173. doi:10.1080/08941920.2010.518582

Mihailovich, P. (2006). Kinship branding: A concept of holism and evolution for the nation brand. *Place Branding*, *2*(3), 229–247. doi:10.1057/palgrave.pb.5990060

Mikkelsen, M. R., & Nørgaard, M. K. (2006). Children's Influence on Family Decision-Making in Food Buying and Consumption. The National Institute of Public Health Denmark and MAPP- Centre for Research on Customer Relations in the Food Sector, Department of Marketing and Statistics, Aarhus School of Business Denmark.

Miletsky, J., & Smith, G. L. (2009). *Perspectives on Branding*. Boston: Course Technology.

Milios, J. (2000). Social Classes in Classical and Marxist Political Economy. *American Journal of Economics and Sociology*, *59*(2), 283–302. doi:10.1111/1536-7150.00027

Miller, G. P., & Basehart, J. (1969). Source trustworthiness, opinionated statements, and response to persuasive communication. *Speech Monographs*, *36*(1), 1–7. doi:10.1080/03637756909375602

Miller, V. (2017). Phatic culture and the status quo: Reconsidering the purpose of social media activism. *Convergence*, *23*(3), 251–269. doi:10.1177/1354856515592512

Milotic, D. (2006). The impact of fragrance on consumer choice. *Journal of Consumer Behaviour, 3*(2), 179–191. doi:10.1002/cb.131

Minahan, S., & Huddleston, P. (2010). Shopping with mum-mother and daughter socialization. *Young Consumers, 11*(3), 170–177. doi:10.1108/17473611011074241

Ming, W. T., & Ting-Jui, C. (2009). Children's influences on family decision making in Hong Kong. Young Consumers. *Insight and Ideas for Responsible Marketers, 10*(2), 146–156. doi:10.1108/17473610910964723

Minkov, M., & Hofstede, G. (2011). The evolution of Hofstede's doctrine. *Cross Cultural Management, 18*(1), 10–20. doi:10.1108/13527601111104269

Mintel. (2012). *The Men's and Women's Fragrance Market: UK, September*. Retrieved July 19, 2015, from www.mintel.com

Misra, S., & Beatty, S. E. (1990). Celebrity spokesperson and brand congruence. An assessment of recall and affect. *Journal of Business Research, 21*(2), 159–173. doi:10.1016/0148-2963(90)90050-N

Mittal, V., & Tsiros, M. (1995). Does Country of Origin Transfer Between Brands? *Advances in Consumer Research: Association for Consumer Research, 22*, 292–296.

Mochiko, T. (2017). *SA's big data rip-off: The #DataMustFall campaign failed to convince SA's biggest phone companies to reduce prices.* Available at: https://www.businesslive.co.za/fm/fm-fox/digital/2017-05-05-sas-big-data-rip-off/

Moerdyk, C. (2013). *Synopsis of Neuromarketing.* South Africa Marketing Association (SAMRA). Retrieved on 20/06/2015 from: www.erikdup.com

Mogaji, E. (2016). *Emotional appeals in UK banks' print advertisement* (Unpublished doctoral dissertation). University of Bedfordshire, Luton, UK.

Mogaji, E., Badejo, A., & Charles, S. (2018). Sportswomen as brand ambassadors: Prospect, challenges. *Project Report.* University of Greenwich. Retrieved from http://gala.gre.ac.uk/id/eprint/20955

Moilanen, T., & Rainisto, S. (2009). *How to Brand Nations, Cities, & Destinations.* Basingstoke, UK: Palgrave. doi:10.1057/9780230584594

Monali, H., & McGuiggan, R. (2006). The relative Influence of Consumer Socialisation agents on Children and Adolescents: Examining the Past and Modeling the Future, European. *Advances in Consumer Research. Association for Consumer Research (U. S.), 7*, 119–124.

Monkhouse, L. L., Barnes, B. R., & Stephan, U. (2012). The influence of face and group orientation on the perception of luxury goods A four market study of East Asian consumers. *International Marketing Review, 29*(6), 647–672. doi:10.1108/02651331211277982

Moore, D. L., Hausknecht, D., & Thamodaran, K. (1988). Time Compression, Response Opportunity, and Persuasion. *The Journal of Consumer Research, 13*, 12–24.

Morin, C. (2011). Neuromarketing: The New Science of Consumer Behaviour. *Society, 48*(2), 131–135. doi:10.100712115-010-9408-1

Morin, S., Dubé, L., & Chebat, J.-C. (2007). The role of pleasant music in servicescapes: A test of the dual model of environmental perception. *Journal of Retailing, 83*(1), 115–130. doi:10.1016/j.jretai.2006.10.006

Moschis, Sim, Anil, Yamashita, & Bouzaglo. (2011). Family and television influences on materialism: a cross cultural life course approach. *Journal of Asia Business Studies, 5*(2).

Moschis, G. P. (1985). The Role of Family Communication in Consumer Socialization of Children and Adolescents. *The Journal of Consumer Research, 11*(4), 898–913. doi:10.1086/209025

Moschis, G. P., & Churchill, G. A. Jr. (1978). Consumer Socialization: A Theoretical and Empirical Analysis. *JMR, Journal of Marketing Research, 15*(4), 599–609. doi:10.2307/3150629

Moschis, G. P., & Mitchell, L. G. (1986). Television advertising and interpersonal influences on teenagers' participation in family consumer decision. *Advances in Consumer Research. Association for Consumer Research (U. S.), 13*(1), 181–186.

Moschis, G. P., & Moore, R. L. (1979). Family communication and consumer socialization. *Advances in Consumer Research. Association for Consumer Research (U. S.), 6*(1), 359–363.

Moschis, G. P., & Moore, R. L. (2001). Decision making among the young: A socialisation perspective. *The Journal of Consumer Research, 6*(2), 101–113. doi:10.1086/208754

Moschis, G. P., Moore, R. L., & Smith, R. B. (1984). The impact of family communication on adolescent consumer socialization. *Advances in Consumer Research. Association for Consumer Research (U. S.), 11*(1), 314–319.

Moschis, G. P., Prahato, A. E., & Mitchell, L. G. (1986). Family Communication Influences on the Development of Consumer Behavior: Some Additional Findings. *Advances in Consumer Research. Association for Consumer Research (U. S.), 13*(1), 365–369.

Mosekwa, K. (2018). *The influence of disposition of trust on the adoption of SARS electronic tax filing in the city of Tshwane* (MTech dissertation). Business School, Tshwane University of Technology.

Mostafa, M. M. (2007). Antecedents of Egyptian consumers' green purchase intentions: A hierarchical multivariate regression model. *Journal of International Consumer Marketing, 19*(2), 97–126. doi:10.1300/J046v19n02_06

Mueller, A., & Schade, M. (2012). Symbols and place identity: A semiotic approach to internal place branding – case study Bremen (Germany). *Journal of Place Management and Development, 5*(1), 81–92. doi:10.1108/17538331211209068

Muhammed, S. I. (1997). *Some Possibilities in Closing Gender Disparities in Education. The Nigerian Academy of Education in Collaboration with the Chris Ogunbanjo Foundation Akoka.* Jas Publishers.

Murphy, P. E., & And Staples, W. A. (1979). A Modernized Family Life Cycle. *The Journal of Consumer Research, 6*(June), 12–22. doi:10.1086/208744

Mutula, S. M., & Mostert, J. (2010). Challenges and opportunities of e-government in South Africa. *The Electronic Library, 28*(1), 38–53. doi:10.1108/02640471011023360

Mybroadband. (2018). *High mobile data prices – operators respond.* Available at: https://mybroadband.co.za/news/cellular/249519-high-mobile-data-prices-operators-respond.html

Myers, J. H., Stanton, R. R., & Haug, F. A. (1971). Correlates of Buying Behaviour: Social Class Vs. Income. *Journal of Marketing, 35*(4), 8–15. doi:10.2307/1250451

Nandonde, F. A., & Kuada, J. (2016). Modern food retailing buying behaviour in Africa: The case of Tanzania. *British Food Journal, 118*(5), 1163–1178.

Narayanan, Y. (2010). Sustainable consumption as a means to self-realization: A Hindu perspective on when enough is enough. *Sustainable Development, 18*(5), 252–259. doi:10.1002d.476

Naresh, G. (2012). Do brand personalities make a difference to consumers? *Procedia: Social and Behavioral Sciences, 37*, 31–37. doi:10.1016/j.sbspro.2012.03.272

Narver, J. C., & Slater, S. (1990). The effect of market orientation on business profitability. *Journal of Marketing*, *54*, 20–35.

Nash, C. (2009). *Parent child purchase relationship* (PhD thesis). Dublin Institute of Technology. Retrieved from http://arrow.dit.ie/cgi/viewcontent.cgi?article=1025&context=busmas

National Pharmaceutical Control Bureau. (2009). *Guidelines for Control of Cosmetics Products in Malaysia*. Malaysia Ministry of Health.

Navimipour, N. J., & Soltani, Z. (2016). The impact of cost, technology acceptance and employees' satisfaction on the effectiveness of the electronic customer relationship management systems. *Computers in Human Behavior*, *55*, 1052–1066. doi:10.1016/j.chb.2015.10.036

NCA. (2016). *Industry information telecom subscriptions for April, 2016*. Accra: National Communication Authority.

Nebenzahl, I. D., & Jaffe, E. D. (2001). Measuring the joint effect of brand and country image in consumer evaluation of global products. *International Marketing Review*, *13*(4), 5–22. doi:10.1108/02651339610127220

Neeley, S. (2005). Influences on Consumer Socialisation. *Young Consumers*, *6*(2), 63–69. doi:10.1108/17473610510701115

Neeley, S. M., & Coffey, T. (2007). Understanding the "Four-Eyed, Four-Legged" Consumer: A Segmentation Analysis of U.S. Moms. *Journal of Marketing Theory and Practice*, *15*(3), 251–261. doi:10.2753/MTP1069-6679150305

Nelson, P. E., & Pearson, J. C. (1988). Understanding and sharing. Dubuque, IA: W.C. Brown Publishers.

Netemeyer, R. G., Durvasula, S., & Lichtenstein, D. R. (1991). A cross-national assessment of the reliability and validity of the CETSCALE. *JMR, Journal of Marketing Research*, *28*(3), 320–327. doi:10.2307/3172867

Neurogadget. (2012). *HeadSpace Agency brings neuromarketing Studies to South Africa*. Retrieved on 20/06/2015 from: http://www.neurogadget.com/2012/08/28/headspace-agency-brings-neuromarketingstudiesto-SA/4603

Newberry, C. R., Klemz, B. R., & Boshoff, C. (2003). Managerial implications of predicting purchase behavior from purchase intentions: A retail patronage case study. *Journal of Services Marketing*, *17*(6), 609–620. doi:10.1108/08876040310495636

New, S., & Ramsay, J. (1997). A critical appraisal of aspects of the lean chain approach. *European Journal of Purchasing and Supply Management*, *3*(2), 93–102. doi:10.1016/S0969-7012(96)00019-6

Nik Abdul Rashid, N. R. (2009). Awareness of eco-label in Malaysia green marketing initiative. *International Journal of Business and Management*, *4*, 132–141.

Nikken, P., & de Haan, J. (2015). Guiding young children's internet use at home: Problems that parents experience in their parental mediation and the need for parenting support. *Cyberpsychology (Brno)*, 44–57. doi:10.5817/CP2015-1-3

Njuguna, P. M. (2015). *Marketing Factors Affecting Consumerism among Urban Household Consumers in Nakuru County, Kenya* (Unpublished PhD Thesis). Jomo Kenyatta University of Agriculture and Technology, Kenya.

Nkamnebe, A. D., Idoko, E., & Kalu, S. E. (2009). Consumer protection in market transactions in Nigeria. *Innovative Marketing*, *5*(4), 89–94.

Norgaard, M., & Brunso, K. (2007). Children's influence and participation in the family decision process during food buying. *Young Consumers*, *8*(3), 197–216. doi:10.1108/17473610710780945

Nørgaard, M., & Brunsø, K. (2011). Family conflicts and conflict resolution regarding food choices. *Journal of Consumer Behaviour*, *10*(3), 141–151. doi:10.1002/cb.361

North & Theuns. (2001). Parents and television advertisements as consumer socialization agents for adolescents: An exploratory study. *Journal of Family Ecology and Consumer Sciences, 29*, 91-99.

North, D. C. (1990). *Institutions, Institutional Change, and Economic Performance*. Cambridge, UK: Cambridge University Press.

Nwankwo, S. (2000). Assessing the marketing environment in sub-Saharan Africa: Opportunities and threats analysis. *Marketing Intelligence & Planning, 18*(3), 144–153. doi:10.1108/02634500010327935

Nworah, U. (2006). *Rebranding Nigeria Critical Perspectives on The Heart Of Africa Image Project*. Available at: http://www.nigerialinks.com/pdf/RebrandingNigeria.pdf

Nworah, U. (2007). Branding Nigeria's Cities. In Advertising News (vol. 2). Lagos: APCON Publications.

Nyarko, I. K., Asimah, V., Agbemava, E., & Tsetse, E.K. (2015). The influence of celebrity endorsement on the buying behaviour of the Ghanaian youth: A study of *fan milk* Ghana ads. *International Journal of Business and Management Review, 3*(10), 83-98.

Nye, J. (2004). *Soft Power: The Means to Success in World Politics*. New York: Perseus Books.

Nze, V. (2010, March 12). Tinapa - Cross River's Gift to Tourism. *Daily Champion*.

O'Cass, A., & Lim, K. (2002). Understanding the Younger Singaporean consumers' View of Western and Eastern Brands. *Asia Pacific Journal of Marketing and Logistics, 14*(4), 54–79. doi:10.1108/13555850210764954

O'Neal, P. W. (Ed.). (2007). *Motivation of Health Behavior*. New York: Nova Science Publishers Inc.

O'Rourke, D., & Lollo, N. (2015). Transforming Consumption: From Decoupling, to Behavior, to Systems Change for Sustainable Consumption. *Annual Review of Environment and Resources, 40*(1), 233–259. doi:10.1146/annurev-environ-102014-021224

Obamuyi, T. M., Iriobe, G. O., Afolabi, T. S., Akinbobola, A. D., Elumaro, A. J., Faloye, B. A., ... Oni, A. O. (2018). Factors Influencing Ponzi Scheme Participation In Nigeria. *Advances in Social Sciences Research Journal, 5*(5), 429–444. doi:10.14738/assrj.55.4547

Ocho, C. (2009). *With 'Good People, Great Nation*. Country Rebrands. Available at http://allafrica.com/stories/200903180560.html

Odiboh, O., Olonode, A., Adesina, E., & Yartey, D. (2018). *Influence of e-communication and digital culture on Nigeria's indigenous socio-cultural systems: A focus on Abeokuta and Ota, Nigeria*. Paper presented at the fourth International *Conference* on Information Management (ICIM), London, UK.

Odiboh, O. O. (2002). *Integrated marketing communication*. Lagos: APCON.

Odunsi, W. (2017, January 1). MMM: Anxiety among participants as January 13 draws close. *Daily Post*.

Offer, A. (2006). *The Challenge of affluence*. New York: Oxford University Press.

Ogbonnikan, F. (2017). *RRS: Rebranding for a Safer Lagos*. Available at: https://www.thisdaylive.com/index.php/2017/03/31/rrs-rebranding-for-a-safer-lagos/

Ogden, Ogden, & Ramzy. (2012). *Perceptions of children's influence on Purchase decisions: A comparison between US and Egypt*. Retrieved from www.wbiconpro.com/516-Denise.pdf

Ohanian, R. (1990). Construction and Validation of A Scale to Measure Celebrity Endorser's Perceived Expertise, Trustworthiness, and Attractiveness. *Journal of Advertising, 19*(3), 39–52. doi:10.1080/00913367.1990.10673191

Ohanian, R. (1991). The Impact of Celebrity Spokesperson's Perceived Image on Consumers' Intention to Purchase. *Journal of Advertising Research*, *31*(1), 46–52.

Ojo, S. (2017). Examining the Impact of Symbolic Capital in Ethnic and Diaspora Entrepreneurship. In S. Ojo (Ed.), *Diaspora and Transnational Entrepreneurship in the Global Contexts* (pp. 66–89). Hershey, PA: IGI Global. doi:10.4018/978-1-5225-1991-1.ch004

Okorie, N., & Agbaleke, D. (2017). Celebrity endorsement influence on brand credibility: A critical review of previous studies. *Online Journal of Communication and Media Technologies.*, *7*(1), 15–20.

Okpara, G., & Onah, J. (2013). The Entrepreneurial Challenge of Consumption Complex Syndrome (CCS) in SSA's MDG – Evidence from Nigeria. *World Review of Business Research*, *3*(3), 30–46.

Ölander, F., & Thøgersen, J. (1995). Understanding of consumer behaviour as a prerequisite for environmental protection. *Journal of Consumer Policy*, *18*(4), 345–385. doi:10.1007/BF01024160

Olatuyi, A., Awoyinka, Y., & Adeniyi, A. (2013). *Nigerian diasporas in the South: Harnessing the potential for national development*. Research Report No. ACPOBS/2013/PUB06. ACP Observatory on Migration and International Organization for Migration.

Olins, W. (1999). *Trading Identities*. London: The Foreign Policy Centre.

OMahony, S., & Meenaghan, T. (1997). The impact of celebrity endorsements on consumers. *Irish Marketing Review*, *10*(2), 15-24.

Omenugha, K. A., Uzuegbunam, C. E., & Ndolo, I. S. (2016). Celebrity culture, media and the Nigerian youth: Negotiating cultural identities in a globalised world. *Critical Arts*, *30*(2), 200–216. doi:10.1080/02560046.2016.1187791

Omidire, D. (2016). *Lagos State Unveils Urban Development Projects for Megacity Initiative*. Available at: https://estateintel.com/lagos-state-unveils-urban-development-projects-for-megacity-initiative/

Ondraczek, J. (2013). The sun rises in the east (of Africa): A comparison of the development and status of solar energy markets in Kenya and Tanzania. *Energy Policy*, *56*, 407–417.

Onyeji, E. (2016, December 1). 7 trending Ponzi schemes in Nigeria in 2016. *Premium Times*.

Onyeji, E. (2017, March 30). MMM, other Ponzi schemes thrive in Nigeria, despite past woes. *Premium Times*.

Ooi, K., Sim, J., Yew, K., & Lin, B. (2011). Exploring factors influencing consumers' behavioral intention to adopt broadband in Malaysia. *Computers in Human Behavior*, *27*(3), 1168–1178. doi:10.1016/j.chb.2010.12.011

Orbaiz, L. V., & Papadopoulos, N. (2003). Toward a model of consumer receptivity of foreign and domestic products. *Journal of International Consumer Marketing*, *15*(3), 101–130. doi:10.1300/J046v15n03_06

Orock, R. T. E. (2007). Gender Equality: Whose Agenda? Observation from Cameroon. *Development in Practice*, *17*(1), 93–97. doi:10.1080/09614520601092220

Orozco, M., & Mills, M. (2007). *Remittances, competition and fair financial access opportunities in Nigeria*. Washington, DC: USAID.

Osborne, G. (2015). *All of Procter & Gamble's fragrance acquisitions and divestures 1990 – 2015*. Retrieved July 19, 2015, from http://www.basenotes.net/features/3165-all-of-procter-and-gambles-fragrance-acquisitions-and-divestures-1990-2015

Osei, C., & Gbadamosi, A. (2011). Re-branding Africa. *Marketing Intelligence & Planning, 29*(3), 284–304. doi:10.1108/02634501111129257

Oslo Roundtable on Sustainable Production and Consumption. (1994). Symposium: *Sustainable Consumption*. Retrieved on December 7th, 2015 from http://www.iisd.ca/consume/oslo004.html

Othman, M. N., Ong, F. S., & Wong, H. W. (2008). Demographic and lifestyle profiles of ethnocentric and non-ethnocentric urban Malaysian consumers. *Asian Journal of Business and Accounting, 1*(1), 5–26.

Overby, J. W., Woodruff, R. B., & Gardial, S. F. (2005). The influence of culture upon consumer's desired value perceptions: A research agenda. *Marketing Theory, 5*(2), 139–163. doi:10.1177/1470593105052468

Owuamanam, J., Alechenu, J. & Onuba, I. (2012). *Bombings threatening our economy*. Academic Press.

Oyeniyi, O. (2014). Celebrity endorsements and product performance: A study of Nigerian consumer markets. *Management & Marketing Journal, 15*(1), 41–51.

Ozer, S. U. (2016). The Role of Culture in City Branding. In A. Bayraktar & C. Uslay (Eds.), *Strategic Place Branding Methodologies and Theory for Tourist Attraction* (pp. 227–244). Hershey, PA: IGI Global.

Özgen, Ö. (2003). An analysis of child consumers in Turkey. *International Journal of Consumer Studies, 27*(5), 366–380. doi:10.1046/j.1470-6431.2003.00306.x

Pagnotta, K. (2012). *Celebrity endorsed perfumes*. Retrieved July 19, 2015, from www.trendhunter.com

Palmatier, R. W., Dant, R. P., Grewal, D., & Evans, K. R. (2006). Factors Influencing the Effectiveness of Relationship Marketing: A Meta-Analysis. *Journal of Marketing, 70*(October), 136–153. doi:10.1509/jmkg.70.4.136

Palmatier, R. W., Jarvis, C. B., Bechkoff, J. R., & Kardes, F. R. (2009). The Role of Customer Gratitude in Relationship Marketing. *Journal of Marketing, 73*(September), 1–18. doi:10.1509/jmkg.73.5.1

Panditbhushan, V., Shastri, S., & Bhat, V. (1946). *Brihat Samhita of Varaha Mihra (with English Translation)*. Electronic Printing Works, Bangalore. Retrieved July 19, 2015, from https://archive.org/details/Brihatsamhita

Parris, T. M., & Kates, R. W. (2003). Characterizing and measuring sustainable development. *Annual Review of Environment and Resources, 28*(1), 559–586. doi:10.1146/annurev.energy.28.050302.105551

Parsons, E., Maclaran, P., & Chatzidakis, A. (2018). *Contemporary Issues in Marketing and Consumer Behaviour* (2nd Ed.). London: Routledge.

Paswan, A. K., & Sharma, D. (2004). Brand-country of origin (COO) knowledge and COO image: Investigation in an emerging franchise market. *Journal of Product and Brand Management, 13*(3), 144–155. doi:10.1108/10610420410538041

Patterson, P. G., Cowley, E., & Prasongsukarn, K. (2006). Service failure recovery: The moderating impact of individual-level cultural value orientation on perceptions of justice. *International Journal of Research in Marketing, 23*(3), 263–277. doi:10.1016/j.ijresmar.2006.02.004

Patton, M. (2002). *Qualitative Research and Evaluation Methods* (3rd ed.). Thousand Oaks, CA: Sage.

Paul, J., & Bhawsar, P. (2011). Japanese acquisition in India's Ranbaxy. *Competitiveness Review, 21*(5), 452–470. doi:10.1108/10595421111171957

Payne, J. W., Bettman, J. R., & Johnson, E. J. (1993). The Adaptive Decision Maker. Cambridge, UK: Academic Press. doi:10.1017/CBO9781139173933

Pearce, P. L. (1982). Perceived changes in holiday destinations. *Annals of Tourism Research*, *9*(2), 145–164. doi:10.1016/0160-7383(82)90044-5

Peattie, K. (2001). Golden goose or wild goose? The hunt for the green consumer. *Business Strategy and the Environment*, *10*(4), 187–199. doi:10.1002/bse.292

Peattie, K., & Collins, A. (2009). Guest editorial: Perspectives on sustainable consumption. *International Journal of Consumer Studies*, *33*(2), 107–112. doi:10.1111/j.1470-6431.2009.00758.x

Peattie, K., & Crane, A. (2005). Green marketing: Legend, myth, farce or prophesy? *Qualitative Market Research*, *8*(4), 357–370. doi:10.1108/13522750510619733

Pechacek, A. (2007). I can't live without my … teens' top ten high-tech gadgets and web sites. *Young Adult Library Services*, *5*(2), 9–16.

Pecotich, A., & Rosenthal, M. J. (2001). Country of Origin, Quality, Brand and Consumer Ethnocentrism. *Journal of Global Marketing*, *15*(2), 31–60. doi:10.1300/J042v15n02_03

Peil, M. (1974). Ghana's aliens. *The International Migration Review*, *8*(3), 367–381. doi:10.1177/019791837400800303

Peirce, S., & Ritchie, B. W. (2007). National Capital Branding: A Comparative Case Study of Canberra, Australia and Wellington, New Zealand. *Journal of Travel & Tourism Marketing*, *22*(3-4), 67–78. doi:10.1300/J073v22n03_06

Penaloza, L. (1994). Atravesando Fronteras/Border Crossings: A Critical Ethnographic Exploration of the Consumer Acculturation of Mexican Immigrants. *Journal of Consumer Research*, *21*(1), 32-54.

Pentz, C., Terblanche, N., & Boshoff, C. (2017). Antecedents and consequences of consumer ethnocentrism: evidence from South Africa. *International Journal of Emerging Markets*, *12*(2), 199-218.

Pérez-Nordtvedt, L., Kedia, B. L., Datta, D. K., & Rasheed, A. A. (2008). Effectiveness and efficiency of cross-border knowledge transfer: An empirical examination. *Journal of Management Studies*, *45*(4), 714–744.

Perraudin, F. (2015). *MPs pass legislation to introduce standardised cigarette packaging*. Retrieved from: http://www.theguardian.com/politics/2015/mar/11/mps-pass-legislation-introduce-standardised-cigarette-packaging

Peter, J. P., & Olson, J. C. (2010). Consumer Behavior and Marketing Strategy (9th ed.). Boston: McGraw-Hill Companies, Inc.

Peter, P. J., & Olson, J. C. (1999). Consumer Behaviour and Marketing Strategy. Irwin/McGraw-Hill.

Peter, J. P., & Olson, J. C. (2008). *Consumer behaviour and marketing strategy* (8th ed.). New York, NY: McGraw-Hill Education.

Peter, R., Ramaseshan, B., & Nayar, C. V. (2002). Conceptual model for marketing solar based technology to developing countries. *Renewable Energy*, *25*, 511–524.

Pettigrew, S., Jongenelis, M., Chapman, K., & Miller, C. (2015). Factors Influencing the Children's Consumption of Soft drinks. *Appetite*, *91*(August), 393–398. doi:10.1016/j.appet.2015.04.080 PMID:25953597

Phau, I., & Cheah, I. (2011). Attitudes towards environmentally friendly products: The influence of ecoliteracy, interpersonal influence and value orientation. *Marketing Intelligence & Planning*, *29*(5), 452–472. doi:10.1108/02634501111153674

Phillips, A., de Savigny, D., & Law, M. (1995). As Canadians butt out, the developing world lights up. *Canadian Medical Association Journal*, *153*(8), 1111–1114. Retrieved from http://www.ncbi.nlm.nih.gov/pmc/articles/PMC1487334/pdf/cmaj00080-0061.pdf PMID:7553519

Pierre, C., Morwitz, V. G., & Reinartz, W. J. (2005). Do intentionss really predict behavior? Self-generated validity effects in survey research. *Journal of Marketing, 69*(2), 1–14. doi:10.1509/jmkg.69.2.1.60755

Pil, H. S., & Shavitt, S. (1994). Persuasion and culture: Advertising appeals in individualistic and collectivistic societies. *Journal of Experimental Social Psychology, 30*(4), 326–350. doi:10.1006/jesp.1994.1016

Pinar, M., Girard, T., & And Eser, Z. (2011). An Exploratory Study Of Consumer-Based Brand Equity In Turkish Banking' Industry. *Services Marketing Quarterly, 32*(4), 282–301. doi:10.1080/15332969.2011.606760

Pitman, S. (2012). *Takasago targets expansion into fast growing India fragrance market*. Retrieved July 19, 2015, http://www.cosmeticsdesign-europe.com/Business-Financial/Takasago-targets-expansion-into-fast-growing-India-fragrance-market

Piyush, M. K. J. (2012). Celebrity endorsements and brand building. *Journal of Advertising*, 1-88. Retrieved from https://openpolicyontario.pbworks.com/f/Celebrity-Endorsements.Report1+%282%29.pdf

Plassman, H., O'Doherty, J., Shiv, D., & Rangel, A. (2008). Marketing actions can modulate neural representations of experienced pleasantness. *Proceedings of the National Academy of Sciences of the United States of America, 105*(3), 1050–1054. doi:10.1073/pnas.0706929105

Pole, S. (2006). *Ayurvedic Medicine: The Principles of Traditional Practice*. Philadelphia, PA: Churchill Livingston Elsevier.

Polya, E. (2012). *Purchase decision making process and roles within the family* (PhD thesis). Szent Istvan University. Retrieved from https://szie.hu//file/tti/archivum/Polya_E_Thesis.pdf

Pornpitakpan, C. (2004). The Effect of Celebrity Endorsers' Perceived Credibility on Product Purchase Intention. *Journal of International Consumer Marketing, 16*(2), 55–74. doi:10.1300/J046v16n02_04

Praet, C. L. C. (2001). Japanese advertising, the world's number one celebrity showcase? A crosscultural comparison of the frequency of celebrity appearances in TV advertising. In *Proceedings of the 2001 Special Asia-Pacific Conference of the American Academy of Advertising*. American Academy of Advertising.

Prahalad, C. K., & Hart, S. L. (2002). The fortune at the bottom of the pyramid. *Strategy Business, 26*, 54–67.

Prasongsukarn. (2009). Validating the Cultural Value scale (CVSCALE) a Case Study of Thailand. *ABAC Journal, 29*(2), 1–13.

Pratkanis, A. R., & Greenwald, A. G. (1993). Consumer involvement, message attention, and the persistence of persuasive impact in a message-dense environment. *Psychology and Marketing, 10*(4), 321–332. doi:10.1002/mar.4220100406

Prayag, A. (2012). *Dubai's Scion Intl to enter India with fragrances in mid-segment*. Retrieved July 19, 2015, http://www.thehindubusinessline.com

Priester, J. R., & Petty, R. E. (2003). The influence of spokesperson trustworthiness on message elaboration, attitude strength, and advertising effectiveness. *Journal of Consumer Psychology, 13*(4), 408–421. doi:10.1207/S15327663JCP1304_08

Pringle, H. (2015). *Stars in your ads: What evidence is there that celebrity sells*. Academic Press.

Pringle, H., & Binet, L. (2005). How marketers can use celebrities to sell more efficiently. *Journal of Consumer Behaviour, 4*(3), 201–214. doi:10.1002/cb.2

Prothero, A., Dobscha, S., Freund, J., Kilbourne, W. E., Luchs, M. G., Ozanne, L. K., & Thøgersen, J. (2011). Sustainable consumption: Opportunities for consumer research and public policy. *Journal of Public Policy & Marketing, 30*(1), 31–38. doi:10.1509/jppm.30.1.31

Purba, D. (2017). The Economics Perspective of The Practice of MMM- Indonesia. *AFEBI Islamic Finance and Economic Review*, *2*(1), 75–91.

PwC. (2015). *Doing Business in the UAE A tax and legal guide.* Available at: https://www.pwc.com/m1/en/tax/documents/doing-business-guides/doing-business-guide-uae.pdf

Qian, W., Rszzaque, M. A., & Keng, K. A. (2007). Chinese cultural values and gift-giving behaviour. *Journal of Consumer Marketing*, *24*(4), 214–228. doi:10.1108/07363760710756002

Quelch, J. A. (1987). Why not exploit dual marketing? *Business Horizons*, *30*(1), 52–60.

Rabbie, F. (2004). Focus-group interview and data analysis. *The Proceedings of the Nutrition Society*, *63*(4), 655–660. doi:10.1079/PNS2004399 PMID:15831139

Raghav, P., & Kumar, A. (2010). The Influence of Television on Children and Adolescents in an Urban Slum. *Indian Journal of Community Medicine*, *35*(3), 447. doi:10.4103/0970-0218.69291 PMID:21031123

Rahbar, E., & Abdul Wahid, N. (2011). Investigation of green marketing tools' effect on consumers' purchase behavior. *Business Strategy Series*, *12*(2), 73–83. doi:10.1108/17515631111114877

Raheja, G. G. (1988). *The poison in the gift: ritual, prestation, and the dominant caste in a north Indian village.* Chigago, IL: University of Chicago Press.

Rahman, S., & Azhar, S. (2011). Xpressions of generation Y: Perceptions of the mobile phone service industry in Pakistan. *Asia Pacific Journal of Marketing and Logistics*, *23*(1), 91–107. doi:10.1108/13555851111100012

Rajagopal, D. (2011). Consumer culture and purchase intentions toward fashion apparel in Mexico. *Journal of Database Marketing and Customer Strategy Management.*, *18*(4), 286–307. doi:10.1057/dbm.2011.33

Rajarathinam, V. (2013). Internet Banking Users' Competence and its Influence On Usage Satisfaction – A View from India. *Journal of Internet Banking and Commerce*, *18*(3), 1–13.

Ramanathan, S., & McGill, A. L. (2007). Consuming with others: Social influences on moment-to-moment and retrospective evaluations of an experience. *The Journal of Consumer Research*, *34*(4), 506–524. doi:10.1086/520074

Ramayah, T., Jason, L. W. C., & Mohamad, O. (2010). Green Product Purchase Intentions: Some Insights from a Developing Country. *Resources, Conservation and Recycling*, *54*(12), 1419–1427. doi:10.1016/j.resconrec.2010.06.007

Ramsey, C. E., & Rickson, R. E. (1976). Environmental knowledge and attitudes. *The Journal of Environmental Education*, *8*(1), 10–18. doi:10.1080/00958964.1976.9941552

Ramsey, J. M. (1993). The effects of issue investigation and action training on eighth-grade students' environmental behavior. *The Journal of Environmental Education*, *2*(3), 31–36. doi:10.1080/00958964.1993.9943501

RAND. (2018). *Developing Countries.* Retrieved from https://www.rand.org/topics/developing-countries.html

Rand, J., & Tarp, F. (2002). Business Cycles in Developing Countries: Are They Different? *World Development*, *30*(12), 2071–2088. doi:10.1016/S0305-750X(02)00124-9

Rangel, A., Camerer, C., & Montague, P. R. (2008, July). Value-based Decision making. *Nature Reviews. Neuroscience*, *9*(7), 545–556. doi:10.1038/nrn2357 PMID:18545266

Ranjbarian, B., Shekarchizade, Z., & Momeni, Z. (2010). Celebrity endorser influence on attitude toward advertisement and brands. *European Journal of Soil Science*, *13*(3), 399–404.

Ranjbarian, B., Shekarchizade, Z., & Momeni, Z. (2010). Celebrity endorser influence on attitude toward advertisements and brands. *European Journal of Soil Science, 13*(3), 399–407.

Rath, J. (2000). *Immigrant business: The economic political, and social environment.* New York, NY: St. Martin's Press. doi:10.1057/9781403905338

Rawlins, N. (2005). The Nervous System. In M. Hewstone, F. D. Fincham, & J. Forster (Eds.), *Psychology* (pp. 42–72). Blackwell Publishing.

Reed, W., Catherine Bate, C., & Simsovic, D. (2003). Kid Law: advertising to children in Canada. In Advertising & Marketing to Children. World Advertising Research Center.

Rehn, A. (2014). *6 Mega Corporations Control Almost the Entire Global Cigarette Industry.* Retrieved from: http://mic.com/articles/81365/6-mega-corporations-control-almost-the-entire-global-cigarette-industry

Reisch, L. (2001). Time and Wealth: The role of time and temporalities for sustainable patterns of consumption. *Time & Society, 10*(2-3), 367–385. doi:10.1177/0961463X01010002012

Reputation Institute. (2013, October 17). *City RepTrak Study* (Press Release). Author.

Reputation Institute. (2017). *2017 Global Reptrak® - Most Reputable Companies in The World.* Available at: https://www.reputationinstitute.com/resources/registered/pdf-resources/2017-global-reptrak-most-reputable-companies-in.aspx

Rettie, R., & Brewer, C. (2000). The verbal and visual components of package design. *Journal of Product and Brand Management, 9*(1), 56–70. doi:10.1108/10610420010316339

Reynolds, M., & Regio, M. (2001). *E-government as a Catalyst in the Information Age.* Microsoft E-Government Initiatives.

Ries, A., & Trout, J. (2001). *Positioning: The Battle for Your Mind Paperback.* New York: McGraw-Hill.

Rina, M. (2010). The influence of vicarious role models on purchase intentions of Botswana teenagers. *Young Consumers, 11*(4), 307–319. doi:10.1108/17473611011093934

Ringle, C. M., Wende, S., & Will, A. (2005). *SmartPLS 2.0 (M3) beta.* Retrieved from http://www.smartpls.de

Ritchie, J., & Spencer, L. (1994). Qualitative data analysis for applied policy research. In A. Bryman & R. Burgess (Eds.), *Analyzing Qualitative Data* (pp. 173–194). London: Sage.

Robenstine, C. (2001). Social Class and the Politics of School Choice. *Journal of Thought, 36*(1), 55–65.

Robert, O. (2012). Young Saudi adults and peer group purchase influence; a preliminary investigation. *Young Consumers, 13*(2), 176–187. doi:10.1108/17473611211233549

Roberts, J. A., & Manolis, C. (2000). Baby boomers and busters: An exploratory investigation of attitudes toward marketing, advertising and consumerism. *Journal of Consumer Marketing, 17*(6), 481–497. doi:10.1108/07363760010349911

Roberts, M., & Pettigrew, S. (2013). Psychological Influences on Children's Food Consumption. *Psychology and Marketing, 30*(2), 103–120. doi:10.1002/mar.20591

Robertson, T. S., & Rossiter, J. R. (1974). Children and Commercial Persuasion: An Attribution Theory Analysis. *The Journal of Consumer Research, 1*(1), 13–20. doi:10.1086/208577

Robinson, R. (1984). Forecasting and Small Business: A study of the strategic planning Process. *Journal of Small Business Management, 22*(2), 19–27.

Roedder & Lakshmi-Ratan. (1992). Age differences in Children's choice Behaviour: The Impact of Available Alternatives. *Journal of Marketing research, 26*, 216-26.

Roedder, D. L. (1981). Age Differences in Children's Responses to Television Advertising: An Information-Processing Approach. *The Journal of Consumer Research*, *8*(2), 144–153. doi:10.1086/208850

Roedder, J. D. (1999). Consumer Socialisation of children: A Retrospective look at twenty five years of research. *The Journal of Consumer Research*, *26*(3), 183–213. doi:10.1086/209559

Roedder-John, D. (2002). Consumer socialization of children: a retrospective look at twenty-five years of research. In F. Hansen, J. Rasmussen, A. Martensen, & B. Tufte (Eds.), *Children: Consumption, Advertising and Media* (pp. 25–89). Copenhagen: Copenhagen Business School Press.

Rogers, E. M. (1995). *Diffusion of innovations: Modifications and model of telecommunications*. New York: Free Press.

Rokeach, M. (1973). *The Nature of Human Values*. New York: Free Press.

Romila, C. (2008). *Tourism Marketing and Crisis Management. Global Media.*

Roozen, I., & Claeys, C. (2010). The relative effectiveness of celebrity endorsement for print advertisement. *Review of Business and Economic Literature*, *55*(1), 76–89.

Roper, S., & Shah, B. (2007). Vulnerable consumers: The social impact of branding on children. *Equal Opportunities International*, *26*(7), 712–728. doi:10.1108/02610150710822339

Rorissa, A., Demissie, D., & Pardo, T. (2011). Benchmarking e-government: A comparison of frameworks for computing e-government index and ranking. *Government Information Quarterly*, *28*(3), 354–362. doi:10.1016/j.giq.2010.09.006

Rose, G. M. (1999). Consumer Socialisation, Parental Style and Developmental Time Tables in the United States and Japan. *Journal of Marketing*, *63*(3), 105–119. doi:10.2307/1251778

Rose, G. M., Boush, D., & Shoham, A. (2002). Family communication and children's purchasing influence: A cross-national examination. *Journal of Business Research*, *55*(11), 867–873. doi:10.1016/S0148-2963(01)00205-3

Rosenberg, N., & Siegel, M. (2001). Use of corporate sponsorship as a tobacco marketing tool: A review of tobacco industry sponsorship in the USA, 1995-99. *Tobacco Control*, *10*(10), 239–246. doi:10.1136/tc.10.3.239 PMID:11544388

Rossi, N. (1989). Dependency Rates and Private Savings Behavior in Developing Countries. *International Monetary Fund, 36*(1), 166-181.

Rossiter, J.R., Percey, L., & Donovan, R.J. (1991, October). A better advertising planning grid. *Journal of Advertising Research*, 11-21.

Roth, K. (2017). *United Arab Emirates: Events of 2016*. Available at: https://www.hrw.org/world-report/2017/country-chapters/united-arab-emirates

Rothschild, M. L. (1979). Advertising Strategies for High and Low Involvement situations. In J. C. Maloney & B. Silverman (Eds.), *Attitude Research Plays for High Stakes* (pp. 74–93). Chicago: American Marketing Association.

Rundh, B. (2005). The multi-faceted dimension of packaging. *British Food Journal*, *107*(9), 670–684. doi:10.1108/00070700510615053

Sabrina, O. S. (2007). *Predicting environmentally purchase behaviour: a test of the value-attitude-behavior hierarchy.* The 2nd Indonesian Business Management Conference, Jakarta, Indonesia.

Saffu, K., & Scott, D. (2009). Developing country perceptions of high- and low-involvement products manufactured in other countries. *International Journal of Emerging Markets*, *4*(2), 185–199.

Sahakian, M., & Wilhite, H. (2014). Making practice theory practicable: Towards more sustainable forms of consumption. *Journal of Consumer Culture*, *14*(1), 25–44. doi:10.1177/1469540513505607

Sahin, S., & Baloglu, S. (2014). City branding: Investigating a brand advocacy model for distinct segments. *Journal of Hospitality Marketing & Management*, *23*(3/4), 239–265. doi:10.1080/19368623.2013.779562

Sajdakowska, M. (2003). Consumer ethnocentrism -Factor influencing consumers' purchasing decisions in the food market. *Acta Scientiarum Polonorum. Technologia Alimentaria*, *2*, 177.

Saleem, M. A., Eagle, L., & Low, D. (2018). Market segmentation based on eco-socially conscious consumers' behavioral intentions: Evidence from an emerging economy. *Journal of Cleaner Production*, *193*, 14–27. doi:10.1016/j.jclepro.2018.05.067

Salmi, A. (2011). International research teams and collective case studies: an abductive approach. In R. Piekkari & C. Welch (Eds.), *Rethinking the Case Study in International Business and Management Research* (pp. 431–452). Cheltenham, UK: Edward Elgar. doi:10.4337/9780857933461.00033

Samarasinghe, R. (2012). The Influence of Cultural Values and Environmental Attitudes on Green Consumer Behaviour. *International Journal of Behavioral Science.*, *7*, 83–98.

Samiee, S., Shimp, T. A., & Sharma, S. (2005). Brand origin recognition accuracy: Its antecedents and consumers' cognitive limitations**.** *Journal of International Business Studies*, *36*(4), 379–397. doi:10.1057/palgrave.jibs.8400145

Sandys, A. (2016). *Place branding: Lagos, Nigeria*. Available at: http://www.transformmagazine.net/articles/2016/place-branding-lagos-nigeria/

Sanne, C. (2002). Willing consumers—or locked-in? Policies for a sustainable consumption. *Ecological Economics*, *42*(1–2), 273–287. doi:10.1016/S0921-8009(02)00086-1

Sanusi. (n.d.). Available at: http://www.punchng.com/news/bombings-threatening-our-economy sanusi/

Sarigollu, E. (2009). A Cross-Country Exploration of Environmental Attitudes. *Environment and Behavior*, *41*(3), 365–386. doi:10.1177/0013916507313920

Sayer, A. (2010). *Method in Social Science: A Realist Approach*. London: Routledge.

Schaefer, M., Berens, H., Heinze, H. J., & Rotte, M. (2006). Neural correlates of culturally familiar brands of car manufacturers. *NeuroImage, 31*(2), 861–865. doi:10.1016/j.neuroimage.2005.12.047

Schaefer, A. (1997). Consumer knowledge and country of origin effects. *European Journal of Marketing*, *31*(1), 56–72. doi:10.1108/03090569710157034

Schaefer, A., & Crane, A. (2005). Addressing sustainability and consumption. *Journal of Macromarketing*, *25*(1), 76–92. doi:10.1177/0276146705274987

Schahn, J., & Holzer, E. (1990). Studies of individual environmental concern: The role of knowledge, gender, and background variables. *Environment and Behavior*, *22*(6), 767–786. doi:10.1177/0013916590226003

Schaninger, C. M. (1981). Social Class versus Income Revisited: An Empirical Investigation. *JMR, Journal of Marketing Research*, *18*(2), 192–208. doi:10.2307/3150954

Schau, H. J., Dang, Y. M., & Zhang, Y. G. (2017). Learning to navigate the American retail servicescape: Online forums as consumer acculturation platforms and consumer gift systems. *Journal of Business Research*, *72*, 178–188. doi:10.1016/j.jbusres.2016.08.031

Schiffman, L., & Kanuk, L. L. (2010). Consumer Behavior (10th ed.). Pearson Education, Inc.

Schiffman, L. G., Kanuk, L. S., & Hansen, H. (2012). *Consumer Behavior: A European Outlook* (2nd ed.). Essex, UK: Pearson Education Limited.

Schlecht, C. (2003). Celebrities' Impact on Branding. Center on Global Brand Leadership, Columbia Business School.

Schmitt, B. (1999). Experiential Marketing. *Journal of Marketing Management*, *15*(1-3), 53–67. doi:10.1362/026725799784870496

Schooler, R. D. (1965). Product bias in the Central American common market. *JMR, Journal of Marketing Research*, *2*(4), 394–397. doi:10.2307/3149486

Schor, J. (2002). Understanding the New Consumerism: Inequality, Emulation and the Erosium of Well Being. *PSW Paper*, *2*(April), 1–13.

Schultz, M., Moritsen, J., & Gabrielsen, G. (2006). Sticky reputation: Analyzing a ranking system. *Corporate Reputation Review*, *4*(1), 24–41. doi:10.1057/palgrave.crr.1540130

Schumacher, E. F. (1973). *Small is Beautiful: Economics as if People Mattered.* London, UK: Blond and Briggs.

Schwartz, J., & Miller, T. (1991). The earth's best friends. *American Demographics*, *13*, 26–35.

Schwartz, S. H. (1994). Are there universal aspects in the structure and contents of human values? *The Journal of Social Issues*, *50*(4), 19–45. doi:10.1111/j.1540-4560.1994.tb01196.x

Schwartz, S. H., & Sagiv, L. (1995). Identifying culture-specifics in the content and structure of values. *Journal of Cross-Cultural Psychology*, *26*(1), 92–116. doi:10.1177/0022022195261007

Scott, K., Martin, D. M., & Schouten, J. W. (2014). Marketing and the New Materialism. *Journal of Macromarketing*, *34*(3), 282–290. doi:10.1177/0276146714532471

Scott, W. (1974). Consumer Socialisation: Initial Study results. *Advances in Consumer Research. Association for Consumer Research (U. S.)*, *1*, 120–125.

Scott, W. R. (2004). Institutional theory. In G. Ritzer (Ed.), *Encyclopaedia of Social Theory* (pp. 408–414). Thousand Oaks, CA: Sage.

SEC. (2016). *Public Alert on the Activities of "MMM Federal Republic of Nigeria" (Nigeria.mmm.net).* Securities & Exchange Commission.

Seelos, C., & Mair, J. (2007). Profitable business models and market creation in the context of deep poverty: A strategic view. *The Academy of Management Perspectives*, *21*, 49–63.

Selles, H. (2013). The relative impact of countries on global natural resource consumption and ecological degradation. *International Journal of Sustainable Development and World Ecology*, *20*(2), 97–108. doi:10.1080/13504509.2013.780190

Selsky, J. W., & Parker, B. (2005). Cross-sector partnerships to address social issues: Challenges to theory and practice. *Journal of Management*, *31*(6), 849–873. doi:10.1177/0149206305279601

Senior, C., & Lee, L. (2008). A Manifesto for Neuromarketing Science. *Journal of Consumer Behaviour*, *7*(4-5), 263–271. doi:10.1002/cb.250

Sertoglu, A., Catli, O., & Korkmaz, S. (2014). Examining the effect of endorser credibility on the consumers' buying intentions: An empirical study in Turkey. *International Review of Management and Marketing*, *4*(1), 66–77.

Sevin, E. (2014). Understanding cities through city brands: City branding as a social and semantic network. *Cities (London, England)*, *38*, 47–56. doi:10.1016/j.cities.2014.01.003

Seyfang, G., & Paavola, J. (2008). Inequality and sustainable consumption: Bridging the gaps. *Local Environment*, *13*(8), 669–684. doi:10.1080/13549830802475559

Shah, D. V., Friedland, L. A., Wells, C., Kim, Y. M., & Rojas, H. (2012). Communication, Consumers, and Citizens Revisiting the Politics of Consumption. *The Annals of the American Academy of Political and Social Science*, *644*(1), 6–19. doi:10.1177/0002716212456349

Shambare, R. (2012). A cold drink for my brother in uniform: Applying the theory of planned behaviour to explain corruption in South Africa. *Proceedings of the 6thIinternational Business Conference.*

Shambare, R. (2016). Consumer Adoption of E-government in South Africa: Barriers, Solutions, and Implications. In A. Gbadamosi (Ed.), Consumerism and Buying Behavior in Developing Nations. Academic Press. doi:10.4018/978-1-5225-0282-1.ch009

Shambare, R. (2014). The adoption of WhatsApp: Breaking the vicious cycle of technological poverty in South Africa. *Journal of Economics and Behavioral Studies*, *6*(7), 542–550.

Shambare, R., & Mvula, A. (2011). South African students' perceptions of Facebook: Some implications for instructors. *African Journal of Business Management*, *5*(26), 10567–10564.

Shanbaug, A. (2012). *Fragrance industry to cross Rs 10,000 crore in next 3 years*. Retrieved May 12, 2015, from http://articles.economictimes.indiatimes.com/2012-05-9/news/31778108_1_perfume-market-fragrance-market-deodorants

Shane, S. (2000). Prior Knowledge and the Discovery of Entrepreneurial Opportunities. *Organization Science*, *11*(4), 448–469. doi:10.1287/orsc.11.4.448.14602

Shane, S., & Cable, D. (2002). Network Ties, Reputation, and the Financing of New Ventures. *Management Science*, *48*(3), 364–381. doi:10.1287/mnsc.48.3.364.7731

Sharma, A. (2009). Role and influence of children in buying children's apparel. *Indian Journal ofMarketing*, *39*(7), 42–46.

Sharma, A. (2011). Role of family in consumer socialization of children: Literature Review.*Journal of Arts. Science and Commerce*, *2*(3), 161–167.

Sharma, A., & Sonwaney, V. (2014). Theoretical Modeling of Influence of children on Family Purcahse Decision Making. *Procedia: Social and Behavioral Sciences*, *133*, 38–46. doi:10.1016/j.sbspro.2014.04.167

Sharma, A., & Sonwaney, V. (2015). Exploring the role of family communication and brand awareness in understanding the influence of child on purchase decisions: Scale development and Validation, *Int. Journal of. Business Excellence*, *8*(6), 748–766. doi:10.1504/IJBEX.2015.072308

Sharma, R., & Dasgupta, P. (2009). Marketing to children: A planning framework. *Young Consumers*, *10*(3), 180–187. doi:10.1108/17473610910985991

Sharma, S., Shimp, T., & Shin, J. (1995). Consumer Ethnocentrism: A Test Antecedents and Moderators. *Journal of the Academy of Marketing Science*, *23*(1), 26–37. doi:10.1007/BF02894609

Shaw, I., & Aldrigde, A. (2003). Consumerism, Health and Social Order. *Social Policy and Society*, *2*(1), 35–43. doi:10.1017/S147474640300109X

Sheth, J. N. (1967). A Review of Buyer Behavior. *Management Science*, *13*(12), 718–786. doi:10.1287/mnsc.13.12.B718

Sheth, J. N., Mittal, B., & Newman, B. I. (1999). *Customer Behaviour. In Consumer Behaviour and Beyond* (pp. 343–355). Orlando: The Dryden Press.

Sheth, J. N., Sethia, N. K., & Srinivas, S. (2011). Mindful consumption: A customer-centric approach to sustainability. *Journal of the Academy of Marketing Science*, *39*(1), 21–39. doi:10.100711747-010-0216-3

Sheth, J. N., & Sisodia, R. S. (2012). *The 4 A's of marketing: Creating value for customers, companies, and society*. Routledge.

Shimp, C. P. (1993). Observation and theory in behavior analysis. *Journal of the Experimental Analysis of Behavior*, *60*(2), 481–484. doi:10.1901/jeab.1993.60-481 PMID:16812715

Shimp, T. (2003). *Advertising, Promotion and Supplemental Aspects of Integrated Marketing Communication* (6th ed.). Fort Worth, TX: The Dryden Press.

Shimp, T., & Sharma, S. (1987). Consumer ethnocentrism: Construction and validation of the CETSCALE. *JMR, Journal of Marketing Research*, *23*, 280–289.

Shimp, T., & Sharma, S. (1987). Consumer Ethnocentrism: Construction and Validation of the CETSCALE. *JMR, Journal of Marketing Research*, *24*(3), 280–289. doi:10.2307/3151638

Shim, S., & Snyder, L. (1995). Parents' Perception Regarding Children's Use of Clothing Evaluative Criteria: An Exploratory Study From the Consumer Socialization Process Perspective. *Advances in Consumer Research. Association for Consumer Research (U. S.)*, *22*(1), 628–632.

Shrivastava, A. (2014). The Earth, not the sky, is the limit: India and 'The Great Transition' to an ecological world. *Futures*, *56*, 87–93. doi:10.1016/j.futures.2013.10.013

Shultz, C. J. II, Deshpandé, R., Cornwell, T. B., Ekici, A., Kothandaraman, P., Peterson, M., ... Veeck, A. (2012). Marketing and Public Policy: Transformative Research in Developing Markets. *Journal of Public Policy & Marketing*, *31*(2), 178–184. doi:10.1509/jppm.11.007

Shyna, N. (2010). *Neutrogena oil moisturizer*. Retrieved July 18, 2015, from http://www.fragrance.org/forum-Fall-Winter-2010/5-profile-indian-fragrance-industry.php

Siamagka, S., & Balabanis, G. (2015). Revisiting Consumer Ethnocentrism: Review, Reconceptualization, and Empirical Testing. *Journal of International Marketing*, *23*(3), 66–86. doi:10.1509/jim.14.0085

Silk Road. (2015). *History of the silk road*. Retrieved April 19, 2015, from http://www.silk-road.com/artl/silkhistory.shtml

Silvera, D. H., & Benedikte, A. (2004). Factors predicting the effectiveness of celebrity endorsement advertisements. *European Journal of Marketing*, *38*(11/12), 1509–1526. doi:10.1108/03090560410560218

Singh, R. (2000). *Entrepreneurial Opportunity Recognition through Social Networks*. Psychology Press.

Sinha, P. (1990). Kolkata and the Currents of History. In Kolkata - The Living City: Vol. 1. The Past. Oxford, UK: Oxford University Press.

Sinha, M., & Sheth, J. (2018). Growing the pie in emerging markets: Marketing strategies for increasing the ratio of non-users to users. *Journal of Business Research*, *86*, 217–224.

Siren, C., Kohtamaki, M., & Kuckertz, A. (2012). Exploration and exploitation strategies, profit performance, and the mediating role of strategic learning: Escaping the exploitation trap. *Strategic Entrepreneurship Journal*, *6*(6), 18–41. doi:10.1002ej.1126

Skirstad, H. (2006). Marketing to children and young people in Norway. *Young Consumers*, *7*(2), 78–80. doi:10.1108/17473610610701529

Skowron, L., & Kristensen, K. (2012). The impact of the recent banking crisis on customer loyalty in the banking sector. *The TQM Journal*, *24*(6), 480–497. doi:10.1108/17542731211270052

Smith, G. H., & Engel, E. (1968). Influence of a female model on perceived characteristics of an automobile. *The 76th Annual Convention of the American Psychological Associations Proceedings*, 681-682.

Smith, E. G., Meurs, L. V., & Neijens, P. C. (2006). Effects of Advertising Likeability: A 10 Year Perspective. *Journal of Advertising Research*, *46*(1), 73–83. doi:10.2501/S0021849906060089

Smith, J. A. (Ed.). (2007). *Qualitative Psychology: A Practical Guide to Research Methods* (2nd ed.). London: Sage Publications Ltd.

Smith, K. H., Stutts, M. A., & Zank, G. M. (2012). An Exploratory Study of the Behavior and Perceptions of College Students with Respect to Regular, Light, and Ultralight Cigarettes. *Journal of Public Policy & Marketing*, *31*(2), 206–222. doi:10.1509/jppm.09.022

Smoke free England. (2007). *A Healthier England.* Available online at: http://www.smokefreeengland.co.uk./

Sneha, K. (2012). *Does celebrity endorsements have an impact or influence the purchase intention or buying behaviour of the youth in India* (Unpublished master's thesis). University of Nottingham, Nottingham, UK.

Solomon, M. R. (1996). *Consumer Behavior: Buying, Having, and Being*. Prentice-Hall.

Solomon, M. R. (2013). *'Consumer Behaviour: Buying, Having, and Being* (10th ed.). Harlow: Pearson Education Ltd.

Solomon, M., Bamossy, G., Askegaard, S., & Hogg, M. (2013). *Consumer behaviour: A European perspective* (5th ed.). Harlow: Prentice Hall.

South Africa. (1997). *Batho Pele — 'People first'*. White paper on transforming public service delivery, Notice 1459 of 1997. Government of South Africa, Department of Public Service and Administration. Pretoria: Government Printer.

South Africa. (2000). *A Green Paper on electronic commerce for South Africa.* Author.

South Africa. (2017). *Telecommunications and Postal Services consults on e-strategy, e-government and ICT SMME support strategies, 8 to 9 May*. Available at: https://www.gov.za/speeches/dtps-consult-nationally-e-strategy-e-government-and-ict-smme-support-strategies-5-may-2017

Spangenberg, J. H. (2002). Environmental space and the prism of sustainability: Frameworks for indicators measuring sustainable development. *Ecological Indicators*, *2*(3), 295–309. doi:10.1016/S1470-160X(02)00065-1

Spangenberg, J. H. (2010). World civilisations at crossroads: Towards an expansionist or a sustainable future—lessons from history. *Futures*, *42*(6), 565–573. doi:10.1016/j.futures.2010.01.007

Spangenberg, J. H. (2014). Institutional change for strong sustainable consumption: sustainable consumption and the degrowth economy. *Sustainability: Science, Practice, & Policy*, *10*(1), 62–77.

Speck, P. S., Schumann, D. W., & Thompson, C. (1988). Celebrity endorsements-scripts, schema and roles: Theoretical framework and preliminary tests. *Advances in Consumer Research. Association for Consumer Research (U. S.)*, *15*(1), 69–76.

Spencer, J. W. (2000). Knowledge flows in the global innovation system: Do U.S. firms share more scientific knowledge than their Japanese rivals? *Journal of International Business Studies*, *31*(3), 521–530.

Srinivasan, S. S., & Till, B. D. (2002). Evaluation of search, experience and credence attributes: Role of brand name and product trial. *Journal of Product and Brand Management*, *11*(7), 417–431. doi:10.1108/10610420210451616

Staniškis, J. K. (2012). Sustainable consumption and production: How to make it possible. *Clean Technologies and Environmental Policy*, *14*(6), 1015–1022. doi:10.100710098-012-0535-9

Starik, M., & Kanashiro, P. (2013). Toward a theory of sustainability management: Uncovering and integrating the nearly obvious. *Organization & Environment*, *26*(1), 7–30. doi:10.1177/1086026612474958

Statista. (2018). *Leading tobacco producing countries worldwide in 2016 (in 1,000 metric tons).* Retrieved from: https://www.statista.com/statistics/261173/leading-countries-in-tobacco-production/

Statistics South Africa. (2015). *Publications.* Available at: http://www.statssa.gov.za/?s=census+2011&sitem=publications

Statt, D. A. (1997). *Understanding the consumer: A psychological Approach.* London: Macmillan Press Ltd. doi:10.1007/978-1-349-25438-5

Stearns, P. N. (2006). Consumerism in world history: The global transformation of desire (2nd ed.; Vol. 1). Routledge. doi:10.4324/9780203969885

Steenkamp, J. B. E. M., Hofstede, F. T., & Wedel, M. A. (1999). Cross-national investigation into the individual and national cultural antecedents of consumer innovativeness. *Journal of Marketing*, *63*(2), 155–169. doi:10.2307/1251945

Stefani, G. (2008). *Harajuku lovers.* Retrieved April 19, 2015, from www.basenotes.net

Sternthal, B., Phillips, L. W., & Dholakia, R. (1978). The persuasive effect of source credibility: A situational analysis. *Public Opinion Quarterly*, *42*(3), 285–314. doi:10.1086/268454 PMID:10297222

Stevens, C. (2010). Linking sustainable consumption and production: The government role. *Natural Resources Forum*, *34*(1), 16–23. doi:10.1111/j.1477-8947.2010.01273.x

Stojanovski, O., Thurber, M., & Wolak, F. (2017). Rural energy access through solar home systems: Use patterns and opportunities for improvement. *Energy for Sustainable Development*, *37*, 33–50.

Stone, M., Stanton, H., Kirkham, J., & Pyne, W. (2001). The digerati: Generation Y finds its voice. Why cannot brands do the same? *Journal of Targeting, Measurement and Analysis for Marketing*, *10*(2), 158–167. doi:10.1057/palgrave.jt.5740042

Straughan, R. D., & Roberts, J. A. (1999). Environmental segmentation alternatives: A look at green consumer behavior in the new millennium. *Journal of Consumer Marketing*, *16*(6), 558–575. doi:10.1108/07363769910297506

Strizhakova, Y., & Coulter, R. (2013). The "green" side of materialism in emerging BRIC and developed markets: The moderating role of global cultural identity. *International Journal of Research in Marketing*, *30*(1), 69–82. doi:10.1016/j.ijresmar.2012.08.003

Suddaby, R., Bruton, G. D., & Si, S. X. (2015). Entrepreneurship through a qualitative lens: Insights on the construction and/or discovery of entrepreneurial opportunity. *Journal of Business Venturing*, *30*(1), 1–10. doi:10.1016/j.jbusvent.2014.09.003

Suki, N.M. (2015). *Customer environmental satisfaction and loyalty in the consumption of green products*. Academic Press.

Sulla, V., & Zikhali, P. (2018, March). *Overcoming Poverty and Inequality in South Africa: An Assessment of Drivers, Constraints and Opportunities*. Washington, DC: The World Bank Group. Retrieved on July, 25th, 2018 from http://documents.worldbank.org/curated/en/530481521735906534/pdf/124521-REV-OUO-South-Africa-Poverty-and-Inequality-Assessment-Report-2018-FINAL-WEB.pdf

Sumner, W. G. (1906). *Folkways: The Sociological Importance of Usages, Manners, Customs, Mores, and Morals*. New York, NY: Ginn and Company.

Sun, X., & Collins, R. (2006). Chinese consumer response to imported fruit: intended uses and their effect on perceived quality. *International Journal of Consumer Studies, 30*(2), 179–188.

Suriano, M. (2011). Hip-Hop and Bongo Flavour in Contemporary Tanzania: Youths' Experiences, Agency, Aspirations and Contradictions. *Africa Development. Afrique et Developpement, 36*(3/4), 113–126.

Susanne, P., Alice, G., & Tino, B.-L. (2012). Family members' roles in healthy-eating socialization based on a healthy-eating intervention. Young Consumers. *Insight and Ideas for Responsible Marketers, 13*(3), 208–223. doi:10.1108/17473611211261610

Sutton, P. (2004). What is sustainability. *Eingana, The Journal of the Victorian Association for Environmental Education*, 1-7.

Suwandinata, H. (2011). *Children's influence on family decision making process in food buying and consumption* (PhD thesis). Retrieved from http://geb.uni-giessen.de/geb/volltexte/2012/8589/pdf/SuwandinataHanny_2012_01_19.pdf

Sweeney, J. C., Hausknecht, D., & Soutar, G. N. (2000). Cognitive Dissonance after Purchase: A Multidimensional Scale. *Psychology and Marketing, 17*(5), 369–385. doi:10.1002/(SICI)1520-6793(200005)17:5<369::AID-MAR1>3.0.CO;2-G

Szmigin, I., & Piacentini, M. (2015). *Consumer Behaviour*. Oxford, UK: Oxford University Press.

Tai, S. H. C., & Wong, Y. H. (1998). Advertising decision making in Asia: "Glocal" versus "regcal" approach. *Journal of Managerial Issues, 10*(3), 318–339.

Talukdar, D., Sudhir, K., & Ainslie, A. (2002). Investigating new product diffusion across products and countries. *Marketing Science, 21*(1), 97–114.

Tan, B. C., & Lau, T. C. (2010). The Influencing Factors of Green Purchase Behaviour: *An Exploratory Study. International Conference on Marketing (ICMAR2010).*

Tan, K. (2011). *Riding on the star power*. The Edge Malaysia.

Tanner, C., & Kast, S. W. (2003). Promoting sustainable consumption: Determinants of green purchase by Swiss consumers. *Psychology and Marketing, 20*(10), 883–902. doi:10.1002/mar.10101

Tantiseneepong, N., Gorton, M., & White, J. (2012). Evaluating responses to celebrity endorsements using projective techniques. *Qualitative Market Research, 15*(1), 57–69. doi:10.1108/13522751211191991

Tanvi, D. (2008). *Children's influence on family purchase decision in India* (MA dissertation). University of Nottingham, Nottingham, UK.

Teas, R. K., & Agarwal, S. (2008). The effects of extrinsic product cues on consumers' perceptions of quality, sacrifice, and value. *Journal of the Academy of Marketing Science, 28*(2), 278–290. doi:10.1177/0092070300282008

Teece, D. J. (2007). Explicating dynamic capabilities: The nature and micro foundations of (sustainable) enterprise performance. *Strategic Management Journal*, *28*(13), 1319–1350.

Temperley, J., & Tangen, D. (2006). The Pinocchio factor in consumer attitudes towards celebrity endorsement: Celebrity endorsement, the Reebok brand, and an examination of a recent campaign. *Journal of Innovative Marketing*, *2*(3), 97–106.

Tesar, G., & Kuada, J. (Eds.). (2013). *Marketing Management and Strategy: An African Casebook*. London: Routledge.

The Balance. (2018). *What is a Developing Country? Developing Countries classification*. Retrieved from https://www.thebalance.com/what-is-a-developing-country-1978982

The Changing face of India. (2012). *Citizen Today*, 8-9. Retrieved from http://www.ey.com/Publication/vwLUAssets/The_changing_face_of_India/$File/The_changing_face_of_India.pdf

The Economist. (2015). *Learning from Lagos*. Available at: https://www.economist.com/news/middle-east-and-africa/21656701-nigerias-commercial-capital-crowded-noisy-violentand-model-rest

The World Bank. (2015). *World Development Indicators database: Gross domestic product 2014, PPP.* Retrieved from December 6th, 2015 databank.worldbank.org/data/download/GDP_PPP.pdf

ThisDaylive.com. (2017). *Lagos Generates More IGR than 30 States Combined*. Available at: https://www.thisdaylive.com/index.php/2017/05/30/lagos-generates-more-igr-than-30-states-combined/

Thomas, S. (2015). *#FeesMustFall: how SA students are using social to subvert traditional media*. Retrieved 19th August 2018 from https://memeburn.com/2015/10/feesmustfall-how-sas-students-are-using-social-to-subvert-traditional-media-narratives/

Thomas, C. D. (2009). Knowing the child consumer: Historical and conceptual insights on qualitative children's consumer research. Young Consumers. *Insight and Ideas for Responsible Marketers*, *10*(4), 269–282. doi:10.1108/17473610911007111

Thompson, N., Kiefer, K., & York, J. (2011). Distinctions not dichotomies: Exploring social, sustainable, and environmental entrepreneurship. In *Social and Sustainable Entrepreneurship* (pp. 205–233). Emerald Group Publishing Limited. doi:10.1108/S1074-7540(2011)0000013012

Thomson, E. S., Laing, A. W., & McKee, L. (2007). Family purchase decision making: Exploring child influence behaviour. *Journal of Consumer Behaviour*, *6*(4), 182–202. doi:10.1002/cb.220

Thongplew, N., Spaargaren, G., & Koppen, V. C. S. A. (2013). Greening consumption at the retail outlet: The case of the Thai appliance industry. *International Journal of Sustainable Development and World Ecology*, *21*(2), 99–110. doi:10.1080/13504509.2013.867551

Till, B. D., & Busler, M. (2000). The Match-up Hypothesis: Physical Attractiveness, Expertise, and the Role of Fit on Brand Attitude, Purchase Intentions, and Brand Beliefs. *Journal of Advertising*, *29*(3), 1–13. doi:10.1080/00913367.2000.10673613

Times Online. (2007). *Tobacco giants targeted African children to boost flagging profits*. Available online at: http://www.timesonline.co.uk/tol/news/world/africa/article2022928.ece

Tisser, B. T. (2010). Who teaches them to consume: A Study of Barzilian youngsters. *International Journal of Consumer Studies*, *34*(3), 298–304. doi:10.1111/j.1470-6431.2009.00857.x

Tocher, N., Oswald, S., & Hall, D. (2015). Proposing social resources as the fundamental catalyst toward opportunity creation. *Strategic Entrepreneurship Journal*, *9*(9), 119–135. doi:10.1002ej.1195

Tomko Paul, R. (2012). *Understanding the factors affecting the influence of children on their parents total purchases* (PhD thesis). Capella University. Retrieved from http://media.proquest.com/media/pq/classic/doc/2662550201/fmt/ai/rep/NPDF?_s=xTqZvWcg%2FEYgxQjxIzJZcW9m7Y4%3D

Toomey Deborah, A., & Francis Alisha, L. (2013). Branded product placement and pre-teenaged consumers: Influence on brand preference and choice. Young Consumers. *Insight and Ideas for Responsible Marketers*, *14*(2), 180–192. doi:10.1108/17473611311325573

Trad, N. G. (2017). *2017 Country Reputation Ranking: Leaders, Highlights and Trends*. Available at: http://placebrandobserver.com/country-reputation-ranking-reptrak-2017/

Treise, D., Weigold, M. F., Conna, J., & Garrison, H. (1994). Ethics in advertising: Ideological correlates of consumer perception. *Journal of Advertising*, *23*(3), 59–69. doi:10.1080/00913367.1994.10673450

Trentmann, F. (2004). Beyond consumerism: New historical perspectives on consumption. *Journal of Contemporary History*, *39*(3), 373–401. doi:10.1177/0022009404044446

Triandis, H. C. (1993). The contingency model in cross-cultural perspective. In M. M. Chemers & R. Ayman (Eds.), *Leadership theory and research: Perspectives and directions* (pp. 167–188). San Diego, CA: Academic Press.

True, J. (2006). Globalisation and Identity. In *Globalisation and Identity* (p. 74). South Melbourne: Oxford University Press.

Tse, D. K., & Gorn, G. J. (1993). An experiment on the salience of country-of-origin in the era of global brands. *Journal of International Marketing*, *1*, 57–76.

Turner, G. M. (2008). A comparison of the Limits to Growth with 30 years of reality. *Global Environmental Change*, *18*(3), 397–411. doi:10.1016/j.gloenvcha.2008.05.001

Turner, L., & Ash, J. (1975). *The golden hordes: International tourism and the pleasure periphery*. London: Constable & Robinson Limited.

Turok, I. (2009). The Distinctive City: Pitfalls in the Pursuit of Differential Advantage. *Environment & Planning A*, *41*(1), 13–30. doi:10.1068/a37379

Twum-Baah, K. A. (2005). Volume and characteristics of international Ghanaian migration. In T. Manuh (Ed.), *At home in the world? International migration and development in contemporary Ghana and West Africa* (pp. 55–77). Accra: Sub-Saharan Publishers.

Tynes, S. R. (2001). Bringing Social Class Home: The Social Class Genealogy and Poverty Lunch Projects. *Teaching Sociology*, *29*(3), 286–298. doi:10.2307/1319188

U.S. Commercial Service Hong Kong. (2014). *Cosmetics and toiletries market overviews*. The U.S. Commercial Service.

Ueltschy, L. (1998). Brand perceptions as influenced by consumer ethnocentrism and country-of-origin effects. *Journal of Marketing Management*, *8*, 12–23.

Umoru, H., Komolafe, B., Ovuakporie, E., Agbakwuru, J., & Asomba, I. (2016). *MMM: How it affects the banks – Bankers*. Vanguard Media Limited.

UN DESA, Population Division. (2015). *World Population Prospects: The 2015 Revision, Key Findings and Advance Tables*. Working Paper No. ESA/P/WP.24. Retrieved December 1, 2015 from esa.un.org/unpd/wpp/publications/files/key_findings_wpp_2015.pdf

UN DESA. (2013). *Report of the World Social Situation 2013: Inequality Matters*. Retrieved December 1, 2015 from www.un.org/esa/socdev/documents/reports/InequalityMatters.pdf

UN Economic and Social Council. (2009). *Africa Review Report on Sustainable Consumption and Production.* Retrieved March 15, 2018 from https://sustainabledevelopment.un.org/content/documents/AfricanReviewReport-on-Sustainable-ConsumptionSummary.pdf

UNEP. (2014). *United Nations Environment Programme Annual Report.* Retrieved January 31st, 2015 from http://www.unep.org/annualreport/2014/en/index.html

UNESCO. (2001). *Youth, sustainable consumption patterns and lifestyles.* Retrieved July 31st, 2018 from http://unesdoc.unesco.org/images/0012/001242/124238e.pdf

United Nations. (2014). *United Nations e-government survey 2014.* Available from: http://unpan3.un.org/egovkb/Portals/egovkb/Documents/un/2014-Survey/E-Gov_Complete_Survey-2014.pdf

United Nations. (2018). *United Nations e-Government Survey 2018.* Available from: https://publicadministration.un.org/egovkb/en-us/Reports/UN-E-Government-Survey-2018

Urs, A. (2015). *eBay emerges largest online perfume mall in India.* Retrieved July 19, 2015, from http://www.thehindubusinessline.com

Usunier, J. C., & Lee, J. A. (2005). *Marketing Across Cultures.* Harlow: Prentice Hall.

Utomi, P. (1985). Legitimacy and Governance: One More Year of Military Rule in Nigeria. *A Journal of Opinion, 14*, 39-42.

Uusitalo & Takala. (1993). Developmental Stage and Children's reaction to T.V advertising. *European Advances in Consumer Research, 1*, 360-365.

Uzuegbunam, C. E. (2017). Between media celebrities and the youth: Exploring the impact of emerging celebrity culture on the lifestyle of young Nigerians. *Mgbakoigba: Journal of African Studies, 6*(2), 130–141.

Vadehra, S. (2004). Advertising to children in India. *Young Consumers, 6*(1), 75–78.

van der Boor, P., Oliveira, P., & Veloso, F. (2014). Users as innovators in developing countries: The global sources of innovation and diffusion in mobile banking services. *Research Policy, 43*(9), 1594–1607. doi:10.1016/j.respol.2014.05.003

Van der Waldt, D., Van Loggerenberg, M., & Wehmeyer, L. (2009). Celebrity Endorsements versus Created Spokespersons in Advertising: A Survey among Students. *SAJEMS, 12*(1), 110–114.

Van Ham, P. (2010). *Social Power in International Politics.* Abingdon, UK: Routledge. doi:10.4324/9780203857847

Van Tosh, L., Ralph, R., & Campbell, J. (2000). The Rise of Consumerism. *Psychiatric Rehabilitation Skills, 4*(3), 383–409. doi:10.1080/10973430008408630

van Weenen, H. (2000). Towards a vision of a sustainable university. *International Journal of Sustainability in Higher Education, 1*(1), 20–34. doi:10.1108/1467 630010307075

Vanguard Newspaper. (2017). *Buhari signs 9 agreements with UAE to strengthen FG's anti-corruption campaign.* Available at: https://www.vanguardngr.com/2017/08/buhari-signs-9-agreements-uae-strengthen-fgs-anti-corruption-campaign/

Varey, R. J. (2011). A sustainable society logic for marketing. *Social Business, 1*(1), 69–83. doi:10.1362/204440811X570563

Vasilchenko, E., & Morrish, S. (2011). The Role of Entrepreneurial Networks in the Exploration and Exploitation of Internationalization Opportunities by Information and Communication Technology Firms. *Journal of International Marketing, 19*(4), 88–105. doi:10.1509/jim.10.0134

Vaughn, R. (1986, February). How Advertising Works: a planning model revisited. *Journal of Advertising Research*, 57-66.

Vaughn, R. (1980). How Advertising Works: A planning model. *Journal of Advertising Research, 20*(5), 27–33.

Veblen, T. (1899). The preconceptions of economic science. *The Quarterly Journal of Economics, 13*(4), 396–426. doi:10.2307/1883645

Verlegh, P., & Steenkamp, J. (1999). A review and meta-analysis of country-of-origin research. *Journal of Economic Psychology, 20*(5), 521–546. doi:10.1016/S0167-4870(99)00023-9

Versus.com. (2018). *Dubai city versus Lagos*. Available at: https://versus.com/en/dubai-city-vs-lagos

Vida, I., Damjan, J., & Fairhurst, A. (1996). Ethnocentric tendencies and consumer purchase behavior in Central and Eastern Europe: the case of Slovenia. *Proceedings of the Academy of Marketing Science: Multicultural Marketing Conference 1996*, 49-55.

Vida, I., & Damjan, J. (2000). The role of consumer characteristics and attitudes in purchase behavior of domestic vs. foreign made products: The case of Slovenia. *Journal of East-West Business, 6*(3), 111–131. doi:10.1300/J097v06n03_06

Vida, I., & Fairhurst, A. (1999). Factors underlying the phenomenon of consumer ethnocentricity: Evidence from four central European countries. *International Review of Retail, Distribution and Consumer Research, 9*(4), 321–337. doi:10.1080/095939699342444

Vida, I., & Reardon, J. (2008). Domestic consumption: Rational, affective or normative choice? *Journal of Consumer Marketing, 25*(1), 34–44. doi:10.1108/07363760810845390

Vien, C. V., Yun, C. T., & Fai, P. L. (2017). The Effect of Celebrity Endorsement on Brand Attitude and Purchase Intention. *Journal of Global Business and Social Entrepreneurship, 1*(4), 141–150.

Vining, J., & Ebreo, A. (1992). Predicting recycling behaviour from global and specific environmental attitudes and changes in recycling opportunities. *Journal of Applied Social Psychology, 22*(20), 1580–1607. doi:10.1111/j.1559-1816.1992.tb01758.x

Von Bormann, T., & Gulati, M. (2014). *The food energy water nexus: Understanding South Africa's most urgent sustainability challenge*. WWF-SA. Retrieved on July 7th, 2018 from http://awsassets.wwf.org.za/downloads/wwf_few_report_3.pdf

Wabwile, M. (2010). Implementing the Social and Economic Rights of Children in Developing Countries: The place of International Assistance and Cooperation. *International Journal of Children's Rights, 18*(3), 355–385. doi:10.1163/157181810X494308

Waldman, D. A. (2013). Interdisciplinary Research is the key. *Frontiers in Human Neuroscience, 7*, 5. doi:10.3389/fnhum.2013.00562 PMID:24062664

Walle, A. H., & Ryans, J. K. (1992). SIA, Developing Countries and Marketing Opportunities: A Primer. *Management Decision, 30*(7), 25–29. doi:10.1108/00251749210019405

Wall, M., Hofstra, G., & Heslop, L. A. (1990). *Imported Versus Domestic Car Owners: Demographic Characteristics and Attitudes*. Paper Presented at the *Conference of the Administrative Sciences Association of Canada.*

Wall, M., Liefeld, J., & Heslop, L. (1991). Impact of country-of-origin cues on consumer judgments in multi-cue situations: A covariance analysis. *Journal of the Academy of Marketing Science, 19*(2), 105–1. doi:10.1007/BF02726002

Wam. (2014). *UAE ranks among most developed countries*. Available at: http://www.emirates247.com/news/emirates/uae-ranks-among-most-developed-countries-2014-12-06-1.572337

Wang, C. K. (1978). *The Effect of Foreign Economics, Political and Cultural Environment on Consumers' Willingness to Buy Foreign Products* (PhD Dissertation).

Wang, D. (2007). *Adolescents perception of their influence in family decision making in China* (Dissertation in MA Marketing). University of Nottingham.

Wang, C. L., Siu, N. Y. M., & Hui, S. Y. (2004). Consumer decision-making styles on domestic and imported brand clothing. *European Journal of Marketing*, *38*(1/2), 436–447. doi:10.1108/03090560410511212

Wang, H., Hsieh, A.-T., Yeh, Y.-C., & Tsai, C.-W. (2004). Who is the decision maker: The parent or the child in group package tour? *Tourism Management*, *25*(2), 183–194. doi:10.1016/S0261-5177(03)00093-1

Wang, S. W., Kao, G. H. Y., & Ngamsiriudom, W. (2017). Consumers' attitude of endorser credibility, brand and intention with respect to celebrity endorsement of the airline sector. *Journal of Air Transport Management*, *60*, 10–17. doi:10.1016/j.jairtraman.2016.12.007

Wanjiru, E. (2006). Branding African countries: A prospect for the future. *Place Branding and Public Diplomacy*, *2*(1), 84–95. doi:10.1057/palgrave.pb.5990047

Warde, A. (2005). Consumption and theories of practice. *Journal of Consumer Culture*, *5*(2), 131–153. doi:10.1177/1469540505053090

Warde, A. (2015). The Sociology of Consumption: Its Recent Development. *Annual Review of Sociology*, *41*(1), 117–134. doi:10.1146/annurev-soc-071913-043208

Ward, S. (1972). Children's reactions to commercials. *Journal of Advertising Research*, *12*, 37–45.

Ward, S. (1974). Consumer Socialization. *The Journal of Consumer Research*, *1*(2), 1–14. doi:10.1086/208584

Ward, S., Wackman, D., & Wartella, E. (1977). The Development of Consumer Information- Processing Skills: Integrating Cognitive Development and Family Interaction Theoris. *Advances in Consumer Research. Association for Consumer Research (U. S.)*, *4*(1), 166–171.

Watne, Lobo, & Brennan.(2011). *Children as agents of Secondary Socialization for their parents, Young Consumers: Insight and Ideas for responsible marketers*. Doi:10.1108/17473611111185841

Watson, J. J., & Wright, K. (2000). Consumer ethnocentrism and attitudes toward domestic and foreign products. *European Journal of Marketing*, *34*(9/10), 1149–1166. doi:10.1108/03090560010342520

Weick, K. (1995). Sensemaking in Organizations. *Administrative Science Quarterly*, *23*(6), 62–83.

Wei, K. K., & Li, W. Y. (2013). Measuring the impact of celebrity endorsement on consumer behavioural intentions: A study of Malaysian consumers. *International Journal of Sports Marketing & Sponsorship*, *14*(3), 157–177.

Welch, C., Piekkari, R., Plakoyiannaki, E., & Paavilainen-Mäntymäki, E. (2010). Theorising from case studies: Towards a pluralist future for international business research. *Journal of International Business Studies*, *42*(5), 740–762. doi:10.1057/jibs.2010.55

Wells, W., & Gubar, G. (1966). Life Cycle concept in Marketing Research. *JMR, Journal of Marketing Research*, *3*(4), 355–363. doi:10.2307/3149851

Werner, J., & Alvensleben, R. V. (2011). Consumer Attitudes towards Organic Food in Germany (F.R.). *Symposium on Horticultural Economics, 8*, 155.

Western Cape. (2001). *The Cape Online E-government Programme*. Provincial Government of the Western Cape. Available from: https://www.westerncape.gov.za/text/2014/October/capeonline_strategy_aug2001.pdf

White, C. (2012). Brands and national image: An exploration of inverse country-of-origin effect. *Place Branding and Public Diplomacy*, *8*(2), 110–118. doi:10.1057/pb.2012.6

Wicker, A. W. (1969). Attitude vs Actions: The relationship of verbal and overt behavioural responses to attitude objects. *The Journal of Social Issues*, *25*, 41–78.

Wilke, W. L., & Dickson, P. R. (1991). Shopping for Appliances: consumers' Strategies and pattern for Information search. In Perspectives in Consumer Behaviour (4th ed.). Englewood Cliffs, NJ: Academic Press.

Wilkues, R. E. (1995). Household Life-Cycle Stages Transitions And Product Expenditures. *The Journal of Consumer Research*, *22*(1), 27–42. doi:10.1086/209433

Williams, L. A., & Burns, A. C. (2000). Exploring the Dimensionality of Children's Direct Influence Attempts. *Advances in Consumer Research. Association for Consumer Research (U. S.)*, *27*(1), 64–71.

Williamson, J. (1978). *Decoding advertisements: Ideology and meaning in advertising* (Vol. 13). London: Marion Boyars.

Wilska, T.-A. (2003). Mobile phone use as part of young people's consumption styles. *Journal of Consumer Policy*, *26*(4), 441–463. doi:10.1023/A:1026331016172

Wilson, C. (2010). Eating, eating is always there: Food, consumerism and cardiovascular disease. Some evidence from Kerala, south India. *Anthropology & Medicine*, *17*(3), 261–275. doi:10.1080/13648470.2010.526699 PMID:21153961

Wilson, G., & Wood, K. (2004). The influence of children on parental purchases during supermarket shopping. *International Journal of Consumer Studies*, *28*(4), 329–336. doi:10.1111/j.1470-6431.2004.00393.x

Wilson, J. A. J., & Liu, J. (2010). Shaping the Halal into a brand? *Journal of Islamic Marketing*, *1*(2), 107–123. doi:10.1108/17590831011055851

Wilson, J. A. J., & Liu, J. (2011). The challenges of Islamic branding: Navigating emotions and halal. *Journal of Islamic Marketing*, *2*(1), 28–42. doi:10.1108/17590831111115222

Wilson, M., Gaines, J., & Hill, R. (2008). Neuromarketing and Consumer Freewill. *The Journal of Consumer Affairs*, *42*(3), 389–410. doi:10.1111/j.1745-6606.2008.00114.x

Wimalasiri, J. (2004). A cross-national study on Children's purchasing behavior and parental response. *Journal of Consumer Marketing*, *21*(4), 274–284. doi:10.1108/07363760410542183

Winston, E., & Dadzie, K. (2002). Market orientation of Nigerian and Kenyan firms: The role of top managers. *Journal of Business and Industrial Marketing*, *17*(6), 471–480.

Wirtz, D., Kruger, J., Scollon, C. N., & Diener, E. (2003). What to do on spring break. *Psychological Science*, *14*(5), 520–524. doi:10.1111/1467-9280.03455 PMID:12930487

Wisenblit, & Priluck, & Pirog. (2013). The influence of parental styles on childrens consumption. *Journal of Consumer Marketing*, *30*(4), 320–327. doi:10.1108/JCM-02-2013-0465

Witt, U. (2001). Learning to consume–A theory of wants and the growth of demand. *Journal of Evolutionary Economics*, *11*(1), 23–36. doi:10.1007/PL00003851

Wo-lap, W. L. (2016). *Getting lost in 'One Belt, One Road'.* Available at: http://www.ejinsight.com/20160412-getting-lost-one-belt-one-road/

Wong, C. Y., Polonsky, M. J., & Garma, R. (2008). The impact of consumer ethnocentrism and country of origin sub-components for high involvement products on young Chinese consumers' product assessments. *Asia Pacific Journal of Marketing and Logistics*, *20*(4), 455–478. doi:10.1108/13555850810909759

Wong, K. K. K. (2013). Partial least squares structural equation modeling (PLS-SEM) techniques using SmartPLS. *Marketing Bulletin*, *24*, 1–23.

Wongtada, N., Rice, G., & Bandyopadhyay, S. K. (2012). Developing and Validating AFFINITY: A New Scale to Measure Consumer Affinity toward Foreign Countries. *Journal of International Consumer Marketing*, *24*(3), 147–167. doi:10.1080/08961530.2012.682037

Wonsun, S. (2010). Consumer Socialization Online: Antecedents And Consequences of Children's Skepticism Toward Online Advertising. *American Academy of Advertising Conference Proceedings, 115*. Retrieved from EBSCOhost

Wonsun, S. (2010). *The role of Parental mediation in children's consumer socialization on the web* (PhD thesis). University of Minnesota. Retrieved from https://conservancy.umn.edu/bitstream/handle/11299/95674/Shin_umn_0130E_11299.pdf?sequence=1

Wood, M., & Mckinley, W. (2010). The production of entreprenurial opportunity: A constructivist perspective. *Strategic Entrepreneurship Journal*, *4*(1), 66–84. doi:10.1002ej.83

Wood, N. T., & Burkhalter, J. N. (2014). Tweet this, not that: A comparison between brand promotions in microblogging environments using celebrity and company-generated tweets. *Journal of Marketing Communications*, *20*(1-2), 129–146. doi:10.1080/13527266.2013.797784

Woodside, A. G., & Lysonski, S. (1989). A General Model of Traveler Destination Choice. *Journal of Travel Research*, *27*(Spring), 8–14. doi:10.1177/004728758902700402

World Advertising Trends . (2001). NTC Publications.

World Bank. (2015). Global Economic Prospect, Middle East and North Africa. World Bank.

World Bank. (2018). *The World Bank Statistics*. Retrieved from www.data.worldbank.org

World Economic Forum. (2013). *Sustainable Consumption: Stakeholder Perspectives*. Retrieved on February, 25th, 2014 from http://www3.weforum.org/docs/WEF_ENV_SustainableConsumption_Book_2013.pdf

World Wide Worx. (2015). *South African Social Media Landscape 2015*. Available at: http://www.worldwideworx.com/wp-content/uploads/2014/11/Exec-Summary-Social-Media-2015.pdf

Wright, A. (2009). *Eco-friendly perfumes: 4 Top Brands*. Retrieved July 2, 2015, from http://voices.yahoo.com/eco-friendly-perfume-4-top-brands-4677815.html?cat=69

Wright, E., & Rogers, J. (2015). *American Society: How it really works* (2nd ed.). Norton Sociology.

WTO. (2018). *Special and differential treatment provisions*. World Trade Organisation. Retrieved from https://www.wto.org/english/tratop_e/devel_e/dev_special_differential_provisions_e.htm#legal_provisions

Wu, C., & Shaffer, D. (1987). Susceptibility to Persuasive Appeals as a Function of Source Credibility and Prior Experience with the Attitude Object. *Journal of Personality and Social Psychology*, *52*(4), 677–688. doi:10.1037/0022-3514.52.4.677

Wu, J. H., Wu, C. W., Lee, C. T., & Lee, H. J. (2015). Green purchase intentions: An exploratory study of the Taiwanese electric motorcycle market. *Journal of Business Research*, *68*(4), 829–833. doi:10.1016/j.jbusres.2014.11.036

Yagci, M. I. (2001). Evaluating the effects of country-of-origin and consumer ethnocentrism: A case of a transplant product. *Journal of International Consumer Marketing*, *13*(3), 63–85. doi:10.1300/J046v13n03_05

Yamoah, F. A. (2005). Role and Impact of Product-Country Image on Rice Marketing: A Developing Country Perspective. *The Journal of American Academy of Business*, *7*(2), 265-276.

Yang, Z., Kim, C., Laroche, M., & Lee, H. (2014). Parental Style and Consumer Socialization among Adolescent: A cross Cultural Investigation. *Journal of Business Research*, *67*(3), 228–236. doi:10.1016/j.jbusres.2013.05.008

Yani-de-Soriano, M., & Slater, S. (2009). Revisiting Drucker's theory: Has consumerism led to the overuse of marketing? *Journal of Management History*, *15*(4), 452–466. doi:10.1108/17511340910987347

Yaveroglu, I. S., & Donthu, J. (2002). Cultural influences on the diffusion of products. *Journal of International Consumer Marketing*, *14*(4), 49–36. doi:10.1300/J046v14n04_04

Ying, F., & Li, Y. (2009). Children's buying behavior in China: A study of their information sources. *Marketing Intelligence & Planning*, *28*(2), 170–187. doi:10.1108/02634501011029673

Yin, R. K. (2003). *Case Study Research Design and Methods*. London: Sage Publications.

Yin, R. K. (2009). *Case Study Research: Design and Methods. Essential guide to qualitative methods in organizational research* (Vol. 5). London: Sage Publications, Inc.

Yolal, M., Emeksiz, M., & Cetinel, F. (2009). Marketing of SMHEs in Turkey: A comparative analysis. *Journal of Hospitality Marketing & Management*, *18*(4), 372–385. doi:10.1080/19368620902799577

Yoo, B., Donthu, B., & Lenartowicz, T. (2011). Measuring Hofstede's Five Dimensions of Cultural Values at the Individual Level: Development and Validation of CVSCALE. *Journal of International Consumer Marketing*, *23*(3/4), 193–210.

Youn, S. (2008). Parental Influence and teen's attitude toward online privacy protection. *The Journal of Consumer Affairs*, *42*(3), 362–388. doi:10.1111/j.1745-6606.2008.00113.x

Yousaf, S., & Huaibin, L. (2013). Profiling Consumer Behavior in the Context of Involvement Level and Demographic Factors: Evidence of Within-Country Differences From a Developing Economy. *Journal of Global Marketing*, *26*(1), 1–17. doi:10.1080/08911762.2013.779404

Zaharah, G. (2011). The influence of Socialisation agents and demographic profiles on brand consciousness. *International Journal of Management and Marketing Research*, *4*(1), 19–29.

Zahid, M., Abdul, R., Jainthy, N., & Samsinar, M. S. (2002). Perceptions of advertising and celebrity endorsement in Malaysia. *Asia Pacific Management Review*, *7*(4), 535–554.

Zahra, S., Rawhouser, H., Bhawe, N., Neubaum, D., & Hayton, J. (2008). Globalisation of Social Entrepreneurship Opportunities. *Strategic Entrepreneurship Journal*, *2*(2), 117–131. doi:10.1002ej.43

Zahrnt, V. (2005). *Enhancing the internal legitimacy of WTO negotiations: Representations of member states through common interest groups and integrated regions*. Working paper.

Zaichkowsky, J. L. (1985). Measuring the Involvement Construct. *The Journal of Consumer Research*, *12*(3), 341–352. doi:10.1086/208520

Zaichkowsky, J. L. (1986). Conceptualizing Involvement. *Journal of Advertising*, *15*(2), 4–14. doi:10.1080/00913367.1986.10672999

Zaidan, E., & Kovacs, J. F. (2017). Resident Attitudes towards Tourists and Tourism Growth: A Case Study from the Middle East, Dubai in United Arab Emirates. *European Journal of Sustainable Development*, *6*(1), 291–307. doi:10.14207/ejsd.2017.v6n1p291

Zaltman, G. (1997). Rethinking Marketing Research: Putting people back in. *JMR, Journal of Marketing Research*, *34*(4), 424–427. doi:10.2307/3151962

Zaltman, G. (2003). *How Consumers think: Essential Insights into the Mind of the Markets*. Boston: Harvard Business School Press.

Zamil, A. (2011). The impact of word of mouth (WOM) on the purchasing decision of the Jordanian consumer. *Research Journal of International Studies*, *20*, 24–29.

Zenker, S., & Braun, E. (2010). The Place Brand Centre – A Conceptual Approach for the Brand Management of Places. In *EMAC (European Marketing Academy), 39th European Marketing Academy Conference*. Brussels: EMAC.

Zhao, W., & Schroeder, P. (2010). Sustainable consumption and production: Trends, challenges and options for the Asia-Pacific region. *Natural Resources Forum*, *34*(1), 4–15. doi:10.1111/j.1477-8947.2010.01275.x

Zinkhan, G. M., & Hong, J. W. (1991). Self Concept and Advertising Effectiveness: A Conceptual Model of Congruency Conspicuousness, and Response Mode. In R. H. Holman & M. R. Solomon (Eds.), *Advances in Consumer Research* (Vol. 18, pp. 348–354). Provo, UT: Association for Consumer Research.

About the Contributors

Ayantunji Gbadamosi (BSc [Hons], MSc, PhD, FHEA, FCIM, FCMI) is the Research Coordinator and The Chair of the Research and Knowledge Exchange Committee at Royal Docks School of Business and Law, University of East London, UK. He received his PhD from the University of Salford, UK and has taught marketing courses at various institutions including University of Lagos (Nigeria), University of Salford (UK), Manchester Metropolitan University (UK), Liverpool Hope University (UK), and various professional bodies. Dr 'Tunji Gbadamosi has several research outputs in the form of Journal articles, chapters in edited books, co-edited books, monograph, conference papers, and Case studies. His papers have been published in a variety of refereed journals including Journal of Brand Management, Thunderbird International Business Review, International Journal of Market Research, International Journal of Retail and Distribution Management, Marketing intelligence and Planning, Social Marketing Quarterly, Nutrition and Food Science, Young Consumers, Journal of Fashion Marketing and Management, Society and Business Review, International Journal of Consumer Studies, The Marketing Review, International Journal of Small Business and Enterprise Development, Entrepreneurship and Regional Development, International Journal of Entrepreneurship and Innovation, Journal of Management Development, Industry and Higher Education, and Journal of Place Branding and Public Diplomacy. He is the author of the book entitled Low-income Consumer Behaviour and the editor of Young Consumer Behaviour (Routledge, 2018) and The Handbook of Research on Consumerism and Buying Behaviour in Developing Nations (IGI Global, 2016). His co-edited books are: (a) Principles of Marketing – A Value-Based Approach (Palgrave, 2013), and (b) Entrepreneurship Marketing: Principles and Practice of SME Marketing (Routledge, 2011). Dr Gbadamosi is a member of the editorial board of several academic journals. He has supervised several undergraduate and postgraduate students including PhD students to successful completion and served as an examiner for several doctorate degree examinations. He is the current Programme Chair of the International Academy of African Business Development (IAABD). His research interest revolves around Consumer Behaviour, SME Marketing, Marketing to Children, and Marketing Communications. He is the author of the paper entitled 'Symbolic Consumption among Black African Women in the UK' that won the EMERLAD Best paper award at the International Academy of African Business Development (IAABD) 2014. He is listed in Who's Who in the World.

* * *

Veronica Adu Brobbey is a lecturer in human resource management at the University of Education, Winneba, Ghana. In her teaching and research work she covers a wide range of topics in human resource and marketing research. She is currently completing her PhD at the Open University of Malaysia through Accra Institute of Technology, Ghana. She has published widely in the field of human resource and marketing. Her research interest focus on counterproductive work behaviour and research methods

Thomas Antwi Bosiakoh is an Honorary Postdoctoral Associate at the Department of Sociology, Macquarie University in Sydney, Australia in recognition for his academic achievement, expertise, and excellence in his field of study. His research and publications intersect migration, criminology, political economy and family studies. He recently completed his doctoral studies on the Mixed embeddedness of Nigerian immigrants informal entrepreneurship in Ghana, receiving the Vice Chancellor's Commendation for academic excellence. He was also the Valedictorian during his graduation in April 2018. Thomas has held teaching positions and delivered conference papers in Ghana and Australia. He has also delivered conference papers in New Zealand, Mali and Morocco.

Stella Aririguzoh obtained her Ph.D in Mass Communication from Covenant University, Canaanland, Ota, Nigeria. She has a B.A (Mass Communication) and M.B.A (Management) degrees from the famed University of Nigeria, Nsukka. She also has the M.A (Broadcasting) and M.Sc. (Industrial Relations/ Personnel Management) from the Abia State University, Uturu and the University of Lagos, Akoka respectively. She has been teaching mass communication since 2000 with emphasis on broadcast courses. She has deep interest in political communication. At present, she teaches in the Department of Mass Communication in Covenant University.

David Bamber is Director of PhD studies, at the University of Bolton, UK. He is Visiting Professor of Management & Education at the Organisational Learning Centre for higher education in Bolton in the UK. He is also Research Fellow at Christ University, Bangalore, India. He is researching aspects of international marketing including the development of Qatar as a destination of choice for global brands and the role of social media on national security in Qatar and. Bamber has an international career in business and academia, and is a management consultant for senior executive clients from developing countries working with with Projacs International and the Organizational Learning Centre Ltd. He has over 15 years experience as a senior lecturer in Marketing, as an External Examiner in several UK Universities, as a reviewer for international journals such as "Studies in Higher Education" and "Social Responsibility Journal". Bamber earned his Ph.D. in "Orgnaizational Learning" at the University of Salford, having co-founded the Centre for Research into Organizational Excellence there. He holds a B.Sc. (Dunelm) from Durham University and a M.Ed. (Ed.Psych.) from the University of Manchester. He has published over 70 peer reviewed articles concerning International Marketing, Place Branding, Corporate Social Responsibility and International Business Ethics in International Journals and at International Conferences. He holds two Emerald Literati Awards.

Jeanne Bentzen is Research Assistant at Aalborg University. Her research interest is in consumer choice theories.

Andreea I. Bujac is an Assistant Professor at the Department of Business and Management, International Business Centre at Aalborg University. Andreea received her PhD in International Marketing from Aalborg University in 2014, and her Msc. in International Business Economics from Aalborg University in 2010. Her primary research interests are in the field of consumer marketing. Specifically, she is interested in branding, consumer behaviour, country-of-origin effects and consumer ethnocentrism. She is the co-author of the paper titled Relationships between Brand Perception, Ideology and Consumer Ethnocentrism in Post-Communist Romania which was published in the Journal of Euromarketing, issue 23, vol.1&2 in 2014.

Cynthia A. Bulley is a senior lecturer and head of Department (Marketing) at the Central University, Ghana. Her current research interests are in the area of consumer behaviour, experiential marketing, and international business.

Brahim Chekima is a Senior Lecturer in the Marketing programme of the Faculty of Business, Economics and Accountancy, Universiti Malaysia Sabah. His research interests include green marketing, consumer behavior, consumer culture and digital marketing. He has published several articles in various international peer-reviewed journals, chapters in edited books and presented at various international and national conferences.

Fatima Zohra Chekima is a faculty member where she is pursuing her Master degree in International Business in the Faculty of Business, Economics and Accountancy, Universiti Malaysia Sabah. She has published in an international peer-reviewed journal and presented at international conferences. Her research interest includes consumer culture, advertising, consumer behaviour, and international marketing.

Khalifa Chekima is a Lecturer at Faculty of Computing and Informatics, Universiti Malaysia Sabah since 2017. Currently he has been appointed as a Researcher at the Center of Data and Information Management, Universiti Malaysia Sabah in January 2018.

Christian Djamgbah holds MPhil in Marketing from the University of Ghana. He is currently pursuing Master of Research in Marketing at Macquarie University in Sydney, Australia. His research interests are in political marketing, branding, and service innovation.

Esther O. Duodu received her BSc degree in administration (marketing option) from the Central University. Following a stint as a research assistant at the Central University, she proceeded to the University of Aberdeen, UK to pursue her master's degree. She gained her MSc degree in Oil and Gas Enterprise Management in 2012. Her current research interests are focused on consumer behaviour, experiential marketing and supply chain management.

Clay Grandsen has been involved with Liverpool Hope University since 2004. His PhD concerns customer delight. Dr. Gransden has over 10 years' experience working in the Hospitality and Marketing sector. Dr. Gransden published in the award-winning text 'Social Media Marketing' titled 'Pokemon Go: A revolution in social gaming'. Currently, Clay is involved in several research and consultancy projects, providing guidance and expertise in marketing and social media at a local, regional and international level.

John Kuada has two doctorate degrees – a PhD from Copenhagen Business School and Dr. Merc from Aalborg University. He is Professor of International Management at the Department of Business and Management, Aalborg University in Denmark. He is author and/or editor of some 20 books on management and internationalization of firms and has written about 150 articles in refereed scholarly and professional journals on issues of enterprise development, management, marketing and cross-border inter-firm relations in Europe and Africa.

Nnamdi O. Madichie is the Director of the Centre for Research & Enterprise at the London School of Business and Management. His research interests straddle the general areas of marketing (consumer behaviour, events, film, music, sports), and entrepreneurship (women, diaspora, international and ethnic entrepreneurship). In addition to having published a textbook on Consumer Behaviour (by Tata McGraw Hill 2012), Dr. Madichie has also contributed materials for leading business and management textbooks used across UK universities – notably Marketing, Real People, Real Decisions (Solomon, 2009); Entrepreneurship Marketing: Principles and Practice of SME Marketing (Nwankwo & Gbadamosi, 2010); International Marketing Strategy (Doole & Lowe, 2012; Doole, Lowe, & Kenyon, 2016); and Strategic Marketing: Creating Competitive Advantage (West, Ford, & Ibrahim, 2015). He has published in reputable business and management journals such as Thunderbird International Business Review, Management Decision, International Journal of Entrepreneurial Behaviour and Research as well as Marketing Intelligence & Planning.

Esther Mensah holds an MSc degree in International Business from Aalborg University. She is currently a management consultant at Premier Resource Consulting in Ghana and an undergraduate thesis supervisor at Valley View University, also located in Ghana. Esther is involved in cutting edge research in international management and has published with Contemporary Social Science: Journal of the Academy of Social Sciences, on the topic "Knowledge transfer in the emerging solar energy sector in Ghana". She is also aspiring to start her doctoral degree in 2019.

Emmanuel Mogaji is a Lecturer in Advertising and Marketing Communications in the Department of Marketing, Events and Tourism, Greenwich University, London. He has a strong focus on service brands. He is a Fellow of the Higher Education Academy.

Odion Odiboh is an acclaimed professional with strong academic drive. His areas of specialization include Integrated Marketing Communication, Advertising, Public Relations and Philosophy of Mass Communication.

Sanya Ojo holds a PhD in Entrepreneurship. He is an accomplished entrepreneur with forty years' experience. This informs his research interests in diaspora/ethnic entrepreneurship, international business strategy and management, and marketing. He has the privilege of mobility in career choices, exploring options critically, establishing educational preferences, and placing bets on multiple knowledge paths, as a consequence of his capacity to benefit from high-end knowledge and research. Currently, he operates a goal-oriented consultancy in business and entrepreneurship both in practice and the academic field. He is a Fellow of Higher Education Academy (FHEA) and a visiting Research Fellow at the University of East London, UK. As an award-winner, he has published in reputable academic journals and resources.

Ayo Oniku teaches Marketing and related business courses at University of Lagos Nigeria. He is a seasoned consultant in Sales and other Marketing and Business areas; a Senior Consultant with Ayo Oniku & Associates. His experiences in recent years cover consulting for Europe-based organisations on market entry into West African markets and training of Sales staff of firms in financial and FMCG sectors.

Abdullah Promise Opute is a Researcher and highly qualified Freelance Academic Consultant. Dr Opute has extensive working experience (industrial and academic) from the UK, Germany and Nigeria. Currently, Dr Opute works as freelance academic consultant. Amongst others, Dr Opute works as Examiner and PhD and Masters theses supervisor at various universities. Dr Opute has a multi-disciplinary academic rooting in the areas of Accounting, Entrepreneurship, Marketing and Organisational Behaviour. His researches have been well-received and recognised at international Conferences. He received the Best Paper Award at the Academy of Marketing Conference in 2007 in Westminster, London, UK. Dr Opute's research interests include (but not limited to) Cross Cultural Management, Relationship Management, Entrepreneurship, Identity Behaviour, Consumer Behaviour, Organisational Socialisation, Strategic Management Accounting, and Strategic Human Resource Management. Dr Opute has published widely and has also served as a reviewer for publishing houses (and Conferences) such as IGI Global Publications, NOVA Science Publishers Inc., Team Performance Management Journal, Australasian Marketing Journal, International Journal of Emerging Markets, African Journal of Business and Economic Research, International Journal of Marketing Studies, Academy of Marketing Conference, European Marketing Academy Conference, European Academy of Management, and British Academy of Management.

Richard Shambare is an Associate Professor in the Department of Business Management at the University of Venda. He teaches business management courses and has a special interest in research in the areas of marketing and entrepreneurship.

Adya Sharma is a professional who has the capability to transform vision into reality. She is a perfect blend of corporate and academic experience. She is a PhD holder, double Post Graduate and an alumna of St. Stephens College. She has been part of the Academic team instrumental in restructuring Marketing syllabus at university level. She brings with her two decades of rich practical experience from the corporate and academic world which perfectly blends with the theories as an academician. She is connected to the corporate industry as a corporate trainer in companies like Goldman Sachs Women Entrepreneurship Program, Tata Motors, Amdocs, McDonalds, Wipro etc. She also has a number of case studies to her credit which are based on real time companies. An avid researcher, she has many acclaimed International Publications to her credit and continues to also write case studies for International Repositories like the Europe based Case Centre. Dr. Sharma has also been the second supervisor for Master thesis of students conducted under Berlin School of Economics and Law, Germany. Her areas of research include Consumer Behaviour, Sales Management and Services Marketing. She has also edited a book titled "Marketing Techniques for Financial Inclusion and Development" with IGI Global – an International Publishing House.

Index

O

P

R

S

T

U

V

W

Y

www.ingramcontent.com/pod-product-compliance
Lightning Source LLC
LaVergne TN
LVHW062110300926
849161LV00010B/2419